From Juvenile Delinquency to Adult Crime

From Juvenile Delinquency to Adult Crime

CRIMINAL CAREERS, JUSTICE POLICY, AND PREVENTION

Edited by Rolf Loeber
and
David P. Farrington

OXFORD
UNIVERSITY PRESS

OXFORD
UNIVERSITY PRESS

Oxford University Press, Inc., publishes works that further
Oxford University's objective of excellence
in research, scholarship, and education.

Oxford   New York
Auckland   Cape Town   Dar es Salaam   Hong Kong   Karachi
Kuala Lumpur   Madrid   Melbourne   Mexico City   Nairobi
New Delhi   Shanghai   Taipei   Toronto

With offices in
Argentina   Austria   Brazil   Chile   Czech Republic   France   Greece
Guatemala   Hungary   Italy   Japan   Poland   Portugal   Singapore
South Korea   Switzerland   Thailand   Turkey   Ukraine   Vietnam

Published by Oxford University Press, Inc.
198 Madison Avenue, New York, New York 10016

www.oup.com

Oxford is a registered trademark of Oxford University Press

Library of Congress Cataloging-in-Publication Data
From Juvenile Delinquency to Adult Crime : criminal careers,
justice policy, and prevention / edited by Rolf Loeber and David P. Farrington.
    p.   cm.
Includes bibliographical references and index.
ISBN 978-0-19-982816-6 (hardback : alk. paper)—ISBN 978-0-19-982818-0 (pbk. : alk. paper)
1. Juvenile delinquency. 2. Juvenile delinquency—Prevention. 3.—Criminal behavior, Prediction of.
4. Criminial justice, Administration of. I. Loeber, Rolf. II. Farrington, David P.
HV9069.T786   2012
364.36—dc23   2011039090

9 8 7 6 5 4 3 2 1

Printed in the United States of America
on acid-free paper

CONTENTS

FOREWORD

Policy-makers and practitioners are turning to science with increasing frequency to answer tough questions about crime and delinquency and to obtain a better understanding of offender motives. One of the excellent developments in our field over the last decade is an expanded dialogue—more consistently sophisticated and mutually more respectful than past conversations—between researchers and those who apply their discoveries. This development is so important, and so welcome, in grasping the link between youthful delinquency and later criminal behavior. Indeed, few public safety issues cry out for a reconciliation of knowledge and practice more loudly than those relating to the germination, continuation, and cessation of juvenile offending.

In my four decades of policy and academic experience, I've observed in the field a fervent hope by many that criminal and juvenile justice practitioners would abandon their reliance on tradition and intuition and turn to research as the foundation for their decisions. I am happy to report that this goal appears closer to reality than in the past. Getting "smart on crime" has become a *cri de cœur* of public safety leaders from the Attorney General of the United States to local elected officials and law enforcement leaders. When I launched my Evidence Integration Initiative at the U.S. Department of Justice's Office of Justice Programs in 2009, I envisioned a prominent role for the federal government in helping translate the evidence derived from research into criminal and juvenile justice practice. After all, success in applying science, in any field, depends on both developing a solid base of knowledge and communicating the relevance of that knowledge. It is welcome news that practitioners and policy-makers are interested in, and even eager for, information researchers have to share. The scientific community must be prepared to meet this demand, especially in the complicated and politically fraught arena of juvenile justice.

The history of our treatment of young offenders in the United States has followed a changing path, from the early paternalistic juvenile courts to the breakthroughs of *In Re Gault* in the 1960s and its demands for greater reliance on due process to the trend toward harsh sanctions in the 1990s. Over the last 15 years, breakthroughs in medical and behavioral science, and an understanding of brain development, have yielded solid empirical evidence that should help reverse this backward trend in juvenile justice. Research in developmental psychology documented by the MacArthur Foundation's Network on Adolescent Development and Juvenile Justice, among others, suggests that children and youth have difficulty grasping the consequences and even motives of their own actions, and further, that they are not fully competent to participate in an adult adjudicative process. This research calls into question the phenomenon of waivers, transfers, exclusions, and other mechanisms propelling young people into a criminal justice system in which they receive punishments they do not comprehend and that often exceed the seriousness of their offending behaviors.

As the contributors to this volume point out, premature exposure to the adult system carries with it many disadvantages, ranging from proximity to seasoned adult offenders to long-term consequences of a criminal record. The question must be asked, is this a wise and cost-effective use of our resources? The Pathways to Desistance Study, an analysis of serious adolescent offenders led by Edward Mulvey and sponsored by OJP's Office of Juvenile Justice and Delinquency Prevention and National Institute of Justice and several other public and private organizations, found the vast majority of youth who commit felonies reduce their offending over time.[1] Juveniles who offend must be held accountable for their actions, but this finding leads us to conclude we expend far too many resources on punishments that yield dubious results and far too few on nurturing positive behavior to steer young people out of criminal involvement. If we are serious about being smarter and more efficient in administering our systems of justice, we must fundamentally re-think our approach to young people who come into contact with those systems.

A critical point in determining the outcome of a criminal career is the period of late adolescence, a stage referred to by Terence Thornberry and his colleagues as a "criminological crossroads."[2] While a growing body of research and programming centered on childhood and early adolescence, we have not paid enough attention to the later teenage and early adult years as a discrete period of social and behavioral development. We should bear in mind that, despite the somewhat arbitrary demarcations of childhood and adulthood affixed by law, cognitive development and brain maturation very often continue beyond the age of legal majority, which varies from state to state. We know too little about factors in an older youth's capacity for desistance and, conversely, what causes him or her to persist in offending into adulthood. If we hope to gain a complete understanding of what works to prevent delinquency from evolving into persistent criminal behavior, we need to look more closely at this critical stage of life and develop our sense of effective interventions and categories of appropriate sanctions.

The authors offer several thoughtful recommendations for changes to legislation and policy to improve our response to these offenders. I am personally intrigued by the notion of creating special courts for young adult offenders. Research has shown diversionary alternatives such as drug courts and other problem-solving specialty approaches can be remarkably successful in curtailing problem behaviors and reducing recidivism. Young Offender Courts, already being implemented in Great Britain, present an innovative model perhaps worth exploring here in the United States. The other recommendations, based in current research, are equally thoughtful and merit consideration.

This volume represents an important effort in determining how we can make wiser, scientifically-based decisions about our approaches to crime and delinquency, particularly, in how to arrest budding criminal careers in a way to maximize—rather than squander—our limited resources. Rolf Loeber and David Farrington, the principal investigators for the National Institute of Justice project of which this book is a product, describe the findings reported herein as "need to know information" that every judge, prosecutor, state legislator, and criminal and juvenile justice professional—along with teachers and others who work with at-risk kids—should find relevant.

My hope is that these chapters will be read and their contents carefully weighed by everyone who designs policies, enacts laws, and makes decisions affecting the operation of our juvenile and criminal justice systems and whose actions influence the lives of our nation's young people.

Assistant Attorney General Laurie O. Robinson
Washington, D.C., June 2011

Acknowledgment

The author wishes to thank Bill Brantley for his assistance in the preparation of this foreword.

Notes

1. Mulvey, E.P. (March, 2011). *Highlights from pathways to desistance: A longitudinal study of serious adolescent offenders.* U.S. Department of Justice, Office of Justice Programs, Office of Juvenile Justice and Delinquency Prevention. Washington, D.C.

2. Thornberry, T.P., Giordano, P.C., Uggen, C., Matsuda, M., Masten, A.S., Bulten, E., & Donker, A.G., Explanations for offending, chapter 3 in this volume.

ACKNOWLEDGMENTS

We are extremely grateful to the National Institute of Justice for funding our study group, and for the great cooperation and advice we received from Carrie Mulford, Social Science Analyst at NIJ, as well as Margaret Zahn and Bernie Auchter. In addition, the writing of this volume was supported by grant MH056630 from the National Institute of Mental Health, and a grant from the Commonwealth of Pennsylvania. We are also very grateful for the cooperation of many scholars who worked as authors on this study group report in such a great spirit of collaboration. In Pittsburgh, we have received great administrative support from Jennifer Wilson, and in Cambridge from Maureen Brown. We also benefitted greatly from the careful editing by Anne Mullin Burnham. The senior editor is much indebted to Lucille Stark for her very kind hospitality in her country home during the many days that he worked there on this volume. Magda Stouthamer-Loeber facilitated the execution of the study group in many ways by her excellent advice and unfaltering support. Maria Ttofi assisted very effectively by taking notes at several of the meetings.

We received expert advice from many individuals outside of the study group. We want to particularly mention our advisors: Alfred Blumstein (Chair), Bob Crutchfield, Candace Kruttschnitt, Ed Mulvey, Peter van der Laan, and James Q. Wilson. Several of the study group meetings were attended by Janet Chiancone (Office of Juvenile Justice and Delinquency Prevention), Akiva Liberman (National Institute of Justice), Jim Mercy (Centers for Disease Control), Richard Morris (Department of Labor), and Howard Snyder (Bureau of Justice Statistics). We much valued their input.

Two most helpful meetings of focus groups took place. One in Washington, DC, included: Debbie Ackerman (Court Service Unit person and Virginia Court Certified Mediator for Alexandria Circuit Court), Lakeesha Bratcher (Juvenile Probation Case Manager), Barry Holman (Office of Research and Quality Assurance, Department of Youth Rehabilitation Services), Roger Rice (Juvenile Probation Case Manager), Tracy Roberts (University of Maryland), Mary Siegfried (Public Defender for Montgomery County), Penelope Spain (Chief Executive Officer and Chief Financial Officer for Mentoring Today), and Chuck Wexler (Executive Director for the Police Executive Research Forum). The focus group in Pittsburgh, PA, included: Judge Donna Joe McDaniel (President Judge), Regina McDonald (Assistant Pittsburgh Police Chief), Charles Moffat (Superintendent of Allegheny County Pittsburgh Police), Jim Rieland (Director of the Juvenile Court), and Eric Woltshock (Deputy District Attorney in charge of Allegheny County Juvenile Unit).

While this book is the product of a great deal of work by many people, we are responsible for its final form and contents. Points of view or opinions in the volume are those of the authors and do not necessarily represent the official position or policies of the U.S. Department of Justice.

Rolf Loeber and David P. Farrington

Pittsburgh, PA, June 2011

CONTRIBUTORS

Steve Aos, Ph.D., is the Director of the Washington State Institute for Public Policy, the non-partisan research unit of the Washington State Legislature.

Erik Bulten, Ph.D., psychologist, is Head of Assessment, Research and Professional Development at the Pompe Foundation, Nijmegen, and senior researcher at the ACSW, Radboud University, Nijmegen.

Andrea Donker, Ph.D. is professor at the University of Applied Sciences, Leiden, Netherlands, and is senior researcher at the University of Applied Sciences, Utrecht.

Finn-Aage Esbensen, Ph.D., is the E. Desmond Lee Professor of Youth Crime and Violence and also serves as Chair of the Department of Criminology and Criminal Justice at the University of Missouri-St. Louis.

David P. Farrington, Ph.D., O.B.E., is Professor of Psychological Criminology at the Institute of Criminology, Cambridge University, and Adjunct Professor of Psychiatry at Western Psychiatric Institute and Clinic, University of Pittsburgh.

Barry C. Feld, Ph.D., is Centennial Professor of Law, University of Minnesota Law School.

Peggy C. Giordano, Ph.D., is Distinguished Research Professor of Sociology at Bowling Green State University.

Patrick Griffin, J.D., is a Program Officer, U.S. Programs, John D. and Catherine T. MacArthur Foundation, Chicago, IL.

Laura S. Guy, Ph.D., is an Assistant Professor in the Center for Mental Health Services Research in the Department of Psychiatry at the University of Massachusetts Medical School (UMMS), Worcester, MA.

J. David Hawkins, Ph.D., is Endowed Professor of Prevention and Founding Director of the Social Development Research Group at the School of Social Work, University of Washington.

Machteld Hoeve, Ph.D., is Assistant Professor of Forensic Child and Youth Care Sciences at the Research Institute Child Development and Education of the University of Amsterdam, Netherlands.

Robert D. Hoge, Ph.D., is Emeritus Professor of Psychology and Distinguished Research Professor, Carleton University.

James C. (Buddy) Howell, Ph.D., worked at the federal Office of Juvenile Justice and Delinquency Prevention (OJJDP) in the U.S. Department of Justice for 21 years, mostly as Director of Research and Program Development.

Lila Kazemian, Ph.D., is an assistant professor in the department of Sociology at the John Jay College of Criminal Justice.

Martin Killias, Ph.D., is professor of criminology and criminal law at the University of Zurich.

Mark W. Lipsey, Ph.D., is Director of the Peabody Research Institute and a Research Professor at Vanderbilt University.

Rolf Loeber, Ph.D., is Distinguished University Professor of Psychiatry, and Professor of Psychology, and Epidemiology at the University of Pittsburgh, Pittsburgh, Pennsylvania, U.S.A., and Professor of Juvenile Delinquency and Social Development at the Free University, Amsterdam, Netherlands.

Ann Masten, Ph.D., is Distinguished McKnight University Professor in the Institute of Child Development at the University of Minnesota.

Mauri Matsuda is a Ph.D student in the Department of Criminology and Criminal Justice at the University of Maryland, College Park. Her research interests include neighborhood dynamics, the life course, macrostructural perspectives, and the role of race, gender, and class inequality in crime and justice.

Daniel P. Mears, Ph.D., is the Mark C. Stafford Professor of Criminology at Florida State University's College of Criminology and Criminal Justice.

Meghan E. Peel, M.Sc., is a doctoral candidate at the School of Criminology and Criminal Justice at Northeastern University and a Research Associate at the Netherlands Institute for the Study of Crime and Law Enforcement.

Alex R. Piquero, Ph.D., is Professor in the Program in Criminology in the School of Economic, Political, and Policy Sciences at the University of Texas at Dallas, Adjunct Professor Key Centre for Ethics, Law, Justice, and Governance, Griffith University, and Co-Editor of the *Journal of Quantitative Criminology*.

Santiago Redondo, Ph.D., is Professor of Criminology at the University of Barcelona (Spain).

Frederick P. Rivara, M.D., M.P.H., is the holder of the Seattle Children's Guild Endowed Chair in Pediatrics, Professor of Pediatrics and adjunct Professor of Epidemiology at the University of Washington.

Richard Rosenfeld, Ph.D., is Curators Professor of Criminology and Criminal Justice at the University of Missouri-St. Louis.

Jerzy Sarnecki, Ph.D., is Professor of General Criminology at Stockholm University, Sweden.

Terence P. Thornberry, Ph.D., is Distinguished University Professor at the Department of Criminology and Criminal Justice at the University of Maryland and the Principal Investigator of the Rochester Youth Development Study.

Patrick H. Tolan, Ph.D., is Director, Youth-Nex: The University of Virginia Center to Promote Effective Youth Development and Professor in the Curry School of Education and Department of Psychiatry and Neurobehavioral Sciences.

Christopher Uggen, Ph.D., is Distinguished McKnight Professor and Chair of Sociology at the University of Minnesota.

Gina M. Vincent, Ph.D., is an Assistant Professor and Director of Translational Law and Psychiatry Research in the Department of Psychiatry at the University of Massachusetts Medical School, Worcester, MA.

David L. Weisburd, Ph.D., is Walter E. Meyer Professor of Law and Criminal Justice and Director of the Institute of Criminology at the Hebrew University Law School, Distinguished Professor in the Department of Criminology, Law and Society, and Director of the Center for Evidence Based Crime Policy at George Mason University.

Brandon C. Welsh, Ph.D., is an Associate Professor in the School of Criminology and Criminal Justice at Northeastern University and a Senior Research Fellow at the Netherlands Institute for the Study of Crime and Law Enforcement.

Helene R. White, Ph.D., is a Professor at the Center of Alcohol Studies and Sociology Department at Rutgers—the State University of New Jersey.

From Juvenile Delinquency to Adult Crime

1 }

Introduction

Rolf Loeber and David P. Farrington

Scholars, professionals, and lay people debate what causes young people to commit crimes. Some argue that there are "bad" individuals who already from childhood are out of control and that many of them become life-course persistent delinquents. Others argue that juvenile delinquents are to a high degree a product of their environment: the worse their environment, the worse their behavior over time. In this volume we present evidence that both positions are tenable, but we also provide evidence that many juvenile delinquents tend to stop offending in late adolescence and early adulthood and that this decrease is accompanied by a decrease in their impulsive behavior and an increase in their self-control.

Since in most states in the United States the legal transition between adolescence and adulthood takes place at age 18 (and less frequently ages 16 or 17), another point of discussion is whether young people by age 18 have full control over their behavior and whether their brain maturation is complete at that age. If so, does this mean that from age 18 onwards we can attribute the causes of offending and culpability to persisting individual difference factors rather than immaturity and disadvantages in families, schools, and social environment?

This volume focuses on the age period between mid-adolescence and early adulthood (roughly ages 15–29)[1] and it addresses what we know about offending careers from the juvenile to the adult years. The volume draws on studies in North America and Europe (Chapter 10). Table 1.1 summarizes the four key groups that we are interested in: juveniles whose offending persists from adolescence into early adulthood (and perhaps later); juvenile offenders who desisted and do not continue to offend into early adulthood; adult-onset offenders who did not offend during adolescence but who became offenders during early adulthood; and, lastly, nonoffenders who do not offend either in adolescence or early adulthood.

We will examine the four groups in general population samples, but we will also focus on special offender groups, such as drug dealers, gang members, homicide offenders, and sex offenders (see Chapter 5).

TABLE 1.1 } Offending in the juvenile and adult years.

	Adult Non-Offender	Adult Offender
Juvenile Non-Offender	Non-Offender	Adult Onset Offender
Juvenile Offender	Adult Desister	Juvenile/Adult Persister

Maturation

Childhood is usually seen as a period in which individuals have not yet fully developed self-control and their impulses tend to lead to misbehavior and acts of delinquency (Jolliffe & Farrington, 2009, 2010; Moffitt, 1993). This is why parents, teachers and other adults during the period from childhood into adolescence help to modulate children's poor internal controls, teach them skills to navigate problems in life, and help them avoid inflicting harm on others. Thus the years across childhood and adolescence are seen as a crucial period in which to bring about in young people a shift from external to internal controls. However, in late adolescence and early adulthood the appearance of physical maturity does not necessarily mean that mental maturity has been fully achieved and that internal controls are completely formed and are regularly exercised by the young person (see, e.g., Steinberg et al., 2009; but see critique by Fischer et al., 2009).[2]

The presence and growth of internal controls can be evidenced in several complementary ways:

- More mature judgment.
- Better decision-making in offending opportunities.
- Better executive functioning, reasoning, abstract thinking, planning.
- Less influence exerted by immediate undesirable consequences than longer-term possible desirable consequences.
- Better impulse control, less likely to take risks and commit crimes for excitement and more likely to make rational prosocial choices.
- Better emotion regulation and self-regulation.
- Less susceptibility to peer influences.
- Avoidance of self-harm.

However, control in one area does not mean necessarily that control in another area is also in place. There is a lack of agreement among scholars regarding the age at which psychosocial maturity and general cognitive capacity reach their maximum values (Steinberg et al., 2009; Fischer, Stein, & Heikkinen, 2009). There are major individual differences in the gradual mastering of internal controls, with some youth maturing early in this respect, and others in more vulnerable populations taking much longer (see Chapter 11). Contrary to legal assumptions, age 18 is not a fixed date of completion of maturational processes for all young people.

All young persons make the transition between adolescence and adulthood, but scholars, prompted by demographic delays in the timing of marriage and parenthood in industrial societies over the past decades, disagree about whether an in-between stage of "emerging adulthood" is a separate stage of development (Arnett, 2000). There is some agreement among scholars that over recent decades "the transition to adulthood has become increasingly prolonged with more youth staying in education longer, marrying later, and having their first child later than in the past" (Hendry & Kloep, 2007, p. 74) and that this applies to several industrialized countries (Blokland et al., in press; Fussell & Furstenberg, 2005). Masten et al. (2004) characterized the transition period as a window of opportunity for individuals to alter their life course and to have second-chance opportunities and turning points in their lives. Other scholars, however, see the transition period as a delayed entry into adulthood, accompanied by delayed outgrowing of adolescent behaviors.

The Age-Crime Curve

Research findings agree that the prevalence of offending increases from late childhood into adolescence, peaks in late adolescence, and decreases subsequently into adulthood. This is generally known as the *age-crime curve* (Farrington, 1986; Tremblay & Nagin, 2005; Laub & Sampson, 2003). An example of such a curve is shown in Figure 1.1. The curve can be observed in all populations of youth. Less well known is the fact that, although an early age of onset, compared to a later age of onset, is associated with a longer criminal career, the highest concentration of desistance takes place during late adolescence and early adulthood *irrespective* of age of onset. This corresponds with the down-slope of the age-crime curve (see Chapter 11). In fact the decrease in prevalence in the down-slope of the age-crime curve is very substantial. In some data sets it goes down from about 50% to about 10% of all persons (e.g., Loeber et al., 2008).[3]

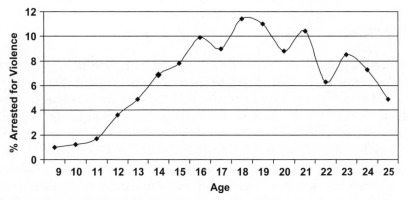

FIGURE 1.1 An example of an age-crime curve.
Loeber & Stallings, 2011.

All available age-crime curves show that the legal age of adulthood at 18 (or for that matter ages 16 or 17 in some states) is not characterized by a sharp change (or decrease) in offending at exactly that age and has no significant relevance to the down-slope of the age-crime curve. Serious offenses (such as rape, robbery, homicide and fraud) tend to emerge after less serious offenses of the late adolescence–early adulthood window. Even for serious offenses, however, there is no clear dividing line at age 18. Steinberg, Cauffman, Woolard, Graham, and Banich (2009) concluded that "The notion that a single line can be drawn between adolescence and adulthood for different purposes under the law is at odds with developmental science" (p. 583).

Offending Careers

This volume addresses what we know about individuals' persistence in offending in contrast to those who desist (see Table 1.1); 30–40% of juvenile offenders recidivate beyond age 18 into adulthood, while other offenders cease offending after adolescence (see Piquero, Hawkins, and Kazemian, Chapter 2, this volume). Piquero and colleagues address the following key questions about delinquency careers: *How common is persistence in and desistance from offending between adolescence and early adulthood?* And *how common is the onset of offending during early adulthood?* The criminal career parameters include prevalence and frequency, continuity, escalation and specialization, types of crimes and criminal careers, co-offending, prediction of offending into adulthood, and prediction of onset of offending in the young adult years. In addition, other chapters in this volume focus on certain categories of offenders (drug dealers, gang members, homicide offenders, and sex offenders) and ask whether they, compared to other offenders, are more likely to persist in offending into adulthood (Chapters 5 and 11).

The Search for Causes

As mentioned, the down-slope of the age-crime curve represents a very substantial decrease in the number of offenders from the peak of the curve in middle to late adolescence. The reason that we emphasize this effect size is because we identify explanations that separately or collectively explain a large portion of the down-slope of the age-crime curve.

Causes (here conservatively called explanations) are reviewed in several chapters and concern persistence in and desistance from offending between adolescence and the onset of offending in early adulthood. These chapters also focus on explanations for the shape of the age-crime curve in different populations. We will consider the following 10 explanatory processes:

1. Early individual differences in self-control (discussed in Chapters 3 and 11).
2. Brain maturation (Chapters 3, 5, 8, and 11).
3. Cognitive changes (e.g., decision making to change behavior; Chapters 3 and 11).
4. Behavioral risk factors (disruptive behavior and delinquency) and behavioral protective factors (nervousness and social isolation; Chapters 3 and 11).
5. Exposure to social risk and protective factors (family, peers, school; Chapters 3 and 11).
6. Mental illnesses and substance use/abuse (Chapters 3 and 11).
7. Life circumstances (e.g., getting married; becoming employed; Chapters 4 and 11).
8. Situational context of specific criminal events, including crime places and routine activities (Chapters 4 and 11).
9. Neighborhood (e.g., living in a disadvantaged neighborhood, and the concentration of impulsive and delinquent individuals in disadvantaged neighborhoods; Chapters 4 and 11).
10. Justice response (e.g., transfer to adult court, longer sentences; Chapter 8).

We will address the following questions: (a) *Does each process explain persistence in offending from adolescence into early adulthood?* (b) *Does each process also explain desistance during that period?* And (c) *Does each process explain the onset of offending during early adulthood?* As will be shown, the explanatory processes tend to operate at different ages of juveniles, some early and some later in offending careers (Figure 1.2).

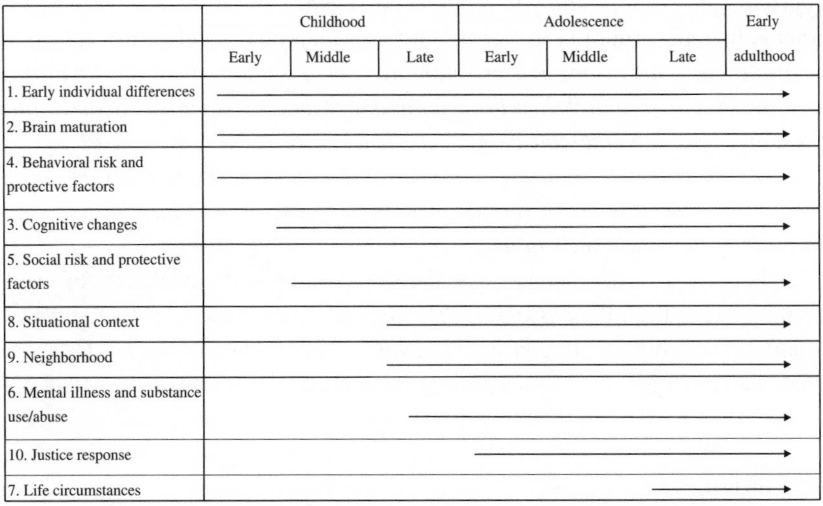

	Childhood			Adolescence			Early
	Early	Middle	Late	Early	Middle	Late	adulthood
1. Early individual differences							
2. Brain maturation							
4. Behavioral risk and protective factors							
3. Cognitive changes							
5. Social risk and protective factors							
8. Situational context							
9. Neighborhood							
6. Mental illness and substance use/abuse							
10. Justice response							
7. Life circumstances							

FIGURE 1.2 Approximate temporal ordering of explanatory processes investigated for persistence in, desistance from, and adult-onset of offending.

Note: Numbers refer to the order in which the explanatory processes are discussed in Chapters 1 and 11.

Justice Response

The justice response to law-breaking by young people is partly specified in the criminal code but partly depends on how that code is interpreted and how much discretion is given to the police, judges, prosecutors, and other justice personnel. In the United States, the justice response is also much influenced by legislators at the federal and state level who, rightly or wrongly, call for harsher and longer sentences for young offenders.

Over the past decades, the juvenile and adult justice systems have become more intertwined and more juveniles are processed in the adult court than previously. The main questions discussed in Chapters 7 and 11 are: *What are the legal age boundaries between juvenile and adult justice systems in different states? How well does the minimum legal age of adulthood map on changes in persistence in and desistance from offending during the transition between adolescence and adulthood?*

As mentioned, there are many explanations of persistence in and desistance from offending between adolescence and early adulthood, and explanations of young adult-onset of offending. These explanations are relevant to legislation and to the administration of juvenile and adult justice. In Chapters 7 and 8 we address the questions: *What are the legal implications of knowledge of explanatory processes in offending from adolescence to adulthood? Are legal boundaries related to young people's maturation and development of cognitive control (or lowered impulsivity)? Does the legal system improve young people's maturation and cognitive control or is young people's cognitive development impervious to the juvenile and adult justice systems?*

In Chapter 11 we also address several questions that pertain to vulnerable categories of youth who come into contact with the law, such as youth who had been in juvenile institutions and youth of low intelligence, but there may very well be other vulnerable groups (Chapter 11). Questions relevant to vulnerable categories of youth are: *Which categories of youth are likely to mature more slowly in their cognitive ability to control their behavior and take longer than others to desist from offending?* And *do vulnerable groups experience more atypical life transitions (e.g., dropping out of school, teenage parenthood) between adolescence and early adulthood? Are vulnerable youth competent enough to understand judicial and court proceedings that affect their future?*

In the current era of evidence-based decision-making, we found that the following questions are critical: *What is known about the relative effectiveness of the juvenile and criminal justice systems in reducing recidivism? What is the justification for special treatment of young persons (and especially young adults) compared to older adults?*

Legislation

There are several other key questions that are relevant for legislation. *What is the usefulness of legislation stipulating minimum or longer sentences for young offenders? Would the lowering of the age of adulthood, for example to age 16, decrease young people's offending and lower the crime rate of populations of young individuals? Would increasing the age of adulthood, for example from age 16 to 18, or for example from age 18 to 21 or higher, decrease young people's offending and lower the crime rate of populations of young individuals? What are the laws in different states regarding transfer of juveniles to the adult criminal court?* In Chapters 8 and 11 we review advantages and disadvantages of several legal and practical options pertaining to young offenders: (a) raising the legal age at which the adult justice system becomes applicable; (b) lowering the legal age at which the adult justice system becomes applicable; (c) increasing sanctions, particularly by means of legislative offense exclusion, minimum length of sentences, and longer incarceration; and (d) the creation of special courts for young adult offenders.

Screening

Increasingly, intake officers, probation officers, and youth workers in the justice system use risk assessment screening instruments (reviewed in Chapter 6) to inform the sentencing of juveniles. Risk assessment instruments are also used with juveniles and adults in institutional settings (including mental health settings) to inform release decisions. We are particularly interested in risk assessment instruments at ages 15–17 that predict persistence or desistance in the young adult years. In addition, Chapter 11 reviews three other types of assessments relevant to young offenders: assessments for mental competence to understand court proceedings; assessments of mental health and the presence of psychiatric disorder(s), and assessments of mental maturity.

Although screening to identify vulnerable youth (i.e., those who are not competent to understand court proceedings) has improved (Chapter 6), screening for youth who are cognitively immature is still under development. While screening for the risk of recidivism has advanced considerably, there are no screening instruments for young adult-onset offending.

Interventions outside of the Justice System

Over the recent decades a range of proven interventions outside of the justice system has become available to reduce and/or prevent conduct problems that often precede delinquency. Chapter 9 reviews the following questions about extrajudicial interventions for different age ranges and target populations of youths: *How effective are family-based programs during toddlerhood in reducing offending during the young adult years? How effective are individually-based programs during childhood in reducing offending during the young adult years? How effective are school-based interventions in reducing young adult offending? How effective are interventions with older juvenile delinquents (ages 14–17) in preventing continuation into young adult offending? How effective are labor market interventions in reducing young adult offending?*

Not all programs are equally effective and not all have a similar effect when applied more broadly (beyond demonstration programs). For that reason we address the following questions: *What is known about the financial benefits and costs of different interventions that might reduce offending in the young adult years? What is known about the success of implementing demonstration programs on a large scale?*

Gender Issues

There is increasing awareness that results obtained with males may not apply to females, and that what may be good for one gender may not necessarily be good for the other (see Chapter 11, this volume). For that reason we address the following questions: *How do criminal career features vary with gender? Are different theories of offending needed for each gender? Are genetic and biological influences the same for each gender? Do life events, life transitions, situational factors, and neighborhood factors have different effects for each gender?*

There are major gender differences in the experience of handicaps and the need for screening to identify these handicaps. For that reason, we address the following questions: *Are psychiatric disorders (e.g., depression, borderline personality disorder) more common among young female than male offenders? How does the predictive accuracy of risk factors, needs, and protective factors vary with gender? How effective is juvenile versus adult court treatment for each gender? Are interventions outside of the justice system differentially effective with each gender?*

Ethnicity

This volume addresses several questions pertaining to ethnicity as it relates to the transition between adolescent and early adult offending. We focus particularly on African-American individuals. For example, we ask: *Is the age-crime curve for African-American males different than that for Caucasians? Are African-American youth more deprived than Caucasian youth in terms of socioeconomic/demographic factors such as a broken home, the family on welfare, a bad neighborhood, and a young mother? Is ethnicity a cause of offending, and does ethnicity explain individual differences in offending once risk factors are taken into account?* We will address also whether screening instruments to assess the risk of recidivism are equally predictive for different ethnic groups, and whether prevention and intervention programs outside of the justice system are equally effective for different ethnic groups.

Headline Conclusions

This volume is largely based on evidence from a wide range of empirical studies and draws from studies conducted all over the world, but particularly in North America and Europe. It contains extensive reviews of the literature and several new data analyses executed especially for this volume. These two aspects present new insights about the interface between offending and the justice system during adolescence and early adulthood. Section III of the concluding chapter (Chapter 11) summarizes the headline findings and arguments that the minimum legal age of adulthood does not relate closely to the age-crime curve or to adolescents' maturation, which leads to less impulsive behavior and more self-control. The findings point to an unplanned overreach of the justice system, particularly when meting out long sentences for young offenders or transferring juveniles from the jurisdiction of the juvenile to the adult court. We consider these matters especially for categories of vulnerable offenders, such as those with low intelligence or mental health problems. Chapter 11 also has major recommendations, such as raising the legal age for juveniles at which adult justice becomes applicable, improved screening of young people in the justice system, and the establishment of Young Adult Offender Courts, which in conjunction with Drug Courts can provide rehabilitation rather than retribution alone, as is common in the adult justice system.

Clearly, there is a major role for the justice system in dealing with known offenders, but the system should not be the first and most expensive resort for dealing with young lawbreakers. We point to major evidence that impulsive behaviors are malleable and that there are programs for juveniles that have demonstrated their effectiveness in reducing impulsivity *and* later offending even into early adulthood.

We posit that the findings reported in this volume are "need to know information" relevant for legislators, judges, prosecutors, and other personnel in the juvenile and adult justice systems, as well as for educators and individuals working in child and adolescent programs to reduce problems of conduct and delinquency, to ensure that today's juvenile delinquents do not become tomorrow's adult criminals.

Acknowledgments

We are much indebted to comments by James C. Howell on an early draft of this chapter.

Notes

1. There are no empirical boundaries for the age range of the period from adolescence to early adulthood. Note that the Transition to Adulthood (T2A) initiative defines early adulthood between "approximately 18 and 24," but acknowledges that this age range is "blurry at

the edges" (Helyar-Cardwell, 2009, p. 12). Our choice of age 29 is based on the fact that the majority of young offenders have outgrown offending by that age.

2. In fact physical growth (bone weight) continues to increase until about age 23 (Doreleijers & Fokkens, 2010).

3. The decrease translates into a very large standardized mean difference effect size of about 1.0.

References

Arnett, J.J. (2000). Emerging adulthood: A theory of development from the late teens through the twenties. *American Psychologist*, 55, 469–480.

Blokland, A.A.J. & Palmen, H. (in press). Criminal career patterns. In R. Loeber, M. Hoeve, N.W. Slot, & P. van der Laan (Eds.), *Persisters and desisters in crime from adolescence into adulthood: Explanation, prevention and punishment*. Aldershot UK: Ashgate.

Doreleijers, T. & Fokkens, J.W. (2010). Minderjarigen en jongvolwassenen: Pleidooi voor een evidence based strafrecht. *Rechtsreeks*, 2, 1–47.

Farrington, D.P. (1986). Age and crime. In M. Tonry, & N. Morris (Eds.), *Crime and justice: An annual review of research* (vol. 7, pp. 189–250). Chicago, IL: Chicago University Press.

Fischer, K.W., Stein, Z., & Heikkinen, K. (2009). Narrow assessments misrepresent development and misguide policy: Comment on Steinberg, Cauffman, Woolard, Graham, and Banich (2009). *American Psychologist*, 64, 595–600.

Fussell, E., & Furstenberg, F.F. (2005). The transition to adulthood during the twentieth century: Race, nativity, and gender. In R.A. Settersten, F.F. Furstenberg, & R.G. Rumbaut (Eds.), *On the frontier of adulthood: Theory, research, and public policy* (pp. 29–75). Chicago, IL: University of Chicago Press.

Helyar-Cardwell, V. (2009). *A new start: Young adults in the criminal justice system*. London, UK: Transition to Adulthood Alliance.

Hendry, L.B., & Kloep, M. (2007). Conceptualizing emerging adulthood: Inspecting the emperor's new clothes? *Child Development Perspectives*, 1, 74–79.

Jolliffe, D., & Farrington, D.P. (2009). A systematic review of the relationship between childhood impulsiveness and later violence. In M. McMurran & R. Howard (Eds.), *Personality, personality disorder, and violence* (pp. 41–61). New York: Wiley.

Laub, J.H., & Sampson, R.J. (2003). *Shared beginnings, divergent lives: Delinquent boys to age 70*. Cambridge, MA: Harvard University Press.

Loeber, R., Farrington, D.P., Stouthamer-Loeber, M., & White, H.R. (2008). *Violence and serious theft: Development and prediction from childhood to adulthood*. Mahwah, NJ: Lawrence Erlbaum.

Loeber, R. & Stallings, R. (2011). Modeling the impact of interventions on local indicators of offending, victimization and incarceration. In R. Loeber & D.P. Farrington, *Young homicide offenders and victims: Risk factors, prediction, and prevention from childhood* (pp. 137–152). New York: Springer.

Masten, A.S., Burt, K.B., Roisman, G.I., Obradovic, J., Long, J.D., & Tellegen, A. (2004). Resources and resilience in the transition to adulthood: Continuity and change. *Development and Psychopathology*, 16, 1071–1094.

Moffitt, T.E. (1993). Adolescence-limited and life-course-persistent antisocial behavior: A developmental taxonomy. *Psychological Review*, 100, 674–701.

Siennick, S.E. (2011). Tough love? Crime and parental assistance in young adulthood. *Criminology*, 49, 163–195.

Steinberg, L., Cauffman, E., Woolard, J., Graham, S., & Banich, M. (2009). Are adolescents less mature than adults?: Minors' access to abortion, the juvenile death penalty, and the alleged APA "flip-flop." *American Psychologist*, 64, 583–594.

Tremblay, R.E., & Nagin, D.S. (2005). The developmental origins of physical aggression in humans. In R.E. Tremblay, W.H. Hartup, & J. Archer (Eds.), *Developmental origins of aggression* (pp. 83–106). New York: Guilford Press.

2

Criminal Career Patterns

Alex R. Piquero, J. David Hawkins, and Lila Kazemian

The empirical study of longitudinal patterns of criminal activity committed by offenders has been a central feature of the criminological discipline. Beginning with the pioneering descriptive work of Quetelet (1842), continuing onto Shaw's (1931) classic *The Jack Roller*, and culminating in Wolfgang et al.'s (1972) pioneering *Delinquency in a Birth Cohort* study, such basic, descriptive accounts about the nature of criminal offending have generated important information regarding the proportion of individuals who offend, the volume of their offending, their participation within and across crime types, patterns of escalation and de-escalation, and the cessation of criminal activity (see reviews in Blumstein et al., 1986; Piquero et al., 2003). Moreover, evidence regarding the nature of criminal careers has also served as an organizing feature of several criminological and especially developmental theories of crime (Farrington, 2005), and has served as an important basis for important methodological/statistical advances for studying changes (both within and between individuals) in criminal activity over the life course (Nagin, 2005).

At the same time, much of the knowledge base regarding criminal careers has emerged from a few select studies, limited in scope by their sample composition, data source, and time observation period. Moreover, even fewer studies have dealt with specific criminal career dimensions that link the important theoretical and policy-oriented transition between juvenile and adult years, a period of the life course when many criminal careers end and a small, select few continue. In this chapter, we review the empirical literature that focuses on several key criminal career dimensions linking offending patterns in adolescence to those in adulthood, including: prevalence, frequency, continuity, adult-onset, specialization, diversification, escalation and de-escalation, stability and change, and co-offending. After each section, we provide a brief summary. The chapter concludes with an overall summary statement, an identification of key research priorities, and some recommendations for practitioners and policy-makers.

Prevalence

As one of the two key dimensions of criminal careers, *prevalence* refers to the proportion of individuals who participate in crime at any given time period. There exist a large number of empirical studies documenting the prevalence of offending in criminal careers. The seminal Philadelphia Birth Cohort Study indicated that about one-third of Philadelphia males born in 1945 had experienced a police contact by age 18 (Wolfgang et al., 1972), a finding which has generally been replicated across most longitudinal studies examining official records. With respect to age-based prevalence estimates, most studies tend to indicate that prevalence peaks in the teenage years (around ages 15–19), and then declines in the early 20s (Blumstein et al., 1986; Piquero et al., 2003). These figures tend to peak earlier in self-reports and later when using official measures (including police contacts, arrests, and then convictions; see Moffitt et al., 2001). Moreover, these findings hold across different samples and time periods. Because space precludes a detailed review of each study regarding offending prevalence, we highlight several studies that are unique with respect to their length (i.e., time period of observation), sample characteristics (i.e., race/gender), measure of crime (i.e., self-reports vs. official records), crime type (i.e., general offending vs. serious-violent offending) and cultural location (i.e., United States, United Kingdom, New Zealand).

Piquero et al. (2007) examined the nature of offending prevalence using the conviction records for over 400 South London males participating in the Cambridge Study in Delinquent Development. Their analyses showed that: (1) the early to middle teenage years saw a steady increase in annual prevalence from 2% to just over 10% at the peak age of 17 (10.7%), only to be followed by a small degree of stability amid a general decline through age 40; (2) the cumulative-prevalence of convictions through age 40 evinced a rapid rise until about age 18, at which point it became asymptotic up to age 40 (39.9% of the sample had at least one conviction); (3) there were very few differences in offending prevalence across offense types, as involvement across most offense types decreased over time (a pattern that was observed both for the number of persons convicted and the sum total number of convictions); and (4) offending prevalence assessed using self-report surveys among the South London males approached 100% by age 40 (Farrington et al., 2001).

Using data from two cohorts of the Pittsburgh Youth Study, Loeber et al. (2008) examined the prevalence of violence and theft from ages 7–25. Generally speaking, about 25% of the study participants in the youngest cohort had been arrested for serious violence at age 19, and about 10% had been convicted for serious violent offending by age 19, while almost 20% had been arrested for serious theft and 20% convicted for serious theft. However, 33% of the subjects in the oldest cohort had been arrested for serious violent offending by age 25, and one in six had been convicted of such offenses. Further, 33% had been arrested for serious theft, and 20% had been convicted of these offenses.

Turning to specific findings, with respect to the (self-reported) prevalence of moderate and serious violence in the youngest cohort, its annual peak (5–6%) was observed in early adolescence (ages 13–16)—higher for moderate compared to serious offending—and then declined soon thereafter to relatively modest to low levels (p. 81). In the oldest cohort, serious violent offending was highest at ages 18–19 (11%), and then declined dramatically thereafter, whereas moderate violence was high at ages 14–15 (17%) then declined. Still, the oldest sample, likely because of the historical time period in which they entered adolescence, evidenced more (serious) violent offending when compared to the youngest cohort. With respect to the prevalence of theft, findings for the youngest cohort indicate that the prevalence of minor theft (stealing outside home or shoplifting) was stable between ages 7–13 (25%), peaked at age 14 (28%), and then decreased by age 19. For moderate theft (more serious stealing), prevalence peaked at ages 14–15 (19%), and then declined, while for serious theft (breaking and entering or auto theft), prevalence was low in middle childhood (1%, ages 7–10), and peaked at ages 14–17 (4–6%), and then declined thereafter. For the oldest cohort (ages 13–25), minor theft decreased from 42% (age 13) to 1% (age 25). For moderate theft a peak was observed at age 15 (32%) and reached a low of 4% by age 25, and for serious theft, it ranged from 8–11% at ages 13–15, and then decreased to 0% by age 25. As was evident for violence, the oldest cohort exhibited a higher level of theft throughout the time period. In both cohorts then, the (self-reported) prevalence of theft was much higher than the prevalence of violence (p. 100), such that by age 19, about 75% of the youngest cohort had engaged in minor theft, compared to about 50% who had engaged in moderate theft, and just fewer than 20% who had engaged in serious theft. Violence was much less common: 33% had engaged in moderate violence and 20% had engaged in serious violence (p. 100).

The PYS analyses reported above relied on self-reports of offending, and it is useful to assess whether the substantive conclusions hold when using official arrests as the outcome criteria. Among the youngest cohort, the (arrest-based) prevalence of serious violence peaks at age 16 (7%) and declines thereafter, while the peak for moderate violence was observed at ages 14 and 18 (both 4%). Among the oldest cohort (first studied at age 13), the prevalence of moderate violent offending peaks at ages 18 and 21 (7%), while it peaks by age 19 (10%) for serious violent offending. Turning to theft, the prevalence of arrest for moderate theft peaks at age 16 (10%) and age 18 (9%), while the peak for serious theft was age 16 (5%) for the youngest cohort, while moderate and serious theft arrests peak at age 16 (moderate 15%, serious 12%) for the oldest cohort (p.109).[1]

In a final analysis, Loeber et al. (2008) developed and examined an all-source measure of serious violence and theft combining self-reported delinquency and official records data to examine the prevalence of violence and theft in the two cohorts (p. 235). These results were substantively similar to those reported above. For violence, the oldest cohort exhibited higher levels at all ages but with a slightly earlier peak for the youngest (ages 13–16) compared to the oldest (ages 18–19) cohort. For theft, there was a higher prevalence at all ages in the oldest cohort, with a peak about ages 14–16 for both cohorts, but with a much more rapid decline in annual prevalence among the youngest cohort.[2]

Moffitt et al. (2001) undertook one of the most comprehensive analyses of gender differences in antisocial behavior within a cohort of 1,000 New Zealand males/females followed to age 21. Participants in the Dunedin Multidisciplinary Health and Human Development Study were given self-report surveys to document their involvement in crime while researchers collected data from the subjects' parents regarding offspring antisocial behavior as well as arrests and convictions from official New Zealand agencies. There was a remarkable consistency in study results across age and data sources (p. 37). First, through age 21 and across multiple data sources, males emerged as more antisocial than females with two exceptions: (a) males and females were most similar in their antisocial behavior during middle adolescence and (b) males and females were most similar in their drug-and alcohol-related offenses. Second, males tended to engage in more serious offenses than females, and not surprisingly tended to be overrepresented in official criminal records. Third, chronic offending was observed among both males and females, but even the most active females offended at a much lower rate than the most active males. Finally, prevalence rises through late childhood into adolescence, peaking in the mid-to-late teens and declining soon thereafter.

Summary. Empirical evidence on ever-prevalence of offending suggests that while most individuals self-report involvement in some form of delinquent or criminal behavior by early adulthood, official records from police contacts, arrests, and convictions show a much smaller estimate (~20–40% depending on data source, follow-up period, etc.), largely because most offenders are not caught. Analyses regarding the prevalence of offending by age indicate a peak in self-reported crime in the early teens and in later adolescence using official records. These figures also vary somewhat according to the crime type analyzed, with more minor crimes peaking earlier and more serious crimes peaking later, suggesting some signs of a change in the mix of offenses and/or escalation in offending across age. In the limited set of studies containing information on offending across race/gender, evidence tends to show that males and minorities (especially African-Americans) show an earlier and higher prevalence peak than females and whites, but data on Hispanics is virtually absent in criminal career research (though see Maldonado-Molina et al., 2009).

Frequency

The second key criminal career dimension, frequency, references the number of crimes committed. To be sure, there exists some debate about the operational definition, with some researchers opting to consider frequency as simply the number of offenses committed by a particular sample (ranging from 0→∞), while others contend that offending frequency should be defined by the number of crimes committed over a particular time period among those offenders who are active (i.e., offending) during the time period being studied (Piquero et al., 2007, p. 46). As could be expected, the evidence on individual offending frequency, especially its overall patterning and stability, is more mixed than the more conclusive and agreed-upon findings emerging from the prevalence estimates reviewed above. Here, we provide a review of two longitudinal studies that have examined the variations in offending frequency trends between adolescence and adulthood.

Using official conviction records, Piquero et al. (2007) examined offending frequency for the South London males through age 40. By age 40, the men had accumulated 760 total convictions, with peaks at ages 17 (69 convictions) and 18 (67 convictions), followed by declines through and into adulthood. When the authors limited their sample to active offenders and examined individual offending frequency (denoted by λ), which is arrived at by taking the total number of offenses at each age divided by the number of offenders at each age, they found that λ peaked at age 16 at 1.78 convictions per offender, remained fairly stable (hovering around 1.50 through age 22), then declined steadily until the late 20s, only to be followed by more erratic downward trends through age 40. Similar substantive conclusions were obtained when the authors examined individual offending frequency across age groups (10–15, 16–20, 21–25, 26–30, 31–35, 36–40), i.e., an early increase followed by a steady decline over time, and also when the authors focused on violence, which revealed much smaller frequency estimates because of its rarity in conviction records among the South London males. Also, prevalence and individual offending frequency closely paralleled one another.

Loeber et al. (2008, p. 85) provided an in-depth analysis of the frequency of violence and theft in the two PYS-based cohorts at different age blocks. Defining the average frequency of self-reported offending by dividing the number of offenses by the number of offenders in each age block, their analysis indicated that the average annual frequency of moderate and serious violence increased over three age blocks (10–12, 13–16, 17–19) among the youngest cohort (peaking around two offenses/offender at ages 17–19 for both moderate/serious violence), while annual reported violence frequency peaked at about four offenses per offender per year during late adolescence (ages 17–19) before dropping off in early adulthood (ages 20–25). Additionally, there were more violent offenders in the oldest cohort, but active offenders in that cohort also committed violence at a higher rate than in the youngest cohort (Loeber et al., 2008, p. 87).

Turning to the theft-frequency analysis, results for the youngest cohort indicate that the annual frequency of self-reported theft increased up to early adolescence (ages 13–16), and then remained stable or decreased in late adolescence. And although there was a gradual increase in frequency from late childhood to early adolescence (especially for moderate theft), serious theft had similar annual frequencies in early and late adolescence (~2.1–2.4 offenses per offender). For all three types of theft among the oldest cohort, the frequency was highest in late adolescence (ages 17–19, 3.5–5.4 offenses per offender), with a much lower frequency of serious theft during early adulthood (ages 20–25, ~2 offenses/offender) (Loeber et al., 2008, p. 87).

To summarize, the annual self-reported frequencies of all thefts were higher among the older PYS cohort and theft-frequency tended to be higher in most comparisons than violence-frequency. Frequent theft was more common in the early part of criminal careers for the oldest cohort while frequent violence was more common in the later part of their careers, and the frequency of offending largely followed an age-crime curve in the oldest but not in the youngest cohort (Loeber et al., 2008, pp. 100–101).

Turning to the frequency of arrests for violence and theft, the results indicated that the annual frequency of arrests for moderate violence in the youngest cohort (using age blocks 10–12, 13–16, 17–19) was stable from late childhood to late adolescence (0.4–0.5), while the annual frequency of arrests for serious violence was similar to that of moderate violence and stable from late childhood to late adolescence (0.5–0.6) (Loeber et al., 2008, p. 110). Among the oldest cohort (using age blocks 13–16, 17–19, 20–25), results for both moderate and serious violence annual arrest frequency was highest during late compared to early adolescence (ages 17–19, 0.6 arrests for moderate and 1.0 arrests for serious violence per offender), while both moderate and serious violence decreased during early adulthood (ages 20–25).

With respect to theft-arrest frequency, among the youngest cohort, the frequency of moderate theft increased from late childhood to late adolescence (to 0.87 arrests in late adolescence) but showed less of a trend for serious theft (to 0.57 arrests in late adolescence) (Loeber et al., 2008, p. 111). For the oldest cohort, frequency of theft arrests was highest for moderate theft during early/late adolescence (~0.9–1.0 arrests per offender), and serious theft also peaked during early/late adolescence (~0.8–0.9 arrests per offender) decreasing significantly from adolescence to early adulthood. Thus, the frequency of arrests did not follow an age-crime curve for the youngest cohort and varied for violence and theft in the oldest cohort, indicating that arrest data, in contrast to self-reported offense data, did not consistently follow an age-crime distribution (p. 112).

Summary. Unlike prevalence trends, which show relatively consistent evidence of peaks in early to late adolescence and a gradual decrease after age 18, individual offending frequency appears to vary according to several characteristics, including sample composition, measures of offending, and time periods observed. That said, a few tentative summary statements can be made. First, annual individual offending frequency appears to peak in late adolescence, and only among a very small and highly select few offenders does it remain stable for a comparably long time (this is because criminal careers are relatively short, on the order of 5–10 years). Second, individual frequencies appear to be higher for nonviolent than violent offenses, but both decline over time. Third, frequency of offending estimates are higher in self-reports than in official records, largely because most individuals do not get caught and/or processed for their offending. Moreover, this is complicated by the fact that studying serious violence with official records is difficult because violence entails a higher likelihood of criminal justice contact and subsequent incapacitation unlike many nonviolent offenses, which are either committed with relative impunity and/or face smaller likelihoods of criminal justice detection and subsequent punishment in the form of incapacitation.

Continuity

There is strong continuity in antisocial behavior from childhood to adolescence to adulthood. As Robins (1978, p. 611) noted "adult antisocial behavior virtually requires childhood antisocial behavior." Yet, there is also significant within-individual change such that most antisocial children and adolescents do not go on to become antisocial adults (Loeber & Le Blanc, 1990; Le Blanc & Loeber, 1998), and even fewer individuals escape adolescence without criminal involvement only to become involved during adulthood (a criminal career dimension which is covered later in this chapter).

In one of the earliest reviews of the persistence literature, where persistence is conceptualized as offending before and after adolescence, Blumstein et al. (1986, pp. 86–89) provided consistent evidence that 30–60% of juvenile delinquents known to the police/juvenile courts persisted as adult offenders with at least one arrest or conviction as an adult for an index or felony offense (see also McCord, 1978; Wolfgang et al., 1987). For three Racine, Wisconsin, birth cohorts, Shannon (1982a) reported that 31%, 44%, and 54% of males with police contacts for nontraffic offenses before age 20 were arrested again as adults by ages 21, 26, and 32.

Using official records collected on over 27,000 individuals from the 1958 Philadelphia Birth Cohort followed from birth to age 26, Tracy and Kempf-Leonard (1996) found more continuity than discontinuity in offending. Among those who were previously recorded as delinquent, 32.5% were also arrested as adults compared to just 7.6% of the cohort subjects who were arrested as adults but had not been officially processed for delinquency as juveniles (p. 80). These figures simultaneously indicate that 67.5% of the cohort juvenile delinquents did not continue their offending as adults, and over 92.4% of the juvenile nondelinquents were nondelinquent as adults (Table 5.1, p. 80).

Tracy and Kempf-Leonard also examined race and gender comparisons with respect to continuity. Blacks were the most likely to have an adult arrest (17.4%) followed by Hispanics (13.1%) and then whites (9.1%). About 23.4% of males and only 3.9% of females had a record of adult crime. Black males had the highest likelihood of adult offender status (44.7% of delinquents and 18.7% of nondelinquents). Among white males, 37% of delinquents and 10.9% of nondelinquents were adult offenders. Among Hispanic males, 36% of delinquents and 17.4% of nondelinquents were adult offenders. With respect to black females, 13.9% of delinquents were adult offenders, compared to 3.9% of nondelinquents. About 8.7% of white female delinquents and 1.2% of white female nondelinquents were adult offenders. Among Hispanic females, 4.8% of delinquents and 2.3% of nondelinquents were adult offenders (Table 5.3, p. 83). As the frequency of officially recorded juvenile delinquency increased from nonoffender to one-time offender to recidivist offender (2–4 offenses) to chronic offender (5+ offenses), the probability of an adult criminal record increased substantially regardless of race/ethnicity group. The smallest percentage of adult offenders was always observed among nondelinquents, and the highest proportion for chronic offenders, regardless of race (Table 5.6, p. 87). This was also true among females as well, but with lower base rates.

Tracy and Kempf-Leonard also examined two "discontinuity" groups: (1) those cohort delinquents who were not recorded as adult offenders (16% of the cohort and two-thirds of the delinquent subset); (2) those cohort members who were first arrested for criminal behavior as adults and had not previously been recorded as juvenile delinquents, who represented 6% of the cohort and about 44% of adult criminals (p. 94). The authors then examined whether adult crime level differed by continuity status by comparing those arrested only as adults to those arrested both as juveniles and as adults (Table 5.11, p. 95). These analyses indicated significant differences between the two continuity groups, regardless of race. For example, among whites, those arrested only as adults (65.5%) were more likely than those arrested both as juveniles and as adults (45.8%) to be arrested for just one adult crime. They were less likely to be adult recidivists (28.4% vs. 37.7%), and much less likely to be chronic adult criminals (6.1% vs. 16.5%). The data for black males also showed that those arrested both as juveniles and as adults were less likely than those arrested only as adults to be arrested only once (34.7% vs. 56.6%), more likely to be recidivists (42.5% vs. 33.3%), and more likely to be chronic adult criminals according to official arrest records (22.8% vs. 9.9%). The data for Hispanic males showed a similar pattern but with less striking differences.

The data for females showed similar findings. However, significant differences between those arrested both as juveniles and as adults and those arrested for the first time as adults emerged only among blacks. About 76.3% of black females arrested for the first time as adults were arrested only once compared to 65.6% of those arrested both as juveniles and as adults. About 21.4% of black females arrested for the first time as adults were recidivists compared to 27.8% of those arrested as juveniles and as adults. About 2.2% of black females arrested for the first time as adults compared with 6.7% of the black females arrested both as juveniles and as adults were chronic offenders according to official records. The data for white females replicated this pattern but differences were not significant because of small cell frequencies, and findings for Hispanic females were inconclusive because of the very small number of cases.

In short, knowledge of official delinquency status helps to assess the prevalence of officially recorded crime in adulthood. About 33% of those arrested for delinquent behavior are also arrested as adults, compared to just 7.6% of those not arrested as juveniles. Delinquency status was associated with adult status among all race groups for males, though, perhaps because of smaller cell sizes, to a lesser extent among females. Those arrested for the first time as adults were considerably less likely than their delinquent counterparts to be arrested frequently and very likely to be arrested only once in adulthood (p. 108). Those arrested only as adults represented 1,526 members of the cohort and exhibited a very low frequency of officially recorded offenses in adulthood by age 26. In short, these findings suggest a considerable degree of continuity in arrests for offending between adolescence and adulthood.

Other relevant findings emerged from this analysis. For example, Tracy and Kempf-Leonard (1996) found that early arrests as well as frequent arrests and arrests over several years for juvenile offenses were significantly associated with adult offender status for both males and females. When they predicted adult crime status from "type of delinquency" they found that for males, arrest for major violence, robbery, and weapon possession as a juvenile predicted adult offender status, as did juvenile co-offending. Among females, arrest for major violence, theft, and drug offending as a juvenile predicted adult offender status but co-offending did not. When the authors examined whether the concentration of delinquency (as a juvenile) in certain offense types significantly predicted adult offender status, they found that high concentration/specialization did not predict adult offender status among females, and it exhibited mixed effects for males (weapon and drug concentration was found to be most important). Lastly, they examined whether officially recorded delinquency careers that exhibited evidence of offense severity escalation demonstrated a higher probability of arrest for adult crime. Among males, delinquency severity predicted adult offender status, but it did not do so among females; the adult offender status effect was also significantly increased by high offense severity early in the career (first three offenses) followed by offense severity escalation shortly thereafter.

Using the longest longitudinal follow-up of criminal offending through age 70, Sampson and Laub (2003, p. 569) selected men who were arrested at least once in each decade of life to age 60, creating a very strict definition of persistence. Forty-six individuals were identified as persistent using these criteria, representing about 10% of the sample, and Sampson and Laub found that their lives were marked by dysfunctional relationships and employment patterns. Subsequent analysis showed that the frequency of crime among these highly persistent offenders declined with age as it did among other offenders in the data. Thus, even among the most active and persistent offenders as indicated by arrests, offending declined with age. Their analyses also showed that persistent offending as indicated by arrests occurred over an extended period of time, across various periods of the life course. Moreover, the lengthier one's juvenile record, the higher the likelihood of being arrested as an adult offender.

Loeber et al. (2008) examined persistence in offending using an all-source measure that combined self-reports and official conviction records, and found that: (1) almost one in five young serious offenders became persistent serious offenders over a period of 6+ years; (2) a higher level of persistence of serious offending (71%) was found for those with an onset during late childhood (ages 10–12, youngest cohort), compared to those with an onset during early adolescence (32%); and (3) 40–50% of the moderate-to-serious offenders early in life persisted in their offending over a period of about 7–9 years. In short, a very small group of persistent offenders offend at a high rate over time. They also found that more African-American youth were involved in serious offending than were white youth, but this difference vanished once controls for risk/protective factors were introduced. Finally, cohort differences were also observed, with persistence of serious offending from early to late adolescence higher for the oldest cohort (47% vs. 32%). For the oldest cohort, persistence in offending was nearly the same in the period from early to late adolescence as in the period from late adolescence to early adulthood (47% vs. 42%) (Loeber et al., 2008, p. 274).

In order to assess continuity in offending, Piquero et al. (2007) examined convictions between different age periods, from 10–15 through 36–40 in the Cambridge Study in Delinquent Development data from males in South London. Excluding the two males who died prior to age 20, they found that 46 of the 69 recorded offenders at 10–15 were recorded offenders at 16–20 (66.7%), whereas 58 out of 340 who were not convicted at 10–15 were recorded offenders at 16–20 (17.1%). The odds ratio, that is, the odds of being convicted for offending at 16–20 for those who were convicted at 10–15 (46/23) divided by the odds of being convicted for offending at 16–20 for those who were not convicted at 10–15 (58/282), was 9.72. Thus, being convicted at 10–15 increased the risk of being convicted for a crime at 16–20 by over nine times. This figure indicates considerable continuity in offending as measured by convictions. It might be expected that odds ratios for adjacent age ranges would be greater than those for nonadjacent age ranges, but this assumption was not invariably true in London, although two adjacent comparisons (16–20 vs. 21–25 and 31–35 vs. 36–40) yielded two of the highest odds ratios. It might also be expected that the two most widely separated age ranges (10–15 vs. 36–40) would yield the lowest odds ratio, and this was true. However, even in this case, the odds ratio (4.16) indicated strong continuity in officially recorded offending over this long time period. Caution should be exercised when interpreting the results among the age 36–40 group because of the very small number of convictions for offenses.

Using official police records obtained for members of three birth cohorts from Racine, Wisconsin, Shannon (1988) examined continuity in police contacts for offending from the juvenile period (age 6–17) to the young adult period (18–20) to the adult period (21+). Looking at total recorded offenses (Table 1, p. 132), continuity in all three periods was observed for 31.2% of the males and 2.2% of the females in the 1942 cohort, with respective percentages of 27.2% and 6.3% for males and females in the 1949 cohort, and 12.3% and 3.2% for males and females in the 1955 cohort. Analyses of those with no delinquency records before age 18 revealed interesting findings. For the 1942 cohort, 7.6% of males and 3.6% of females did not have a contact prior to age 18 but did so at ages 18–20 and 21+. In the 1949 cohort, the respective percentages were 4.9% and 3.6%, and for the 1955 cohort, the percentages were 3.3% and 1.4% for males and females, respectively. Given the small window for 21+ offending in the 1955 cohort, it is not surprising that exclusion of the 21+ period yielded more recorded offending, including a higher percentage of adult-onset, that is, no recorded offending before age 18 but recorded offending between ages 18–20. Additionally, it should be noted that, when traffic offenses are excluded, the corresponding percentages are reduced but the substantive story generally remains the same (with respect to persistence and adult-onset) for both males and females.

Other findings showed that the likelihood of an adult police contact was predicted by contacts during the juvenile and young adult periods (which was true across both gender and race/ethnicity, p. 134), that a high frequency and seriousness of police contacts in one period predicted the number of contacts in the next period (pp. 134–135), that discontinuity rather than continuity in contacts was the usual pattern (p. 151), and that seriousness of crimes for which people had a police contact peaked in the mid-teens, and very few individuals progressed toward contacts for more serious crime with age.

Summary. Across most studies, there exists strong continuity in offending, particularly in adjacent time periods, and the strength of this continuity increases linearly with the number of offenses previously committed; that is, the most frequent offenders tend to exhibit the strongest and longest continuity in their offending behavior. At the same time, there does exist a pattern of discontinuity such that not all offenders have continuous and persistent criminal careers, a finding that is in a large part a function of the number of offenses committed (i.e., less frequent offenders are less likely to continue offending). In general, these findings hold across samples, demographic characteristics (race/gender), time periods, and the length of observations.

Still, some evidence suggests that the measurement of offending continuity may lead to some bias in the conclusions reached. For example, not all offenders who commit crimes are detected and subsequently punished by the criminal justice system. To the extent that high-rate offenders engage in a high frequency of offenses without detection, there is the effect of underestimating the level of continuity. On the other hand, it is possible that official crime data overestimates continuity. If police think someone is an offender, they may be more likely to arrest that person. They are more likely to think that those whom they have already arrested when they were teenagers are criminals, so they are more likely to suspect them as adults and to try to build cases that lead to arrest. Thus, exploring the nature and level of continuity in offending over the life course across multiple sources of crime measurement remains a high priority, especially because most continuity-based analyses use official records.

Studying issues of continuity independent of crime, that is, conduct disorder and other antisocial behaviors, is difficult however because of researchers' limited ability to recognize heterogeneity in antisocial behavior at a very young age, as well as the lack of similarity in measurement strategies and theoretical/operational definitions over time and across studies (cf. Tremblay et al., 2006). Clearly, some individuals engage in certain forms of conduct disorder/antisocial activity early in the life course that are akin to criminal behavior but not technically so. Research does show that children exhibiting serious conduct disorder often "graduate" into other forms of antisocial behavior such that the underlying propensity is the same but the manifestation of the "crime" is a changing function of the age-appropriateness of the behavior, opportunity for certain age-appropriate acts, and official criminal justice reactions to the acts.

In particular, this line of research focuses on developmental sequences of offending, which conceptualizes antisocial behavior over time via a stepping-stone approach that can be differentiated in many ways, i.e., from minor to serious offenses (Le Blanc & Fréchette, 1989). There has been only minimal analysis of this issue (Loeber et al., 1999; Tolan & Gorman-Smith, 1998), but it tends to show a relationship between onset age and involvement in serious and violent offending with escalation toward more serious offenses as (certain kinds of) delinquents transition from childhood to adolescence. However, much more remains to be done in terms of replication across data sources, incorporation of multiple sources of data on antisocial and criminal behavior, and especially whether there is a similar set of de-escalation patterns as (most) delinquents transition out of crime in early adulthood (see also Kazemian et al., 2009).

Adult-Onset

Perhaps on the heels of scholars noting the rarity of adult-onset offending (Moffitt et al., 2001; Le Blanc, 1998), there have been only a handful of empirical studies examining adult-onset offending. This is somewhat surprising given that in a very important review of criminal careers, Blumstein et al. (1986, p. 88) concluded that "40–50% of adult offenders do not have records of juvenile police contacts." Here, we provide an overview of some recent investigations into the adult-onset question.

Kratzer and Hodgins (1999) identified a sizeable group of adult-onset offenders in the Swedish Project Metropolitan, a longitudinal study of over 14,000 males and females born in Stockholm in 1953 and followed until age 30. Their analysis indicated that 78% of the females and 55% of the males convicted as adults were adult-onset offenders, who did not have records of either official or unofficial delinquency (arrests which did not lead to prosecution) during adolescence. Findings regarding the predictors of adult-onset offending indicated that measures of childhood and adolescent characteristics, specifically intelligence test scores, could be important predictors of adult-onset offending.

Eggleston and Laub (2002) used data from the 1942 and 1949 Racine, Wisconsin, birth cohorts to examine whether there was (1) onset in adulthood and (2) if

so, whether the processes relating to adult-onset differed from the processes relating to persistence in officially recorded offending from the juvenile to adult
years. After reviewing the extant knowledge base, the authors conclude that
adult-onset involves a nontrivial percentage of cases, regardless of time period,
country, and measurement of crime (i.e., with an average adult-onset estimate of
50%), but that information regarding the distinguishing characteristics of adult-
onset vis-à-vis persistent offenders is scarce. These authors defined late- or adult-
onset as age 18 or older. After data reductions, the final sample consisted of 732
individuals followed from age 6 to age 25 (for the 1949 cohort) and 32 (for the 1942
cohort) and for whom nontraffic/nonstatus officially recorded police contact data
were obtained.

The authors identified 83 late-/adult-onsetters (or 11.3% of the 732 cases), of
which 55.4% were male and 75.9% were white, compared to the 96 persistent offenders, or 13.1% of the 732 cases, of which 69.8% were white and 87.5% were male.
Turning to their prediction analysis of the characteristics that they were able to
distinguish between adult offending with (persisters) and without (adult-onset) juvenile offending, the authors found more similarities than differences in the effect
of predictor variables on adult offending among juvenile- and adult-onset offenders.
In fact, the only variable to significantly discriminate between the two groups was
employment, which suggested that having more continual employment from high
school increased the probability of officially recorded offending among late-/adult-
onsetters. Although limited by the number of covariates available, the conclusion
reached is that the determinants of officially recorded adult-onset offending appear
to be similar to the determinants of continuation of criminal behavior from the
juvenile to adult years.

Gomez-Smith and Piquero (2005) used data from the Philadelphia Perinatal
Birth Cohort Project to examine the prevalence of—and correlates associated
with—officially recorded adult-onset offending. An important aspect of their
study was that it was the first investigation of the adult-onset question with an
African-American sample. Among the 987 subjects followed through the mid-30s,
the authors found 78 (or 7.9% of the sample) individuals who were classified as
adult-onset (i.e., no police contact prior to age 18 but who had at least one criminal
conviction at/after age 18), with more males (25.9%) than females (5.6%) in the
adult-onset group. These authors had a wide array of individual and family characteristics collected in the first dozen years of the subjects' (and mothers') lives
with which to investigate the correlates of adult-onset offending, but they did not
have any measures after adolescence. Their analysis, comparing adult-onsetters to
nonoffenders, juvenile-only offenders, and persistent (juvenile and adulthood) offenders using official records indicated that three variables distinguished between
adult-onset and nonoffenders (and to a lesser extent desisters): sex (males more
likely to be adult-onset offenders), maternal cigarette smoking (subjects whose
mothers smoked during pregnancy were more likely to be adult-onset offenders),
and the total score on the California Achievement Test (subjects who scored

higher on the test were less likely to be adult-onset offenders). Finally, and similar to the results of Eggleston and Laub, no variable distinguished adult-onset offenders from persisters.

Zara and Farrington (2009) used conviction data through age 50 from over 400 South London males participating in the Cambridge Study in Delinquent Development to examine adult criminal careers. Defining adult-onset as a first conviction at/after age 21, the authors identified 35 individuals (~8%). When these individuals were compared to early-starters and nonoffenders, the results showed that several early childhood and adolescent characteristics significantly distinguished the adult-onset group. In general, adult-onsetters were able to operate socially in an acceptable manner before adulthood but were inadequately equipped to cope with adult life demands and adversities. Moreover, early-life characteristics such as nervousness, anxiousness, social isolation, and inhibition were related to adult-onset.

Summary. One overall conclusion regarding adult-onset is that there is a non-negligible amount of adult-onset offenders, but that there do not appear to be many unique predictors for adult-onset offending (though this may have more to do with the lack and type of variables available for study in the adult period, as most studies have had to use childhood/adolescent variables, which are not very proximate to offending).

Still, there only exists a very small knowledge base regarding the empirical study of post-juvenile/adult-onset, and a number of issues limit the conclusions to be reached from these prior studies. First, there has been very little investigation of adult-onset among females. This is unfortunate because some research has suggested that females tend to initiate offending in early adulthood (Kratzer & Hodgins, 1999). Second, most studies do not generally contain variables drawn from the early-adult time period that may be more proximate to adult-onset offending. These are likely to be more situationally-based variables that consider the likelihood of crime as a problem-solving tactic (i.e., theft to make ends meet). Third, few studies have been able to distinguish between official and self-report records in adulthood, with most adult-onset studies using official records to measure crime. In the context of findings from Nagin et al. (1995), who observed that while some offenders continued to offend in adulthood according to self-reports but not conviction records, it is important that adult-onset studies collect self-report data as well as information from other sources, including spouses and children. This is especially important given that in some longitudinal studies (Elliott et al., 1989; Farrington, 2001; Moffitt et al., 2001), virtually all subjects have engaged in some form of illegal behavior by the late teenage years. Thus, self-report data are critical for the identification of adult-onset.

Finally, a specific accounting of the type of offense serving as adult-onset appears important, largely because some crime types appear more often, likely because of opportunity factors in adulthood including tax evasion, spousal assault, and white-collar/corporate crimes. For example, Weisburd and Waring (2001) reported that the average age of onset in their sample of convicted white-collar offenders was 35 years, but an earlier age was observed if the offender had a higher number of previous offenses. Also, there is some research on sex offenders that deals with adult-onset offending but such studies tend to be based on very highly selected samples. For example, Smallbone and Wortley (2004) studied the offending histories (official and self-report) of 207 adult male child molesters and found an average age of first sexual contact with a child of 32 years of age, a mean age at first conviction for any offense of 30 years, and a mean age at first conviction for a sexual offense of 37 years.

Trends in Specialization, Diversification, and Escalation from Adolescence into Adulthood

The study of specialization has been the focus of much criminological theory and empirical research, and, in fact, the notion that there are "specialists-in-crime," especially corporate and sex offenders, has been a consistent source of debate. In general, two large-scale literature reviews converge on three overall conclusions from the knowledge base regarding the involvement of offenders within and across offense categories and types (Blumstein et al., 1986; Piquero et al., 2003). First, most studies indicate that frequent offenders engage in a wide variety of crimes over their criminal career, with only a few concentrating on a select set of crime types. Second, those offenders who show some evidence of specialization appear to concentrate their offending within a large category of offenses (e.g., property crimes) and appear to switch within these larger categories (e.g., from theft to burglary to fencing). Third, there is some minimal evidence regarding a slight trend toward increasing specialization with age, but it is premature to draw any definitive conclusion regarding this finding.

Although these general observations present a portrait of the current state of specialization research, there are a small handful of studies that have examined the nature of offense patterning from the juvenile to adult periods. In one of the first studies to examine this issue, Piquero et al. (1999) used data from the 1958 Philadelphia Birth Cohort, covering the period from ages 8–26, and found a relationship between onset age and officially recorded offending versatility (i.e., earlier onset→less specialization) but the association disappeared after controlling for age, suggesting that offenders tend to become somewhat more specialized in crimes for which they were apprehended over time regardless of the age at which they initiated offending. Also using the same Philadelphia data, Mazerolle and colleagues (2000) further investigated the interrelationships between gender, onset age, persistence, and specialization in officially recorded offending and found that male and female offenders who began their offending early in life and persisted into adulthood were arrested for more diverse offenses.

Three other studies provide long-term analyses of the specialization question. First, using conviction records from the South London male cohort through age 40, Piquero et al. (2007) found little evidence of specialization-in-violence, and also concluded that the strongest predictor of a violent conviction over the course of a career was the number of convictions. More frequent offenders had a higher likelihood of conviction for a violent crime. In the second study, Nieuwbeerta et al. (2009) introduced and applied a new method for studying individual offender specialization over the life course, based on the diversity index, to data on a sample of Dutch offenders through age 72. Three specific findings emerged from their analysis. First, there was much diversity in individual, officially recorded offending patterns over the life course. Second, the authors found evidence of an age-diversity curve, in which there was increasing diversity between early adolescence and young adulthood but then specialization during adulthood. Finally, when they isolated frequent offenders and further disaggregated the age-diversity curve, they found that high diversity was the most common pattern during adulthood, followed by a pattern of specialization. Very few frequent offenders remained highly specialized throughout the lifespan, and when offenders did specialize during adulthood they tended to specialize in property crimes. In the third investigation, Armstrong (2008) used longitudinal data from a cohort of California parolees followed from release into adulthood and found that trends in specialization over arrest/conviction number were more likely to reflect changes in specialization over age.

In another investigation, Loeber et al. (2008) examined specialization in serious, violent offending using data from two (youngest and oldest) cohorts from the Pittsburgh Youth Study and approached the study of specialization in two different ways. First, using an all-source measure of offending based on self-reported delinquency and convictions, they found that, while most offenders were versatile in committing theft and violence, a nontrivial proportion committed only theft or only violence. In fact, about one-half of violent offenders were specialists, that is, they did not commit theft, compared to one-third of the serious theft offenders who did not commit violent offenses (p. 317). Second, they found mixed evidence regarding changes in specialization across age. Based on the all-source measure of offending, offense specialization for theft and violence in the youngest cohort was curvilinear—highest at ages 10–12 and 17–19, but lowest at ages 13–16. For the oldest cohort specialization in violence increased with age from 53% in early adolescence (ages 13–16) to 83% in early adulthood (ages 20–25), whereas theft specialization was curvilinear, lowest during late adolescence (ages 17–19) and increasing during early adulthood (p. 130). Third, when they examined the specialization question through the lens of dual-trajectory analysis, they found that boys who follow a specific trajectory in one form of serious delinquency also tended to follow a similar trajectory in the other forms of serious delinquency. However, while the trajectory analysis detected more violence than theft specialization, in both cohorts there were groups of violent offenders who were low in theft, but serious theft offenders who did not engage in violence were exceedingly rare. In other words, serious theft offenders were also in most cases violent offenders (p. 265).

Aside from the specialization question, the issue of escalation and de-escalation is also of central import to criminal careers. Escalation refers to an increase in the severity of offenses committed by individuals over time while de-escalation relates to the opposite process, a progression from serious to minor offending over time. Many developmental models advance a stepping-stone approach toward the escalation question, oftentimes assuming that lengthy criminal careers are marked by a general trend toward escalation in the severity of offenses over the course of a career (Elliott, 1994; Loeber et al., 1999). Because data requirements for the escalation/de-escalation question require information on the nature of each offense committed by individuals over the course of their criminal careers, there have not been many empirical investigations of this question (Blumstein et al., 1988). Two recent efforts however, are illustrative.

Using self-report data from the Pittsburgh Youth Study referenced above, Loeber et al. (2008, p. 101) assessed developmental sequences in offending and found that, in general, theft preceded violence but the pattern was more common for the youngest cohort. Further, they found that the probability of progression to the next level of seriousness decreased with increasing seriousness and that there was little escalation to serious forms of violence. Finally, among the oldest cohort, the movement toward a higher prevalence of serious offending appears to have been due to a higher prevalence of the precursors of minor and moderate offending.

In the second study, Kazemian et al. (2009) undertook a comparative analysis of de-escalation patterns between ages 17–18 and 32, based on self-report and official records data from the Cambridge Study in Delinquent Development and the Montreal Two Samples Longitudinal Study (a sample of 470 adjudicated French-Canadian males). In addition to studying within-individual changes in escalation/de-escalation, they also investigated the extent to which cognitive predispositions and social bonds related to patterns of de-escalation and whether it was possible to make predictions over a 15-year period about offending in adulthood. Although the within-individual analysis showed that the key predictors measured at ages 17–18 were weakly related to de-escalation up to age 32, the measures were stronger predictors of between-individual differences in offending gravity.

Summary. The analyses of specialization in criminal careers suggest that there is little specific concentration within offense types among most offenders. This overall conclusion holds with respect to different samples, measures of offending (including the incorrect presumption of specialization among sex offenders; Zimring et al., 2008, 2009), time periods, and different measurement strategies. However, because few specialization studies have linked the juvenile and early adult periods, and linked across the full life course in particular, it is premature to draw any firm conclusion regarding the nature of specialization with age and over time. Moreover, because of data limitations, there is much less research on patterns of escalation and de-escalation within criminal careers over the life course, and even less is known about the predictors of potential changes in the severity of offenses over time.

More specifically, there are a series of methodological issues and decisions that may influence the conclusions drawn about changes in offending patterns over time. First, the decision regarding the number and type of offense categories is critical because it will necessarily influence the amount of switching that is detected, across and within categories. Traditionally, researchers have employed broad categories (violent, property, drug, other), but some researchers focus specifically on specific crime types (sex offending, robbery, assault, etc.; Francis et al., 2004; Sullivan et al., 2006; Soothill, Francis, Ackerley, & Humphreys, 2008), how much time is needed in order to detect changes in an offender's offense mix, and whether issues of aggregation (whether to study offense mix at the weekly, monthly, or yearly levels) impact findings (McGloin et al., 2007). For instance, criminal careers may be characterized by short-term specialization (in the form of crime sprees and the like), but long-term versatility.

Second, studies have tended to study specialization primarily with official records of arrests and/or convictions which, because of the inherent biases associated with official records, may have a tendency to capture only more serious crimes (and/or identify those more frequent offenders who have a higher likelihood of drawing attention from the criminal justice system; see Lynam et al., 2004). Third, there exist a number of statistical approaches to examine specialization, for example, Forward Specialization Coefficient, Diversity Index, Proportion of Certain Crimes Belonging to a Certain Category, Item Response Theory, etc., all of which have been used and critiqued, and all of which, to some degree, have properties that may influence the conclusions drawn from the study (Osgood & Schreck, 2007). Fourth, largely due to data limitations, few efforts have examined the correlates associated with specialization; thus, it remains unknown how specialization may develop over the life course (McGloin et al., 2007). Finally, very few studies have investigated specialization across demographic groups, especially race and gender, as well as the differential degrees of specialization according to neighborhood and opportunity structures (e.g., Armstrong & Britt, 2004; Schreck, McGloin, & Kirk, 2009). These issues offer researchers valuable insight as they investigate the specialization issue, especially in how specialization increases across the juvenile/adult time periods, as well as the issue of escalation and de-escalation over time, a much less-studied research question.

Stability and Change

One of the most important and well-documented of all criminological facts is the strong correlation between prior and future criminal activity. Two prominent explanations have been put forth to account for this strong relationship, population heterogeneity and state dependence (Nagin & Paternoster, 1991, 2000). The former explanation suggests that the correlation is due to time-stable population differences in the underlying proclivity to crime. Here, individuals are believed to vary in their propensity to commit crime and this (typically unobserved) propensity explains the strong link between past and future criminal conduct. The latter explanation suggests that crime exerts an undesirable effect on social bonds, conventional attachments, and so forth. In this context, the experience of crime materially influences the individual in such a way as to engender more crime in the future. A third explanation combines the two perspectives and suggests that both processes relate to future criminal activity in varying respects and magnitude over the life course.

Various studies have demonstrated that offending patterns are characterized by both stability and change in offending over the life course, and there is some evidence regarding the degree of continuity between juvenile delinquency and criminal behavior in early adulthood. One noteworthy descriptive account was conducted by Stattin and Magnusson (1991), who studied the stability/change relationship between childhood (up to age 14), adolescence (ages 15–20), and early adulthood (ages 21–30) using longitudinal data for 709 Swedish males. A number of findings emerged from their analysis. First, they observed modest correlations reflecting the stability of officially recorded criminal activity (i.e., .40 between childhood and adolescence, .34 between childhood and early adulthood, and .38 between adolescence and early adulthood). Second, there was little evidence of specialization in crime across the time periods and into adulthood, even among those individuals who offended across time periods. Finally, as found in many other criminological studies, a small number of males who offended in all three time periods were responsible for most of the crime in the sample, and showed little specialization.

Other studies have moved beyond descriptive analyses of the relationship between past and future offending and have examined the predictors associated with this association, as well as the degree to which each perspective accounts for the relationship. Using a sample of high school students from South Carolina, Nagin and Paternoster's (1991) analysis of self-report data indicated that, even after accounting for unobserved heterogeneity, there still remained a significant correlation between prior and future criminal activity. Nagin and Farrington (1992a) used conviction records for the South London males in the Cambridge Study in Delinquent Development and, although their analysis revealed support for both explanations, the evidence in favor of the persistent heterogeneity explanation was quite strong, so much so that once unobserved heterogeneity was considered, the state dependence effect was greatly diminished. In a follow-up study, these same authors examined an age-at-onset state dependence effect and found once again that, after controlling for persistent unobserved heterogeneity, the once significant age-at-onset effect was reduced to insignificance, suggesting that the association between prior and future convictions was largely due to persistent unobserved heterogeneity (Nagin & Farrington, 1992b).

In a series of analyses using data from the Glueck study, Sampson and Laub (1993; Laub et al., 1998; Laub & Sampson, 2003; Sampson, Laub, & Wimer, 2006) have examined the linkages between prior and future arrests across time periods, especially those between the second and third decade of life. The authors have consistently found evidence in favor of a mixed perspective combining aspects of population heterogeneity and state dependence, even after controlling for unobserved heterogeneity. Key findings from their combined studies show that life events such as (a good) marriage—especially one's attachment/investment associated with the marriage—relate to (dis-)continued crime over the life course in addition to other observed and unobserved heterogeneity.

Similar findings for the importance of a combined perspective have been observed. For example, Paternoster et al. (1997) examined the offending patterns of 838 male offenders released from North Carolina (juvenile) training schools and followed into adulthood. In an analysis controlling only for observed heterogeneity, the authors found a strong and significant state dependence effect (i.e., whether the male was arrested in the previous year); this effect was substantially reduced (by 64%) but remained significant in a model controlling for unobserved heterogeneity. Paternoster and colleagues also examined whether there were differences across two distinct groups of offenders, differentiated by age at first adjudication. Findings indicated mixed evidence regarding the usefulness of splitting the sample into offender groups and assessing the past versus future crime relationship, but an age-15 cut-point for early-/late-starting offenders yielded findings consistent with a state dependence explanation. Further, in a very comprehensive analysis of two longitudinal cohorts of California parolees (released in 1981–2 and in 1986–7), Ezell and Cohen (2005) found: (1) a positive association between past and future arrests; (2) after controlling for persistent unobserved heterogeneity using both parametric and non-parametric methods, there was still a significant relationship between prior and future offending, i.e., a state dependence effect; and (3) the state dependence effect did not vary across distinct latent classes of offenders.

Other studies have found support for a mixed model of population heterogeneity and state dependence using both self-report and officially recorded crime. For example, Horney et al. (1995), using self-reported life calendar data from Nebraska felons; Piquero et al. (2002), using a longitudinal cohort of California parolees followed into their 20s; and Theobald and Farrington (2009), using the South London male cohort followed to age 48 all report findings of a crime-inhibiting effect of marriage over and above observed and unobserved heterogeneity. However, Paternoster and Brame (1997), using self-report data from the National Youth Survey (NYS), found that both prior delinquency and exposure to delinquent peers were significantly related to crime, even after controlling for unobserved heterogeneity. After dividing the NYS sample into two groups based on offending propensity at age 12, the authors found no evidence that prior offending or delinquent peers exerted differential effects on future crime across the two offender groups. Cernkovich and

Giordano (2001) used data from two samples (a sample of individuals in Ohio households and a sample of institutionalized offenders, both interviewed as adolescents in 1982, 1992, and 1995, when both groups were young adults) in order to investigate stability and change patterns between adolescence and early adulthood. Their analysis indicated that there was a strong linkage between prior and future crime in both samples, but that social bonding levels were associated with adult crime only in the household sample (supporting a combined population heterogeneity/state dependence explanation), perhaps in large part because there was little change in the bonding measures among the serious, institutionalized offenders.

Two final studies are noteworthy in that they expressly investigated the linkage between adolescent and adult offending using novel methodological approaches. In the first study, Paternoster et al. (2001) analyzed convictions through age 40 for the South London male sample and found that variations in adult offending were consistent with a random process after conditioning on adolescent offending. In other words, variations in adult convictions could be attributed to two primary sources: the adolescent's conviction history and Poisson variations (in a Poisson process events are assumed to arrive randomly in time and at a constant rate) in adult convictions. Substantively, this finding suggests that additional information based on time trends and/or life experiences during adulthood is unnecessary to fit the adult conviction distribution, and all that is necessary for understanding the adult conviction distribution is knowledge of the individual's convictions during adolescence. In an important replication and extension, Piquero et al. (2005) conducted an analysis of the official conviction records from the ~1,000 males and females participating in the Dunedin Multidisciplinary Health and Human Development Study through age 26. Not only did these authors replicate the substantive finding from the earlier Paternoster et al. investigation, they also detected similar findings for both males and females. In short, both studies provide very strong evidence of a persistent heterogeneity explanation of crime.

Of course, even the strongest designed study cannot take into consideration every possible observed individual characteristic related to criminal activity, which presents a significant limitation to previous investigations because unmeasured sources of persistent heterogeneity may relate to future crime in important ways. This was recognized in an important methodological study by Bushway et al. (1999), who examined the relationship between past and future crimes while controlling for unmeasured sources of persistent heterogeneity. These authors used offending data from 13,160 males in the 1958 Philadelphia Birth Cohort study through age 26 and applied three different statistical approaches (random effects, semiparametric random effects, and fixed effects models), all of which make a series of different statistical assumptions. They found that, while both population heterogeneity and state dependence effects were important, unobserved heterogeneity exerted an important and rather strong effect on future crime. Thus, failing to account for unobserved heterogeneity can produce biased estimates in favor of a state dependence argument compared with a persistent heterogeneity argument.

Summary. The issue of stability versus change strikes at the core of several important theoretical debates in criminology regarding the relationship between past and future crimes. The empirical knowledge base is starting to accumulate and coalesce on a few key conclusions. First, across most studies, using different types of samples, measures of criminal activity, and time periods, there is strong evidence regarding a population heterogeneity explanation linking past to future crime. Second, with the exception of the Paternoster et al. (2001) and Piquero et al. (2005) investigations, which were based on a unique methodological approach, most studies report evidence of a state dependence effect linking a series of different life events to subsequent criminal activity, even after controlling for observed and unobserved population heterogeneity. Taken together, these findings offer strong evidence of a mixed population heterogeneity/state dependence perspective linking prior and future crimes.

At the same time, some issues that are worthy of theoretical and methodological attention remain. Theoretically, criminologists need to move beyond their focus, largely due to data constraints, on a select few life events (marriage, jobs, peers) and onto the effects of other life circumstances such as parenting children, incarceration, and mobility. Also, theorists need to seriously consider if the state dependence effects vary across different periods of the life course and/or across different demographic groups. Methodologically, researchers need to continue their work exploring the consequences associated with the initial conditions assumption, or the focus on criminal activity measured in the initial observation (which is required so that the model is able to obtain an unbiased estimate of the individual-specific component of the error term; Ezell and Cohen, 2005, p. 75), as well as the distributional form of the unobserved heterogeneity effects (Brame et al., 1999; Bushway et al., 1999). On this latter point, more work is needed regarding whether these assumptions vary according to sample characteristics and across different types of crime measures, as well as the degree of (true) skewness of unobserved heterogeneity in the population generally, and across different offender samples in particular. There is a pressing need for more attention and research on these and related issues (Nagin & Paternoster, 2000; Cernkovich and Giordano, 2001).

Co-Offending

The state of knowledge on co-offending patterns remains underdeveloped in criminology, in large part because of the lack of individual-level longitudinal data necessary to study offending and co-offending patterns within persons over time (Sarnecki, 2001; McCord & Conway, 2002; McGloin & Piquero, 2009; Goldweber et al., 2011). Moreover, most information that exists with respect to co-offending has been available for the juvenile period only, and very few studies have linked offending and co-offending patterns from the juvenile to adult years. Because of this sizeable gap in the research literature, we highlight three studies that have examined co-offending using different data sources and time periods.

Stolzenberg and D'Alessio (2008) used data from the National Incident Based Reporting System (NIBRS), which contains over 466,000 criminal arrests from seven states, in order to examine the relationships between age, offending, and co-offending. Two key findings emerged from their study. First, co-offending arrest patterns by age do not offer much insight into why the classic aggregate age-crime curve appears the way it does, as results indicate that the age-crime curve appears the same for both solo- and co-offending. Further, most offending in the NIBRS data is comprised of solo- and not co-offending, regardless of age. Second, a supplemental analysis using crimes reported to the police replicated the arrest-based results reported above. Importantly, although these results are based on an analysis of official record data that does not include longitudinal information about co-offending at the individual-level, they cast some doubt on the view that most juvenile offenses are characterized by co-offending.

Extending previous co-offending analyses by Reiss and Farrington (1991), Piquero et al. (2007) used data from the Cambridge Study in Delinquent Development of South London males through age 40 to examine the nature and extent of co-offending. These authors found that: (1) like the age/crime curve, the age/co-offending curve peaked in the late teenage years; (2) the incidence of co-offending decreased with age primarily because individual offenders changed and became less likely to offend with others, rather than because of selective attrition of co-offenders or greater persistence of those who offend primarily alone; (3) co-offending appeared more common for some crimes (burglary, robbery) than others; (4) there was a relationship between the total number of co-offenders in a person's career and career length, such that individuals with short career lengths (<5 years) tended to associate with fewer co-offenders, and individuals with very lengthy careers (20+ years) had many co-offenders throughout their criminal careers (averaging over 10 co-offenders), likely because this reflected a larger number of offenses; (5) there was a strong relationship between age at first conviction and the mean total number of co-offenders in a person's career; offenders with an early age at first conviction tended to have, on average, a higher total mean number of co-offenders throughout their careers while individuals with a later age at first conviction tended to have, on average, fewer co-offenders; and, as expected, co-offending varied with age of onset (early-onset offenders had a significantly higher number of co-offenders than late-onset offenders); (6) the relationship between co-offending and offense type, with a few exceptions (fraud and robbery) was independent of age, and reflected more of a change in offense type over age than a pattern based on age within offense type; (7) the relationship between career length and co-offending indicated that, while those with shorter career lengths had little experience with co-offending, the mean number of co-offenders per offense stayed relatively constant with career length; (8) when examining persistent offenders (those 24 males who had each committed at least 10 offenses by age 40), the analyses indicated that 52.5% of the total crimes committed by persistent offenders were committed alone; only one person was exclusively a solo offender, three persons were predominantly solo offenders, and one was predominantly a co-offender; and (9) overall, exclusive solo-offending was rare (only one person offended only alone) and exclusive co-offending was uncommon at all ages.

It is important to note that Stolzenberg and D'Alessio (2008) and Piquero et al. (2007) arrive at very different conclusions regarding the nature of co-offending. This is likely the case because of the data used to examine the issue. In the former study, arrest and offense information based on aggregate, cross-sectional data was used, while in the latter study, longitudinal individual-level information was employed.

In the third study, van Mastrigt and Farrington (2009) used the universe of officially recorded offenses (105,348 offenses, 61,646 offenders, 120,274 offense participations examined) that were cleared by a large metropolitan police force located in the North of England between 2002 and 2005 to examine the interrelationships between co-offending and age, gender, and crime type. Several important results emerged from their study. First, a minority of detected official crime involved multiple offenders. Second, much like the age-crime relationship, co-offending decreased with age. Third, co-offending was greater for females than males. Fourth, co-offending varied by crime type, and was most common for burglary and robbery.

Summary. There is an absence of empirical studies regarding co-offending generally, and co-offending patterns between the juvenile and adult periods in particular. The lack of co-offending studies is directly a function of lack of data on the characteristics of individual offenses. For example, very few of the longitudinal offending data sources in criminology contain detailed information for each individual offense committed by each individual offender. Moreover, the extent to which such data is available in official record sources is highly variable across police and correctional departments, such that there are important data quality concerns. To the extent that self-report data can be collected at the individual level with respect to the nature and characteristics of each criminal event over time, much needed information will be provided on co-offending. This is a key priority for future research, especially because of the importance of shifts in peer relationships and peer contexts in the transition from adolescence to adulthood (Moffitt, 1993; Laub and Sampson, 2003, p.146).

Conclusions and Recommendations

This chapter provided an overview of some of the main findings from criminal career research, with a particular emphasis on changes observed in criminal career dimensions between adolescence and adulthood. These findings have been an important source of background information regarding the nature of offending, with respect to the modification and formulation of developmental/life-course criminology theories, and for consideration in public policy decision-making regarding system responses to child and adolescent offenders, including decisions associated with sentence selection and prevention/intervention efforts. The review of extant research presented in this chapter has led us to formulate some key recommendations for future research as well as to provide some recommendations for practitioners and policy-makers.

Research recommendations. First, there is a need to study criminal careers with more comprehensive data that include long follow-ups that extend well into adulthood, that include both self-reports and official records in order to distinguish between individuals who commit crimes either as juveniles or as adults but who are or are not apprehended (Brame et al., 2004; Blumstein et al., 2010), that include additional measures of changes in life circumstances such as living with children or moving to a different neighborhood, and that are appropriate for studying within-individual change in criminal behavior. These data are indispensable for the study of changes in criminal career trends in the transition between adolescence and adulthood, namely patterns of stability and change in offending behavior generally, and the stops and starts (i.e., intermittency) that characterize many criminal careers (Laub & Sampson, 2003; Piquero, 2004). Second, research is needed on the criminal career trends of different demographic groups. For example, there is a need for comparisons of offending patterns over time across gender and race (Farrington et al., 2007; Piquero & Brame, 2008). Future analyses should extend beyond the black/white dichotomy, and explore criminal career trends for other ethnic and racial groups, including Hispanics and Asians. These studies will need to investigate heterogeneity within these broad categories given the cultural differences within them (Maldonado-Molina et al., 2009) and the likely relationships between immigration status—including recency of immigration and number of generations in the United States—and criminal behavior (Sampson et al., 2005). Further, it will be important to gather criminal career information in new data sources—both in the United States and abroad—so as to not rely on the same handful of longitudinal studies to provide baseline criminal career data. This will be important for purposes of generalization. Finally, comparison of criminal career offending patterns among individuals living in the same city, but born during different time and historical periods, would be important not only to examine how age-crime relations change over time in the same locale, but also how age of onset, crime type mix, and system responses vary over time in the same locale. The Pittsburgh Youth Study has served as the sole—but very important—exemplar of the importance of this issue and associated findings.

Third, it is essential to acquire a better understanding of the processes underlying changing criminal career patterns (specialization, de-escalation, deceleration, etc.) in order to better grasp the structure of criminal careers in terms of length, intensity, and seriousness. This knowledge is particularly crucial in the transition from adolescence to adulthood, as this coincides with the peak in the age-crime curve, and would offer some valuable insight for incapacitation and reentry policies (Blumstein & Piquero, 2007).

Fourth, while there has been an abundance of studies on juvenile onset, it is also important to advance knowledge about adult-onset offending, to examine the predictors of adult-onset offending based on individual and social measures in adulthood, and to identify the dimensions of the transition from adolescence to adulthood that may contribute to adult-onset offending.

Fifth, as articulated throughout this chapter, much of the knowledge base has been garnered from either official or self-report records, with very few efforts combining both sources of information (Lidz et al., 2007). An understanding of the probability of an official record given self-reported offending is important not only for the relationship between age and crime (Kirk, 2006), but also with respect to policy because it provides an estimate of the amount of antisocial behavior that does not get officially processed (Babinski et al., 2001; Blumstein et al., 2010). Additionally, other reports of offending from sources other than the main respondent, to include parent-, teacher-, and peer-informants, may also be beneficial with respect to providing a more complete account of the nature of offending. Further, it would be important to gather qualitative information on offending—especially the circumstances associated with offending and offending decisions—so as to provide some context for understanding the quantitative data.

Sixth, there are several difficulties associated with studying persistence, which include the theoretical and empirical definitions associated with the term (Soothill et al., 2009; Piquero, 2009), and many studies do not use similar definitions, making it difficult to compare across studies. For example, is a persistent offender one who offends 10 times in one year or once a year for 10 years (Piquero, Sullivan, & Farrington, 2010); do these two definitions identify the same person and do the same risk factors relate to both identifications equally well?

Finally, very little is known about changes in patterns of co-offending over time. More research is needed on changes in co-offending trends between adolescence and adulthood, a topic that is likely to inform both theory and policy.

Policy recommendations. The study of criminal careers has the potential to provide useful information to practitioners and policy-makers in order to make better decisions regarding prediction, punishment, and prevention/intervention efforts. With respect to predicting which offenders will be the most serious and long-term and how best to punish such offenders, studying the continuity of offending from adolescence to adulthood is critical because this is the period when many policy officials will make decisions regarding the incarceration of offenders—some of whom will curtail their offending naturally and some of whom will persist into adulthood. Because continuity in offending behavior across periods of the life course is so strong, a natural question is whether prediction of adult offending depends on offending as a juvenile (Robins, 1978).

Recently, Blumstein and Nakamura (2009) studied the key question of: "how long does it take for an individual with a prior criminal record and no subsequent criminal involvement to be of no greater risk than persons of the same age in the general population, and does this time vary by crime type and age at the prior arrest?" Using data from a sample of individuals arrested for the first time as adults in New York State in 1980 (allowing for a 27-year follow-up), and focusing on 16, 18, and 20 year-olds arrested for robbery, burglary, and aggravated assault, the authors examined the "close enough" issue. They found that the risk of recidivism decreased monotonically with time clean. There is some point at which one can be confident that redemption has occurred, where the risk of re-offending has subsided to the level of a reasonable comparison group (i.e., T^{**}, or the number of years that those who have a prior arrest need to stay clean to be considered "close enough" to those who have never been arrested). Results also showed that T^{**} varied with age and crime type; younger starters and violent offenders have to wait longer to be comparable with a person of the same age from the general population and to meet the criterion of redemption. In short, knowledge about the continuity of offending from adolescent to early adult years generally can provide important information regarding the ability of criminal justice personnel to make effective decisions in light of scarce resources.

In this regard, knowledge about (average) criminal career length also offers useful information to assist decision-makers when planning and meting out sentences of varying durations. To the extent that criminal careers are short on average, then this would call for shorter sentences, whereas if knowledge emerges regarding longer average career lengths, then longer sentences may be necessary (Blumstein & Piquero, 2007). Yet, in the few career length studies that exist, it has been found that criminal careers are of a short duration (typically under 10 years), which calls into question many of the long-term sentences that have characterized American penal policy.

Aside from prediction/punishment policy decisions, other policy options focus on preventing criminal career onset and persistence. Here, two recent meta-analyses have provided strong evidence that very early child prevention programming offers an effective tactic at preventing delinquency and crime. In the first study, Piquero et al. (2009) conducted a meta-analysis of 55 early family/parent training studies in the United States and abroad and showed that such programs were a very effective intervention for reducing behavior problems among young children. In the second study, Piquero et al. (2010) conducted a meta-analyses of 34 programs designed to improve self-control up to age 10 among children and adolescents and found that the programs improved a child/adolescent's self-control and that the interventions also reduced delinquency.

Practitioners and policymakers have a range of options when deciding what to do with current and future (serious) offenders. These options include both short-term and long-term decisions and investments. Criminal career data can provide useful information about the longitudinal patterning of criminal activity so as to make informed and competent decisions given the limited resources available to the various systems that have to deal with delinquent/criminal offending and its consequences.

Notes

1. One of the key features of the PYS is its incorporation of both self-reported and official measures of offending. In general, the findings indicate that a larger proportion of subjects engage in serious offenses during early adolescence (via self-reports) without being arrested than during later adolescence (p.121), and conviction records show even less prevalence than arrest-based official measures because of the filtering process of the criminal justice system. In general, subsequent analyses by Loeber et al. (2008, pp. 124–125) lead to the conclusion that some misclassification may occur if serious violent offenders and serious theft offenders are identified solely via official records, for as many as 70% of the serious violent offenders in the two cohorts were not convicted for their violence. Longitudinal data containing repeated self-report and official measures are the exception and not the norm in criminology (Blumstein et al., 2010).

2. Researchers have recently employed semi-parametric mixture models to examine prevalence/frequency of offending over the life course (Nagin, 2005). These models parcel out distinct offending groups based on their offending careers, with evidence showing unique age/crime curves for the various latent classes as well as unique predictors associated with latent class memberships (see review in Piquero, 2008). Loeber et al. (2008, pp. 236–245) also performed this type of analytic technique for trajectories of violence and theft for both cohorts, the results of which indicated that, while the trajectories varied mostly by their peak age, all of them eventually declined (see also Laub and Sampson, 2003).

References

Armstrong, T.A. (2008). Exploring the impact of changes in group composition on trends in specialization. *Crime and Delinquency*, 54, 366–389.

Armstrong, T.A., & Britt, C. (2004). The effect of offender characteristics on offense specialization and escalation. *Justice Quarterly*, 21, 843–876.

Babinksi, L.M., Hartsough, C.S., & Lambert, N.M. (2001). A comparison of self-report of criminal involvement and official arrest records. *Aggressive Behavior*, 27, 44–54.

Blumstein, A., Cohen, J., Piquero, A.R., & Visher, C.A. (2010). Linking the crime and arrest processes to measure variations in individual arrest risk per crime. *Journal of Quantitative Criminology*, 26, 533–548.

Blumstein, A., Cohen, J., Roth, J.A., & Visher, C.A. (1986). *Criminal careers and "career criminals."* Washington, DC, National Academy Press.

Blumstein, A., & Nakamura, K. (2009). Redemption in the presence of widespread criminal background checks. *Criminology*, 47, 327–360.

Blumstein, A., & Piquero, A.R. (2007). Criminal careers research and rational sentencing policy. *Criminology and Public Policy*, 6, 679–688.

Brame, R., Bushway, S., & Paternoster, R. (1999). On the use of panel research designs and random effects models to investigate static and dynamic theories of criminal offending. *Criminology*, 37, 599–641.

Brame, R., Fagan, J., Piquero, A.R., Schubert, C., & Steinberg, L. (2004). Criminal careers of serious delinquents in two cities. *Youth Violence and Juvenile Justice*, 2, 256–272.

Bushway, S., Brame, R., & Paternoster, R. (1999). Assessing stability and change in criminal offending: A comparison of random effects, semiparametric, and fixed effects modeling strategies. *Journal of Quantitative Criminology*, 15, 23–61.

Cernkovich, S.A. & Giordano, P.C. (2001). Stability and change in antisocial behavior: The transition from adolescence to early adulthood. *Criminology*, 39, 371–410.

Eggleston, E., & Laub, J.H. (2002). The onset of offending: A neglected dimension of the criminal career. *Journal of Criminal Justice*, 30, 603–622.

Elliott, D.S. (1994). Serious violent offenders: Onset, developmental course, and termination–The American Society of Criminology 1993 Presidential Address. *Criminology*, 32, 1–21.

Elliott, D.S., Huizinga, D., & Menard, S. (1989). *Multiple problem youth: Delinquency, substance use, and mental health problems*. New York: Springer.

Ezell, M.E., & Cohen, L.E. (2005). *Desisting from crime: Continuity and change in long-term crime patterns of serious chronic offenders*. Oxford: Oxford University Press.

Farrington, D.P. (2005). *Integrated developmental and life-course theories of offending*. New Brunswick, NJ: Transaction.

Farrington, D.P., Coid, J.W., Harnett, L., Jolliffe, D., Soteriu, N., Turner, R., & West, D.J. (2006). *Criminal careers up to age 50 and life success up to age 48. New findings from the Cambridge Study in Delinquent Development*. Home Office Research Study 299. London, UK: Home Office Research, Development and Statistics Directorate.

Farrington, D.P., Jolliffe, D., Hawkins, J.D., Catalano, R.F., Hill, K.G., & Kosterman, R. (2007). Why are boys more likely to be referred to juvenile court? Gender differences in official and self-reported delinquency. *Victims and Offenders*, 3, 123–145.

Farrington, D.P., Jolliffe, D., Loeber, R., Stouthamer-Loeber, M., & Kalb, L. (2001). The concentration of offenders in families, and family criminality in the prediction of boys' delinquency. *Journal of Adolescence*, 24, 579–596.

Francis, B., Soothill, K., & Fligelstone, R. (2004). Identifying patterns of offending behaviour: A new approach to typologies of crime. *European Journal of Criminology*, 1, 47–87.

Goldweber, A., Dmitrieva, J., Cauffman, E., Piquero, A.R., & Steinberg, L. (2011). The development of criminal style in adolescence and young adulthood: Separating the lemmings from the loners. *Journal of Youth and Adolescence*, 40, 332–346.

Gomez-Smith, Z. & Piquero, A.R. (2005). An examination of adult onset offending. *Journal of Criminal Justice*, 33, 515–525.

Horney, J., Osgood, D.W., & Marshall, I.H. (1995). Criminal careers in the short-term: Intra-individual variability in crime and its relation to local life circumstances. *American Sociological Review*, 60, 655–673.

Kazemian, L., Farrington, D.P., & Le Blanc, M. (2009). Can we make long-term accurate predictions about patterns of de-escalation in offending behavior? *Journal of Youth and Adolescence*, 38, 384–400.

Kirk, D.S. (2006). Examining the divergence across self-report and official data sources on inferences about the adolescent life-course of crime. *Journal of Quantitative Criminology*, 22, 107–129.

Kratzer, L., & Hodgins, S. (1999). A typology of offenders: A test of Moffitt's theory among males and females from childhood to age 30. *Criminal Behaviour and Mental Health*, 9, 57–73.

Laub, J.H., Nagin, D.S., & Sampson, R.J. (1998). Trajectories of change in criminal offending: Good marriages and the desistance process. *American Sociological Review*, 63, 225–238.

Laub, J.H., & Sampson, R.J. (2003). *Shared beginnings, divergent lives*. Cambridge, MA: Harvard University Press.

Le Blanc, M. (1998). Screening of serious and violent juvenile offenders: Identification, classification, and prediction. In R. Loeber & D.P. Farrington (Eds.), *Serious and violent juvenile offenders: Risk factors and successful interventions*. Thousand Oaks, CA: Sage.

Le Blanc, M., & Fréchette, M. (1989). *Male criminal activity from childhood through youth: Multilevel and developmental perspectives*. New York: Springer.

Le Blanc, M. & Loeber, R. (1998). Developmental criminology updated. In M. Tonry (Ed.), *Crime and Justice* (Vol. 23, pp. 115–197). Chicago IL: Chicago University Press.

Lidz, C.W., Banks, S., Simon, L., Schubert, C., & Mulvey, E.P. (2007). Violence and mental illness: A new analytic approach. *Law and Human Behavior*, 31, 23–31.

Loeber, R., Farrington, D.P., Stouthamer-Loeber, M., & White, H.R. (2008). *Violence and serious theft: Development and prediction from childhood to adulthood*. New York: Routledge.

Loeber, R., & Le Blanc, M. (1990). Toward a developmental criminology. In M. Tonry & N. Morris (Eds.), *Crime and Justice* (Vol. 12, pp. 375–473). Chicago IL: University of Chicago Press.

Loeber, R., Wei, E., Stouthamer-Loeber, M., Huizinga, D., & Thornberry, T.P. (1999). Behavioral antecedents to serious and violent offending: Joint analysis from the Denver Youth Study, Pittsburgh Youth Study, and the Rochester Youth Development Study. *Studies on Crime and Crime Prevention*, 8, 245–263.

Lynam, D.R., Piquero, A.R., & Moffitt, T.E. (2004). Specialization and the propensity to violence: Support from self-reports but not official records. *Journal of Contemporary Criminal Justice*, 20, 215–228.

Maldonado-Molina, M.M., Piquero, A.R., Jennings, W.G., Bird, H., & Canino, G. (2009). Trajectories of delinquency among Puerto Rican children and adolescents at two sites. *Journal of Research in Crime and Delinquency*, 46, 144–181.

Mazerolle, P., Brame, R., Paternoster, R., Piquero, A., & Dean, C. (2000). Onset age, persistence, and offending versatility comparisons across gender. *Criminology*, 38, 1143–1172.

McCord, J. (1978). A thirty-year follow-up of treatment effects. *American Psychologist*, 33, 284–289.

McCord, J., & Conway, K.P. (2002). Patterns of juvenile delinquency and co-offending. In R. Waring & D. Weisburd (Eds.), *Crime and social organization* (pp. 15–30). New Brunswick, NJ: Transaction.

McGloin, J.M., & Piquero, A.R. (2009). "I wasn't alone": Collective behaviour and violent delinquency. *Australian and New Zealand Journal of Criminology*, 42, 336–353.

McGloin, J.M., Sullivan, C.J., Piquero, A.R., & Pratt, T.C. (2007). Local life circumstances and offending specialization/versatility—comparing opportunity and propensity models. *Journal of Research in Crime and Delinquency*, 44, 321–346.

Moffitt, T.E. (1993). Adolescence-limited and life-course-persistent antisocial behavior: A developmental taxonomy. *Psychological Review*, 100, 674–701.

Moffitt, T.E., Caspi, M., Rutter, P., & Silva, A. (2001). *Sex differences in antisocial behaviour: Conduct disorder, delinquency, and violence in the Dunedin Longitudinal Study*. Cambridge, UK: Cambridge University Press.

Nagin, D.S., & Farrington, D.P. (1992a). The stability of criminal potential from childhood to adulthood. *Criminology*, 30, 235–260.

Nagin, D.S., & Farrington, D.P. (1992b). The onset and persistence of offending. *Criminology*, 30, 501–524.

Nagin, D.S., Farrington, D.P., & Moffitt, T.E. (1995). Life-course trajectories of different types of offenders. *Criminology*, 33, 111–139.

Nagin, D.S. (2005). *Group-based modeling of development*. Cambridge, MA: Harvard University Press.

Nagin, D.S., & Paternoster, R. (1991). On the relationship of past to future participation in delinquency. *Criminology*, 29, 163–189.

Nagin, D.S., & Paternoster, R. (2000). Population heterogeneity and state dependence: State of the evidence and directions for future research. *Journal of Quantitative Criminology*, 16, 117–144.

Nieuwbeerta, P., Blokland, A.A.J., Piquero, A.R., & Sweeten, G. (2009). A life-course analysis of offense specialization across age: Introducing a new method for studying individual specialization over the life course. *Crime & Delinquency*, 57, 3–28.

Osgood, D.W., & Schreck, C.J. (2007). A new method for studying the extent, stability, and predictors of individual specialization in violence. *Criminology*, 45, 273–312.

Paternoster, R., Brame, R., & Farrington, D.P. (2001). On the relationship between adolescent and adult convictions. *Journal of Quantitative Criminology*, 17, 201–225.

Paternoster, R., Dean, C.W., Piquero, A., Mazerolle, P., & Brame, R. (1997). Generality, continuity, and change in offending. *Journal of Quantitative Criminology*, 13, 231–266.

Piquero, A.R. (2004). The intermittency of criminal careers. In S. Maruna & R. Immarigeon (Eds.), *Offender re-entry and desistance* (pp. 102–129). Albany: SUNY Press.

Piquero, A.R. (2008). Taking stock of developmental trajectories of criminal activity over the life course. In A. Liberman (Ed.), *The long view of crime: A synthesis of longitudinal research* (pp. 23–78). New York: Springer.

Piquero, A.R. (2009). Methodological issues in the study of persistence in offending. In J. Savage (Ed.), *The development of persistent criminality* (pp. 271–287). New York: Oxford University Press.

Piquero, A.R., & Brame, R. (2008). Assessing the race-/ethnicity-crime relationship in a sample of serious adolescent delinquents. *Crime & Delinquency*, 54, 390–422.

Piquero, A.R., Brame, R., Mazerolle, P., & Haapanen, R. (2002). Crime in emerging adulthood. *Criminology*, 40, 137–169.

Piquero, A.R., Brame, R., & Moffitt, T.E. (2005). Extending the study of continuity and change: Gender differences in the linkage between adolescent and adult offending. *Journal of Quantitative Criminology*, 21, 219–243.

Piquero, A.R., Farrington, D.P., & Blumstein, A. (2003). The criminal career paradigm: Background and recent developments. In M.H. Tonry (Ed.), *Crime and justice: A review of research* (Vol. 30, pp. 359–506). Chicago, IL: University of Chicago Press.

Piquero, A.R., Farrington, D.P., & Blumstein, A. (2007). *Key issues in criminal career research: New analyses of the Cambridge study in delinquent development*. Cambridge, UK: Cambridge University Press.

Piquero, A.R., Farrington, D.P., Welsh, B.C., Tremblay, R., & Jennings, W. (2009). Effects of early family/parent training programs on antisocial behavior and delinquency. *Journal of Experimental Criminology*, 5, 83–120.

Piquero, A.R., Jennings, W., & Farrington, D.P. (2010). On the malleability of self-control: Theoretical and policy implications regarding a general theory of crime. *Justice Quarterly*, 27, 803–834.

Piquero, A.R., Paternoster, R., Brame, R., Mazerolle, P., & Dean, C.W. (1999). Onset age and specialization in offending behavior. *Journal of Research in Crime and Delinquency*, 36, 275–299.

Piquero, A.R., Sullivan, C., & Farrington, D.P. (2010). Assessing differences between short-term, high-rate offenders and long-term, low-rate offenders. *Criminal Justice and Behavior*, 37, 1309–1329.

Quetelet, A. (1842). *A treatise on man and the development of his faculties*. Edinburgh: Chambers.

Reiss, A.J., & Farrington, D.P. (1991). Advancing knowledge about co-offending: Results from a prospective longitudinal survey of London males. *Journal of Criminal Law and Criminology*, 82, 360–395.

Robins, L.N. (1978). Sturdy childhood predictors of adult antisocial behaviour: Replications from longitudinal studies. *Psychological Medicine*, 8, 611–622.

Sampson, R.J., & Laub, J.H. (1993). *Crime in the making: Pathways and turning points through life*. Cambridge, MA: Harvard University Press.

Sampson, R.J., & Laub, J.H. (2003). Life-course desisters? Trajectories of crime among delinquent boys followed to age 70. *Criminology*, 41, 555–592.

Sampson, R.J., Laub, J.H., & Wimer, C. (2006). Does marriage reduce crime? A counterfactual approach to within-individual causal effects. *Criminology*, 44, 465–508.

Sampson, R.J., Morenoff, J.D., & Raudenbush, S. (2005). Social anatomy of racial and ethnic disparities in violence. *American Journal of Public Health*, 95, 224–232.

Sarnecki, J. (2001). *Delinquent networks: Youth co-offending in Stockholm*. Cambridge, UK: Cambridge University Press.

Schreck, C.J., McGloin, J.M., & Kirk, D.S. (2009). On the origins of the violent neighborhood: A study of crime type differentiation across Chicago neighborhoods. *Justice Quarterly*, 26, 771–794.

Shannon, L.W. (1982). *Assessing the relationship of adult criminal careers to juvenile careers*. Washington, DC: Office of Juvenile Justice and Delinquency Prevention.

Shannon, L.W. (1988). *Criminal career continuity: Its social context*. New York: Human Sciences Press.

Shaw, C. (1931). *The jack-roller*. Chicago, IL: University of Chicago Press.

Smallbone, S.W., & Wortley, R.K. (2004). Onset, persistence, and versatility of offending among adult males convicted of sexual offenses against children. *Sexual Abuse: A Journal of Research and Treatment*, 16, 285–298.

Soothill, K., Fitzpatrick, C., & Francis, B. (2009). *Understanding criminal careers*. Cullompton, Devon, UK: Willan.

Soothill, K., Francis, B., Ackerley, E., & Humphreys, L. (2008). Changing patterns of offending behaviour among young adults. *British Journal of Criminology*, 48, 75–95.

Stattin, H., & Magnusson, D. (1991). Stability and change in criminal behaviour up to age 30. *British Journal of Criminology*, 31, 327–346.

Stolzenberg, L., & D'Alessio, S.J. (2008). Co-offending and the age-crime curve. *Journal of Research in Crime and Delinquency*, 45, 65–86.

Sullivan, C.J., McGloin, J.M., Pratt, T.C., & Piquero, A.R. (2006). Rethinking the norm of offender generality: Investigating specialization in the short term. *Criminology*, 44, 199–233.

Theobald, D., & Farrington, D.P. (2009). Effects of getting married on offending: Results from a prospective longitudinal survey of males. *European Journal of Criminology*, 6, 496–516.

Tolan, P.H., & Gorman-Smith, D. (1998). Development of serious and violent offending careers. In R. Loeber and D.P. Farrington (Eds.), *Serious and violent juvenile offenders: Risk factors and successful interventions* (pp. 68–85). Newbury Park, CA: Sage.

Tracy, P.E., & Kempf-Leonard, K. (1996). *Continuity and discontinuity in criminal careers.* New York: Plenum.

Tremblay, R.E., Japel, C., Perusse, D., Mcduff, P., Boivin, M., Zoccolillo, M., & Montplaisir, J. (2006). The search for the age of onset of physical aggression: Rousseau and Bandura revisited. *Criminal Behaviour and Mental Health*, 9, 8–23.

van Mastrigt, S.B., & Farrington, D.P. (2009). Co-offending, age, gender, and crime type: Implications for criminal justice policy. *British Journal of Criminology*, 49, 552–573.

Weisburd, D., & Waring, E. (2001). *White-collar crime and criminal careers.* New York: Cambridge University Press.

Wolfgang, M., Figlio, R.M., & Sellin, T. (1972). *Delinquency in a birth cohort.* Chicago, IL: University of Chicago Press.

Wolfgang, M.E., Thornberry, T.P., & Figlio, R.M. (1987). *From boy to man, from delinquency to crime.* Chicago, IL: University of Chicago Press.

Zara, G., & Farrington, D.P. (2009). Childhood and adolescent predictors of late onset criminal careers. *Journal of Youth and Adolescence*, 38, 287–300.

Zimring, F., Jennings, W., & Piquero, A.R. (2008). Juvenile and adult sexual offending in Racine, Wisconsin: Does early sex offending predict later sex offending in youth and young adulthood? *Criminology and Public Policy*, 6, 507–534.

Zimring, F., Jennings, W.G., Piquero, A.R., & Hays, S. (2009). Investigating the continuity of sex offending: Evidence from the Second Philadelphia Birth Cohort. *Justice Quarterly*, 26, 58–76.

3

Explanations for Offending

Terence P. Thornberry, Peggy C. Giordano,
Christopher Uggen, Mauri Matsuda, Ann S. Masten,
Erik Bulten, and Andrea G. Donker

In recent decades, criminologists have mapped trajectories of criminal activity in ever-sharper detail. As this volume's chapters make clear, this work has yielded a wealth of information about offending during the critical transition from adolescence to adulthood. Yet advancement in science hinges on the construction of theoretical models as well as quantitative observation. And criminology today is confronted with explanations as divergent as the earth-centered and sun-centered views of the cosmos competing in the sixteenth century. It took a century to settle that dispute empirically—for Ptolemy's predictions were just as accurate as those of Copernicus—despite their fundamentally different explanations of the world. In criminology, as in astronomy, clear thinking about theory is needed for the field to advance. We here describe some of the major theoretical models that have been offered to explain variation in trajectories of offending during the transition to adulthood, followed by a discussion of the empirical evidence related to them.

The transition from adolescence to adulthood is one of the most important stages of the life-course. Rindfuss, Swicegood, and Rosenfeld (1987) have referred to it as a "demographically dense" period because it involves transitions, and often multiple transitions, on major life course trajectories including education, work, residence, family formation, and parenthood. The timing and success of these transitions has important consequences for the long-term development both of the individual and his or her family (Elder, 1997). The transition from adolescence to adulthood also has been described as a window of opportunity or vulnerability when developmental and contextual changes converge to support positive turnarounds and redirections of the life course (Masten, Long, Kuo, McCormick, & Desjardins, 2009; Masten, Obradović, & Burt, 2006). The transition years also are a criminological crossroads, as major changes in criminal careers often occur at these ages as well. For some who began their criminal careers during adolescence, offending continues and escalates; for others involvement in crime wanes; and yet others only begin serious involvement in crime at these ages. In this chapter we review several major theoretical explanations for criminal offending during the transition years, as well as the empirical support associated with these theories. We begin by specifying the patterns of offending that seem to be the most salient for theories to explain, and we identify key questions that theories should address with respect to these patterns.

Patterns of Offending

As described in detail in Chapter 2, there are distinctive patterns of offending that emerge during the transition from adolescence to adulthood. In this chapter we focus on three notable trajectories of offending during this developmental stage. One shows a rise of offending in adolescence and persistence of high crime rates into adulthood; one reflects the overall age-crime curve pattern of increasing offending in adolescence followed by desistance during the transition years; and the third group shows a late onset of offending relative to the age-crime curve. Developmental theories of offending ought to be able to account for such markedly different trajectories.

With respect to persistence, theories should be able to explain why some juveniles persist in offending during the early adult years and to identify factors associated with continuity in offending at this particular developmental stage. Three issues about desistance seem particularly salient: to identify what causes offenders to move from active involvement in offending to a zero or near-zero rate; to identify the factors that maintain offending at a near-zero rate over time; and to examine if these processes vary developmentally. Two theoretical questions seem particularly important for understanding late onset cases: to identify the assets and protective factors that prevented involvement in delinquency earlier during childhood and adolescence, and to identify the developmental processes that are associated with the onset of offending during the transition to adulthood, when the normative trend is declining rates.

Theoretical Models

A number of theoretical perspectives have been proffered to explain patterns of offending over the life course and, in particular, during the transition from adolescence to adulthood. While it is beyond the scope of this chapter to review all of these theories, we provide an overview of five broad theoretical perspectives that currently inform the field's understanding of these patterns of offending. They are: static or population heterogeneity models, dynamic or state dependence models, social psychological theories, the developmental psychopathology perspective, and the biopsychosocial perspective.

The static or population heterogeneity models adopt an ontogenetic perspective to explain offending across the life course. They view human development ". . . as a process of maturational unfolding" in which behavior, including criminal behavior, emerges in a uniform sequence contingent upon age so that patterns of behavioral change unfold at roughly the same ages for all individuals (Dannefer, 1984, p. 103). There are three defining aspects to static theories of crime. First, the basic causes of criminal behavior, and changes in offending over time, are to be found in individual endowments that are established relatively early in the life course. Second, these early endowments create inter-individual (or relative) stability in the behavior. That is, across the life course individuals are generally expected to maintain their position relative to other individuals with respect to their levels of offending. Third, changing levels of offending are a product of maturational unfolding, that is, normative changes in the behavior that naturally occur as individuals age. Maturation accounts well for intra-individual change across time, for example, the elevation in offending during mid-adolescence that is observed in the general age-crime curve, but that does not fundamentally disturb inter-individual stability. There are several theories of criminal behavior that adopt this approach, including the works of Glueck and Glueck (1950), Mednick (1977), Wilson and Herrnstein (1985), Gottfredson and Hirschi (1990), Moffitt (1993), and Patterson, Capaldi, and Bank (1991).

A second group of theories, often referred to as dynamic or life-course developmental models, adopts a sociogenetic (or epigenetic) approach. In these models, human behavior is never viewed as set or established, inevitably flowing forth from early endowments. Sociogenesis emphasizes ". . . the uniquely 'open' or 'unfinished' character of the human organism in relation to its environment" (Dannefer, 1984, p. 107), a plasticity that persists across the full life course. As a result, one would expect neither inter-individual stability nor uniform intra-individual change. As individuals confront different social environments and experiences over the life course, the plasticity of human development generates varying responses that result in inter-individual change. Moreover, the tremendous variability in social experiences and environments combined with the variation among individuals of the same age that interact with those environments minimizes the chances of observing a universal pattern of intra-individual change. As with the ontogenetic approach, there are several sociogenetic theories of delinquency, as found in the works of such theorists as Akers (1998), Catalano and Hawkins (1986), Farrington (2003), Elliott, Huizinga, and Ageton (1985), Sampson and Laub, (1993, 2003), and Thornberry and Krohn (2001, 2005).

The third perspective we discuss, a social psychological perspective, also has sociogenetic underpinnings. These theories focus on subjective aspects of life experiences as the key to understanding behavioral continuity and change. These experiences include cognitive and emotional processes, issues of identity, and human agency. These subjective phenomena are not fixed (as reflected in the notion of stable traits that foster particular worldviews or emotional responses), but instead arise from the accumulation of social experiences that inevitably occur as individuals move forward in the life course. Moreover, the social psychological perspective also stresses the interplay of structure and these subjective processes. As with the other general orientations, there are several social psychological theories of criminal behavior, for example as proposed by Giordano, Cernkovich, and Rudolph (2002), Matsueda and Heimer (1997), and Massoglia and Uggen (2010).

The fourth perspective we discuss, developmental psychopathology, is an integrative framework that brings together ideas from the sciences of human development, general systems theory, clinical psychology, psychiatry, sociology, pediatrics, neuroscience, behavior genetics, and other disciplines concerned with good and poor adaptation over the life course (Cicchetti, 2006; Masten, 2006; Sroufe, 2007). In this perspective, the life-course trajectory is always influenced by antecedent development (as reflected in current structure and function of the organism, in personality, memories, knowledge, reputation, etc.) as well as the current interactions among systems of the person and context. Early experiences can be carried forward, sometimes with profound consequences on the life course, while at the same time the possibility of change continues throughout the lifespan. The developmental psychopathology perspective also underscores the possibility of concentrated windows of opportunity or vulnerability over the life course, when change and turning points are more likely, including the transition to the adulthood period.

The fifth perspective, the biopsychosocial perspective regards aggressive behavior as a result of interacting mechanisms at biological, psychological, interpersonal, and environmental levels. Determinants from all levels are regarded as dimensional, gradual, and dynamic. As a multilevel approach, it argues that a single level explanatory framework is probably insufficient. The empirical support for the biopsychosocial perspective has increased considerably over the years in many scientific domains. Studies have shown, for instance, the dynamics of the brain (experience-independent, experience-dependent, and experience-expectant plasticity), are closely shaped by life experiences and are physically changing due to life experiences (Draganski et al., 2004; Peters et al., 2010).

Explanations for Offending

We now discuss how each of these perspectives explains offending patterns during the transition years. We pay particular attention to issues of persistence, desistance, and late onset of offending across the juvenile–early adult years.

Static theories. One of the most prominent theories of crime to adopt a population heterogeneity perspective is Gottfredson and Hirschi's (1990) self-control theory. In this theory, the propensity to engage in crime is viewed as a product of the person's level of self-control, which is established roughly by age 8 (Hirschi & Gottfredson, 2001). According to their theory this propensity ". . . is stable through life, and consequently is unaffected by events that occur in life" (Warr, 2002, p. 99). Youth who are exposed to effective parenting styles at early ages and who have positive relations with their parents are likely to have high levels of self-control and therefore low rates of offending at all ages; in contrast, youth who experience poor parenting styles and have harsh, brittle relationships with their parents are likely to have low levels of self-control and therefore high levels of offending at all ages. While some individuals are more involved in crime than others, the overall shape of offending careers is universal, follows the general age-crime curve, and reflects the ontogenetic assumption of inter-individual stability (Gottfredson & Hirschi, 1990, p. 132).

Typological theories, for example those presented by Moffitt (1993) and Patterson and colleagues (1991), present a related view of offending across the life course. They identify two major groups of offenders, early-starters (Patterson, Capaldi, and Bank, 1991) or life-course persistent offenders (Moffitt, 1993), and late starters (Patterson et al., 1991) or adolescence-limited offenders (Moffitt, 1993). The former group, which is relatively small, has a childhood onset of offending. In the theory of Patterson and his colleagues this is largely due to ineffective parenting styles and to the coercive exchanges that develop in distressed families. In Moffitt's theory, early onset is primarily due to the interplay between individual deficits, especially neuropsychological deficits, and ineffective parenting styles. In both of these theories, early problems set the stage for high levels of continuity in offending across the life course, a condition aptly captured in Moffitt's designation of "life-course persistent offenders." In contrast, the second group—late starters or adolescence-limited offenders—has an onset of offending during the adolescent years and delinquent careers that tend to be relatively short. For this group, both theories focus on challenges associated with adolescent development—such as association with delinquent peers, failure in school, and the difficulty in adjusting to the maturity gap—to explain involvement in delinquency.

The basic premises of these theories provide a set of expectations about changing patterns of offending during the transition years from adolescence to adulthood. First, with respect to persistence, in Gottfredson and Hirschi's theory (1990), individuals with low levels of self-control are expected to have high levels of offending at all ages. Their low levels of self-control cause high levels of offending during adolescence and the general stability of self-control over the life course increases the likelihood of continuity in offending into the adult years.

The typological theories offer a somewhat different explanation for persistence. To illustrate we focus on Moffitt's model in which persistence is caused by two general developmental processes. The first, contemporary continuity, refers to the relatively strong continuity in the original problem behaviors, "such as high activity level, irritability, poor self-control, and low cognitive ability" (Moffitt, 1993, p. 683). As these individual deficits persist, they lead to persistently high levels of offending across the life course. The second process, cumulative continuity, refers to the consequences of earlier antisocial behavior such as isolation in delinquent peer groups, school failure, and ultimately difficulty in the transition to adult roles, such as failure to finish school, teen parenthood, and unemployment. These consequences of earlier offending make it difficult for the individual to escape involvement in antisocial behavior, and they increase the persistence of delinquent careers. Patterson and colleagues (1991) offer a similar explanation. Early problems arising in family interactions, particularly from coercive interactional styles, are reinforced and persist as the child enters the school context, where progressive problems arise in relationships with normative peers and academic achievement. Progressive failures in key developmental tasks lead to a cascade of subsequent problems, including deviant peer affiliations, with growing risk for persistent offending.

Although the processes that account for persistence differ somewhat between self-control theory and the typological theories, they share one central feature: persistence is almost entirely associated with early onset of offending and its theorized consequences. That is, those who start offending at relatively young ages, primarily during childhood, are likely to maintain their high levels of offending at the transition from adolescence to adulthood and, indeed, beyond.

In the typological theories, desistance is primarily associated with the other, numerically larger, group of offenders referred to as late starters by Patterson and colleagues (1991) and as adolescence-limited offenders by Moffitt (1993). Their offending typically starts during early adolescence and they are likely to desist from offending by early adulthood. For Moffitt, for example, their offending is largely a product of the gap between the onset of sexual and physical maturity and the onset of social maturity or adult roles and privileges in advanced industrial societies. Given that all adolescents confront this gap to some degree, peer influences may contribute a strong motivating influence for delinquency. However, when the frustration associated with the maturity gap wanes as individuals age, the motivating forces supporting delinquency diminish considerably and desistance becomes quite likely. Desistance is also aided by the fact that cumulative continuity is less likely for these offenders and they are more apt to make successful transitions to adult roles such as partner, parent, and employee.

For Gottfredson and Hirschi, desistance is entirely a function of maturational reform and ". . . maturational reform is just that, change in behavior that comes with maturation; . . . spontaneous desistance is just that, change in behavior that cannot be explained and change that occurs regardless of what else happens" (Gottfredson & Hirschi, 1990, p. 136). A similar view was presented by Glueck and Glueck: ". . . the biological process of maturation is the chief factor in the behavior changes of criminals" (1940, p. 107). Age of onset and the early characteristics associated with onset are fully capable of predicting desistance. Youth with low self-control begin offending early, and their low self-control prevents them from escaping the lures of crime. Youth with high levels of self-control will start later (if at all) and end earlier. "Combining little or no movement from high self-control to low self-control with the fact that socialization continues to occur throughout life produces the conclusion that the proportion of the population in the potential offender pool should tend to decline as cohorts age" (Gottfredson & Hirschi, 1990, p. 107). Developmental variables, such as association with delinquent peers, gang membership, and, at later ages, marriage and employment exert no causal impact on the likelihood or timing of desistance; relationships between these variables and desistance are entirely spurious (Gottfredson & Hirschi, 1990). Much like Gottfredson and Hirschi, Moffitt argues that "the taxonomy accepts that antisocial participation declines markedly in mid-life, but, nonetheless, it expects rank-order stability, particularly on age-relevant measures of antisocial activity" (2006, p. 294).

Overall, these theories suggest that the processes of persistence and desistance are likely to occur to different groups of offenders. For Gottfredson and Hirschi (1990), those with lower self-control are likely to start offending earlier and to persist while those with higher levels of self-control are likely to start later and to desist earlier. For the typological theories, one type of offender has an early onset and life-course persistent pattern while the other type has a more age normative onset and a high likelihood of desistance at the transition from adolescence to adulthood.

Neither the static nor typological theories of offending anticipate the presence of late onset cases as a meaningful portion of the population. For example, Moffitt's theory (1993) identifies only three groups in the population, nonoffenders, adolescence-limited offenders, and life-course persistent offenders. There are no late-onset cases because, as Moffitt, Caspi, Rutter, and Silva state, the "onset of antisocial behavior after adolescence is extremely rare" (2001, pp. 84–85). A similar view is presented by Patterson et al. (1991). Even though they discuss "late starters," that is actually a residual category defined as anyone who is not an "early starter," and generally refers to onset in adolescence. Their theory does not posit the existence of a late-onset group as defined above—offenders who initiated their criminal careers after the age normative period of onset.

The rarity or absence of late onset offending is also evident in Gottfredson and Hirschi's (1990) self-control theory. If offenders initiate offending at unusually late ages, that could only be because their high levels of self-control prevented their involvement in adolescent delinquency, but that same high level of self-control would also cause them to desist very quickly should they begin. Thus, it is highly unlikely that individuals would begin a career of persistent offending later in the life course. Doing so is logically inconsistent with the expectation of inter-individual stability in offending.

Empirical support for static theories. Gottfredson and Hirschi (1990) explained onset and persistence in crime and analogous behaviors by the absence of self-control, a trait established in early childhood that exhibits relative stability across the life course. Gottfredson (2006) cites a considerable body of research in support of self-control theory, tested on diverse samples and utilizing various outcome measures. Further, a meta-analysis (Pratt & Cullen, 2000) shows support for the effect of low self-control on crime and analogous behaviors. In general, the prediction that low self-control is associated with higher rates of offending is borne out by the empirical literature, especially when attention focuses on explanations of onset and persistence. Even so, the support for self-control theory is weaker in studies that utilize a longitudinal design (Pratt & Cullen, 2000).

According to Moffitt (1993), life-course persistent offenders experience several neuropsychological and family-environmental risk factors in early childhood. Longitudinal data from a sample of New Zealanders indicate that the following risk factors predicted life-course persistent offending: "undercontrolled temperament measured by observers at age three, neurological abnormalities and delayed motor development at age three, low intellectual ability, reading difficulties, poor scores on neuropsychological tests of memory, hyperactivity, and slow heart rate" and "teenaged single parents, mothers with poor mental health, mothers who were observed to be harsh or neglectful, as well as by experiences of harsh and inconsistent discipline, much family conflict, many changes of primary caretaker, low family socio-economic status, and rejection by peers in school" (Moffitt, 2006, pp. 279–280). Moffitt (1993) also predicted that the dispositions of life-course persistent offenders will be stable throughout life, though the expressions of this disposition may change with age. For example, these offenders may switch to family abuse and neglect in later adulthood; thus, they may exhibit continuity in behavior even if self-report and official measures give the impression of a decline in offending over time. In the Dunedin cohort, Moffitt (2006) found that, at age 26, life-course persistent offenders were involved in more serious and violent behavior, had mental health and substance abuse problems, financial and employment problems, and committed domestic abuse of women and children.

Although this perspective enjoys empirical support at this general level, there is somewhat less support for it when the specific issues about offending during the transition years are considered. One of the basic assertions of this approach is that there will be high levels of relative, or inter-individual, stability in offending across the life course. Indeed, this expectation generates the perspective's explanation with respect to persistence, desistance, and late-onset offending. One way of assessing relative stability is to rely upon recently developed mixture models (Nagin & Land, 1993; Nagin, 2005) to differentiate patterns of offending trajectories across the life course. These models identify a finite number of discrete groups in the population, each having its own offending trajectory with distinct intercepts and slopes. If the static theories are correct there should be relatively few points of intersection among the trajectory curves. That is, high-rate offenders should almost always be high-rate offenders and low-rate offenders should almost always be low-rate offenders. By and large the results of the trajectory literature are not consistent with this expectation. Figure 3.1 presents trajectory results for the Rochester Youth

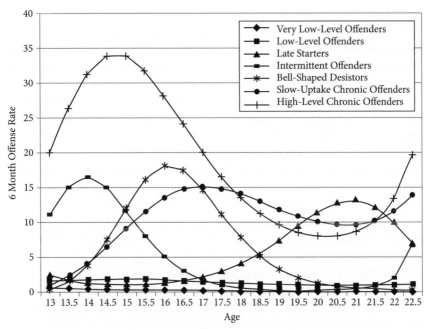

FIGURE 3.1 Trajectories of offending from the Rochester Youth Development Study.
Bushway et al., 2003, p. 144.

Development Study for general offending (see Bushway, Thornberry, & Krohn, 2003). For example, the group labeled "late starters" has a very low rate of offending to age 17.5 but then crosses three other groups to have the highest offending rate observed between ages 20 and 21.5. In contrast, the groups labeled "bell-shaped desisters" and "intermittent offenders" have relatively high rates at earlier ages but cross two other groups to have low rates by the end of the observation period. Laub and Sampson (2003) estimated trajectory models for general, violent, property, and alcohol/drug crimes to age 70. In all four models, they found multiple groups and multiple points at which the various groups intersected with respect to offending. None of these results in which different groups intersect with others over time is consistent with the expectation of rank-order stability.

Piquero (2008) presented a very thorough review of the trajectory literature. The results from the studies included in that review are quite consistent with the results from the Rochester data and the Glueck data. The vast majority of the trajectory models fail to support the notion of relative stability. This result is observed for both official and self-report data, for general and serious offending, and for studies that end in adolescence and those that extend into adulthood. This result is fundamentally inconsistent with the ontogenetic claim of universal, maturational unfolding which generates inter-individual stability.

Static theories also predict that late-onset offending will be extremely rare. There is, in fact, very little empirical evidence with regard to the issue of late starters. Wolfgang, Thornberry, and Figlio (1987) examined late starters in the Philadelphia Birth Cohort Study. They found that 24% of the offenders were arrested for the first time during their adult years. This group committed quite serious offenses, having a higher average seriousness score for their offenses (368) than even the persistent offenders (281; Wolfgang et al., 1987, p. 23). Eggleston and Laub (2002) defined late bloomers as those who begin their criminal careers when they are 18 or older and found that, across 18 studies, an average of 17.2% of nondelinquents begin offending in adulthood. They comprise about half of the adult offender population and are typically serious offenders who continue to offend well into their adult years. In Chapter 2, Piquero, Hawkins, and Kazemian summarized their general review of this literature by saying that: "one overall conclusion regarding adult-onset is that there is a nonnegligible amount of adult onset. . . ." Although the empirical literature on this issue is sparse it is certainly plausible that there is a noticeable group of late-onset offenders whose adult criminal careers are nontrivial.

A second way to examine empirical support for static theories with respect to offending during the transition years is to examine the relative importance of age of onset and early characteristics in predicting persistence and desistance. Recall that the explanation for persistent offending in this perspective is to be found primarily in risk factors such as low self-control, family dysfunction, and neuro-psychological deficits that are established during childhood. A large literature shows that early characteristics such as these predict levels of offending (several excellent reviews are available such as Farrington, 2000; Hawkins et al., 1998; Lipsey & Derzon, 1998). Youth with deficits in domains such as individual charac-teristics, family, school, and peer relations are more likely to be delinquent and to have higher lifetime levels of offending. Do these early characteristics also predict later change?

Farrington and Hawkins (1991) found that several factors, such as family and educational variables measured at ages 8 and 10, predicted desistance. Piquero, Farrington, and Blumstein (2007) found that higher levels of self-control mea-sured at ages 3 to 11 predicted desistance from crime between ages 18 and 26. The effect reported by Piquero et al. (2007) is modest, however, and when measures of social bonds are added to the model (Wright, Caspi, Moffitt, & Silva, 1999) the effect is reduced. Also, as noted above, Moffitt (2006) reported that many early characteristics are related to persistent offending.

In contrast, however, many studies find that early background factors are not good predictors of changes in offending. Nagin, Farrington, Moffitt (1995) reported that background variables have a limited capacity to predict desistance, as do Laub and Sampson (2003). White, Xie, Thompson, Loeber, and Stouthamer-Loeber (2001) found that only conduct disorder predicted change in alcohol use and none of the other early adolescent psychopathology measures they investigated pre-dicted change in marijuana use (see also Loeber, Slot, van der Laan, and Hoeve, 2008). Childhood and adolescent factors did not discriminate among six trajectory classes of offending, leading Wiesner and Capaldi (2003) to conclude that adolescent problem behaviors are not manifestations of criminal propensity established early in life. Similarly, Chung, Hill, Hawkins, Gilchrist, and Nagin (2002) found that few characteristics measured at ages 10–12 could distinguish between late starters and nonoffenders or between escalators and desisters. Laub and Sampson concluded that ". . . group membership is not easily, if at all, predictable from individual, childhood, and adolescent risk factors" (2003, p. 110; see also, Sampson & Laub, 2009), a conclusion echoed by Morizot and Le Blanc that ". . . the overall pattern [of results] suggests that self- and social control variables do not seem to possess the ability to make long-term predictions about desistance" (2007, p. 65).

In sum, the empirical support for static theories is somewhat mixed. On the one hand, as demonstrated by Paternoster, Brame, and Farrington (2001) and Piquero, Brame, and Moffitt (2005) individual differences matter. In addition, many of the causal factors identified by these theories are related to offending. On the other hand, there is little empirical support for its core notion of relative stability, and many studies find that early characteristics do not effectively predict changing patterns of offending such as persistence and desistance during the transition years.

Dynamic theories. Theories that adopt a developmental, life-course perspective of crime present a different explanation for these patterns of offending during the transition years. They do not deny the importance of early individual or parenting differences, such as temperament or emotion regulation in the child, or early parenting styles. Behaviors established early continue to influence behavior over the life course (e.g., Sampson & Laub, 1993; Thornberry, 2005). Nevertheless, while these early characteristics retain some explanatory importance, the primary explanation for later offending is to be found in the changing social environment that individuals confront as they traverse the life course. For example, changing relationships with parents and peers, the timing and success of transitions along major life-course trajectories such as family, school, and work, and the consequences of earlier involvement in delinquency and contact with the juvenile justice system are all expected to exert a strong influence on diverging patterns of offending such as persistence and desistance (Akers, 1998; Catalano & Hawkins, 1986; Farrington, 2003; Laub & Sampson, 2003; Thornberry & Krohn, 2005).

At least three general developmental processes have been identified to account for persistence during the transition years. The first stems from the stability of the causal factors that are associated with the onset of offending. Developmental theories posit that negative temperamental traits, ineffective parenting styles, poverty and structural disadvantage, school failure, and association with delinquent peers are all linked to the onset and maintenance of delinquent careers (Catalano & Hawkins, 1996; Thornberry & Krohn, 2005). In turn, each of these attributes exhibits some stability over the life course. For example, it is often difficult for families who experience extreme levels of poverty and structural adversity to escape that adversity, and the development of adolescents raised in those families is constantly compromised. Similarly, ineffective parenting styles are often evi-dent both in childhood and in adolescence (Patterson, Reid, & Dishion, 1992), leading to hostile, brittle relationships between parent and child during the tran-sition years. The absence of strong social and emotional support from parents decreases the likelihood of escaping from involvement in crime and increases levels of persistence. More generally, if deficits that were associated with earlier involvement in delinquency persist, they are likely, to some extent, to maintain persistent involvement in offending.

The second developmental process has to do with the negative consequences of the earlier involvement in antisocial behavior. As is true of all state dependence models (Nagin & Paternoster, 1991), dynamic theories assume that involvement in delinquency disrupts later life-course development, especially if it is prolonged and serious. Thornberry's (1987) interactional theory views delinquency as embedded in mutually reinforcing causal relationships. Delinquency attenuates bonds to conventional people and institutions, increases subsequent involvement in delinquent peer networks and street gangs, and strengthens delinquent belief systems (see also, Akers, 1998). Individuals who have weakened prosocial bonds and are enmeshed in delinquent behaviors and networks are likely to experience high levels of persistence in offending.

Life-course theories also emphasize the impact of earlier offending on transi-tions along major life-course trajectories. Delinquency disrupts the successful completion of the developmental challenges of adolescence. As just noted, delin-quents are likely to become alienated from parents and family, fail at school, and become enmeshed in delinquent peer groups. All of these factors have been shown to be related to disorderly and unsuccessful transitions to adult roles. For example, they are associated with increased levels of school dropout, teen parenthood, unstable employment records, and marital instability (Krohn, Lizotte, & Perez, 1997). In turn, failure to make timely and successful transitions from adolescent to adult roles reduces both human and social capital and increases the likelihood of persistent involvement in offending.

A third general process has to do with involvement in the juvenile justice system (Bernburg & Krohn, 2003; Paternoster & Iovanni, 1989; Sampson & Laub, 1997). Official records of arrest and incarceration have long-term consequences for the individual. Official labeling increases embeddedness in criminal social net-works which increases persistence in offending (Bernburg, Krohn, & Rivera, 2006). Similarly, official labels increase the likelihood of school dropout and unstable employment, both of which are associated with increased persistence in offending (Bernburg & Krohn, 2003).

Overall, developmental life-course theories point to at least three processes that are associated with persistence in offending from adolescence to adult-hood: the stability of earlier deficits, the life-course consequences of delin-quency, and official labeling. Thus, persistence is not primarily an outcome of early endowments as it is in static theories. Quite the contrary; in dynamic theories, persistence is primarily an outcome of more proximal developmental processes that were often set in motion by earlier development including earlier involvement in delinquent behavior.

In dynamic theories, desistance is largely explained by the re-establishment of bonds to conventional society (Sampson & Laub, 1993; Thornberry, 1987) and by concordant changes in the individual's social networks (Warr, 1998). Desistance is more likely to occur when the causal factors that created delinquency in the first place ". . . are less numerous, less extreme, and less intertwined" (Thornberry & Krohn, 2005:201), but it is not predetermined by age of onset. Offenders who increase attachment to conventional others and commitment to prosocial activities like school and work are more likely to escape persistent involvement in criminal behavior: ". . . a cascade of successful relationships and acceptance by conventional people can result in stronger social bonds, and this process can, in turn, lessen the propensity for crime" (Cohen & Vila, 1996, p. 139). The changing network constellation provides both new sources of control and new opportunity structures (Warr, 1998) that channel behavior away from crime.

For example, in Farrington's theory, desistance is related to "changes in socialization influences (decreasing importance of peers, increasing importance of the female partners and children), and life events such as getting married, having children, moving home and getting a steady job" (2003, p. 235). Sampson and Laub's social control theory (1993) emphasizes the importance of adult social bonds such as marital attachments in accounting for desistance during the transition years. Farrington and West (1995) also highlight the importance of stable marriages in accounting for desistance from offending. Part of this effect is direct; a "quality" marriage increases attachment to others thereby increasing social control and reducing offending. But part of this effect is indirect; marriage alters the nature of routine activities (Horney, Osgood, & Marshall, 1995), for example, by reducing time spent on street corners and in bars, and also decreases time spent with delinquent peer networks (Warr, 1998). All of these changes reduce opportunities and reinforcements for criminal behavior, thereby enhancing the likelihood of desistance.

The other primary source of social bonding that is linked to desistance during the transition years is commitment to conventional activities such as marriage (King, Massoglia, & Macmillan, 2007), military service (Bouffard & Laub, 2004), and work (Uggen, 2000). The hypothesized mechanisms linking these activities to cessation in crime include financial incentives, direct supervision or control, and a generalized stake in conformity (Toby, 1957).

Relatively little theoretical attention has been paid to late onset offending (as described in Chapter 2) in these dynamic models. Thornberry and Krohn (2005) hypothesize that these offenders are unlikely to have the multiple causal factors that are associated with early onset offending—for example, negative temperamental traits, ineffective parenting, and structural disadvantage—in their backgrounds. They are, however, likely to have less human capital—for example, lower intelligence and academic competence and fewer social skills—than other adolescents (Nagin, Farrington, & Moffitt, 1995). At earlier ages they are buffered from the effects of these deficits by strong social bonds. The family is hypothesized to provide a supportive environment in part because of their more advantageous structural position; family resources and attachments (Mannheim, 1967) provide both social control and social support to constrain their behavior. During early adulthood, however, individuals begin to leave the protective environments of the family and school to seek employment and independence. Given the freedom and instability of this developmental stage, deficits in human capital become a serious impediment for acquiring meaningful employment and establishing stable partner relationships. The difficulty experienced during the transition years also makes them more vulnerable to the influence of deviant friends and to the consequences of alcohol and drug use which often escalate at these ages. The combination of a stressful transition to adult statuses and emerging substance use increases the probability of both the onset and continuation of offending.

Empirical support for dynamic theories. At a general level, both the static and dynamic approaches to explaining criminal offending enjoy some degree of empirical support for their theoretical positions. For example, both theories are supported by the robust positive association between past and future offending and the consistent finding that criminal behavior is relatively stable over time (see also, Piquero et al., Chapter 2, this volume). Robins (1978) found that childhood antisocial behaviors predict high levels of adult antisocial behavior in samples that vary by race, historical period, geographic area, and age at follow-up. According to these findings, childhood antisocial behavior was a necessary condition of adult antisocial behavior.

Nagin and Paternoster (1991) compared the evidence for population heterogeneity and state dependence arguments by examining the effect of unobserved and observed heterogeneity relative to prior participation in crime on later offending in a three-wave panel study of juvenile delinquency. They found that prior participation in offending had a positive and significant effect on later offending, controlling for persistent unobserved heterogeneity, thus providing greater evidence for the state dependence effect. Paternoster, Dean, Piquero, Mazerolle, and Brame (1997) found support for both population heterogeneity and state dependence arguments in their longitudinal examination of a sample of North Carolina juvenile training school releasees. Although the effect of prior arrests is reduced after individual differences are controlled, lending support to the population heterogeneity position, prior arrest maintained a positive, significant effect on future arrests, bolstering the state dependence position. Consistent with these latter findings, Nagin and Paternoster (2000) summarize the decade of empirical research on both perspectives with two conclusions: First, individual differences (i.e., population heterogeneity arguments) do play a significant role in the propensity to offend; second, time-varying characteristics (i.e., state dependence arguments) are also implicated in criminal offending in the long run. Although these results suggest that both perspectives are important for understanding offending, there is also a robust empirical literature within each tradition. We began our discussion by focusing first on the static theories.

According to the state dependence position, the relationship between past and future offending is causal, such that involvement in offending changes the likelihood of future offending. These theories are also dynamic, assuming that individual differences are not fixed and are likely to change over time. Persistence is attributed to the negative consequences of delinquent behavior and official sanctioning by the justice system, as well as the maintenance of causal factors, or continuity in individual differences (Thornberry, 2005; Sampson & Laub, 1997). Desistance is attributed to positive life events, such as marriage and work, changes in causal factors, and the direct effect of age on crime (see Piquero et al., Chapter 2, this volume). Finally, dynamic theories allow for late onset offending.

Using data originally collected by Sheldon and Eleanor Glueck, Sampson and Laub (1993) show that family process variables (such as supervision, attachment, and discipline), as well as school attachment, significantly predicted delinquency in a sample of lower class Boston youth. In addition, they found that antisocial behavior in childhood and in adolescence predicted arrest, military offenses, and a range of negative family, school, and work outcomes in adulthood. In other words, continuity—both homotypic and heterotypic—is partially explained by early childhood behavior.

Despite finding considerable evidence of continuity, Sampson and Laub (1993) and Laub and Sampson (2003) examined the role of change and desistance in adulthood. Job stability, commitment, and marital attachment in young and middle adulthood reduced the likelihood of future offending for the Glueck men (1993). In addition, follow-up life history interviews of the sample show that men who desisted were more likely to have experienced positive turning points, such as marriage and military service. For example, being in the state of marriage reduced the likelihood of offending by over 30% controlling for both between individual (e.g., criminal propensity) and within individual (e.g., age) factors (Laub & Sampson, 2003).

Other research lends support to the premise that later life events serve as turning points that alter trajectories of offending. Uggen (2000) found that assignment to an experimental work program reduced recidivism for older offenders, though it had no significant effect on younger offenders. Thus, age may be an important condition that moderates the effects of social control variables such as work and marriage. Farrington, Gallagher, Morley, St. Ledger, and West (1986) found that unemployment increased involvement in crimes that led to financial gain but did not increase other types of crimes.

School and family ties, religion, and work identify youth who desist from using cocaine (Hamil-Luker, Land, & Blau, 2003). Moffitt, Caspi, Harrington, and Milne (2002) found that, while early factors did not substantially differentiate the trajectories of adolescence-limited and life-course persistent offenders, more proximal factors did. Similarly, Wiesner and Silbereisen (2003) reported that time-averaged covariates were more effective in predicting trajectory group membership than were initial status covariates. Finally, Simons, Johnson, Conger, and Elder (1998) show that there is no direct effect of early conduct problems on adolescent delinquency after family, school, and peer influences are considered.

In addition, studies of desistance have attempted to "unpack" the specific mechanisms that explain why change occurs (see also Horney et al., Chapter 4, this volume). Horney, Osgood, and Marshall (1995) found that changes in "local life circumstances" (p. 658)—such as onset of illegal drug use, heavy drinking, cohabitation with a wife or girlfriend, and school attendance—significantly affected the probability of monthly offending in a sample of incarcerated male offenders. Specifically, illegal drug use, heavy drinking, and living with a girlfriend lead to increases in short-term offending whereas living with a wife and attending school lead to reductions in short-term offending; contrary to expectations, work had either a weak or positive effect on offending. That life events such as marriage and school modify the likelihood of offending in the short-term is consistent with the arguments of dynamic theories regarding long-term trajectories. It is also suggestive of rational choice and routine activities perspectives, which emphasize the role that life events play in structuring daily activities that are conducive to either desistance or continuation of offending.

Using data from the National Youth Study, Warr (1998) found that the marriage effect is mediated by reductions in time spent with delinquent peers. The marriage effect has also been demonstrated in a more contemporary sample from the Netherlands that also includes females (Bersani, Laub, & Nieuwbeerta, 2009). Farrington and West (1995) found that getting married decreased involvement in crime while later separation increased involvement in crime.

Finally, there is a very sparse empirical literature on the issue of adult-onset offending. Eggleston and Laub (2002) did not find any significant differences in the effect of various independent variables (measured at childhood, adolescence, and adulthood) for the adult-onset offenders, relative to other offender categories (i.e., nondelinquent, juvenile only, and persistent). Gomez-Smith and Piquero (2005) found three variables that discriminated between late onset offenders and others: gender (with males more likely to be adult-onset offenders than females), maternal cigarette smoking during pregnancy, and low scores on the California Achievement Test. Finally, Zara and Farrington (2009) found characteristics such as nervousness, anxiousness, social isolation and social inhibition to be associated with a late onset pattern of offending.

Overall, the weight of the evidence from these studies is consistent with the basic expectations of dynamic theories of crime. More proximal, dynamic factors are strongly related to patterns of offending, whereas age of onset and early endowments are less important during the transition years. In general, strong social bonds, movement away from deviant peer groups, and successful transitions to adulthood in such crucial areas as school, work, and family are associated with desistance from crime. In contrast, failure to make successful and orderly transitions from adolescence to adulthood, and the related failure to establish strong prosocial bonds are associated with persistent offending across this stage of the life course.

Social psychological theories focus on subjective aspects of life experiences as key to understanding behavioral continuity as well as change, including cognitive and emotional processes, issues of identity, and the idea of human agency. Although some theoretical formulations focus on subjective processes that appear to be fixed, (i.e., the notion that stable traits foster worldviews or emotional responses that continuously increase the propensity for crime), more often, social psychological perspectives emphasize the malleability of these processes. Accordingly, social psychological theories have often been used to explain changes over the life course in the individual's level of involvement in criminal activity. Life-course theories that focus on the impact of a small set of transition events (e.g., the 'good marriage effect') place most of the conceptual attention on the actions of the change agent. For example, the spouse has an important role in structuring the individual's routine activities, "knifing off" relationships with bad companions, and monitoring the partner's actions (Laub & Sampson, 2003). In contrast, social psychological theories, especially theories of symbolic interaction (Mead, 1934), thrust the actor and actor-based changes into the foreground (Matsueda & Heimer, 1997; Giordano, Schroeder, & Cernkovich, 2007; Maruna, 2001). But while social psychological theories to a greater extent explore individual-level changes, they nevertheless focus heavily on the reciprocal relationship between actor and environment. Thus, sociologically oriented social psychological perspectives in particular highlight the role of social experiences and structural contingencies in fostering cognitions or emotions, or changes in these aspects of the self.

The concept of "hostile attributional bias" provides one example of a cognitive process that is theorized to result in life-course continuity in aggressive behavior. Scholars such as Dodge, Price, Bachorowski, and Newman (1990) argue that more aggressive individuals are more likely than their nonaggressive counterparts to possess a particular type of social information processing deficit, the tendency to overattribute negative intentions of others, even in ambiguous situations. This attributional style emerges early and, as it is an individual difference, it may be linked with a lifelong pattern of aggressive actions. Researchers in this tradition have discussed some social origins of this cognitive bias (see, e.g., Dodge, 2006), and have also developed interventions designed to alter this cognitive distortion, but have more often emphasized the stability of this personality style and its long-term effects on aggressive tendencies (Huessman, Eron, Lefkowitz & Walder, 1984).

Sociologically oriented social psychological theories have focused more attention on life-course changes in crime, especially desistance, although these theories can be extended to understand late onset or more episodic patterns of offending and even continuity/persistence. Giordano et al. (2002) developed a "theory of cognitive transformation," that focused attention on cognitive shifts that precede, accompany, and follow desistance from crime. Many scholars have noted that a basic motivation to change is a first step in affecting sustained behavior change, but Giordano et al. (2002) emphasize that individuals also vary in their openness and receptivity to particular catalysts or "hooks for change." For example, faith-based interventions with offenders are common in prison settings, but some individuals will be more receptive to these efforts than others, and this may also be the case for the same individual at different points in the life course. A variety of experiences can operate as successful hooks for change, but social psychological perspectives emphasize that these are important not only as a source of social control, but because they foster new definitions of the situation (attitudes), a blueprint for how to succeed as a changed individual, and a satisfying and achievable replacement self (see also Maruna, 2001; Matsueda & Heimer, 1997). A final cognitive shift involves a redefinition of one's former criminal actions as no longer desirable and fundamentally incompatible with one's new identity. This emphasis also differs from the social control framework, where motivation is assumed to be constant, but it is the degree of social control over individual conduct that influences variations in criminalinvolvement.

It is useful to distinguish subjective changes that can be tied to particular transition events from those that appear to unfold somewhat independently of these role transitions. For example, a prosocial spouse may well foster more negative attitudes about the desirability of affiliating with certain friends—yet decreased susceptibility to peer pressure is a broader phenomenon that accompanies movement from the period of adolescence to young adulthood, and that is also implicated in the declines in criminal activity that typically occur across this transition (Thornberry, 1987; Giordano, Cernkovich, & Rudolph, 2002). Giordano, Schroeder, and Cernkovich (2007) recently focused on both types of emotional changes, suggesting that an exclusive focus on cognitive processes does not provide a comprehensive treatment of criminal continuity and change (Agnew, 1997). The adolescent to adult transition may result in a diminution of the negative emotions originally connected to criminal behavior (e.g., as engendered by conflict with parents), a diminution of positive emotions connected to crime (what was once a source of thrills and excitement begins to lose its luster; see Shover, 1996; Steffensmeier & Ulmer, 2005), and increased ability to regulate or manage the emotions in socially acceptable ways. These forms of emotional mellowing are likely interrelated. For example, young adults who are no longer as hostile toward their parents (the original source of their negative emotions) may be more likely to turn to them for support (emotion-coping/ management).

Emotions are also implicated in changes that tie more directly to particular transitions such as marriage. Emotions can be seen as providing energy or valence to new lines of action (Collins, 2004; Frijda, 2002). Thus while an ongoing marriage provides a measure of social control over individual conduct, the initial move in the direction of this prosocial terrain is not well explained, or is attributed to chance or luck (Laub, Nagin, & Sampson, 1998). The positive emotions that connect to a new love relationship are, however, available early on and may contribute to the actor's motivation to embark on a self-improvement project. Emotional processes and transformations are also likely integral to the success of other catalysts for change. For example, spiritual transformations are associated with new attitudes and behaviors, but as Pargament (1997) notes, emotions are also central to the conversion process and, for some offenders spirituality has proven an effective vehicle for emotion coping (see Terry, 2003). Maruna (2001) focuses heavily on desisters' feelings of redemption, even beyond the specifically religious connotations of the term (see also McAdams, Diamond, de St. Aubin, & Mansfield, 1997). Persisters believe they are stuck in their current circumstances, while desisters have more positive, agentic worldviews, including feelings of pride that they have been able to put considerable distance between the old criminal self and the one they have crafted around the process of "making good." More recently, Maruna and Mann (2006) extend this notion, suggesting that the tendency within criminal justice and other therapeutic environments to require offenders to take full responsibility for their actions may be misguided, and that doing so is not necessarily a positive step in the desistance process. Instead, offenders' beliefs that the negative behavior was the result of particular external factors may facilitate the process of distancing from these actions, and carve out more productive future goals and actions (see also Mischkowitz, 1994; Vaughan, 2007).

Rational choice theories also focus on subjective, social psychological processes, and have been applied to explorations of the desistance process. For example, Shover's (1996) discussion of desistance theorizes that over time the offender recalibrates the costs and benefits of crime, and many of the changes in perspective (e.g., an increased reluctance to participate in the riskier and more dangerous forms of crime, such as robbery, and increased awareness of time as a diminishing resource) do not fundamentally depend on external catalysts such as a spouse.

Although the above perspectives on desistance vary in emphasis, all tend to highlight the distinctively human capacity for reflection and ability to develop a future plan that diverges from prior habitual actions (Mead, 1934). Thus, human agency is a key concept for social psychological treatments of the desistance process. This need not lead to individualistic theorizing (wherein the individual simply decides to quit crime and sets about doing so); social experiences are critical to initial changes in attitudes and emotions associated with behavior change, and also provide reinforcement during later phases of this process. Some subjective changes (e.g., reduced interest in pleasing one's peers, tired of being tired) may set the stage for the actor to make an "agentic move" (e.g., search for a prosocial romantic partner) that will have the positive effects described in social control and social learning frameworks. Although the spouse can be effective as a monitor and role model, agentic moves are an important part of the entire sequence. Particularly in the contemporary context, marriage is not an inevitable or automatic feature of the transition from adolescence to adulthood, and the choice of a prosocial partner in particular reflects choice-making and the actor's own desire to shift identities and shape a different way of life. As Emirbayer and Goodwin (1994) suggest in their treatment of the agency concept, individuals have an important role in creating the very networks that influence them in turn.

Although most researchers interested in social psychological factors have focused on desistance processes, subjective processes may also be implicated in the late onset pattern. For example, disadvantaged youth may focus heavily on lofty occupational aspirations (e.g., becoming a professional football player) that in the long run prove to be unattainable. For adults with more adult needs and responsibilities, however, feelings of demoralization and even anger about these circumstances, and changing attitudes (cognitions) can support movement into illegal activities or drug use (MacLeod, 1995; Zhang, Loeber, & Stouthamer-Loeber, 1997). The social psychological realm is important because these attitudes and emotions are important mediators—it is the individual's reaction to accumulated structural disadvantage that is key. A concrete example of the late-starter pattern is provided by research that shows that African-American youth have generally low rates of drug and alcohol use, but later on in the life course this early advantage fades (a kind of late onset).

The notion of human agency may also be implicated in late-onset processes. Thus, we noted above that individuals have agency with respect to their choice of social networks and behaviors they pursue. The meanings of these actions may, however, change as individuals mature, and adulthood provides more "degrees of freedom" than adolescence for the pursuit of agentic moves. For example, the youth who is protected by a restrictive family in adolescence may later gravitate toward delinquent companions, get in bar fights, or take advantage of illegal opportunities. Theoretically, this could be conceptualized as simply a reduction in social control, yet more than this absence of social control is required since other individuals are likely to turn away from the wild party or street life even when opportunities for involvement are presented. Actions are always identity-relevant—that is they support one's view of self. However, consistent with a symbolic interactionist perspective, this identity is constantly evolving and the individual has agency with respect to moving toward, as well as away from, different identities as the life course continues to unfold.

A social psychological approach to late onset also includes a role for emotional processes. While the idea of accumulated feelings of demoralization discussed above conveys the notion of a gradual erosion of early "protective" factors, adult relationships and situations may be associated with strong emotional experiences that result in a late onset of some forms of antisocial behavior (e.g., a couple's escalating conflicts that result in eventual violence, or involvement in heavy drinking/drug use). Intimate partner violence is associated with longer duration relationships, cohabitation (Brown & Bulanda, 2008), and other dimensions of relationship "seriousness," all of which are more typical of young adult than adolescent dating patterns (Giordano, Flanigan, Manning, & Longmore, 2009).

Social psychological perspectives also offer an explanation for episodic or intermittent patterns of offending that are common in long-term follow-up studies of delinquent youths (see, e.g., Bushway, Piquero, Broidy, Cauffman, and Maze-rolle, 2001) but that represent embarrassing negative cases for extant theories of desistance, particularly when acts are committed by those who have developed strong bonds or have clearly expressed a strong commitment to turning their lives around (a cognitive transformation). However, a focus on emotional processes provides one conceptual bridge between these broader life-course trends and situated actions that come to be associated with specific derailment experiences. Although it is traditional to focus on aspects of identity that correspond to one's major roles (e.g., family man, good mother, reliable worker), it is also useful to consider that the individual possesses an emotional self that is constantly evolving along with these other identity statuses and, while influenced by the latter, exists somewhat independent of them (Engdahl, 2004; Lupton, 1998). Symbolic interaction theories also stress that past selves are never completely discarded (Mattley, 2002). Thus, when confronted with what are perceived as particularly stressful or trying circumstances, some individuals may draw on earlier forms of emotion-coping (e.g., violence, drug/alcohol use). Indeed, Shover's (1996) rational choice theory seems most amenable to the behavior he focused upon—theft—while violence and drug relapses may be more intimately linked to emotional processes and features of the immediate social context. This does not imply, however, that emotions and cognitions are opposites, but instead that they are intimately related. Thus, even if an individual "flies off the handle" and gets involved in a fight, these strong emotions and associated actions are supported by a set of cognitions that "make sense" or have meaning in light of the current circumstances. In this case, the family man concerns or religious teachings have receded, and other concerns have come to the foreground. Symbolic interaction theories have frequently focused on these situational variables (e.g., factors associated with violence escalation), but to date most of this work has not linked up to the broader life-course tradition and the individual's longer-term pattern of offending.

Developmental psychopathology is a fourth broad perspective for understanding and addressing criminal offending during the transition from adolescence to adulthood. This framework emphasizes the role of development for understanding, preventing, and treating problems of human behavior or adaptation (Cicchetti, 2006; Masten, 2006; Sroufe, 2007). At the heart of this perspective are core tenets of developmental systems theory, in which development is viewed as a dynamic process emerging from complex interactions and co-actions over time involving genes and many interdependent systems from the cellular to the social and societal levels. Because so many interactions are involved in development, across the multiple levels of genes, the developing organism, and experience, the life course is probabilistic. No two individuals will be alike because even identical twins (who have an identical genetic make-up) will have different experiences. Any individual will have the potential to develop in multiple directions, depending on experiences and their timing, as well as stochastic events, while individuals with disparate beginnings also have the potential to develop in similar directions as a result of their life experiences. Thus, there are multiple pathways to similar endpoints (equifinality) and branching pathways from similar starting points (multifinality). Evidence on gene-expression and brain plasticity in relation to experience increasingly underscores the potential for diversity in human development and its dynamic nature. Forks and turning points along developmental pathways hold great interest in developmental psychopathology because they may illuminate key causal processes (e.g., contextual or developmental changes or critical life events) or key windows of plasticity when a system is more likely to change. Positive development, desistance, and resilience all hold as much interest as psychopathology, accelerating problems, and vulnerability. Not surprisingly, problems and disorders with striking developmental patterns also hold great interest for developmental psychopathologists.

The age-crime curve and the varying pathways toward and away from offending are intriguing to consider from the perspective of developmental psychopathology, for reasons very similar to the interest in underage drinking and substance use disorders (Masten, Faden, Zucker, & Spear, 2008). In both cases, individuals, families, and societies have a stake in preventing or reducing the problematic behavior. Both kinds of problems show striking "average" developmental patterns, as well as striking individual trajectories over the life course. Both kinds of problems have interesting linkages and parallels with respect to other behavior problems or competencies, suggesting that there may be some common causes, consequences, or influences that account for continuity and change in both kinds of behaviors.

Rates of drinking, binge drinking, and substance use disorders, for example, also show rapid escalation on average during adolescence, peak in early adulthood, and then decline (Masten et al., 2008). At the same time, there are widely varying individual trajectories of binge and nonbinge drinking observed from adolescence into adulthood, with some individuals abstaining altogether from drinking, others rising and persisting, while others drink more in the early adulthood window or during the college years (Masten et al., 2008; Schulenberg & Maggs, 2002). Use and abuse of other substances show similar patterns (Jackson, Sher, & Schulenberg, 2005). Additionally, the pathways to various substance use problems and antisocial behavior appear to be intertwined, with similar risk factors and high rates of co-occurrence (Zucker, Donovan, Masten, Mattson, & Moss, 2008), for example, the activation of violence as a result of heavy alcohol consumption.

In developmental theory, early onset of problems often implicates either serious problems in the early caregiving environment (e.g., maltreatment, neglect, malnutrition, inconsistent care, exposure to toxicants), a nonnormal organism (e.g., a genetic abnormality), or some combination of vulnerability or sensitivity in the organism and negative experiences. There is great current interest in genetic polymorphisms that may moderate the impact of negative experiences on development, and broadly in the interplay of genes and experience in shaping development (Rutter, Moffitt, & Caspi, 2006). Additionally, there is considerable interest in the possibility that negative early experiences can become biologically embedded in a child who then carries forward a vulnerability in the form of altered brain development or stress reactivity that subsequently contributes to problems (Obradović & Boyce, 2009). High levels of stress with poor parenting, for example, could result in dysregulation of stress response systems and altered brain development leading to poor executive functioning skills. Such individuals enter school and subsequently adolescence with high reactivity and poor impulse control. As a result, they are more likely to be rejected by prosocial peers, do poorly in school, and fall in with deviant peers. When the engines of adolescence turn on as a result of pubertal changes, in the context of poor parenting and deviant peers, these young people are more likely to engage in risky or thrill-seeking behavior, as well as early sexual activity, smoking, and alcohol and drug use.

In addition, evidence is growing that early self-control and antisocial behaviors may initiate a cascade of subsequent problems over time and contexts (Burt & Roisman, 2010; Masten et al., 2005; Obradović, Burt, & Masten, 2010). Early antisocial behavior, in effect, spreads to other domains of function over time, yielding numerous indirect consequences. Cascade effects explain in part why early prevention programs, which often target or alter aggressive, disruptive, impulsive and inattentive behavior, have such a high rate of return on investment (Heckman, 2006). Successful efforts to interrupt these cascades through intervention require good timing and the right targets, and hold the potential of positive cascading effects (see Masten et al., 2009). Patterson and colleagues (Patterson, Forgatch, & DeGarmo, 2010) have demonstrated successful interventions of this kind, with spreading treatment effects over time, in their intervention experiments to prevent or reduce antisocial behavior through improved parenting skills.

In developmental psychopathology, it also has been noted that there are general windows of "vulnerability and opportunity" when the likelihood of change increases (Dahl & Spear, 2004; Masten et al., 2006; Steinberg et al., 2006). Some windows of change may open as a result of development (e.g., puberty) or contextual transitions (e.g., entering or leaving school, leaving home), although some appear to reflect a confluence of developmental and contextual changes.

Early adolescence is widely viewed as a vulnerability window for multiple forms of problems and disorders, when developmental changes and contextual challenges converge to accelerate certain problems, such as risk taking behavior, depression, and delinquency, particularly when parenting quality is poor (Dahl & Spear, 2004; Masten, 2007; Steinberg et al., 2006). In developmental psychopathology, adolescence represents a maturity gap not only because of the interval between sexual maturation and adult social roles, but also because of a gap in developmental systems related to motivation, self-control, and brain development. There is a maturational gap in the timing of "go" systems in the brain that motivate sensation seeking and risky behavior, maturing in early adolescence as a result of puberty, and the "stop and think" systems of the prefrontal cortex, maturing much later in early adulthood. This gap results in a period of vulnerability that has been described as "starting the engines without a skilled driver" (Steinberg et al., 2006). Many societies provide protective monitoring, rituals, and other forms of "scaffolding" to support, protect, and shape the young adolescent in directions approved by the community or society during this window of vulnerability. Young people who enter this period with ineffective parenting and supports, alienated from mainstream society, and in the company of peers who encourage antisocial behavior and impulsive risk-taking behavior, have accelerating risk for a variety of problems and precocious adult behaviors.

The transition to adulthood also is a period of concentrated change when young people are leaving home and striking out on their own. For young people with little or no family support and poor prospects for work or higher education, this can be another time of great challenge and vulnerability. Youth aging out of foster care, or emancipated early due to family conflict, for example, may face the challenges of this transition with very little support. Nonetheless, there is accumulating evidence that this period affords new opportunities more often than new vulnerabilities.

The transition to adulthood often appears to be an opportunity window, when development and context converge to support positive change, including desistance from criminal behavior (Masten, 2007; Masten et al., 2006). It is probably not a coincidence that longitudinal studies of resilience have observed a pattern of development in which individuals turn their lives in a dramatically positive direction or "stage a recovery" during this window (Masten et al., 2006). For most individuals, brain development in this period yields growing capabilities for planning and taking action on those plans, and more reflective decision-making. Societies often provide chances to move into new contexts with supports and opportunities to gain skills and self-efficacy (e.g., apprenticeships, military service, college) and mentors outside the family begin to open new doors for the future. It also is unlikely to be a coincidence that many societies afford these opportunities (with scaffolding) for novice adults at this particular time. During this period, young people are gaining cognitive capacity from the myelination and functional maturation of the prefrontal cortex. Concomitantly, expectations are also increasing for mature behavior and the stakes for offending rise with legal adult status. Romantic relationships are maturing in ways that may foster law-abiding behavior (e.g., growing closeness and intimacy, settling down, diversion and time away from deviant peers). As a result of these developments, the capacity for change increases along with the motivation and opportunities to move toward positive adult roles.

Normative growth in the potential and opportunities for change does not, of course, assure positive change, as many observers and investigators have noted in developmental psychopathology, as well as the dynamic developmental models of offending described above. The brain may be "hijacked" by drug addiction, the culture of college may be conducive to binge drinking, a young person may be recruited by an anti-social or anti-society organization (there are dangerous 'mentors'), and discrimination may lead a young person away from mainstream goals. Some young people are cut off from societal opportunities because of lingering consequences of earlier missteps (e.g., school dropout or a criminal record). And some young people may simply be unlucky in that the consequences of their behavior alter their opportunities or potential (e.g., a person becomes pregnant or is injured in an accident). A combination of these factors could increase the probability of persistent involvement in offending for some, or late onset of offending for others, resulting in a variety of offending trajectories over the course of adolescence and early adulthood that do not follow a decline of criminal behavior in the transition to adulthood observed in general age-crime curves.

The biopsychosocial model. Neural development during early childhood is characterized by massive changes that support the development of mature regulation of emotion and behavior. Early neural development is characterized by an initial exuberant increase in synaptic connections followed by pruning and synaptic elimination that improve the efficiency of brain connectivity (Huttenlocher, 1979; Huttenlocher, 1990; Ramakers, 2005). Anatomic neuroimaging studies are now providing *in vivo* evidence of these dramatic maturational changes that highlight differences in the developmental trajectories across brain regions. In particular, frontal regions involved in executive functioning and attentional processes mature later than regions involved in more basic functions such as motor or sensory cortices. Giedd et al. (1996) demonstrated that by age 6, total brain volume has attained approximately 95% of the lifetime peak volume. White matter volume, at least when quantified without reference to newer diffusion-based techniques, increases linearly with age without discernible variation across brain regions. In contrast, cortical gray matter changes are nonlinear and show substantial regional differences (Giedd et al., 1999). Frontal gray matter increases from childhood through early adolescence and then declines towards early adulthood. Similar patterns have been observed in the developmental trajectories of cortical thickness (Shaw et al., 2008).

Age-related changes in brain activity accompany these anatomic shifts across development. For example, changes in regional cerebral glucose metabolism across early development mirror the phases of synaptic excess and elimination observed in anatomical studies (Chugani, Phelps, and Mazziotta, 1987). Specifically, glucose metabolism increases from birth, peaks around age 9, and declines to adult levels through adolescence. Functional magnetic resonance imaging (fMRI) studies suggest that cortical functional development is characterized by a shift from diffuse to focal cortical responses when performing tasks requiring attentional control (Casey et al., 1997; Bunge, Dudukovic, Thomas, Vaidya, and Gabrieli, 2002; Durston, Mulder, Casey, Ziermans, and van Engeland, 2006; Tamm, Menon, and Reiss, 2002). A similar pattern of more diffuse local functional connectivity has been documented in examinations of spontaneous fluctuations of hemodynamic activity (Fair et al., 2008; Fair et al., 2009; Kelly et al., 2009; Supekar, Musen, and Menon, 2009).

This pattern of diffuse activation in children suggests that local functional networks are immature and inefficient while more focal activations in adults are presumed to be a consequence of synaptic elimination and improved efficiency. Convergent methods demonstrate that brain circuits involved in cognitive control, attention, and emotion regulation are actively developing throughout late childhood and adolescence. Thus, decreases in risk behaviors and conduct problems that occur starting in middle to late adolescence are likely related to maturity of the brain and associated regulation.

With regard to externalizing problems such as aggression, recent studies have demonstrated altered structure of dorsal anterior cingulate cortex and amygdala (Whittle et al., 2008; Boes, Tranel, Anderson, and Nopoulos, 2008). In a study of 117 nonreferred children (ages 7–17), Boes et al., (2008) found a significant negative partial correlation between aggressive behaviors in boys, as measured by parent and teacher report, and the volume of the right anterior cingulate cortex. A study of adolescent aggression during parent-child interactions found amygdala volume correlated positively with duration of aggressive behaviors, suggesting an inability to down-regulate quickly (Whittle et al., 2008). Alterations in anterior cingulate cortex function associated with aggression have also been observed in a study of healthy adults stratified based on a common polymorphism in the monoamine oxidase A (MAOA) gene which has been associated with impulsive aggression in humans and animals (Meyer-Lindenberg et al., 2006). Individuals with the low-expression variant that is associated with increased risk of violent behavior showed significant reductions in anterior cingulate cortex and amygdala volumes and increased amygdala response to emotional stimuli, compared to those with the high-expression allele. Men with the low-expression variant showed deficient activation of dorsal anterior cingulate cortex during an inhibitory control task (Meyer-Lindenberg et al., 2006). Taken together, these findings suggest that the anterior cingulate cortex may not effectively regulate amygdala activity in individuals who are genetically predisposed towards impulsivity and aggression.

In summary, compelling evidence from clinical studies of adults and adolescents implicates altered function in the anterior cingulate cortex–amygdala circuit in the pathophysiology of emotion and behavioral dysregulation. Reduced activation of the anterior cingulate cortex and increased reactivity of the amygdala in depressed and aggressive individuals suggests that the regulatory function of the anterior cingulate cortex is compromised in many of these individuals.

Socialization depends, in part, on the ability of the child to learn from reward and punishment (e.g., fear conditioning) within proper conditions (social, economic, psychological, etc.). Neurobiologically based malfunctions of those learning abilities create a neurobiological base for a failing process of socialization. For instance, in participants with early- and adolescence-onset forms of conduct disorder (CD), fear conditioning deficits were observed (Fairchild et al., 2008). Compromised fear conditioning contributes to antisocial behavior and probably to a lack of conscience. This is illustrated by a longitudinal study of Gao, Raine, Venables, Dawson, and Mednick (2010), which demonstrated that poor fear conditioning at age 3 predisposes to crime at age 23 because individuals who lack fear are less likely to avoid situations and events associated with future punishment. Several parts of the cortex and the amygdala-hippocampal complex are involved in this process of socialization and social learning, building up "morality" and the sensitivity for reward and punishment (Van Overwalle & Baetens, 2009; Schug, Gao, Glenn, Yang, and Raine, 2010).

Early in adolescence, a dramatic remodeling of the reward circuitry occurs, resulting in "go" systems in the brain that fuel sensation seeking and risky behavior as a result of puberty (Van Leijenhorst et al., 2009, 2010). A more gradual and lengthier maturation of brain systems involved in self-regulation has also been demonstrated (Steinberg, 2010). For instance, "stop and think" systems in the prefrontal cortex will not mature before early adulthood (Van Leijenhorst et al., 2009, 2010). These pace differences create a kind of maturational gap: reward-seeking tends to increase between preadolescence and mid-adolescence and declines thereafter in a curvilinear pattern. Level of impulsivity, on the other hand, follows a linear pattern, declining steadily from age 10 on. The combination of relatively higher tendencies to seek reward and still maturing capacities for self-control may be responsible for the heightened vulnerability to risk-taking in middle adolescence (Steinberg, 2010).

It seems plausible that improvement in self-control during adolescence partly underlies desistance from delinquent behavior. Maturation of impulse control and suppression of aggression is, however, also associated with other brain systems involved in the maturation of personal responsibility, resistance to peer influence, and consideration of others. Maturation of these two brain systems (the 'cognitive-control' one and 'socio-emotional' one) may be differentially related to desistance from antisocial behavior (Monahan, Steinberg, Cauffman, & Mulvey, 2009).

As adolescence is a critical developmental period for the maturation of neurobiological processes, substance abuse also typically emerges during this stage. An imbalance between cognitive controls in the face of appetitive cues may be predictive for a greater risk for alcohol and substance dependence (Casey & Jones, 2010). Substance abuse can influence the regulatory function of the brain negatively. Diminished self-control not only increases the imbalance between the reward and regulatory functions in the brain but also decreases the threshold towards criminal behavior. As substance abuse is associated with the risk of criminal behavior it might indirectly explain to some extent late-onset antisocial behavior.

Psychophysiological features are also of interest in explaining behavior during the transition from adolescence into adulthood since these features seem to be associated with aggression and criminal behavior. Low heart rate in childhood has been demonstrated to be predictive for aggression during adolescence, while high heart rate "protected" against it (Ortiz & Raine, 2004). Antisocial adolescents who desisted from criminal offending showed higher heart rates. In a Dutch study, young delinquents in the age range of 12–14 consistently had lower overall levels of arousal as measured by heart rate (Popma and Raine, 2006). In general, a low heart rate (HR) and reduced skin conductance (SC) are considered to be factors associated with antisocial behavior in children and adolescents (Ortiz & Raine, 2004). How-ever, whether higher HR and normal SC can function as protective factors remains to be seen (Loeber, Pardini, Stouthamer-Loeber, and Raine, 2007).

Genetic research focuses on heritability estimates of antisocial behavior as well as on candidate genes for antisociality, in interaction with the environment. Twin studies provided substantial evidence for these genetic influences of aggressive and antisocial behavior (Popma & Raine, 2006; Schug et al., 2010). Some genes seem to influence antisocial behavior across the entire lifespan, whereas others only appear to operate in adolescence or adulthood. There is some preliminary evidence that specific candidate genes are associated with adolescent-onset anti-social behavior (Burt & Mikolajewski, 2008) and also persistence is theoretically associated with genetic approaches (Silberg, Rutter, Tracy, Maes, and Eaves, 2007).

Undoubtedly, the expression of genes is embedded in complex gene-environ-ment interactions and the initiation and maintenance of aggression is influenced by the family environment. Within such a complex interaction the explanatory power of these biological predispositional variables may be relatively greater in more or less "healthy" family circumstances where the "social push" towards anti-social behavior is low (Schug et al., 2010; Popma & Raine 2006). During adoles-cence, negative peer influences form an example of such a "social push."

Conclusions and Future Directions

Several theoretical models offer clear, coherent explanations for offending in the transition from adolescence to adulthood. As noted above, these theories also en-joy considerable empirical support. It appears that, while stable, individual differ-ences retain some importance for explaining offending during the transition years, changing life circumstances in such areas as family formation, work, and social network affiliations are also quite important.

The theories discussed in this chapter focus on broad developmental patterns to explain offending during the transition from adolescence to adulthood. For example, some of the theories, especially those that adopt a static orientation, focus on the impact of early characteristics on offending that occurs between the ages of 15 and 29. The dynamic theories focus on changes that occur along major life-course trajectories such as education, work, and family formation. For example, the order and timing of transitions along these trajectories are used to provide explanations for persistence and for desistance as individuals move from adoles-cence, through early adulthood, to the greater stability of the adult years.

The theories that are discussed in Chapter 4 complement this broad develop-mental perspective. They focus on the short-term effects that life circumstances can have on offending. For example, they examine whether offending increases or decreases during periods when the individual is unemployed, or whether parent-hood and living with a child leads to changes in offending patterns. That chapter also discusses the moderating influence that neighborhood and place characteristics can have on these processes. Clearly, a complete theory of criminal offending during the transition years would incorporate both the long-term developmental processes that are the focus of this chapter and the short-term changes in life circumstances that are the focus of Chapter 4. Indeed, the systematic incorporation of both of these influences into one conceptual framework is a crucial next step for theory development in this area. Doing so will provide both a more comprehensive theoretical explanation for offending and more precise recommendations for policy and practice.

Although life-course criminology has made considerable progress in refining theoretical explanations, there are still many topics that require additional attention. Among them are the following:

1. Much more is known about persistence and desistance as compared to late-onset offending. Late onset is an important pattern of offending, both theoretically and in terms of policy implications, and deserves more explicit theoretical attention.

2. Several researchers have pointed to intermittent patterns of offending where offenders stop for a period of time and then relapse to continue their involvement in offending. Very little attention, either theoretically or empirically, has been devoted to this pattern. One of the few exceptions is Laub and Sampson (2003). Longitudinal studies should describe this pattern more precisely and theoretical models should explain the factors associated with why offenders stop and then reinitiate offending after some period of time.

3. Criminological theories have focused more attention on explaining broad patterns of persistence versus desistance and less attention on explaining finer-grained distinctions in criminal careers. For example, there are fewer explanations of escalation versus de-escalation (but see Le Blanc, 1997) or of the different factors associated with the drop in offending and in the maintenance of the near-zero offending for the study of desistance. Movement toward investigation of these fine-grained processes will yield more detailed understanding of offending during the transition years as well as more refined policy implications.

Although these and other topics need to be addressed in future theoretical development, it is important to note that they will start from a solid theoretical base. Current theories clearly provide helpful, even if incomplete, explanations for offending and changes in offending. The task for the future is to build upon the considerable progress that has been made in the past quarter century.

The theories discussed in this chapter have numerous implications for policy and practice. One of the strong themes to emerge from these conceptual models is the long-term negative consequences of disorderly transitions that can occur during this developmental stage. For example, failure to complete high school and teen parenthood have important effects on the individual and his or her family. This suggests the importance of developing effective prevention programs to reduce the occurrence of these precocious transitions in the first place. Doing so will not only improve the level of educational attainment and the process of family formation in general, but it is also likely to have secondary effects such as reducing the prevalence and frequency of criminal offending during the early adult years. Obviously, these prevention efforts will not be entirely successful. Thus, it is also vitally important to develop effective services to reduce the future negative consequences that are likely to befall high school dropouts and teen parents. At the same time, the theories discussed here also point to the long-term benefits of early intervention programs. Offending during the transition years is not entirely explained by proximal life-course circumstances; early influences such as the quality of parenting practices and the level of school disengagement also play a role. As a result, effective early intervention programs are likely to have benefits that are evident even during the early adult years (see also Welsh et al., Chapter 9, this volume).

Finally, we note that contemporary criminology offers a full spectrum of well-developed static and dynamic theories to explain differences in trajectories of offending during the transition to adulthood. Yet the very fact of these differing trajectories calls out for theories that can account for malleability or change. While academic criminologists now take dynamic theories for granted, such accounts are only beginning to diffuse into public discourse and policy. For these latter audiences, the notion of dramatic change in offending trajectories has important, if not revolutionary, implications. To the extent that we can observe and explain malleability or change in criminal behavior during the teens and twenties, it becomes progressively more difficult to justify applying permanent sanctions to young offenders. Policies such as life sentences without possibility of parole or the lifelong application of civil disabilities such as disenfranchisement assume that criminality is a fixed trait that crystallizes early in the life course and is all but immutable thereafter. Our review of criminological theory and the available empirical evidence call such dour assumptions into question, suggesting instead that change is common if not ubiquitous.

References

Agnew, R. (1997). Stability and change over the life course: A strain theory explanation. In T.P. Thornberry (Ed.), *Developmental theories of crime and delinquency* (pp. 101–132). New Brunswick, NJ: Transaction.

Akers, R.L. (1998). *Social learning and social structure: A general theory of crime and deviance.* Boston: Northeastern University Press.

Bernburg, J.G. & Krohn, M.D. (2003). Labeling, life chances, and adult crime: The direct and indirect effects of official intervention in adolescence on crime in early adulthood. *Criminology*, 41, 1287–1318.

Bernburg, J.G., Krohn, M.D., & Rivera, C.J. (2006). Official labeling, criminal embedded-ness, and subsequent delinquency: A longitudinal test of labeling theory. *Journal of Research in Crime and Delinquency*, 43, 67–88.

Bersani, B., Laub, J.H., & Nieuwbeerta, P. (2009). Marriage and desistance from crime in the Netherlands: Do gender and socio-historical context matter? *Journal of Quantitative Criminology*, 25, 3–24.

Boes, A.D., Tranel, D., Anderson, S.W., & Nopoulos, P. (2008). Right anterior cingulate: A neuroanatomical correlate of aggression and defiance in boys. *Behavioral Neuroscience*, 122, 677–684.

Bouffard, L.A. & Laub, J. (2004). Jail or the army: Does military service facilitate desistance? In S. Maruna & R. Immarigeon (Eds.), *After crime and punishment: Pathways to offender reintegration* (pp. 129–151). Portland, OR: Willan Publishing.

Brown, S.L., & Bulanda, J.R. (2008). Relationship violence in early adulthood: A compari-son of daters, cohabitors, and marrieds. *Social Science Research*, 37, 73–87.

Bunge, S.A., Dudukovic, N.M., Thomason, M.E., Vaidya, C.J., & Gabrieli, J.D.E. (2002). Immature frontal lobe contributions to cognitive control in children: Evidence from fMRI. *Neuron*, 33, 301–311.

Burt, S.A., & Mikolajewski, A.J. (2008). Preliminary evidence that specific candidate genes are associated with adolescent-onset antisocial behavior. *Aggressive Behavior*, 34, 437–445.

Burt, K.B., & Roisman, G.I. (2010). Competence and psychopathology: Cascade effects in the NICHD Study of Early Child Care and Youth Development. *Development and Psychopathology*, 22, 557–567.

Bushway, S.D., Piquero, A.R., Broidy, L. Cauffman, E., & Mazerolle, P. (2001). An empirical framework for studying desistance as a process. *Criminology*, 39, 491–516.

Bushway, S.D., Thornberry, T.P., & Krohn, M.D. (2003). Desistance as a developmental process: A comparison of static and dynamic approaches. *Journal of Quantitative Criminology*, 19, 129–153.

Casey, B.J., & Jones, R.M. (2010). Neurobiology of the adolescent brain and behavior: Impli-cations for substance use disorders. *Journal of the American Academy of Child & Adoles-cent Psychiatry*, 49, 1189–1201.

Casey, B.J., Trainor, R.J., Orendi, J.L., Schubert, A.B., Nystrom, L.E., Giedd, J.N., Castella-nos, F.X., Haxby, J.V., Noll, D.C., Cohen, J.D., Forman, S.D., Dahl, R.E., & Rapoport, J.L. (1997). A developmental functional MRI study of prefrontal activation during perfor-mance of a go-no-go task. *Journal of Cognitive Neuroscience*, 9, 835–847.

Catalano, R.F., & Hawkins, J.D. (1986). *The social development model: A theory of antisocial behavior*. Paper presented at the Safeco Lectureship on Crime and Delinquency, School of Social Work, University of Washington, Seattle, WA.

Catalano, R.F., & Hawkins, J.D. (1996). The social development model: A theory of antisocial behavior. In J.D. Hawkins (Ed.), *Delinquency and crime: Current theories* (pp. 149–197). New York: Cambridge University Press.

Chugani, H.T., Phelps, M.E., & Mazziotta, J.C. (1987). Positron emission tomography study of human brain functional development. *Annals of Neurology*, 22, 487–497.

Chung, I.-J., Hill, K.G., Hawkins, J.D., Gilchrist, L.D., & Nagin, D.S. (2002). Childhood predictors of offense trajectories. *Journal of Research in Crime and Delinquency*, 39, 60–90.

Cicchetti, D. (2006). Development and psychopathology. In D. Cicchetti & D. Cohen (Eds.), *Developmental psychopathology: Vol. 1. Theory and method (2nd ed.,* pp. 1–23). Hoboken, NJ: Wiley.

Cohen, L.E. & Vila, B.J. (1996). Self-control and social control: An exposition of the Gottfredson-Hirschi/Sampson-Laub debate. *Studies on Crime and Crime Prevention,* 5, 125–150.

Collins, R. (2004). *Interaction ritual chains.* Princeton, NJ: Princeton University Press.

Dahl, R.E., & Spear, L.P. (2004). (Eds.). Adolescent brain development: Vulnerabilities and opportunities. *Annals of the New York Academy of Sciences,* 1021.

Dannefer, D. (1984). Adult development and social theory: A paradigmatic appraisal. *American Sociological Review,* 49, 100–116.

Dodge, K.A. (2006). Translational science in action: Hostile attributional style and the development of aggressive behavior problems. *Developmental Psychopathology,* 18, 791–814.

Dodge, K.A., Price, J.M., Bachorowski, J., & Newman, J.P. (1990). Hostile attributional biases in severely aggressive adolescents. *Journal of Abnormal Psychology,* 99, 385–392.

Draganski, B., Gaser, C., Busch, V., Schuierer, G., Bogdahn, U., & May, A. (2004). Changes in grey matter induced by training. *Nature,* 427, 311–312.

Durston, S., Mulder, M., Casey, B.J., Ziermans, T., & van Engeland, H. (2006). Activation in ventral prefrontal cortex is sensitive to genetic vulnerability for attention deficit hyperactivity disorder. *Biological Psychiatry,* 60, 1062–1070.

Eggleston, E.P., & Laub, J.H. (2002). The onset of adult offending: A neglected dimension of the criminal career. *Journal of Criminal Justice,* 30, 603–622.

Elder, G.H. (1997). The life course and human development. In R.M. Lerner (Ed.), *Handbook of child psychology, volume 1: Theoretical models of human development* (pp. 939–991). New York: Wiley.

Elliott, D.S., Huizinga, D., & Ageton, S.S. (1985). *Explaining delinquency and drug use.* Beverly Hills, CA: Sage.

Emirbayer, M., & Goodwin, J. (1994). Network analysis, culture, and the problem of agency. *American Journal of Sociology,* 99, 1411–1454.

Engdahl, E. (2004). *A theory of the emotional self: From the standpoint of a neo-Meadian.* Unpublished doctoral dissertation, Örebro University, Sweden.

Fair, D.A., Cohen, A.L., Dosenbach, N.U.F., Church, J.A., Miezin, F.M., Barch, D.M., Raichle, M.E., Petersen, S.E., & Schlaggar, B.L. (2008). The maturing architecture of the brain's default network. *Proceedings of the National Academy of Sciences of the United States of America,* 105, 4028–4032.

Fair, D.A., Cohen, A.L., Power, J.D., Dosenbach, N.U.F., Church, J.A., Miezin, F.M., Schlaggar, B.L., & Petersen, S.E. (2009). Functional brain networks develop from a "local to distributed" organization. *PLos Computational Biology,* 5, e1000381.

Fairchild, G., van Goozen, S.H.M., Stollery, S.J., Brown, J., Gardiner, J., Herbert, J., & Goodyer, I.M. (2008). Cortisol diurnal rhythm and stress reactivity in male adolescents with early-onset or adolescence-onset conduct disorder. *Biological Psychiatry,* 64, 599–606.

Farrington, D.P. (2000). Explaining and preventing crime: The globalization of knowledge—The American Society of Criminology 1999 Presidential Address. *Criminology,* 38, 1–24.

Farrington, D.P. (2003). Developmental and life-course criminology: Key theoretical and empirical issues—The 2002 Sutherland Address. *Criminology*, 41, 221–255.

Farrington, D.P., Gallagher, B., Morley, L., St. Ledger, R.J., & West, D.J. (1986). Unemployment, school leaving, and crime. *British Journal of Criminology*, 26, 335–356.

Farrington, D.P., & Hawkins, J.D. (1991). Predicting participation, early onset and later persistence in officially recorded offending. *Criminal Behaviour and Mental Health*, 1, 1–33.

Farrington, D.P., & West, D.J. (1995). Effects of marriage, separation and children on offending by adult males. In J. Hagan (Ed.), *Current perspectives on aging and the life cycle, vol. 4: Delinquency and disrepute in the life course* (pp. 249–281). Greenwich, CT: JAI Press.

Frijda, N.H. (2002). Emotions as motivational states. In E. Pacherie (Ed.), *European review of philosophy: Emotion and action* (Vol. 5, pp. 11–32). Stanford, CA: CSLI.

Gao, Y., Raine, A., Venables, P.H., Dawson, M.E., & Mednick, S.A. (2010). Reduced electrodermal fear conditioning from ages 3 to 8 years is associated with aggressive behavior at age 8 years. *Journal of Child Psychology and Psychiatry*, 51, 550–558.

Giedd, J.N., Blumenthal, J., Jeffries, N.O., Castellanos, F.X., Liu, H., Zijdenbos, A., Paus, T., Evans, A.C., & Rapoport, J.L. (1999). Brain development during childhood and adolescence: A longitudinal MRI study. *Nature Neuroscience*, 2, 861–863.

Giedd, J.N., Vaituzis, C., Hamburger, S.D., Lange, N., Rajapakse, J.C., Kaysen, D., Vauss, Y.C., & Rapoport, J.L. (1996). Quantitative MRI of the temporal lobe, amygdale, and hippocampus in normal human development: Ages 4–18 years. *The Journal of Comparative Neurology*, 366, 223–230.

Giordano, P.C., Cernkovich, S.A., & Rudolph, J.L. (2002). Gender, crime, and desistance: Toward a theory of cognitive transformation. *American Journal of Sociology*, 107, 990–1064.

Giordano, P.C., Flanigan, C.M., Manning, W.D., & Longmore, M.A. (2009). *Developmental shifts in romantic relationships from adolescence to early adulthood.* Paper presented at the annual meeting of the American Sociological Association, San Francisco, California.

Giordano, P.C., Schroeder, R.D., & Cernkovich, S.A. (2007). Emotions and crime over the life course: A neo-Meadian perspective on criminal continuity and change. *American Journal of Sociology*, 112, 1603–1661.

Glueck, S., & Glueck, E.T. (1940). *Juvenile delinquents grown up.* New York: The Commonwealth Fund.

Glueck, S., & Glueck, E.T. (1950). *Unraveling juvenile delinquency.* Cambridge, MA: Harvard University Press.

Gomez-Smith, Z., & Piquero, A.R. (2005). An examination of adult onset offending. *Journal of Criminal Justice*, 33, 515–525.

Gottfredson, M.R. (2006). The empirical status of control theory in criminology. In F.T. Cullen, J.P. Wright, & K.R. Blevins (Eds.), *Taking stock: The status of criminological theory* (pp. 77–100). New Brunswick, NJ: Transaction.

Gottfredson, M.R., & Hirschi, T. (1990). *A general theory of crime.* Stanford, CA: Stanford University Press.

Hamil-Luker, J., Land, K.C., & Blau, J. (2003). Diverse trajectories of cocaine use through early adulthood among rebellious and socially conforming youth. *Social Science Research*, 33, 300–321.

Hawkins, J.D., Herrenkohl, T., Farrington, D.P., Brewer, D., Catalano, R.F., & Harachi, T.W. (1998). A review of predictors of youth violence. In R. Loeber & D.P. Farrington (Eds.),

Serious and violent juvenile offenders: Risk factors and successful interventions (pp. 106–146). Thousand Oaks, CA: Sage.

Heckman, J.J. (2006). Skill formation and the economics of investing in disadvantaged children. *Science, 312,* 1900–1902.

Hirschi, T., & Gottfredson, M.R. (2001). Self-control theory. In R. Paternoster & R. Bachman (Eds.), *Explaining criminals and crime: Essays in contemporary criminological theory* (pp. 81–96). Los Angeles, CA: Roxbury Publishers.

Horney, J., Osgood, D.W., & Marshall, I.H. (1995). Criminal careers in the short-term: Intraindividual variability in crime and its relation to local life circumstances. *American Sociological Review, 60,* 655–673.

Huesmann, L.R., Eron, L.D., Lefkowitz, M.M., & Walder, L.O. (1984). Stability of aggression over time and generations. *Developmental Psychology, 20,* 1120–1134.

Huttenlocher, P.R. (1979). Synaptic density in human frontal cortex: Developmental changes and effects of aging. *Brain Research, 163,* 195–205.

Huttenlocher, P.R. (1990). Morphometic study of human cerebral cortex development. *Neuropsychologia, 28,* 517–552.

Jackson, K.M., Sher, K.J., & Schulenberg, J.E. (2005). Conjoint developmental trajectories of young adult alcohol and tobacco use. *Journal of Abnormal Psychology, 114,* 612–626.

Kelly, A.M.C., Di Martino, A., Uddin, L.Q., Shehzad, Z., Gee, D.G., Reiss, P.T., Margulies, D.S., Castellanos, F.X., & Milham, M.P. (2009). Development of anterior cingulate functional connectivity from late childhood to early adulthood. *Cerebral Cortex, 19,* 640–657.

King, R., Massoglia, M., & MacMillan, R. (2007). The context of marriage and crime: Gender, the propensity to marry, and offending in early adulthood. *Criminology, 45,* 33–65.

Krohn, M.D., Lizotte, A.J., & Perez, C.M. (1997). The interrelationship between substance use and precocious transitions to adult statuses. *Journal of Health and Social Behavior, 38,* 87–103.

Laub, J.H., Nagin, D.S., & Sampson, R.J. (1998). Trajectories of change in criminal offending: Good marriages and the desistance process. *American Sociological Review, 63,* 225–238.

Laub, J.H., & Sampson, R.J. (2003). *Shared beginnings, divergent lives: Delinquent boys to age 70.* Cambridge, MA: Harvard University Press.

Le Blanc, M. (1997). A generic control theory of the criminal phenomenon: The structural and dynamic statements of an integrated multilayered control theory. In T.P. Thornberry (Ed.), *Developmental theories of crime and delinquency* (pp. 215–285). New Brunswick, NJ: Transaction.

Lipsey, M.W., & Derzon, J.H. (1998). Predictors of violent or serious delinquency in adolescence and early adulthood: A synthesis of longitudinal research. In R. Loeber & D.P. Farrington (Eds.), *Serious and violent juvenile offenders: Risk factors and successful interventions* (pp. 86–105). Thousand Oaks, CA: Sage.

Loeber, R., Pardini, D.A., Stouthamer-Loeber, M., & Raine, A. (2007). Do cognitive, physiological, and psychosocial risk and promotive factors predict desistance from delinquency in males? *Development and Psychopathology, 19,* 867–887.

Loeber, R., Slot, N.W., van der Laan, P., & Hoeve, M. (2008). Tomorrow's criminals: The development of child delinquency and effective interventions. Burlington, VT: Ashgate Publishing Company.

Lupton, D. (1998). *The emotional self: A sociocultural exploration.* London: Sage.

MacLeod, J. (1995). *Ain't no makin it: Aspirations and attainment in a low-income neighborhood.* Boulder, CO: Westview Press.

Mannheim, H. (1967). *Comparative criminology.* Boston: Houghton Mifflin Company.

Maruna, S. (2001). *Making good: How ex-convicts reform and rebuild their lives.* Washington, DC: American Psychological Association Books.

Maruna, S., & Mann, R. (2006). Fundamental attribution errors? Re-thinking cognitive distortions. *Legal and Criminological Psychology,* 11, 155–177.

Massoglia, M., & Uggen, C. (2010). Settling down and aging out: Toward an interactionist theory of desistance and the transition to adulthood. *American Journal of Sociology,* 116, 543–582.

Masten, A.S. (2006). Developmental psychopathology: Pathways to the future. *International Journal of Behavioral Development,* 31, 46–53.

Masten, A.S. (2007). Competence, resilience and development in adolescence: Clues for prevention science. In D. Romer & E.F. Walker (Eds.), *Adolescent psychopathology and the developing brain: Integrating brain and prevention science* (pp. 31–52). New York: Oxford University Press.

Masten, A.S., Faden, V.B., Zucker, R.A., & Spear, L.P. (2008). Underage drinking: A developmental framework. *Pediatrics, 121, Supplement* 4, S235–S251.

Masten, A.S., Long, J.D., Kuo, S. I-C., McCormick, C.M., & Desjardins, C.D. (2009). Developmental models of strategic intervention. *European Journal of Developmental Science,* 3, 282–291.

Masten, A.S., Obradović, J., & Burt, K. (2006). Resilience in emerging adulthood: Developmental perspectives on continuity and transformation. In J.J. Arnett & J.L. Tanner (Ed.), *Emerging adults in America: Coming of age in the 21st Century* (pp. 173–190). Washington, DC: American Psychological Association Press.

Masten, A.S., Roisman, G.I., Long, J.D., Burt, K.B., Obradović, J., Riley, J.R., Boelcke-Stennes, K., & Tellegen, A. (2005). Developmental cascades: Linking academic achievement, externalizing and internalizing symptoms over 20 years. *Developmental Psychology,* 41, 733–746.

Matsueda, R.L., & Heimer, K. (1997). A symbolic interactionist theory of role-transitions, role-commitments, and delinquency. In T.P. Thornberry (Ed.), *Developmental theories of crime and delinquency* (pp. 162–213). New Brunswick, NJ: Transaction.

Mattley, C. (2002). The temporality of emotion: Constructing past emotions. *Symbolic Interaction,* 25, 363–378.

McAdams, D.P., Diamond, A., de St. Aubin, E., & Mansfield, E.D. (1997). Stories of commitment: The psychosocial construction of generative lives. *Journal of Personality and Social Psychology,* 72, 678–694.

Mead, G.H. (1934). *Mind, self, and society from the standpoint of a social behaviorist.* Chicago: University of Chicago Press.

Mednick, S.A. (1977). A biosocial theory of the learning of law-abiding behavior. In S.A. Mednick & K.O. Christiansen (Eds.), *Biosocial bases of criminal behavior* (pp. 1–8). New York: Gardner Press.

Meyer-Lindenberg, A., Buckholtz, J.W., Kolachana, B., Hariri, A.R., Pezawas, L., Blasi, G., Wabnitz, A., Honea, R., Verchinski, B., Callicott, J.H., Egan, M., Mattay, V., & Weinberger, D.R. (2006). Neural mechanisms of genetic risk for impulsivity and violence in humans. *Proceedings of the National Academy of Sciences of the United States of America*, 103, 6269–6274.

Mischkowitz, R. (1994). Desistance from a delinquent way of life? In E.G.M. Weitekamp & H.-J. Kerner (Eds.), *Cross-national longitudinal research on human development and criminal behavior* (pp. 303–330). Boston: Kluwer Academic.

Moffitt, T.E. (1993). Adolescence-limited and life-course-persistent antisocial behavior: A developmental taxonomy. *Psychological Review*, 100, 674–701.

Moffitt, T.E. (2006). A review of research on the taxonomy of life-course persistent versus adolescence-limited antisocial behavior. In F.T. Cullen, J.P. Wright, & K.R. Blevins (Eds.), *Taking stock: The status of criminological theory* (pp. 277–312). New Brunswick, NJ: Transaction.

Moffitt, T.E., Caspi, A. Harrington, H., & Milne, B.J. (2002). Males on the life-course-persistent and adolescence-limited antisocial pathways: Follow-up at age 26 years. *Development and Psychopathology*, 14, 179–207.

Moffitt, T.E., Caspi, A., Rutter, M., & Silva, P.A. (2001). *Sex differences in antisocial behaviour: Conduct disorder, delinquency, and violence in the Dunedin longitudinal study*. Cambridge, UK: Cambridge University Press.

Monahan, K.C., Steinberg, L., Cauffman, E., & Mulvey, E.P. (2009). Trajectories of antisocial behavior and psychosocial maturity from adolescence to young adulthood. *Developmental Psychology*, 45, 1654–1668.

Morizot, J., & Le Blanc, M. (2007). Behavioral, self, and social control predictors of desistance from crime: A test of launch and contemporaneous effect models. *Journal of Contemporary Criminal Justice*, 23, 50–71.

Nagin, D.S. (2005). *Group-based modeling of development*. Cambridge, MA: Harvard University Press.

Nagin, D.S., Farrington, D.P., & Moffitt, T.E. (1995). Life-course trajectories of different types of offenders. *Criminology*, 33, 111–139.

Nagin, D., & Land, K.C. (1993). Age, criminal careers, and population heterogeneity: Specification and estimation of a nonparametric, mixed Poisson model. *Criminology*, 31, 327–362.

Nagin, D.S., & Paternoster, R. (1991). On the relationship of past and future participation in delinquency. *Criminology*, 29, 163–189.

Nagin, D.S., & Paternoster, R. (2000). Population heterogeneity and state dependence: State of the evidence and directions for future research. *Journal of Quantitative Criminology*, 16, 117–145.

Obradović, J.J., & Boyce, W.T. (2009). Individual differences in behavioral, physiological, and genetic sensitivities to contexts: Implications for development and adaptation. *Developmental Neuroscience*, 31, 300–308.

Obradović, J.J., Burt, K.B., & Masten, A.S. (2010). Testing a dual cascade model linking competence and symptoms over 20 years from childhood to adulthood. *Journal of Clinical Child and Adolescent Psychology*, 39, 90–102.

Ortiz, J., & Raine, A. (2004). Heart rate level and antisocial behavior in children and adolescents. *Journal of the American Academy of Child & Adolescent Psychiatry*, 43, 154–162.

Pargament, K.I. (1997). *The psychology of religion and coping: Theory, research, practice*. New York: Guilford Press.

Paternoster, R., Brame, R., & Farrington, D.P. (2001). On the relationship between adolescent and adult convictions. *Journal of Quantitative Criminology*, 17, 201–225.

Paternoster, R., Dean, C.W. Piquero, A.R., Mazzerolle, P., & Brame, R. (1997). General-ity, continuity, and change in offending. *Journal of Quantitative Criminology*, 13, 231–266.

Paternoster, R. & Iovanni, L. (1989). The labeling perspective and delinquency: An elabora-tion of the theory and assessment of the evidence. *Justice Quarterly*, 6, 359–394.

Patterson, G.R., Capaldi, D., & Bank, L. (1991). An early starter model for predicting delin-quency. In D.J. Pepler & K.H. Rubin (Eds.), *The development and treatment of childhood aggression* (pp. 139–168). Hillsdale, NJ: Erlbaum.

Patterson, G.R., Forgatch, M., & DeGarmo, D. (2010). Cascading effects following interven-tion. *Development and Psychopathology*, 22, 949–970.

Patterson, G.R., Reid, J.B., & Dishion, T.J. (1992). *Antisocial boys*. Eugene, OR: Castalia.

Peters, J.C., Jans, B., van de Ven, V., De Weerd, P., & Goebel, R. (2010). Dynamic brightness induction in V1: Analyzing simulated and empirically acquired fMRI data in a "common brain space" framework. *NeuroImage*, 52, 973–984.

Piquero, A.R. (2008). Taking stock of developmental trajectories of criminal activity over the life course. In A. Liberman (Ed.), *The long view of crime: A synthesis of longitudinal research* (pp. 23–78). New York: Springer.

Piquero, A.R., Brame, R., & Moffitt, T.E. (2005). Extending the study of continuity and change: Gender differences in the linkage between adolescent and adult offending. *Jour-nal of Quantitative Criminology*, 21, 219–243.

Piquero, A.R., Farrington, D.P., & Blumstein, A. (2007). *Key issues in criminal career research: New analyses of the Cambridge study in delinquent development*. Cambridge, UK: Cambridge University Press.

Popma, A., & Raine, A. (2006). Will future forensic assessment be neurobiologic? *Child and Adolescent Psychiatric Clinics of North America*, 15, 429–444.

Pratt, T.C., & Cullen, F.T. (2000). The empirical status of Gottfredson and Hirschi's general theory of crime: A meta-analysis. *Criminology*, 38, 931–964.

Ramakers, G. (2005). Wat gebeurt er in het hoofdje van een baby? Over hersenontwikkeling en intelligentie. *Neuropraxis*, 9, 142–148.

Rindfuss, R.R., Swicegood, C.G., & Rosenfeld, R.A. (1987). Disorder in the life course: How common and does it matter? *American Sociological Review*, 52, 785–801.

Robins, L.N. (1978). Sturdy childhood predictors of adult antisocial behavior: Replications from longitudinal studies. *Psychological Medicine*, 8, 611–622.

Rutter, M., Moffitt, T.E., & Caspi, A. (2006). Gene-environment interplay and psychopa-thology: Multiple varieties but real effects. *Journal of Child Psychology and Psychiatry*, 47, 226–261.

Sampson, R.J., & Laub, J.H. (1993). *Crime in the making: Pathways and turning points through life*. Cambridge, MA: Harvard University Press.

Sampson, R.J., & Laub, J.H. (1997). A life-course theory of cumulative disadvantage and the stability of delinquency. In T.P. Thornberry (Ed.), *Developmental theories of crime and delinquency* (pp. 133–162). New Brunswick, NJ: Transaction.

Sampson, R.J., & Laub, J.H. (2003). Life-course desisters? Trajectories of crime among delinquent boys followed to age 70. *Criminology*, 41, 555–592.

Sampson, R.J., & Laub, J.H. (2009). A life-course theory and long-term project on trajec-tories of crime. *Monatsschrift fur Kriminologie und Strafrechtsreform (Journal of Crimi-nology and Penal Reform)*, 92, 226–239.

Schug, R.A., Gao, Y., Glenn, A.L., Yang, Y., & Raine, A. (2010). The developmental evidence base: neurobiological research and forensic applications. In G.L. Towl, & D.A. Crighton (Eds.), *Forensic psychology* (pp. 73–94). Hoboken, NJ: Wiley-Blackwell.

Schulenberg, J.E., & Maggs, J.L. (2002). A developmental perspective on alcohol use and heavy drinking during adolescence and the transition to young adulthood. *Journal of Studies on Alcohol*, S14, 54–70.

Shaw, P., Kabani, N.J., Lerch, J.P., Eckstrand, K., Lenroot, R., Gogtay, N., & Greenstein, D. (2008). Neurodevelopmental trajectories of the human cerebral cortex. *Journal of Neuroscience*, 28, 3586–3594.

Shover, N. (1996). *Great pretenders: Pursuits and careers of persistent thieves.* Boulder, CO: Westview Press.

Silberg, J.L., Rutter, M., Tracy, K., Maes, H.H., & Eaves, L. (2007). Etiological heterogeneity in the development of antisocial behavior: The Virginia Twin Study of Adolescent Behavioral Development and the young adult follow-up. *Psychological Medicine*, 37, 1193–1202.

Simons, R.L., Johnson, C., Conger, R.D., & Elder, G.H. (1998). A test of latent trait versus life course perspectives on the stability of adolescent antisocial behavior. *Criminology*, 36, 217–241.

Sroufe, L.A. (2007). The place of development in developmental psychopathology. In A.S. Masten (Ed.), *Multilevel dynamics in developmental psychopathology: Pathways to the future. The Minnesota Symposia in child psychology* (pp. 285–298). Vol. 34. Mahwah, NJ: Erlbaum.

Steffensmeier, D., & Ulmer, J.T. (2005). *Confessions of a dying thief: Understanding criminal careers and criminal enterprise.* New Brunswick, NJ: Transaction Aldine.

Steinberg, L. (2010). A dual systems model of adolescent risk-taking. *Developmental Psychobiology*, 52, 216–224.

Steinberg, L., Dahl, R., Keating, D., Kupfer, D.J., Masten, A.S., & Pine, D.S. (2006). Psychopathology in adolescence: Integrating affective neuroscience with the study of context. In D. Cicchetti and D. Cohen (Eds.). *Developmental psychopathology, Vol. 2: Developmental neuroscience* (2nd ed., pp. 710–741). New York: Wiley.

Supekar, K., Musen, M., & Menon, V. (2009). Development of large-scale functional brain networks in children. *PLos Biology*, 7, e1000157.

Tamm, L., Menon, V., & Reiss, A.L. (2002). Maturation of brain function associated with response inhibition. *Journal of the American Academy of Child & Adolescent Psychiatry*, 41, 1231–1238.

Terry, C.M. (2003). *The fellas: Overcoming prison and addiction.* Belmont, CA: Wadsworth.

Thornberry, T.P. (1987). Toward an interactional theory of delinquency. *Criminology*, 25, 863–891.

Thornberry, T.P. (2005). Explaining multiple patterns of offending across the life course and across generations. In R.J. Sampson & J.H. Laub (Eds.), *Developmental criminology and its discontents: Trajectories of crime from childhood to old age* (pp. 156–195). Thousand Oaks, CA: Sage.

Thornberry, T.P., & Krohn, M.D. (2001). The development of delinquency: An interactional perspective. In S.O. White (Ed.), *Handbook of youth and justice* (pp. 289–305). New York: Plenum.

Thornberry, T.P., & Krohn, M.D. (2005). Applying interactional theory to the explanation of continuity and change in antisocial behavior. In D.P. Farrington (Ed.), *Integrated developmental and life-course theories of offending* (pp. 183–209). New Brunswick, NJ: Transaction.

Toby, J. (1957). Social disorganization and stake in conformity. *Journal of Criminal Law, Criminology, and Police Science*, 48, 12–17.

Uggen, C. (2000). Work as a turning point in the life course of criminals: A duration model of age, employment, and recidivism. *American Sociological Review*, 67, 529–546.

Van Leijenhorst, L., Moor, B.G., Op de Macks, Z.A., Rombouts, S.A., Westenberg, P.M., & Crone, E.A. (2010). Adolescent risky decision-making: Neurocognitive development of reward and control regions. *NeuroImage*, 51, 345–355.

Van Leijenhorst, L., Zanolie, K., Van Meel, C.S., Westenberg, P.M., Rombouts, S.A., & Crone, E.A. (2009). What motivates the adolescent? Brain regions mediating reward sensitivity across adolescence. *Cerebral Cortex*, 20, 61–69.

Van Overwalle, F., & Baetens, K. (2009). Understanding others' actions and goals by mirror and mentalizing systems: A meta-analysis. *NeuroImage*, 48, 564–584.

Vaughan, B. (2007). The internal narrative of desistance. *British Journal of Criminology*, 47, 390–404.

Warr, M. (1998). Life-course transitions and desistance from crime. *Criminology*, 36, 183–216.

Warr, M. (2002). *Companions in crime*. New York: Cambridge University Press.

White, H.R., Xie, M., Thompson, W., Loeber, R., & Stouthamer-Loeber, M. (2001). Psychopathology as a predictor of adolescent drug use trajectories. *Psychology of Addictive Behavior*, 15, 210–218.

Whittle, S., Yap, M.B.H., Yücel, M., Fornito, A., Simmons, J.G., Barrett, A., Sheeber, L., & Allen, N.B. (2008). Prefrontal and amygdale volumes are related to adolescents' affective behaviors during parent-adolescent interactions. *Proceedings of the National Academy of Sciences of the United States of America*, 105, 3652–3657.

Wiesner, M., & Capaldi, D.M. (2003). Relations of childhood and adolescent factors to offending trajectories of young men. *Journal of Research in Crime and Delinquency*, 40, 231–262.

Wiesner, M., & Silbereisen, R.K. (2003). Trajectories of delinquent behaviour in adolescence and their covariates: Relations with initial and time-averaged factors. *Journal of Adolescence*, 26, 753–771.

Wilson, J.Q., & Herrnstein, R.J. (1985). *Crime and human nature*. New York: Simon & Schuster.

Wolfgang, M.E., Thornberry, T.P., & Figlio, R.M. (1987). *From boy to man, from delinquency to crime*. Chicago: University of Chicago Press.

Wright, B.R.E., Caspi, A., Moffitt, T.E., & Silva, P.A. (1999). Low self-control, social bonds, and crime: Social causation, social selection, or both? *Criminology*, 37, 479–514.

Zara, G., & Farrington, D.P. (2009). Childhood and adolescent predictors of late onset criminal careers. *Journal of Youth and Adolescence*, 38, 287–300.

Zhang, Q., Loeber, R., & Stouthamer-Loeber, M. (1997). Developmental trends of delinquent attitudes and behaviors: Replications and synthesis across domains, time, and samples. *Journal of Quantitative Criminology*, 13 (2), 181–215.

Zucker, R.A., Donovan, J.E., Masten, A.S., Mattson, M.E., & Moss, H.B. (2008). Early developmental processes and the continuity of risk for underage drinking and problem drinking. *Pediatrics*, 121, Supplement 4, S252–S272.

4

Contextual Influences

Julie Horney, Patrick Tolan, and David Weisburd

In this chapter we address three important contextual influences on the onset, continuation, or escalation of offending during the transition from adolescence to adulthood. We begin the chapter by considering the context of those individual life circumstances that make emerging adulthood such an important time in the life course (see Chapter 1, Introduction, this volume). We then consider the situational context of specific criminal events, including crime places, and consider how different situational aspects may be of particular relevance at different ages. Finally we turn to the broad context of neighborhood and community, how it sets the stage for the transition from adolescence to adulthood, and how it may moderate the effects of individual life circumstances.

Individual Life Circumstances

As many have pointed out, the transition from adolescence into adulthood typically involves major changes in many of the most important life circumstances that shape individual behavior (see Siennick & Osgood, 2008). This is the time when most young people move away from living with their families, when they either end their formal schooling or begin new kinds of schooling, when they first become involved in serious romantic relationships, when some become parents for the first time, when employment plays a more major role in their lives, and when they change their patterns of leisure activities. Our focus here is on the circumstances that have received the most research attention—marriage and romantic relationships, parenthood, employment, and leisure activities.

Many scholars view these changes in circumstances as major life turning points and as representing the entry into new, relatively permanent roles. We believe it is important to consider the reality that for many young adults these transitions may be transitory. More young people are moving back to live with parents after periods of schooling or employment, schooling may proceed in fits and starts, marriages end in divorce, some parents lose children through divorce, abandonment, or state action, and employment patterns may be unstable as economies falter or the demand for certain goods and services shifts. The lives of offenders are likely to be particularly chaotic, with frequent changes in these major life circumstances. Consequently we suggest that it is important to consider potential short-term effects of these life circumstances as well as the long-term changes in offending trajectories that they may engender.

As we discuss the impact of changes in life circumstances that accompany the transition to adulthood, it will be important to be mindful of historic changes in the normative patterning of many of these circumstances. Changes in the institution of marriage and in the age of first giving birth are particularly noteworthy. In addition it will be important to consider the meaning of the life transitions to different groups; we will give special attention to the potential moderating effects of race and gender as we consider how life circumstances are related to offending patterns in this important transition period.

We will proceed by reviewing what is known about the impact of each of the key life circumstance changes on offending continuity or discontinuity from adolescence to early adulthood as well as the evidence for mechanisms of impact. We begin by considering the change that has received most attention as an important determinant of offending patterns.

ROMANTIC RELATIONSHIPS

The effect of marriage on offending has perhaps been studied more than any other life circumstance. Cross-sectional studies showing lower crime rates among married individuals suffer from potential selection bias because it is likely that individuals higher in criminal potential are less likely than others to marry (see Siennick & Osgood, 2008). Siennick and Osgood (2008) discussed this problem and described recent techniques designed to address the selection problem. We will focus here on the considerable evidence for the importance of marriage that has been amassed from studies using techniques such as within-person analyses and propensity score matching.

Effects of Marriage

For males, marriage has been associated with reduced involvement in substance use (Duncan, Wilkerson, & England, 2006; Fleming, White, Oesterle, Haggerty, & Catalano, 2010; Staff, Schulenberg, Maslowski, Bachman, O'Malley, Maggs, & Johnston, 2010) and with reductions in criminal behavior (Blokland & Nieuwbeerta, 2005; Capaldi, Kim, & Owen, 2008; Farrington & West, 1995; Horney, Osgood, & Marshall, 1995; King, Massoglia, & MacMillan, 2007; Laub, Nagin, & Sampson, 1998; Laub & Sampson, 2003; Piquero, MacDonald, & Parker, 2002; Sampson & Laub, 1993; Sampson, Laub, & Wimer, 2006; Simons, Stewart, Gordon, Conger, & Elder, 2002; Theobald & Farrington, 2009, 2011). These marriage effects have been found with nationally representative samples (Duncan et al., 2006; King et al., 2007; Staff et al., 2010); with samples of at-risk youth (Capaldi et al., 2008) and incarcerated juveniles (Laub et al., 1998; Laub & Sampson, 2003; Piquero et al., 2002; Sampson & Laub, 1990, 1993; Sampson et al., 2006); and with samples of incarcerated adults (Horney et al., 1995).

The evidence for marriage effects for males has been found in studies that have controlled for selection with statistical techniques such as propensity score matching (King et al., 2007; Theobald & Farrington, 2009) and inverse probability of treatment weighting (Sampson et al., 2006), and with techniques that measure within-person change across observations, thus ruling out any time-stable characteristics of individuals as competing explanations (Horney et al., 1995; Laub & Sampson, 2003; Theobald & Farrington, 2009, 2011; also see Siennick & Osgood, 2008, for a thorough discussion of methods of controlling selection effects).

The evidence of marriage effects for females is less clear, in part because fewer studies have focused on women and because female samples have typically been smaller. Declines in substance use similar in magnitude to those found for males have been found for females in two nationally representative samples (Duncan et al., 2006; Staff et al., 2010). Fleming et al. (2010) failed to find a significant interaction between gender and marriage in their study of substance use, but their sample included a very small number of married individuals. In two studies of criminal behavior, results for males and females clearly differed. With a national household survey sample, King, Massoglia et al. (2007) found either no marriage effects for females or effects that were much smaller than those for males. Bersani, Laub, and Nieuwbeerta (2009), studying Dutch citizens convicted of crimes, found a significant interaction between gender and marriage, with smaller negative associations between marriage and crime for females than for males. They suggested that these differences could reflect the greater likelihood of women being married to criminal men, but they had no data on the criminality of spouses. However, Theobald and Farrington (2010) found that an enduring first marriage was followed by a decrease in offending of convicted women.

In the one study that has considered possible racial differences in the impact of marriage, Piquero et al. (2002) found that, while marriage was associated with lower rates of nonviolent arrests for both white and nonwhite male parolees from the California Youth Authority, the pattern for violent arrests was different. Marriage had no significant association with arrests for nonwhites, whereas for whites it was associated with an *increase* in violent arrests.

In summary, studies that have addressed selection biases have still found considerable evidence of marriage inhibiting crime and substance use in males. Fewer studies of marriage effects on females have been conducted, and results have been mixed. The single study asking whether marriage effects were the same for whites and nonwhites found that results differed by crime type.

Effects of Nonmarital Relationships

Although the greatest attention has been paid to the institution of marriage as a factor leading to desistance from deviance and crime, some studies have addressed other forms of relationships that play important roles in the transition from adolescence to young adulthood. These other forms take on increasing significance given dramatic changes in the institution of marriage in recent years. Divorce rates have increased, and young adults have been marrying at later ages (Amato, Booth, Johnson, & Rogers, 2007). Cohabitation was rare in the 1960s, but by 2002, 60% of women age 25–39 in the United States had been involved in at least one cohabiting relationship (Smock, Casper, & Wyse, 2008). That number represented a striking increase even since 1995 when 48% of women in that age group reported having been in a cohabiting relationship (Bumpass & Lu, 2000). As cohabitation has increased, fewer cohabiting relationships have ended in marriage (Manning & Smock, 2002).

Whereas some studies have aggregated various kinds of relationships and assessed the effects of "romantic relationships" (Simons et al., 2002; Stouthamer-Loeber, Wei, Loeber, & Masten, 2004), others have explicitly addressed a variety of relationship types, including cohabiting relationships, dating relationships, and engagements (both cohabiting and non-cohabiting). Although cohabitation was rare in their sample of white men born in the 1920s, Sampson et al. (2006) found that, similar to marriage, cohabitation was associated with a decrease in offending. Two studies with nationally representative samples of young adults found mixed results for substance abuse being associated with relationships other than marriage. Staff et al. (2010) found reductions in marijuana use associated with being engaged, but the effects were smaller than those found with marriage. Cohabitation without being engaged was not related to reductions in either marijuana or cocaine use. Duncan et al. (2006) found declines in binge drinking for women who were cohabiting (but no declines in marijuana use) and found no declines in substance use for cohabiting men. Fleming et al. (2010), with a community sample of young adults, found that cohabiting was related to lower frequencies of heavy drinking and marijuana use, but that the effects were smaller than those of marriage. Dating relationships were also associated with lower substance use but with even smaller effects than cohabitation.

Quite different results were found by Horney et al. (1995) and Piquero et al. (2002), who both studied samples of criminal offenders. These two studies found that cohabitation did not have the same crime-reduction effect as marriage; indeed, cohabitation was associated with increases in criminal behavior or arrests.

Taken together, the studies examining type of relationship have shown greater reductions in crime and deviance with more formalized relationships. In order to understand the reasons for effects varying by type of relationship, it is necessary to explore the basic mechanisms accounting for the influence of relationships on offending.

Mechanisms of Romantic Relationship Effects

The dominant explanation for marriage effects has been the social bonding explanation set forth by Sampson and Laub (1993) in their age-graded theory of informal social control. In their view marriage represents an investment in social capital, and "adult social ties are important insofar as they create interdependent systems of obligation and restraint that impose significant costs for translating criminal propensities into action" (p. 141). They suggest that the social bonds that lead to reduction in offending are created when there are strong emotional ties to a spouse. Laub et al. (1998) elaborated on the social bonding notion by stressing the importance of an enduring attachment. Looking across time, they found that in the periods following "good marriages" (those which at age 32 had a marriage quality score above the median), men were significantly less likely than those not married or not in good marriages to be involved in crime, and that the effects of good marriage increased across time. Marriage alone did not result in the same crime reduction effects. However, in later analyses that more closely tracked within-individual change over time, Sampson et al. (2006) found crime reduction effects of marriage even after between-person measures of marital attachment were controlled.

Maume, Ousey, and Beaver (2005), in a study of marijuana use, measured marital attachment using items from the National Youth Survey that assessed general satisfaction, spousal support, encouragement and warmth, and level of marital stress. They found that those who got married and were rated "high" in marital attachment were more likely to desist from marijuana use across two waves of the study than those who remained single. Those who got married but were rated "low" in marital attachment, however, did not differ from those who did not marry. Although their results lend support to the notion that the quality of a marriage is an important determinant of its effects on offending, the small numbers who married and the fact that their sample combined males and females, call for some caution in interpreting results.

Simons et al. (2002) took a different approach to studying relationship quality and its association with offending. In an Iowa sample of young adults and their romantic partners (including spouses, cohabiting partners, and partners in continuing, exclusive romantic relationships), they videotaped couples working on assigned tasks and, using the tapes, had trained observers rate relationship quality on a number of dimensions, including physical affection, communication, and support. They used structural equation modeling to test their hypotheses that the quality of the romantic relationship should have a direct effect on crime because a high-quality relationship should increase stakes in conformity and have an indirect influence by increasing the individual's job commitment. For males, they found the indirect effect they had posited, but no evidence of a direct effect of relationship quality on offending. For females, in contrast, a significant negative relationship was found between the quality of the romantic relationship and involvement in offending, but there was no indirect relationship through job commitment. The authors observed that, as their respondents were only in their early to mid-20s, it is possible that the effect of romantic relationships "will emerge as these men grow older and spend more years with their romantic partners" (p. 430).

It is notable that the measure of spousal attachment employed by Sampson, Laub and colleagues was constructed so that separations and divorces were indicators of weak attachment. Thus the "good marriage" effect could represent overall time spent in a marital relationship and thus result from other aspects of marriage besides emotional attachment. Capaldi et al. (2008) studied the possibility that the stability of a relationship, rather than attachment to the partner, might be most important in reducing participation in crime. Stability could reflect factors other than emotional attachment, "such as a lack of better alternatives or financial dependency" (p. 3). In within-individual analyses of the Oregon Youth Study community sample of at-risk men who were participating in a couples study, they found that being in a continuing romantic relationship was associated with desistance from offending among men with a previous arrest, whereas time-varying measures of the man's attachment to his partner had no significant association with continued offending.

Warr (1998) challenged the social bonding explanation for marriage effects and proposed instead that marriage lowers the rate of offending through reducing the time that individuals spend with delinquent or criminal friends. In an analysis of National Youth Survey data, he found significant differences between married and unmarried respondents in the amount of time spent with friends; those who were married spent half as much time with friends and reported fewer friends who were involved in delinquent acts. When desistance from delinquency was regressed on marital status, marriage effects disappeared when number of delinquent friends and time spent with friends were controlled.

Additional support for friends as a mediating variable for relationship effects was reported by Staff et al. (2010), who controlled for the number of nights out socializing in their study of the effects of relationships on substance use; they found that marriage and cohabitation were still associated with reductions in substance use, although the associations were somewhat less strong. Simons et al. (2002), in their structural equation model, found for males that higher quality romantic relationships were associated with fewer delinquent friends, which was associated with less offending. For females, however, the association between quality of relationship and delinquent friends was not significant.

Although these results suggest that time spent with friends is an important mediator of the marriage effect, the findings are not necessarily incongruent with a social bonding explanation. The social investment in marriage could lead to spending less time with friends, and particularly delinquent friends, in order to avoid potential trouble that would put the relationship at risk.

Partner Deviance

An important question about relationship effects is whether they are moderated by the deviance of the romantic partner. Assortative mating suggests that those with a propensity for crime and deviance would also tend to choose romantic partners with similar tendencies. Sampson and Laub (1993) found evidence of differential partner selection: whereas 19% of the control-group men had wives with a prior criminal history, 50% of the men in the delinquent group were married to women with a criminal background. However, they found that when marital attachment was controlled, the wife's criminal history was not significantly related to offending during ages 25–32.

Contrary results were found by Simons et al. (2002), who reasoned that the deviance of a romantic partner could matter in at least two ways: First, through direct influence, "conventional partners are apt to oppose and punish involvement in deviant behavior, whereas antisocial partners are likely to promote and reinforce such actions" (p. 404). Second, in an indirect manner, deviant partners would be more likely than conventional partners to encourage, rather than discourage, spending time with deviant friends. In their SEM analysis, Simons and colleagues found for males a direct and significant positive association between having an antisocial partner and criminal behavior, and also found that an antisocial partner was negatively associated with the quality of the romantic relationship, which, in turn, influenced offending through deviant friends and job attachment. For females, there was an even stronger direct association between antisocial partners and criminal behavior and also a negative association with relationship quality, which, in turn, directly affected criminal behavior.

Capaldi et al. (2008) also emphasized the importance of a partner's antisocial tendencies. They found that young men with previous arrests had higher arrest counts in the year following being with a romantic partner if that partner was antisocial. Antisocial partners were also associated with first arrests among young men who had not been arrested before being in a serious romantic relationship, suggesting that involvement with an antisocial partner might be an important factor in adult onset of offending. However, Theobald and Farrington (2010) found that offending diminished after marriage for men whether or not they married a convicted woman.

Summary and Future Directions

Increasingly strong evidence for the existence of marriage effects on crime and substance use suggests that understanding how romantic relationships develop and evolve during the transition from adolescence to adulthood is important for understanding whether offending persists or not during this key period or whether there may even be an onset of deviant behavior during the transition. In light of differences in marriage effects that have been found for males and females, and of theoretical perspectives predicting gender differences, we advise that future studies should include separate analyses for males and females. Employing combined samples with no check for interactions is likely to make interpretation of results problematic.

Similarly, we believe there is a need for more research to sort out the effects of marriage, cohabitation, and other romantic relationships. It is important to know if these kinds of relationships have different implications for offending and if so, why. Again, failing to distinguish among them is likely to produce misleading results. Research that compares the quality of relationships, the time spent with deviant friends, and the nature of leisure activities for individuals across these different kinds of romantic relationships should be helpful in explaining their differential associations with offending. Another influence on relationship effects may be the characteristics of partners who are involved in these relationships. If men, for example, tend to choose dating or cohabiting partners with greater tendencies toward criminal behavior than the partners they choose for marriage, we would expect marriage to be more closely linked to desistance than the other types of relationships.

In spite of the fairly consistent crime reduction effects shown for romantic relationships, we have some concern that little attention has been paid to the opportunity for violence provided by romantic relationships. Few studies have disaggregated

crimes by type, and none that we are aware of has been able to separate out interpersonal violence directed at the romantic partner. In light of concerns about the
prevalence of domestic violence, we hope that future researchers will be able to
address the possibility that marriage and other romantic relationships may also
have such very specific crime enhancing effects. Moffitt (1993, p. 684) suggested
that, for those she labeled lifetime persistent offenders, "opportunities for change
will often be actively transformed . . . into opportunities for continuity," as when "a
new romance provides a partner for abuse." Moffitt's statement implies continuity
in offending in the transition from adolescence to adulthood, with either a new
type of offending or perhaps just a new target for offending. But it is also possible
that the opportunity provided by a romantic relationship actually leads to early
adult onset of offending when an individual lacks the pro-social skills to deal with
domestic conflict. These are issues that need attention in future research.

PARENTHOOD

Although it is arguably one of the most dramatic role transitions in an individual's
life, parenthood has been studied far less than the institution of marriage in relationship to offending in the transition from adolescence to adulthood. It is notable
that Sampson and Laub (1993) and Laub and Sampson (2003), who were so instrumental in stressing the importance of adult social bonds for desistance from crime,
have paid relatively little attention to parenthood.

Most studies of parenthood effects on criminal activity of the parent have used
cross-sectional designs. Even in those studies, researchers have failed to find strong
relations with criminal offending for males (Graham & Bowling, 1995; Uggen &
Kruttschnitt, 1998). The level of parenthood is high among known serious male delinquents; however, many of these males do not become active, involved parents and
often do not live with their children, and thus parenthood might not be expected to
have a major impact on their lives (Wei, Loeber, & Stouthamer-Loeber, 2002).

Although we might expect larger effects for females because of their typically
greater involvement with their children, studies of female parenthood have produced inconsistent results. Uggen and Kruttschnitt (1998), analyzing data from the
National Supported Work Demonstration Project (Hollister, Kemper, & Maynard,
1984), found that women who had children at the time of assignment to the program remained free from earning illegal income longer than women without children, but having children was not related to the time to an arrest. Blokland and
Nieuwbeerta (2005) conducted within-person analyses for four groups of Dutch
convicted offenders with different offending trajectories and found few and inconsistent effects of parenthood. In a Dutch general population study, they found no
significant relationship of parenthood to offending.

Stronger, more consistent results have been found in two longitudinal studies focusing on young women. In a study of adolescent girls (using Add Health data),
Hope, Wilder, and Watt (2003) found evidence of a parenthood effect when they
compared different options for dealing with a pregnancy. They found significantly

lower rates of delinquency among girls who kept their baby than among girls who had abortions or gave the baby up for adoption. Results were unchanged when they controlled for the number of delinquent friends (friends who smoked or used marijuana). In order to address selection effects they conducted a limited analysis of girls who became pregnant between the first and second waves of the survey. They found that those who kept their babies had higher rates of smoking and marijuana use than the never-pregnant girls during the first wave, but their rates were almost 45% lower in the second wave, after the birth of their children, thus indicating real effects, not just selection artifacts. In a more extended longitudinal study with data from the Denver Youth study, Kreager et al. (2010) used fixed-effects models to address selection effects and found that both teenage motherhood and young-adult motherhood were significantly related to decreases in overall delinquency, in fighting, and in stealing, as well as in drug use. These results persisted when marriage and race were controlled.

The preceding studies measured parenthood by whether and when individuals were known to have had children but did not have data on whether parents were living with their children or on the relationship between parents and children. Others have used more refined measures to assess parenthood effects, but again results have been mixed. Griffin and Armstrong (2003) studied women probationers and determined whether they were living with children during particular months. They found that, in months when women were living with children, their involvement in drug dealing decreased by 35%, even after employment, relationships, and stable living situations were controlled. Living with children, however, was not significantly related to their involvement in nondrug crimes. Yule (2010) employed a similar within-person analysis of month-to-month variation in life circumstances in a sample of jailed women in a study that focused specifically on motherhood and found similarly mixed results, but results also inconsistent with those of Griffen and Armstrong. During the months living with children, the women in her study were less likely to use drugs and to be involved in property crime, showed no change in their involvement with dealing drugs or in "mutual" violence with intimate partners, and were somewhat more likely to be involved in "sole" violence against mutual partners.

In their study of substance use with Monitoring the Future data, Staff et al. (2010) measured whether respondents had children or were expecting a child (respondent or partner was pregnant) and whether the respondent was living with the children. Using within-person analyses, they found declines in alcohol use by pregnant women and by their male partners, and that women with children used fewer substances, especially if they were living with their children. Males living with their children also used less alcohol and other substances.

Giordano et al. (2002) reasoned that measuring attachment to children would provide a truer picture of the social bonding that would be expected to lead to reductions in offending. In their study of adults with serious offending histories they asked respondents to agree or disagree with the statement "I'm closer to my kid(s) than a lot of people my age are to theirs." However, they found no relationship between this variable and self-reported criminal involvement and no interaction of gender with attachment to children.

Future Directions

Although findings on parenthood are mixed, a few patterns have emerged. Associations of parenthood with desistance from crime have been more likely when researchers have measured living with children than when simply considering that individuals have had children, and they have been found more often in studies of females than of males. Results also seem to be more consistent for substance use than for other types of offending. In order to reconcile inconsistencies, more studies of males as parents are needed, as are better measures of the nature of parent-child relationships, especially for men. Null findings for men may simply reflect the fact that many more men than women are living apart from their children. Most studies have not included measures of the stresses of parenthood, which may balance or outweigh the effects of positive social bonds in determining the course of criminal behavior in the transition from adolescence to adulthood (see Giordano et al. 2002; Yule, 2010). Assessing the impact of parenthood is likely to be a substantially more complex endeavor than assessing the impact of marriage.

Generally, the results on parenthood effects have not been as robust as those on marriage effects. Fewer studies of parenthood have been conducted, and fewer have adequately addressed selection issues. Selection issues for parenthood are more complicated than those for marriage. Those who marry are expected to have a lower criminal propensity than those who do not, but the relationship between propensity and parenthood is expected to vary with age. Teenage parenthood has been viewed as a negative outcome occurring in those who are at a higher risk for delinquent behavior, substance abuse, and school failure. For example, Bardone, Moffitt, Caspi, Dickson and Silva (1996) found that girls with adolescent conduct disorder were far more likely to become pregnant by age 21 than those girls without conduct disorders. The recent study by Kreager et al. (2010), showing parenthood having positive effects for disadvantaged teenage mothers, illustrates the importance of and need for within-person studies in order to control for complex selection patterns.

EMPLOYMENT

Besides entry into marriage or other serious romantic relationships, another major change that comes with the transition from adolescence to adulthood is entry into the world of work. As with marriage, numerous cross-sectional studies have found more criminal offending among the unemployed than among the employed, but selection effects have been difficult to rule out. Again, we focus in this chapter on recent studies using newer techniques to effectively address the problem that individual characteristics affect both the likelihood of being employed and the likelihood of being involved in criminal behavior.

Because young people typically enter the work sphere long before they enter into marriage, and because young people work fewer hours than adults and at different kinds of jobs, the literature on employment is strongly stratified by age. Studies can be grouped by their focus on the teen years (Apel, Bushway, Raymond, Brame, & Sweeton, 2008; Farrington, Gallagher, Morley, St. Ledger, & West, 1986;

Paternoster, Bushway, Brame, & Apel, 2003), on the young adult years (Crutchfield & Pitchford, 1997; Thornberry & Christenson, 1984; Wadsworth, 2006), or on the full range of adult years (Horney et al., 1995; Laub & Sampson, 2003; Piquero et al., 2002; Sampson & Laub, 1993; Uggen, 2000).

In the young adult and adult years, employment has been associated with a reduction in crime in studies using nationally representative data sets such as the National Longitudinal Study of Youth (NLSY) (Crutchfield & Pitchford, 1997; Wadsworth, 2006) as well as in specialized data sets such as the Philadelphia Birth Cohort (Thornberry & Christenson, 1984), the Glueck and Glueck (1950) sample of institutionalized youth as reanalyzed by Sampson and Laub (1993) and Laub and Sampson (2003), and the Supported Work Experiment sample of convicted offenders, addicts, and school drop-outs with arrest histories (Uggen, 2000). Reductions in substance use associated with employment have also been found (Staff et al., 2010) in the Monitoring the Future follow-up of a nationally representative sample of high school seniors. These studies have addressed selection problems through experimental designs (Uggen 2000), within-person analyses (Laub & Sampson 2003; Staff et al., 2010), and controls for prior delinquent or criminal involvement (Thornberry & Christenson, 1984; Crutchfield & Pitchford, 1997; Wadsworth, 2006).

Research on employment among adolescents in the 1990s provided a different picture of the effects of employment. A number of studies indicated that working extended hours was associated with adolescent problem behaviors, including delinquency, substance use, and poor grades (see Greenberger & Steinberg, 1986). The negative impact was attributed to work taking students away from their studies and their families and providing them with the resources that allowed them to be more independent and engage in unsupervised activities. More recent studies with methodological improvements (within-person analyses and instrumental variables analyses) suggest, however, that the earlier results reflected selection effects whereby youth already exhibiting problem behaviors were more likely than others to work long hours. These studies have either found no deleterious effects of work (Apel et al., 2007; Paternoster et al., 2003; Staff, Osgood, Schulenberg, Bachman, & Messersmith, 2010) or a beneficial effect in an associated reduction in offending (Apel et al., 2008). The studies suggest that the transition from adolescence to adulthood, instead of representing a turning point at which work shifts from a negative to a positive influence, may instead be seen as a time when the continuously beneficial effect of work comes to play an increasingly important role in the individual's life.

Job Stability

Sampson and Laub (1993) emphasized the social bonding aspects of work to explain its crime reduction benefits over the life course, and their original employment measure included not only an indicator of whether or not the man was employed in a particular year, but also measures of his job stability (how long he had held the job) and of job attachment (a three-point scale of his work habits as reported by his employer). However, in a more conservative (within-person) analysis Laub and Sampson (2003) used a simple measure of employed versus un-employed and found that periods of unemployment were still associated with a substantial increase in offending.

In attempting to explain the link between employment and crime, other re-searchers have considered the role of job stability, which has been measured as time spent in a particular job (Sampson & Laub, 1993; Uggen, 1999), as the number of months employed at all in the previous year (Crutchfield & Pitchford, 1997; Wadsworth, 2006), and as expectations regarding keeping a job (Crutchfield & Pitchford, 1997; Giordano et al., 2002). The evidence for the importance of stability is mixed. Crutchfield and Pitchford (1997) found stability to have a significant neg-ative relationship with crime, and Uggen (1999) found stability to be a marginally significant predictor. In contrast, neither Wadsworth (2006) nor Giordano et al. (2002) found any significant relationships between job stability and offending.

Job Quality

Many have asserted that the quality of employment should be an important deter-minant of the relationship between employment and criminal involvement. As Allan and Steffensmeier (1989) observed, "where jobs are insecure, with low pay, few benefits, and minimal opportunities for advancement, work may provide fewer incentives for young people to form lasting commitments to conventional life-styles." Job characteristics that have been considered in individual level studies in-clude the level of pay, the benefits available, the occupational status, and other rewarding aspects of the job. The level of income seems to be the least important of these. Crutchfield and Pitchford (1997) and Wadsworth (2006), studying young adults, and Uggen (1999), whose sample included a wide range of ages, found no significant relationship between the amount of income earned when employed and criminal offending. In contrast, Wadsworth (2006), while controlling for previous delinquency and suspension/expulsion from school, found that receiving benefits with a job (health insurance and paid vacation leave) was associated with lower rates of offending. Wadsworth also found such a relationship with an employment quality variable that included respondents' ratings of job security, good pay, being able to do things they do best, chances of promotion, and significance of the job in the broader scheme of things. Although suggestive of the importance of job quality, this study was not able to rule out selection effects whereby those who were less likely to offend are more likely to have jobs of higher quality, such as with benefits.

Occupational status is another aspect of job quality that is thought to be relevant to reducing criminal behavior. Staff et al. (2010) found that compared to men who were not working, men in professional jobs were less likely to drink heavily, use marijuana, and use cocaine. In contrast, men in nonprofessional jobs did not differ significantly in their substance use from those with no jobs. For women, whether jobs were professional or nonprofessional made no difference to substance use.

Uggen (1999) measured quality of work by matching job satisfaction scores from the Quality of Employment Survey (Quinn & Staines, 1979) of a national sample of workers to categories of occupations held by ex-offenders involved in the National Supported Work Demonstration Project (Piliavin & Gartner, 1981). He found that holding higher quality jobs was associated with lower rates of self-reported offending, even when controls were entered for prior crime and substance use, job tenure and pay, and individual characteristics including age, race, experience, and prior earnings. The job quality results persisted even when the model included unmeasured characteristics that were predictive of being employed. As with the Wadsworth (2006) study described above, it was not possible in this study to rule out differential selection into quality jobs by those who were less likely to offend, but a number of these studies taken together indicate that job quality may play an important role in the link between employment and crime. A stronger within-person design was used by Blokland and Nieuwbeerta (2005) who analyzed data from a nationally representative sample of Dutch citizens for whom life-event calendars had been used to record employment histories. They assigned an occupational status score to each respondent for each year covered in the study and found that occupational status was unrelated to offending. Rates of offending in their sample were quite low, however, so their results may not have been sensitive to effects of life circumstances.

Whereas Uggen (1999) measured job quality by average satisfaction scores of a national sample of workers employed in particular kinds of jobs, Simons et al. (2002) employed a Job Satisfactions Scale based on responses of the young adults in their study to 23 items assessing their perceptions of positive and negative aspects of their own jobs. In a path model of factors mediating the stability of offending from adolescence to adulthood, higher subjective perceptions of job quality were associated with lower rates of offending for males, but the relationship between adolescent delinquency and adult crime was not shown to be mediated by job attachment. Citing past research showing "that work and financial problems are more strongly related to the physical and psychological well-being of males than of females," Simons et al. (2002) predicted that job satisfaction would be less important for females, and they indeed found that for females there was no association between job satisfaction and offending.

Although most of the literature supports the importance of employment in fostering desistance from crime and substance use, a few studies have reported results at odds with the majority of studies. In a study focused on marriage effects, Maume et al. (2005) controlled for the move into full-time employment across two waves of the National Youth Survey for those who used marijuana at the first wave and found that employment was not related to the likelihood of desistance from marijuana use. Results did not change when the authors substituted a measure of job stability. When they narrowed their sample to include only those who were not married and were not in college during either wave, they found that full-time employment was associated with a *decrease* in the likelihood of desistance.

In an analysis of seven-year follow-up data on male parolees from the California Youth Authority, Piquero et al. (2002) found that whether or not a man was employed full-time during a particular year was not related to arrests during that year. Horney, Osgood, and Marshall (1995), who used a life-event calendar to obtain month-by-month reports of employment and crime, found that being employed was associated with a 28% *increase* in the odds of committing a property crime in that month. Although both of these two studies employed strong within-person designs that could control for all time-stable individual differences, the measures of employment in both were relatively crude, capturing neither stability nor quality of employment. Both of these studies also involved samples of serious offenders, and it is possible that employment effects are conditioned by criminal propensity. As observed earlier, Moffitt (1993) has suggested that where others find opportunities for desistance from offending, persistent offenders sometimes find opportunities for offending, as when "a new job furnishes the chance to steal" (p. 684). Theft from an employer may be a more ubiquitous problem that complicates the research findings on employment. Nagin, Farrington, and Moffitt (1995), in a study of offending trajectories of working-class London males, found that the group identified from their offending pattern as "adolescence-limited," after a peak conviction rate at age 16, reached a conviction rate of zero by age 22. By age 32 their job stability was no different from the group of "never convicted." However, self-reports indicated that this group continued to be involved in property crime; in particular, 43% of them admitted to stealing from an employer during the preceding five years.

Future Directions

Findings on the relationship between employment and crime are somewhat less consistent than findings on marriage. Although work generally seems to be associated with lower levels of offending, contradictory results call for a better understanding of the role of work. Studies on the role of work characteristics have produced mixed results. It is unclear whether objective characteristics of jobs or individuals' perceptions of quality are more important. Research has focused on traditional measures used in the study of labor markets, such as pay and benefits, but the role of bonds with colleagues, commitment to keeping a job, or the match between the realities of a job and an individual's expectations for employment have received little attention. In light of what we know about the importance of structure in leisure activities (Osgood, Wilson, O'Malley, Bachman, & Johnston, 1996), it may also be important to consider the degree of structure inherent in different kinds of employment. Some jobs may provide many more opportunities for offending than others. It is especially important that we understand how they provide opportunities for stealing from the employer (Osgood & Wilson, 1996).

The current high levels of unemployment in this country are making the transition to adult employment more challenging for many young people, as uncertainties about the type of work and the dependability of employment confront more and more individuals. The impact of this period of severely reduced employment opportunities on desistance from offending versus continuing involvement in criminal activity or even early adult-onset offending is as yet unknown but should be a productive topic for future research.

LEISURE ACTIVITIES

Although the routine activities perspective was developed in relation to victimization, it has also been applied, although much less frequently, to individual offending. Because major changes in leisure activities typically occur with the transition from adolescence to adulthood, this perspective is likely to be important for understanding changes in offending patterns during that critical period. Using data from a longitudinal study following high school seniors from age 18 to 26, Osgood et al. (1996) found age-related changes in most of their activities. They reported significant declines across those years in riding in a car for fun, visiting with friends, going to parties, spending evenings out for fun and recreation, going on dates, going to movies, participating in community affairs, participating in active sports, and relaxing alone. In contrast, they found increases in at-home activities, including working around the house, watching TV, and reading books or magazines. The only activity among those asked about that did not change over this period was going shopping.

A number of studies have reported links between leisure activity and offending (Agnew & Petersen, 1989; Anderson & Hughes, 2009; Bernburg & Thorlindsson, 2001; Hawdon, 1996, 1999; Mahoney & Stattin, 2000; Riley, 1987; Vazsonyi, Pickering, Belliston, Hessing, & Junger, 2002). Although these studies have found increased offending linked to unstructured kinds of socializing across a wide range of cultural contexts, most have involved cross-sectional analyses that cannot rule out selection problems. Osgood et al. (1996), however, provided a within-person analysis across the ages 18 to 26 that showed that individuals were more likely to be involved in criminal behavior, heavy alcohol use, marijuana use, other drug use, and dangerous driving when they spent more time in unstructured socializing such as riding in a car for fun, visiting with friends, going to parties, and spending evenings out for fun and entertainment. Other activities outside the home such as going on dates, going to movies, and participating in active sports were not related to criminal behavior or drug use.

Osgood et al. (1996) focused on unstructured activities with peers outside the presence of authority figures, observing that "the lack of structure leaves time available for deviance; the presence of peers makes it easier to participate in deviant acts and makes them more rewarding; and the absence of authority figures reduces the potential for social control responses to deviance" (p. 651). Anderson and Hughes (2009) additionally considered how the availability of transportation facilitates such activities; they found that access to private transportation (driving more than one mile per week) was associated with significant increases in property crime, violence, heavy drinking, and marijuana use.

It is conceivable that the effects of time spent socializing with peers could reflect the influence of deviant peers rather than participation in the activities. However, Haynie and Osgood (2003) were able to control for the deviance of peers as reported by peers themselves in a network study and found that, although deviant peers led to more delinquency, there was an independent contribution to offending of time spent in unstructured socializing.

Important connections exist between leisure activities and the major role transitions of marriage, parenthood, and work across the ages 18 to 30. Osgood and Wilson (1996) found, in a within-person analysis, that the amount of unstructured socializing was significantly reduced for both males and females when they lived with a spouse, cohabited with an intimate partner, lived with children of their own, or were engaged, even when age was controlled. They did not find similar changes for working either part-time or full-time. They also found that the activities were important mediators of the negative relationship between marriage or engagement and violent offending, accounting for a substantial portion, although far from all, of the relationship. Osgood and Wilson's sample was a nationally representative sample of high school seniors. Horney, Johnson, and Hassell (2000) found similar results with a sample of males incarcerated for serious offenses: leisure activities reflecting unstructured socializing accounted for a substantial portion of the reduction in offending associated with living with a wife.

Conclusions and Future Directions

Consistent findings on the relationship between leisure activities and offending have emerged even though activities have typically been only loosely defined. Standard survey questions have measured nights out for fun and entertainment or time spent hanging out with friends. Researchers have made assumptions about the degree of structure involved in the activities and about the presence of authority figures, but they have seldom directly measured structure or the presence of authority figures. It is thus possible that the size of leisure activity effects has been underestimated. More precise measurement of the nature of activities and the circumstances surrounding them may be a productive direction for future research. We also have little evidence to show that the crimes at issue actually occur during these leisure activities. Most of the research in this area has focused on adolescents and the role of parental supervision of activities. More research is needed on young adults, with attention paid to the shifts in the meaning of structure and supervision of activities.

The Situational Context of Criminal Events

An understudied aspect of criminology is the immediate situational context of criminal events (see reviews by Birkbeck & LaFree, 1993; Monahan & Klassen, 1982; Sampson & Lauritsen, 1994). Generally, studies of situational factors have not specifically addressed the age of offenders, so there is currently little that the situational or event perspective can offer to aid the understanding of offending in relation to the transition from adolescence to adulthood. However, because many situational contexts are likely to change during that transition and because age may moderate the effects of situational factors, we suggest this as a promising area for future research.

EVENTS AS SITUATIONS

The situational perspective has usually been applied to violence, with a focus on factors such as the presence of third parties or bystanders (Felson & Steadman, 1983), the presence of weapons (Kleck & McElrath, 1991; Wells & Horney, 2002), and resistance by a victim (Felson & Steadman, 1983). The kind of bystanders present (e.g., peers versus others) in high-risk situations is likely to change across the years of transitioning into adulthood and the presence of particular types of bystanders may have different effects on individuals at different stages of the transition. Weapons may become more available as adolescents age, but the maturity of event participants may lessen their impact in a particular situation. There is a need to know more about how violent events unfold and also to expand the situational perspective to a broader range of crime types. An integration of the routine activities perspective and its emphasis on unstructured socializing with the situational perspective that focuses on actual crime events could be especially productive.

PLACE AS A CONTEXT FOR OFFENDING

Criminologists have had a long and enduring interest in the idea of place and its role in the production of crime (Weisburd & McEwen, 1997; Weisburd, Bruinsma & Bernasco, 2009). In recent years, there has been growing interest in looking at the distribution of crime at smaller geographic units of place such as addresses or street segments, or clusters of these micro units of geography (Eck & Weisburd 1995; Sherman, 1995; Taylor 1997; Weisburd & Green 1995). A number of studies have shown significant clustering of crime in "hot spots" (Brantingham & Brantingham, 1999; Crow & Bull, 1975; Pierce, Spaar, & Briggs, 1986; Roncek, 2000; Sherman, Gartin, & Buerger, 1989; Weisburd, Maher, & Sherman, 1992; Weisburd & Green, 1994).

CRIME "HOT SPOTS," "ACTIVITY SPACES," AND CRIME

There is strong reason to believe that the concept of crime hot spots is a useful concept for understanding patterns of offending in relation to the transition from adolescence to adulthood. We have discussed above important findings on the role of leisure activities in providing opportunities for crime. We believe that those activities are strongly concentrated in particular places because adolescents are encouraged and often required to be at certain places at specific times. Schools, for example, provide a very strong nexus for routine activities of adolescents. Schools and other areas of juvenile activity (e.g., community centers, movie theaters, or malls) are places where potential offenders and victims come into close contact in contexts where supervision by authorities may not always be high. Roman (2002, 2005) has found evidence suggesting that the presence of a school in an area increases the probability of violent crimes, even more so around those times of day that are associated with high levels of activity by young people (Snyder & Sickmund, 2006).

The routine activities of offenders and victims are also affected by routes of travel to and from school. Students are likely to wait at specific bus stops, or take specific paths to schools. In the course of these activities they are also likely to identify opportunities for crime both in regard to other students and to the community at large. Thus the concentration of teenage students in large middle and high schools likely serves to reinforce the role of schools as "focal points" of crime since they increase the concentration of potential offenders and victims in areas proximate to schools and on travel routes to and from schools (Brantingham & Brantingham, 1995).

Adolescents are also assumed to be attracted to very specific types of activities, which in turn influence their "activity spaces" (Felson, 2006). Malls and movie theaters for example, are well-known "hang outs" for youth, and indeed such businesses seek to attract young people as customers. The fact that young people are most likely to victimize other young people (Snyder, 2003) reinforces the importance of such activity spaces as providing opportunities for crime. Empirical evidence on the concentration of youth crime in hot spots is provided by Weisburd, Morris, and Groff (2009), who studied crime in the city of Seattle between 1989 and 2002. They found that less than 1% of the total street segments in Seattle accounted for 50% of the arrest incidents in any given year. Data drawn from incident reports allowed Weisburd et al. (2009) to provide confirmation of the relevance of youth activity spaces to understanding crime patterns. High concentrations of crime were found in schools and/or youth centers, and in shops/malls and restaurants. Prior research on crime at place points to the centrality of such adult activity spaces as bars (Roncek, 1981; Roncek & Maier, 1991) and transit points to work for adult crime (Block & Davis, 1996; Brantingham & Brantingham, 1990, 1995). The comparatively insignificant role of bars in the Weisburd et al. (2009) study suggests that the transition of juvenile offenders and victims from adolescence to adulthood involves not only changes in conventional life patterns such as marriage or work, but a corresponding change in opportunity settings for involvement in crime (Wikström & Butterworth, 2006).

CONCLUSIONS

Given the exploratory findings from the Weisburd et al. (2009) Seattle study, and the well-established literature on routine activities and crime, it is reasonable to speculate on the impact of transitions in activity spaces as adolescents make the transition to adulthood. It is clear that activity spaces change with the movement of young people from high schools to work or colleges, or with their transition from single to marital status. Some transitions in activity spaces from youth to adulthood may lead to decreases in risk of criminal behavior, but others may lead to increased risk or at least continued risk of criminal involvement. The example of bars seems particularly important in this regard. But we think that other adult activity spaces are also important in the development of crime events. For example, it is likely that specific types of adult entertainment areas are related to crime events. In turn, even in the ordinary commute of adults to work or leisure, there are transit nodes that evidence a higher risk of criminal offending. We suggest that, along with additional research on leisure activities, research on activity spaces will be useful in further elucidating the changes in offending that occur with the transition from adolescence to adulthood.

Neighborhoods and Communities

Relative social and economic disadvantage as experienced in communities and neighborhoods has been a central issue since the early days of modern criminology (Shaw & McKay, 1942). The focus on residence location affecting risk for delinquency has also commanded considerable recent research interest (Bursik & Grasmick, 1993; Sampson, 1997). In formulating an understanding of how community characteristics might affect risk, two distinct but related considerations are commonly emphasized: structural characteristics thought to represent the economic and political resources of a given community and social processes thought to represent the personal relationships and group cohesion among those residing in a given neighborhood or community (Leventhal & Brooks-Gunn, 2000). Both can be reliably correlated with delinquency and criminal behavior across the lifespan (Crane, 1991) and have a substantial relation to each other; however, structural and social characteristics are not synonymous and do not consistently have the same relationship with delinquency (Tolan, Gorman-Smith, & Henry, 2003). It is necessary to consider both structural characteristics and social processes as interrelated but distinct community/neighborhood influences.

Structural characteristics are usually measured by demographic characteristics, average income level, home ownership levels, and other indicators of economic well-being and social integration into the larger economy and political sphere (Bursik & Grasmick, 1993). Social processes are measured by indicators of the quality of relationships among neighbors, the felt ownership of the community, perceptions of well-being in the community, and perceptions of efficacy in being able to manage problems in the community such as deviant behavior and conditions conducive to crime (Gorman-Smith, Tolan, & Henry, 2000; Leventhal & Brooks-Gunn, 2000).

LINKS TO OFFENDING IN ADOLESCENCE

Numerous studies empirically link low average income and higher levels of community crime to youth violence (Sampson, Raudenbush, & Earls, 1997; Tolan et al., 2003) and a host of other related outcomes including academic achievement (Brooks-Gunn, Duncan, & Aber, 1997; Coulton, Pandey, & Chow, 1990), social competence (Dornbusch, Ritter, & Steinberg, 1991), aggression (Chung & Steinberg, 2006), and serious offending (Wikström & Loeber, 2000). It should be noted that these studies vary in how criminality is measured and rarely consider more specific aspects such as onset age, seriousness, or persistence of offending (see Loeber, Pardini, Stouthamer-Loeber, & Raine, 2007 for one of the few exceptions).

However, two recent studies shed some light on how neighborhoods can influence persistence. Kubrin and Stewart (2006) demonstrated that the socioeconomic status of neighborhoods accounts for recidivism even after individual predictors have been controlled. Similar results on recidivism in drug offending by juveniles were found by Grunwald, Lockwood, Harris, and Mennis (2010). Thus, there is good reason to consider community structural characteristics as important for understanding the continuation of criminal behavior beyond adolescence, but the current empirical evidence bearing on this topic is limited.

The most commonly held perspective is that structural characteristics, particularly concentrated poverty, in some urban communities are likely to contribute to people's risk of involvement in delinquency and of continuation of offending. This impact is primarily through blocked or limited access to critical developmental resources such as quality schools, safe recreational spaces, opportunities for noncriminal income-producing activities, and means for achieving status with peers (Wilson, 1987). Second, and closely related to the concentration of poverty, social impediments and cultural strain that are legacies of segregation and other discriminatory patterns are thought to carry structurally based risk (Jencks & Meyer, 1990). Third, these structural characteristics are seen as creating stress, isolation, uncertainty, and pessimism about opportunity, social justice, neighborhood social relationships and related informal controls (Tolan et al., 2003). Finally, these features may promote or support norms of being fatalistic about crime and violence or of accepting such behavior as useful and perhaps even valuable (Guerra, Huesmann, Tolan, VanAcker, & Eron, 1995).

Thus, as exemplified in the work of Sampson and others (Sampson, 1997; Sampson et al., 1997), the structural characteristics of a neighborhood can impede the development of the kind of social organization that can reduce crime levels. The potential effects on offending are illustrated in a study by Furstenberg (1993), which found that mothers residing in the most dangerous poor-urban neighborhoods isolated their family from the neighborhood as a way to protect their children from feared negative influences and potential direct harm. While this increased the mothers' perceptions of safety, it also cut the mother and children off from local resources and potential social support that could help with the many challenges of raising children. Thus, the characteristics of the community led to parenting behavior that could decrease the social functioning of children and increase their risk for delinquency. Another example is found in a study of differences in parenting practice effects on delinquency in poor and extremely poor neighborhoods. Gorman-Smith, Tolan and Henry (2000) confirmed the known protective effect of parenting practices such as close monitoring and consistent discipline in mitigating the relation of higher life stress to delinquency of the child in poor neighborhoods. However, this protective mitigation was not found in neighborhoods that were extremely impoverished, thus indicating that structural factors can affect delinquency in diverse ways.

At the same time, neighborhood social processes can vary substantially even among structurally impaired communities, and those neighborhood social processes can still be effective in reducing the risk of delinquency. For example, Gorman-Smith, Tolan, and Henry (2000) found in a sample of poor Chicago neighborhoods that neighborhoods clustered into three types. There were two types with very serious structural impairment, but they differed in levels of social organization. One neighborhood type had low levels of social organization, but the other, in spite of extreme poverty and other types of impairment, had very high levels of social organization. A third type of neighborhood had somewhat less structural impairment but had lower levels of social organization. Patterns of family functioning varied across neighborhoods. The key finding from this study was that high levels of neighborhood social organization mitigated the negative impact of structural disadvantage and poor family functioning on delinquency. It is also the case that low neighborhood social organization can relate to increased risk for a variety of problem behaviors even if structural risk is not particularly elevated (Elliott et al., 1996; Tolan et al., 2003).

These are but a few examples of how structural aspects of neighborhoods and neighborhood social organization are both important to understanding criminal behavior. While these studies have focused on delinquency, it is likely that similar influences affect the probability of continuation of offending beyond adolescence.

CONTINUATION OF OFFENDING INTO ADULTHOOD

A small number of studies have explicitly assessed neighborhood influence as they considered the continuation of adolescent offending into adulthood. These studies have varied, however, in the centrality or thoroughness of the focus on neighborhoods. Stouthamer-Loeber, Wei, Loeber, and Masten (2004) analyzed the Pittsburgh Youth Study sample of urban males, primarily sampled from lower socioeconomic areas of that city and designed to overrepresent those with elevated early aggression, to examine the process of desistance from criminal behavior in early adulthood (ages 20–25). Desistance in young adulthood by those with delinquent involvement throughout their adolescent years was related to a variety of personal and family variables but not to the perception of neighborhood disadvantage during adolescence. Persisters were found to be of lower economic status, but the authors interpreted this as an outcome of criminal involvement rather than a cause. It should be noted this study was not designed to assess neighborhood and community effects and included limited measurement of such constructs. Thus, the study is unable to clearly differentiate individual and neighborhood socioeconomic influences.

In a subsequent analysis of the Pittsburgh sample, Loeber, Pardini, Stouthamer-Loeber, and Raine (2007) included housing quality and community crime level as two indicators of community influence on delinquency and persistence into early adulthood. In bivariate analyses they found that good housing quality and low community crime were protective against involvement in delinquency but were unrelated to persistence in offending beyond adolescence. In multivariate logistic regression models that included individual, familial, peer, and school factors, housing quality and community crime level were not significantly related to any crime outcomes.

Kosterman, Graham, Hawkins, Catalano, and Herrenkohl (2001) undertook a similar evaluation, focusing specifically on violence perpetration among Seattle youth in neighborhoods marked by elevated crime levels. While there was some relationship between family socioeconomic status and violent behavior during adolescence, there was no relationship to adult continuation of violence. This study did not directly evaluate community or neighborhood characteristics. However, one variable that related to persistence in offending was the quality of school engagement, which has been linked to the structural factor of underlying school resources (Herrenkohl, Hawkins, Chung, Hill, & Battin-Pearson, 2000).

One study providing results very specific to the role of neighborhoods in the persistence of delinquency was conducted by Tolan, Schoeny, Gorman-Smith, and Henry (2006), using the Chicago Youth Development Study sample of adolescent males residing in high-crime, high-poverty Chicago communities, with overrepresentation of those with elevated aggression. They differentiated four trajectories of delinquency involvement during adolescence: minimal or nondelinquency (26% of the sample), minor but chronic involvement (34%), escalators who showed no involvement early in adolescence but serious and frequent involvement by the end of adolescence (12%), and serious and chronic offenders throughout adolescence (28%). Moderate but consistent relations were found between these adolescent patterns and several indicators of functioning measured when the young men were 23 to 25 years old. As would be expected, those with the serious and chronic offending pattern during adolescence as well as those with escalating patterns showed significantly poorer functioning on adult indicators such as educational achievement and criminal involvement. All four groups, including those with little delinquency, had some members who exhibited criminal behavior during young adulthood.

The study then examined the potential moderating effects of community structural characteristics and neighborhood social relationships. Structural characteristics were not found to moderate any of the relations; however, there was an interesting finding for neighborhood social relationships. Specifically, and pertinent to the focus of this chapter, involvement in criminal behavior in young adulthood (whether measured by self-reports of seriousness and frequency of criminal acts or by legal convictions), for the group with little or no adolescent delinquency involvement, was significantly lower when the quality of neighborhood social relationships was higher. This negative relation suggests a protective influence against what might otherwise be a post-adolescent pattern of increasing criminal behavior. It seems that, in impoverished urban communities, neighborhood processes may save youth who, although able to avoid offending involvement during adolescence, may otherwise get pulled into it as they make the transition to adulthood.

NEIGHBORHOODS AND COMMUNITIES AS MODERATORS OF TRANSITIONS FROM ADOLESCENCE TO ADULTHOOD

Neighborhoods and communities may also play an important role in determining the extent to which adolescent offending persists into adulthood because of the way in which they either facilitate or make more difficult the role transitions that are associated with desistance. For example, in areas with high unemployment rates, job stability will be more difficult to achieve, leading either to more pull toward crime or less pull toward desistance during the transition to young adulthood. Similarly, in areas where marriage is less plausible or less expected, individuals may be less likely to form the kinds of attachments that result in lower rates of offending. One particular effect, which needs better documentation but is suggested by recent studies, is the concentration of returning incarcerated delinquents in lower socio-economic communities where opportunities for employment are lower and opportunities for crime may be higher, and where resources for successful reentry are likely to be strained (Kubrin & Stewart, 2006).

Neighborhoods and communities may also be influential through moderating the effects of social bonds that are typically associated with adult roles. Crutchfield and Pitchford (1997, p. 98) theorized that "the effect of marginal employment on stakes in conformity is conditional on opportunities for interaction with others 'in the same boat.'" Specifically, they hypothesized that individuals with marginal, secondary labor market jobs would feel they had less to lose by activities such as staying out late drinking with friends—activities which often lead to criminal involvement. They would be even more likely to choose to engage in these activities if more of their acquaintances were also in marginal jobs and thus participating in these activities. Using the National Longitudinal Surveys of Youth (NLSY) Labor Market Experience data, in which respondents' residences were geo-coded, Crutchfield and Pitchford (1997) were able to examine the role of county labor markets as a context for the impact of employment on individual behavior. In support of their hypothesis, they found a significant interaction for involvement in violence, whereby individuals out of the labor force for longer times were more likely to engage in violent behavior when they resided in counties in which larger proportions of the population were also out of the labor force.

Another intriguing example of the possible moderating effects of neighborhoods on the relationship between major role transitions and criminal involvement is found in the recent study of motherhood by Kreager, Matsueda, and Erosheva (2010), described earlier in this chapter. They tested the hypothesis derived from qualitative studies (e.g., Edin & Kefalas, 2005) that single motherhood could lead to desistance from criminal offending in poor urban neighborhoods. Using fixed-effects models with longitudinal data from the Denver Youth study, collected in the most disadvantaged neighborhoods of Denver, they found that parenthood was significantly related to decreases in delinquency and substance use. Although these researchers did not directly compare disadvantaged and advantaged neighborhoods, their results contrast sharply with those of many earlier studies of general populations. The authors suggest that "within a context of bleak conventional prospects and ample illicit alternatives, having a child in the absence of the father can provide meaning and fulfillment for an otherwise empty and hollow life" (p. 250). In this case, it appears that this role transition may have protective benefits that it would not have in other communities with less dire social circumstances. Thus, in communities with structural characteristics related to greater delinquency and adult crime risk, social relationships may play a particularly pivotal role in the continuity of criminal involvement from adolescence into young adulthood.

CONCLUSIONS AND FUTURE DIRECTIONS

This set of findings outlines the potential importance of neighborhood structural and social relationship factors in affecting youth development generally as well as continuation of delinquency in the transition to adulthood. Despite the longstanding interest in community and neighborhood factors as influences on criminality, there is a notably thin literature that considers their role in continuation of offending or in late onset of criminality. We are thus limited in reaching any substantial conclusions about the level of importance of these factors, how they might act in concert with or as frames for other influences, and how any impact might be dependent on other individual and family risk and protective factors. The little available research suggests that neighborhood social processes may be more directly influential than economic and other structural factors, although through restricted resources structural characteristics can affect social processes. However, structural characteristics may act to affect other developmental influences such as ease of role transition and support for timely and adequate attainment of key adult role status features.

We suggest the value of further research that applies a theoretical formulation that connects neighborhood and community characteristics with individual and family risk characteristics through systematic hypothesis testing. For example, some studies conceive of neighborhood and community factors as potentiating individual risk, leading those who might escape delinquency elsewhere to develop such problems in poorer functioning neighborhoods (Loeber & Farrington, 2001). Others conceive of neighborhood and community characteristics as a larger system, in which individual and family risk factors are nested (Tolan, Gorman-Smith, & Henry, 2003). Multivariate, multilevel models with specific processes of interrelation are needed for explaining risk during this transition period.

We see a need for research that examines how neighborhoods/communities affect the likelihood that adolescents make successful transitions into adult roles (marriage, parenthood, employment) that can lead to desistance from crime, as well as the likelihood that they will be able to maintain those beneficial statuses. We also suggest that researchers should study how neighborhood/community context may moderate the effects of life circumstances that seem to be important determinants of continuity or discontinuity in offending. Although nationally representative samples can be important for assessing the generality of relations, it is also important to study samples that allow for assessing important neighborhood/community contextual effects.

Relevance of Findings for Practitioners and Policy-Makers

The transition from adolescence to adulthood is a critical time for determining the future trajectory of criminal offending. Programs and policies that can assist young people in this transition would have great promise both for reducing crime and for reducing the harmful effects of crime that can ruin lifetime prospects for those involved in criminal behavior. Findings on the importance of successful transitions into institutions such as marriage, parenthood, and employment suggest that programs and policies related to social supports for these institutions have the potential to facilitate desistance from criminal behavior. These would include programs designed to teach relationship skills, parenting skills, and skills related to finding and keeping a job. They would also include programs providing economic safety nets that are often critical to families staying together during difficult economic times. Additionally, efforts directed at educating youth about the challenges of the transition to adulthood and about how to prepare for adult roles may be useful. Programs of any of these types would be of particular importance for youth who have already been caught up in either the juvenile justice or the criminal justice system, as their options for successful transition into adulthood have already been seriously limited (see Altschuler, 2005; Chung, Little, & Steinberg, 2005; Travis & Visher, 2005; Uggen & Wakefield, 2005).

In the case of situational interventions, much more needs to be learned. Nonetheless, our work suggests that there is significant opportunity in focusing interventions on altering situational opportunities for offending in the contexts in which young people are found. Crime prevention of this sort not only reduces crime in the community, it also keeps youth from experiencing incarceration during the important transition to adulthood.

In the area of micro places or crime hot spots, we think there are particularly promising possibilities for the design of interventions. If a very small number of places are responsible for a large proportion of crime during the years of transition from adolescence to adulthood, a focus on those places provides much promise for assisting the successful navigation of that transition. Although the hot spots concept has become an important policing strategy more generally (Eck & Weisburd, 2004), to date neither practitioners nor policy-makers have used the concept to focus on juvenile or young adult crime. We think that the identification of such hot spots, combined with interventions that are not simply enforcement based, has particular promise. In this regard, the use of teachers, parents, social workers, and other community workers might allow cities to increase supervision at problem places, without encouraging incarceration.

We have seen evidence of the importance of the neighborhood and community context in which the transition from adolescence to adulthood occurs. The findings in this area point to the value of concentrating attention on neighborhoods marked by high poverty and high crime. Such areas not only place youth at higher risk for criminal involvement, but they also typically have fewer resources to aid healthy and effective youth development. The lack of resources in such communities may make the transition to adult employment, successful intimate relationships, and parenthood even more difficult than usual. Development of the kinds of programs described above will be particularly important in these communities. Programs designed to manage post-incarceration adjustment will be critical in these communities in light of the concentration of formerly incarcerated youth who are more likely to continue criminal behavior beyond adolescence in neighborhoods with lower economic and social bonding opportunities. A focus on programs in these locations should have the dual value of efficiently reaching the largest numbers of those in need and blunting any increase in individual risk related to residence in communities with many other at-risk youth.

References

Agnew, R., & Petersen, D.M. (1989). Leisure and delinquency. *Social Problems*, 36, 332–350.

Allan, E.A., & Steffensmeier, D.J. (1989). Youth, underemployment, and property crime: Differential effects of job availability and job quality on juvenile and young adult arrest rates. *American Sociological Review*, 54, 107–123.

Altschuler, D.M. (2005). Policy and program perspectives on the transition to adulthood for adolescents in the juvenile justice system. In D.W. Osgood, E.M. Foster, C. Flanagan & G.R. Ruth (Eds.), *On your own without a net: The transition to adulthood for vulnerable populations* (pp. 92–113). Chicago IL: University of Chicago Press.

Amato, P.R., Booth, A., Johnson, D.R., & Rogers, S.J. (2007). *Alone together: How marriage in America is changing*. Cambridge, MA: Harvard University Press.

Anderson, A.L., & Hughes, L.A. (2009). Exposure to situations conducive to delinquent behavior: The effects of time use, income, and transportation. *Journal of Research in Crime and Delinquency*, 46, 5–34.

Apel, R., Bushway, S.D., Brame, R., Haviland, A.M., Nagin, D.S., & Paternoster, R. (2007). Unpacking the relationship between adolescent employment and antisocial behavior: A matched samples comparison. *Criminology*, 45, 67–97.

Apel, R., Bushway, S.D., Raymond, P., Brame, R., & Sweeton, G. (2008). Using state child labor laws to identify the causal effect of youth employment on deviant behavior and academic achievement. *Journal of Quantitative Criminology*, 24, 337–362.

Bardone, A.M., Moffitt, T.E., Caspi, A, Dickson, N., Silva, P.A. (1996). Adult mental health and social outcomes of adolescent girls with depression and conduct disorder. *Development and Psychopathology*, 8, 811–829.

Bernburg, J.G., & Thorlindsson, T. (2001). Routine activities in social context: A closer look at the role of opportunity in deviant behavior. *Justice Quarterly*, 18, 543–567.

Bersani, B.E., Laub, J.H., & Nieuwbeerta, P. (2009). Marriage and desistance from crime in the Netherlands: Do gender and socio-historical context matter? *Journal of Quantitative Criminology*, 25, 3–24.

Birkbeck, C., & LaFree, G. (1993). The situational analysis of crime and deviance. *Annual Review of Sociology*, 19, 113–137.

Block, R.L., & Davis, S. (1996). The environs of rapid transit stations: A focus for street crime or just another risky place? In R.V. Clarke (Ed.), *Preventing mass transit crime* (Vol. 6, pp. 237–257). Monsey, New York: Criminal Justice Press.

Blokland, A.A.J., & Nieuwbeerta, P. (2005). The effects of life circumstances on longitudinal trajectories of offending. *Criminology*, 43, 1203–1240.

Brantingham, P.J., & Brantingham, P.L. (1990). *Environmental criminology*. Prospect Heights: Waveland Press.

Brantingham, P.J., & Brantingham, P.L. (1995). Criminality of place: Crime generators and crime attractors. *European Journal on Criminal Policy and Research*, 3, 5–26.

Brantingham, P.J., & Brantingham, P.L. (1999). Theoretical model of crime hot spot genera-tion. *Studies on Crime and Crime Prevention*, 8, 7–26.

Brooks-Gunn, J., Duncan, G.J., & Aber, J.L. (1997). *Neighborhood poverty: Policy implica-tions in studying neighborhoods*. New York: Russell Sage Foundation.

Bumpass, L., & Lu, H-h. (2000). Trends in cohabitation and implications for childrens' family contexts in the United States. *Population Studies*, 54, 29–41.

Bursik, R.J., & Grasmick, H. (1993). *Neighborhoods and crime: The dimensions of effective community control*. New York: Lexington.

Capaldi, D.M., Kim, H.K., & Owen, L.D. (2008). Romantic partners' influence on men's likelihood of arrest in early adulthood. *Criminology*, 46, 269–299.

Chung, H.L., Little, M., & Steinberg, L. (2005). The transition to adulthood for adolescents in the juvenile justice system: A developmental perspective. In D.W. Osgood, E.M. Fos-ter, C. Flanagan & G.R. Ruth (Eds.), *On your own without a net: The transition to adult-hood for vulnerable populations* (pp. 68–91). Chicago IL: University of Chicago Press.

Chung, H.L., & Steinberg, L. (2006). Relations between neighborhood factors, parenting behaviors, peer deviance, and delinquency among serious juvenile offenders. *Develop-mental Psychology*, 42, 319–331.

Coulton, C.J., Pandey, S., & Chow, J. (1990). Concentration of poverty and the changing ecology of low-income, urban neighborhoods: An analysis of the Cleveland area. *Social Work Research and Abstracts*, 26, 5–16.

Crane, J. (1991). The epidemic theory of ghettos and neighborhood effects on dropping out and teenage childbearing. *American Journal of Sociology*, 96, 1226–1259.

Crow, W., & Bull, J. (1975). *Robbery deterrence: An applied behavioral science demonstration (Final report)*. La Jolla, CA: Western Behavioral Science Institute.

Crutchfield, R.D., & Pitchford, S.R. (1997). Work and crime: The effects of labor stratifica-tion. *Social Forces*, 76, 93–118.

Dornbusch, S.M., Ritter, P.L., & Steinberg, L. (1991). Community influences on the relation of family statuses to adolescent school performance: Differences between African Americans and non-hispanic whites. *American Journal of Education*, 99, 543–567.

Duncan, G.J., Wilkerson, B., & England, P. (2006). Cleaning up their act: The effects of marriage and cohabitation on licit and illicit drug use. *Demography*, 43, 691–710.

Eck, J.E., & Weisburd, D. (1995). Crime places in crime theory. In J.E. Eck & D. Weisburd (Eds.), Crime and place (Vol. 4, pp. 1–33). Monsey, NY: Willow Tree Press.

Eck, J.E., & Weisburd, D. (2004). What can the police do to reduce crime, disorder, and fear? *Annals of the American Academy of Political and Social Science*, 593, 42–65.

Edin, K., & Kefalas, M. (2005). *Promises I can keep: Why poor women put motherhood before marriage*. Berkeley: University of California Press.

Elliott, D.S., Wilson, W.J., Huizinga, D., Sampson, R.J., Elliott, A., & Rankin, B. (1996). The effects of neighborhood disadvantage on adolescent development. *Journal of Research in Crime and Delinquency*, 33, 389–426.

Farrington, D.P., Gallagher, B., Morley, L., St. Ledger, R.J., & West, D.J. (1986). Unemploy-ment, school leaving, and crime. *British Journal of Criminology*, 26, 335–356.

Farrington, D.P. & West, D.J. (1995). Effects of marriage, separation and children on offend-ing by adult males. In J. Hagan (Ed.), *Current perspectives on aging and the life cycle, vol. 4. Delinquency and disrepute in the life course* (pp. 249–281). Greenwich, CT: JAI Press.

Felson, M. (2006). *Crime and nature*. Thousand Oaks, CA: Sage.

Felson, R.B., & Steadman, H.J. (1983). Situational factors in disputes leading to criminal violence. *Criminology*, 21, 59–74.

Fleming, C.B., White, H.R., Oesterle, S., Haggerty, K.P., & Catalano, R.F. (2010). Romantic relationships and substance use in early adulthood: An examination of the influences of relationship type, partner substance use, and relationship quality. *Journal of Studies on Alcohol and Drugs*, 71, 847–856.

Furstenberg, F.F. (1993). How families manage risk and opportunity in dangerous neighborhoods. In W.J. Wilson (Ed.), *Sociology and the public agenda*. Newbury Park, CA: Sage.

Giordano, P.C., Cernkovich, S.A., & Rudolph, J.L. (2002). Gender, crime, and desistance: Toward a theory of cognitive transformation. *American Journal of Sociology*, 107, 990–1064.

Glueck, S., & Glueck, E. (1950). *Unraveling juvenile delinquency*. Cambridge, MA: Harvard University Press.

Gorman-Smith, D., Tolan, P.H., & Henry, D. (2000). A developmental-ecological model of the relation of family functioning to patterns of delinquency. *Journal of Quantitative Criminology*, 16, 169–198.

Graham, J., & Bowling, B. (1995). *Young people and crime*. London: Home Office.

Greenberger, E., & Steinberg, L. (1986). *When teen-agers work: The psychological and social costs of adolescent employment*. New York: Basic Books.

Griffin, M.L., & Armstrong, G.S. (2003). The effect of local life circumstances on female probationers' offending. *Justice Quarterly*, 20, 213–239.

Grunwald, H.E., Lockwood, B., Harris, P.W., & Mennis, J. (2010). Influences of neighborhood context, individual history and parenting behavior on recidivism among juvenile offenders. *Journal of Youth and Adolescence*, 39, 1067–1079.

Guerra, N.G., Huesmann, L.R., Tolan, P.H., VanAcker, R.V., & Eron, L.D. (1995). Stressful events and individual beliefs as correlates of economic disadvantage and aggression among urban children. *Journal of Consulting and Clinical Psychology*, 63, 518–528.

Hawdon, J.E. (1996). Deviant lifestyles: The social control of daily routines. *Youth and Society*, 28, 162–188.

Hawdon, J.E. (1999). Daily routines and crime: Using routine activities as measures of Hirschi's involvement. *Youth and Society*, 30, 395–415.

Haynie, D.L. & Osgood, D.W. (2005). Reconsidering peers and delinquency: How do peers matter? *Social Forces*, 84, 1109–1130.

Herrenkohl, T.I., Hawkins, J.D., Chung, I.-J., Hill, K.G., & Battin-Pearson, S.R. (2000). School and community risk factors and interventions. In R. Loeber & D.P. Farrington (Eds.), *Child delinquents: Development, intervention, and service needs* (pp. 211–246). Thousand Oaks, CA: Sage.

Hollister, R.G., Kemper, P., & Maynard, R.A. (1984). *The national supported work demonstration*. Madison, WI: University of Wisconsin Press.

Hope, T.L., Wilder, E.I., & Watt, T.T. (2003). The relationship among adolescent pregnancy, pregnancy resolution, and juvenile delinquency. *Sociological Quarterly*, 44, 555–576.

Horney, J., Osgood, D.W., & Marshall, I.H. (1995). Criminal careers in the short-term: Intra-individual variability in crime and its relation to local life circumstances. *American Sociological Review*, 60, 655–673.

Horney, J., Roberts, J.J., & Hassell, K. (2000). The social control function of intimate partners. Paper presented to the annual meeting of the American Society of Criminology, San Francisco.

Jencks, C., & Meyer, S.E. (1990). The social consequences of growing up in a poor neighbor-hood. In L.E. Lynn & M.G.H. McGeary (Eds.), *Inner-city poverty in the United States* (pp. 111–186). Washington, DC: National Academies Press.

King, R., Massoglia, M., & MacMillan, R. (2007). The context of marriage and crime: Gen-der, the propensity to marry, and offending in early adulthood. *Criminology*, 45, 33–66.

Kleck, G., & McElrath, K. (1991). The effects of weaponry on human violence. *Social Forces*, 69, 669–692.

Kosterman, R., Graham, J.W., Hawkins, J.D., Catalano, R.F., & Herrenkohl, T.I. (2001). Childhood risk factors for persistence of violence in the transition to adulthood: A so-cial development perspective. *Violence and Victims*, 16, 355–369.

Kreager, D.A., Matsueda, R.L., & Erosheva, E.A. (2010). Motherhood and criminal desis-tance in disadvantaged neighborhoods. *Criminology*, 48, 221–258.

Kubrin, C.E., & Stewart, E.A. (2006). Predicting who reoffends: The neglected role of the neighborhood in recidivism studies. *Criminology*, 44, 165–197.

Laub, J.H., Nagin, D.S., & Sampson, R.J. (1998). Trajectories of change in criminal offending: Good marriages and the desistance process. *American Sociological Review*, 63, 225–238.

Laub, J.H., & Sampson, R.J. (2003). *Shared beginnings, divergent lives: Delinquent boys to age 70.* Cambridge, MA: Harvard University Press.

Leventhal, T., & Brooks-Gunn, J. (2000). The neighborhoods they live in: The effects of neigh-borhood residence on child and adolescent outcomes. *Psychological Bulletin*, 126, 309–337.

Loeber, R., & Farrington, D.P. (Eds.) (2001). *Child delinquents: Development, intervention, and service needs.* Thousand Oaks, CA: Sage.

Loeber, R., Pardini, D., Stouthamer-Loeber, M., & Raine, A. (2007). Do cognitive, physio-logical, and psychological risk and promotive factors predict desistance from delin-quency in males? *Development and Psychopathology*, 19, 867–887.

Mahoney, J.L., & Stattin, H. (2000). Leisure activities and adolescent antisocial behavior: The role of structure and social context. *Journal of Adolescence*, 23, 113–127.

Manning, W.D., & Smock, P.J. (2002). First comes cohabitation and then comes marriage? A research note. *Journal of Family Issues*, 23, 1065–1087.

Maume, M.O., Ousey, G.C., & Beaver, K. (2005). Cutting the grass: A reexamination of the link between marital attachment, delinquent peers, and desistance from marijuana use. *Journal of Quantitative Criminology*, 21, 27–53.

Moffitt, T.E. (1993). Adolescence-limited and life-course-persistant antisocial behavior: A developmental taxonomy. *Psychological Review*, 100, 674–701.

Monahan, J., & Klassen, D. (1982). Situational approaches to understanding and predicting individual violent behaviors. In M.E. Wolfgang & N. Weiner (Eds.), *Criminal violence* (pp. 292–319). Beverly Hills, CA: Sage.

Nagin, D.S., Farrington, D.P., & Moffitt, T.E. (1995). Life-course trajectories of different types of offenders. *Criminology*, 33, 111–139.

Osgood, D.W., & Wilson, J.K. (1996). Violence, routine activities, and the transition from adolescence to adulthood. Paper presented to the annual meeting of the American Soci-ety of Criminology, Chicago.

Osgood, D.W., Wilson, J.K., O'Malley, P.M., Bachman, J.G., & Johnston, L.D. (1996). Routine activities and individual deviant behavior. *American Sociological Review*, 61, 635–655.

Paternoster, R., Bushway, S.D., Brame, R., & Apel, R. (2003). Effect of teenage employment on delinquency and problem behaviors. *Social Forces*, 82, 297–335.

Pierce, G., Spaar, S., & Briggs, L.R. (1986). *The character of police work: Strategic and tactical implications*. Boston, MA: Center for Applied Social Research, Northeastern University.

Piliavin, I., & Gartner, R. (1981). *The impact of supported work on ex-offenders*. New York: Institute for Research on Poverty and Mathematica Policy Research.

Piquero, A.R., MacDonald, J.M., & Parker, K.F. (2002). Race, local life circumstances, and criminal activity. *Social Science Quarterly*, 83, 654–670.

Quinn, R.P., & Staines, G.L. (1979). *The 1977 quality of employment survey*. Ann Arbor, MI: University of Michigan.

Riley, D. (1987). Time and crime: The link between teenager lifestyle and delinquency. *Journal of Quantitative Criminology*, 3, 339–354.

Roman, C.G. (2002). *Schools as generators of crime: Routine activities and the sociology of place*. Unpublished Dissertation, American University, Washington, D.C.

Roman, C.G. (2005). Routine activities of youth and neighborhood violence: Spatial modeling of place, time, and crime. In F. Wang (Ed.), *Geographic information systems and crime analysis* (pp. 293–310). Hershey, PA: Idea Group.

Roncek, D.W. (1981). Bars, blocks, and crimes. *Journal of Environmental Systems*, 11, 35–47.

Roncek, D.W. (2000). Schools and crime. In V. Goldsmith, P.G. McGuire, J.H. Mollenkopf & T.A. Ross (Eds.), *Analyzing crime patterns: Frontiers of practice* (pp. 153–165). Thousand Oaks, CA: Sage.

Roncek, D.W., & Maier, P.A. (1991). Bars, blocks, and crime revisited: Linking the theory of routine activities to the empiricism of "hot spots." *Criminology*, 29, 725–753.

Sampson, R.J. (1997). The embeddedness of child and adolescent development: A community-level perspective on urban violence. In J. McCord (Ed.), *Violence and childhood in the inner city* (pp. 31–77). New York: Cambridge University Press.

Sampson, R.J., & Laub, J.H. (1990). Crime and deviance over the life course: The salience of adult social bonds. *American Sociological Review*, 55, 608–627.

Sampson, R.J., & Laub, J.H. (1993). *Crime in the making: Pathways and turning points through the life course*. Cambridge, MA: Harvard University Press.

Sampson, R.J., Laub, J.H., & Wimer, C. (2006). Does marriage reduce crime? A counterfactual approach to within-individual causal effects. *Criminology*, 44, 465–508.

Sampson, R.J., & Lauritsen, J.L. (1994). Violent victimization and offending: Individual-, situational-, and community-level risk factors. In A.J. Reiss & J.A. Roth (Eds.), *Understanding and preventing violence: Social influences* (Vol. 3, pp. 1–114). Washington, D.C.: National Academy Press.

Sampson, R.J., Raudenbush, S.W., & Earls, F.J. (1997). Neighborhoods and violent crime: A multilevel study of collective efficacy. *Science*, 277, 918–924.

Shaw, C.R., & McKay, H.P. (1942). *Juvenile delinquency and urban areas*. Chicago IL: University of Chicago Press.

Sherman, L.W. (1995). Hot spots of crime and criminal careers of places. In J.E. Eck & D. Weisburd (Eds.), *Crime and place* (Vol. 4, pp. 35–52). Monsey, NY: Willow Tree Press.

Sherman, L.W., Gartin, P., & Buerger, M.E. (1989). Hot spots of predatory crime: Routine activities and the criminology of place. *Criminology*, 27, 27–55.

Siennick, S.E., & Osgood, D.W. (2008). A review of research on the impact on crime of transitions to adult roles. In A.M. Liberman (Ed.), *The long view of crime: A synthesis of longitudinal research* (pp. 161–187). New York: Springer.

Simons, R.L., Stewart, E., Gordon, L.C., Conger, R.D., & Elder, G.H. (2002). A test of life-course explanations for stability and change in antisocial behavior from adolescence to young adulthood. *Criminology*, 40, 401–434.

Smock, P.J., Casper, L., & Wyse, J. (2008). *Nonmarital cohabitation: Current knowledge and future directions for research (No. 08-648)*. Ann Arbor, MI: Population Studies Center, University of Michigan, Institute for Social Research.

Snyder, H.N. (2004). *Juvenile arrests 2001*. Washington, D.C.: Office of Juvenile Justice and Delinquency Prevention, U.S. Department of Justice.

Snyder, H.N., & Sickmund, M. (2006). *Juvenile offenders and victims: 2006 national report*. Washington, D.C.: Office of Juvenile Justice and Delinquency Prevention, U.S. Department of Justice.

Staff, J., Osgood, D.W., Schulenberg, J.E., Bachman, J.G., & Messersmith, E.E. (2010). Explaining the relationship between employment and juvenile delinquency. *Criminology*, 48, 1101–1131.

Staff, J., Schulenberg, J.E., Maslowski, J., Bachman, P.M., Maggs, J.L., & Johnston, L.D. (2010). Substance use changes and social role transitions: Proximal developmental effects on ongoing trajectories from late adolescence through early adulthood. *Development and Psychopathology*, 22, 917–932.

Stouthamer-Loeber, M., Wei, E., Loeber, R., & Masten, A.S. (2004). Desistance from persistent serious delinquency in the transition to adulthood. *Development and Psychopathology*, 16, 897–918.

Taylor, R.B. (1997). Social order and disorder of street blocks and neighborhoods: Ecology, microecology, and the systemic model of social disorganization. *Journal of Research in Crime and Delinquency*, 34, 113–155.

Theobald, D. & Farrington, D.P. (2009). Effects of getting married on offending. Results from a prospective longitudinal survey of males. *European Journal of Criminology*, 6, 496–516.

Theobald, D. & Farrington, D.P. (2010). Should policy implications be drawn from the effects of getting married on offending? *European Journal of Criminology*, 7, 239–247.

Theobald, D. & Farrington, D.P. (2011). Why do the crime reducing effects of marriage vary with age? *British Journal of Criminology*, 51, 136–138.

Thornberry, T.P., & Christenson, R.L. (1984). Unemployment and criminal involvement: An investigation of reciprocal causal structures. *American Sociological Review*, 49, 398–411.

Tolan, P.H., Gorman-Smith, D., & Henry, D. (2003). The developmental-ecology of urban males' youth violence. *Developmental Psychology*, 39, 274–291.

Tolan, P.H., Schoeny, M., Gorman-Smith, D., & Henry, D. (2006, November). Predictors of successful development in high risk inner-city males. Paper presented as part of Symposium on Normality and Psychopathology in Adolescent Development: Current Issue and Future Pathways. A Festschrift in Honor of Daniel Offer, M.D., Chicago, IL.

Travis, J., & Visher, C.A. (2005). Prisoner reentry and the pathways to adulthood: Policy perspectives. In D.W. Osgood, E.M. Foster, C. Flanagan & G.R. Ruth (Eds.), *On your own without a net: The transition to adulthood for vulnerable populations* (pp. 145–177). Chicago IL: University of Chicago Press.

Uggen, C. (1999). Ex-offenders and the conformist alternative: A job quality model of work and crime. *Social Problems*, 46, 127–151.

Uggen, C. (2000). Work as a turning point in the life course of criminals: A duration model of age, employment, and recidivism. *American Sociological Review*, 65, 529–546.

Uggen, C., & Kruttschnitt, C. (1998). Crime in the breaking: Gender differences in desistance. *Law and Society Review*, 32, 339–366.

Uggen, C., & Wakefield, S. (2005). Young adults reentering the community from the criminal justice system: The challenge of becoming an adult. In D.W. Osgood, E.M. Foster, C. Flanagan & G.R. Ruth (Eds.), *On your own without a net: The transition to adulthood for vulnerable populations* (pp. 114–144). Chicago IL: University of Chicago Press.

Vazsonyi, A.T., Pickering, L., Belliston, L.M., Hessing, D., & Junger, M. (2002). Routine activities and deviant behaviors: American, Dutch, Hungarian, and Swiss youth. *Journal of Quantitative Criminology*, 18, 397–422.

Wadsworth, T. (2006). The meaning of work: Conceptualizing the deterrent effect of employment on crime among young adults. *Sociological Perspectives*, 49, 343–368.

Warr, M. (1998). Life-course transitions and desistance from crime. *Criminology*, 36, 183–216.

Wei, E.H., Loeber, R., & Stouthamer-Loeber, M. (2002). How many of the offspring born to teenage fathers are produced by repeat serious delinquents? *Criminal Behaviour and Mental Health*, 12, 83–98.

Weisburd, D., Bruinsma, G.J.N., & Bernasco, W. (2009). Units of analysis in geographic criminology: Historical development, critical issues, and open questions. In D. Weisburd, W. Bernasco & G.J.N. Bruinsma (Eds.), *Putting crime in its place: Units of analysis in spatial crime research* (pp. 3–31). New York: Springer-Verlag.

Weisburd, D., & Green, L. (1994). Defining the drug market: The case of the Jersey City DMA system. In D.L. MacKenzie & C.D. Uchida (Eds.), *Drugs and crime: Evaluating public policy initiatives* (pp. 61–76). Newbury Park, CA: Sage.

Weisburd, D., & Green, L. (1995). Policing drug hot spots: The Jersey City drug market analysis experiment. *Justice Quarterly*, 12, 711–736.

Weisburd, D., Maher, L., & Sherman, L.W. (1992). Contrasting crime general and crime specific theory: The case of hot spots of crime. In F. Adler & W.S. Laufer (Eds.), *Advances in criminological theory* (Vol. 4, pp. 45–70). New Brunswick, NJ: Transaction.

Weisburd, D., & McEwen, T. (1997). Introduction: Crime mapping and crime prevention. In D. Weisburd & T. McEwen (Eds.), *Crime mapping and crime prevention* (Vol. 8, pp. 1–23). Monsey, NY: Criminal Justice Press.

Weisburd, D., Morris, N.A., & Groff, E.R. (2009). Hot spots of juvenile crime: A longitudinal study of arrest incidents at street segments in Seattle, Washington. *Journal of Quantitative Criminology*, 25, 443–467.

Wells, W., & Horney, J. (2002). Weapon effects and individual intent to do harm: Influences on the escalation of violence. *Criminology*, 40, 265–296.

Wikström, P.O., & Butterworth, D.A. (2006). *Adolescent crime: Individual differences and lifestyles*. Portland, OR: Willan.

Wikström, P.O., & Loeber, R. (2000). Do disadvantaged neighborhoods cause well-adjusted children to become adolescent delinquents: A study of male juvenile serious offending, individual risk and protective factors, and neighborhood context. *Criminology*, 38, 1109–1142.

Wilson, W.J. (1987). *The truly disadvantaged: The inner city, the underclass and public policy*. Chicago IL: University of Chicago Press.

Yule, C.F. (2010). *Mothering in the context of criminalized women's lives: Implications for offending*. Unpublished Dissertation, University of Toronto, Toronto.

5

Special Categories of Serious and Violent Offenders

DRUG DEALERS, GANG MEMBERS, HOMICIDE
OFFENDERS, AND SEX OFFENDERS

Richard Rosenfeld, Helene R. White, and Finn-Aage Esbensen

Theft and violent offending have been linked to many other illegal behaviors, including drug dealing and gang membership. We refer to drug dealers and gang members in this chapter as "special" categories of offenders. We also consider homicide and sex offenders as special offenders, although limited data and space preclude extensive treatment of these categories. This chapter summarizes existing research and introduces new data on drug dealing, gang membership, homicide, and sex offending. As in Chapter 2, we examine ages of onset and desistance, common and unique correlates, predictors of persistence and desistance, and the generality versus specificity of offending, but here we focus on these special categories of offenders. We are particularly interested in the transition from adolescence into young adulthood when examining persistence and desistance and the generality and specificity of offending. General forms of offending (i.e., property and violent offending) drop off for most offenders during this critical transition period. In this chapter we examine whether this transition period is also important for special categories of offenders. We also assess how drug use and gun carrying influence patterns of special offending from adolescence into young adulthood.

Drug Use, Drug Dealing, and Other Types of Offending

Although we refer to these four categories of offenders as in some sense "special," at the outset it is important to emphasize the connections and commonalities, as well as the differences, among them. For example, in many studies each of these special types of offenders has been linked to drug use as well as to other forms of criminal offending (for reviews see White, in press; White & Gorman, 2000). In general, the research shows that, compared with nonoffenders, criminal offenders report higher rates of substance use, and substance users and abusers report higher rates of offending compared to nonusers (White & Gorman, 2000). Whether substance use *causes* specific instances of criminal offending depends on individual and contextual factors, as well as on the type of substance examined (White, in press). For many individuals, substance use and offending are not causally related but rather are linked because common predictors are related to both, although there are also unique predictors of drug use compared to serious and violent offending (White & Gorman, 2000; White & Labouvie, 1994).

Drug dealing is also connected to drug use and nondrug offending and has been a major illegal activity for drug-involved criminals (Lipton & Johnson, 1998), probably because dealing is a source for needed drugs or income to buy drugs (Harrison, 1992). Nonetheless, the prevalence of drug use varies considerably among dealers. Many dealers do not use drugs or do so only moderately (Hunt, 1990; Lipton & Johnson, 1998) and high-frequency dealers often engage in other illegal activities (Inciardi & Pottieger, 1998; Lipton & Johnson, 1998; Van Kammen & Loeber, 1994; see below).

Goldstein (1985) labeled the violence connected with the illegal drug market as "systemic violence." Systemic violence emerges from conflicts among drug sellers or between sellers and buyers over price, purity, quantity, territory, and other conditions of distribution and exchange. Systemic violence probably accounts for most drug-related violence and an appreciable fraction of all serious violence, especially homicides, among youths in inner cities (Blumstein, 1995; Fagan & Chin, 1990; Inciardi & Pottieger, 1991). Most of the drug-related homicides in inner cities during the crack cocaine epidemic of the late 1980s and early 1990s have been attributed to systemic violence (Goldstein, Brownstein, Ryan, & Bellucci, 1989). At least during that period, a strong link existed among illegal drug use (demand), dealing (supply), and homicide. Other homicides are related to the commission of another felony (e.g., robbery), gang activity, and interpersonal disputes. Further, a large fraction of homicides occur while perpetrators are under the influence of substances, especially alcohol (White & Gorman, 2000).

Some researchers have attributed violence associated with drug dealing to youth gangs. In general, however, studies show that there are numerous types of gangs, some of which do not sell or use drugs (Levine & Rosich, 1996). With respect to drug dealing by individual gang members, a large body of research indicates that the prevalence and level of dealing are greater among gang members than non-gang involved youth (Bjerregaard, 2010; Esbensen & Huizinga 1993; Esbensen, Peterson, Freng & Taylor, 2002; Fagan 1996; Thornberry 1998). This relationship, however, is refuted by other research which suggests that dealing is just as prevalent among youth who do not belong to gangs as among gang members, and there is little evidence that drug-related activities increase gang violence (Fagan, 1989; Inciardi, 1990; Levine & Rosich, 1996; Moore, 1990).[1]

Sexual assaults are often related to alcohol or drug use at the time of the assault (Abbey, Zawacki, Buck, Clinton, & McAuslan, 2001; Ullman, Karabastos, & Koss, 1999). In a national study of college students, Koss (1988) found that about three-fourths of the rape perpetrators had been drinking alcohol (with or without use of another drug). Sexual assaults that are alcohol-related, compared to those that are not, are more likely to occur between men and women who do not know each other well and tend to occur outside the home (Abbey et al., 2001).

Prior research therefore documents strong *prima facie* connections among drug use, drug dealing, violent behavior, and gang membership, although the causal significance of these relationships is uncertain. We build on existing research with new data, drawn primarily from the Pittsburgh Youth Study (PYS; see Chapter 2 for a description of this sample and its strengths and limitations) to examine the transition of special offending from adolescence to young adulthood. The current analyses focus on the youngest cohort born primarily in 1980–1981 (from approximately age 6 through age 19; $N = 503$) and the oldest cohort born primarily in 1973–1975 (from approximately age 12 through age 25; $N = 506$). For these analyses, data were coded by participant age at each assessment.

Given its rarity and other distinctive characteristics, homicide cannot be studied with the self-report and longitudinal datasets used to investigate gang and drug offending—an exception is the PYS, although the small number of homicide offenders in the sample ($N = 37$ as of 2009) limits the kinds of analyses that can be done on these offenders (see Loeber et al., 2005; Loeber & Farrington, 2011). The PYS also permits limited analyses of violent sex offenders (Van Wijk et al., 2005). We can gain additional insight into the sequencing of homicide over the life course, for those offenders who commit more than a single homicide, by examining the criminal histories and recidivism of persons sentenced to prison for homicide. We analyze data from the Bureau of Justice Statistics' *Recidivism of Prisoners Released in 1994* dataset (see Langan & Levin, 2002; Rosenfeld, Wallman, & Fornango, 2005) on the criminal records and recidivism rates of a sample of persons released from 15 state prisons in 1994 who were sentenced to prison for homicide and other offenses (N = 33,625). These analyses compare the recidivism rates and criminal histories of homicide offenders, sex offenders, other violent offenders, drug offenders, and property offenders. Our assessment of recidivism is restricted to offenders who were under age 30 when released from prison, and our analysis of criminal histories is based on all released prisoners in the sample regardless of age.

Typical Age of Onset

Determining the average age of onset of problem behaviors is fraught with numerous methodological problems (Golub, Labouvie, & Johnson, 2000). First, age of onset depends on the age range of the sample studied. For example, if the sample is composed of adolescents, then data are right censored because some adolescents may not have begun to engage in a specific behavior at the time of data collection. On the other hand, if one studies adults, age of onset may have been many years prior, and retrospective reporting may not be accurate (Golub et al., 2000). Besides age, initiation of problem behaviors depends on cohort and historical factors. For example, when comparing two cohorts of youths aged 13–19, one born in approximately 1980–1981 and the other born in approximately 1973–1975 from the PYS, White, Loeber, and Farrington (2008) found that among marijuana users, the average age of onset was 17.0 years for the older cohort compared to 14.8 years for the younger cohort. This difference could reflect changes in availability or acceptance of marijuana (Bachman, Johnston, & O'Malley, 1998). In addition, there are regional, racial/ethnic, and gender differences in age of onset for many problem behaviors (Wallace, Bachman, O'Malley, Schulenberg, Cooper, & Johnston, 2003). For example, Esbensen and Elliott (1994) found that the age of onset of marijuana use peaked earlier for females than males. The data we report below should be interpreted with these caveats in mind.

White, Loeber, and Farrington (2008, pp. 149–150) examined the mean age of onset for gang membership, drug dealing, marijuana use, hard drug use, and gun carrying in both cohorts of the PYS sample. This information is summarized in Figure 5.1. In the younger cohort gang membership (mean age = 12.3) occurred first. A year and a half later came gun carrying (13.9), followed by marijuana use (14.8), drug dealing (14.8), and finally hard drug use (15.7). It should be noted that drug dealing began approximately a year before hard drug use. In the older cohort, the sequence was gang membership (15.9), marijuana use (16.5), drug dealing (17.0), gun carrying (17.3) and hard drug use (17.5). The age of onset of gang membership was much later in the older than the younger cohort, which may reflect a period effect, that is, the differing conditions associated with the historical periods during which each cohort reached a given age. It also may be attributable to a cohort effect, the differing conditions associated with the average birth year of the two cohorts. The fact that the average age of onset across behaviors was generally later in the older than younger cohort also could reflect right censoring given that the younger cohort was followed until age 19 and the older cohort until age 25. However, when the analysis was limited to those in both cohorts who began each behavior by age 19, the age of onset for all behaviors was still significantly earlier in the younger than older cohort (also shown in Figure 5.1).

White et al. (2008, p. 151) also examined where serious theft (i.e., breaking and entering and auto theft) and violence (i.e., robbery, attacking to hurt or kill, and forced sex) fit within this sequence of other problem behaviors (also shown in Figure 5.1). They found that, in the younger cohort, serious theft preceded all behaviors except gang membership; serious violence began before gun carrying, marijuana use, drug dealing, and hard drug use. In the older cohort, serious theft began before all problem behaviors, while serious violence began before gang

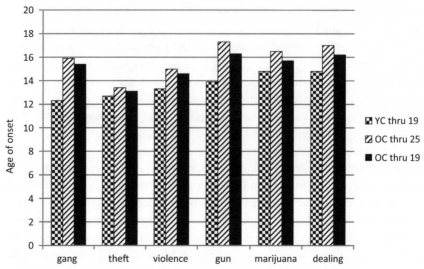

FIGURE 5.1 Average age of onset for the PYS Youngest (YC) and Oldest (OC) Cohorts.
(Adapted from White et al. [2008], Table 6.1.)

membership, illegal drug use, gun carrying and drug dealing. Thus, in both cohorts, serious violence preceded drug dealing.

White and colleagues (2008, p. 153-154) reanalyzed the mean ages of onset comparing two behaviors for those who engaged in both of them (whereas the previous analysis examined means for everyone who engaged in each behavior; see Table 5.1). In the younger cohort, marijuana was first used more than one year earlier than hard drugs. Gang membership was significantly more likely to precede illegal drug use and drug dealing. Illegal drug use (including marijuana use) was significantly more likely to precede dealing. Onset of gun carrying followed gang membership, but occurred around the same time as illegal drug use and dealing. The same sequential order was replicated in the older cohort except that gun carrying preceded dealing.

When serious violence was examined, youth in both cohorts "were equally as likely to first use illegal drugs as they were to first engage in serious violence and the mean age of onset of serious violence preceded the mean age of onset of illegal drug use by only a few months" (p. 156). The mean age of violence was also about one year earlier than dealing. There were a few cohort differences. In the younger cohort, "gang membership preceded serious violence by less than one year," whereas in the older cohort "the mean age of onset of serious violence preceded gang membership by a few months" (p. 156). In the older cohort, a greater proportion of youth was first violent before they carried a gun, whereas in the younger cohort they were equally likely to be violent first or carry a gun first. In both cohorts, the onset of serious theft preceded the onset of illegal drug use, gun carrying, and dealing. "As with violence, the sequencing of gang

TABLE 5.1 } Ages of onset comparing two types of offending and/or drug use in the PYS sample.

		Mean Age	
Earlier[a]	Later	Earlier	Later
Youngest Cohort			
Marijuana	Hard	14.4	15.8
Gang	Drug	12.3	13.7
Gang	Deal	12.5	14.4
Drug	Deal	13.9	14.8
Drug	Gun	13.8	13.8
Gun	Deal	13.9	14.3
Gang	Gun	12.4	13.6
Violence	Drug	13.4	13.6
Gang	Violence	12.3	13.0
Violence	Deal	13.6	14.6
Violence	Gun	13.5	13.9
Theft	Drug	12.9	13.7
Gang	Theft	12.2	12.6
Theft	Deal	13.0	14.3
Theft	Gun	12.9	13.7
Oldest Cohort			
Marijuana	Hard	15.3	17.4
Gang	Drug	15.9	16.1
Gang	Deal	16.0	16.4
Drug	Deal	15.9	16.9
Drug	Gun	15.8	17.2
Deal	Gun	16.7	17.1
Gang	Gun	16.1	17.0
Violence	Drug	14.9	15.5
Violence	Gang	15.5	15.9
Violence	Deal	15.2	16.3
Violence	Gun	15.3	16.9
Theft	Drug	13.4	15.5
Theft	Gang	13.6	15.9
Theft	Deal	13.8	16.3
Theft	Gun	13.9	16.7

[a]Each row is based on the same individuals who at some time engaged in both behaviors with the earlier age being the behavior that generally comes first for those who engage in both, but not for everyone (for greater detail, see White et al., 2008).

Gun = Gun Carrying; Gang = Gang Membership; Marijuana = Marijuana Use; Hard = Hard Drug Use; Drug = younger age of Marijuana and Hard Drug Use; Deal = Drug Dealing.

Source: Adapted from White et al. (2008), Tables 6.2 and 6.3.

membership and serious theft differed between the cohorts" (p. 157). In the younger cohort, boys were as likely to join gangs before they committed their first serious theft offense as afterward, whereas in the older cohort a significantly greater proportion were first serious theft offenders before they were gang members.

In an examination of the initiation of drug use, drug sales, violent offending, and gang joining, Esbensen and colleagues (2002) reported results from their six-city longitudinal study. They found that "when the gang youth initiated the behavior in question, the most common pattern was for the behavior in question to be initiated during the same year the youth reported joining the gang. For example, 47% reported joining a gang the same year they started using drugs. Similarly 35% initiated violence and drug sales the same year of gang joining" (p. 48).

With respect to youth gang initiation, many of the recent studies that include younger cohorts have found that gang membership generally starts with the transition to middle school (and also the onset of puberty). In their Rochester sample, Thornberry, Krohn, Lizotte, Smith, and Tobin (2003) found that there was a general clustering of gang involvement in the younger ages (around age 12). Similar findings were reported by Esbensen and Huizinga (1993) in Denver and by Peterson, Taylor, and Esbensen (2004) in their 11-city cross-sectional study as well as in their six-city longitudinal sample.

Further, it should be noted that most longitudinal studies examining the effect of joining a gang on illegal activity have been supportive of an enhancement effect, a combination of selection and social facilitation. That is, gang members report higher levels of involvement in delinquency, relative to non-gang youth, prior to joining the gang (selection effect). But gang members become more criminally active while in the gang (facilitation effect).[2]

Some research points to an earlier age of onset for sex offenders who aggress against female peers or adult women than among those who aggress against children. In this and other respects, as reported below, male adolescents who aggress against female peers or adults are more similar to other offenders than to those who aggress against children (Lussier, 2005).

With rare exceptions, such as mass and serial murderers, homicide is overwhelmingly a one-time event. In 2005 the mean age of homicide offenders was 28 (in incidents with a known offender) and the mean age of victims was 32. The average age of homicide offenders and victims dropped between the mid-1970s and the mid-1990s and has risen since then (Fox & Zawitz, 2007). For both victims and offenders, aggregate homicide rates peak in young adulthood (see Table 5.2). The age distribution of homicide offenders differs by homicide circumstance. Offenders in gang-related homicides are younger than those in drug or felony homicides. In 2005 about 29% of the offenders in gang-related homicides were under age 18, compared with 15% of those in felony homicides and 11% of those in drug-related homicides (Fox & Zawitz, 2007).

TABLE 5.2 } Age-specific homicide offending and victimization rates per 100,000 population, 2005.

Age	Offender[a]	Victim
Under 14	0.1	1.4
14-17	9.3	4.8
18-24	26.5	14.9
25-34	13.5	11.6
35-49	5.1	5.7
50 and over	1.4	2.6

[a] For incidents with known offender.

Source: Supplementary Homicide Reports (Fox & Zawitz, 2007).

Although most offenders begin offending in adolescence, using data from the PYS we examined the prevalence of special categories of offending in young adulthood among those who did not offend in adolescence. In other words, this analysis examined the onset of special offending during the transition from adolescence into young adulthood. Based on weighted data from the PYS oldest cohort, we found that 29.7% of those who did not deal drugs in adolescence (before age 18) began dealing in young adulthood (at age 18 or later). In comparison, only 6.2% of young men first joined gangs in young adulthood. Whereas only 3.8% of those who did not commit a serious theft offense in adolescence committed one in young adulthood, 15% committed their first serious violent offense in young adulthood. Thus, there appears to be some initiation of dealing and serious violence during the transition from adolescence into young adulthood, but very little later initiation of gang membership and serious theft (see Chapter 2 for a discussion of late-onset offending).

Within the PYS oldest cohort, 58.4% (based on self-reported weighted data) had not engaged in serious offending, dealing, or gang membership during adolescence (prior to age 18). In young adulthood, 23.8% of this group first began dealing, 3.1% first joined a gang, 7.8% committed their first serious violent offense, and 2.6% committed their first serious theft offense.

Duration and Age of Desistance

Dealing, gun carrying, and gang membership appear to follow a maturation process similar to violent offending, although dealing persists longer (White et al., 2008; see, also Piquero et al., Chapter 2, this volume). That is, the annual prevalence of these behaviors tends to peak in late adolescence and then drops off rapidly. These findings are in contrast to substance use, which persists much longer. White and colleagues (2008, pp. 158-159) examined the duration of problem behaviors into young adulthood among those who engaged in them in adolescence. In the older cohort, marijuana use persisted on average for six years (see Figure 5.2). Dealing came next for about three-and-a-half years, hard drug use and gun

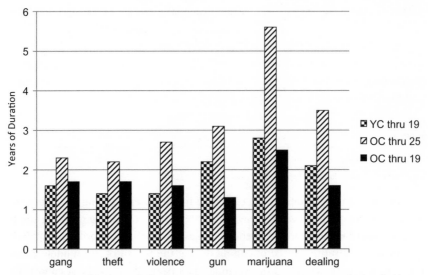

FIGURE 5.2 Years of duration of offending and substance use for the PYS Youngest (YC) and Oldest (OC) Cohorts.

Adapted from White et al. (2008), Table 6.4.

carrying for three years, and gang membership for two years. The only behavior that was likely to have ceased prior to age 20 was gang membership, which reflects the transitory nature of adolescent gang membership (Thornberry et al., 2003). White et al. (2008) also found that, in the older cohort followed through age 25, marijuana use persisted two to four times longer than serious theft and violence. Dealing also persisted longer than serious offending in both cohorts. Thus, it appears that gang membership is primarily limited to the adolescent years and is quite transitory (see below), whereas dealing is the special type of offending that is most likely to persist from adolescence into young adulthood.

As indicated in the preceding section, youth join gangs at relatively early ages, generally in the years associated with entry into middle school (ages 10–12). Longitudinal research has documented that youth gang membership is usually transitory, with the majority of youth belonging to a gang for less than one year (Bendixen et al., 2006; Esbensen & Huizinga, 1993; Gatti et al., 2005; Peterson et al., 2004; Thornberry et al., 1993). In the Thornberry et al. (2003) study, 76 of 151 male gang members were identified as "short-term" gang members (less than one year), while 38 of the 57 female gang members were short-term. Analyses of the Rochester (Thornberry et al., 2003) and Denver (Esbensen & Huizinga, 1993) samples suggested that there appears to be a gender difference in persistence of gang membership, with a smaller proportion of girls still active by middle to late adolescence. That is, there is evidence to suggest that females age out of gangs at an earlier age than their male peers. In their multisite study, Peterson et al. (2004) found that 69% of gang-involved youth were members for only one reporting year.

As a consequence of this transiency, most gang-involved youth are no longer gang-involved by middle to late adolescence. Thornberry and colleagues (2003) reported that 12.6% of their sample was gang-involved at Wave 2 and only 4.6% were gang members at Wave 9. Similarly, Bellair and McNulty (2009) analyzed the National Longitudinal Survey of Youth and found annual prevalence rates of gang membership to be 2.3% for age 12 and 1% when the sample was age 16.

To date there has been limited research examining the process of desistance from gangs. In a notable exception, Decker and Lauritsen (2002, p. 53) emphasized the importance of viewing desistance as "a process not dissimilar to that which they used in entering the gang—a gradual series of steps and commitments." While some researchers suggest that, to exit the gang, members must be "beat out" (e.g., Vigil, 1988), research on younger samples indicates that the more common path to leaving the gang is simply aging out or changing peer group affiliation (e.g., Peterson, 2012; Thornberry et al., 2003).

Given its relative rarity, especially in general population longitudinal studies, little reliable evidence exists regarding desistance in sex offending. Generally speaking, however, it appears that those who aggress against children persist in sex offending for a longer period beyond adolescence than those who aggress against female peers or adult women (Langan, Schmitt, & Durose, 2003; Lussier, 2005).

As noted above, except for the unusual subtypes of serial and mass murder, which are not well-documented in the research literature, homicide is typically a one-time occurrence and therefore the ages of onset and desistance are the same. But some evidence is available on repeat homicide offending over the life course for persons imprisoned for homicide. We present that evidence when discussing offense persistence and specialization below.

Causes and Correlates of Special Categories of Offending

Drug dealing. Given that many drug dealers are also delinquent and use drugs, the correlates of drug dealing are similar to those found for delinquency and drug use (Altschuler & Brounstein, 1991; Van Kammen & Loeber, 1994). Compared to non-dealers, dealers are more likely to engage in several high-risk behaviors including weapon carrying, truancy, violence, and high-risk sexual behaviors (Centers & Weist, 1998; De Li, S., Priu, H., & Mackenzie, D., 2000; Li & Feigelman, 1994). According to Centers and Weist (1998), one of the most consistent findings is that drug dealers do more poorly in school than nondealers and they suggest that drug-dealing youth may have deficits in cognitive and emotional processes. In addition, studies find that, compared to nondealers, dealers report lower levels of parental monitoring and are less likely to come from intact families (Li, Stanton, & Feigelman, 2000; Little & Steinberg, 2006; Van Kammen & Loeber, 1994). Little and Steinberg (2006) found that drug dealers reported higher peer resistance than nondealers. This finding may be unique to drug dealing given that adolescent drug users often have low peer resistance skills (Pandina, Johnson, & White, 2009; Steinberg & Monahan, 2007).

Gang membership. The phenomenon of gangs is subject to a number of definitional issues. Most research has focused on youth gangs, which are substantively different from adult gangs, motorcycle gangs, prison gangs, and major drug-dealing gangs (Klein & Maxson, 2006). Unfortunately, reference is often made to gangs without specifying the type of gangs of interest. Given the topic of this book, our comments are specific to youth gangs, members of which may eventually become involved in the other types of gangs as they transition from adolescence into young adulthood.

Stereotypical descriptions of youth gang members focus on demographics, including age, gender, and race. The belief is that gang members are disproportionately male (some law enforcement data suggest virtually exclusively male), older, and members of racial/ethnic minority groups. Surveys suggest that membership is not quite this demographically restricted. Girls comprise a significant proportion of gang members; youths first join gangs as early as age 10 to 12; and gang members tend to reflect the racial/ethnic composition of the neighborhood (Esbensen & Lynskey, 2001).

The community is the domain that has been examined most frequently in regard to both the emergence of gangs and the factors associated with joining gangs. Numerous studies indicate that poverty, unemployment, the absence of meaningful jobs, and social disorganization contribute to the presence of gangs (Curry & Thomas, 1992; Fagan, 1990; Hagedorn, 1988; Huff, 1990; Vigil, 1988). There is little debate that gangs are more prominent in urban than rural or suburban areas and that they are more likely to emerge in economically distressed neighborhoods. However, recent surveys conducted by the National Youth Gang Center have identified youth gangs in rural and suburban communities (e.g., Egley, Howell, & Moore, 2010; Starbuck, Howell, & Lindquist, 2001). Nonetheless, the traditional image of American youth gangs remains one characterized by urban social disorganization and economic marginalization; the housing projects or barrios of Los Angeles, Chicago, and New York are viewed as the stereotypical homes of youth gang members.

Social structural conditions alone, however, cannot account for the presence of gangs. Fagan (1990, p. 207) commented that "inner-city youths in this study live in areas where social controls have weakened and opportunities for success in legitimate activities are limited. Nevertheless, participation in gangs is selective, and most youths avoid gang life." Factors associated with gang emergence and gang joining must therefore be examined.

A large array of risk factors associated with gang joining/involvement has been identified in the literature (Esbensen, Peterson, Taylor, & Freng, 2009; Howell & Egley, 2005; Klein & Maxson, 2006; Thornberry et al., 2003), with considerable overlap in factors identified. However, researchers have tended to include different risk factors in their studies or have measured the risk factors differently, so a lack of consensus remains about which risk factors are most strongly related to gang affiliation. Howell and Egley (2005), for example, provided a lengthy list of risk factors associated with gang membership. At the other extreme, Klein and Maxson (2006) reported a very limited set of risk factors associated with gang joining. In their systematic review, Klein and Maxson reviewed 20 studies published since 1990 that met their inclusion criteria: studies limited to adolescent samples; that compared youth who joined gangs to youth who did not; that used data derived directly from youth and family members versus police records; and that were cross-sectional or longitudinal. Klein and Maxson summarized their systematic review by classifying risk factors on a continuum of support, ranging from consistently supported, mostly supported, inconclusive, and mostly not supported. Based on this strategy, only three risk factors received consistent support across numerous studies: two at the individual-level (negative life events and nondelinquent behavior problems) and one in the peer domain (characteristics of the peer network). An additional three risk factors were identified as being mostly supported: delinquent beliefs in the individual domain, parental supervision in the family domain, and affective dimensions of the peer network in the peer domain. It is also instructive to identify those risk factors that were *not* supported in the research: low self-esteem, family poverty/disadvantage, family structure, family attachment, unsafe school environment, and criminogenic neighborhood indicators (Klein & Maxson, 2006, pp. 144–146).

While there is little consensus regarding which specific risk factors are predictive of gang joining, greater consensus exists regarding the substantive effect of cumulative risk factors, especially in multiple domains. As is the case for other adolescent problem behaviors, the relationship between the number of risk factors and gang joining is not linear, rather it is geometric (e.g., Esbensen, Peterson, Taylor, & Freng, 2010; Thornberry et al., 2003). For example, in their examination of risk factors associated with violent offending and gang membership, Esbensen and colleagues (2009) reported that approximately 25% of violent offenders have between zero and five risk factors, 39% have between six and 10, and 36% have 11 or more. Among gang members, however, the pattern differed with only 13% having zero to five risk factors, 35% possessing six to ten, and 52% reporting 11 or more risk factors.

Sexual assault. Studies of college men who have sexually assaulted women have identified the following characteristics: hostility toward women, strong masculine gender role identity, low empathy, having experienced violence as a child, delinquency, strong peer influences (e.g., members of fraternities that encourage hostility toward women), and having experienced early and frequent sex (Abbey, 2002). Men who report having perpetrated sexual assault are more like to be heavy drinkers than those who do not perpetrate sexual assault (Abbey et al., 2001). In addition, men who commit sexual assault report relatively high rates of alcohol and drug dependence, although their rates are lower than for other types of offenders (Karberg & James, 2005). Testa (2002) suggested that the higher rates of alcohol dependence among men who commit sexual assault might simply reflect higher levels of psychopathology and deviance.

In one of the few general population studies comparing violent sex offenders with other violent offenders, Van Wijk et al. (2005) found few risk factors that reliably distinguished the two categories of offenders in the PYS data. Compared with other violent offenders, sex offenders were significantly more likely to have run away from home, have higher academic achievement, have lived in better neighborhoods (but poorer housing), have younger, poorly educated mothers, and have experienced inconsistent discipline. Nevertheless, on the large majority of the risk factors considered, the violent sex offenders did not differ from other violent offenders, and the differences that did emerge are not easily interpreted.

Homicide. Only limited data are available that can be used to compare the correlates of homicide offending and other types of offending. Here we present Uniform Crime Reports data on the race, gender, and age distribution of persons arrested for homicide, rape, other violent crimes (robbery, aggravated assault), drug offenses, and property crimes (burglary, larceny, and motor vehicle theft). These data provide a reasonably accurate indication of the demographic correlates of homicide offending because most homicides are cleared by an arrest. They offer a less accurate demographic picture of other types of offending for which clearance rates are much lower (see Table 5.3).

As shown in Table 5.3, males constitute the great majority of persons arrested for homicide, other violent offenses, and drug offenses. Just over a third of arrests for property crimes involve females. Although African-Americans, who constitute about 13% of the U.S. population, are disproportionately represented in arrests for all of the crime types shown in Table 5.3, African-Americans constitute a much smaller proportion of arrestees for property crime (30.1%) than for homicide (50.1%). Finally, the age distribution of arrestees differs somewhat by offense type. Compared with those arrested for rape and other violent crimes, persons arrested for homicide are less likely to be juveniles and more likely to be young adults. Over

TABLE 5.3 } Gender, race, and age distribution of persons arrested by offense type, 2008.

	% Homicide	% Rape	% Other Violent[a]	% Drug	% Property[b]
Male	89.2	98.8	81.5	81.6	65.2
Female	10.8	1.2	18.5	18.4	34.8
Black	50.1	32.2	39.2	34.8	30.1
White	47.9	65.2	58.5	63.8	67.4
Other	2.1	2.6	2.3	1.3	2.5
Under 18	9.8	14.8	16.3	10.6	26.1
18-24	40.0	28.4	29.4	35.8	29.8
25 and over	50.1	56.8	54.3	53.6	44.0

[a] Robbery, aggravated assault.

[b] Burglary, larceny, motor vehicle theft.

Source: Uniform Crime Reports.

a quarter of property crime arrestees and 10.6% of persons arrested for drug crimes are juveniles. Young adults constitute 29.8% of persons arrested for property crimes and 35.8% of those arrested for drug offenses.

In one of the very few prospective longitudinal studies of homicide offenders based on a general population sample, Loeber et al. (2005) reported an average age of just under 19 for the 33 male homicide offenders in the sample; 88% were under age 21 when they committed homicide. Nearly all of the homicide offenders had engaged in violence prior to committing homicide. Compared with other study participants who had engaged in serious violence (rape, robbery, aggravated assault) but had not committed a homicide, the homicide offenders were significantly more likely to carry a weapon, sell hard drugs, and report involvement in gang fighting. In addition, they were more likely than other violent offenders to have a conduct disorder diagnosis, have delinquent peers, be held back in school, have a family on welfare. These results, while based on a small number of homicide offenders and requiring replication, suggest that homicide offenders differ from other violent offenders with respect to both proximate risk factors (e.g., drug selling, weapon carrying, gang involvement) and long-term risk factors (e.g., socioeconomic disadvantage, conduct disorder). But the differences are quantitative rather than qualitative. Homicide offenders, it appears, are like other violent offenders, but with higher levels on most risk factors.

Predictors of Persistence and Desistance

For this chapter we examined the self-reported prevalence of drug dealing and gang membership, as well as serious theft and violent offending in the PYS oldest cohort (for an extended treatment of these issues, see Loeber, Farrington, Stouthamer-Loeber, & White, 2008). These data were weighted back to the original screening sample to compensate for the over-sampling of high-risk youth and, thus, can be generalized to youth who began the seventh grade in the Pittsburgh Public Schools during the late 1980s. In the PYS oldest cohort, the weighted prevalence in adolescence (ages 13–17) was 24.6% for drug dealing and 16.8% for gang membership. This compares to 21.0% for serious violence and 20.2% for serious theft. In young adulthood, prevalence of dealing (42.4%) increased; violence (22.1%) remained the same; gang membership (12.6%) decreased somewhat, and theft (7.9%) decreased substantially. Note that these prevalence rates are for the total sample and do not necessarily reflect within-individual change from adolescence into young adulthood.

Table 5.4 shows within-individual change in persistence of drug use, gun carrying, drug dealing, gang membership, serious violence, and serious theft in the PYS oldest cohort. (These data were weighted.) Those youth who were involved in each behavior in adolescence (ages 13–17) who also engaged in the behavior in

TABLE 5.4 } Percent of PYS oldest cohort who engaged in each behavior during adolescence and persisted in the same behavior into young adulthood (weighted).

Behavior	Percent
Marijuana Use	90.3
Hard Drug Use	60.5
Drug Dealing	80.0
Gang Membership	36.0
Gun Carrying	77.7
Serious Violence	45.1

TABLE 5.5 } Odds of committing a serious theft or violent offense in young adulthood if engaged in other offenses during adolescence in the oldest cohort in the PYS (unweighted).

Type of Offense during Adolescence	No Serious Offense in Adolescence (N=277) OR[a] (CI)[b]	At Least One Serious Offense in Adolescence (N=229) OR (CI)
Gun Carrying	3.25 (1.20-8.79)*	1.74 (1.01-3.01)*
Dealing	3.77 (1.64-8.68)*	2.30 (1.34-3.96)*
Gang Membership	3.11 (0.74-13.00)	1.53 (0.76-3.08)
Marijuana Use	3.01 (1.52-5.97)*	1.56 (0.90-2.68)
Hard Drug Use	3.20 (1.19-8.58)*	1.13 (0.69-3.16)

[a]OR = Odds Ratio

[b]CI = Confidence Interval

*$p < .05$

young adulthood (ages 18–25) were considered to be persisters. Persistence was highest for drug dealing (80.0%) and gun carrying (77.7%). In contrast, less than half (45.1%) of seriously violent adolescents continued violent offending in young adulthood. About one-third (36.0%) of adolescent gang members persisted into young adulthood and one-fourth (23.5%) of adolescent serious theft offenders persisted.

We were also interested in whether being a special offender in adolescence or using drugs (marijuana or hard drugs) and carrying a gun in adolescence would increase the risk of serious offending in early adulthood. To address this question, we divided youth from the PYS oldest cohort into those who committed a serious offense and those who did not during adolescence and conducted logistic regression analyses to determine the increased risks of serious offending in young adulthood based on categories of behaviors in adolescence. For these analyses we combined serious theft (burglary and motor vehicle theft) and serious violence (robbery, aggravated assault, aggravated indecent assault, homicide, forcible rape, involuntary deviate sexual intercourse, and spousal sexual assault) based on both self-report data and official records for convictions. These results (unweighted) are shown in Table 5.5.

Among those youth who did not commit a serious offense in adolescence, carrying a gun (OR [Odds Ratio] = 3.25), dealing drugs (OR = 3.77), using marijuana (OR = 3.01), and using hard drugs (OR = 3.20) in adolescence significantly increased the odds of their committing a serious offense in early adulthood. Only gang membership in adolescence did not significantly predict serious offending in young adulthood. Among those youth who had committed at least one serious offense in adolescence, carrying a gun (OR = 1.74) and drug dealing (OR = 2.30) during adolescence significantly increased the odds of also committing at least one serious offense in young adulthood. Marijuana use, hard drug use, and gang membership in adolescence did not significantly predict persistence of adolescent serious offending into young adulthood.

We also looked at the effect of various combinations of adolescent gun carrying, dealing, gang membership, and hard drug use (two at a time, three at a time, and all four at once) on serious offending in young adulthood for adolescents who did and did not commit serious offenses in adolescence. In general, hard drug use and dealing during adolescence in combination with other behaviors were significant predictors of later serious offending for those who did not seriously offend during adolescence. Dealing in combination with other problem behaviors during adolescence was a particularly strong and consistent predictor of the persistence of serious offending from adolescence into young adulthood (these data are not shown but available from the authors upon request).

As noted above, we can use the Bureau of Justice Statistics (BJS) prisoner release dataset to gain some insight into patterns of persistence and desistance

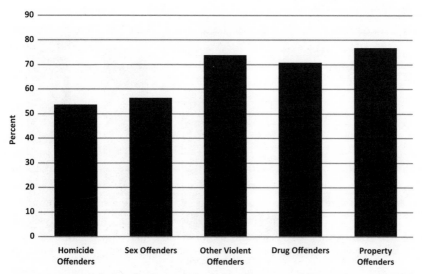

FIGURE 5.3 Percent of released prisoners under the age of 30 rearrested for any offense within three years.

Source: Recidivism of Prisoners Released in 1994.

among persons imprisoned for homicide. The BJS data include several measures of recidivism. Here we define recidivism as an arrest for a new crime within three years after release from prison in 1994. Our analysis is limited to prisoners under age 30 when released. About 54% of imprisoned homicide offenders were rearrested within three years after release from prison (see Figure 5.3). Although that is a sizeable recidivism rate, it is considerably smaller than the recidivism rates of those imprisoned for other violent crimes (74%), drug offenses (71%), and property crimes (77%). The recidivism rate of sex offenders (57%) is only slightly greater than that of homicide offenders (see Langan et al., 2003, for a detailed analysis of the recidivism rates of persons imprisoned for sex offenses).

These results refer to arrests for any crime. Figure 5.4 compares the *crime-specific* recidivism rates of released prisoners under age 30 according to the offense for which they were imprisoned—that is, the percentage of those imprisoned for homicide who were rearrested for homicide, the percentage of those imprisoned for a sex offense who were rearrested for a sex offense, etc. The marked contrast in persistence between offenders imprisoned for homicide and those imprisoned for other types of crime is evident from the figure. Only 0.2% of persons imprisoned for homicide were rearrested for homicide within three years after release. (Again, these results are limited to persons less than age 30 at release.) Sex offenders also exhibit a comparatively low crime-specific recidivism rate (6%). The comparable figures (i.e., the prevalence of rearrest for the same type of crime for which the individual was sentenced to prison) for the other offense categories are 33% for other violent offenders, 42% for drug offenders, and 44% for property offenders.

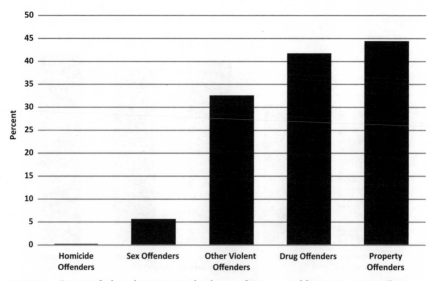

FIGURE 5.4 Percent of released prisoners under the age of 30 rearrested for imprisonment offense within three years.

Source: Recidivism of Prisoners Released in 1994.

Therefore, if we define persistence, albeit over a short follow-up period, as continuing involvement in criminal activity, regardless of offense type, persons imprisoned for homicide and sex offending are somewhat less persistent offenders than those imprisoned for other types of crime. But if persistence is defined as continuing involvement in the *same* type of crime, imprisoned homicide and sex offenders are far less likely to persist than are those imprisoned for other violent, drug, and property crimes.

The limitations of using data on released prisoners to estimate offense persistence or versatility, especially the much greater likelihood that homicide offenders will be arrested and sentenced to prison than other offenders and the use of a follow-up period of only three years to measure recidivism, must be kept in mind when interpreting these results. Nonetheless, our results are similar to those from other studies. For example, in a study of imprisoned homicide offenders in New Jersey, Roberts, Zgoba, and Shahidullah (2007) found that none had committed another murder during a minimum follow-up period of five years after release from prison. They also found that homicide offenders varied in their commission of drug and other violent crimes during the follow-up period, depending on the circumstances of the homicide for which they were imprisoned. For example, those sentenced to prison for the commission of a homicide during another felony were more likely to commit a drug offense after release than those imprisoned for domestic homicide.

The BJS dataset does not contain indicators of gang affiliation. A study of prisoners released from Illinois prisons, however, reports higher rearrest rates within approximately two years after release for gang members than nonmembers (Olson, Dooley, & Kane, 2004). The difference in recidivism between gang members and other released prisoners is attenuated but remains statistically significant with age, gender, race, and other correlates of both gang membership and recidivism controlled.

Specialized and General Offending[3]

There is a lack of consensus regarding the generality versus specificity of criminal offending. Some researchers contend that all types of deviance are constituent behaviors of a more general problem behavior syndrome (Jessor & Jessor 1977; Jessor, Donovan, & Costa 1991) or a general criminal propensity (Gottfredson & Hirschi, 1990). Much of the research on offending patterns among youth gang members supports the notion of a "cafeteria style" of offending (see Klein 1995); that is, gang members engage in a wide variety of offenses and, for the most part, do not specialize in a specific type of criminal activity. Whereas some studies have found that a single latent variable is sufficient to account for the covariance among different forms of deviant behavior (e.g., Dembo et al., 1992; Donovan & Jessor, 1985; Jessor et al. 1991; Osgood, Johnston, O'Malley, & Bachman, 1988), other studies have found that problem behaviors constitute several distinct factors (e.g., Fagan, Weis, Cheng, & Watters, 1987; Gillmore et al., 1991; White, 1992; White, Pandina, & LaGrange, 1987). White and Labouvie (1994) argued that the concept of a problem behavior syndrome is applicable for only a minority of adolescents because: (1) there are generally low correlations among problem behaviors, (2) various problem behaviors follow different developmental paths, (3) problem behaviors do not cluster together for all adolescents; and (4) there are several independent influences on each behavior. Overall, the degree of overlap depends on the types of behaviors included and the types of samples examined.

Nevertheless, drug dealing tends to overlap considerably with drug use and other types of offending. For example, studies in the late 1980s and early 1990s found that crack users were heavily involved in dealing, but they also participated in nondrug offending (Johnson, Natarajan, Dunlap, & Elmoghazy, 1994; Inciardi & Potteiger, 1994). Among a sample of in-custody, inner-city male adolescents, large percentages of dealers did not use cocaine or crack. On the other hand, few crack or cocaine users did not also deal (Lipton & Johnson, 1998; see also Inciardi & Potteiger, 1998). Johnson, Williams, Dei, and Sanabria (1990) found that violence was related to crack selling rather than use, and those selling in groups had higher rates of violence than those selling alone. Studies of dealing support a selection effect. That is, most dealers are already violent and delinquent before they begin dealing drugs (Inciardi & Potteiger, 1991; Johnson et al., 1994; Johnson et al., 1990; Van Kammen & Loeber, 1994).

Figure 5.5 shows the weighted percentage of the PYS oldest cohort who engaged in one type of offending in adolescence and who also engaged in another during

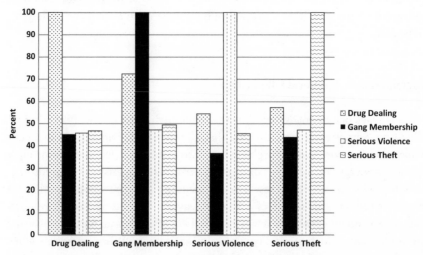

FIGURE 5.5 Percent co-occurrence of adolescent drug dealing, gang membership, serious violence, and serious theft in the PYS Oldest Cohort (weighted data).

Pittsburgh Youth Study (Loeber et al., 2008) data analyzed for this chapter.

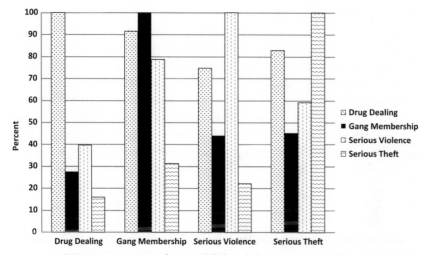

FIGURE 5.6 Percent co-occurrence of young adult drug dealing, gang membership, serious violence, and serious theft in the PYS Oldest Cohort (weighted data).
Pittsburgh Youth Study (Loeber et al., 2008) data analyzed for this chapter.

adolescence. Almost half of drug dealers were also gang members and more than four in 10 dealers committed serious violent or serious theft offenses. Almost three-fourths of the gang members also dealt drugs and about half engaged in serious violence or serious theft. Thus, these findings indicate a high degree of overlap between special category offenders and serious theft and violent offenders during adolescence.

Figure 5.6 shows the weighted percentage of the PYS oldest cohort who engaged in each type of offense during young adulthood and also engaged in another type of offense. Rates are very high for the overlap between gang membership and drug dealing. In addition, a large proportion of young adult gang members were also violent offenders. In contrast, young adult dealers were not necessarily involved in other types of offending. However, serious violent offenders were also likely to deal. Whereas only 22.2% of the serious violent offenders also committed serious theft offenses, 59.2% of the serious theft offenders also committed serious violence. The relatively high degree of overlap among these offenses in young adulthood indicates that most young adult offenders are generalists rather than specialists.

Table 5.4 above shows generality of problem behaviors from adolescence into young adulthood. Figure 5.7 reproduces these data for the special categories of offenders and also displays the percentage of adolescents who engage in a given type of offense during adolescence and a different type of offense as young adults. Overall, these data indicate that those youth who commit offenses in adolescence are likely to also offend in young adulthood, although the nature of the specific offense may change over time.

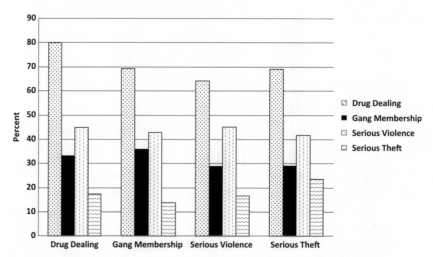

FIGURE 5.7 Percent of adolescents in the PYS Oldest Cohort who report selected behaviors in adolescence and continue into young adulthood (weighted data).
Pittsburgh Youth Study (Loeber et al., 2008) data analyzed for this chapter.

Public perception and policy portray sex offenders as specialists who require specific forms of treatment and control. The research literature, however, offers a more nuanced view. Those who aggress against children are more likely to specialize in sex offending than those who aggress against adolescent or adult females (Lussier, 2005, p. 274). The general portrait of sex offenders that emerges from research indicates elements of both generality and specialization in their offense repertoires. Sex offenders have higher recidivism rates for nonsex offenses than for sex offenses, which is evidence of versatility in offending. But sex offenders have higher rates of recidivism for sex offenses than do other types of offenders, which is evidence of relative specialization (see Waite et al., 2005). Lussier (2005, p. 288) concluded from his research review that the criminal behavior of sex offenders "is characterized by a certain tendency to specialize in sexual crime over time against the backdrop of much versatility."

Allowing for the rarity of lethal violence and consequent data limitations, a similar pattern characterizes homicide offenders. Some studies find that homicide offenders also commit other violent offenses (e.g., Loeber et al., 2005). Are homicide offenders specialists? According to the persistence measure reported above, in a limited sense they are; we might term them "one-time specialists." Very few prisoners sentenced for homicide and then released commit another homicide during the next three years. When it comes to other types of offending, the recidivism rates of homicide offenders are lower than those of other types of offenders, albeit still substantial (see Roberts et al., 2007). Again, this pattern is suggestive of somewhat greater specialization, or less offense versatility, among homicide offenders. Another way to measure offense specialization with these data, however, is to examine the prior arrests of imprisoned offenders who were released in 1994.

TABLE 5.6 } Prior arrests of released prisoners by imprisonment offense (%)

	Imprisonment Offense			
Prior arrest for:	Homicide	Other Violence	Drug	Property
Homicide	9.6	7.2	3.3	3.5
Other Violence	57.1	61.4	51.8	57.1
Drug	32.0	49.5	79.1	57.9
Property	51.2	70.8	70.2	88.1

Source: Recidivism of Prisoners Released in 1994.

In the 1994 cohort of released prisoners, 22.6% of those imprisoned for homicide had no arrests prior to imprisonment,[4] which is a much higher percentage with no prior arrests than the comparable percentages for those imprisoned for other violent offenses (10.7%), drug offenses (6.0%), and property offenses (4.0%). These figures reflect to some degree the differing imprisonment risks across offense types. The imprisonment risk for homicide offenders is much greater than that for other offenders, who typically must accumulate several prior arrests before they face a substantial risk of imprisonment. Even so, most imprisoned homicide offenders had a record of prior arrests. Keeping in mind the differing imprisonment risks across the offense categories, we can ask whether persons imprisoned for a given crime are more likely than others to have a prior arrest for that crime. The answer is clearly yes, as shown in Table 5.6.

For each crime type, the modal offense category of prior arrests is the offense for which the individual was imprisoned (the main diagonal in the table). But the variation in offense specialization by this measure is substantial. About 88% of those imprisoned for property crime had a prior arrest for property crime. The comparable percentage for imprisoned homicide offenders is 9.6%. But that is a higher percentage of prior homicide arrests than we observe for the other offense categories. Homicide offenders were just about as likely as other offenders to have a prior arrest for a violent offense, but were less likely to have been arrested for a property or drug offense. By this measure, imprisoned homicide offenders are less versatile than other imprisoned offenders with respect to committing nonviolent crime. The degree to which this pattern reflects selection into the sample of released prisoners associated with the comparatively greater imprisonment risk of homicide offenders, however, remains uncertain.

Conclusions and Discussion

In this chapter we have examined drug dealing and gang membership, and to a lesser extent sex offending and homicide, with respect to the age of onset and desistance, correlates and causes, and offense specialization and persistence during the transition from adolescence into young adulthood. We have characterized these types of offending as "special," but how special or distinct are they compared with other types of offending in terms of onset, desistance, correlates, specialization, and persistence? And are the differences between special and nonspecial offending numerous or important enough to warrant classifying those who engage in special offending as a particular type of offender? That is, is there something special about the kinds of individuals who engage in special types of offending?

In a technical sense, every type of delinquent or criminal offending is special; if it were not, there would be no reason to give it a distinct label and description. But in this volume special offending and offenders are treated separately from other offending and offenders because, in principle, they exhibit differing empirical patterns along the key dimensions of the delinquent or criminal career. They begin and end earlier (or later) in the life course; have different causes and correlates; involve more (or less) specialization; persist for a longer (or shorter) period of time. Such differing patterns are important because, once established, they may call for special theories, explanations, and prevention and intervention programs.

Summary of results. We found some evidence of differing behavioral patterns for some, but not all, types of special offenders with respect to some, but not all, dimensions of the delinquent or criminal career. Although not given extended consideration in this chapter, drug use is common among nearly all types of offending and offenders, whether special or not. Interestingly, drug dealing is a common criminal activity of drug users, but a sizeable fraction of drug dealers report little to no drug use. In this somewhat ironic sense, drug dealers at the higher levels in the dealing hierarchy are special in their lower propensity to use drugs than some other criminally involved adolescents and young adults who do not sell drugs.

With respect to the age of onset of criminal offending, a general pattern that emerges from our review of prior research and new analyses is that the initiation of criminal activity is not rigidly fixed in enduring biological or developmental processes, but is contingent on crime type, time period, and perhaps other features of social context. Consistent with prior research, we do find that initiation is much more likely to occur during adolescence than adulthood, but gang involvement, weapon carrying, and drug dealing began considerably earlier in adolescence during the 1990s than during the 1980s. That difference is likely a result of both contemporary developments (period effects) and conditions specific to the birth and early development of differing cohorts (cohort effects). Whatever those conditions might be, it is clear that the age of onset of criminal activity can vary meaningfully over a brief period of time.

Extensive evidence indicates that gang members have higher rates of offending prior to joining a gang than do same-age, non-gang youth and that gang membership increases their rate of offending. But the age of onset of gang membership tends to precede the age of onset of other criminal activities, on average occurring in early adolescence. Homicide offending, overwhelmingly a one-time event, occurs in late adolescence or early adulthood, but the age of homicide offenders varies according to the circumstance of the killing, with gang killings more likely than other kinds to take place during adolescence. We also find an earlier age of onset for sex offenders who victimize peers or adults than for those who victimize children. Although most criminal offending begins in adolescence, we do find some evidence of initiation of serious violence and drug dealing in early adulthood, whereas gang membership almost always begins during adolescence.

In general, drug dealing and serious violence follow an age-crime curve characteristic of general delinquency, peaking in late adolescence and dropping off sharply in young adulthood. Nevertheless, dealing is the most persistent form of special offending we examined and often extends from adolescence into young adulthood. Furthermore, there is greater young adult onset of dealing than gang membership, serious theft, or serious violence. Gang membership tends to peak in mid-adolescence and there is little onset of gang membership during the transition from adolescence into young adulthood. Much evidence points to gang involvement as a transient experience, with some studies showing that more than half of gang members remain in the gang for a year or less. This result underscores the importance of a leading gang researcher's recommendation to avoid gang suppression strategies that may solidify gang identification beyond the period in which most gang members would otherwise cease involvement (Klein, 1995).

Prior research has uncovered few correlates of special offending that are not also associated with violent and general delinquency. Even the risk factors associated with sex offending, which is widely viewed as qualitatively distinct from other types of offending, are similar to those for other violent offending. In this context, the finding of Loeber et al. (2005) that some of the correlates of homicide differ from those of other serious violence, in magnitude if not in kind, assumes special importance. It is perhaps not surprising that PYS participants who committed homicide were more likely than other violent offenders to carry weapons, report gang involvement, and deal drugs—all are proximal or situational factors found in prior research to elevate risk for lethal violence. But evidence that homicide offenders also are more likely to have a diagnosis for conduct disorder, do less well in school, and have grown up in families with higher rates of welfare dependency, if replicated in future research, suggests there may be more enduring characteristics that distinguish the homicide *offender*, and not simply the offense, from those who have engaged in serious nonlethal violence.

We also find variation among the several types of special offenders in the degree to which they persist from adolescence to young adulthood. Our analysis of PYS data indicates comparatively strong persistence from adolescence into young adulthood of drug dealing and gun carrying, themselves highly correlated, less persistence in serious violence and theft, and little persistence in gang involvement. In addition, drug dealing increases the odds of persistence of other forms of serious offending into young adulthood, but gang membership does not. Sex offending against children not only begins later in adolescence than sex offending against peers or adults does, but it persists for a longer period in adulthood. Finally, persons imprisoned for homicide are less likely than those imprisoned for drug, property, or other violent offenses to commit another crime within three years after release from prison—and very few commit another homicide.

The evidence on specialization in offending is consistent with that on persistence. We find a high degree of overlap among different types of offending during both adolescence and young adulthood and from adolescence into young adulthood, with drug dealers especially likely to engage in violent and other types of offending. In other words, the evidence points toward offense generality over specialization. Although the research is more limited, we observe elements of both offense generality and specialization in sex and homicide offending. Persons imprisoned for a sex offense or homicide are far more likely to be arrested for another type of crime than for a sex offense or a homicide within three years of release from prison, strong evidence of general rather than specialized offending. But they are also more likely to be arrested for another sex offense or homicide than are persons who were imprisoned for some other offense. Prior research does indicate somewhat greater specialization among sex offenders who victimize children than those who victimize adults. In this and other respects, those who aggress against children stand out from other special offenders, including other sex offenders.

Research recommendations. So, in the end, how special is special offending during the transition from adolescence into young adulthood? A judicious conclusion from prior research and our own analyses presented here suggests that drug dealing does not differ markedly from other types of offending in onset, desistance, or covariates. But, much like gang membership, drug dealing appears to increase the risk for other types of offending. Unlike gang membership, however, drug dealing tends to persist from adolescence into adulthood. Why drug dealing is more persistent and less transient than gang involvement during this developmental period is an important topic for future research, particularly in light of the evidence suggesting that both are risk factors for homicide.

A second conclusion from our review is that sex offenders who victimize peers and adults resemble nonsex offenders in onset, persistence, and other aspects of their criminal careers more than do those who aggress against children. If there is a special type of offender that emerges from the research literature, it is the sex offender who victimizes children. Additional research is needed to formulate effective interventions for these special offenders.

Policy recommendations. Three major policy implications emerge from our review. Given the strong evidence regarding the transiency of gang membership, the first principle of gang prevention programs should be to "do no harm." As mentioned, a veteran gang researcher has warned against engaging in a gang suppression strategy (e.g., enhanced penalties for crimes committed by gang members) or prevention activity that solidifies gang identity, which is often weak and ephemeral, or strengthens gang cohesiveness, which is typically exaggerated by the popular media and, all too often, by law enforcement (Klein, 1995). Gang prevention specialists should also clarify the objectives of prevention programs, especially with respect to *reducing gang membership* as opposed to *reducing gang-related crime and violence.* They are not the same. The well-known Boston Ceasefire initiative, for example, did not attempt to reduce gang membership but nonetheless achieved sharp reductions in gang-related violence, including homicides (Kennedy, Braga, Piehl, & Waring, 2001). Policy interventions that reduce gang membership may or may not lead to reductions in gang violence, and vice versa. Policy-makers must be clear about which of these objectives is paramount and tailor intervention strategies accordingly.

A second policy implication from our review of special categories of offenders concerns the troubling persistence of drug dealing in the transition from adolescence into adulthood, especially when compared with the markedly lower rate of persistence among theft offenders. Drug dealing and theft are both acquisitive offenses; their purpose is to make money. Why, then, are adolescent dealers more likely than thieves to persist in the activity as young adults? One reason may be the widespread—and largely false—perception among disadvantaged adolescents that dealing drugs is an especially good way to make "big" money (Reuter, MacCoun, Abrahamse, & Simon, 1990). This suggests that interventions with drug dealers should impart credible and realistic information about the payoffs of drug dealing, perhaps in connection with employment counseling and job placement efforts.

Third, although our review of the existing research has not been extensive, it appears that interventions for those who aggress against children should differ from those directed at other types of offenders, including other sex offenders. Given the similarities between sex offenders who victimize peers or adults and nonsex offenders in age of onset, offense generality, persistence, and other characteristics, interventions that prove successful with general offenders may prove as effective with this category of sex offender. On the other hand, specialized interventions should be reserved for sex offenders who aggress against children.

Finally, at present we do not have sufficient evidence to recommend special theories or interventions for homicide offenders as distinct from other violent offenders. But the emerging evidence suggests that homicide offenders may differ from those who commit serious nonlethal violence beyond their greater involvement in gangs, drug selling, and other aspects of situational risk. It is difficult to imagine a more important issue for future research on violent offending and offenders during the transition to young adulthood than to identify distinct predictors—particularly those that are modifiable—of homicide.

Acknowledgments

The Preparation of this chapter was supported in part by grants from the National Institute of Alcohol Abuse and Alcoholism (ARRA R01 AA016798), and the National Institute of Mental Health (P30 MH079920).

Notes

1. For greater detail on gangs, violence, drug use, and drug dealing, see Bjerregaard, 2010; Esbensen & Huizinga, 1993; Esbensen, Peterson, Freng, & Taylor, 2002; Klein, Maxson, & Miller, 1995; Moore, 1990; Thornberrry, Krohn, Lizotte, Smith, & Tobin, 2003.

2. See, for example, Bendixen et al., 2006; Esbensen & Huizinga, 1993; Gatti, Tremblay, Vitaro, & McDuff, 2005; Gordon, Lahey, Kawai, Loeber, Stouthamer-Loeber, & Farrington, 2004.

3. See Chapter 2 and Loeber et al. (2008) for extended treatments of offense specialization and generality.

4. These results are for prisoners of all ages. Sex offenders are included with other violent offenders.

References

Abbey, A. (2002). Alcohol-related sexual assault: A common problem among college students. *Journal of Studies on Alcohol*, 14, 118–128.

Abbey, A., Zawacki, T., Buck, P.O., Clinton, A.M., & McAuslan, P. (2001). Alcohol and sexual assault. *Alcohol Research and Health*, 25, 43–51.

Altschuler, D.M., & Brounstein, P.J. (1991). Patterns of drug use, drug trafficking, and other delinquency among inner-city adolescent males in Washington, D.C. *Criminology*, 29, 589–621.

Bachman, J.G., Johnston, L.D., & O'Malley, P.M. (1998). Explaining recent increases in students' marijuana use: Impacts of perceived risks and disapproval, 1976 through 1996. *American Journal of Public Health*, 88, 887–892.

Bellair, P., & McNulty, T.L. (2009). Gang membership, drug selling, and violence in neighborhood context. *Justice Quarterly*, 26, 644–669.

Bendixen, M., Endresen, I.M., & Olweus, D. (2006). Joining and leaving gangs: Selection and facilitation effects on self-reported antisocial behaviour in early adolescence. *European Journal of Criminology*, 3, 85–114.

Bjerregaard, B. (2010). Gang membership and drug involvement: Untangling the complex relationship. *Crime and Delinquency*, 56, 3–34.

Blumstein, A. (1995). Youth violence, guns, and the illicit drug industry. *Journal of Criminal Law and Criminology*, 86, 10–36.

Centers, N., & Weist, M. (1998). Inner city youth and drug dealing: A review of the problem. *Journal of Youth and Adolescence*, 27, 395–411.

Curry, G.D., & Thomas, R.W. (1992). Community organization and gang policy response. *Journal of Quantitative Criminology*, 8, 357–374.

De Li, S., Priu, H., & Mackenzie, D. (2000). Drug involvement, lifestyles, and criminal activities among probationers. *Journal of Drug Issues*, 30, 593–619.

Decker, S.H., & Lauritsen, J.L. (2002). Leaving the gang. In C.R. Huff (Ed.), *Gangs in America*, 3rd edition (pp. 51–67). Thousand Oaks, CA: Sage.

Dembo, R., Williams, L., Wothke, W., Schmeidler, J., Getreu, A., Berry, E., & Wish, E. (1992). The generality of deviance: Replication of a structural model among high-risk youths. *Journal of Research in Crime and Delinquency*, 29, 200–216.

Donovan, J.E., & Jessor, R. (1985). Structure of problem behavior in adolescence and young adulthood. *Journal of Consulting and Clinical Psychology*, 53, 890–904.

Egley, A., Howell, J.C., & Moore, J.P. (2010). *Highlights of the 2008 National Youth Gang Survey*. Washington, DC: US Department of Justice, Office of Justice Programs.

Esbensen, F.-A., & Elliott, D.S. (1994). Continuity and discontinuity in illicit drug use: Patterns and antecedents. *Journal of Drug Issues*, 24, 75–97.

Esbensen, F.-A., & Huizinga, D. (1993). Gangs, drugs, and delinquency in a survey of urban youth. *Criminology*, 31, 565–589.

Esbensen, F.-A., & Lynskey, D.P. (2001). Youth gang members in a school survey. In M.W. Klein, H-J. Kerner, C.L. Maxson, & E.G.M. Weitekamp, (Eds.) *The Eurogang paradox: Street gangs and youth groups in the U.S. and Europe* (pp. 93–114). Amsterdam NL: Kluwer Academic.

Esbensen, F.-A., Peterson, D., Freng, A., & Taylor, T.J. (2002). Initiation of drug use, drug sales, and violent offending among a sample of gang and nongang youth. In C.R. Huff (Ed.) *Gangs in America*, 3rd edition (pp. 37–50). Thousand Oaks, CA: Sage.

Esbensen, F.-A., Peterson, D., Taylor, T.J., & Freng, A. (2009). Similarities and differences in risk factors for violent offending and gang membership. *Australian and New Zealand Journal of Criminology*, 42, 310–335.

Esbensen, F.-A., Peterson, D., Taylor, T.J., & Freng. A. (2010). *Youth violence: Sex and race differences in offending, victimization, and gang membership*. Philadelphia, PA: Temple University Press.

Fagan, J. (1989). The social organization of drug use and drug dealing among urban gangs. *Criminology*, 27, 633–667.

Fagan, J. (1990). Intoxication and aggression. In M. Tonry & J.Q. Wilson (Eds.), *Drugs and crime* (pp. 241–320). Chicago, IL: University of Chicago Press.

Fagan, J. (1990). *Social processes of delinquency and drug use among urban gangs*. In C.R. Huff (Ed.), *Gangs in America*, 1st edition (pp. 183–222). Newbury Park, CA: Sage.

Fagan, F. (1996). Gangs, drugs, and neighborhood change. In C.R. Huff (Ed.) *Gangs in America*, 2nd edition (pp. 39–74). Thousand Oaks, CA: Sage.

Fagan, J., & Chin, K. (1990). Violence as regulation and social control in the distribution of crack. In M. De La Rosa, E.Y. Lambert, & B. Gropper (Eds.), *Drugs and violence: Causes, correlates, and consequences (Research Monograph 103*, pp. 8–43). Rockville, MD: US Department of Health and Human Services, National Institute on Drug Abuse.

Fagan, J., Weis, J.G., Cheng, Y., &. Watters, J.K. (1987). *Drug and alcohol use, violent delinquency and social bonding: Implications for theory and intervention*. San Francisco, CA: The URSA Institute.

Fox, J.A., & Zawitz, M.W. (2007). *Homicide trends in the United States*. Washington, DC: U.S. Department of Justice. http://bjs.ojp.usdoj.gov/content/homicide/homtrnd.cfm.

Gatti, U., Tremblay, R.E., Vitaro, F., & McDuff, P. (2005). Youth gangs, delinquency, and drug use: A test of selection, facilitation, and enhancement hypotheses. *Journal of Child Psychology and Psychiatry*, 46, 1178–1190.

Gillmore, M.R., Hawkins, J.D., Catalano, R.F., Day, L.E., & Moore, M. (1991). Structure of problem behavior in preadolescence. *Journal of Consulting and Clinical Psychology*, 59, 499–506.

Goldstein, P.J. (1985). The drugs/violence nexus: A tripartite conceptual framework. *Journal of Drug Issues*, 15, 493–506.

Goldstein, P.J., Brownstein, H.H., Ryan, P.J., & Bellucci, P.A. (1989). Crack and homicide in New York City, 1988. A conceptually based event analysis. *Contemporary Drug Problems*, 16, 651–687.

Golub, A., Labouvie, E.W., & Johnson, B.D. (2000). Response reliability and the study of adolescent substance use progression. *Journal of Drug Issues*, 30, 103–118.

Gordon, R.A., Lahey, B.B., Kawai, E., Loeber, R., Stouthamer-Loeber, M., & Farrington, D.P. (2004). Antisocial behavior and youth gang membership: Selection and socialization. *Criminology*, 42, 55–87.

Gottfredson, M.R., & Hirschi, T. (1990). *A general theory of crime*. Stanford, CA: Stanford University Press.

Hagedorn, J.M. (1988). *People and Folks: Gangs, Crime and the Underclass in a Rustbelt City*. Chicago, IL: Lake View Press.

Harrison, L.D. (1992). The drug-crime nexus in the USA. *Contemporary Drug Problems*, 19, 203–245.

Howell, J.C., & Egley, A. (2005). Moving risk factors into developmental theories of gang membership. *Youth Violence and Juvenile Justice*, 3, 334–354.

Huff, C.R. (1990). *Gangs in America*. Newbury Park, CA: Sage.

Hunt, D. (1990). Drugs and consensual crimes: Drug dealing and prostitution. In M. Tonry & J.Q. Wilson (Eds.), *Drugs and crime* (pp. 159–202). Chicago, IL: University of Chicago Press.

Inciardi, J.A. (1990). The crack-violence connection within a population of hard-core adolescent offenders. In M. De La Rosa, E.Y. Lambert, & B. Gropper (Eds.), *Drugs and violence: Causes, correlates, and consequences* (NIDA Research Monograph 103, pp. 92–111). Rockville, MD: NIDA.

Inciardi, J.A., & Pottieger, A.E. (1991). Kids, crack, and crime. *Journal of Drug Issues*, 21, 257–270.

Inciardi, J.A., & Pottieger, A.E. (1994). Crack-cocaine use and street crime. *Journal of Drug Issues*, 24, 273–292.

Inciardi, J.A., & Pottieger, A.E. (1998). Drug use and street crime in Miami: An (almost) twenty-year retrospective. *Substance Use and Misuse*, 33, 1839–1870.

Jessor, R., Donovan, J.E., & Costa, F.M. (1991). *Beyond adolescence: Problem behavior and young adult development*. New York: Cambridge University Press.

Jessor, R., & Jessor, S. (1977). *Problem behavior and psychosocial development: A longitudinal study of youth*. New York: Academic Press.

Johnson, B.D., Natarajan, M., Dunlap, E., & Elmoghazy, E. (1994). Crack abusers and non-crack abusers: Profiles of drug use, drug sales and nondrug criminality. *Journal of Drug Issues*, 24, 117–141.

Johnson, B.D., Williams, T., Dei, K.A., & Sanabria, H. (1990). Drug abuse in the inner city. Impact on hard-drug users and the community. In M. Tonry & J.Q. Wilson (Eds.), *Drugs and crime* (pp. 9–67). Chicago, IL: University of Chicago Press.

Karberg, J.C., & James, D.J. (2005). *Substance dependence, abuse, and treatment of jail inmates, 2002*. Washington, DC: US Department of Justice, Office of Justice Programs, Bureau of Justice Statistics.

Kennedy, D.M., Braga, A.A., Piehl, A.M., & Waring, E.J. (2001). *Reducing gun violence: The Boston Gun Project's Operation Ceasefire*. Washington, D.C.: National Institute of Justice.

Klein, M.W. (1995). *The American street gang.* New York: Oxford University Press.

Klein, M.W., & Maxson, C. (2006). *Street gang patterns and policies.* New York: Oxford University Press.

Koss, M.P. (1988). Hidden rape: Sexual aggression and victimization in a national sample of students in higher education. In A.W. Burgess (Ed.), *Rape and sexual assault* (pp. 3–25). New York: Garland.

Langan, P.A., & Levin, D.J. (2002). *Recidivism of prisoners released in 1994.* Washington, DC: United States Department of Justice, Bureau of Justice Statistics.

Langan, P.A., Schmitt, E.L., & Durose, M.R. (2003). *Recidivism of sex offenders released from prison in 1994.* Washington, DC: United States Department of Justice, Bureau of Justice Statistics.

Levine, F.J., & Rosich, K.J. (1996). *Social causes of violence: Crafting a science agenda.* Washington, DC: American Sociological Association.

Li, X., & Feigelman, S. (1994). Recent and intended drug trafficking among male and female urban African-American early adolescents. *Pediatrics,* 93, 1044–1099.

Li, X., Stanton, B., & Feigelman, S. (2000). Impact of perceived parental monitoring on adolescent risk behavior over four years. *Journal of Adolescent Health,* 27, 49–56.

Lipton, D.S., & Johnson, B.D. (1998). Smack, crack, and score: Two decades of NIDA-funded drugs and crime research at NDRI 1974–1994. *Substance Use and Misuse,* 33, 1779–1815.

Little, M., & Steinberg, L. (2006). Psychosocial correlates of adolescent drug dealing in the inner city. *Journal of Research in Crime and Delinquency,* 43, 357–386.

Loeber, R., & Farrington, D.P. (2011). *Young homicide offenders and victims: Development, risk factors and prediction from childhood.* New York: Springer.

Loeber, R., Farrington, D.P., Stouthamer-Loeber, M., & White, H.R. (2008). *Violence and serious theft: Development and prediction from childhood to adulthood.* New York: Routledge.

Loeber, R., Homish, D.L., Wei, E.H., Pardini, D., Crawford, A.M., Farrington, D.P., Stouthamer-Loeber, M., Creemers, J., Koehler, S.A., & Rosenfeld, R. (2005). The prediction of violence and homicide in young males. *Journal of Consulting and Clinical Psychology,* 73, 1074–1088.

Lussier, P. (2005). The criminal activity of sexual offenders in adulthood: Revisiting the specialization debate. *Sexual Abuse: A Journal of Research and Treatment,* 17, 269–292.

Moore, M.H. (1990). Supply reduction and drug law enforcement. In M. Tonry & J.Q. Wilson (Eds.), *Drugs and Crime* (pp. 109–157). Chicago, IL: University of Chicago Press.

Olson, D.E., Dooley, B., & Kane, C.M. (2004). The relationship between gang membership and inmate recidivism. *Illinois Criminal Justice Information Authority Research Bulletin,* 2, 1–12.

Osgood, D.W., Johnston, L.D., O'Malley, P.M., & Bachman J.G. (1988). The generality of deviance in late adolescence and early adulthood. *American Sociological Review,* 53, 81–93.

Pandina, R.J., Johnson, V.L., & White, H.R. (2009). Peer influences on substance use during adolescence and emerging adulthood. In L.M. Scheier (Ed.), *Handbook of drug use etiology* (pp. 383–401). Washington, D.C.: American Psychological Association.

Peterson, D. (2012). Girlfriends, gun-holders, and ghetto rats? Moving beyond narrow views of girls in gangs. In S. Miller, L.D. Leve, & P.K. Kerig (Eds.), *Delinquent girls: Contexts, relationships, and adaptation* (pp. 71–84). New York: Springer.

Peterson, D., Taylor, T.J., & Esbensen, F.-A. (2004). Gang membership and violent victimization. *Justice Quarterly*, 21, 793–816.

Reuter, P.H., MacCoun, R.J., Murphy, P., Abrahamse, A., & Simon, B. (1990). *Money from crime: A study of the economics of drug dealing in Washington D.C.* Santa Monica, CA: Rand.

Roberts, A.R., Zgoba, K.M., & Shahidullah, S.M. (2007). Recidivism among four types of homicide offenders: An exploratory analysis of 336 homicide offenders in New Jersey. *Aggression and Violent Behavior*, 12, 493–507.

Rosenfeld, R., Wallman, J., & Fornango, R. (2005). The contribution of ex-prisoners to crime rates. In J. Travis & C. Visher (Eds.), *Prisoner reentry and crime in America* (pp. 80–104). New York: Cambridge University Press.

Starbuck, D., Howell, J.C., & Linquist, D.J. (December, 2001). *Hybrid and other modern gangs*. Washington, DC: Office of Juvenile Justice and Delinquency Prevention, Juvenile Justice Bulletin.

Steinberg, L., & Monaghan, K. C. (2007). Age differences in resistance to peer influence. *Developmental Psychology*, 43, 1531–1543.

Testa, M. (2002). The impact of men's alcohol consumption on perpetration of sexual aggression. *Clinical Psychology Review*, 22, 1239–1263.

Thornberry, T.P. (1998). Membership in youth gangs and involvement in serious violent offending. In R. Loeber & D.P. Farrington (Eds.) *Serious and violent juvenile offenders: Risk factors and successful interventions* (pp. 147–166). Thousand Oaks, CA: Sage.

Thornberry, T.P., Krohn, M.D., Lizotte, A.J., & Chard-Wierschem, D. (1993). The role of juvenile gangs in facilitating delinquent behavior. *Journal of Research in Crime and Delinquency*, 30, 55–87.

Thornberry, T.P., Krohn, M.D., Lizotte, A.J., Smith, C.A., & Tobin, K. (2003). *Gangs and delinquency in developmental perspective*. New York: Cambridge University Press.

Ullman, S.E., Karabastos, G., and Koss, M.P. (1999). Alcohol and sexual assault in a national sample of college women. *Journal of Interpersonal Violence*, 14, 603–625.

Van Kammen, W., & Loeber, R. (1994). Are fluctuations in delinquent activities related to the onset and offset in juvenile illegal drug use and drug dealing? *Journal of Drug Issues*, 24, 9–24.

Van Wijk, A., Loeber, R., Vermeiren, R., Pardini, D. Bullens, R., & Doreleijers, T. (2005). Violent juvenile sex offenders compared with violent juvenile nonsex offenders: Explorative findings from the Pittsburgh Youth Study. *Sexual Abuse: A Journal of Research and Treatment*, 17, 333–352.

Vigil, J.D. (1988). *Barrio gangs: Street life and identity in Southern California*. Austin, TX: University of Texas Press.

Waite, D., Keller, A., McGarvey, E.L., Wieckowski, E., Pinkerton, R., & Brown, G.L. (2005). Juvenile sex offender re-arrest rates for sexual, violent nonsexual and property crimes: A 10-year follow-up. *Sexual Abuse: A Journal of Research and Treatment*, 17, 313–331.

Wallace, J.M., Bachman, J.G., O'Malley, P.M., Schulenberg, J., E., Cooper, S.M., & Johnston, L.D. (2003). Gender and ethnic differences in smoking, drinking, and illicit drug use among American 8th, 10th, and 12th grader students, 1976–2000. *Addiction*, 98, 225–234.

White, H.R. (1992). Early problem behavior and later drug problems. *Journal of Research in Crime and Delinquency*, 29, 412–429.

White, H.R. (in press). Substance use and crime. In K. Sher (Ed.), *Psychology and substance abuse*. Oxford: Oxford University Press.

White, H.R., & Gorman, D.M. (2000). Dynamics of the drug-crime relationship. In G. LaFree (Ed.), *Criminal Justice 2000: The nature of crime. Continuity and change* (pp. 151–218). Washington, DC: US Department of Justice.

White, H.R., & Labouvie, E.W. (1994). Generality versus specificity of problem behavior. Psychological and functional differences. *Journal of Drug Issues*, 24, 55–74.

White, H.R., Loeber, R., & Farrington, D.P. (2008). Substance use, drug dealing, gang membership, and gun carrying and their predictive associations with serious violence and serious theft. In R. Loeber, D.P. Farrington, M. Stouthamer-Loeber & H.R. White, *Violence and serious theft: Development and prediction from childhood to adulthood* (pp. 137–166). New York: Routledge.

White, H.R., Pandina, R.J., & LaGrange, R.L. (1987). Longitudinal predictors of serious substance use and delinquency. *Criminology*, 25, 715–740.

6

Prediction and Risk/Needs Assessments

Robert D. Hoge, Gina M. Vincent, and Laura S. Guy

This chapter provides a review of available knowledge regarding the prediction of early adult offending (focusing on the age range of 18 to 29) on the basis of information available during the juvenile years and of assessment tools for formulating these predictions (see Vincent, Terry, & Maney [2009] for a review of juvenile instruments and meta-analyses cited in this chapter for reviews of adult instruments). The chapter begins with a discussion of general issues regarding prediction and assessment, including the parameters of risk prediction and legal and ethical issues associated with risk assessment. We then provide a brief summary of risk factors associated with criminal activity. Technical issues in the conduct of risk assessments are discussed, followed by reviews of the major established juvenile and adult risk assessment tools. The chapter concludes with research and clinical recommendations relating to risk assessment and prediction.

Parameters of Risk Prediction and Assessment with Youth

The prediction of the onset and persistence of criminal activity depends on early identification of serious and violent individuals and circumstantial factors that facilitate such identification. Three concepts are relevant to our analysis of risk assessment and prediction. Risk factors refer to characteristics of youths or their circumstances that increase the likelihood that they will engage in delinquency (e.g., a history of conduct disorder). *Criminogenic need* factors (also known as dynamic risk factors) are risk factors that can be changed, and, if changed, could reduce the likelihood of engagement in antisocial behaviors (e.g., antisocial peer associations). Strength or protective factors are features of the youth or his or her situation that can buffer the effects of risk factors (e.g., a positive bond between youth and parent can reduce the impact of negative peer associations).

The identification of the risk, need, and protective factors is both a theoretical and empirical issue (see Thornberry et al., Chapter 3, this volume; also, Farrington,

2005; Guerra, Williams, Tolan, & Modecki, 2008; Rutter, Giller, & Hagell, 1998) and will be explored in more detail later in this chapter. However, several points need to be stressed here. First, different risk and protective factors may predict the onset of and desistance from delinquency. For example, early drug abuse may be associated with the onset of criminal activities, but the establishment of a positive social bond may be associated with desistance from such activities. Second, the relative importance of risk, need, and protective factors may vary with developmental age. For example, some drug and alcohol use assumes decreasing influence through adolescence, whereas peer group influences assume increasing importance. This presents a challenge to assessing risk for delinquency during late adolescence because we are dealing with a period of transition between older adolescence and early adulthood. However, much of the available research focuses either on adolescents or adults, and relatively little information is available for the transition years.

The Contexts of Risk Assessments

Risk assessments are relevant in a range of criminal and civil legal decisions, such as pre-charge diversion, pre-trial detention, eligibility for alternative measures programs, and waivers to adult and mental health proceedings, sentencing, and dispositions (see Howell et al., Chapter 8, this volume). While some of these decision contexts may call for a narrow focus on risk for future delinquency because a quick decision needs to be made, most decisions require an assessment of criminological needs as well. As we noted earlier, criminogenic needs are essentially dynamic risk factors that are driving individuals' offending. Assessing the criminogenic need factors underlying risk is important in any decision where a disposition or intervention is to be provided to address the risk factor. If, for example, negative peer associations and substance abuse are major risk factors for delinquency, then these factors can be identified as criminogenic need factors to be addressed in any intervention effort. The term *risk management* will be used when referring to the identification of criminogenic needs for purposes of reducing risk.

The selection of the risk assessment tool, and consequently the amount of information needed from the tool, depends on the nature of the decision in question. Pre-trial detention or classification decisions will often require an estimate of the likelihood of committing a violent offense over some short period of time. Similarly, decisions such as those relating to eligibility for pre-charge diversion or pre-trial alternative measures may call for general predictions of the likelihood of re-offending. However, longer-term decisions, such as disposition, case planning, or management may call for an assessment of the likelihood of re-offending, in addition to the criminogenic needs underlying the risk of offending. Also, longer range planning like this can benefit from risk assessment tools that contain strength or protective factors.

Another aspect of this issue concerns the relation between the assessment and the ultimate legal question. As Heilbrun (2010) stresses, a direct link does not always exist between the two. A prediction of the likelihood of engaging in a violent sexual assault is directly linked with a designation of a violent sexual predator. However, an estimate of the likelihood of engaging in a criminal act might be only one consideration in a decision about placement within an institutional or community program. Care must always be taken in evaluating the relevance of the assessment to the judicial decision to be made.

Considerable variability exists in the way in which risk/needs assessments are formulated and reported. Variations occur, first, in the source of the assessment. In many cases a mental health professional will conduct the assessment. This is particularly true for waiver or civil commitment proceedings requiring a professional psychological assessment. Personnel other than mental health professionals, such as probation officers, intake officers, correctional officers, or youth workers, also conduct risk/needs assessments; these individuals should have received specialized training.

Variability also exists in the procedures employed to conduct the assessments. Some judicial and correctional systems employ no formal or structured assessment procedures. For example, a correctional officer may interview the youth and on the basis of his or her experience form a judgment about the risk level. In other cases more or less structured procedures might be employed. These would normally be based on clinical interviews and possibly the use of standardized tests. Tests are common in the case of psychologists or psychiatrists assigning mental health diagnoses. However, and as we will see below, a number of standardized and validated procedures have been developed to guide the collection and synthesis of information to yield estimates of risk and needs. These are often suitable for use by both mental health professionals and trained judicial and correctional personnel.

Relatively little information is available regarding the frequency of use of standardized risk/needs assessment procedures in correctional or forensic decision contexts. Informal observations would suggest that many systems employ only unstructured assessments or locally developed and nonvalidated instruments. Mulvey and Iselin (2008) have suggested that many of the reports provided to judges to aid in disposition decisions are based on informal assessment procedures. This is unfortunate because, as we will see below, a number of validated, standardized instruments are available to guide such decisions.

Legal and Ethical Considerations

Legal and ethical issues arise in connection with many forensic risk assessments (Grisso & Applebaum, 1992; Heilbrun, 2001, 2010; Heilbrun, Grisso, & Goldstein, 2008; Melton, Petrila, Poythress, & Slobogin, 2007). For example, in the United

States the Federal Rules of Evidence specify criteria relevant to the admissibility of expert testimony, and this includes testimony based on risk assessments. Other sources of guidance are from professional practice and ethical guidelines (Heilbrun, 1992, 2010; Melton et al., 2007). The American Psychological Association's (APA) *Ethical Principles of Psychologists and Code of Conduct* (APA, 2002) provides a broad range of guidelines regarding psychological practice. A group within a division of APA, the Committee on Ethical Guidelines for Forensic Psychologists (1991), provides standards specifically applicable to forensic practices, including the conduct and reporting of risk assessments.

Practice guidelines regarding the use of tools for conducting risk assessments also are available. Heilbrun (1992) offered the following recommendations regarding the selection and use of such instruments: they should be commercially available, have a manual, and be critically reviewed in the literature; have adequate reliability and validity demonstrated; be relevant to the forensic decision; be administered using standard procedures; scores should be interpreted with reference to populations and contexts that are similar to that of the evaluee; when possible, objective tests and actuarial procedures should be used; and response style should be considered, as distorted responding may negate the results of the assessment. Importantly, it must be kept in mind that practice and ethics guidelines only govern the actions of the relevant mental health providers. Other professionals such as probation or correctional officers may not be affected by any professional guidelines relevant to conducting risk assessments.

A second source of guidance in the conduct of risk or risk/needs assessments may be found in policy statements and practice guidelines developed in specific jurisdictions. Many agencies in the United States have adopted standardized tools to guide the conduct of these assessments and an increasing number have developed case planning and management procedures directly tied to the assessments.

Current Knowledge Regarding the Prediction of Offending in Early Adulthood

Three related areas of theory and research relevant to the prediction of late or early adult-onset offending have emerged: (a) analyses of the trajectories of criminal offending, (b) identification of risk and protective factors, and (c) a developmental life-course perspective integrating these two areas. We will provide only brief summaries of these literatures in this chapter but will refer the reader to more comprehensive reviews as well as to Piquero et al. (Chapter 2, in this volume).

Efforts to identify stable trajectories of criminal careers have focused on two patterns labeled life-course persistent delinquency and adolescent-limited delinquency (Loeber, Slot, & Stouthamer-Loeber, 2006; Loeber & Stouthamer-Loeber, 1998; Moffitt, 2003; Thornberry, 2005). The life-course persistent pattern describes cases where evidence of conduct problems appears during the preschool years, escalates through early childhood and adolescence, and persists into adulthood. Adult offenders convicted of very serious crimes often exhibit this pattern. The adolescent-limited pattern on the other hand describes cases where antisocial acts first appear in adolescence. The criminal activity in this case is generally not of a serious nature and the individual usually desists by later adolescence.

The issue of trajectories is of particular concern in the present case because of our focus on ages 18 to 29. This is the period when youth with early signs of a life-course persistent pattern either persist or desist in these activities. The first appearance of criminal activities after age 18 has generally been considered relatively rare, but it does occur and can be considered an extension of the adolescent-onset pattern. Although the available evidence is equivocal regarding the number or nature of the trajectories (Piquero, Farrington, & Blumstein, 2007; Piquero et al., Chapter 2, this volume; Sampson & Laub, 2003), the information provides some guidance regarding the prediction of criminal activity during the early adult years.

The second area of relevance to prediction concerns the identification of risk and protective factors associated with the onset, persistence, and desistance from criminal activity (see Hoge & Andrews, 2010; Lipsey & Derzon, 1998; Loeber & Stouthamer-Loeber, 1987; Thornberry & Krohn, 2003). A large and growing literature on these factors derives from both cross-sectional and longitudinal studies. Of particular value are the long-term longitudinal studies such as the Cambridge Study in Delinquent Development (Farrington, 2004; Farrington et al., 2006), the Pittsburgh Youth Study (Loeber, Stouthamer-Loeber, & Farrington, 2008) and the Rochester Youth Development Study (Thornberry, 2005; Thornberry, Ireland, & Smith, 2001). A wide range of contextual (e.g., criminality in family of origin, high crime neighborhood) and individual (e.g., antisocial attitudes, negative peer associations) factors have been identified in this research.

Several cautions should be noted. First, conceptual and methodological issues persist in this research (O'Connor & Rutter, 1996; Rutter et al., 1998). Conceptual issues relate to the difficulty of identifying causal factors among the correlates identified. Methodological problems involve subject loss and the comparability of measures at different points in data collection. Second, the applicability of the risk factors across gender, cultural group, and age has not always been well established. Another issue is that few efforts have been developed to identify strength or protective factors. These are important because they represent potential moderators of the effects of risk and are associated with desistance from criminal activity. Two categories of potential risk factors are worthy of further discussion and will be described later: mental health and personality variables.

The third relevant development is represented in efforts to formulate a developmental life-course perspective on the prediction of criminal behavior (Catalano & Hawkins, 1996; Farrington, 2004, 2005; Guerra et al., 2008; Thornberry, 2005). Evaluating risk requires consideration of the developmental stage and social context (Mulvey, 2005). Even the relevance of risk factors can change across time (for a review see Odgers, Vincent, & Corrado, 2002). For example, smoking prior to age 12 is a significant risk factor, but smoking at age 15 when experimentation is a normal part of development, or in early adulthood when smoking is legal, would not be risk factors for offending.

Another key developmental concept for assessments of risk for violence and serious offending is the impact of maturation on the time frame for which predictions remain accurate. A significant limitation on attempts to identify youth who will become chronic and violent offenders is the potential for a high false positive rate. A significant number of youth who engage in violent behavior at one stage of development do not continue to do so as their development proceeds. Indeed, at least 50% of children who initiate pervasive and serious antisocial behavior between ages 6 and 12 do not develop into seriously antisocial adults (Patterson et al., 1998; Robins, 1974), and an even greater portion of serious offending adolescents do not develop into antisocial adults (Moffitt & Caspi, 2001; see also Piquero et al., Chapter 2, this volume). The National Youth Survey (Elliott, Huizinga, & Menard, 1989) found that, for about 50% of youths, violent behavior persisted into adulthood if their first violent acts occurred before age 11, about 30% persisted if their violence started between ages 11 and 13, and about 10% persisted if their first violent acts occurred in adolescence. Taken as a whole, the research suggests that even youth who engage in the most serious violence or antisocial behavior at a young age have only a 50–50 chance of persisting.

Mental Health Variables in Risk Assessment

The relation of mental health problems to offending and violence is complicated. On the one hand, many individuals with mental disorders do not have a violent or delinquent history. On the other hand, many individuals with a mental disorder are involved in the justice system. Single-site studies using forms of the Diagnostic Interview for Children (DISC) suggest that about two-thirds of youths involved with the juvenile justice system meet criteria for one or more psychiatric disorders, even after excluding conduct disorder (Atkins, Pumariega, & Rogers, 2003; Teplin, Abram, McClelland, Dulcan, & Mericle, 2002; Wasserman, McReynolds, Lucas, Fisher, & Santos, 2002). This is substantially higher than prevalence rates found in youths in the general population (around 14 to 22%; Kazdin, 2000). More recently, a nationwide study of self-reported mental health symptoms among justice-involved youth found that 72% of girls and 63% of boys had at least one clinically significant mental health problem (Vincent, Grisso, Terry, & Banks, 2008). Further, in a complex analysis of longitudinal data, researchers reported that 19.5% of adult crime among women and 28.7% of adult crime among men was attributable to individuals with childhood psychiatric disorders, and those diagnosed with multiple disorders were at even greater risk for later criminal behavior (Copeland, Miller-Johnson, Keeler, Angold, & Costello, 2007). The percentages remained significant even after adjustments removing conduct disorder and juvenile offense history (20.6% for females and 15.3% for males, respectively).

There are several potential explanations for this relation between mental disorder and offending, and possibly even persistent offending, into early adulthood. First, some child and adolescent mental disorders, or symptoms of mental disorder, may be causally connected to violence and antisocial behavior, namely, disruptive behavior disorders and attention deficit–hyperactivity disorder (ADHD). This potential causal connection is evidenced in a concept known as a hyperactive-impulsive-attention deficit (HIA) syndrome (Loeber, 1990), which when combined with conduct problems, seems to be found in children with early initiation of antisocial behavior that is frequent and severe (Lynam, 1996).

With respect to other types of disorders, mood disorders may relate to violent offending in cases where the mood disorders manifest in anger or hostility (Vincent & Grisso, 2005). Many youths with conduct problems have some form of anxiety (Frick, Lilienfeld, Ellis, Loney, & Silverthorn, 1999), and post-traumatic stress disorder in particular can underlie tendencies to react aggressively (Charney, Deutch, Krystal, Southwick, & Davis, 1993). Less is known about the connection between psychosis and offending or violence among youth.

In some cases, mental disorder may not be connected to actual offending, but youths and adults with mental health problems wind up in the justice system as a consequence of the lack of community mental health services. Until further research can disentangle the relationships, the evidence implies that most risk assessment schemes should contain an item or items related to attention problems and impulsive behavior. Further, until we know more about the connection between other symptoms of mental illness and offending among youth, consideration should be given to risk assessment tools, including those that contain some form of override feature for use with cases for which examiners have reason to believe that symptoms of mental illness are connected to violent or antisocial outcomes for a particular youth.

Personality and Callous-Unemotional Traits in Risk Assessment

The features of some personality disorders (e.g., Borderline, Narcissistic, Antisocial) are likely to get some individuals in trouble with the law. Given that these disorders tend to have their roots in childhood and adolescence, these personality traits may be related to early offending and may be a good predictor of offending into early adulthood. Psychopathic personality disorder probably has been the most widely studied with respect to its relation to future offending, particularly violent offending (for a review see Hare, 2003). The association between psychopathic personality and later offending and violence among adults has been documented in a number of meta-analyses of prospective studies (e.g., Hemphill, Hare, & Wong, 1998; Leistco, Salekin, DeCoster & Rogers, 2008). Many psychopathic features get people in trouble with the law, including impulsive and sensation-seeking behavior, callous and guiltless emotions, and an arrogance characterized by a desire to exert power over others.

The relation between psychopathy and early adult offending is more complicated when assessing young people. Many scholars acknowledge that diagnosing or labeling a youth as a "psychopath" is inappropriate given developmental changes that affect personality through adolescence. There is a youth psychopathy assessment tool designed to assess psychopathic traits among adolescents (reviewed later), which has demonstrated a small to moderate effect for prediction of violence and re-offending, but most research has not examined its prediction of offending into early adulthood.

Instead, the focus for youth has been on a "syndrome" that involves the combination of *callous-unemotional traits AND serious conduct problems*, referred to as CU-CD. Callous-unemotional traits distinguish sub-groups of seriously conduct-disordered children and adolescents who experience minimal distress when engaging in criminal behaviors (Frick, O'Brien, Wootton, & McBurnett, 1994) and are more severe and stable in their offending patterns. In a prospective study, Frick, Kimonis, Dandreaux, and Farell (2003) discovered that callous-unemotional features were relatively stable during childhood for children who had CU scores falling in the lower or upper quartiles at age 6 if they also had serious conduct problems. Parent and teacher ratings of Interpersonal Callousness (IC) in children ages 7 to 12 appear to predict adult psychopathy ratings in the same youths at ages 18 to 19 (Burke, Loeber, & Lahey, 2007).

The stability of these traits from childhood or adolescence into adulthood has proven still to be only modest. Longitudinal studies examining measurement invariance in measures of IC or psychopathic features indicate that there is measurement invariance from late adolescence to young adulthood (6 years, Loney, Taylor, Butler, & Iacono, 2007). However, one longitudinal study found that, of the juveniles who scored in the top 20% of psychopathic traits at age 13, the vast majority (86%) did not score above a diagnostic threshold on a measure of psychopathic traits as adults 11 years later (Lynam, Caspi, Moffitt, Loeber, & Stouthamer-Loeber, 2007). Although the fact that 14% continued to score high as adults makes this construct relatively stable as far as youth disorders are concerned, practically speaking, use of assessments of these traits in childhood and adolescence to predict who would be psychopathic as adults would lead to a large number of false predictions. This body of literature indicates that it is crucial for risk assessment schemes to contain an item or items related to impulsivity, attention problems, sensation-seeking, and low empathy and remorse or callousness, all of which are strongly related to chronic offending.

Risk/Needs Assessment Formats

The four types of assessment formats are unstructured clinical, static actuarial, static/dynamic actuarial, and structured professional judgment, although this categorization is something of an oversimplification (Borum & Verhaagen, 2006;

Hoge, 2008). *Unstructured clinical assessments* depend on the unguided collection of information and the formulation of a judgment about level of risk through subjective interpretation of the information. For example, a psychologist may interview the client in an unstructured manner and, on the basis of his or her education and experience, will formulate a judgment about the likelihood that the individual will engage in violence or an antisocial act. Research has shown that unstructured clinical assessments are associated with poor levels of reliability and validity. Indeed, when mental health professionals make specific, unstructured predictions that a person "will" or "will not" be violent, they will likely be accurate in no more than one-third of cases (Grisso & Tomkins, 1996; Monahan, 1996; Rubin, 1972).

The different approaches to assessing risk can vary in terms of the amount of structure imposed on the three central decisions that arise in the assessment process: 1) which risk factors to consider and how to measure them; 2) how to combine the risk factors; and 3) how to generate the final risk estimate (Monahan, 2008). Standardized risk assessments are based on structured procedures for the collection and synthesis of information. *Actuarial measures* constitute a specific type of standardized measure. Structure is imposed on each of the three major decisions in the actuarial assessment approach, there is no discretion in terms of selecting, measuring, or combining risk factors, and the final risk estimate is determined by a priori, fixed rules. Items on these measures are often empirically derived using a construction sample with known outcomes (the developers know who recidivated and who did not) to identify the factors that predicted re-offending in that group. An algorithm is created to categorize people according to the likelihood of reoffending.

Actuarial decision-making means that specific risk predictions are formulated based on a statistical formula. Static actuarial measures include only historical and invariant items. Bonta (1996) described these as second-generation risk assessment instruments (unstructured clinical procedures constitute the first generation). Although scholars asserted that actuarial tools are superior to clinical judgment in the prediction of violence and re-offending (Grove & Meehl, 1996; Quinsey, Harris, Rice, & Cormier, 1998), the incremental gain in predictive validity is minimal (Litwack, 2001). Moreover, Bonta and several other critics have cautioned that static actuarial instruments are for the most part atheoretical, cover only a limited range of predictor variables, and are not useful for intervention planning or reassessments to measure individual progress (Borum, 1996; Dvoskin & Heilbrun, 2001; Hart, 2003; Hoge & Andrews, 2010).

Static/dynamic actuarial measures, termed third-generation measures by Bonta (1996), incorporate both static and dynamic risk factors. For the most part, these tools include static and dynamic risk factors that were selected due to a known empirical association with later offending, as opposed to selecting items that were predictive in a particular construction sample. As such, these tools are generally theoretically and empirically grounded. In the juvenile offender area, these instruments are often referred to as risk/need actuarial tools. These tools can be used for reassessment and for intervention planning. They often include an override procedure to the final risk level to account for idiosyncratic factors that may affect an individual's risk level but would not be reflected in the overall score.

The fourth category of risk assessment tools is *structured professional judgment* (SPJ). In this approach to assessing risk for violence, structure is imposed on which risk factors should be considered and how they should be measured, but the way in which factors are combined is left to the discretion of the evaluator. The evaluator's discretion similarly is valued in terms of generating the final estimate of risk. Like the static/dynamic actuarial tools, SPJ tools are informed by the state of the discipline in clinical theory and empirical research on static and dynamic factors to include factors that guide decisions about risk and treatment planning. The intent was to improve human judgment by adding structure, and to improve actuarial decision-making by adding more rater discretion (Borum & Douglas, 2003). These instruments emphasize "prevention" as opposed to "prediction." They contain static and dynamic risk factors and protective factors, assuming that risk can change as a result of treatment quality and quantity, developmental factors, protective factors, context, and the passage of time. The difference between SPJ tools and the static/dynamic actuarial tools is that SPJ tools lead to a final judgment by the rater regarding the overall level of risk (typically communicated as low, moderate, or high) based on a combination of risk factors, protective factors, and idiosyncratic factors present. No algorithm is used to produce a quantitative index of risk level.

Summarizing Debates

Considerable research has been conducted on the relative efficacy of unstructured clinical judgment versus standardized assessments (Baird & Wagner, 2000; Bonta, Law, & Hanson, 1998; Grove & Meehl, 1996; Grove, et al., 2000). The research consistently demonstrates that standardized assessments, whether based on actuarial or structured judgment procedures, yield better predictions of future behavior than unstructured clinical assessments. This evidence is strong and at this point is rarely disputed. However, some disagreements in the field remain.

The first disagreement is the issue of actuarial versus SPJ tools for estimates of an individual's risk level. There is an accumulating body of literature regarding adult populations that suggests that SPJ-based decisions about risk may have incremental predictive validity over simple score-based decisions (Douglas, Yeoman, & Boer, 2005). The validity or reliability of actuarial overrides is still largely unknown. More recently, a very comprehensive meta-analysis of adult risk assessment tools indicated that, on average, when compared directly within the same sample, SPJ and actuarial tools have equivalent predictive validity for re-offending (Guy, 2008).

Another related debate is the value of including criminogenic need factors in risk tools. One argument is that the inclusion of these dynamic variables in determinations of risk level (e.g., low, moderate, or high risk) can diminish the predictive accuracy of risk tools and, therefore, should be in a separate tool. The premise of this argument is that the goal of a risk assessment should be prediction. Of course, research has demonstrated that certain dynamic risk factors or criminogenic needs can elevate risk for delinquency (e.g., Farrington & West, 1993; Moffitt & Caspi, 2001), which suggests that they should be included in any risk tools (Austin, 2006). Further, the inclusion of these criminogenic need factors is essential for measuring changes or progress in risk level and for case management.

Statistically speaking, the debate revolves around whether dynamic risk or criminogenic need factors add incremental predictive value to quantitative risk levels. Practically speaking, however, this debate should consider that once an offender is labeled as high-risk by a tool with unchangeable factors, there is no room for documenting developmental changes.

One issue that continues to complicate this discussion is the definition of "needs." Dynamic risk factors would be considered *criminogenic needs* when they have a causal connection with the individual's risk for re-offending. Criminogenic needs theoretically are changeable. This is in contrast to other types of *needs* an offender may have that have not shown a significant relation to later offending, such as depression. One might refer to these as *well-being needs*. In our view, criminogenic needs are an essential feature of any comprehensive risk assessment tool; however, well-being needs belong in a separate assessment tool or, at the least, may be included within a risk assessment tool but should not be included in quantitative estimates of risk.

Review of Risk Assessment Instruments

Tools were selected for inclusion in this chapter if they: (1) were developed to assess risk for general antisocial behavior or violence in the community; (2) were designed to be generalizable rather than jurisdiction- or sample-specific (this excludes tools that are modified for each site, such as the Wisconsin classification system, Baird, 1981); (3) are administered by a trained rater/examiner or professional (i.e., not self-report inventories); and (4) have enough research evidence (including peer-reviewed research) to be considered *evidence-based* or *promising* at the time of this review. We defined evidence-based and promising as having some evidence of inter-rater reliability (IRR) and predictive validity for re-offending and enough information for replicable assessments, such as having a test manual. Categorization of a tool as evidence-based (versus promising) requires reliability evidence and validation from an independent party that receives no economic gain from the tool (Austin, 2006). We review tools used with youth (ages 12–17) and adults (aged 18 and older); no instrument has been developed specifically for the transition-ages (18 to 29). Table 6.1 provides a summary of the measures reviewed and identifies the variables included.

TABLE 6.1 } Empirically-based risk factors contained in each risk assessment tool reviewed.

Risk Factors	Youth Tools					Adult Tools				
	WSJCA	YASI	YLS/CMI	SAVRY	NCAR	LSI/CMI	SIR	VRAG	HCR-20	COVR
PERSONAL RISK FACTORS - STATIC										
History of joblessness	X	X	X			X			X	X
History of school suspensions/ expulsions	X	X		X	X	X			X	
Early school leaving	X	X		X	X					
History of homelessness			X		X	X				
Early conduct problems									X	
Early age of onset for offending	X	X			X	X	X	X	X	X
Early violence/ aggression				X					X	
Prior probation/ custody	X	X	X	X	X	X	X	X	X	X
Exposure to violence (early)	X	X	X	X	X				X	
Early caregiver disruption	X			X					X	
History of violence	X	X		X	X	X	X	X	X	X
History of nonviolent delinquency/ offending	X	X	X	X	X	X	X	X		X
History of abuse/ maltreatment	X	X	X	X	X				X	X
CONTEXTUAL RISK FACTORS - STATIC										
Antisocial attitudes, values, beliefs, family	X	X	X	X						
Criminality in family	X	X	X	X	X	X				X
Mental illness in family	X	X	X							
Marital conflicts in family	X	X	X		X	X				
Joblessness in family	X		X							
Low family income	X		X			X				
Inadequate family housing			X		X					

(*continued*)

TABLE 6.1 (*continued*)

Risk Factors	Youth Tools					Adult Tools				
	WSJCA	YASI	YLS/CMI	SAVRY	NCAR	LSI/CMI	SIR	VRAG	HCR-20	COVR
Dysfunctional neighborhood/community disorganization				X		X				
High crime neighborhood				X		X			X	
PERSONAL RISK FACTORS - DYNAMIC										
Antisocial attitudes, values, beliefs	X	X	X	X		X			X	
Attentional disorder	X		X	X						
Psychopathy (adult tools)								X	X	X
Low empathy/remorse			X	X						
Inflated self-worth	X		X	X						
Sensation seeking				X	X					
Impulsivity	X		X	X	X				X	
Chronic lying										
Hostile, aggressive, violent	X	X	X	X	X	X			X	X
Anger management issues	X	X	X	X						
Lack of motivation			X	X						
Drug abuse	X	X	X	X	X	X			X	X
Alcohol abuse	X	X	X	X	X	X		X	X	X
Poor school adjustment	X	X	X	X	X	X		X	X	
Poor school performance	X	X	X	X	X	X		X		
Poor coping ability	X		X	X		X			X	
Mental illness/health	X	X			X	X		X	X	X
CONTEXTUAL RISK FACTORS - DYNAMIC										
Dysfunctional family environment	X	X	X	X	X	X				
Ineffective parenting	X	X	X	X	X					
Parent-youth conflicts/attachment problem	X	X	X		X	X			X	
Lack of family supports	X	X		X					X	

TABLE 6.1 (*continued*)

Risk Factors	Youth Tools					Adult Tools				
	WSJCA	YASI	YLS/CMI	SAVRY	NCAR	LSI/CMI	SIR	VRAG	HCR-20	COVR
Maternal/paternal poor coping										
Negative peer associations	X	X	X	X	X	X			X	X
PERSONAL FACTORS (POSITIVE/STRENGTHS)										
Emotional maturity				X						
Positive, prosocial attitude	X	X	X	X		X				
Good problem-solving skills	X	X		X						
Good social skills	X	X		X		X				
Motivation to address personal issues/Readiness		X		X						
Job stability	X	X	X			X			X	X
Educational commitment/ achievement	X	X	X	X		X				
Positive hobby/ sport involvement	X	X	X	X		X				
Intelligence				X	X					
Positive attitude toward authority/ treatment	X	X		X		X				
Resilient personality traits				X						
CONTEXTUAL FACTORS (POSITIVE/STRENGTHS)										
Stable & cohesive family unit	X	X	X		X	X				
Supportive parent	X	X	X	X	X	X				
Supportive other adult	X	X		X		X				
Stable marital/ partner relation- ship	X					X			X	
Positive peer associations	X	X	X	X	X	X				
Strong attachment and bonds	X	X		X						

Risk Assessment Instruments Created for Adolescents

Each of the tools reviewed below is completed based on an interview with the youth and collateral contacts, and a review of file information. While reviewing the evidence, it is important to note that most studies of adolescent tools have used short follow-up periods of approximately one year. A few have tracked arrest rates after three to three-and-a-half years. This means the research, as it stands, offers little in terms of prediction of young adulthood/late-onset offending.

Youth Level of Service/Case Management Inventory (YLS/CMI). The YLS/CMI (Hoge & Andrews, 2006) is a static/dynamic actuarial instrument for assessing risk for recidivism for male and female juvenile offenders aged 12 to 17. The instrument uses an "adjusted actuarial approach," meaning that it has a total score used to determine risk level, but the evaluator can override. IRR between professionals and probation officers report good ICCs (Intraclass Correlation Coefficients) on most subscales (.71 to .85; Schmidt, Hoge, & Robertson, 2005) and .75 for the Total Risk score (Poluchowiz, Jung, & Rawana, 2000).

Predictive validity has been studied prospectively using both file-based and probation-officer completed assessments. A recent meta-analysis of multiple studies, many from independent researchers, confirmed that there was a substantial amount of variability in effect sizes across predictive validity studies for the YLS/CMI. On average, the effect size (weighted r) was .29 for nonviolent re-offending (based on three samples) and .26 for violent re-offending (based on nine samples; Olver, Stockdale, & Wormith, 2009). Areas under the ROC curve (AUCs) have ranged around .57 to .75 (Schwalbe, 2007). Based on a limited number of studies, Olver et al. (2009) noted that the YLS/CMI seems to predict re-offending equally well across genders and for minority youth in U.S. and Canadian settings.

The Structured Assessment of Violence Risk in Youth (SAVRY). The SAVRY (Borum, Bartel, & Forth, 2006) is an SPJ tool comprising static and dynamic risk factors and protective factors for male and female young offenders aged 12 to 18. The ultimate determination of an examinee's overall level of violence risk is communicated via the Summary Risk Rating (SRR), which is rated as low, moderate, or high, based on the examiner's judgment as informed by a systematic appraisal of relevant factors. The IRR is good (e.g., ICCs for total scores around .81 and .77 for SRR, Catchpole & Gretton, 2003) as demonstrated by many studies. Predictive validity for both violent and nonviolent offending has been demonstrated in forensic and young offender populations across multiple studies (for a review, see Olver et al., 2009), including circumstances where the assessment was completed by masters-level clinicians or juvenile justice personnel (Vincent, Chapman, & Cook, 2005).

A recent meta-analysis reported weighted rs of .38 for nonviolent re-offending (based on two samples) and .30 for violent re-offending (based on nine samples) for total scores (Olver et al., 2009) with no statistically significant variability in effect sizes across studies. It should be noted that the meta-analysis summarized the predictive accuracy of SAVRY total scores rather than the SRR, which is how the tool is used in practice. Studies examining the prediction of the SRR also have reported high accuracy (AUC = .71 for violent re-offending; Lodewijks, Doreleijers, & de Ruiter, 2008). AUCs for the total score have ranged from .65 to .89 among studies with a follow-up period of one year or more (for a review, see Borum, Lodewijks, Bartel, & Forth, 2010).

The Washington State Juvenile Court Assessment (WSJCA) and Youth Assessment and Screening Instrument (YASI). The WSJCA (Barnoski, 2004) is a risk for re-offending assessment tool for use with offenders aged 12 to 18. Most users utilize a computer-based program referred to as the Back on Track, or, more recently, the Positive Achievement Change Tool (PACT). Another adaptation of this tool is the YASI, which was created by Orbis Partners by expanding the WSJCA to include mental health items. These tools come in three parts: a pre-screen, full assessment, and reassessment. The pre-screen is an actuarial tool comprising mostly static items whereas the other tools contain static and dynamic items. Using a sample of 20,339 pre-screen assessments and 12,187 full assessments for youths on probation, Barnoski (2004) found that the felony recidivism rate and violent recidivism rate of the high-risk group were about three times that of the low-risk group after an 18-month follow-up. The AUC was .64 for both violent and nonviolent recidivism. The predictive validity is good for minority groups and girls, but weaker than the predictive validity for whites and boys (Washington State Institute for Public Policy, 2004) and, therefore, a different item-weighting system is recommended for these groups. One study of the PACT, conducted by an independent examiner using a one-year follow-up, indicated that as the overall level of risk for youth arrestees increased, the odds of rearrest increased by 1.5 times (Baglivio, 2009). The AUC, however, was only .59. The IRR has not been reported for any of the measures, so it is unknown if the lower AUC in this study was due to diminished IRR.

North Carolina Assessment of Risk (NCAR). The NCAR is a brief, actuarial tool designed to evaluate risk for re-offending among juvenile offenders. It consists of nine risk items that together comprise a total risk score. The tool, which can be completed easily by juvenile justice personnel, comprises primarily static risk factors, but also contains a few dynamic risk items. Although the name implies that the NCAR is jurisdiction-specific, it is likely to generalize because the items were selected according to general delinquency research and theory rather than statistical associations between indicators and recidivism in this jurisdiction. To our knowledge, there are no rigorous studies of the tool's inter-rater agreement, but estimates suggest it is adequate (Schwalbe, Fraser, Day, & Arnold, 2004). Schwalbe, Fraser, Day, and Cooley (2006) examined the predictive validity of the NCAR using a sizeable sample of 9,534 delinquent offenders (*M* = 13.7 years) over an average one-year follow-up. Cox regressions resulted in a hazard ratio of 1.08, meaning that a one-point increase in the NCAR score would be associated with an additional 8% chance of recidivism. The NCAR was predictive among both white and black boys and black girls, but did not differentiate recidivists among white girls. A meta-analysis with three studies indicated AUCs ranged from .60–.68 (Schwalbe, 2007).

Psychopathy Checklist: Youth Version (PCL:YV). The PCL:YV (Forth, Kosson, & Hare, 2003) is a downward extension of the Psychopathy Checklist-Revised

(PCL-R) for adults that is used to provide a dimensional assessment of the "proto-typical" psychopath among adolescents aged 12 to 18. The PCL:YV is an expert symptom-rating scale that defines psychopathy along interpersonal, affective, and behavioral symptom clusters. Scoring of the tool's 20 items is based on each symptom's pervasiveness, severity, and chronicity. Total and factor (i.e., symptom cluster) scores are dimensional, meaning that they represent the level or severity of psychopathic traits. The PCL:YV is not a risk assessment tool per se but is used in risk assessments in light of research that indicates that youth who score high on the PCL:YV have more serious and persistent criminal histories with an earlier onset than those who score low (e.g., Brandt, Wallace, Patrick, & Curtin, 1997). A meta-analysis (Edens, Campbell, & Weir, 2007) of PCL:YV total scores yielded medium effect sizes for general ($r = .26$) and violent recidivism ($r = .23$). PCL:YV total scores have high IRR ($r = .90-.96$) across the various populations (i.e., institutional, probation, or community) tested by many independent researchers.

Generally, high PCL:YV scores in youth may compel a conclusion of high risk over short periods of time. However, given that adolescence is a time of extreme developmental change and most studies employing PCL:YV have not used follow-up periods into adulthood, risk and psychopathic characteristics should be reassessed routinely in high-risk youth to determine if maturation attenuates risk. Since the PCL:YV is not a diagnostic tool, there are no established valid cutoffs for making categorical decisions of whether someone is, or is not, a psychopath (Forth et al., 2003). Other cautions about use of the PCL:YV is that in girl samples there is not yet good evidence that the tool predicts rearrest well (Odgers, Moretti, & Reppucci, 2005; Vincent, Odgers, McCormick, & Corrado, 2008).

Risk Assessment Instruments Created for Adults

Classification of Violence Risk (COVR). The COVR (Monahan et al., 2005) is an interactive software program developed to estimate the risk that a psychiatric in-patient will be violent towards others in the community. In contrast to most actuarial tools that are created using a regression approach, the COVR is based on a multiple iterative classification tree (ICT) method. As such, individuals can be classified at the same level of risk based on different combinations of risk factors. The particular questions administered to an individual depend on the answers given to prior questions. The software can assess 40 risk factors, but in practice only enough risk factors necessary to classify the patient's violence risk are considered. In the development sample, psychiatric subjects were placed into one of five risk groups whose likelihood of violence to others over the next 20 weeks ranged from 1% (the 'low-risk' group) to 76% (the 'high-risk' group), with a resulting AUC of .88. The recidivism rates for the low- and high-risk groups in a cross-validation analysis were respectively 9% and 35% and the AUC was .63. An AUC of .70 was obtained when a modified follow-up procedure was used. Despite the relatively large drop in predictive accuracy (which is to be expected to some extent when any actuarial method is cross-validated), results indicated that the COVR's use of multiple ICT models was a useful aid in decision-making.

Historical-Clinical-Risk Management-20 (HCR-20). The HCR-20 (Webster, Douglas, Eaves, & Hart, 1997) adheres to the SPJ model of risk assessment and was developed to facilitate assessments of risk for violence. The tool comprises 20 items across three scales, including an historical scale, which is static, and clinical and risk scales, which are dynamic. Like the SAVRY, evaluators provide SRRs after considering all the factors. Research from independent parties provides support for the use of the HCR-20 across both genders with forensic and civil psychiatric patients, mentally disordered offenders, and general correctional offenders. The median IRR coefficient for the HCR-20 total score across 25 studies was .85 (Douglas & Reeves, 2009). Fewer studies have reported IRR for SRRs; across nine values (from five studies), the median ICC was .65. This is expected to be lower relative to the multi-item index because the SRR is a single item. There have been over 50 evaluations of the tool's predictive validity across approximately a dozen countries (Guy, 2008). Overall, findings indicate that HCR-20 numeric total scores, numeric scale scores, and SRRs are associated with violence with average effect sizes of moderate to large magnitude, and that the tool performs comparably across genders and countries. In a recent meta-analysis (Guy, 2008), the weighted mean AUC for the numeric total score for violence was .73 (based on 14 effect sizes). Across the six studies that have investigated SRRs, results indicate the categorical estimates are as or more strongly related to violence than are the numeric total, with four studies demonstrating that the SRR added incrementally to the numeric total.

Violence Risk Appraisal Guide (VRAG). The VRAG (Harris, Rice, & Quinsey, 1993; Quinsey et al., 1998) is an actuarial tool developed to assess the risk of violence among male forensic populations. There have been few studies done with women. Most of the tool's 12 items are static risk factors that in multiple regression analyses made independent and incremental contributions to predictive accuracy among approximately 50 variables that were available in institutional records. Several reliability and validity studies have been conducted by independent examiners. Harris et al. (1993) reported a high IRR ($r = .90$). The AUC for violent recidivism in the development sample was .76. Among the over 30 independent replications of the VRAG (see www.mhcp-research.com), typically moderate to high predictive accuracy for violent recidivism has been obtained, although the average of cross-validated effect sizes is lower (as expected based on the actuarial derivation approach). Campbell, French, and Gendreau (2009) reported a weighted mean correlation of .32 for violent recidivism (based on 14 effect sizes). Predictive accuracy is not moderated by nationality (there are replications in seven countries), length of follow-up (mean durations have ranged from 12 weeks to 10 years), or how violent recidivism has been operationalized (Quinsey et al., 1998).

Level of Service Inventory-Revised (LSI-R). The LSI-R (Andrews & Bonta, 1995) is an actuarial tool developed according to the principles advanced by the Risk/Needs/Responsivity framework (Andrews & Bonta, 2006). It comprises 54 items primarily representing dynamic risk factors (i.e., criminogenic needs), across 10 domains. It is distinct from other actuarial tools in that its items were selected rationally, rather than statistically, on the basis of prior evidence of their association with recidivism. Another unique feature is that it was developed using a gender-balanced sample (40% male; Andrews et al., in press). Although the LSI was developed for use with general offender populations, research also supports its use with mentally disordered offenders and forensic psychiatric patients.

A large body of research supports the reliability and predictive utility of the LSI-R for general recidivism among men and women. For example, when the reassessment interval was less than a month, the mean inter-rater reliability across six samples was .92 (Andrews, Bonta & Wormith, in press). Based on 19 prospective studies, Campbell et al. (2009) reported a weighted mean correlation of .28 for violent recidivism. Gendreau, Goggin, and Smith (2002) meta-analyzed 33 effect sizes and reported the aggregate correlation between the LSI-R and general recidivism to be .37. Meta-analytic evidence (Smith, Cullen, & Latessa, 2009) from 27 effect sizes yielded an association of a similar magnitude ($r = .35$), and gender did not moderate predictive accuracy in this research.

A revised version of the tool, the *Level of Service/Case Management Inventory* LS/CMI; Andrews, Bonta, & Wormith, 2004), has been developed in which the 54 LSI-R items were refined and combined into 43 items. The LS/CMI is unique in that it is a fully functioning case management tool.

Statistical Information for Recidivism Scale (SIR). The SIR (Nuffield, 1982) is an actuarial tool developed by the National Parole Board of Canada in 1975 (originally referred to as the *General Information for Recidivism Scale*, or GSIR) to assess risk for recidivism among offenders released from Canadian penitentiaries. The tool comprises 15 primarily static risk variables covering demographic characteristics and criminal history. Satisfactory levels of inter-rater agreement have been reported. For example, Wormith and Goldstone (1984) reported an 85% agreement rate when comparing parole officer and researcher scores. Adequate levels of predictive validity have also been reported for men, although validity coefficients for female samples tend to be lower than for male samples. Campbell et al. (2009) reported a weighted correlation of .22 based on 17 effect sizes for the prospective prediction of violent recidivism in male offenders from SIR scores. At present, research supports the use of the SIR only with men from nonaboriginal ethnic backgrounds.

Psychopathy Checklist—Revised (PCL-R). The PCL-R (Hare, 1991, 2003) is a structured measure of psychopathic traits that often is used as a risk prediction tool in light of its strong association with future offending (especially violent offending). Its items are organized into two correlated factors representing Affective/Interpersonal (Factor 1) and Socially Deviant/Impulsive Lifestyle (Factor 2) characteristics.

The PCL-R manual reports adequate IRR ratings for pooled samples of male offenders (ICC_1 = .86, ICC_2 = .92), male forensic patients (ICC_1 = .88, ICC_2 = .93), and female offenders (ICC_1 = .94, ICC_2 = .97). As noted earlier, several meta-analyses reported strong associations between PCL-R scores and violence in institutions (e.g., Guy, Edens, Anthony, & Douglas, 2005) and the community (e.g., Leistico et al., 2008) with Factor 2 being a stronger predictor of recidivism than Factor 1. In the most recent and comprehensive quantitative synthesis, Leistico and colleagues (2008) aggregated effect sizes from 95 nonoverlapping studies (representing 15,826 individuals). The median weighted Cohen's *d* values for the total, Factor 1,and Factor 2 scores were .57, .38, and .58, respectively. Importantly, in this and previous meta-analyses, substantial heterogeneity in effect sizes was observed, which suggests that it is likely that the association between PCL-R scores and recidivism is moderated by several factors (e.g., race, gender, institutional setting, and country in which data were collected).

Review of Meta-Analyses Comparing Risk Assessment Instruments

Several meta-analyses have compared one or more risk assessment instruments used with juveniles (Olver, Stockdale, & Wormith, 2009; Schwalbe, 2007, 2008) or adults (Campbell et al., 2009; Gendreau, Goggin, & Little, 1996; Gendreau, Goggin, & Smith, 2002; Guy, 2008; Hanson & Morton-Bourgon, 2009; Walters, 2006). Taken together, the studies comparing the aggregate predictive validity of various actuarial and SPJ tools indicate that there often is no definitive advantage to either approach with respect to predicting who will re-offend. When differences are observed, they most often are in the direction of the actuarial approach; the magnitudes of the differences, however, typically are small. For example, examining all available studies in which an SPJ and an actuarial measure were studied in the same sample, Guy (2008) found that, regardless of whether the predictor for the SPJ tool was the SRR or the numeric rating, the mean-weighted effect sizes for the SPJ and actuarial approaches were moderate in size and virtually identical for all comparisons. For violent (including sexual) recidivism, the mean-weighted AUC values in the SRR versus actuarial comparison were both .61, and for the SPJ numeric total score versus actuarial comparison, the corresponding mean-weighted AUC values were .71 and .68, respectively.

Examining several tools for use with adults with respect to their predictive validity for general recidivism, Gendreau, Goggin, and Little (1996) reported that the LSI-R had a slightly larger mean effect size (.33, *k* = 28) compared to the Wisconsin Classification System (Baird, 1981 .32, *k* = 14) or PCL-R (.29, *k* = 9). Gendreau and colleagues later compared the predictive validity of the LSI/LSI-R relative to the PCL/PCL-R for violent recidivism (Gendreau, Goggin, & Smith, 2002) and found that the effect sizes were highly similar in studies in which both tools were used in the same sample. Mean correlations for the LSI-R and the

PCL-R for general recidivism were .37 and .26, respectively, and for violent recidivism were .24 and .22, respectively. A similar pattern was observed for between-study comparisons of the tools.

Campbell et al. (2009) examined prospective evaluations of forensic psychiatric patients and general offenders in which the HCR-20, LSI/LSI-R, PCL/PCL-R, SIR, or VRAG was used. The authors concluded that each tool predicted violent recidivism with at least a moderate magnitude of success, and that although the LSI-R, PCL-R, and SIR yielded the most precise point estimates, no one measure should be singled out as being most effective in predicting violent recidivism. Importantly, the authors did not evaluate the performance of the only SPJ tool included (the HCR-20) as it was intended to be used in clinical practice (i.e., SRRs were not included, which, as noted above, consistently yield larger effect sizes as compared to the numeric total scores for the HCR-20).

With respect to youth instruments, examining the predictive validity of 42 effect sizes coded from 33 samples that reported on 28 risk assessment instruments (primarily actuarial tools), Schwalbe (2007) reported that the mean-weighted AUC for all tools versus recidivism was .64; substantial variability was observed (range of AUCs: .55–.78). Relative to "first" or "second" generation tools, higher levels of accuracy were observed among "third generation" tools, such as the YLS/CMI. Similar to findings for the overall sample, the weighted mean AUC value (derived from 11 effect sizes) for the YLS/CMI was .64 (95% C.I. = .51–.78).

In a more recent meta-analysis of the YLS/CMI, PCL:YV, and SAVRY from 44 samples that represented 8,746 youth, Olver et al. (2009) found that all three measures were significantly associated with general, nonviolent, and violent recidivism with comparable, moderate degrees of accuracy. In head-to-head comparisons of tools used in the same sample, mean effect sizes were comparable for the YLS/CMI and PCL:YV/SAVRY comparisons. Of the two studies in which the YLS and SAVRY were compared directly, predictive accuracy was comparable in one study (Catchpole & Gretton, 2003), and the SAVRY was more predictive in the other (Welsh et al., 2008). However, it is important to note that in the latter study the SAVRY was completed by trained masters level research assistants retrospectively based on file reviews whereas the YLS/CMI had been completed by probation officers in the field. Thus, comparisons should be made with caution. The weighted mean correlation from these two studies was .43 for the SAVRY and .29 for the YLS.

Secondary Analyses

Our review indicates that there has been considerable progress in the area of risk assessment to predict and prevent later offending among offending populations. However, whether these tools maintain their relevance (or predictive accuracy) during different developmental periods is unknown. In other words, the question is whether tools are as adept at predicting re-offending behavior occurring during early adulthood as tools are at predicting re-offending behavior during adolescence (for youth tools, which are generally valid for ages 12 to 17) or later adulthood (for adult tools, valid for ages 18 and older).

The co-authors and colleagues conducted a very preliminary investigation into the validity of assessment tools for assessing risk at different developmental periods (Vincent, Fusco, Gershenson, & Guy, 2010, unpublished data). This involved a search of all publications and unpublished datasets known to the authors which, (a) included one of the assessment tools reviewed in this chapter, (b) studied an offender (corrections, pre-trial detention, or probation) or forensic psychiatric population (civil psychiatric samples were not included), and (c) had a measure of re-offending in the community (self-report or official records). The researchers requested datasets from the authors to be used in a secondary data analysis. The datasets obtained and included in these analyses are described in Table 6.2. Follow-up periods for these datasets spanned one to seven years. Data sets were then combined by risk tool to examine the following recidivism outcomes: (1) *any re-offending*, which includes violent re-offending and all other crime types (except status offenses), and (2) *violent re-offending* only. Studies varied in the manner that they operationalized recidivism (see Table 6.2).

The first question was whether the tools were accurate at predicting re-offending during early adulthood (defined as ages 18 to 25), relative to adolescent re-offending (for youth tools) or later adult re-offending (for adult tools). This required generating sub-samples that included only cases that had a follow-up period spanning early adulthood. Thus, the researchers included only cases that had been assessed on an instrument (or released from an institution where applicable) prior or equal to age 23, which would provide at least one or two years follow-up into early adulthood. Cases that were not tracked until age 19 or older also were excluded from the analyses. As such, a considerable number of cases were dropped from many of the datasets. The final samples used in subsequent analyses are provided in Table 6.3 for the youth tools and Table 6.4 for the adult tools.

The researchers used Receiver Operator Characteristic (ROC) curves, calculated in SPSS, to examine the predictive accuracy of each instrument for any re-offending (includes all types of offenses) and for violent re-offending specifically. Tables 6.3 and 6.4 report the AUC and confidence intervals for each instrument as a function of the developmental period during which cases committed their first re-offense. The tables provide AUCs for both any re-offending and violent re-offending for each tool as the data permitted. AUCs ranged from non-significant at .53 (for the SAVRY's prediction of any re-offending) to .82 (for the HCR-20's prediction of violent offending during early adulthood). The MedCalc software was used to test whether AUCs differed significantly between the early adult and other developmental periods for each risk assessment tool. None of the AUCs were significantly different.

What can be said from the findings is that tools with statistically significant accuracy maintain that accuracy regardless of the developmental period in which

TABLE 6.2 } Descriptions of studies included in the secondary data analysis.

	n	% Female	% Minority	Instrument	Recidivism: Charges or Convictions
North Carolina Department of Juvenile Justice (unpublished data)	6,751	27.0	58.6	NCAR	Charges
de Vogel, de Ruiter, Hildebrand, Bos, & van de Ven (2004)	119	10.9	18.5	HCR-20	Convictions
Douglas, Ogloff, Nicholls, & Grant (1999); Nicholls, Ogloff, & Douglas (2004)	279	40.1	21.5	HCR-20	Other
Harris, Rice, & Cormier (2002)	1,190	NR	NR	VRAG	Charges
Lodewijks, de Ruiter, & Doreleijers (2008)	82	42.7	37.8	SAVRY	Charges
Loza, Villeneuve, & Loza-Fanous (2002)	278	0.0	NR	VRAG	Charges
Rowe (2002)	408	19.9	NR	YLS	Charges
Vincent, Quinlan, Nitschelm, & Ogloff (2003)	248	12.0	26.6	HCR-20; VRAG	Convictions
Vincent, Chapman, & Cook (under review)	757	30.7	64.1	SAVRY	Charges
Welsh, Schmidt, McKinnon, Chattha, & Meyers (2008)	133	37.6	31.6	SAVRY; YLS	Charges

Note: NCAR = North Carolina Assessment of Risk; HCR-20 = Historical Clinical Risk Management- 20; VRAG = Violence Risk Appraisal Guide; YLS/CMI = Youth Level of Service/Case Management Inventory; SAVRY = Structured Assessment of Violence Risk for Youth; NR = Not Recorded.

TABLE 6.3 } AUCs and Cox regressions for risk assessment tools for adolescent populations by developmental period of first re-offense.

Whole Usable Sample				Recidivists During Early Adulthood				Recidivists During Adolescence			
	n	Base rate Re-offense	Base rate Violence	Base rate Re-offense	AUC (CI)	Base rate Violence	AUC (CI)	Base rate Re-offense	AUC (CI)	Base rate Violence	AUC (CI)
NCAR	2129	17%	MIS	NA			NA	17%	.61*** (.58-.64)	MIS	
SAVRY	786	84%	41%	7%	.59 (.50-.69)	7%	.63** (.56-.71)	77%	.53 (.48-.58)	34%	.56* (.52-.60)
YLS	425	61%	26%	4%	.67* (.52-.82)	3%	NV	57%	.74** (.69-.80)	23%	.67*** (.60-.73)

COX REGRESSIONS

NCAR		Re-offense- $\chi^2(1) = 40.31$; $Exp(\beta)$ = 1.07***
SAVRY	Re-offense- $\chi^2(1) = 3.80$; $Exp(\beta) = 1.04^*$ Violence - $\chi^2(1) = 11.89$; $Exp(\beta) = 1.07^{***}$	Re-offense- $\chi^2(1) = 4.20$; $Exp(\beta)$ = 1.01* Violence - $\chi^2(1) = 18.09$; $Exp(\beta)$ = 1.03*
YLS	Re-offense- $\chi^2(1) = 5.82$; $Exp(\beta)$ = 1.06*	Re-offense- $\chi^2(1) = 69.17$; $Exp(\beta)$ = 1.06*** Violence- $\chi^2(1) = 23.82$; $Exp(\beta)$ = 1.06***

Note: The recidivist columns include only samples of cases that committed their first re-offense during that time period. No early adulthood analyses are provided for the NCAR sample because all recidivists committed their first offense during adolescence. AUC = Area Under the Curve. CI = 95% Confidence Interval. NA = not applicable. NV = cannot provide a valid calculation due to low sample sizes. MIS = cannot provide a calculation due to considerable missing data or information unavailable for all data sets. * = $p < .05$, ** = $p < .01$, *** = $p < .001$.

TABLE 6.4 } AUCs and Cox regressions for risk assessment tools for early to older adult populations by developmental period of first re-offense.

	Whole Usable Sample			Recidivists During Early Adulthood				Recidivists During Adulthood			
	n	Base rate Re-offense	Base rate Violence	Base rate Re-offense	AUC (CI) Re-offense	Base rate violence	AUC (CI) violence	Base rate Re-offense	AUC (CI) Re-offense	Base rate violence	AUC (CI) violence
VRAG	589	MIS	44%	MIS		15%	.68* (.58-.78)	MIS		30%	.71** (.65-.77)
HCR-20	127	49%	39%	43%	.73** (.65-.89)	34%	.82*** (.72-.93)	6%	NV	5%	NV

COX REGRESSIONS

VRAG — Violence - $\chi^2(1) = 7.6$; $Exp(\beta) = 1.04^{**}$ | Violence - $\chi^2(1) = 30.71$; $Exp(\beta) = 1.05^{***}$

HCR-20 — Re-offense - $\chi^2(1) = 19.31$; $Exp(\beta) = 1.15^{***}$; Violence - $\chi^2(1) = 15.87$; $Exp(\beta) = 1.14^{***}$ | NV

Note: The recidivist columns include only samples of cases that committed their first re-offense during that time period. AUC = Area Under the Curve. CI = 95% Confidence Interval. NV = cannot provide a valid calculation due to low sample sizes. MIS = cannot provide a calculation due to considerable missing data or information unavailable for all data sets. * = $p < .05$, ** = $p < .01$, *** = $p < .001$.

re-offending occurred. Although we can compare AUCs (a measure of effect size) within tools, one should not try to interpret differences between tools. The analyses reported here did not account for confounding variables that would affect outcomes across studies, such as length of follow-up, operational definition of recidivism, and sample demographics (e.g., gender, race).

A significant limitation of ROC analyses is that they do not account for the length of time in which individuals had an opportunity to re-offend (time at risk). Therefore, the researchers conducted a second set of analyses using Cox Proportional-Hazards Regressions for each tool in each time period in which samples permitted a valid analysis in order to account for the potential confounding effects of time at risk. Cox regression is a semi-parametric test that models the relation between predictor variables and an *event* (i.e., any re-offense or violent re-offense) while accounting for time to the occurrence of the event. The dependent variable, *time at risk to re-offend*, is based on the *cumulative survival function*; that is, the proportion of cases "surviving" (i.e., not charged with or convicted of a new offense) at a particular point in time. The Cox regressions included all cases regardless of whether they had re-offended by estimating time to a hypothetical event for these *censored cases*. Inclusion of censored cases is essential because each released individual who has not recidivated theoretically could still be arrested in the future. The preferred index for interpretation is the Hazard function ($Exp[\beta]$), a measure of the likelihood (odds) of a case experiencing an event, given it has survived that long. For example, an $Exp[\beta]$ of 1.40 indicates that a one-unit increase in the risk assessment total score would result, on average, in a 40% increase in the odds of a rearrest, given a case has survived this long.

Time at risk was calculated separately for any re-offense and violent re-offense based on the days between the adjudication for the index offense (the offense that resulted in the subject being included in the sample and when the risk assessment was completed) or release from an institution (for samples from correctional or forensic hospital settings) and the first rearrest. For nonrecidivists, time at risk was calculated according to the final follow-up date for the whole sample. Results of the Cox regressions are provided in Tables 6.3 and 6.4. The tables show that the risk tools were significant predictors of both violent and any re-offending after taking time at risk into account, regardless of the developmental period in which the offense occurred. The odds were similar for early adult recidivists and adolescent recidivists for most adolescent tools, with the exception of the SAVRY. For the adult tools, odds were also similar for early adult and adult recidivists.

In sum, risk assessment tools predicted re-offending during early adulthood as well as or better than re-offending that occurred during adolescent years for individuals who were first assessed and first offended during adolescence. Adult risk assessment tools conducted during early adulthood also were adept at predicting re-offending during this developmental period. This was true even after controlling for the amount of time an individual had to re-offend.

Unfortunately, there are several constraints on these analyses that limit the conclusions. Because of the selection of participants, the datasets cannot be used to determine what variables predict early adult-onset offending. Risk assessment tool validation studies tend to include only cases that committed an offense in a set time period onward. For many of the offenders in these studies, their index offense in the study would not be the first offense they ever committed in their life. It would be necessary to use data from longitudinal studies of young community samples in order to determine which variables predicted early adult-onset offending. Risk assessment validation studies tend not to gather data from people before they have ever offended. A second limitation is that the data did not permit examination of *continued* offending into early adulthood for adolescent samples. The datasets contained each case's first re-offense (any type), first violent re-offense, and in some instances the first nonviolent re-offense specifically. Therefore, we do not have information about continued offending. The only exception was the NCAR data set. Unfortunately, analyses for early adulthood could not be conducted for the NCAR dataset because a very small number of youth re-offended in early adulthood during the two-year follow-up period (approximately 20).

Conclusions and Recommendations

Recommendations for research. The most important conclusion from our review of the literature concerns the need for more information about the risk, need, and protective factors associated with criminal activity occurring during ages 18 to 29.

We already have considerable information about factors influencing antisocial be-haviors during childhood and adolescence and for ages 18 and older. However, infor-mation about the specific periods of later adolescence and early adulthood is sparse. Likewise, information about factors that can identify those who will initiate offend-ing during this age period is very sparse. In addition, there is no evidence yet to show that risk screening instruments can differentiate between different developmental trajectories of offending during the transition between adolescence and adulthood (for trajectories see Piquero et al., Chapter 2, this volume). Researchers are encour-aged to focus more carefully on that period and investigate screening instruments that can distinguish between different developmental trajectories of offending.

Of particular concern in assessments is the influence of normative life events for the early adult period, including school and work experiences, changes in bonds with parents, and the establishment of new relationships (see Horney et al., Chapter 4, this volume; Thornberry et al., Chapter 3, this volume). Contacts with the juvenile and adult justice and correctional systems are also of relevance for many youth. These variables are often not represented in the research, or, if they are, interactions among them are often not explored. For example, it is possible that forming a positive romantic relationship during early adulthood can mediate the effects of early school drop-out and criminal convictions on later offending. It is this type of interaction that must be explored before definitive answers can be found to the question of variables influencing early adult persistence and desis-tance (Thornberry, 2005).

The validity of generalizing current knowledge about the risk, need, and strength factors associated with early adult offending is also of concern. Much of the research is based on samples of American, Canadian, and British males from the majority culture. Our knowledge of the dynamics of early adult crime among females and those from minority ethnic and cultural groups is limited.

Limitations to our knowledge of the factors affecting early adult offending im-pact, of course, the validity of our assessment tools. We have seen that consider-able progress has been made in developing and evaluating instruments for assessing risk, need, and strength factors in youth and in adults. Further, most of these measures display construct validity to the extent that they include the major risk factors associated with criminal activity. Indeed, the meta-analyses reviewed indicate that all the tools selected for review in this chapter are comparable in terms of their predictive accuracy.

The secondary analyses provide some important additional insights into the ability of risk assessment tools to predict re-offending occurring at different devel-opmental periods, especially early adulthood. The tentative conclusion is that these tools predict re-offending during early adulthood as well as other time pe-riods. Future analyses should use longitudinal studies of community samples that would permit *post hoc* scoring of risk assessment tools using variables available in the dataset (although a limitation of this approach would be that the investigation would be retrospective in nature). Additionally, risk assessment researchers could start recording data for every re-offense occurring during their follow-up periods so trajectory analyses can be conducted in the future, permitting examination of the prediction of continued offending versus desistance in early adulthood. Future efforts also could determine whether specific risk and criminogenic need factors within these risk assessment tools differentially predict continued offending.

Implications for practitioners. The conclusions of this review provide some important guidelines for practitioners and policy-makers. First, based on a wealth of findings, there are specific risk factors that arguably should be contained in any risk assessment tool for youth in order to maximize its effectiveness. These factors include impulsivity, remorselessness, callousness-unemotional traits, inconsistent or lax parental discipline, and early onset violence. However, the relevance of these risk factors to the onset of offending or continued offending in early adulthood (ages 18 to 29) is not well established. Further research on the issue of early adult-onset offending may lead to the development of a new instrument or the modification of an existing measure.

Second, it should not be assumed that the factors associated with the initiation in or desistance from criminal activity are the same for early adulthood as for earlier or later developmental stages. In particular, normative transitions relating to school, work, parental bonds, and the establishment of new relationships often assume unique importance during this period. For example, risk assessment tools for adults should contain a measure of psychopathic personality or Cluster B-type personality traits, given the moderate association with violence, yet it is unlikely that psychopathy would be a good predictor of early adult-onset offending since these individuals tend to initiate offending behavior much earlier in life.

We have seen that existing youth and adult risk/needs prediction instruments are of roughly equal value in terms of construct and predictive validity. However, instruments do vary somewhat in the variables represented, and the instrument selected should include variables identified as having particular relevance for the early adult period.

There also may be implications for interventions geared towards risk management or prevention of continued offending. Treatment strategies that lead to desistance among adolescents may not work for those initiating offending later in life. For example, standard adolescent treatment programs for attitude change, peer group affiliation, or family therapies may not address the criminogenic needs of individuals initiating offending in early adulthood.

Finally, lessons for broad systemic changes exist. The period of early adulthood has been traditionally neglected when it comes to educational, vocational, mental health, and social services. Within most systems, individuals aged 17 to 21 are shifted out of the adolescent services systems, and there is often little to replace those services. Counseling and other treatment/support services, to assist individuals to cope with substance abuse, employment, and relationship issues arising during this period, could ease the transition and help individuals avoid the problems that often characterize these years.

References

American Psychological Association (2002). Ethical principles of psychologists and code of conduct. *American Psychologist*, 57, 1060–1073.

Andrews, D.A. & Bonta, J. (1995). *Level of Service Inventory-Revised*. Toronto, ON: Multi-Health Systems.

Andrews, D.A., Bonta, J., & Wormith, S. (2004). *Manual for the Level of Service/Case Management Inventory (LS/CMI)*. North Tonawanda, NY: Multi-Health Systems.

Andrews, D.A., Bonta, J., & Wormith, S.J. (in press). *The Level of Service/RNR*. Toronto, ON: Multi-Health Systems.

Atkins, D., Pumariega, W., & Rogers K. (1999). Mental health and incarcerated youth. In: Prevalence and nature of psychopathology. *Journal of Child and Family Studies*, 8, 193–204.

Austin, J. (September, 2006). How much risk can we take? The misuse of risk assessment in corrections. *Federal Probation*, 70, 58–63.

Baglivio, M. (2009). The assessment of risk to recidivate among a juvenile offending population. *Journal of Criminal Justice*, 37, 596–607.

Baird, C.S. (1981). Probation and parole classification: The Wisconsin model. *Corrections Today*, 43, 36–41.

Baird, C., & Wagner, D. (2000). The relative validity of actuarial- and consensus-based risk assessment systems. *Children and Youth Services Review*, 22, 839–871.

Barnoski, R. (2004). *Washington State Juvenile Court Assessment manual, Version 2.1 (Report No. 04-03-1203)*. Olympia, WA: Washington State Institute for Public Policy.

Boccaccini, M.T., Turner, D.B., & Murrie, D.C. (2008). Do some evaluators report consistently higher or lower PCL-R scores than others? Findings from a statewide sample of sexually violent predator evaluations. *Psychology, Public Policy, and Law*, 14, 262–283.

Bonta, J. (1996). Risk-needs assessment and treatment. In A.T. Harland (Ed.), *Choosing correctional options that work: Defining the demand and evaluating the supply* (pp.18–32). Thousand Oaks, CA: Sage.

Bonta, J.S., Law, M, & Hanson, R.K. (1998). The prediction of criminal and violent recidivism among mentally disordered offenders: A meta-analysis. *Psychological Bulletin*, 122, 123–142.

Borum, R. & Douglas K. (2003). New directions in violence risk assessment. *Psychiatric Times*, 20, 102–103.

Borum, R. (1996). Improving the clinical practice of violence risk assessment: Technology, guidelines, and training. *American Psychologist*, 51, 945–956.

Borum, R., Bartel, P., & Forth, A. (2006). *Structured Assessment of Violence Risk in Youth (SAVRY)*. Lutz, FL: Psychological Assessment Resources.

Borum, R., Lodewijks, H., Bartel, P., & Forth, A. (2010). Structured Assessment of Violence Risk in Youth (SAVRY). In R.K. Otto & K.S. Douglas (Eds.), *Handbook of violence risk assessment* (pp. 63–80). New York: Routledge.

Borum, R., & Verhaagen, D. (2006). *Assessing and managing violence risk in juveniles*. New York: Guilford Press.

Brandt, J.R., Wallace, A.K., Patrick, C.J., & Curtin, J.J. (1997). Assessment of psychopathy in a population of incarcerated adolescent offenders. *Psychological Assessment*, 9, 429–435.

Burke, J., Loeber, R., & Lahey, B. (2007). Adolescent conduct disorder and interpersonal callousness as predictors of psychopathy in young adults. *Journal of Clinical Child and Adolescent Psychology*, 36, 334–346.

Campbell, M.A., French, S., & Gendreau, P. (2009). The prediction of violence in adult offenders. *Criminal Justice and Behavior, 36*, 567–590.

Catalano, R.F., & Hawkins, 1996. The social development model: A theory of antisocial behaviour. In J.D. Hawkins (Ed.), *Delinquency and crime: Current theories* (pp. 149–197). Cambridge, UK: Cambridge University Press.

Catchpole, R., & Gretton, H. (2003). The predictive validity of risk assessment with violent young offenders: A 1-year examination of criminal outcome. *Criminal Justice and Behavior, 30*, 688–708.

Charney, D., Deutch, A., Krystal, J., Southwick, S., & Davis, M. (1993). Psychological mechanisms of posttraumatic stress disorder. *Archives of General Psychiatry, 50*, 294–305.

Committee on Ethical Guidelines for Forensic Psychologists (1991). Specialty guidelines for forensic psychologists. *Law and Human Behavior, 15*, 655–665.

Copeland, W.E., Miller-Johnson, S., Keeler, G., Angold, A., & Costello, E.J. (2007). Childhood psychiatric disorders and young adult crime: A prospective, population-based study. *American Journal of Psychiatry, 164*, 1668–1675.

de Vogel, V., de Ruiter, C., Hildebrand, M., Bos, B., & van de Ven, P. (2004). Type of discharge and risk of recidivism measured by the HCR-20: A retrospective study in a Dutch sample of treated forensic psychiatric patients. *International Journal of Forensic Mental Health, 3*, 149–165.

Douglas, K.S., Ogloff, J.R.P., Nicholls, T.L., & Grant, I. (1999). Assessing risk for violence among psychiatric patients: The HCR-20 Violence Risk Assessment Scheme and the Psychopathy Checklist: Screening Version. *Journal of Consulting and Clinical Psychology, 67*, 917–930.

Douglas, K.S., & Reeves, K. (2009). The HCR-20 violence risk assessment scheme: Overview and review of the research. In R.K. Otto & K.S. Douglas (Eds.), *Handbook of violence risk assessment* (pp. 147–186). Oxford UK: Routledge.

Douglas, K.S., Yeoman, M., & Boer, D.P. (2005). Comparative validity analysis of multiple measures of violence risk in a sample of criminal offenders. *Criminal Justice and Behavior, 32*, 479–510.

Dvoskin, J.A., & Heilbrun, K. (2001). Risk assessment: Release decision-making toward resolving the great debate. *Journal of the American Academy of Psychiatry and the Law, 29*, 6–10.

Edens, J., Campbell, J. & Weir, J. (2007). Youth psychopathy and criminal recidivism: A meta-analysis of the Psychopathy Checklist measures. *Law and Human Behavior, 31*, 53–75.

Elliott, D.S., Huizinga, D., & Menard, S. (1989). *Multiple problem youth: Delinquency, substance use and mental health problems.* New York: Springer-Verlag.

Farrington, D.P. (2004). Conduct disorder, aggression, and delinquency. In R.M. Lerner, & L. Steinberg (Eds.), *Handbook of adolescent psychology* (2nd ed.; pp. 627–624). New York: Wiley.

Farrington, D.P., & West, D.J. (1993). Criminal, penal, and life histories of chronic offenders: Risk and protective factors and early identification. *Criminal Behaviour and Mental Health, 3*, 492–523.

Farrington, D.P. (2005). (Ed.) *Integrated developmental and life-course theories of offending.* New Brunswick, NJ: Transaction.

Frick, P., J. Kimonis, E., Dandreaux, D., & Farell, J. (2003). The 4-year stability of psychopathic traits in non-referred youth. *Behavioral Sciences and the Law, 21*, 713–736.

Frick, P.J., Lilienfeld, S.O., Ellis, M., Loney, B., & Silverthorn, P. (1999). The association between anxiety and psychopathy dimensions in children. *Journal of Abnormal Child Psychology, 27,* 383–392.

Frick, P., O'Brien, B., Wotton, J., & McBurnett, K. (1994). Psychopathy and conduct problems in children. *Journal of Abnormal Psychology,* 103, 700–707.

Forth, A.E., Kosson, D.S., & Hare, R.D. (2003). *Hare Psychopathy Checklist: Youth Version.* Toronto, ON: Multi-Health Systems.

Gendreau, P., Goggin, C., & Smith, P. (2002). Is the PCL-R really the "unparalleled" measure of offender risk? A lesson in knowledge cumulation. *Criminal Justice and Behavior,* 29, 397–426.

Gendreau, P., Little, T., & Goggin, C.E. (1996). A meta-analysis of the predictors of adult offender recidivism: What works! *Criminology,* 34, 401–433.

Grisso, T., & Appelbaum, P. (1992). Is it unethical to offer predictions of future violent behavior? *Law and Human Behavior,* 16, 621–633.

Grisso, T., & Tomkins, A.J. (1996). Communicating violence risk assessments. *American Psychologist,* 51, 928–930.

Grove, W.M., & Meehl, P.E. (1996). Comparative efficiency of informal (subjective, impressionistic) and formal (mechanical, algorithmic) prediction procedures: The clinical-statistical controversy. *Psychology, Public Policy, and Law,* 2, 293–323.

Guerra, N.G., Williams, K.R., Tolan, P.H., & Modecki, K.L. (2008). Theoretical and research advances in understanding the causes of juvenile offending. In R.D. Hoge, N. Guerra, & P. Boxer (Eds.), *Treating the juvenile offender* (pp. 33–53). New York: Guilford Press.

Guy, L.S. (2008). *Performance indicators of the structured professional judgment approach for assessing risk for violence to others: A meta-analytic survey.* Doctoral dissertation, Simon Fraser University, Burnaby, BC.

Guy, L.S., Edens, J.F., Anthony, C., & Douglas, K.S. (2005). Does psychopathy predict institutional misconduct among adults? A meta-analytic investigation. *Journal of Consulting and Clinical Psychology,* 73, 1056–1064.

Hanson, R.K., & Morton-Bourgon, K.E. (2009). The accuracy of recidivism risk assessments for sexual offenders: A meta-analysis. *Psychological Assessment,* 21, 1–21.

Hare, R.D. (1991). *Manual for the Hare Psychopathy Checklist—Revised.* Toronto, ON: Multi-Health Systems.

Hare, R.D. (2003). *Manual for the Hare Psychopathy Checklist—Revised* (2nd ed.). Toronto, ON: Multi-Health Systems.

Harris, G., Rice, M., & Cormier, C. (2002). Prospective replication of the Violence Risk Appraisal Guide in predicting violent recidivism among forensic patients. *Law and Human Behavior,* 26, 377–394.

Harris, G., Rice, M., & Quinsey, V. (1993). Violent recidivism of mentally disordered offenders: The development of a statistical prediction instrument. *Criminal Justice and Behavior,* 20, 315–335.

Hart, S.D. (2003). Actuarial risk assessment: commentary on Berlin, et al. *Sexual Abuse,* 15, 377–382.

Heilbrun, K. (1992). The role of psychological testing in forensic assessment. *Law and Human Behavior,* 16, 257–272.

Heilbrun, K. (2001). *Principles of forensic mental health assessment.* New York: Kluwer Academic/Plenum.

Heilbrun, K. (2010). *Violence risk assessment in adults.* Oxford, UK: Oxford University Press.

Heilbrun, K., Grisso, T., & Goldstein, A. (2008). *Foundations of forensic mental health assessment*. New York: Oxford University Press.

Hemphill, J.F., Hare, R.D., & Wong, S. (1998). Psychopathy and recidivism: A review. *Legal and Criminological Psychology*, 3, 139–170.

Hoge, R.D. (2008). Assessment in juvenile justice systems. In R.D. Hoge, N. Guerra, & P. Boxer (Eds.), *Treating the juvenile offender* (pp. 54–75). New York: Guilford Press.

Hoge, R.D., & Andrews, D.A. (2006). *Youth Level of Service/Case Management Inventory: User's manual*. North Tonawanda, NY: Multi-Health Systems.

Hoge, R.D., & Andrews, D.A. (2010). *Evaluation of risk for violence in juveniles*. New York: Oxford University Press.

Kazdin A. (2000). *Psychotherapy for children and adolescents: Directions for research and practice*. New York: Oxford University Press.

Leistico, A.R., Salekin, R.T., DeCoster, J., & Rogers, R. (2008). A large-scale meta-analysis relating the Hare measures of psychopathy to antisocial conduct. *Law and Human Behavior*, 32, 28–45.

Lipsey, M.W., & Derzon, J.H. (1998). Predictors of violent or serious delinquency in adolescence and early adulthood: A synthesis of longitudinal research. In R. Loeber & D.P. Farrington (Eds.), *Serious and violent juvenile offenders: Risk factors and successful interventions* (pp. 86–105). Thousand Oaks, CA: Sage.

Lipsey, M.W., & Wilson, D.B. (2001). *Practical meta-analysis*. Thousand Oaks, CA: Sage.

Litwack, T.R. (2001). Actuarial versus clinical assessments of dangerousness. *Psychology, Public Policy, and Law*, 7, 409–443.

Lodewijks, H., de Ruiter, C., & Doreleijers, T. (2008). Gender differences in violent outcome and risk assessment in adolescent offenders after residential treatment. *International Journal of Forensic Mental Health*, 7, 133–146.

Lodewijks, H.P.B., Doreleijers, T.A.H., & de Ruiter, C. (2008). SAVRY risk assessment in violent Dutch adolescents: Relation to sentencing and recidivism. *Criminal Justice and Behavior*, 35, 696–709.

Loeber, R., & Stouthamer-Loeber, M. (1998). Development of juvenile aggression and behavior: Some common misconceptions and controversies. *American Psychologist*, 53, 242–259.

Loeber, R. (1990). Development and risk factors of juvenile antisocial behavior and delinquency. *Clinical Psychology Review*, 10, 1–41.

Loeber, R., & Stouthamer-Loeber, M. (1987). Prediction. In H.C. Quay (Ed.), *Handbook of juvenile delinquency* (pp. 325–382). New York: Wiley.

Loeber, R., Slot, N.W., & Stouthamer-Loeber, M. (2006). A three-dimensional, cumulative developmental model of serious delinquency. In P.O.H. Wikström & R. Sampson (Eds.), *The explanation of crime: Contexts and mechanisms* (pp. 153–194). Cambridge, UK: Cambridge University Press.

Loney, B., Taylor, J., Butler, M., & Iacono, W. (2007). Adolescent psychopathy features: 6-year temporal stability and the prediction of externalizing symptoms during the transition to adulthood. *Aggressive Behavior*, 33, 242–252.

Loza, W., Villeneuve, D., & Loza-Fanous, A. (2002). Predictive validity of the Violence Risk Appraisal Guide: A tool for assessing violent offender's recidivism. *International Journal of Law and Psychiatry*, 25, 85–92.

Lynam, D. (1996). Early identification of chronic offenders: Who is the fledgling psychopath? *Psychological Bulletin*, 120, 209–234.

Lynam, D. R., Caspi, A., Moffitt, T.E., Loeber, R., & Stouthamer-Loeber, M. (2007). Longitudinal evidence that psychopathy scores in early adolescence predict adult psychopathy. *Journal of Abnormal Psychology*, 116, 155–165.

Melton, G., Petrila, J., Poythress, N., & Slobogin, C. (2007). *Psychological evaluations for the courts: A handbook for mental health professionals and lawyers* (3rd ed.). New York: Guilford Press.

Moffitt, T.E. (2003). Life-course-persistent and adolescence-limited antisocial behavior: A 10-year research review and research agenda. In B.B. Lahey, T.E. Moffitt, & A. Caspi (Eds.), *Causes of conduct disorder and juvenile delinquency* (pp. 49–75). New York: Guilford Press.

Moffitt, T.E., & Caspi, A. (2001). Childhood predictors differentiate life-course persistent and adolescence-limited antisocial pathways among males and females. *Development and Psychopathology*, 13, 355–375.

Monahan, J. (1996). Violence prediction: The last 20 years and the next 20 years. *Criminal Justice and Behavior*, 23, 107–120.

Monahan, J. (2008). Structured risk assessment of violence. In R.I. Simon, & K. Tardiff (Eds.), *Textbook of violence assessment and management* (pp. 17–33). Arlington, VA: American Psychiatric Publishing.

Monahan, J., Steadman, H.J., Robbins, P.C., Appelbaum, P., Banks, S., & Grisso, T., et al. (2005). An actuarial model of violence risk assessment for persons with mental disorders. *Psychiatric Services*, 56, 810–815.

Mulvey, E.P. (2005). Risk assessment in juvenile justice policy and practice. In K. Heilbrun, N.E.S. Goldstein, & R.E. Redding (Eds.), *Juvenile delinquency: Prevention, assessment, and intervention* (pp. 209–231). New York: Oxford University Press.

Mulvey, E.P., & Iselin, A.R. (2008). Improving professional judgments of risk and amenability in juvenile justice. *The Future of Children*, 18, 35–57.

Murrie, D.C., Boccaccini, M.T., Johnson, J.T., & Janke, C. (2008). Does interrater (dis) agreement on psychopathy checklist scores in sexually violent predator trials suggest partisan allegiance in forensic evaluations? *Law and Human Behavior*, 32, 352–362.

Nicholls, T.L., Ogloff, J.R.P., & Douglas, K.S. (2004). Assessing risk for violence among male and female civil psychiatric patients: The HCR-20, PCL:SV, and VSC. *Behavioral Sciences and the Law*, 22, 127–158.

Nuffield, J. (1982). *Parole decision-making in Canada: Research towards decision guidelines*. Ottawa, ON: Supply and Services Canada.

O'Connor, T.G., & Rutter, M. (1996). Risk mechanisms in development: Some conceptual and methodological considerations. *Developmental Psychology*, 32, 787–795.

Odgers, C.L., Moretti, M., & Reppucci, N.D. (2005). Examining the science and practice of violence risk assessment with female adolescents. *Law and Human Behavior*, 29, 7–27.

Odgers, C., Vincent, G.M., & Corrado, R.R. (2002). A preliminary conceptual framework for the prevention and management of multi-problem youth. In R.R. Corrado, R. Roesch, S.D. Hart, & Gierowski, J.K. (Eds.), *Multi-problem violent youth: A foundation for comparative research on needs, interventions and outcomes* (pp. 302–329). Amsterdam NL: IOS Press.

Olver, M.E., Stockdale, K.C., & Wormith, J.S. (2009). Risk assessment with young offenders: A meta-analysis of three assessment measures. *Criminal Justice and Behavior*, 36, 329–353.

Patterson, G.R., Forgatch, M.S., Yoerger, K.L., & Stoolmiller, M. (1998). Variables that initiate and maintain an early-onset trajectory of offending. *Developmental Psychopathology*, 10, 531–547.

Piquero, A.R., Farrington, D.P., & Blumstein, A. (2007). *Key issues in criminal career re-search: New analyses of the Cambridge Study in Delinquent Development*. Cambridge, UK: Cambridge University Press.

Poluchowicz, S., Jung, S., & Rawana, E.P. (2000, June). The interrater reliability of the Ministry Risk/Needs Assessment Form for juvenile offenders. Paper presented at the Annual Conference of the Canadian Psychological Association, Montreal, QC.

Quinsey, V.L., Harris, G.T., Rice, M.E., & Cormier, C.A. (1998). *Violent offenders: Appraising and managing risk*. Washington, DC: American Psychological Association.

Robins L.N. (1974). Antisocial behaviour disturbances of childhood: Prevalence, prognosis, and prospects. In E.J. Anthony & C. Koupernik (Eds.), *The child in his family: Children at psychiatric risk*. Oxford, UK: Wiley.

Rowe, R.C. (2002). *Predictors of criminal offending: Evaluating measures of risk/needs, psychopathy, and disruptive behaviour disorders*. Unpublished doctoral thesis. Carleton University, Ottawa, ON.

Rubin, B. (1972). Prediction of dangerousness in mentally ill criminals. *Archives of General Psychiatry*, 27, 397–407.

Rutter, M., Giller, H., & Hagell, A. (1998). *Antisocial behaviour by young people*. Cambridge, UK: Cambridge University Press.

Sampson, R.J., & Laub, J.H. (2003). A life-course view of the development of crime. *Annals of the American Academy of Political and Social Science*, 602, 12–45.

Schmidt, F., Hoge, R., & Robertson, L. (2005). Reliability and validity analyses of the Youth Level of Services/Case Management Inventory. *Criminal Justice and Behavior*, 32, 329–344.

Schwalbe, C.S. (2007a). A meta-analysis of juvenile justice risk assessment instruments: Predictive validity by gender. *Criminal Justice and Behavior*, 35, 1367–1381.

Schwalbe, C.S. (2007b). Risk assessment for juvenile justice: A meta-analysis. *Law and Human Behavior*, 31, 449–462.

Schwalbe, C.S., Fraser, M.W., Day, S.H., & Arnold, E. (2004). North Carolina Assessment of Risk (NCAR): Reliability and predictive validity with juvenile offenders. *Journal of Offender Rehabilitation*, 40, 1–22.

Schwalbe, C.S., Fraser, M.W., Day, S.H., & Cooley, V. (2006). Classifying juvenile offenders according to risk of recidivism: Predictive validity, race/ethnicity, and gender. *Criminal Justice and Behavior*, 33, 305–324.

Smith, P., Cullen, F.T., & Latessa, E.J. (2009). Can 14,737 women be wrong? A meta-analysis of the LSI-R and recidivism for female offenders. *Criminology and Public Policy*, 8, 183–208.

Teplin, L., Abram K., McClelland, G., Dulcan, M., & Mericle, A. (2002). Psychiatric disorders in youth and juvenile detention. *Archives of General Psychiatry*, 59, 1133–1143.

Thornberry, T.P. (2005). Explaining multiple patterns of offending across the life course and across generations. *Annals of the American Academy of Political and Social Science*, 602, 156–195.

Thornberry, T.P., & Krohn, M.D. (2003). (Eds.). *Taking stock of delinquency: An overview of findings from contemporary longitudinal studies*. New York: Kluwer/Plenum.

Upperton, R, A., & Thompson, A.P. (2007). Predicting juvenile offender recidivism: Risk-need assessment and juvenile justice officers. *Psychiatry, Psychology and Law*, 14, 138–146.

Vincent, G.M., Chapman, J., & Cook, N.E. (2005). Risk/needs assessment in juvenile justice: Predictive validity of the SAVRY, racial differences, and contributions of needs factors. *Criminal Justice and Behavior*, 32, 42–62

Vincent, G.M., Fusco, S.L., Gershenson, B.G. & Guy, L.S., (2010). Secondary analyses for the prediction and assessment of early adult criminal activity. Unpublished report to the National Institute of Justice.

Vincent, G.M., Grisso, T., Terry, A., & Banks, S. (2008). Gender and race differences in mental health symptoms in juvenile justice. *Journal of the American Academy of Child and Adolescent Psychiatry, 47*, 282–290.

Vincent, G.M., Odgers, C.L., McCormick, A., & Corrado, R.R. (2008). The PCL:YV and recidivism in male and female juveniles: A follow-up into young adulthood. *International Journal of Law and Psychiatry, 31*, 287–296.

Vincent, G.M., Quinlan, J. C, Nitschelm, S., & Ogloff, J.R.P. (2003, April). Differential recidivism prediction by mental disorder. Paper presented at the 2003 annual conference of the International Association of Forensic Mental Health Services, Miami, FL.

Vincent, G.M., Terry, A., & Maney, S. (2009). Risk/needs tools for antisocial behavior and violence among youthful populations. In J. Andrade (Ed.), *Handbook of violence risk assessment and treatment for forensic mental health practitioners* (pp. 337–424). New York: Springer.

Walters, G. (2006). Risk-appraisal versus self-report in the prediction of criminal justice outcomes: A meta-analysis. *Criminal Justice and Behavior, 33*, 279–304.

Washington State Institute for Public Policy. (March, 2004). *Assessing risk for re-offense: Validating the Washington State Juvenile Court Assessment* (Document No. 04-03-1201). Olympia, WA: WSIPP.

Wasserman, G., McReynolds, L., Lucas, C., Fisher, P., & Santos L. (2002). The Voice DISC-IV with incarcerated male youths: Prevalence of disorder. *Journal of the American Academy of Child & Adolescent Psychiatry, 41*, 314–321.

Webster, C.D., Douglas, K., Eaves, D. & Hart, S. (1997). *HCR-20: Assessing risk for violence, Version 2*. Burnaby, BC: Simon Fraser University.

Welsh, J., Schmidt, F., McKinnon, L., Chattha, H., & Meyers, J. (2008). A comparative study of adolescent risk assessment instruments: Predictive and incremental validity. *Assessment, 15*, 104–115.

Wormith, J.S., & Goldstone, C.S. (1984). The clinical and statistical prediction of recidivism. *Criminal Justice and Behavior, 11*, 3–34.

7 }

Legal Boundaries Between the Juvenile and Criminal Justice Systems in the United States

Patrick Griffin

In responding to law-violating behavior, every U.S. state[1] distinguishes between juveniles and adults. Each state maintains one court and correctional system for juveniles, and another for adults. And each state sets limits on eligibility for juvenile handling—boundaries where childhood ends and adult criminal responsibility begins. But no two states draw these boundaries in precisely the same way.

States draw their juvenile-adult boundaries by means of three basic types of laws:

- *Jurisdictional age* laws set general upper-age limits to the original jurisdiction of juvenile courts. They may also set age-determined limits on juvenile courts' retention of authority over individuals already under their jurisdiction.
- *Transfer* laws in all states provide for exceptions to the general jurisdictional age rules—allowing or requiring certain categories of juvenile-age offenders to be prosecuted "as adults" in criminal court.
- In some states, *blended sentencing* laws further complicate the juvenile-adult boundaries. Some of these laws provide juvenile courts with criminal sentencing powers. Others allow criminal courts dealing with juvenile-age offenders to impose sanctions in the juvenile correctional system.

Jurisdictional Age Boundaries

In most states, the upper age of delinquency jurisdiction is 17—meaning that youth accused of violating the law before turning 18 come under the original jurisdiction of the juvenile courts, while those accused of violating the law on or after their 18th birthdays are handled in criminal courts. But a substantial minority

TABLE 7.1 } Upper age of original juvenile court jurisdiction.

State	Age 15	Age 16	Age 17	State	Age 15	Age 16	Age 17
Alabama			▪	Montana			▪
Alaska			▪	Nebraska			▪
Arizona			▪	Nevada			▪
Arkansas			▪	New Hampshire		▪	
California			▪	New Jersey			▪
Colorado			▪	New Mexico			▪
Connecticut*			▪	New York	▪		
Delaware			▪	North Carolina	▪		
District of Columbia			▪	North Dakota			▪
Florida			▪	Ohio			▪
Georgia		▪		Oklahoma			▪
Hawaii			▪	Oregon			▪
Idaho			▪	Pennsylvania			▪
Illinois**		▪		Rhode Island			▪
Indiana			▪	South Carolina		▪	
Iowa			▪	South Dakota			▪
Kansas			▪	Tennessee			▪
Kentucky			▪	Texas		▪	
Louisiana		▪		Utah			▪
Maine			▪	Vermont			▪
Maryland			▪	Virginia			▪
Massachusetts		▪		Washington			▪
Michigan		▪		West Virginia			▪
Minnesota			▪	Wisconsin		▪	
Mississippi			▪	Wyoming			▪
Missouri		▪					

Note: Table information is as of the end of the 2009 legislative session.

* Connecticut's upper age of original jurisdiction is being raised in stages from 15 to 17, with the transition to be completed by 2012.

** In Illinois, the upper age rose from 16 to 17 for those accused of misdemeanors only, effective 2010.

have an upper age of 16—meaning that they hold all 17-year-old offenders criminally responsible—and a few have an upper age of 15 (Table 7.1). Generally, for purposes of determining whether a youth is to be handled as a juvenile or an adult, the age that counts is the age at the time of the offense.

Laws drawing bright-line age boundaries between the juvenile and adult systems do not necessarily erase all age-based distinctions among those on the

TABLE 7.2   }   Age limits on retention of juvenile court jurisdiction.

State	Prior to 21st birthday	21st birthday	Beyond 21st birthday	State	Prior to 21st birthday	21st birthday	Beyond 21st birthday
Alabama		▪		Montana			▪
Alaska	▪			Nebraska	▪		
Arizona		▪		Nevada		▪	
Arkansas		▪		New Hampshire		▪	
California			▪	New Jersey			▪
Colorado			▪	New Mexico		▪	
Connecticut		▪		New York		▪	
Delaware		▪		North Carolina		▪	
District of Columbia		▪		North Dakota	▪		
Florida			▪	Ohio		▪	
Georgia		▪		Oklahoma	▪		
Hawaii			▪	Oregon			▪
Idaho		▪		Pennsylvania		▪	
Illinois		▪		Rhode Island*	▪		
Indiana		▪		South Carolina		▪	
Iowa	▪			South Dakota		▪	
Kansas			▪	Tennessee	▪		
Kentucky	▪			Texas		▪	
Louisiana		▪		Utah		▪	
Maine		▪		Vermont**		▪	
Maryland		▪		Virginia		▪	
Massachusetts		▪		Washington		▪	
Michigan		▪		West Virginia		▪	
Minnesota		▪		Wisconsin			▪
Mississippi	▪			Wyoming		▪	
Missouri		▪					

Note: Extended jurisdiction may be restricted to certain offenses or juveniles. Table information is as of the end of the 2009 legislative session.

* In 2007, Rhode Island lowered its jurisdictional retention limit from the 21st to the 19th birthday.

** In 2008, Vermont raised its jurisdictional retention limit for certain juveniles from the 18th to the 21st birthday.

adult side of the line. Many states have ameliorative sentencing provisions, special holding or programming requirements, or separate correctional institutions for young adult offenders.

Laws that set an upper age limit to the original jurisdiction of juvenile courts must be distinguished from laws that dictate how long juvenile courts may retain jurisdiction over delinquent youth already under their supervision. In most states, a juvenile court may continue to exercise dispositional jurisdiction over an adjudicated youth until the youth reaches age 21 (Table 7.2).

Transfer Boundaries

In addition to general jurisdictional age boundaries between the juvenile and adult justice systems, all states have transfer laws that alter these boundaries in exceptional cases, and allow or require criminal prosecution of some offenders who would otherwise fall on the juvenile side of the jurisdictional age line.

Transfer laws could be found in some of the earliest juvenile codes. In the last three decades of the 20th century, however, they became far more sweeping in their coverage and inflexible in their operation.

Transfer Mechanisms

There are three basic kinds of transfer law. All states now have one or another of these kinds of laws, and most have more than one kind (Table 7.3).

- *Judicial waiver laws* allow juvenile courts to waive jurisdiction over individual cases. A case subject to waiver begins in juvenile court, and may be transferred only after a judge's approval, based on articulated standards, following a formal hearing. While all states set minimum thresholds for waiver and prescribe standards that must be consulted in waiver decision-making, most leave the waiver decision largely to the judge's discretion. However, some set up presumptions in favor of waiver in certain classes of cases, and some even specify circumstances under which waiver is mandatory.
- *Statutory exclusion laws* grant criminal courts exclusive original jurisdiction over cases meeting certain statutorily defined age/offense thresholds. If a case comes within a statutory exclusion category, it must be filed originally in criminal court.
- *Prosecutorial discretion* or *concurrent jurisdiction laws* define a class of cases in which prosecutors may decide whether to proceed in juvenile or criminal court. No hearing is held to determine the appropriate forum, and there may be no formal standards for deciding between them.

There are two other common kinds of laws that serve to regulate movement across transfer boundaries in many states:

- "Once an adult/always an adult" laws mandate criminal handling for accused juveniles who have been criminally prosecuted in the past, regardless of the seriousness of the current offense.
- Reverse waiver laws allow juveniles whose cases are in criminal court to petition to have them transferred to juvenile court.

TABLE 7.3 } Transfer mechanisms.

State	Judicial Waiver			Prosecutorial Discretion	Statutory Exclusion	Reverse Waiver	Once an Adult Always an Adult
	Discretionary	Presumptive	Mandatory				
Number of states	45	15	15	15	29	24	34
Alabama	■				■		■
Alaska	■	■			■		
Arizona	■			■	■	■	■
Arkansas	■			■		■	
California	■	■		■	■	■	■
Colorado	■	■		■		■	
Connecticut			■			■	
Delaware	■		■		■	■	■
Dist. of Columbia	■	■		■			■
Florida	■			■	■		■
Georgia	■		■	■	■	■	
Hawaii	■						■
Idaho	■				■		■
Illinois	■	■	■		■		■
Indiana	■		■		■		■
Iowa	■				■	■	■
Kansas	■	■					■
Kentucky	■		■			■	
Louisiana	■		■	■	■		
Maine	■	■					■
Maryland	■				■	■	■
Massachusetts					■		
Michigan	■			■			■
Minnesota	■	■			■		■
Mississippi	■				■	■	■
Missouri	■						■
Montana				■	■	■	
Nebraska				■		■	
Nevada	■	■			■	■	■
New Hampshire	■	■					■
New Jersey	■	■	■				
New Mexico					■		
New York					■	■	
North Carolina	■		■				■
North Dakota	■	■	■				■
Ohio	■		■				■
Oklahoma	■			■	■	■	■
Oregon	■				■	■	■
Pennsylvania	■	■			■	■	■

TABLE 7.3 (*continued*)

State	Judicial Waiver			Prosecutorial Discretion	Statutory Exclusion	Reverse Waiver	Once an Adult Always an Adult
	Discretionary	Presumptive	Mandatory				
Rhode Island	■	■	■				■
South Carolina	■		■		■		
South Dakota	■				■	■	■
Tennessee	■					■	■
Texas	■						■
Utah	■	■			■		■
Vermont	■			■	■	■	
Virginia	■		■	■		■	■
Washington	■				■		■
West Virginia	■		■				
Wisconsin	■				■	■	■
Wyoming	■			■		■	

Note: Table information is as of the end of the 2009 legislative session.

Transfer Thresholds

Judicial waiver. Judicial waiver is the oldest and still the most common form of transfer law, but it is no longer the sole means by which juvenile-age offenders reach criminal court in most of the country. In comparison with other transfer mechanisms, judicial waiver procedures are both individualized and transparent, but they are also time- and resource-intensive.

A total of 45 states have *discretionary waiver laws* designating a class of cases in which waiver of jurisdiction may be considered, generally on the prosecutor's motion (Table 7.4). Most states set a minimum threshold for waiver-eligibility—generally a minimum age, a specified type or level of offense, and/or a sufficiently serious record of previous delinquency—but it is often quite low. In a few states, prosecutors may ask the court to waive virtually any juvenile delinquency case. As a practical matter, however, even in these states, waiver proceedings are likely to be relatively rare. Nationally, the proportion of juvenile cases in which prosecutors *seek* waiver is not known, but waiver is *granted* in less than 1% of petitioned delinquency cases (Adams & Addie, 2009).

Presumptive waiver laws in 15 states designate a category of cases in which waiver to criminal court must be presumed appropriate (Table 7.5). A juvenile meeting age, offense, or other statutory thresholds triggering presumptive waiver must rebut the presumption in favor of transfer, or the case will be sent to criminal court.

Mandatory waiver laws in 15 states *require* juvenile courts to transfer certain kinds of cases for criminal prosecution (Table 7.6). Proceedings against juveniles meeting criteria for mandatory waiver must be initiated in juvenile court, but the transfer outcome in such cases is automatic. At most, the juvenile court's role is to

TABLE 7.4 } Discretionary waiver thresholds.

State	Any Criminal Offense	Certain Felonies	Capital Crimes	Murder	Certain Person Offenses	Certain Property Offenses	Certain Drug Offenses	Certain Weapon Offenses
Alabama	14							
Alaska	NS							
Arizona		NS						
Arkansas		14	14	14	14			14
California	16							
Colorado		12		12	12			
Delaware	NS							
Dist. of Columbia	16	15						NS
Florida	14							
Georgia	15		13		13			
Hawaii		14		NS				
Idaho	14	NS		NS	NS	NS	NS	
Illinois	13							
Indiana		14		10			16	
Iowa	14							
Kansas	10							
Kentucky		14	14					
Louisiana				14	14			
Maine		NS						
Maryland	15		NS					
Michigan		14						
Minnesota		14						
Mississippi	13							
Missouri		12						
Nevada		14						
New Hampshire	15			13	13			
New Jersey	14			14	14	14	14	14
North Carolina		13						
North Dakota	16				14			
Ohio		14						
Oklahoma		NS						
Oregon		15		NS	NS	15		
Pennsylvania		14						
Rhode Island	16		NS					
South Carolina	16	14		NS	NS		14	14
South Dakota	NS							
Tennessee	16			NS	NS			
Texas		14	14				14	

TABLE 7.4   (*continued*)

State	Any Criminal Offense	Certain Felonies	Capital Crimes	Murder	Certain Person Offenses	Certain Property Offenses	Certain Drug Offenses	Certain Weapon Offenses
Utah		14						
Vermont				10	10	10		
Virginia		14						
Washington	NS							
West Virginia		NS		NS	NS	NS	NS	
Wisconsin	15	14		14	14	14	14	
Wyoming	13							

Notes: An entry in the column below an offense category means that there is some offense or offenses in that category for which a juvenile may be waived for criminal prosecution. The number indicates the youngest possible age at which a juvenile accused of an offense in that category may be waived. "NS" means no age restriction is specified for an offense in that category. Table information is as of the end of the 2009 legislative session.

make a probable cause determination, and perhaps issue preliminary orders related to pre-trial holding, appointment of counsel, and so on, before transferring the case to criminal court. Because a mandatory waiver law functions like a statutory exclusion, removing a predetermined category of cases from juvenile court jurisdiction, age/offense/prior record thresholds for mandatory waiver tend, like exclusion thresholds, to be higher.

Statutory exclusion. A total of 29 states have *statutory exclusion laws*, limiting the juvenile court's original jurisdiction in such a way as to leave out certain kinds of cases involving juvenile-age offenders (Table 7.7). Typically, the term "delinquency" is defined to exclude certain offenses or age/offense/prior record combinations. Because accused juveniles in such cases are outside the juvenile court's original jurisdiction, they are instead handled in criminal court. When the states that legislatively exclude a class of offenders from juvenile court jurisdiction are combined with those that *mandate* judicial waiver in some cases (as described above), the resulting total is 38 states that provide for "automatic transfers."

Prosecutorial discretion. Prosecutorial discretion or concurrent jurisdiction laws in 15 states define a category of cases in which both criminal and juvenile courts are given jurisdiction, each concurrent with the other (Table 7.8). In such cases, it is up to prosecutors to decide whether to proceed initially in juvenile or criminal court. Generally, the choice is entirely discretionary—few states make any effort to guide or limit prosecutors' decisions, or to specify any general principle or specific factors to be considered. Because no hearing is held and no evidentiary record created, defendants have no opportunity to test the basis for prosecutors' decisions or to present counter-evidence of their own. And afterwards, there is nothing to review to determine whether decisions were made appropriately. As a result, prosecutorial discretion laws in some places may operate more like statutory exclusions, sweeping wholesale categories of cases into criminal court, with little or no individualized consideration.

TABLE 7.5 } Presumptive waiver thresholds.

State	Any Criminal Offense	Certain Felonies	Capital Crimes	Murder	Certain Person Offenses	Certain Property Offenses	Certain Drug Offenses	Certain Weapon Offenses
Alaska					NS			
California		14		14	14	14	14	
Colorado*		12		12	12			
Dist. of Columbia**	15			15	15	15		
Illinois		15					15	
Kansas**	14	14			14		14	
Maine				NS	NS			
Minnesota		16						
Nevada**	14				14			
New Hampshire	15			15	15		15	
New Jersey		14		14	14	14	14	14
North Dakota		14		14	14		14	
Pennsylvania				14	14			
Rhode Island*	NS							
Utah		16		16	16	16		16

Notes: An entry in the column below an offense category means that there is some offense or offenses in that category for which a juvenile is presumed to be an appropriate candidate for waiver to criminal court. The number indicates the youngest possible age at which a juvenile accused of an offense in that category is subject to the presumption. "NS" means no age restriction is attached to the presumption for an offense in that category. Table information is as of the end of the 2009 legislative session.

* In Colorado and Rhode Island, the presumption is applied against juveniles with certain kinds of previous histowries.

** In the District of Columbia, Kansas, and Nevada, the presumption applies to any offense committed with a firearm.

In all, 44 states have laws—including prosecutorial discretion, statutory exclusion and/or mandatory waiver laws—that either dictate criminal handling of certain defined categories of juvenile offenders, or else place decisions about that handling solely in the hands of prosecutors.

Juvenile Blended Sentencing

Although they do not provide for the criminal *prosecution* of juveniles, *juvenile blended sentencing laws* bear a functional resemblance to transfer laws in that they expose some categories of serious juvenile offenders to criminal *penalties*. A total of 14 states empower their juvenile courts to impose criminal sanctions under some circumstances (Table 7.9). The most common type of juvenile blended sentencing scheme allows juvenile court judges to impose both juvenile and suspended adult sanctions on certain categories of offenders. A juvenile subject to

TABLE 7.6 } Mandatory waiver thresholds.

State	Certain Felonies	Capital Crimes	Murder	Certain Person Offenses	Certain Property Offenses	Certain Drug Offenses	Certain Weapon Offenses
Connecticut	14	14	14				
Delaware	15		NS	NS	16	16	
Georgia			14	14	15		
Illinois	15						
Indiana	NS					16	
Kentucky	14						
Louisiana			15	15			
New Jersey	16		16	16	16	16	16
North Carolina		13					
North Dakota			14	14		14	
Ohio	14		14	16	16		
Rhode Island			17	17			
South Carolina	14						
Virginia			14	14			
West Virginia	14		14	14	14		

Notes: An entry in the column below an offense category means that there is some offense or offenses in that category for which waiver to criminal court is mandatory. The number indicates the youngest possible age at which a juvenile accused of an offense in that category is subject to mandatory waiver. "NS" means no age restriction is specified for an offense in that category. Table information is as of the end of the 2009 legislative session.

such a combination sentence remains in the juvenile correctional system only conditionally, with a criminal sentence dangling overhead as a way of encouraging cooperation and discouraging future misconduct.

Age, offense, and prior record criteria qualifying juveniles for blended sentencing treatment are similar to—but generally broader than—criteria for transfer to criminal court. Although they remain in juvenile court, juveniles subject to blended sentencing are entitled to the basic procedural rights afforded to criminal defendants, including at a minimum the right to be tried by a jury, and often the right to be indicted by a grand jury as well.

Individualized Judicial Corrective Mechanisms

Even juveniles subject to automatic or prosecutor-controlled transfer mechanisms may be afforded a chance, at some point in the process, to make an individualized showing that they belong in the juvenile system. There are two kinds of judicial

TABLE 7.7 } Statutory exclusion thresholds.

State	Any Criminal Offense	Certain Felonies	Capital Crimes	Murder	Certain Person Offenses	Certain Property Offenses	Certain Drug Offenses	Certain Weapon Offenses
Alabama		16	16				16	
Alaska					16	16		
Arizona		15		15	15			
California				14	14			
Delaware		15						
Florida				16	NS	16	16	
Georgia				13	13			
Idaho				14	14	14	14	
Illinois		15		13	15			15
Indiana		16		16	16		16	16
Iowa		16					16	16
Louisiana				15	15			
Maryland			14	16	16			16
Massachu-setts				14				
Minnesota				16				
Mississippi		13	13					
Montana				17	17	17	17	17
Nevada	16*	NS		NS	16			
New Mexico				15				
New York				13	13	14		14
Oklahoma				13				
Oregon				15	15			
Pennsylva-nia				NS	15			
South Carolina		16						
South Dakota		16						
Utah		16		16				
Vermont				14	14	14		
Washington				16	16	16		
Wisconsin				10	10			

Note: An entry in the column below an offense category means that there is some offense or offenses in that category that is excluded from juvenile court jurisdiction. The number indicates the youngest possible age at which a juvenile accused of an offense in that category is subject to exclusion. "NS" means no age restriction is specified for an offense in that category. Table information is as of the end of the 2009 legislative session.

* In Nevada, the exclusion applies to any juvenile with previous felony adjudication, regardless of the current offense charged, if the current offense involves the use or threatened use of a firearm.

TABLE 7.8 } Prosecutorial discretion thresholds.

State	Any Criminal Offense	Certain Felonies	Capital Crimes	Murder	Certain Person Offenses	Certain Property Offenses	Certain Drug Offenses	Certain Weapon Offenses
Arizona		14						
Arkansas		16	14	14	14			
California		14	14	14	14	14	14	
Colorado		14		14	14	14		14
Dist. of Columbia				16	16	16		
Florida	16	16	NS	14	14	14		14
Georgia			NS					
Louisiana				15	15	15	15	
Michigan		14		14	14	14	14	
Montana				12	12	16	16	16
Nebraska	16	NS						
Oklahoma		16		15	15	15	16	15
Vermont	16							
Virginia				14	14			
Wyoming	13	14		14	14	14		

Notes: An entry in the column below an offense category means that there is some offense or offenses in that category that is subject to criminal prosecution at the option of the prosecutor. The number indicates the youngest possible age at which a juvenile accused of an offense in that category is subject to criminal prosecution. "NS" means no age restriction is specified for an offense in that category. Table information is as of the end of the 2009 legislative session.

corrective or "fail-safe" mechanisms that serve to inject individualized consideration into what would otherwise be automatic or inflexible transfer processes. *Reverse waiver laws* permit criminal courts to restore transferred youth to juvenile court for trial or disposition. *Criminal blended sentencing laws* authorize criminal courts to impose juvenile dispositions rather than criminal ones in sentencing transferred youth.

A total of 24 states have reverse waiver laws that allow juveniles subject to prosecution in criminal court to petition to have their cases transferred to juvenile court (Table 7.10). Generally, in such cases the criminal court is guided by the same kinds of broad standards and considerations as a juvenile court in a waiver proceeding. In most cases, the reverse waiver hearing is held prior to trial, and if the reverse waiver is granted, the case is adjudicated in juvenile court. But sometimes the offender's guilt must be established first, and reverse waiver is for disposition purposes only.

A total of 18 states have criminal blended sentencing laws, authorizing criminal courts to sentence juveniles who have been tried and convicted as adults to supervision, treatment, and rehabilitative programs available only in the juvenile system (Table 7.10). In other words, while the youth may have been *convicted* as an adult,

TABLE 7.9 } Juvenile blended sentencing age thresholds.

State	Any Criminal Offense	Certain Felonies	Capital Crimes	Murder	Certain Person Offenses	Certain Property Offenses	Certain Drug Offenses	Certain Weapon Offenses
Alaska					16			
Arkansas		14		NS	14			14
Colorado		NS			NS			
Connecti-cut		14			NS			
Illinois		13						
Kansas	10							
Mas-sachusetts		14			14			14
Michigan	NS	NS		NS	NS	NS	NS	
Minnesota		14						
Montana		12		NS	NS	NS	NS	NS
New Mexico		14		14	14	14		
Ohio		10		10				
Rhode Island		NS						
Texas		NS		NS	NS		NS	

Notes: Numbers represent the youngest possible age at which juvenile blended sentences may be imposed for offenses in each category. "NS" indicates that in at least one of the offense restrictions indicated, no minimum age is specified. Table information is as of the end of the 2009 legislative session.

he or she will be *sanctioned* as a juvenile. The juvenile disposition may be imposed by itself or in combination with a suspended criminal sentence to ensure cooperation with the dispositional program.

A total of 15 states have no fail-safe laws at all, though juveniles in these states may either be categorically excluded from juvenile court jurisdiction or subject to criminal handling at the unreviewable discretion of prosecutors. In 14 other states, fail-safe mechanisms either are not available in every case subject to categorical transfer rules, or else restrict judges' authority to make individual exceptions to those rules (Table 7.10).

Summary and Conclusions

Across the United States, a complex patchwork of jurisdictional age, transfer, and blended sentencing laws determines where, in any given place, the juvenile justice system leaves off and the adult criminal justice system begins. Transfer laws, which provide for offense-based exceptions to the usual age rules for determining responsibility for criminal acts, vary considerably from state to state, but

TABLE 7.10 } Individualized Judicial Corrective Mechanisms.

State	Automatic ProsecutorControlled Transfer	Reverse Waiver Available	Criminal Blended Sentencing Available	Not Available in All Cases	No Judicial Corrective Available
Number of States	44	24	18	15	14
Alabama	▪				▪
Alaska	▪				▪
Arizona	▪	▪		▪	
Arkansas	▪	▪	▪		
California	▪	▪	▪	▪	
Colorado	▪	▪	▪		
Connecticut	▪	▪		▪	
Delaware	▪	▪			
Dist. of Columbia	▪				▪
Florida	▪		▪	▪	
Georgia	▪	▪		▪	
Idaho	▪		▪		
Illinois	▪		▪	▪	
Indiana	▪				▪
Iowa	▪	▪	▪		
Kentucky	▪	▪	▪	▪	
Louisiana	▪				▪
Maryland	▪	▪		▪	
Massachusetts	▪		▪	▪	
Michigan	▪		▪	▪	
Minnesota	▪				▪
Mississippi	▪	▪			
Missouri			▪		
Montana	▪	▪			
Nebraska	▪	▪	▪		
Nevada	▪	▪		▪	
New Jersey	▪				▪
New Mexico	▪		▪	▪	
New York	▪	▪		▪	
North Carolina	▪				▪
North Dakota	▪				▪
Ohio	▪				▪
Oklahoma	▪	▪	▪		
Oregon	▪	▪		▪	
Pennsylvania	▪	▪			
Rhode Island	▪				▪
South Carolina	▪				▪
South Dakota	▪	▪			
Tennessee		▪			

(*continued*)

TABLE 7.10 *(continued)*

State	Automatic ProsecutorControlled Transfer	Reverse Waiver Available	Criminal Blended Sentencing Available	Not Available in All Cases	No Judicial Corrective Available
Utah	▪				▪
Vermont	▪	▪	▪		
Virginia	▪	▪	▪	▪	
Washington	▪				▪
West Virginia	▪		▪		
Wisconsin	▪	▪	▪		
Wyoming	▪	▪			

Note: Table information is as of the end of the 2009 legislative session.

collectively form a very prominent feature of America's approach to serious juvenile offending. In recent decades transfer laws have become far more common, more sweeping in their coverage, and more automatic in their operation. A total of 44 states now have laws that either dictate criminal handling of certain kinds of juvenile offenders, or allow prosecutors unfettered discretion to opt for such handling. While states with automatic, inflexible, or prosecutor-driven transfer laws often retain some sort of corrective mechanism to ensure individualized judicial consideration of the appropriateness of criminal handling, a substantial minority do not, and others restrict judicial review so that it is not available in all cases subject to transfer.

Research recommendations. More research on the criminal justice processing of juvenile-age offenders in the United States is urgently needed. There are currently no national datasets tracking youth who are prosecuted and sanctioned as adults, and state reporting in this area is inconsistent and incomplete. As a result, the most basic questions about the operation of these laws—including the total number of young people affected, their offenses, their ages and other demographic characteristics, the way their cases are handled, the kinds of sentences they receive, and their post-sentencing outcomes—cannot now be answered. Practitioners and researchers are unable to test the assumptions behind the laws, and policy-makers and the public lack information with which to judge their workings and effectiveness.

One part of the solution would be an improved national data collection effort capable of yielding reliable national estimates regarding criminally processed youth in general. But improved research and reporting at the state level is clearly needed as well in order to inform comparisons of the operation and impact of individual state transfer, blended sentencing, and jurisdictional age laws.

Policy recommendations. Our ignorance regarding the actual workings of transfer laws should give us pause. There is a substantial likelihood that many of these laws are not working fairly, not working as originally intended, or quite simply not working—especially in view of the available research, which has for the most part failed to establish the effectiveness of transfer laws in deterring youth crime generally, or in reducing the likelihood that transferred youth will commit further crimes. At the very least, states should be considering ways of narrowing the scope of laws that expose broad categories of young offenders to criminal prosecution, providing more safeguards to prevent unforeseen and unintended results, and introducing more flexibility and transparency into the process in order to ensure that an individual youth's history and background, degree of culpability, treatment and service needs, and amenability to rehabilitation are appropriately taken into account in transfer decision-making.

Note

1. For purposes of this discussion, the term "states" includes the District of Columbia. Except where otherwise noted, state laws summarized here are as amended through 2009.

References

Adams, B., & Addie, S. (June 2009). "Delinquency Cases Waived to Criminal Court, 2005." *OJJDP Fact Sheet*. Washington, DC: U.S. Department of Justice, Office of Justice Programs, Office of Juvenile Justice and Delinquency Prevention.

8

Young Offenders and an Effective Justice System Response

WHAT HAPPENS, WHAT SHOULD HAPPEN, AND WHAT WE NEED TO KNOW

James C. Howell, Barry C. Feld, and Daniel P. Mears

For the juvenile and criminal justice systems in the United States, the past half century was a tumultuous period. Beginning in the 1960s, the national crime rate sharply increased, prompting some criminologists to join with political forces to reject the rehabilitative ideal in favor of a "justice model" that would limit corrections officials' discretion with offenders and institute due process rights and determinate sentencing. This pendulum swing from treatment to punishment was buttressed by a negative review of program evaluations in juvenile and criminal justice systems. Some analysts warned of a coming generation of juvenile "superpredators" that was projected to occur between about 1995 and 2010.

Although this dire prediction never materialized, the more punitive philosophy of the criminal justice system filtered down to the juvenile justice system and ushered in significant changes in the boundaries of the juvenile justice system and in policies and procedures for handling juvenile offenders within it. Large numbers of juvenile offenders have been removed from the juvenile justice system and placed in the criminal justice system. Blended sentence provisions have been enacted into law along with offense-based determinant and mandatory minimum sentences. Punitive measures are used more widely than ever before. New laws have designated more juveniles as serious offenders, brought more minor offenders into the system, and extended periods of confinement in juvenile correctional facilities.

The period of overreaction to juvenile crime appears to be coming to a close. Both the juvenile and criminal justice systems are returning to an emphasis on rehabilitation and evidence-based practices. Moreover, there is considerable optimism that we can hold juveniles accountable, manage the risks they pose to others, and provide them with "room to reform" without "permanently damaging their lives."

Against this backdrop, we examine juvenile and criminal justice policies and practices with respect to young offenders who cross over from the juvenile to the criminal justice system. We divide this chapter into four sections. In the first, we discuss differences between the juvenile and adult justice system responses to juveniles, inconsistencies in both the juvenile and criminal justice systems, actual versus ideal justice system responses to young offenders, and the effectiveness of these responses. The second section considers key contextual factors and special considerations when deciding how to respond to young offenders. In the third, we discuss effective programs, and we follow this with highlighted research gaps. The chapter concludes with the presentation of a range of critical policy recommendations.

Intended Versus Actual Justice System Responses to Young Offenders

The shift from rehabilitative to punitive justice policies. During most of the twentieth century, state sentencing policies were primarily offender-oriented and based on a rehabilitative model of individualized sentencing (Tonry, 2009; Warren, 2007). Beginning in the 1960s, the national crime rate increased sharply. At the same time, evaluations of correctional interventions during the rehabilitative period claimed that "nothing works" (Lipton, Martinson, & Wilks, 1975; Martinson, 1974) and cast a negative shadow over therapeutic criminal and juvenile justice policy and practice (Garland 2001; Tonry 2004). This assessment led the federal government and many states to turn to offense-based sentencing policies and to embrace more punitive measures. Martinson's (1974) conclusion—'"with few isolated exceptions, the rehabilitative efforts that have been reported so far have no appreciable effect on recidivism'" (p. 25)—provided a critical foundation from which to advocate such changes. The claim that "nothing works" persisted throughout the 1970s and 1980s until sophisticated scholars used advanced analytical tools to examine the evidence to date. The results refuted Martinson's negative assessment and showed that well-implemented rehabilitative programs can substantially reduce recidivism (Cullen, 2005; Lipsey & Cullen, 2007).

The pendulum swing from treatment to punishment filtered down from the criminal justice to the juvenile justice system (Feld, 1988; Howell, 2003b). Two compelling images in the 1990s buttressed policies to enhance punishment of juvenile offenders. First, as mentioned, analysts warned of a coming generation of juvenile "superpredators" (DiIulio, 1995a) whom they characterized as a "new breed" of cold-blooded killers (DiIulio, 1995b, p. 23). Second, DiIulio and Wilson predicted a new "wave" of juvenile violence to occur between about 1995 and 2010, which they based in part on a projected increase in the under age 18 population (DiIulio, 1996, 1997; Wilson, 1995). The sharp increase in adolescent and young adult homicides in the late 1980s and early 1990s (Blumstein, 1995a, 1995b; Cook & Laub, 1998; Fox, 1996) was tied to the presumed new wave of juvenile "superpredators." Such dire warnings, which helped to promote punitive policies, rested on three assumptions: that the relative proportion of serious and violent offenders among all juvenile delinquents was growing; that juvenile offenders were becoming younger and younger; and that juveniles were committing more and more violent crimes.

None of these assumptions proved to be correct. Several researchers have debunked the superpredator myth and doomsday projections (Howell, 2003b, 2009; Males, 1996; Snyder, 1998; Snyder & Sickmund, 2000; Zimring, 1998). A new wave of minority superpredators did not develop, nor did a general wave of juvenile violence occur. To be sure, rates of violent juvenile behavior increased in some cities in the 1980s and early 1990s, including Pittsburgh (Loeber, Farrington, Stouthamer-Loeber, White, & Wei, 2008) and Denver (Huizinga, Weiher, Espiritu, & Esbensen, 2003). However, analysis of national self-report and victimization data showed that the anticipated increase in juvenile violence was exaggerated (Howell, 2009, pp. 39–55). Because of juveniles' low base rate of serious and violent crime, the "tyranny of small numbers" affects analyses and interpretations of serious juvenile violence (Snyder, Sickmund, & Poe-Yamagata, 1996). When a small increase occurs in a small number of cases, it appears as a large percentage increase. Even at the height of the juvenile crime increase (1993), "only about 6% of all juvenile arrests were for violent crimes and less than one-tenth of one percent of their arrests were for homicides" (McCord, Widom, & Crowell, 2001, p. 33).

The one notable exception that provided some support for the doomsday predictions involved homicide. From the mid-1980s to the early-1990s, there was an increase in homicide involving firearms that involved both juveniles and young adults (Cook & Laub, 1998). However, the biggest absolute change was for young adults (p. 60). Studies conducted by the National Center for Juvenile Justice have shown that adults, not juveniles, accounted for two-thirds of the increase in murders in the late 1980s and early 1990s, and that the adults were responsible for nearly three-fourths of the increase in violent crime arrests during this period (Snyder et al., 1996, p. 20). Public policy analysts and the research communities attribute the dramatic growth in homicide largely to the availability of firearms—primarily handguns—the recruitment of young people into illicit drug markets (Decker, 2007; Blumstein, 1995b), and, more importantly, increased gang homicide (Howell, 1999; Howell & Decker, 1999).

Scholars have offered several explanations for the adoption of extremely punitive crime and delinquency policies and practices in the United States that began in the 1970s (cf. Beckett & Sasson, 2003; Bishop, 2006; Cullen, 2005; Feld, 1999; Feld, 2003; Garland, 2001; Mears, 2006; Tonry, 2009). Martinson's (1974) negative assessment of the effectiveness of rehabilitation provided one impetus. In addition, arrest, prosecution, and confinement rates for juveniles and adults increased dramatically in the 1980s and 1990s, driven by a succession of four domestic U.S. "wars": the "war on crime," the "war on drugs," the "war on gangs," and the "war on juveniles" (Howell, 2003b). The centerpiece of the war on drugs was the battle against the perceived crack cocaine epidemic (Brownstein, 1996; Hartman & Golub, 1999; Reeves & Campbell, 1994). According to these sources, no one has presented convincing empirical evidence that a nationwide crack cocaine epidemic in fact occurred (see also Howell, 2012). The mass media, politicians, and law enforcement attributed escalating violent youth crime to a gun violence and crack cocaine epidemic, a claim that fueled support for more punitive sentencing policies (Brownstein, 1996; Reeves & Campbell, 1994). Other scholars have argued that racial animus contributed to "get tough" policies in both the juvenile and criminal justice system (Feld, 1999; Tonry, 2009; Tonry & Melewski, 2008). In turn, such policies have contributed to disproportionate minority confinement (Feld, 1999; 2003; Snyder & Sickmund, 2006).

Inconsistencies in the juvenile and adult justice systems. By the end of the 1990s, all states had enacted laws to make their juvenile justice systems more punitive or eased transfer of more juveniles to the criminal justice system and to confine them in adult prisons (Howell, 2009, pp. 288–290). Juvenile courts designated larger proportions of juveniles as serious and violent offenders and incarcerated more juveniles. States abandoned rehabilitative programs and used boot camps—military-style regimented discipline, "Scared Straight" programs, and increased confinement in detention centers and juvenile reformatories (Males, 1996; Roush & McMillen, 2000).

Some observers erroneously declared that the rehabilitative mission of juvenile courts had "collapsed" (Scott & Steinberg, 2008, pp. 88–95). Although many state legislatures rewrote their juvenile codes to endorse punitive objectives in the 1990s, virtually all of them maintained allegiance to juvenile courts' traditional rehabilitative mission (Bishop, 2006; Tanenhaus, 2002, 2004). Bishop's review of laws enacted during 2003–2005 observed that "efforts are underway to mitigate or even abandon punitive features [of juvenile laws enacted in the past decade and] to address the treatment needs of most juvenile offenders" (p. 660; see also Butts & Mears, 2001).

By contrast, in the criminal justice system, retributive policies continue to predominate, as evidenced by the dramatic increase in persons under probation or parole supervision (Glaze & Palla, 2005), the growth of state prisons (Mears, 2008; Irwin, 2005) and supermax prisons (Mears, 2005). At the beginning of 2008, for the first time in our nation's history, one out of every 100 Americans was confined in state or federal prisons and jails and the U.S. incarceration rate was five or more times higher than in any other Western country (Tonry 2004; Tonry & Farrington 2005). The absence of a clear or consistent emphasis on rehabilitation or on evidence-based practices has led some scholars to observe that "what is done in corrections would be grounds for malpractice in medicine" (Latessa, Cullen, & Gendreau, 2002). Since 2000, 20 *Civil Rights of Institutionalized Persons Act* (42 U.S.C. § 1997a et seq.), investigations have been made of 23 juvenile justice facilities in more than a dozen states (U.S. Department of Justice, 2007).

Research consistently shows lower recidivism rates in the juvenile justice system than in the criminal justice system, but the prospect of released youth or adults going on to lead crime-free lives leaves considerable room for improvement. For example, one large-scale study found that 27% of released youth were readmitted within one year of their release; male readmission rates were much higher than for females (28% and 16%, respectively), and a strong relationship existed between prior correctional commitments and readmission rates (Krisberg & Howell, 1998). A recent survey of juvenile correctional administrative agencies (Virginia Department of Juvenile Justice, 2005), included 33 states. Some states measured recidivism by rearrests (nine states), others used reconvictions (12 states), and still others measured reincarceration (12 states). The average recidivism rates suggest room for improvement with this population: rearrests (57%), reconvictions (33%), and reincarceration (22%). Outcomes for adults are worse. About two-thirds of adult probationers commit other crimes within three years of their sentences, and many of them are serious (Manhattan Institute, 1999). Analysts report similar recidivism rates from prisons, with two-thirds of released prisoners rearrested within three years (Langan & Levin, 2002).

In sum, the shift from rehabilitative to punitive justice policies has not produced the anticipated results. Although offense-oriented sentencing policies did result in longer sentences for juvenile offenders, these did not lower recidivism, and they may well have produced an increase among juveniles sentenced to adult prisons where recidivism rates are higher. The next section explores in more detail the disjunction between ideal and actual juvenile justice practices.

Ideal versus actual responses to young offenders. As a result of the changes during the past 30 years, young people today face a bewildering and inconsistent array of juvenile and adult justice system responses. Broadly speaking, the juvenile justice system is tougher today than it was in the past, but it remains more rehabilitative than the adult justice system. As a result of inconsistencies in juvenile and criminal justice processing, whether youths receive treatment depends fortuitously on which system handles them. This creates a substantial disjunction between ideal and actual responses to young offenders. In what follows, we discuss some of the processing and sentencing decisions and policies that affect young people. The discussion serves (1) to illuminate the inconsistency in the processing and sentencing of young people, (2) to highlight the disjunction between ideal and actual practice, and (3) to draw attention to critical issues (e.g., racial and ethnic variation in the use and effects of sentencing laws, sentencing of the most serious juvenile offenders). The flowchart shown in Figure 8.1 illustrates the juvenile justice system's processing stages and the decision points at which juvenile offenders can be transferred into the criminal justice system, beginning at the prosecution stage, following arrest.

Arrests. Criminologists have long assumed that arrests contribute to desistance during and after the juvenile years (Blumstein, Cohen, Roth, & Visher, 1986; but

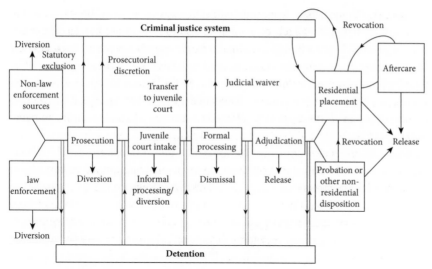

FIGURE 8.1 Juvenile justice system flowchart.
Source: Snyder and Sickmund, 2006, p. 107.

see Zimring & Hawkins, 1973). This decision point of course precedes any sentencing decision, but nonetheless is critical for young people. Ideally, arrest alone would have a deterrent value for juveniles. However, at least in some locations, arrest may exacerbate a youth's future involvement in the justice system (Bernburg & Krohn, 2003, Bernburg, Krohn, & Rivera, 2006; Huizinga & Henry, 2008).

Effects of prosecution practices on persistence or desistance after the juvenile years. No studies exist that systematically examine the effects of different prosecution practices on offenders' persistence or desistance during the juvenile through post-adolescent years. Recidivism studies typically rely on limited operationalizations of recidivism. For example, they do not examine the effects of sanctions on trajectories of offending or the persistence in or desistance from offending. Persistence and desistance refer to patterns of offending that occur over a period of time. By definition, then, they are established through multiple observation points. For example, some youth may fit a "frequent offender" profile and their desistance is defined by a reduction in the level or rate of offending (Piquero, Farrington, & Blumstein, 2007). Traditional recidivism studies which operationalize recidivism as "offended/did not offend" at one point in time provide little to no insight into how adjudicatory and correctional practices amplify or suppress desistance.

Studies rarely examine the impact of prosecutorial practices on recidivism. Instead, they focus simply on the end outcome—that is, the effects of receiving a given sanction. Studies of transfer, for example, examine the impact of sending youth to adult prisons. They typically show that this practice can actually increase rather than decrease recidivism (see, e.g., Winner, Lanza-Kaduce, Bishop, & Frazier, 1997; see, more generally, Bishop & Frazier, 2000; Feld, 2009; Hahn et al., 2007; Kupchik,

2006; Lanza-Kaduce, Lane, Bishop, & Frazier, 2005; Mears, 2003). However most of the studies to date do not adequately control for selection effects, nor do they examine the practice of threatening to invoke transfer laws or the use of such laws for specific cases (Podkopacz & Feld, 2001). Accordingly, we know little about the full impact of transfer laws as they are used in practice (Mears, 2003), and much less about their effects on persistence or desistance after the juvenile years. However, it is clear that punishment per se has little or no effect on recidivism for juvenile offenders (Lipsey, 2009; Lipsey & Cullen, 2007).

Effects of prosecution practices on different ethnic minorities. A voluminous literature exists on court and correctional decision-making and its impact on racial and ethnic minorities (see, e.g., Hawkins & Kempf-Leonard, 2005). The literature on front-end decision-making finds that "minority youths are more likely than whites to be arrested, referred to court, and detained by police" (Bishop, 2005, p. 45). However, relatively little attention has been given to subsequent decision-making by prosecutors. Bishop's (2005) review found that "relatively few studies have explored the influence of race/ethnicity on prosecutorial decisions to file formal charges" (p. 52). Some studies reported that prosecutors are more likely to charge minorities than white youths while others find the opposite (p. 52; see also Tracy, 2005). In some cases, direct effects largely disappear once researchers control for type of offense or offense severity (Podkopacz & Feld, 1995). By and large, however, we know little about how race and ethnicity affect formal charging practices and plea negotiations.

The impact of targeted prosecution on conviction of offenders ages 15–29. Targeted prosecution involves selective identification and prosecution of serious, chronic, or violent offenders, sometimes coupled with efforts to enhance treatment or intervention. Little research has directly examined prosecutorial practices and their impact on juveniles' transition into early adulthood. However, some studies suggest that selective prosecution—for example, vertical prosecution, which involves assigning an experienced prosecutor to handle juveniles' cases from charging through disposition (Backstrom & Walker, 2006)—can produce more rapid court processing, more convictions, more placements in secure confinement, and less plea bargaining (Office of Juvenile Justice and Delinquency Prevention, 1988). Even so, we know little about the gap between ideal and actual practice, much less how the level and quality of implementation can influence the impact of vertical prosecution on recidivism.

Transfer methods. Every state in the United States uses one or more statutory approaches to prosecute some juveniles as adults (Feld, 2000; Snyder & Sickmund, 2006; Griffin, 2008, and Chapter 7, this volume). Although the details of states' transfer laws vary considerably, all rely on variations of three general strategies to prosecute children in criminal courts: judicial waiver, legislative offense exclusion, and prosecutorial direct-file (Snyder & Sickmund, 2006; Griffin, 2008, and Chapter 7, this volume). Because transfer served as a central focus of juvenile justice reforms in recent decades, and because it illustrates the "get tough" trend in juvenile justice, we discuss it in more detail than we do the other decision-making points and sentencing policies in juvenile and criminal justice.

Judicial waiver statutes represent the most prevalent transfer mechanism used in 45 states (Griffin, 2008, and Chapter 7, Table 7.3, this volume), although it accounts for the fewest number of youths tried in adult criminal courts. Judicial waiver laws allow a juvenile court judge to waive jurisdiction after conducting a hearing to determine whether a youth is "amenable to treatment" or poses a danger to public safety (*Kent v. United States* 1966; Feld, 2000; Zimring, 2000). These assessments reflect the individualized sentencing discretion characteristic of juvenile courts and consider clinical evidence and a youth's social background as well as the offense and criminal history (Feld, 1999, 2000). Although 14 is the minimum age for transfer in most jurisdictions, some states permit waiver of youths as young as age 10 or specify no minimum age, and others require adult prosecution of children as young as age 13 (Snyder & Sickmund, 2006; Griffin, 2008, and Chapter 7, Table 7.4, this volume).

The number of delinquency cases judicially waived to criminal court peaked at 13,200 in 1994 (Snyder & Sickmund, 2006, p. 186). By 2001, waived cases were down to 6,300—below the 1985 level. We attribute the overall decline in judicially waived youths since the mid-1990s to states' adoption of offense exclusion and prosecutorial direct-file laws that shifted discretion from the judicial branch to the executive branch—to prosecutors making offense charging decisions that determine jurisdiction. These changes eliminated the need for judicial hearings and increased the number of youths transferred to criminal courts by other methods (Feld, 2008; Griffin, 2008, and Chapter 7, Tables 7.7 and 7.8, this volume).

Although 45 states have judicial waiver statutes, statutory exclusion and prosecutorial direct-file laws account for most of the juveniles tried as adults (see Feld, 2008; Griffin, 2008, and Chapter 7, Tables 7.7 and 7.8, this volume). Analysts estimate that states annually try more than 200,000 juveniles under age 18 as adults simply because juvenile court jurisdiction ends at age 15 or 16, rather than at age 17 (Butts & Mitchell, 2000; Feld, 2008; Snyder & Sickmund, 2006). "If only half of these cases actually went forward for criminal court processing, they would still far exceed the number of juveniles ending up in adult court by all other methods combined" (Butts & Mitchell, 2000, p. 186). Analysts estimate that states try an additional 55,000 youths a year in criminal courts who were within the age jurisdiction of juvenile courts through transfer mechanisms (Human Rights Watch, 2005; Snyder & Sickmund, 2006).

Legislative offense exclusion frequently supplements judicial waiver provisions (Griffin, 2008, and Chapter 7, Table 7.7, this volume). This approach emphasizes the seriousness of the offense, rather than characteristics of the offender, and reflects the retributive values of the criminal law (Feld, 2000, 2008). Because legislatures create juvenile courts, they may define their jurisdiction simply to exclude youths charged with serious offenses from their jurisdiction without any hearing (Feld, 2000; Griffin, 2008). For example, several states exclude from juvenile court jurisdiction youths aged 16 or older charged with first-degree murder (Griffin, 2008, and Chapter 7, Table 7.7, this volume).

In 15 states, juvenile and criminal courts share concurrent jurisdiction over certain ages and offenses, typically older youths and serious crimes (Griffin, 2008, and Chapter 7, Table 7.8, this volume). Prosecutors can direct-file or charge youths in either the juvenile or criminal justice system without any judicial review of their charging/forum-selection decision (Snyder & Sickmund, 2006; Griffin, 2008; *Manduley v. Superior Court of San Diego*, 2002). A prosecutor's decision to charge a youth in criminal rather than juvenile court determines which court has jurisdiction (Feld, 1999, 2008). Analysts estimate that prosecutors determine the adult status of 85% of all youths tried as adults based on age and the offense charged (Juszkiewicz, 2000, pp. 13–14).

The exact number of juveniles transferred to the criminal justice system each year remains unknown. Criminal justice authorities do not maintain these data because the age at which an offender committed his or her crime is not a crucial fact for adult correctional authorities' decision-making. In addition, the juvenile justice system does not systematically compile data on the various types of transfer proceedings because most of these decisions are made by prosecutors. In addition, two key actors—legislators (statutory exclusion) and prosecutors (direct-file authority)—have created a "dark figure of waiver" in the transfer picture (Mears, 2003, p. 159). The data on judicial waiver indicates that between 1985 and 2002, judges were most likely to transfer person offense cases to criminal court, except between 1989–1991, when they most frequently waived drug offense cases (Snyder & Sickmund, 2006, p. 186). It remains unknown to what extent transfer laws are used to plea bargain cases to traditional juvenile court sanctions (Mears, 2003). Below, we discuss research on the effectiveness of transfer laws.

Sentencing of the most serious juvenile offenders. No standard sentencing approach governs states' criminal justice systems. Thirty years ago, indeterminate sentencing was the prevailing model, but this has given way to a wide variety of sentencing options, including determinate and mandatory minimum sentences, three-strikes laws (designed to increase prison terms for repeat offenders), and "truth in sentencing" laws (which require offenders to serve some specified proportion of their sentences). The result is "a national crazy quilt made up of piecemeal sentencing reforms—without a public rationale that would explain the relationship between imprisonment and release" (Travis & Petersilia, 2001, p. 296).

In the 1980s, the punish-rehabilitate pendulum began to swing toward punishment for juvenile offenders and this trend accelerated in the 1990s. New state laws generally increased eligibility for criminal court processing and adult correctional sanctioning and reduced confidentiality protections for some juvenile offenders. Between 1992 and 1997, all but three states changed laws in one or more of the following areas (Snyder & Sickmund, 2006, pp. 96–97):

- Transfer provisions—Laws made it easier to transfer juvenile offenders from the juvenile justice system to the criminal justice system (45 states).
- Sentencing authority—Laws gave criminal and juvenile courts expanded sentencing options (31 states).
- Confidentiality—Laws modified or removed traditional juvenile court confidentiality provisions by making records and proceedings more open (47 states).

These laws increased sentences for a broader range of juvenile offenses and transferred more juveniles to criminal courts for sentencing as adults, especially those charged with violent and drug offenses (Torbet & Szymanski, 1998). Another purpose of these legal reforms was to "criminalize" juvenile courts. In Texas, for example, the legislature created a "determinate sentencing" law that permitted the juvenile court to impose lengthier terms of confinement than otherwise would be allowed, depending on a youth's age and the type of offense committed (Mears, 1998). In addition, youth incarcerated in juvenile justice facilities could complete their sentences in adult prisons, subject to judicial review. In essence, prosecutors gained an additional tool with which to seek tougher sentences that would extend beyond the age limits of the juvenile justice system. Many other sentencing reforms nationally aimed at enhancing the penalties that youth could receive in juvenile court (Mears, 2002).

In sum, the disjunction between intended and actual system responses—arrest, prosecution, transfer, and sentencing—and our limited knowledge about the nature or magnitude of the disjunction pose enormous problems for policy-makers who wish to improve the transition of young offenders into law-abiding adulthood. The legal responses are highly variable and inconsistently applied. Moreover, there is a lack of research (and knowledge of the consequences) of different prosecutorial strategies. At the same time, evidence suggests that many of the responses are applied more intensively to racial and ethnic minorities and in ways that exceed what might be anticipated from potential differences in the level or severity of offending. These same issues arise even when the focus is on the most serious and violent young offenders. Against that backdrop, we turn now to several changes that further highlight the complexity of, and inconsistency in, how society responds to young offenders.

The Effectiveness of Transfer and New Approaches to Sanctioning Young Offenders

This section examines research on the effectiveness of transfer laws while emphasizing new studies addressing the impact of transfer laws.

Transfer laws: new research on their effectiveness. Earlier reviews of transfer studies reported that transferred youths are more likely to re-offend, re-offend more quickly and at higher rates, and commit more serious offenses following release from prison than do juveniles retained in the juvenile justice system (Bishop & Frazier, 2000; Fagan, 2007; Howell, 1996; Howell & Howell, 2007). A more recent and systematic review of transfer studies conducted by the Community Preventive Services Task Force of the Centers for Disease Control and Prevention (McGowan et al., 2007) synthesizes the cumulative findings. The Task Force examined whether trying juveniles in the adult criminal justice system prevented or reduced interpersonal violence. It found that transferring juveniles to the adult justice system generally increases, rather than decreases, rates of violence—that is, waiver had an iatrogenic effect. The Task Force (2007) found that transferred juveniles are 34% more likely to be rearrested for a violent or other crime than are juveniles retained in the juvenile justice system (McGowan et al., 2007, p. S14). In other words, "available evidence indicates that juveniles who experience the adult justice system, on average, commit more subsequent violent crime following release than juveniles retained in the juvenile justice system" (p. S5). Evidence was insufficient for the Task Force to determine the effect of such laws and policies in reducing violent behavior in the overall juvenile population. Other studies buttress the CDC's negative findings. Prior work indicates that changes in transfer laws or practices do not produce a specific or a general deterrent effect (Bishop & Frazier, 2000; Fagan, 2007; Steiner & Wright, 2006). There appear to be collateral consequences of criminal convictions (Mauer & Meda, 2003), including an elevated risk of violent victimization in adult jails and prisons (Bishop & Frazier, 2000; Forst, Fagan, & Vivona, 1989; Parent, Lieter, Kennedy, Livens, Wentworth, & Wilcox, 1994). In addition, transfer of youth may be developmentally disruptive because it interferes with acquisition of crucial educational, vocational, and social skills (Scott & Steinberg, 2008). Not least, concerns have been raised about the potential net-widening effects (transfer of less serious offenders) that transfer laws, as well as blended sentencing (Cheesman, Green, Cohen, Dancy, Kleiman, & Mott, 2002; Podkopacz & Feld, 2001), create (Mears, 2003).

Transfer laws, if implemented as intended, should result in youth being processed in adult court and sentenced to adult prisons. Prior theory and research suggests that such exposure likely increases offending. Prison environments can serve as "schools for crime" (Irwin, 1980; Nagin, Cullen, & Jonson, 2009). Indeed, Bishop and Frazier (2000) found that "youths in prison were exposed to an inmate subculture that taught criminal motivations as well as techniques of committing crime and avoiding detection" (pp. 263–64). In addition, "youths were more likely to learn social rules and norms that legitimated domination, exploitation, and retaliation. They routinely observed both staff and inmate models who exhibited these behaviors, and they observed these illegitimated norms being reinforced" (ibid.). Not least, youths reflected on their experiences of being prosecuted and confined as adults rather than as juveniles and expressed "very negative reactions to criminal court processing. Many youths experienced the court process not so much as a condemnation of their behavior as a condemnation of them" (p. 263). Once in adult prison, facilities provided fewer than 10% with any type of counseling or treatment program. They viewed correctional officers as "hostile and derisive. Many respondents reported feeling threatened by correctional staff, both physically and emotionally" (p. 266).

The efficacy of criminal, juvenile, and blended sentencing on future offending. Many new sentencing laws have "criminalized" juvenile courts and changed their procedures to operate more like adult criminal courts. The changes have included expanding adversarial procedures, increasing the role for prosecutors, formalizing due process, eliminating confidentiality, routinely gathering fingerprints, using "blended sentencing," and emphasizing offense-based sanctions rather than rehabilitative dispositions in juvenile courts (Fagan & Zimring, 2000; Feld, 1993, 1998; Singer, 1996). The increased criminalization of juvenile courts has proceeded without any evidence that it effectively reduces crime or recidivism and runs counter to the traditional mission of the juvenile court (Butts & Mitchell, 2000; Feld, 1999; Mears, 2000, 2001). To illustrate, 15 states, including Texas (Mears, 2000; Mears & Field, 2000), Florida (Bishop & Frazier, 1996), and Minnesota (Podkopacz & Feld, 1995, 1996, 2001), have introduced blended sentencing laws without any obvious improvement of recidivism outcomes or enhanced ability of either the juvenile or adult justice systems to manage better the youth with whom they come into contact. Because blended sentencing laws are now ubiquitous and affect large swathes of the young offender population, these bear further discussion, as follows.

Some have described "blended sentencing" legislation as "a marriage of convenience between those that [*sic*] want to punish more and those that [*sic*] want to give kids one more chance" (John Stanoch, chief juvenile court judge for Hennepin County, Minnesota, quoted in Belluck, 1998, p. A26). In blended sentencing systems, youths are entitled to receive all adult criminal procedural safeguards, including the right to a jury trial. Following conviction, judges may combine a sentence in the juvenile system with an adult criminal sentence, which is stayed pending successful completion of the juvenile disposition. If a youth violates conditions of probation or re-offends, then a judge may revoke the juvenile's probation and execute the criminal sentence. There are five versions of blended sentencing law—three based in juvenile courts and two based in criminal court. The five models vary according to the authority vested in the respective courts.

Zimring (2000) has described the "Byzantine complexity" of blended sentencing laws (p. 215). In Kansas, judges can impose a blended sentence on a youth as young as age 10 for any offense, and several states specify no, or a very low, minimum age (e.g., 12 or 13) for imposition of a blended sentence (see the state-by-state discussion of blended sentencing provisions in Griffin, 2008, and Chapter 7, Table 7.9, this volume). Many youths who receive blended sentences fail their juvenile probation, which then leads the courts to execute the adult criminal sentences. This process can result in "net widening" and, in particular, criminal sentences for youths convicted of less serious offenses. Net widening occurs when a new sanction that was intended to serve as an alternative to a given level of system processing brings more youths into the system's net (Merlo, Benekos, & Cook, 1997).

Torbet and colleagues (1996) have observed that "confusion exists about [blended sentencing] statutes and the rules and regulations governing them, especially with respect to the juvenile's status during case processing and subsequent placement" (p. 15). They found that the selection of sentencing options is confusing "for all system actors, including offenders, judges, prosecutors, and corrections administrators" (p. 15). Thus they conclude that "blended sentencing initiatives may cause more confusion than good" (p. 15; see also Mears, 1998). In addition to procedural confusion, system ambivalence about what to do with serious and violent juvenile offenders is evident (Torbet, Gable, Hurst, Montgomery, Szymanski, & Thomas, 1996).

Specialized courts. Juxtaposed against a clear "get tough" trend in juvenile justice stands a countervailing trend toward embracing sanctioning options that include both punishment and rehabilitation as central guiding tenets (Butts & Mears, 2001; Mears, 2002). Specialized courts—including at least 840 juvenile or family drug courts and more than 125 mental health courts—are operating in both the juvenile and adult justice systems (personal communication, National Council of Juvenile and Family Court Judges, August 16, 2010). In addition, more than 1,000 youth courts are now operating in the United States according to the National Youth Court Center (http://www.youthcourt.net/). However, as with the "get tough" trends, little is known about the implementation or impact of these courts. Several studies that have focused on teen courts and drug courts, respectively, nonetheless bear mention.

Butts, Buck, & Coggeshall (2002) evaluated four youth courts and found that recidivism rates among teen court youth were lower than those of youth in the regular juvenile justice system in all four sites and significantly lower in two of the four sites. Researchers have studied drug courts more than any other kind of specialized court. A recent meta-analysis tentatively suggests that drug offenders participating in a drug court are less likely to re-offend than similar offenders sentenced to traditional correctional options (Wilson, Mitchell, & Mackenzie, 2006). However, the equivocal conclusion stems from the weak methodological research in this area (Butts & Roman, 2004). Although there are too few studies on juvenile drug courts to draw any conclusions at this time, the studies to date suggest that courts are less effective with juvenile offenders than with older ones (Shaffer, Hartman, Listwan, Howell, & Latessa, 2011). A very recent evaluation of the Akron, Ohio, Municipal Drug Court for adults found that it reduced recidivism among different types of drug users, although the sample was primarily composed of low-to moderate low-risk clients (Shaffer et al., 2011).

Special Considerations When Deciding How to Respond to Young Offenders

Culpability. Culpability focuses on an actor's blameworthiness and degree of de-served punishment. Youths' diminished responsibility requires mitigated sanctions to avoid permanently life-changing penalties and provide room to reform. Compared with adults, youths' immature judgment reflects differences in appreciation of risk, appraisal of short- and long-term consequences, self-control, and susceptibility to negative peer influences (Scott & Steinberg, 2008). The Supreme Court's 2005 decision in *Roper v. Simmons* (543 U.S. 551), to abolish executions of juvenile offenders in the United States, provides the backdrop for our discussion of adolescents' reduced criminal responsibility.

In *Roper v. Simmons*, the Supreme Court conducted a proportionality analysis of adolescents' culpability to determine whether the death penalty ever could be an appropriate punishment for juveniles. A majority of the Court offered three reasons why states could not punish as severely as adults youths found to be criminally responsible (*Roper*, 2005). First, juveniles' immature judgment and lesser self-control caused them to act impulsively and without full appreciation of the consequences of their actions and thus reduced their culpability. Second, juveniles are more susceptible than adults to negative peer influences. In addition, juveniles' greater dependence on parents and community extends some responsibility for their crimes to others, which further diminishes their criminal responsibility. Third, juveniles' personalities are more in flux and less well-formed than those of adults and their crimes provide less reliable evidence of "depraved character." Although the differences between adolescents and adults seem intuitively obvious, *Roper* provided minimal scientific evidence to support its conclusions (Denno, 2006).

The Court's *Roper* decision (2005, p. 569) also attributed youths' diminished culpability to a "lack of maturity and . . . underdeveloped sense of responsibility . . .[that] often result in impetuous and ill considered actions and decisions." *Roper* focused on adolescents' immature judgment, rather than the narrower criminal law inquiry into the ability to distinguish right from wrong, and concluded that their immaturity reduced culpability. The Court's rationale recognized both adolescents' reduced moral culpability and their greater capacity for growth and change—that is, their diminished responsibility for past offense, and their unformed and perhaps redeemable character. In sum, the Supreme Court concluded that juveniles' reduced culpability warranted a categorical prohibition of execution (Feld, 2008; Johnson & Tabriz, 2010).

Although *Roper* barred the death penalty for juveniles, the Court's rationale has wider implications for sentencing adolescents. The Court's capital punishment jurisprudence insisted that "death is different" (*Eddings*, 1982; *Harmelin*, 1991; *Graham*, 2010). However, youths' diminished criminal responsibility is just as relevant when states seek to impose life without parole (LWOP) or other lengthy sentences as it is when they seek to execute them (Johnson & Tabriz, 2010; Logan, 1998;

Feld, 2008). The same developmental psychological characteristics and penal considerations that distinguish youths' criminal responsibility for purposes of execution reduce their culpability and warrant mitigated sentences (Zimring, 1998). Despite youths' diminished responsibility, 42 states permit judges to impose an LWOP sentence on any offender—adult or juvenile—convicted of serious offenses, for example murder or rape, and 27 states require mandatory sentences for offenders convicted of those crimes. And, of course, judges may impose very lengthy or consecutive terms that create the functional equivalent of life sentences.

Mandatory LWOP sentences preclude consideration of youthfulness as a mitigating factor (Human Rights Watch, 2005; Johnson & Tabriz, 2010). Several states abrogated the common-law infancy defense for very young children and removed the only substantive criminal law protections for youth (Carter, 2006). Appellate courts regularly uphold LWOP sentences and long terms of imprisonment imposed on youths as young as age 12 and reject juveniles' pleas to consider youthfulness as a mitigating factor (Feld, 2008; Human Rights Watch, 2005; Deitch, 2009). About one of every six juveniles who received an LWOP sentence was age 15 or younger when they committed their crimes (Human Rights Watch, 2005). More than half (59%) of these juveniles received an LWOP sentence for their first-ever criminal conviction (Human Rights Watch, 2005). More than one-quarter (26%) of these youths received an LWOP sentence for a felony—murder to which they were an accessory rather than the principal (Human Rights Watch, 2005).

Although the Court's death penalty jurisprudence treats youthfulness as a mitigating factor, trial courts perversely treat it as an aggravating factor and sentence juveniles more severely than their adult counterparts (Snyder & Sickmund, 2006). Perhaps the clearest example is the "juvenile penalty" that researchers have discovered—that is, *juvenile offenders sent to adult court are more likely to be incarcerated and to receive lengthier sentences compared with their young adult counterparts* (Kurlychek & Johnson, 2004, 2010; Steiner, 2009; see also Kupchik, 2006, 2007). In addition, a larger proportion of juveniles convicted of murder receive LWOP sentences than do adult murderers (Feld, 2008). The "juvenile status" penalty can be seen in nationwide sentencing patterns. In a federal Bureau of Justice Statistics study (Brown & Langan, 1998), transferred juveniles convicted of felonies were given longer prison sentences than adults. Transferred juveniles were sentenced to prison for a maximum of nine years on average, compared to seven years for adults under age 18 (as defined by state statutes) and five years for adults aged 18 and older. Similar disparities persist in more recent studies (Fagan, 2007; Johnson & Tabriz, 2010; Kurlychek & Johnson, 2010).These inequities demonstrate the inability of the criminal justice system to treat juvenile offenders fairly and apply a reasonable measure of proportionality to their cases.

In *Graham v. Florida* (2010), the Court applied *Roper's* diminished responsibility rationale to youths convicted of non-homicide crimes sentenced to life without parole. Historically, the Court's Eighth Amendment proportionality analyses had distinguished between capital sentences and long terms of imprisonment and deferred to legislative decisions about deserved punishments. However, *Graham v. Florida* (2010) concluded that offenders who did not kill were "categorically less deserving of the most serious forms of punishment than are murderers." Because of juveniles' diminished responsibility, those who did not kill have "twice diminished moral culpability. . . . The age of the offender and the nature of the crime" categorically precluded the penultimate penalty for non-homicide crimes as well. *Graham* emphasized youths' immature judgment and reduced self-control, susceptibility to negative peer influences, and transitory character development. *Graham* asserted that subsequent research in developmental psychology and neuroscience bolstered *Roper's* conclusion that adolescents' reduced culpability required somewhat mitigated sentences in that studies show marked differences between juvenile and adult minds. Most noteworthy, it is well established that sections of the brain that control behavior generally do not mature until late adolescence. *Graham's* Eighth Amendment analyses referred to many factors—penal justifications for sentencing practices, the *Roper* conclusion about adolescent developmental differences, states' laws and sentencing practices, and international law—and neuroscience provided one more piece of confirming data in the Court's holding (Maroney, 2009).

To what extent do the Supreme Court's views conform to the scientific study of child and adolescent development? For many years, developmental psychologists focused on logical reasoning capacity as the linchpin of maturity. A new perspective on adolescent risk-taking has emerged that begins with "the premise that risk taking in the real world is the product of both logical-reasoning and psychosocial factors" (Steinberg, 2007, p. 56; see also Steinberg, 2004). "However, unlike logical-reasoning abilities, which appear to be more or less fully developed by age 15, psychosocial capacities that improve decision-making and moderate risk-taking—such as impulse control, emotion regulation, delay of gratification, and resistance to peer influence—continue to mature well into young adulthood" (Steinberg, 2004; Steinberg & Monahan, 2007; see Figure 8.2).

Developmental psychologists have described many aspects of mental immaturity (Steinberg, 2004), yet "trying to understand why risk taking is more common during adolescence has challenged psychologists for decades" (Steinberg, 2007, p. 55). What stymied them most, Steinberg suggests, is that the logical-reasoning abilities of mid-adolescents are comparable to those of adults (see also Scott, 2000; Steinberg & Cauffman, 2000; Scott & Steinberg, 2008). This is where neuroscience has made an important contribution. As Steinberg (2007) explains, "advances in developmental neuroscience provide support for [a] new way of thinking about adolescent decision making" (p. 56). Specifically, it "appears that heightened risk taking in adolescence is the product of the interaction between two brain networks. The first is a socio-emotional network that is especially sensitive to social and emotional stimuli, that is particularly important for reward processing, and that is remodeled in early adolescence by the hormonal changes of puberty" (ibid). "The second network is a cognitive-control network that [supports] executive

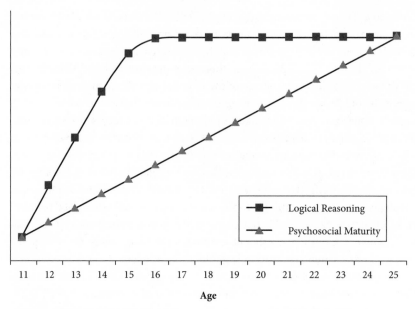

FIGURE 8.2 The reasoning-maturity gap.
Source: Steinberg, 2007, p. 56.

functions such as planning, thinking ahead, and self-regulation, and that matures gradually over the course of adolescence and young adulthood largely independently of puberty" (ibid; see also Steinberg, 2004). Thus risk-taking is the product of a competition between the socio-emotional and cognitive-control networks. The implication is that adolescence is a period in which the socio-emotional network abruptly becomes more assertive (i.e., at puberty) while the cognitive-control network gains strength only gradually, over a longer period of time, as illustrated in Figure 8.2.

The importance of this reasoning-maturity gap is buttressed by developmental neuroscience studies undertaken in recent years. Researchers at the Harvard Medical School, the National Institute of Mental Health, the UCLA School of Medicine, and others have collaborated to map the development of the brain from childhood to adulthood and to examine its implications (Juvenile Justice Center, 2004; National Institute of Mental Health, 2001). Their research used magnetic resonance imaging (MRI) to measure brain development. Until recently, most neuroscientists believed that the essential "wiring" of the brain was completed very early—perhaps by age 6—and that the brain matured fully in childhood, certainly by early adolescence. However, neuroscientists have discovered a second spurt in brain development, one that occurs during the adolescent years. In other words, the teen brain is not a finished product but a work in progress, with maturation continuing well into the 20s (Giedd et al., 1999; Paus et al., 1999; Sowell, Thompson, Jernigan, & Toga, 1999; Sowell, Thompson, Tessner, & Toga, 2001).

Many of the differences between adolescents' and adults' thinking and behaving reflect these developmental differences in the human brain. Adolescents simply do not have the physiological capacity of adults to exercise judgment or control impulses (Gruber & Yurgelun-Todd, 2006). The prefrontal cortex (PFC) of the frontal lobe of the brain operates as the "chief executive officer" to control advanced cerebral activities (Gruber & Yurgelun-Todd, 2006; Kandel et al., 2000). Executive functioning includes reasoning, abstract thinking, planning, anticipating consequences, and impulse control (Aronson, 2007; Sowell et al., 1999; Sowell et al., 2001). During adolescence and into the early 20s, increased myelination of the prefrontal cortex improves cognitive function, reasoning ability, and executive functioning in general (Paus et al., 1999; Sowell et al., 2001). By contrast, the amygdala—the limbic system located at the base of the brain—controls instinctual behavior, such as the "fight or flight" response. Adolescents rely more heavily on the amygdala and less heavily on the PFC than do adults when they experience stressful situations (Baird et al., 1999). Their impulsive behavior reflects a "gut reaction" rather than sober reflection. Novel circumstances and aroused emotions especially challenge youths' ability to exercise self-control and to resist impulsive decisions. Building on these discoveries, behavioral scientists have developed a more explicit explanation of the gap between reasoning capacity and psychosocial maturity in adolescents.

Established in 1997, the MacArthur Foundation's research network on Adolescent Development and Juvenile Justice (ADJJ) has studied juveniles' decision-making and judgment, adjudicative competence, and criminal culpability (Feld, 2008; Scott & Steinberg, 2008). The ADJJ research reports a disjunction between youths' cognitive abilities and their maturity of judgment. Even though adolescents may exhibit intellectual and cognitive abilities comparable with adults, they do not develop the psychosocial maturity, ability to exercise self-control, and competence to make adult-quality decisions until their early 20s (Feld, 2008; Scott & Steinberg, 2003). The "immaturity gap" represents the cleavage between cognitive maturity—the ability to distinguish right from wrong—which reaches near-adult levels by age 16, and adolescents' psychosocial maturity of judgment, risk assessment, and self-control, which may not emerge fully for nearly another decade (Feld, 2008). This latter deficit provides the basis for finding reduced criminal responsibility in youths. Youths' immature judgment in several areas—perceptions of risk, appreciation of future consequences, self-management, and ability to make autonomous choices—distinguishes them from adults (Scott & Steinberg, 2003). As *Roper* concluded, youths' characteristically bad choices are categorically less blameworthy than those of adults because differences in knowledge and experience, short-term versus long-term time perspectives, attitude toward risk, and impulsivity are features of normal adolescent development (Scott & Grisso, 1997; Scott & Steinberg, 2003).

The ADJJ researchers also studied juveniles' ability to evaluate risks and to delay gratification (Feld, 2008). This research suggests that adolescents' risk perception actually *declines* during mid-adolescence and then gradually increases into adulthood, and that 16- and 17-year-old youths perceive fewer risks than do either younger or older research subjects. Mid-adolescents are the most "present-oriented" of all the age groups studied, with future orientation gradually increasing into the early 20s (Feld, 2008). Youths weigh costs and benefits differently than adults and give different subjective values to outcomes, which affect their ultimate choices (Scott, 2000; Scott & Steinberg, 2008). In a study of individuals' ability to delay gratification, adolescents more often opted for an immediate but smaller reward, whereas adults delayed a reward unless the immediate value was only slightly discounted (Feld, 2008). Youths also view *not* engaging in risky behaviors differently than adults, which also leads to riskier choices by adolescents (Scott, 2000; Scott & Steinberg, 2003, 2008). Youths engage in risky behavior because it provides heightened sensations, excitement, and an "adrenaline rush" (Scott & Grisso, 1997; Spear, 2000). The widest divergence between the perception of and the preference for risk occurs during mid-adolescence when youths' criminal activity also increases. Youths' feelings of invulnerability and immortality heighten these risk proclivities.

To calculate risks, an individual has to identify potential positive and negative outcomes, estimate their likelihood, and then apply value preferences to optimize outcomes (Furby & Beyth-Marom, 1992). To a greater extent than adults, adolescents underestimate the amount and likelihood of risks, employ a shorter time frame in their calculus, and focus on gains rather than losses (Furby & Beyth-Marom, 1992; Grisso, 2000; Scott, 2000). Juveniles aged 15 and younger act more impulsively than do older adolescents, but even 16- and 17-year old youths fail to exhibit adult levels of self-control (Feld, 2008). Because of youth and inexperience, adolescents may possess less information or consider fewer options than adults when they make decisions (Scott, 2000). Although youths and adults use similar amounts of time to solve simple problems, the length of time used to solve complex problems increases with age.

Adjudicative competence. The same developmental characteristics that diminish youths' criminal responsibility also adversely affect their adjudicative competence. Competence is the constitutional prerequisite to the exercise of other procedural rights. Due process requires a defendant to be competent to assure a fair trial. To be competent to stand trial, a criminal defendant must have "sufficient present ability to consult with his lawyer with a reasonable degree of rational understanding [and have a] rational as well as factual understanding of the proceedings against him," as well as the capacity "to assist in preparing his defense" (Dusky, 1960). Adjudicative competence involves a defendant's ability to communicate with lawyers or aid in his or her defense, make legal decisions and understand and participate in such legal procedures, and to waive *Miranda* rights, waive or assist counsel, to stand trial, and to exercise other constitutional protections. Judges evaluate a youth's competence by assessing his or her ability to: "1) understand the charges and the basic elements of the adversary system (understanding),

2) appreciate one's situation as a defendant in a criminal prosecution (appreciation), and 3) relate pertinent information to counsel concerning the facts of the case (reasoning)" (Bonnie & Grisso, 2000, p. 76).

Developmental psychologists have examined adolescents' adjudicative competence, their capacity to exercise or waive *Miranda* rights or the right to counsel, and their ability to participate in legal proceedings. This research strongly questions whether juveniles possess the cognitive ability, psychosocial maturity, and judgment necessary to exercise legal rights. Many young offenders, especially those under age 16 and those confronted with the complexities of criminal courts, are unable to meet the legal standards for competence (Grisso et al., 2003; Scott & Grisso, 2005; Scott & Steinberg, 2008). Developmental psychologists argue that immaturity per se produces the same deficits of understanding, impairment of judgment, and inability to assist counsel as does severe mental illness, and renders many juveniles legally incompetent (Grisso, 1997, 2000; Scott & Grisso, 2005). This vulnerability is enhanced for certain juvenile categories: (a) those who are marginal or weak in intelligence, (b) those who are mentally ill, and (c) those who are otherwise mentally impaired from injury or child abuse. For adolescents, generic developmental limitations, rather than mental illness or mental retardation, adversely affect their ability to understand legal proceedings, to receive information, communicate with and assist counsel, and to make rational decisions (Grisso, 1997; Scott & Grisso, 2005; Redding & Fuller, 2004).

Despite clear developmental differences between adolescents and adults, the Court and most states' laws do not provide youths with additional procedural safeguards to protect them from their own immaturity and vulnerability. About half of the states address juveniles' competency to stand trial in statutes, court rules of procedure, or case law and conclude that delinquents have a fundamental right not to be tried while incompetent (Scott & Grisso, 2005; Feld, 2009). However, states use adult legal standards to gauge juveniles' competence to stand trial and ability to waive *Miranda* rights and counsel. Because of developmental differences, formal legal equality results in practical inequality for juveniles in the justice system.

Developmental psychologists contend that all children and adolescents younger than age 16 should receive automatic competency assessments and express serious reservations about the competency of 16- and 17-year-olds (Scott & Steinberg, 2003). Although older adolescents may have adult-like cognitive capacities for reasoning, their ability to exercise sound judgment in ambiguous or stressful situations may be limited (Scott, 2000). A critical challenge to assessing competency is the fact that many jurisdictions do not provide adequate or appropriate youth competency assessments (Grisso, 2004).

Reentry challenges and contexts unique to young people. An estimated 200,000 juveniles and young adults ages 24 and younger leave secure juvenile correctional facilities or state and federal prisons and return home each year (Mears & Travis, 2004). Most reentry research has focused on adults, and we know little about the reentry of young people. This deficiency is critical because it would be risky to assume that the challenges young offenders face upon returning to society are the same as those for adults. Despite some overlap, substantial differences exist. For example, young people who are released from secure confinement confront several barriers unique to their age group:

- School systems may not be receptive to working with them and may warehouse them in special classrooms or alternative schools.
- Developmental disabilities may have gone undiagnosed, or untreated, or mistreated.
- Family settings may include violence and drug-dealing.
- Peer networks may foster criminality, a particular concern because of the greater importance of peer association among adolescents.
- They are likely to be unemployed, because they typically will not have graduated from high school, will be less likely to complete school, and will have a limited, if any, employment history. One-third of the general population had received a high school diploma versus only 21% of state prison inmates (Harlow, 2003).
- They have little experience in what it means to have positive, prosocial experiences with (a) friends, (b) recreation, (c) intimate emotional relationships, (d) the self-discipline needed for employment, etc.

These constitute but some of the broad array of challenges young people face upon reentry into society, and if unaddressed are likely to contribute to a trajectory of criminal involvement. Because parole/probation violations account for a large proportion of all incarcerations, states need to use proven techniques more widely to reduce violations or keep parole/probation violators out of prison. Nationwide, the vast majority (about 80%) of released prisoners are subject to a period of supervision in the community. Large numbers of parolees return to prison for new crimes or technical violations of their parole and account for 35% of new prison admissions nationally (Baer et al., 2006, p. 18). Juvenile parole violations are governed by the same impairments that affect offending.

A major obstacle to successful offender reentry are civil disqualifications that affect offenders after incarceration. The Urban Institute's *Returning Home* study documented the pre-release needs and post-release experiences of prisoners in Illinois, Maryland, Texas, and Ohio (Baer et al., 2006; see also Annie E. Casey Foundation, 2005). Even so, few studies have systematically compared these needs and experiences among youth populations.

A few effective post-release programs are available for young adult offenders. A systematic review of prisoner reentry programs (Seiter & Kadela, 2003) indicated a positive result for several of them, including vocational training and/or work release, drug rehabilitation, education programs (to some extent), halfway house programs, pre-release programs, and promising results for sex- and violent-offender programs. Another review of adult inmate programs found small but positive benefits for work release programs (versus in-prison incarceration) and job counseling/search for inmates leaving prison (Aos, Phipps, Barnoski, & Lieb, 2001). Once again, however, few studies exist that have systematically compared the effectiveness of reentry programs among youth versus adult offender populations.

International law and practice. The United States is the only developed nation that tries its youngest offenders in regular criminal courts without modified procedures.[1] Until *Roper v. Simmons* (2005) banned executions of adolescents who commit capital murder before age 18, the United States was the only country in the world that gave official sanction to the juvenile death penalty.

The U.N. Convention on the Rights of the Child (CRC) codified the basic human rights of children and was adopted by the United Nations General Assembly in 1989. The United States and Somalia are the only U.N. member countries that have not ratified this convention. Other international covenants provide special protections to juvenile offenders around the world. These include Articles VII (right to special protection), XXV (right to due process), and XXVI (right to protection against cruel, infamous, or unusual punishment) of the American Declaration of the Rights and Duties of Man.

Race, ethnicity, and gender. The disproportionate overrepresentation of racial and ethnic minorities in the juvenile and adult criminal justice systems raises issues of justice, fairness, and equity. Although a few earlier studies have found no race effect in arrests (Pope & Snyder, 2003), most research reports that minority youth are overrepresented in all stages of juvenile and criminal justice processing from arrests to confinement (Feld, 1999; Hawkins & Kempf-Leonard, 2005; Hawkins, Laub, Lauritsen, & Cothern, 2000; Howell, 2003b, 2006; Liebman, Fagan, & West, 2000; Snyder & Sickmund, 2006; Tonry, 1994, 2009). Disproportionate minority contact with the justice system occurs even when self-reported delinquency is taken into account (Huizinga et al., 2007). In particular, black youths are disproportionately arrested and processed in the juvenile and criminal justice systems for drug offenses in comparison with white offenders, even though their drug use rates are no higher than those of white youths (Centers for Disease Control and Prevention, 2006). Latino youth are also overrepresented in the U.S. juvenile and criminal justice systems and receive harsher treatment than white youth (Arya, Villarruel, Villanueva, & Augarten, 2009; Villarruel & Walker, 2002). Disparities associated with defendants' race or ethnicity occur at all stages of the criminal justice system: arrest, pre-trial release, prosecutor decision-making, sentencing, imprisonment, and prison release decision-making (Howell, 2009, p. 297). More attention is needed to understanding why such differences exist and to reducing minority youth overrepresentation in juvenile and adult justice systems.

Gender disparities exist in juvenile and criminal justice administration. It is an accepted fact in criminology that in both the juvenile and adult criminal justice systems "official female criminality, as well as self-reported delinquency, is less serious, begins later in adolescence, and is less persistent than male criminality and delinquency [and that] the gap is largest for serious offenses" (Cernkovich, Lanctôt, & Giordano, 2008, p. 4; see also Feld, 2006; Lanctôt & Le Blanc, 2002; Steffensmeier, Schwartz, Zhong, Ackerman, & Ackerman, 2005). Although relatively more girls are present in the juvenile justice system than in previous years, it is not presently flooded with them (Snyder & Sickmund, 2006). Similarly, more women are now present in the adult criminal justice system, particularly for violent assault, but "we have changed our laws, police practices, and policies in other ways toward enhanced identification and criminalization of violence in general and of women's violence in particular" (Steffensmeier, Zhong, Ackerman, Schwartz, & Agha, 2006, p. 94). The evidence is persuasive that "it is the cumulative effect of policy shifts, rather than a change in women's behavior toward more violence, that accounts for their higher arrest rates and the narrowing gender gap in official counts of criminal assault" (ibid). Studies of gender differences in juvenile courts attribute some of the perceived increases in girls' violent offending to a relabeling of former status offenders, charging them instead with simple assault, and thereby allowing their institutional confinement (Feld, 2009).

This does not mean, however, that public policy should ignore the progression from juvenile careers to involvement in adult criminality among females. In a Philadelphia study, Kempf-Leonard, Tracy, and Howell (2001), found that violent and chronic female delinquents constituted just 2% of all the female delinquents in the sample, but 44% of this subgroup had adult careers in crime, accounting for 11% of the total number of police encounters. Here, the violent and chronic female share is 5.5 times as great as parity would suggest. This study suggests that serious, violent, and chronic female offender careers deserve far more attention in research concerning criminal careers than they have received in the past, particularly with respect to the role of mental health problems in offending careers. Girls are at significantly higher risk (80%) than boys (67%) for a mental health disorder, with girls demonstrating higher rates than boys of internalizing disorders (Shufelt & Cocozza, 2006). Separate from a focus on recidivism, there is a need to better understand the processing, sanctioning, and effects of sanctions on young women.

Effective Programs for Juvenile Offenders

Effective programs for both juvenile and young adult offenders are reviewed by Welsh et al. in Chapter 9 of this volume. However, much of the delinquency intervention research involves rather generic kinds of programs not likely by themselves to attract the attention of a reviewer performing program-by-program reviews. Meta-analysis has many advantages. As Lipsey (1999) notes, "Most striking, perhaps, is the power of meta-analysis to identify intervention effects not clearly visible to traditional reviewers" (p. 619; see also Lipsey & Wilson, 1998). Lipsey's (1999) discovery of the delinquency reduction potential of "practical" juvenile justice program interventions is an excellent example. Another advantage of meta-analysis is that this technique enables users to easily assess program effectiveness on a number of other dimensions, such as the types of offenders with whom program interventions work best, gender effects of different interventions, and supplementary program interventions that work well with particular interventions. These are features that cannot be assessed comprehensively in program-by-program reviews. Thus the narrative review method lacks the scope and depth of meta-analysis procedures.

In a comprehensive meta-analytic review of more than 600 controlled studies on various interventions conducted in English-speaking countries from 1958 to 2002, Lipsey (2009) found that the most consistently effective generic types of services (i.e., those with the largest mean recidivism reductions) are cognitive-behavioral therapy (26% reduction), behavior management services (22%), group counseling (22%), mentoring (21%), and case management (individually tailored service plans) (20%)—provided that these services are implemented with high fidelity and target high-risk offenders (p. 142). Importantly, these evidence-based program services are about equally effective with girls and boys and both minority and nonminority offenders (Lipsey, 2009)—and also with serious and violent offenders (Lipsey & Wilson, 1998).[2]

Research-based program guidelines have been incorporated into a Standardized Program Evaluation Protocol (SPEP), which allows juvenile justice agencies to compare their current services to best practices shown in the research to improve outcomes for youth involved with juvenile justice. More specifically, the SPEP creates a metric by assigning points to programs according to how closely their characteristics match those associated with the best recidivism outcomes for similar programs, as identified in Lipsey's large (2009) meta-analysis of evaluation studies. Programs are scored along four critical dimensions: (1) type of program, (2) amount of treatment, (3) quality of treatment, and (4) youth risk level. Viewed from a diagnostic and program improvement perspective, low ratings on any of these factors identify aspects of a program that, if improved, should improve effectiveness. The SPEP is thus designed not only to evaluate each program against an evidence-based best practice profile, but to provide guidance for improving programs that fall short in that evaluation. As Lipsey (2009, p. 145) says, "It does not take a magic bullet program to impact recidivism, only one that is well made and well aimed."

The success of this approach to evidence-based practice can be increased by embedding it in a forward-looking administrative model, a system organized around risk management. The Office of Juvenile Justice and Delinquency Prevention's Comprehensive Strategy for Serious, Violent, and Chronic Juvenile Offenders (Wilson & Howell, 1993; Howell, 2003a, 2003b, 2009) is a framework for putting research into practice in the juvenile justice and human service field in order to improve outcomes. More specifically, it involves applying "best practices" derived from sound program evaluation research and the use of advanced management tools into state and local prevention and intervention systems. The key management tools in this framework are validated risk and needs assessment instruments, a disposition matrix that guides placements in a manner that protects the public, and protocols for developing comprehensive treatment plans that facilitate matching effective services with offender treatment needs and evaluating those services on an ongoing basis (using the SPEP instrument described above). Use of this forward-looking administrative framework and advanced management tools should increase the capacity of state juvenile justice systems to more effectively control and rehabilitate adolescents on the verge or at high risk of becoming transition offenders (Howell, 2009). It has been implemented successfully in a number of states (Howell, 2003a, 2003b, 2009).

A promising forward-looking model for offenders who are candidates for transitioning into the criminal justice system is specialized services for young adult offenders by an intervention team of professionals. The British T2A (Transition to Adulthood) initiative is particularly noteworthy (Helyar-Caldwell, 2010). Experimental pilot programs were recommended by the Barrow Cadbury Commission on Young Adults and the Criminal Justice System (2005). The Barrow Cadbury Trust then established three pilot programs (in London, Worcestershire, and Birmingham). Each is implementing a team approach to sentencing and to meeting the specific needs of 18–24-year-olds, to build support for desistance (see Helyar-Caldwell, 2010, pp. 8–9 for the 10 guiding recommendations and descriptions of the three programs). Sentencing and placements are based on maturity assessments. A Maturity Assessment Framework is outlined in the Marburg Guidelines. This tool and additional information on the pilot programs can be accessed at the T2A Alliance Web site: http://www.t2a.org.uk/. These programs are being evaluated by the Oxford Centre for Criminological Research. Preliminary research findings would be instructive in developing an American model in jurisdictions where American courts are inclined to consider such factors as maturity assessments in the administration of justice for young transition offenders.

Future Research

We must acknowledge that little research has evaluated the performance of state systems in handling serious and violent juvenile offenders. Hence, several fundamental questions remain to be answered:

- In what important ways do state juvenile justice systems differ in their handling of serious and violent juvenile offenders? Similarly, how do state criminal justice systems differ in their handling of their youngest serious and violent juvenile offenders? How can the chasm between these systems be bridged in a way that mirrors the research link between juvenile delinquency and adult crime?
- Which combinations of sentences and interventions work best and for whom to reduce recidivism and shorten serious and violent juvenile

offender careers? Which ones produce the greatest improvements, not only in recidivism and criminal careers but also in other important outcomes, including education, housing, employment, and mental health?

- Which correctional system approaches in either juvenile or criminal justice are most effective? At present, states vary greatly in the upper age of juvenile court jurisdiction that they use, the upper ages of jurisdiction for youth sentenced to juvenile justice custodial facilities, and the ages at which youth can be transferred to adult court for various offenses. The result is a situation of enormous complexity, with youth between ages 15 and 21 being handled in markedly different ways within and across juvenile and criminal justice systems and within and across states. As a result, similar youth can and do receive highly different types of correctional intervention. At the same time, the variation affords an opportunity to investigate whether some types of intervention are more effective than others for reducing persistent offending.

- How, if at all, does the effectiveness of different sanctioning, treatment, and correctional system approaches vary by age, gender, and race and ethnicity? System-wide client flow studies would be required to assess this vitally important issue. Some research studies suggest that arrest and juvenile court exposure (Bernburg & Krohn, 2003, Bernburg, Krohn, & Rivera, 2006; Huizinga & Henry, 2008) may produce an unintended criminogenic effect. Yet these studies do not control for risk level. If a juvenile justice system was doing its job in protecting public safety, higher-risk offenders would penetrate the system more deeply and have higher recidivism rates.

- What, if any, are the unintended consequences of the many large-scale efforts to address crime among young people? Some recent efforts appear to have produced unintended outcomes. For example, substantial evidence suggests that transfer laws may actually increase rather than decrease recidivism (Hahn et al., 2007; McGowan et al., 2007) and blended sentences may produce net-widening and consign younger, less-sophisticated offenders to prison (Podkopacz & Feld 2001). Any adequate assessment of juvenile justice reforms therefore requires systematically identifying the full range of intended and unintended effects of these reforms (Mears, 2000).

- Of the many new initiatives and laws enacted annually to address crime among young people, which are effective and feasible to implement on a large-scale basis? For example, specialized courts (drug, teen, mental health) exist but, to be effective, require sustained funding and quality implementation over the long term (Butts & Roman, 2004). Such efforts may be feasible in large metropolitan communities but typically will not be feasible in those that are smaller. Other efforts, such as the widespread use of validated screening and assessment instruments to guide the selection of appropriate interventions, are now feasible on a statewide basis.

- Alongside efforts to improve system responses to serious and violent juvenile offending, how do we ensure that both the juvenile and adult justice systems afford adequate due process protections to youth and that they accommodate, where appropriate, developmental differences in the emotional, cognitive, and psychosocial development of young people?

Critical importance of rigorous evaluations of new initiatives. Evaluation of juvenile and young adult court processing, treatment, and sanctioning is critical for identifying problem areas, programs and policies that are effective, and ways to introduce efficiencies and fairer, more just, and cost-effective processing (Mears, 2010). The recommended evaluation design for outcome measurement should incorporate a system flow perspective, using a system-wide framework that encompasses the entire juvenile justice system from primary prevention to discharge from post-dispositional placement (Figure 8.3). In this evaluation scheme, developed by Lipsey (see Howell, 2009, p. 251), youths who enter the juvenile justice system are viewed as moving along alternative pathways of services and sanctions, during which they interact with juvenile justice service programs and supervision contexts. This figure can also be viewed in relation to the juvenile justice system flowchart (Figure 8.1), which illustrates processing stages in the middle of the figure: that is prosecution, juvenile court intake, formal processing, adjudication, and residential placement. In that figure, juvenile justice system program evaluation would commence when the offender advances to the intake stage, the point at which services are more likely to be provided. Multiple services are even more likely at the next stage, following adjudication, because this is the point at which comprehensive treatment plans are often developed and intensive services are provided, including "intensive supervision" in conjunction with graduated sanctions (possibly detention) and particularly close surveillance and home visits by a probation officer. It is here and in residential placement that an array of services is commonly provided, as shown in Lipsey's evaluation design (Figure 8.3).

Each of the pathways taken is associated with certain outcomes and costs, with the outcomes themselves entailing later costs or cost savings according to how positive they are. The key concept of the evaluation design is to use the automated state data systems and Lipsey's SPEP to continuously evaluate and monitor outcomes and costs in a way that will allow periodic assessment of the effectiveness of service and sanctions combinations and, collectively, the overall juvenile justice system. The critical data elements of this evaluation design are risk and needs information for each juvenile at entry, program ratings, recidivism outcomes after completion of a pathway, service and supervision costs, and expected costs associated with recidivism and reentry into the juvenile justice system. This evaluation design can easily be extended to encompass the adult criminal justice system.

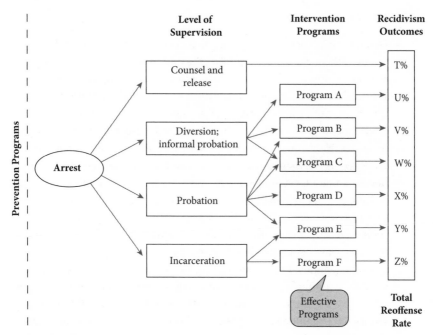

FIGURE 8.3 System-wide evaluation design.

Source: Lipsey, 2006.

Application of research on systems to the target age group. This model permits an examination of the impacts of system interventions on various subgroups, males versus females, minorities versus nonminorities, low-risk versus moderate-and high-risk offenders, and among various age groups. Two of these groups are of priority interest, characterized here as the "target age group." By this, we refer to young offenders in the juvenile justice system who are prime candidates for continuing their criminal careers into adulthood. This group is distinguished by age (older offenders) and risk level (who are persistent serious and violent offenders). The system flow evaluation design can be employed to examine system effectiveness in providing services and sanctions to this group in both the juvenile and adult criminal justice systems.

Policy Recommendations

We cannot overstate the sense of urgency surrounding the need to reform juvenile and criminal justice policies and practices with respect to the transitioning young offender group. In some instances, this transition can have life or death implications. For this reason, we urge state legislators, judges, and policy-makers to implement the following actions immediately.

IMMATURITY DISCOUNTS

- Given the evidence to date, policy-makers should revisit waiver laws and policy with an eye towards limiting the option of transfer for youth.[3] Waiver constitutes a less-than-ideal option, and we emphasize that waiver should be used only in the most serious cases and for older youth; it is these youth who, on average, would be more culpable and who would spend less time incarcerated in juvenile justice facilities. In limited instances, waiver may be appropriate with youth who have extensive records of recidivism or unsuccessful treatment. It bears emphasizing, however, that repeated recidivism may stem from poor treatment, and so it is important that, when considering waiver in such cases, there is careful assessment of the quality of prior treatment. Waiver criteria should identify those combinations of serious present offenses, offense histories, offender culpability, criminal participation, clinical evaluations, and other aggravating and mitigating factors that some advocates insist deserve "real time" sentences substantially longer than those available in juvenile court. Because an "immaturity discount" should substantially reduce the length of adult sentences, only extraordinarily serious cases should warrant consideration for transfer. An adversarial waiver hearing at which both the state and defense can present evidence about the offense, culpability, and clinical responsiveness will produce more accurate and fair transfer decisions than prosecutors will make in their offices without access to clinical information and subject to political considerations (e.g., Feld, 1999, 2003a; Zimring, 1998a, 2000; Bishop, 2000a, 2004; Kupchik, 2006; Scott & Steinberg, 2008). Finally, in cases where waiver occurs, youth who are sent to adult facilities should be housed primarily with younger offenders and offered similar services and treatment to what they would receive in the juvenile justice system. The separate housing and greater emphasis on treatment reflects an evidence-based approach to sanctioning young offenders (Lipsey & Cullen, 2007) and accords with the tenets of the juvenile court and with public opinion (Mears, 2001; Cullen, 2007).
- When sentencing youth, judges should apply an "immaturity discount" to the sentence that he or she would impose on an adult offender. A categorical "immaturity discount" would provide adolescents who are sentenced as adults with fractional reductions in sentence-lengths and would use age as a proxy for culpability (Feld, 1997, 1999, 2008; Scott & Steinberg, 2003, 2008; Tanenhaus & Drizin, 2002). In addition to recognizing youths' diminished responsibility, an "immaturity discount" provides a corrective that addresses the fact that same-length sentences exact a greater "penal bite" from younger offenders than from older ones (Von Hirsch, 2001). The "immaturity discount" includes a sliding scale of

diminished responsibility and gives the largest sentence reductions to the youngest, least mature offenders (Scott & Steinberg, 2003; Tanenhaus & Drizin, 2002). The deeper discounts for younger offenders correspond with their greater (on average) developmental differences in maturity of judgment and self-control.

- Legislatures should abolish life without parole sentences and instead apply immaturity discounts. Realistically, life without parole sentences for juveniles are but a "slower form of death" (Feld, 2008; Johnson & Tabriz, 2010). By definition, an immaturity discount would preclude imposing life without parole sentences and other "virtual life" sentences. Apart from adolescents' diminished responsibility, the likelihood of recidivism decreases with age and the costs of confining geriatric inmates increase substantially (ibid. p. 63).

CATEGORICAL RULE OF YOUTHFULNESS

- A categorical rule of youthfulness as a mitigating factor in sentencing is preferable to individualized discretion. The *Roper* court opted to treat adolescents' diminished responsibility categorically rather than individually. It adopted a categorical prohibition because "the differences between juvenile and adult offenders are too well marked and well understood to risk allowing a youthful person to receive the death penalty despite insufficient culpability" (*Roper*, 2004, pp. 572–573). *Roper* concluded that neither clinicians nor jurors could accurately distinguish between the vast majority of immature juveniles who deserve leniency, and the rare youth who might possess adult-like culpability. Despite individual variability, the Court reasoned that a rule which occasionally "under-punishes the rare, fully-culpable adolescent still will produce less aggregate injustice than a discretionary system that improperly, harshly sentences many more undeserving youths" (*Roper*, 2004, p. 573).

CULPABILITY AND COMPETENCE

- Adolescents' reduced culpability should be incorporated in sentencing decisions. This recommendation is supported by two observations. The first is our inability either to define or identify what constitutes adult-like culpability among offending youths. Despite adolescents' developmental differences, clinicians lack the tools with which to assess youths' impulsivity, foresight, or preference for risks in ways that relate to maturity of judgment and criminal responsibility (*Roper*, 2005; Zimring, 1998). Development and validation of such tools is a top priority. The second reason to treat youthfulness categorically is the inability of judges or juries to fairly weigh an abstract consideration of youthfulness as a mitigating factor against the aggravating reality of a horrific crime.

TOOLS AND PROTOCOLS FOR ASSESSING ADJUDICATIVE COMPETENCE

- Tools and protocols are available to assess objectively adjudicative competence, and these should be further tested and moved into more widespread use. Many youths in the juvenile and criminal justice systems lack adjudicative competence because of developmental immaturity (Grisso et al., 2003). Moreover, the prevalence of mental illness among young offenders heightens concerns about their ability to understand and participate in legal proceedings or to assist counsel (Grisso, 2004). In some young offenders, reasoned judgments may be impaired by incomplete brain maturation. The combination of generic developmental immaturity and mental illness requires the development of protocols to assess adolescents' competence. Depending on whether states try youths in juvenile or criminal courts, this requires clarification of the operative legal standard—adult standard or juvenile-normed standard (Scott & Grisso, 2005). It requires training of judges and lawyers to recognize the developmental limitations of younger offenders (Grisso, 2004). It also poses a challenge for mental health clinicians who evaluate juveniles' competence (Kruh & Grisso, 2009). It is important to focus on individual differences in maturation.

With the support of the MacArthur Foundation Research Network on Adolescent Development and Juvenile Justice, the MacArthur Competency Assessment Tool-Criminal Adjudication (MacCAT-CA; Hoge, Bonnie, Poythress, & Monahan, 1999) was developed to assess an individual's competency to stand trial. MacCAT-CA consists of three scales, Understanding, Reasoning, and Appreciation, along with several other variables (age, IQ, achievement level, experience with the juvenile justice system, and a screen for psychopathology) that may be related to competence to stand trial. Results of a validation study suggest that performance on the MacCAT-CA varied with age, with younger participants performing significantly worse than older juveniles (Ficke, Hart, & Deardorff, 2006). The most extensive data on application of the MacCAT-CA, reported by Grisso, Steinberg, Woolard, and colleagues (2003), gathered data on approximately 1,400 adolescents and adults in pre-trial detention/jail and community settings at four sites (Los Angeles, Philadelphia, northern Florida, and Virginia). This study indicated that the MacCAT-CA can be successfully administered to adolescents and that it discriminated well among age groups. Woolard & Harvell (2005) remind us that this instrument is intended to serve as one tool for making a comprehensive forensic evaluation that should include a social history, mental status exam, and personal interviews with the client and collateral informants, among other components.

However, research on developmental immaturity (incompetence) of judgment and decision-making suggests that adolescents may differ from adults in important ways that compromise their effectiveness as defendants but are not included in adult assessment instruments or protocols (Woolard & Harvell, 2005). The Virginia Juvenile Competence Program of the Institute of Law, Psychiatry, and Public Policy (ILPPP) provides court ordered services to all youth found incompetent to stand by juvenile court judges in each of the court jurisdictions throughout the state (http://ilppp.virginia.edu/research-initiatives/policy-development/restoring-juveniles-found-incompetent-to-stand-trial.html). In addition, the ILPPP conducts a training program on principles and practices of juvenile forensic evaluation.

COMMUNITY PROGRAMS

- Expenditures saved from lower custody rates should be reinvested in front-end, evidence-based community programs that address the specific needs of young adults and the causes of their offending. Community-based programs are far more cost-effective than correctional institutions. Moreover, the earlier successful intervention occurs in offender careers, the greater the cost savings (Cohen, Piquero, & Jennings 2010; Welsh et al., Chapter 9, this volume).

YOUNG OFFENDER COURTS

- Consideration should be given to establishing in the United States Young Offender Courts for transitioning offenders that are more focused on rehabilitation. Pilot programs should be tested for the utility of this structure for bridging the gap between the U.S. juvenile justice and criminal justice systems.

A forward-looking administrative model. Both the juvenile and criminal justice systems in every state should be developing forward-looking organizational models that are built around risk management, using offender management tools that increase the capacity of state justice systems to more effectively control and rehabilitate transition offenders. The Comprehensive Strategy for Serious, Violent, and Chronic Juvenile Offenders (Howell, 2003a, 2003b; Howell, 2009; Wilson & Howell, 1993) is a user-friendly forward-looking administrative framework that promotes system-wide management of juvenile offenders, services, and resources. The necessary tools are available (validated risk and needs assessment instruments, a disposition matrix that guides placements in a manner that protects the public, and protocols for developing comprehensive treatment plans that improve the matching effective services with offender treatment needs) to make system-wide improvements and to perform state-wide evaluations of all service programs against research-based guidelines (Howell, 2009; Lipsey, 2009; Lipsey, Howell, Kelly et al., 2010). This framework can easily be adapted within the criminal justice system.

Conclusions

This chapter has addressed what happens with older adolescents who transition into the criminal justice system, what should happen, and what we need to know. On the first topic, our review emphasizes that neither the juvenile nor the criminal justice system handles this offender group well. The wide diversity of measures that have been introduced has not been found to be effective, and little research has accompanied them. The states are left with dysfunctional—and sometimes contradictory—policies and practices that would be very challenging to isolate and evaluate, if not impossible in some instances. What *should* happen is systematic adoption of research-based policies. We need to know if these work, but this cannot be accomplished without a major investment in evaluation of experimental policies and practices.

We recommend several specific reforms pertaining to young offenders in the criminal justice system:

- An "immaturity discount" should be taken off the appropriate sentence that judges would impose on an adult offender.
- A categorical rule of youthfulness as a mitigating factor in sentencing is preferable to individualized discretion.
- Adolescents' reduced culpability should be incorporated in sentencing decisions. Development and validation of tools to assess young offenders' maturity of judgment and criminal responsibility is a top priority.
- Tools and protocols that are available to assess objectively competence to stand trial should be further tested and moved into more widespread use.
- Expenditures saved from lower custody rates should be reinvested in evidence-based community programs that address the specific needs of young adults and the causes of their offending.
- States should develop or expand forward-looking administrative models organized around risk management, using advanced tools that increase system capacity to more effectively control and rehabilitate transition offenders.

Notes

1. Sweden, Norway, and Denmark do not have juvenile courts but try youths aged 15 or older in the adult criminal justice system, albeit with modified procedures and social welfare alternative sentencing options to adult sentences (Tonry & Doob, 2004).

2. But adolescent girls may need tailored multi-component programs that address unique problems (particularly relational aggression) and co-morbid treatment needs (Hipwell & Loeber, 2006).

3. The first author does not support transfer of any juvenile offenders to the U.S. criminal justice system nor any legal jurisdiction of criminal courts over them. The U.S. criminal justice system has demonstrated that it is unqualified as a model that should be used for juvenile offenders (Brown & Langan, 1998; Hahn et al., 2007; Howell, 2009, pp. 296–97; Howell & Howell, 2007; Kurlychek & Johnson, 2010; Liebman, Fagan, & West, 2000; Tonry, 2007). Juveniles should never, under any circumstances, be placed in adult prisons. This is inhumane and counterproductive in that violent recidivism is more likely. Neither short nor long prison terms reduce crime (Lipsey & Cullen, 2007). Older dangerous adolescent offenders who require secure confinement should be placed in youthful offender facilities. Existing facilities could be made available for this purpose if juvenile and adult correctional systems were to rigorously apply risk assessment and classification procedures and reduce current excessive populations in prisons and juvenile correctional facilities. The cost savings should be reinvested in expanded and improved rehabilitative services.

References

Annie E. Casey Foundation. (2005). *Reentry: Helping former prisoners return to communities, a guide to key ideas, effective approaches, and technical assistance resources for making connections.* Baltimore, MD: Annie E. Casey Foundation.

Aronson, J.D. (2007). Brain imaging, culpability and the juvenile death penalty. *Psychology, Public Policy and Law*, 13, 115–142.

Aos, S., Phipps, P., Barnoski, R., & Lieb, R. (2001). *The comparative costs and benefits of programs to reduce crime.* Olympia, WA: Washington State Institute for Public Policy.

Arya, N., Villarruel, F., Villanueva, C., & Augarten, I. (2009). *America's invisible children: Latino youth and the failure of justice.* Policy Brief, Race and Ethnicity Series. Washington, DC: Campaign for Youth Justice and National Council of La Raza.

Backstrom, J.C., & Walker, G.L. (2006). The role of the prosecutor in juvenile justice: Advocacy in the courtroom and leadership in the community. *William Mitchell Law Review*, 32, 963–988.

Baer, D., Bhati, A., Brooks, L., Castro, J., La Vigne, N., Mallik-Kane, K., Naser, R., Osborne, J., Roman, C., Roman, J., Rossman, S., Solomon, C.V., & Winterfield, L. (2006). *Understanding the challenges of prisoner reentry.* Washington, DC: Urban Institute.

Baird, A.A., Gruber, S.A., Fein, D.A., Mass, L.C., Steingard, R.J., Renshaw, P.F., Cohen, B.M., & Yurgleun-Todd, D.A. (1999). Functional magnetic resonance imaging of facial affect recognition in children and adolescents. *Journal of the American Academy of Child and Adolescent Psychiatry* 38, 195–199.

Barrow Cadbury Commission on Young Adults and the Criminal Justice System. (2005). *Lost in transition*. London, UK: Barrow Cadbury Trust.

Beckett, K., & Sasson, T. (2003). *The politics of injustice: Crime and punishment in America* (2nd ed.). Thousand Oaks, CA: Pine Forge Press.

Belluck, P. (February 11, 1998). Fighting youth crime, some states blend adult and juvenile justice. *The New York Times*, pp. A1, A26.

Bernburg, J.G., & Krohn, M.D. (2003). Labeling, life chances, and adult crime: The direct and indirect effects of official intervention in adolescence on crime in early adulthood. *Criminology*, 41, 1287–1318.

Bernburg, J.G., Krohn, M.D., & Rivera, C.J. (2006). Official labeling, criminal embeddedness, and subsequent delinquency. *Journal of Research in Crime and Delinquency*, 43, 67–88.

Bishop, D.M. (2004). Injustice and irrationality in contemporary youth policy. *Criminology and Public Policy*, 3, 633–644.

Bishop, D.M. (2005). The role of race and ethnicity in juvenile justice processing. In D.F. Hawkins & K. Kempf-Leonard (Eds.), *Our children, their children: Confronting racial and ethnic differences in American juvenile justice* (pp. 23–82). Chicago, IL: University of Chicago Press.

Bishop, D.M. (2006). Public opinion and juvenile justice policy: Myths and misconceptions. *Criminology and Public Policy*, 5, 653–664.

Bishop, D.M., & Frazier, C.E. (1996). Race effects in juvenile justice decision-making: Findings of a statewide analysis. *Journal of Criminal Law and Criminology*, 86, 392–413.

Bishop, D.M. & Frazier, C.E. (2000). Consequences of transfer. In J.A. Fagan & F.E. Zimring (Eds.), *The changing borders of juvenile justice: Transfer of adolescents to the criminal court* (pp. 227–276). Chicago, IL: University of Chicago Press.

Blumstein, A. (1995a). Violence by young people: Why the deadly nexus? *National Institute of Justice Journal*, 229, 2–9.

Blumstein, A. (1995b). Youth violence, guns, and the illicit-drug industry. *Journal of Criminal Law and Criminology*, 86, 10–36.

Blumstein, A., Cohen, J., Roth, J.A., & Visher, C.A. (Eds.). (1986). *Criminal careers and career criminals*. Washington, DC: National Academy Press.

Bonnie, R.J., & Grisso, T. (2000). Adjudicative competence and youthful offenders. In T. Grisso & R.G. Schwartz (Eds.), *Youth on trial: A developmental perspective on juvenile justice* (pp. 70–103). Chicago, IL: University of Chicago Press.

Brown, J., & Langan, P. (1998). *State court sentencing of convicted felons, 1994*. Washington, DC: U.S. Department of Justice, Bureau of Justice Statistics.

Brownstein, H. (1996). *The rise and fall of a violent crime wave: Crack cocaine and the social construction of a crime problem*. Guilderland, NY: Harrow and Heston.

Butts, J., Buck, J., & Coggeshall, M. (2002). *The impact of teen court on young offenders*. Washington, DC: The Urban Institute.

Butts, J.A. & Mears, D.P. (2001). Reviving juvenile justice in a get-tough era. *Youth and Society*, 33, 169–198.

Butts, J.A., & Mitchell, O. (2000). Brick by brick: Dismantling the border between juvenile and adult justice. In C.M. Friel (Ed.), *Criminal justice 2000: Boundary changes in criminal justice* (Vol. 2, pp. 167–213). Washington, DC: National Institute of Justice.

Butts, J.A. & Roman, J. (Eds). (2004). *Juvenile drug courts and teen substance abuse*. Washington, DC: The Urban Institute.

Carter, A.M. (2006). Age matters: The case for a constitutionalized infancy defense. *University of Kansas Law Review*, 54, 687–714.

Centers for Disease Control and Prevention. (2006). Youth risk behavior surveillance: United States, 2005. *Prevention Morbidity and Mortality Weekly Report*, 55, 1–108.

Cernkovich, S.A., Lanctôt, N., & Giordano, P.C. (2008). Predicting adolescent and adult antisocial behavior among adjudicated delinquent females. *Crime and Delinquency*, 54, 3–33.

Cheesman, F., Green, H., Cohen, T., Dancy, D., Kleiman, M., & Mott, N. (2002). *Blended sentencing in Minnesota: On target for justice and public safety?* Williamsburg, VA: National Center for State Courts.

Cohen, M.A., Piquero, A.R., & Jennings, W.G. (2010). Estimating the costs of bad outcomes for at-risk youth and the benefits of early childhood interventions to reduce them. *Criminal Justice Policy Review*, 21, 391-434.

Cook, P.J., & Laub, J.H. (1998). The unprecedented epidemic of youth violence. In M. Tonry & M.H. Moore (Eds.), *Youth violence* (pp. 27–64). Chicago, IL: University of Chicago Press.

Cullen, F.T. (2005). The twelve people who saved rehabilitation: How the science of criminology made a difference. *Criminology*, 43, 1–42.

Cullen, F.T. (2007). Make rehabilitation corrections' guiding paradigm. *Criminology and Public Policy*, 6, 717–728.

Decker, S.H. (2007). Youth gangs and violent behavior. In D.J. Flannery, A.T. Vazsonyi, & I.D. Waldman (Eds.), *The Cambridge handbook of violent behavior and aggression* (pp. 388–402). Cambridge, UK: Cambridge University Press.

Deitch, M. (2009). *From time out to hard time: Young children in the adult criminal justice system*, Austin, TX: The University of Texas at Austin, LBJ School of Public Affairs.

Denno, D. (2006). The mind of a child: The relationship between brain development, cognitive functioning, and accountability under the law: The scientific shortcomings of Roper v. Simmons. *Ohio State Journal of Criminal Law*, 3, 380–396.

DiIulio, J.J. (1995a). The coming of the super-predators. *The Weekly Standard*, 1, [November 27], p. 23.

DiIulio, J.J. (1995b). Arresting ideas. *Policy Review*, 74, 12–16.

DiIulio, J.J. (1996). They're coming: Florida's youth crime bomb. *Impact*, (Spring), 1, 25–27.

DiIulio, J.J. (1997). Reinventing parole and probation. *Brookings Review*, 15, 40–42.

Dusky v. United States, 362 U.S. 402 (1960).

Fagan, J. (2007). End natural life sentences for juveniles. *Criminology and Public Policy*, 6, 735–746.

Fagan, J., & Zimring, F.E. (2000). *The changing borders of juvenile justice*. Chicago, IL: University of Chicago Press.

Feld, B.C. (1988). The juvenile court meets the principle of offense: Punishment, treatment and the difference it makes, *Boston University Law Review*, 68, 821–915.

Feld, B.C. (1993). Criminalizing the American juvenile court. In M. Tonry (Ed.), *Crime and Justice: A review of research* (Vol. 7, pp. 197–280). Chicago, IL: University of Chicago Press.

Feld, B.C. (1997). Abolish the juvenile court: Youthfulness, criminal responsibility, and sentencing policy. *Journal of Criminal Law and Criminology*, 88, 68–136.

Feld, B.C. (1998). Juvenile and criminal justice systems' responses to youth. In M. Tonry & M.H. Moore (Eds.), *Youth violence* (pp. 189–262). Chicago, IL: University of Chicago Press.

Feld, B.C. (1999). *Bad kids: Race and the transformation of the juvenile court.* New York: Oxford University Press.

Feld, B.C. (2003). The politics of race and juvenile justice: The "due process revolution" and the conservative reaction. *Justice Quarterly, 20,* 765–800.

Feld, B.C. (2000). Legislative exclusion of offenses from juvenile court jurisdiction: A history and critique. In J.A. Fagan & F.E. Zimring (Eds.), *Changing borders of juvenile justice: Transfer of adolescents to the criminal court* (pp. 83–144). Chicago, IL: University of Chicago Press.

Feld, B.C. (2006). *Final report of the Girl's Study Group.* Washington, DC: Office of Juvenile Justice and Delinquency Prevention.

Feld, B.C. (2008). A slower form of death: Implications of Roper v. Simmons for juveniles sentenced to life without parole. *Notre Dame Journal of Law, Ethics, and Public Policy, 22,* 9–65.

Feld, B.C. (2009). *Cases and materials on juvenile justice administration* (3rd ed.). St. Paul, MN: West.

Ficke, S.L., Hart, K.J., & Deardorff, P.A. (2006). The performance of incarcerated juveniles on the MacArthur Competence Assessment Tool-Criminal Adjudication (MacCAT-CA). *Journal of the American Academy of Psychiatry and Law, 34,* 360–373.

Forst, M., Fagan, J., & Vivona, T.S. (1989). Youth in prisons and training schools: Perceptions and consequences of the treatment-custody dichotomy. *Juvenile and Family Court Journal, 40,* 1–14.

Fox, J.A. (1996). *Trends in juvenile violence: A report to the United States Attorney General on current and future rates of juvenile offending.* Boston, MA: Northeastern University Press.

Furby, L., & Beyth-Marom, R. (1992). Risk taking in adolescence: A decision-making perspective. *Developmental Review, 12,* 1–44.

Garland, D. (2001). *The culture of control: Crime and social order in contemporary society.* Chicago, IL: University of Chicago Press.

Giedd, J.N., Blumenthal, J., Jeffries, N.O., Castellanos, F.X., Liu, H., Zijdenbos, A., Paus, T., Evans, A.C., & Rapoport, J.L. (1999). Brain development during childhood and adolescence: A longitudinal MRI study. *Nature Neuroscience, 2,* 861–863.

Glaze, L.E., & Palla, S. (2005). *Probation and parole in the United States, 2004.* Washington, DC: U.S. Department of Justice, Bureau of Justice Statistics.

Griffin, P. (2008). *Different from adults: An updated analysis of juvenile transfer and blended sentencing laws, with recommendations for reform.* Pittsburgh, PA: National Center for Juvenile Justice and the John D. and Catherine T. MacArthur Foundation.

Grisso, T. (1997). The competence of adolescents as trial defendants. *Psychology, Public Policy, and Law, 3,* 3–32.

Grisso, T. (2000). Forensic clinical evaluations related to waiver of jurisdiction. In J. Fagan & F.E. Zimring (Eds.), *The changing borders of juvenile justice: Transfer to criminal court* (pp. 321–352). Chicago, IL: University of Chicago Press.

Grisso, T. (2004). *Double jeopardy: Adolescent offenders with mental disorders.* Chicago, IL: University of Chicago Press.

Grisso, T., Steinberg, L., Woolard, J., Cauffman, E., Scott, E., Graham, S., Lexcen, F., Reppucci, N.D., & Schwartz, R. (2003). Juveniles' competence to stand trial: A comparison of adolescents' and adults' capacities as trial defendants. *Law and Human Behavior, 27,* 333–363.

Gruber, S.A. &. Yurgelun-Todd, D.A. 2006. Neurobiology and the law: A role in juvenile justice. *Ohio State Journal of Criminal Law*, 3, 321–340.

Hahn, R.A., McGowan, A., Liberman, A., Crosby, A., Fullilove, M., Johnson, R., Moscicki, E., Price, L., Snyder, S., Tuma, F., Lowy, J., Briss, P., Cory, S., & Stone, G. (2007). *Effects on violence of laws and policies facilitating the transfer of youth from the juvenile to the adult justice system*. Atlanta, GA: Centers for Disease Control.

Harlow, C.W. *(2003). Education and correctional populations.* Washington, DC: U.S. Department of Justice, Bureau of Justice Statistics.

Hartman, D.A., & Golub, A. (1999). The social construction of the crack epidemic in the print media. *Journal of Psychoactive Drugs*, 31, 423–433.

Hawkins, D.F., & Kempf-Leonard, K. (2005). *Our children, their children: Confronting racial and ethnic differences in American juvenile justice.* Chicago, IL: University of Chicago Press.

Hawkins, D.F., Laub, J.H., Lauritsen, J.L., & Cothern, L. (2000). *Race, ethnicity, and serious and violent juvenile offending.* Washington, DC: U.S. Department of Justice, Office of Juvenile Justice and Delinquency Prevention.

Helyar-Caldwell, V. (2010). *Young adult manifesto.* London, UK: Barrow Cadbury Trust.

Hipwell, A.E., & Loeber, R. (2006). Do we know which interventions are effective for disruptive and delinquent girls? *Clinical Child and Family Psychology Review*, 9, 221–255.

Hoge, S.K., Bonnie, R.J., Poythress, N., & Monahan, J. (1999). *MacArthur Competence Assessment Tool-Criminal Adjudication (MacCAT-CA).* Odessa, FL: Psychological Assessment Resources.

Howell, J.C. (Ed.) (1995). *Guide for implementing the comprehensive strategy for serious, violent, and chronic juvenile offenders.* Washington, DC: U.S. Department of Justice, Office of Juvenile Justice and Delinquency Prevention.

Howell, J.C. (1996). Juvenile transfers to the criminal justice system: State-of-the-art. *Law and Policy*, 18, 17–60.

Howell, J.C. (1999). Youth gang homicides: A literature review. *Crime and Delinquency*, 45, 208–241.

Howell, J.C. (2003a). Diffusing research into practice using the Comprehensive Strategy for Serious, Violent, and Chronic Juvenile Offenders. *Youth Violence and Juvenile Justice: An Interdisciplinary Journal*, 1, 219–245.

Howell, J.C. (2003b). *Preventing and reducing juvenile delinquency: A comprehensive framework.* Thousand Oaks, CA: Sage.

Howell, J.C. (2006). Review of our children, their children: Confronting racial and ethnic differences in American juvenile justice. *Social Service Review*, 80, 750–753.

Howell, J.C. (2009). *Preventing and reducing juvenile delinquency: A comprehensive framework* (2nd ed.). Thousand Oaks, CA: Sage.

Howell, J.C. (2012). Gangs in America's communities. Thousand Oaks, CA: Sage.

Howell, J.C., & Decker, S.H. (1999). *The youth gangs, drugs, and violence connection.* Washington, DC: Office of Juvenile Justice and Delinquency Prevention, Juvenile Justice Bulletin. Office of Justice Programs. U.S. Department of Justice.

Howell, J.C., & Howell, M.Q. (2007). Violent juvenile delinquency: Changes, consequences, and implications. In D. Flannery, A. Vazonsyi, & I. Waldman (Eds.), *Cambridge handbook of violent behavior and aggression* (pp. 501–518). Cambridge, UK: Cambridge University Press.

Huizinga, D., & Henry, K.L. (2008). The effect of arrest and justice system sanctions on subsequent behavior: Findings from longitudinal and other studies. In A.M. Liberman (Ed.), *The long view of crime: A synthesis of longitudinal research* (pp. 220–254). New York: Springer.

Huizinga, D., Thornberry, T., Knight, K., Lovegrove, P., Loeber, R., Hill, K., & Farrington, D.P. (2007). *Disproportionate minority contact in the juvenile justice system: A study of differential minority arrest/referral to court in three cities. A report to the Office of Juvenile Justice and Delinquency Prevention*. Rockville, MD: National Criminal Justice Reference Service.

Huizinga, D., Weiher, A.W., Espiritu, R., & Esbensen, F. (2003). Delinquency and crime: Some highlights from the Denver Youth Survey. In T.P. Thornberry & M.D. Krohn (Eds.), *Taking stock of delinquency: An overview of findings from contemporary longitudinal studies* (pp. 47–91). New York: Kluwer Academic/Plenum.

Human Rights Watch and Amnesty International. (2005). *The rest of their lives: Life without parole for child offenders in the United States*. New York: Human Rights Watch/Amnesty International.

Irwin, J. (1980). *Prisons in turmoil*. Boston: Brown.

Irwin, J. (2005). *The warehouse prison: Disposal of the new dangerous class*. Los Angeles: Roxbury.

Johnson, R., & Tabriz, S. (2010). Death by incarceration as a cruel and unusual punishment when applied to juveniles: Extending *Roper* to life without parole, our other death penalty. *University of Maryland Law Review*, 9, 241-258.

Juszkiewicz, J. (2000). *Youth crime/adult time: Is justice served? Building blocks for youth report*. Washington, DC: Pretrial Services Resource Center.

Juvenile Justice Center. (2004). *Adolescence, brain development, and legal culpability*. Washington, DC: Juvenile Justice Center, American Bar Association.

Kandel, E.R., Schwartz, J.H., & Jessell, T.M. (2000). *Principles of neuroscience* (4th ed.). New York: McGraw-Hill.

Kempf-Leonard, K., Tracy, P.E., & Howell, J.C. (2001). Serious, violent, and chronic juvenile offenders: The relationship of delinquency career types to adult criminality. *Justice Quarterly*, 18, 449–478.

Krisberg, B., & Howell, J.C. (1998). The impact of the juvenile justice system and prospects for graduated sanctions in a comprehensive strategy. In R. Loeber & D.P. Farrington (Eds.), *Serious and violent juvenile offenders: Risk factors and successful interventions* (pp. 346–366). Thousand Oaks, CA: Sage.

Kruh, I., & Grisso, T. (2009). *Evaluation of juveniles' competence to stand trial*. New York: Oxford University Press.

Kupchik, A. (2006). *Judging juveniles: Prosecuting adolescents in adult and juvenile courts*. New York: New York University Press.

Kupchik, A. (2007). The correctional experiences of youth in adult and juvenile prisons. *Justice Quarterly*, 2, 247–270.

Kurlychek, M.C., & Johnson, B.D. (2004). The juvenile penalty: A comparison of juvenile and young adult sentencing outcomes in criminal court. *Criminology*, 42, 485–517.

Kurlychek, M.C., & Johnson, B.D. (2010). Juvenility and punishment: Sentencing juveniles in adult criminal court. *Criminology*, 48, 725–758.

Lanctôt, N., & Le Blanc, M. (2002). Explaining deviance by adolescent females. In M. Tonry (Ed.), *Crime and justice: A review of research* (Vol. 29, pp. 113–202). Chicago, IL: University of Chicago Press.

Langan, P.A., & Levin, D.J. (2002). *Recidivism of prisoners released in 1994.* Special Report. Washington, DC: U.S. Department of Justice, Bureau of Justice Statistics.

Lanza-Kaduce, L., Lane, J., Bishop, D.M. & Frazier, C.E. (2005). Juvenile offenders and adult felony recidivism: The impact of transfer. *Journal of Crime and Justice,* 28, 59–77.

Latessa, E.J., Cullen, F.T., & Gendreau, P. (2002). Beyond correctional quackery: Professionalism and the possibility of effective treatment. *Federal Probation,* 66, 43–49.

Liebman, J.S., Fagan, J., & West, V. (2000). *A broken system: Error rates in capital cases, 1973–1995.* New York: School of Law, Columbia University.

Lipsey, M.W. (1999). Can rehabilitative programs reduce the recidivism of juvenile offenders? An inquiry into the effectiveness of practical programs. *Virginia Journal of Social Policy and the Law,* 6, 611–641.

Lipsey, M.W. (2009). The primary factors that characterize effective interventions with juvenile offenders: A meta-analytic overview. *Victims and Offenders,* 4, 124–147.

Lipsey, M.W., & Cullen, F.T. (2007). The effectiveness of correctional rehabilitation: A review of systematic reviews. *Annual Review of Law and Social Science,* 3, 297–320.

Lipsey, M.W., Howell, J.C., Kelly, M.R., Chapman, G., & Carver, D. (2011). *Improving the effectiveness of juvenile justice programs: A new perspective on evidence-based practice.* Washington, DC: Georgetown University, Center for Juvenile Justice Reform.

Lipsey, M.W., & Wilson, D.B. (1998). Effective intervention for serious juvenile offenders: A synthesis of research. In R. Loeber & D.P. Farrington (Eds.), *Serious and violent juvenile offenders: Risk factors and successful interventions* (pp. 313–345). Thousand Oaks, CA: Sage.

Lipton, D., Martinson, R., & Wilks, J. (1975). *The effectiveness of correctional treatment: A survey of treatment evaluation studies.* New York: Praeger.

Loeber, R., Farrington, D.P., Stouthamer-Loeber, M., White, H.R., & Wei, E. (2008). *Violence and serious theft: Development and prediction from childhood to adulthood.* New York: Routledge.

Logan, W.A. (1998). Proportionality and punishment: Imposing life without parole on juveniles. *Wake Forest Law Review,* 33, 681–725.

Manhattan Institute (1999). *"Broken windows" probation: The next step in fighting crime.* New York: Center for Civic Innovation, Manhattan Institute.

Males, M.A. (1996). *The scapegoat generation: America's war on adolescents.* Monroe, ME: Common Courage Press.

Maroney, T.A. (2009). The false promise of adolescent brain science in juvenile justice. *Notre Dame Law Review,* 85, 89–176.

Martinson, R. (1974). What works? Questions and answers about prison reform. *Public Interest,* 35, 22–54.

Mauer, M., & Meda, C.E. (2003). *Invisible punishment: The collateral consequences of mass imprisonment.* New York: The New Press.

McCord, J., Widom, C.S., & Crowell, N.A. (2001). *Juvenile crime, juvenile justice.* Washington, DC: National Academy Press.

McGowan, A., Hahn, R., Liberman, A., Crosby, A., Fullilove, M., Johnson, R., Moscicki, E., & et al. (2007). Effects on violence of laws and policies facilitating the transfer of juveniles from the juvenile justice system to the adult justice system: A systematic review. *American Journal of Preventive Medicine,* 32, 7–28.

Mears, D.P. (1998). The sociology of sentencing: Reconceptualizing decisionmaking processes and outcomes. *Law and Society Review,* 32, 667–724.

Mears, D.P. (2000). Assessing the effectiveness of juvenile justice reforms: A closer look at the criteria and the impacts on various stakeholders. *Law and Policy,* 22, 175–202.

Mears, D.P. (2001). Getting tough with juvenile offenders: Explaining support for sanctioning youths as adults. *Criminal Justice and Behavior*, 28, 206–226.

Mears, D.P. (2002). Sentencing guidelines and the transformation of juvenile justice in the twenty-first century. *Journal of Contemporary Criminal Justice*, 18, 6–19.

Mears, D.P. (2003). A critique of waiver research: Critical next steps in assessing the impacts of laws for transferring juveniles to the criminal justice system. *Youth Violence and Juvenile Justice*, 1, 156–172.

Mears, D.P. (2005). A critical look at supermax prisons. *Corrections Compendium*, 30, 6–7, 45–49.

Mears, D.P. (2006). Exploring state-level variation in juvenile incarceration rates: symbolic threats and competing explanations. *Prison Journal*, 86, 470–490.

Mears, D.P. (2008). Accountability, efficiency, and effectiveness in corrections: Shining a light on the black box of prison systems. *Criminology and Public Policy*, 7, 143–152.

Mears, D.P. (2010). *American criminal justice policy: An evaluation approach to increasing accountability and effectiveness*. New York: Cambridge University Press.

Mears, D.P., & Field, S.H. (2000). Theorizing sanctioning in a criminalized juvenile court. *Criminology*, 38, 983–1019.

Mears, D.P., & Travis, J. (2004). Youth development and reentry. *Youth Violence and Juvenile Justice*, 2, 3–20.

Merlo, A.V., Benekos, P.J., & Cook, W.J. (1997). "Getting tough" with youth legislative waiver as crime control. *Juvenile and Family Court Journal*, 48, 1–15.

Nagin, D.S., Cullen, F.T., & Jonson, C.L. (2009). Imprisonment and reoffending. *Crime and Justice*, 38, 115–200.

National Institute of Mental Health. (2001). Teenage Brain. http://www.nimh.nih.gov/health/publications/teenage-brain-a-work-in-progress.shtml (accessed March 6, 2010)

Office of Juvenile Justice and Delinquency Prevention. (1988). *Targeting serious juvenile offenders can make a difference*. Washington, DC: Office of Juvenile Justice and Delinquency Prevention.

Parent, D.G., Lieter, V., Kennedy, S., Livens, L., Wentworth, D., & Wilcox, S. (1994). *Conditions of confinement: Juvenile detention and corrections facilities*. Washington, DC: Office of Juvenile Justice and Delinquency Prevention.

Paus, T., Zijdenbos, A., Worsley, K., Collins, D.L., Blumenthal, J., Giedd, J.N., Rapoport, J.L., & Evans A.C. (1999). Structural maturation of neural pathways in children and adolescents: In vivo study. *Science*, 283, 1908–1911.

Piquero, A.R., Farrington, D.P., & Blumstein, A. (2007). *Key issues in criminal career research: New analyses of the Cambridge Study in Delinquent Development*. New York: Cambridge University Press.

Podkopacz, M.R., & Feld, B.C. (1995). Judicial waiver policy and practice: Persistence, seriousness and race. *Law and Inequality*, 14, 101–207.

Podkopacz, M.R., & Feld, B.C. (1996). The end of the line: An empirical study of judicial waiver. *Journal of Criminal Law and Criminology*, 86, 449–492.

Podkopacz, M.R., & Feld, B.C. (2001). The back-door to prison: Waiver reform, "blending sentencing," and the law of unintended consequences. *Journal of Criminal Law and Criminology*, 91, 997–1071.

Pope, C.E., & Snyder, H.N. (2003). *Race as a factor in juvenile arrests*. Washington, DC: U.S. Department of Justice, Office of Juvenile Justice and Delinquency Prevention.

Redding, R.E. (2008). *Juvenile transfer laws: An effective deterrent to delinquency?* Washington, DC: U.S. Department of Justice, Office of Juvenile Justice and Delinquency Prevention.

Redding, R.E., & Fuller, E.J. (2004). What do juvenile offenders know about being tried as adults? Implications for deterrence. *Juvenile and Family Court Journal*, 55, 35–44.

Reeves, J.L., & Campbell, R. (1994). *Cracked coverage: Television news, the anti-cocaine crusade, and the Reagan legacy.* Durham, NC: Duke University Press.

Roush, D., & McMillen, M. (2000). *Construction, operations, and staff training for juvenile confinement facilities.* Washington, DC: U.S. Department of Justice, Office of Juvenile Justice and Delinquency Prevention.

Scott, E.S. (2000). Criminal responsibility in adolescence: Lessons from developmental psychology. In T. Grisso & R.G. Schwartz (Eds.), *Youth on trial: A developmental perspective on juvenile justice* (pp. 291–324). Chicago, IL: University of Chicago Press.

Scott, E.S. and Grisso, T. (1997). The evolution of adolescence: A developmental perspective on juvenile reform. *Journal of Criminal Law and Criminology*, 88, 137–189.

Scott, E.S., & Grisso, T. (2005). Developmental incompetence, due process, and juvenile justice policy. *North Carolina Law Review*, 83, 793–845.

Scott, E.S., & Steinberg, L. (2003). Blaming youth. *Texas Law Review*, 81, 799–840.

Scott, E.S., & Steinberg, L. (2008). *Rethinking juvenile justice.* Boston, MA: Harvard University Press.

Shaffer, D.K., Hartman, J.L., Listwan, S.J., Howell, T., & Latessa, E.J. (2011). Outcomes among drug court participants: Does drug of choice matter? *International Journal of Offender Therapy and Comparative Criminology*, 55, 155–174.

Seiter, R.P., & Kadela, K.R. (2003). Prisoner reentry: What works, what does not, and what is promising. *Crime and Delinquency*, 49, 360–388.

Shufelt, J.S., & Cocozza, J.C. (2006). *Youth with mental health disorders in the juvenile justice system.* Delmar, NY: National Center for Mental Health and Juvenile Justice.

Singer, S.I. (1996). Merging and emerging systems of juvenile and criminal justice. *Law and Policy*, 18, 1–15.

Smith, P., Cullen, F.T., & Latessa, E.J. (2009). Can 14,737 women be wrong? A meta-analysis of the LSI-R and recidivism for female offenders. *Criminology and Public Policy*, 8, 183–208.

Snyder, H.N. (1998). Serious, violent and chronic juvenile offenders: An assessment of the extent of and trends in officially-recognized serious criminal behavior in a delinquent population. In R. Loeber & D.P. Farrington (Eds.), *Serious and violent juvenile offenders: Risk factors and successful interventions* (pp. 428–444). Thousand Oaks, CA: Sage.

Snyder, H.N., & Sickmund, M. (2000). *Challenging the myths.* Washington, DC: U.S. Department of Justice, Office of Juvenile Justice and Delinquency Prevention.

Snyder, H.N., & Sickmund, M. (2006). *Juvenile offenders and victims: 2006 National Report.* Washington, DC: U.S. Department of Justice, Office of Juvenile Justice and Delinquency Prevention.

Snyder, H.N., Sickmund, M., & Poe-Yamagata, E. (1996). *Juvenile offenders and victims: 1996 Update on violence.* Washington, DC: U.S. Department of Justice, Office of Juvenile Justice and Delinquency Prevention.

Sowell, E.R., Thompson, H.C.J., Jernigan, T.L., & Toga, A.W. (1999). In vivo evidence for post-adolescent brain maturation in frontal and striatal regions. *Nature Neuroscience*, 2, 859–861.

Sowell, E.R., Thompson, P.M., Tessner, K.D., & Toga, A.W. (2001). Mapping continued brain growth and gray matter density reduction in dorsal frontal cortex: Inverse relationships during postadolescent brain maturation. *Journal of Neuroscience*, 21, 8819–8829.

Spear, P. (2000). The adolescent brain and age-related behavioral manifestations. *Neuroscience and Biobehavioral Reviews*, 24, 417–463.

Steffensmeier, D., Schwartz, J., Zhong, H., & Ackerman, J. (2005). An assessment of recent trends in girls' violence using diverse longitudinal sources: Is the gender gap closing? *Criminology*, 43, 355–405.

Steffensmeier, D., Zhong, H., Ackerman, J., Schwartz, J., & Agha, S. (2006). Gender gap trends for violent crimes, 1980 to 2003: A UCR-NCVS comparison. *Feminist Criminology*, 1, 72–98.

Steinberg, L. (2004). Risk-taking in adolescence: What changes, and why? *Annals of the New York Academy of Sciences*, 1021, 51–58.

Steinberg, L. (2007). Risk taking in adolescence: New perspectives from brain and behavioral science. *Current Directions in Psychological Science*, 16, 55–59.

Steinberg, L., & Cauffman, E. (2000). A developmental perspective on jurisdictional boundary. In J.A. Fagan & F.E. Zimring (Eds.), *Changing borders of juvenile justice: Transfer of adolescents to the criminal court* (pp. 379–406). Chicago, IL: University of Chicago Press.

Steinberg, L., & Monaghan, K.C. (2007). Age differences in resistance to peer influence. *Developmental Psychology*, 43, 1531–1543.

Steiner, B. (2009). The effects of juvenile transfer to criminal court on incarceration decisions. *Justice Quarterly*, 26, 77–106.

Steiner, B., & Wright, E. (2006). Assessing the relative effects of state direct file waiver laws on violent juvenile crime: Deterrence or irrelevance? *Journal of Criminal Law and Criminology*, 96, 1451–1477.

Tanenhaus, D.S. (2002). The evolution of juvenile courts in the early twentieth century: Beyond the myth of immaculate construction. In M.K. Rosenheim, F.E. Zimring, & D.S. Tanenhaus (Eds.), *A century of juvenile justice* (pp. 42–73). Chicago, IL: University of Chicago Press.

Tanenhaus, D.S. (2004). *Juvenile justice in the making.* New York: Oxford University Press.

Tanenhaus, D.S., & Drizen, S.A. (2002). Owing to the extreme youth of the accused: The changing legal response to juvenile homicide. *Journal of Criminal Law & Criminology*, 92, 641–706.

Task Force on Community Preventive Services. (2007). Recommendation against policies facilitating the transfer of juveniles from juvenile to adult justice systems for the purpose of reducing violence. *American Journal of Preventive Medicine*, 32, 5–6.

Tonry, M. (1994). Racial politics, racial disparities, and the war on crime. *Crime and Delinquency*, 40, 475–494.

Tonry, M. (2004). *Thinking about crime: Sense and sensibility in American penal culture.* New York: Oxford University Press.

Tonry, M. (2007). Treating juveniles as adult criminals: An iatrogenic violence prevention strategy if ever there was one. *American Journal of Preventive Medicine*, 32, 3–4.

Tonry, M. (2009). Explanations of American punishment policies: A national history. *Punishment and Society*, 11, 377–394.

Tonry, M. & Doob, A. (Eds). (2004) *Youth crime and youth justice: Comparative and cross-national perspectives.* Chicago, IL: Chicago University Press.

Tonry, M., & Farrington, D.P. (2005). *Crime and punishment in western countries 1980–1999.* Chicago IL: University of Chicago Press.

Tonry, M., & Melewski, M. (2008). The malign effects of drug and crime control policies on black Americans. In M. Tonry (Ed.), *Crime and justice: A review of research* (Vol. 37, pp. 1–44). Chicago, IL: University of Chicago Press.

Torbet, P., Gable, R., Hurst, H., Montgomery, I., Szymanski, L., & Thomas, D. (1996). *State responses to serious and violent juvenile crime.* Washington, DC: U.S. Department of Justice, Office of Juvenile Justice and Delinquency Prevention.

Torbet, P., & Szymanski, L. (1998). *State legislative responses to violent juvenile crime: 1996–1997 update.* Washington, DC: U.S. Department of Justice, Office of Justice Programs, Office of Juvenile Justice and Delinquency Prevention.

Tracy, P.E. (2005). Race, ethnicity, and juvenile justice: Is there bias in postarrest decision making? In D.F. Hawkins and K. Kempf-Leonard (Eds.), *Our children, their children: Confronting racial and ethnic differences in American juvenile justice* (pp. 300–347). Chicago, IL: University of Chicago Press.

Travis, J., & Petersilia, J. (2001). Reentry reconsidered: A new look at an old question. *Crime and Delinquency, 47,* 291–313.

U.S. Department of Justice (2007). *Department of Justice activities under the Civil Rights of Institutionalized Persons Act: Fiscal year 2006.* Washington, DC: Office of the Attorney General, U.S. Department of Justice.

Villarruel, F.A., & Walker, N.E. (2002). *Donde esta la justicia? A call to action on behalf of Latino and Latina youth in the U.S. justice system.* Washington, DC: Building Blocks for Youth.

Virginia Department of Juvenile Justice. (2005). Juvenile recidivism in Virginia. *DJJ Research Quarterly, 3,* 1–12.

Visher, C.A., Lattimore, P.L., & Linster, R.L. (1991). Predicting the recidivism of serious youthful offenders using survival models. *Criminology, 29,* 329–366.

Von Hirsch, A. (2001). Proportionate sentences for juveniles: How different than for adults? *Punishment and Society, 3,* 221–236.

Warren, R. (2007). *Evidence-based practice to reduce recidivism: Implications for state judiciaries.* Williamsburg, VA: National Center for State Courts, National Institute of Corrections.

Wilson, D.B., Mitchell, O., & Mackenzie, D.L. (2006). A systematic review of drug court effects on recidivism. *Journal of Experimental Criminology, 2,* 459–487.

Wilson, J.J., & Howell, J.C. (1993). *A comprehensive strategy for serious, violent and chronic juvenile offenders.* Washington, DC: U.S. Department of Justice, Office of Juvenile Justice and Delinquency Prevention.

Wilson, J.Q. (1995). Crime and public policy. In J.Q.Wilson & J. Petersilia (Eds.), *Crime* (pp. 489–507). San Francisco, CA: ICS Press.

Winner, L., Lanza-Kaduce, L., Bishop, D., & Frazier, C. (1997). The transfer of juveniles to criminal court: Reexamining recidivism over the long term. *Crime and Delinquency, 43,* 548–563.

Woolard, J.L., & Harvell, S. (2005). The MacArthur Competence Assessment Tool—Criminal Adjudication. In T. Grisso & G. Vincent (Eds.), *Handbook of mental health screening and assessment for juvenile justice* (pp. 370–383). New York: Guilford Press.

Zahn, M.A., Day, J.C., Mihalic, S.F., & Tichavsky, L. (2009). Determining what works for girls in the juvenile justice system: A summary of evaluation evidence. *Crime and Delinquency*, 55, 266–293.

Zavlek, S. (2005). *Planning community-based facilities for violent juvenile offenders as part of a system of graduated sanctions*. Washington, DC: U.S. Department of Justice, Office of Juvenile Justice and Delinquency Prevention.

Zimring, F.E. (1998). Toward a jurisprudence of youth violence. In M. Tonry & M.H. Moore (Eds.), *Youth violence* (pp. 477–501). Chicago, IL: University of Chicago Press.

Zimring, F.E. (2000). The punitive necessity of waiver. J. Fagan & F.E. Zimring (Eds.), *The changing borders of juvenile justice: Transfer to criminal court* (pp. 207–226). Chicago, IL: University of Chicago Press.

Zimring, F.E. (2002). The common thread: Diversion in the jurisprudence of juvenile courts. In M.K. Rosenheim, F.E. Zimring, & D.S. Tanenhaus (Eds.), *A century of juvenile justice* (pp. 142–157). Chicago, IL: University of Chicago Press.

Zimring, F.E. (2007). Protect individual punishment decisions from mandatory penalties. *Criminology and Public Policy*, 6, 881–886.

Zimring, F.E., & Hawkins, G.J. (1973). *Deterrence*. Chicago, IL: University of Chicago Press.

9

Promoting Change, Changing Lives

EFFECTIVE PREVENTION AND INTERVENTION TO
REDUCE SERIOUS OFFENDING

Brandon C. Welsh, Mark W. Lipsey, Frederick P. Rivara,
J. David Hawkins, Steve Aos, and Meghan E. Hollis-Peel

After decades of rigorous study in the United States and across the Western world—using prospective longitudinal studies—a great deal is known about risk factors for delinquency and later criminal offending. These studies have found factors in neighborhoods and communities, families, schools, and peer groups, as well as characteristics of individuals themselves, that increase the probability of offending. They have also demonstrated that many of the same factors predict substance abuse, teenage pregnancy, dropping out of school, and other behavior problems during adolescence and young adulthood (Rutter et al., 1998; Howell, 2009). Because they predict future criminal behavior among those not yet involved in crime, risk factors are potential targets for prevention and intervention programs. No less important, these longitudinal studies have also identified protective factors that inhibit the development of criminal behavior, the misuse of drugs, and other risky behaviors of adolescents and young adults (Catalano et al., 2005; Loeber et al., 2008).

There is also a growing body of high-quality scientific evidence on the effectiveness of prevention and intervention programs that address these risk factors (and in some cases protective factors). Randomized controlled trials and rigorous quasi-experimental comparison group studies have shown that many such programs have positive effects on subsequent offending and a range of other outcomes (Farrington & Welsh, 2007; Greenwood, 2006; Lipsey & Cullen, 2007). Moreover, prevention scientists have used this evolving knowledge to design new and better interventions aimed at criminal and delinquent behavior, and have subjected them to rigorous evaluation. Ample evidence now supports the conclusion that there are programs at different targeting levels—universal, selected, and indicated—that are effective for preventing or reducing subsequent criminal behavior (Catalano, 2007).

These prevention and intervention programs, and the research on their effectiveness, however, largely divide along the same lines as the juvenile and criminal justice systems. Programs are targeted either at juveniles (typically defined as under age 18) or adults, and they are evaluated by assessing the effects on later offending during the juvenile or adult years, respectively. Much less is known about the effectiveness of prevention and intervention modalities that are targeted at the transitional stage from adolescence to early adulthood. As has been established throughout this volume, the transition from adolescence to early adulthood marks an important stage in the life course (see Chapters 1, 2, and 3), one that holds important implications for the prevention of persistence, encouragement of desistance, the prevention of adult-onset offending, and the escalation of criminal offending.

The main aim of this chapter is to review the scientific evidence on effective prevention and intervention programs—across the major domains of individual, family, school, peers, community, and labor market—to reduce serious offending in early adulthood. Also important is a focus on interventions that seek to enhance desistance in a period in which desistance naturally occurs, as well as decrease persistence in offending from adolescence into early adulthood. Specifically, it was the charge of this chapter to assess:

- Programs implemented during the later juvenile years (ages 15–17) that have measured the impact on offending in early adulthood (ages 18–29).
- Programs implemented in early adulthood that have measured the impact on offending up to age 29.
- Programs implemented in early childhood that have measured the impact on offending in early adulthood.

The organization of this chapter is as follows. The first section describes the methodology that guides our reviews of prevention and intervention programs. The next section presents reviews of the evidence for the effects on the transitional age group of particular intervention modalities targeted at the major risk factors for offending—divided into six parts. The first five of these cover the major domains in which prevention and intervention programs take place. These include family, school, peers and community, individual, and labor market. In an additional part we review the effectiveness of restorative justice programs. The next section draws on meta-analyses of the effects of interventions with juvenile and adult offenders to examine the extent to which those effects vary by age group. This is followed by a description of the results of an analysis of the benefits and costs of selected evidence-based programs for juvenile and young adult offenders conducted by the Washington State Institute for Public Policy. The final section brings together the main conclusions and identifies gaps in knowledge and priorities for research.

Methodology

The vast majority of prevention and intervention programs have not been evaluated adequately. In this chapter, we focus on the highest quality research studies (i.e., randomized experiments and non-randomized quasi-experiments that establish equivalence between groups), as well as the most rigorous research reviews (i.e., systematic and meta-analytic reviews) that include only high-quality studies. We further restricted our criteria for inclusion of evaluation studies to those with a sample size of no less than 50 individuals and an outcome measure of criminal offending (a program would not be included if it only had outcome measures of risk factors). This ensures that our conclusions are based on the best available evidence.

An evaluation of a prevention or intervention program is considered to be high quality if it possesses a high degree of internal, construct, and statistical conclusion validity (Cook & Campbell, 1979; Shadish et al., 2002). Internal validity refers to how well the study unambiguously demonstrates that an intervention (e.g., parent training) had an effect on an outcome (e.g., offending). Here, some kind of control condition is necessary to estimate what would have happened to the experimental units (e.g., people or areas) if the intervention had not been applied to them— termed the "counterfactual inference." Construct validity refers to the adequacy of the operational definition and measurement of the theoretical constructs that underlie the intervention and the outcome. Statistical conclusion validity is concerned with whether the relationship between the presumed cause (the intervention) and the presumed effect (the outcome) is statistically reliable.

Put another way, researchers and policy-makers can have a great deal of confidence in the observed effects of an intervention if it has been evaluated with a design that controls for the major threats to these three forms of validity. Randomized experiments (see Farrington & Welsh, 2005, 2006) and rigorous quasi-experimental research designs are the types of evaluation designs that can best achieve high internal validity in particular (i.e., control groups are needed to counter threats to internal validity). While randomized experiments have higher internal validity, quasi-experiments go a long way toward countering many threats to internal validity. Because of this they are considered the minimum research design for assessing intervention effects that is interpretable (Cook & Campbell, 1979; Shadish et al., 2002).

It is also important that the most rigorous methods be used to assess the available research evidence. Systematic reviews and meta-analyses are the most rigorous methods for assessing effectiveness. These use rigorous methods for locating, appraising, and synthesizing evidence from prior evaluation studies, and they are reported with the same level of detail that characterizes high-quality reports of original research. They have explicit objectives, explicit criteria for including or excluding studies, extensive searches for eligible evaluation studies, careful extraction and coding of key features of studies, and a structured and detailed report of the methods and conclusions of the review. All of this contributes greatly to the ease of their interpretation and replication by other researchers.

A meta-analysis involves the statistical or quantitative analysis of the results of prior research studies (Lipsey & Wilson, 2001). Since it involves the statistical summary of data (in particular, effect sizes), it requires a reasonable number of intervention studies that are sufficiently similar to be grouped together. When there is sufficient diversity in the settings, participants, and methods used in those studies, meta-analysis can yield conclusions about the external validity (i.e., generalizability) of findings about program effects as well as summarizing their average effects.

Specific Program Effects for the Transitional Age Group

FAMILY

Family-based prevention and intervention programs target risk factors for offending that are associated with the family, such as poor child rearing, poor supervision, and inconsistent or harsh discipline. Broadly speaking, family-based prevention programs have developed along the lines of two major fields of study: psychology and public health. When delivered by psychologists, these programs are often classified into parent management training, functional family therapy, or family preservation (Wasserman & Miller, 1998). Typically, they attempt to change the social contingencies in the family environment so that children are rewarded in some way for appropriate or prosocial behaviors and punished in some way for inappropriate or antisocial behaviors. Family-based programs delivered by health professionals such as nurses are typically less behavioral, mainly providing advice and guidance to parents or general parent education. More often this type of family prevention is provided in the early years of the life course.

Early family prevention. Farrington and Welsh (2007) and Piquero et al. (2009) found that early parent education—in the context of home visitation—and parent management training (PMT) are effective intervention modalities for preventing offending in the juvenile years. Only two early family-based prevention programs have measured the impact on offending in early adulthood. Long et al. (1994) evaluated a PMT program, tracking their experimental children for 14 years after the completion of the program. Seventy-three young children (between ages 2 and 7) who were referred to the researcher's clinic for noncompliance (to parent requests) and their mothers were randomly allocated to an experimental group that received PMT or to a control group that received no services. Over the course of eight to 10 sessions, mothers were taught to attend to and reward appropriate behavior and to use clear commands and time-out for noncompliance. At the completion of treatment, it was found that children in the experimental group, compared to the controls, were less likely to exhibit "deviant" behavior and were more compliant.

At the latest follow-up of 26 experimental group participants (from the original 47 in this condition), when they were between ages 16 and 21, Long et al. found that they were similar on delinquency, emotional adjustment, and academic progress compared to controls retrospectively matched on age, gender, ethnicity, and family socioeconomic status. A new control group, comprising 26 young adults, was used as the basis of comparison, presumably because the researchers did not have follow-up data for the original controls.

The best known home visiting program, and the only one with a direct measure of delinquency, is the Nurse-Family Partnership (NFP) initially carried out in Elmira, New York, by David Olds (see Olds et al., 2007). Four hundred first-time mothers were randomly assigned to receive home visits from nurses during pregnancy, to receive visits both during pregnancy and during the first two years of their child's life, or to a control group who received no visits. Each visit lasted just over one hour and the mothers were visited on average every two weeks. The home visitors gave advice about prenatal and postnatal care of the child, about infant development, and about the importance of proper nutrition and of avoiding smoking and drinking during pregnancy.

The results of the experiment showed that postnatal home visits caused a significant decrease in recorded child physical abuse and neglect during the first two years of life, especially by poor, unmarried, teenage mothers (Olds et al., 1986), and in a 15-year follow-up, significantly fewer experimental compared to control group mothers were identified as perpetrators of child abuse and neglect (Olds et al., 1997). At age 15, children of the higher risk mothers who received home visits incurred significantly fewer arrests than controls (Olds et al., 1998). In the latest follow-up at age 19, compared to their control counterparts, girls of the full sample of mothers had incurred significantly fewer arrests and convictions and girls of the higher risk mothers had significantly fewer children of their own and less Medicaid use; few program effects were observed for the boys (Eckenrode et al., 2010).

Family interventions for adjudicated delinquents. Greenwood (2006) identified three effective family interventions for adjudicated delinquents that operate outside of the justice system: multisystemic therapy (MST), functional family therapy (FFT), and multidimensional treatment foster care (MTFC). Woolfenden et al. (2002a, b) carried out a systematic review of the effectiveness of family and parenting interventions, including MST, FFT, and MTFC with mostly delinquent children and adolescents (in seven of the eight randomized studies all of the participants were chronic offenders, serious offenders, or both). Woolfenden et al. found that family and parenting interventions for juvenile delinquents and their families led to a significant effect size in rearrest rates.

> a. Multisystemic therapy. MST is a multi-modal intervention designed for serious juvenile offenders (Henggeler et al., 1998). The particular type of treatment is chosen according to the needs of the young person, and it may include individual, family, peers, school, and community interventions (including parent training and skills training); more often though, it is referred to as a family-based treatment. Three unique MST programs have measured the impact on offending in early adulthood.

Henggeler et al. (2002) carried out a long-term follow-up of a randomized experiment of MST versus usual community services (UCS) for 118 substance-abusing juvenile offenders. The mean age at treatment was 15.7 and the mean age at follow-up was 19.6. Compared to those who received UCS, MST participants had significantly lower yearly conviction rates for aggressive criminal activity (0.15 vs. 0.57), but not for property crimes. Treatment effects on long-term illicit drug use were mixed, with biological measures indicating significantly higher rates of marijuana abstinence for MST participants (55% vs. 28%), but no effect on cocaine use.

Schaeffer and Borduin (2005) carried out a particularly long-term follow-up of a randomized experiment of MST versus individual therapy (IT) for 176 serious and violent juvenile offenders. The mean age at treatment was 13.7 and the mean age at follow-up was 28.8. Compared to those who received IT, MST participants had significantly lower recidivism rates (50% vs. 81%), including lower rates of rearrest for violent offenses (14% vs. 30%). MST participants also had 54% fewer arrests and 57% fewer days of confinement in adult detention facilities.

Borduin et al. (2009) carried out another long-term follow-up of a randomized experiment of MST versus UCS for 48 high risk juvenile sex offenders. The mean age at treatment was 14 and the mean age at follow-up was 22.9. Compared to those who received UCS, MST participants reported lower recidivism rates for sexual (8% vs. 46%) and nonsexual (29% vs. 58%) crimes. As well, MST participants had 70% fewer arrests for all crimes and spent 80% fewer days in detention facilities compared to UCS participants.

b. Functional Family Therapy. FFT involves modifying patterns of family interaction—by modeling, prompting, and reinforcement—to encourage clear communication of requests and solutions between family members, and to minimize conflict (Alexander & Parsons, 1973). Only one known FFT program has measured the impact on offending in early adulthood in recent years.

Gordon et al. (1995) carried out a long-term follow-up of an experiment of FFT compared to probation services for 54 juvenile offenders. The mean age at treatment was 15.4 for the experimental group and 15.3 for the control group. Most of the experimental and control group members were between the ages of 20 and 22 at follow-up. FFT participants reported a lower rate of rearrests compared to their control counterparts (9% vs. 41%). Published data is expected to be available in the near future on a longer-term follow-up of a large-scale randomized experiment of FFT in Washington State (Barnoski, 2002).

c. Multidimensional Treatment Foster Care. MTFC involves individual-focused therapeutic care (e.g., skill building in problem solving) for adolescents in an alternative, noncorrectional environment (foster care) and parent management training (Chamberlain & Reid, 1998). Only two MTFC programs have measured the impact on offending in early adulthood.

Chamberlain et al. (2007) carried out a short-term follow-up of a randomized experiment of MTFC compared to group care for 81 serious and chronic female juvenile offenders. The age at treatment was between 13 and 17, and the age at follow-up was between 15 and 19. Analyses showed that MTFC was more effective than group care, as measured by days in locked settings, number of criminal referrals, and self-reported delinquency. Further analyses revealed that older MTFC participants exhibited less delinquency relative to younger participants in both conditions.

Eddy et al. (2004) carried out a two-year follow-up of a randomized experiment of MTFC compared to services-as-usual group home care for 79 adolescent males under the control of the juvenile justice system. The age at treatment was between 12 and 17 (mean age 14.9) and the age at follow-up was between 16 and 19 (mean age 16.9). The results show that MTFC was significantly more effective than group home care, as measured by referrals for violent offending and self-reports of violent behavior. Twenty-four percent of the group home care condition had two or more criminal referrals for violent offenses compared to only 5% in the MTFC condition. Rates of self-reported violent offending were four to nine times higher among group home care participants compared to those who received MTFC.

SCHOOL

Schools are a critical social context for crime prevention efforts from the early to later grades (Elliott et al., 1998). All schools work to produce vibrant and productive members of society. According to Gottfredson et al. (2002, p. 149), "students who are impulsive, are weakly attached to their schools, have little commitment to achieving educational goals, and whose moral beliefs in the validity of conventional rules for behavior are weak are more likely to engage in crime than those who do not possess these characteristics." The school's role in influencing these risk factors and preventing offending in both school and the wider community (the focus here) differs from situational and administrative measures taken to make the school a safer place (e.g., through metal detectors, police in school, or video surveillance cameras). We do not focus on situational interventions in this chapter (see Horney et al., Chapter 4, this volume).

The meta-analyses of Wilson et al. (2001) and Gottfredson et al. (2006) identified four school interventions that were effective in preventing delinquency among youths in middle school and high school: school and discipline management, classroom or instructional management, reorganization of grades or classes, and increasing self-control or social competency with cognitive behavioral or behavioral instructional methods. In a meta-analysis of the effects of school-based psychosocial prevention programs on aggressive and disruptive behavior, Wilson and Lipsey (2007) found that the most effective approaches (across all ages) were universal programs and targeted programs for selected and indicated children.

Only three school-based prevention programs have measured the impact on offending in early adulthood, and each one of these began in the early grades.

The Seattle Social Development Project (Hawkins et al., 1991) is a multi-component program combining parent training, teacher training, and skills training for children. About 500 first grade children (aged 6) in 21 classes were randomly assigned to be in experimental or control classes in the original study. The parents and teachers of children in the experimental classes received instruction in methods of child management and instruction, which were designed to increase children's attachment to their parents and their bonding to school, based on the assumption that delinquency is inhibited by the strength of social bonds. The children also were trained in interpersonal cognitive problem-solving. Their parents were trained to notice and reinforce socially desirable behavior in a program called "Catch Them Being Good." Their teachers were trained in classroom management, for example, to establish rules and routines at the beginning of the school year, to provide children with clear instructions and expectations, to reward children for participation in desired behavior, to use methods least disruptive to instruction to maintain order in the classroom, and to teach children prosocial methods of solving problems.

In a follow-up when the study participants were aged 18, Hawkins et al. (1999) found that the full intervention group who received the intervention from grades 1–6 reported significantly less violence, less alcohol abuse, and fewer sexual partners than a late intervention group (grades 5–6 only) or controls. In the latest follow-up, which included 93% of the original sample, Hawkins et al. (2008b) found that the full intervention group (compared to the comparison groups) reported significantly better educational and economic attainment, mental health, and sexual health by age 27, but no effects were found for substance abuse and criminal activity at ages 24 or 27.

The Montreal Longitudinal-Experimental Study (Tremblay et al., 1992) is also a multi-component program that combines skills training, parent training, and teacher support. Beginning with a large sample of disruptive (aggressive/hyperactive) children (age six) from low socio-economic neighborhoods in Montreal, the researchers randomly allocated 250 of them to experimental or control conditions. Between ages 7 and 9, the experimental group received training designed to foster social skills and self-control. Coaching, peer modeling, role playing, and reinforcement contingencies were used in small group sessions at school on such topics as "how to help," "what to do when you are angry," and "how to react to teasing." Also, their parents were trained using the parent management training techniques developed by Patterson (1982). Parents were taught how to provide positive reinforcement for desirable behavior, to use nonpunitive and consistent discipline practices, and to develop family crisis management techniques.

By age 12 (3 years after treatment), the experimental boys committed significantly less burglary and theft, were significantly less likely to get drunk, and were significantly less likely to be involved in fights than the controls. Also, the experimental boys had significantly higher school achievement (Tremblay et al., 1992). At every age from 10 to 15, the experimental boys had significantly lower self-reported delinquency scores than the control boys. Interestingly, the differences in delinquency between experimental and control boys increased as the follow-up progressed. However, the experimental boys were only slightly less likely to have a juvenile court record up to age 15 (7% compared with 9% of the controls). The experimental boys were also less likely to be gang members, to get drunk, or take drugs, but they were not significantly different from the controls on having sexual intercourse by age 15 (Tremblay et al., 1995, 1996).

In the latest follow-up, when the study participants were aged 24, Boisjoli et al. (2007) conducted criminal records searches of all 250 of the original participants. They found that those in the experimental group were only less likely to have a criminal record than their control counterparts (22% compared with 33%).

The final school-based prevention program is the Good Behavior Game (GBG; Kellam & Rebok, 1992). It uses a universal classroom behavior management strategy that is designed to foster learning by teaching children to regulate their own and their classmates' behavior. Teachers are trained in the curriculum and receive supportive monitoring throughout the school year. In an experimental study in 19 urban elementary schools in Baltimore, Maryland, first grade students were randomly assigned to heterogeneous groups that included equal numbers of aggressive and disruptive children. While GBG was in progress, teachers monitored the behavior of students in each group. Misbehavior of any student in a group resulted in a check mark being placed on the chalkboard for that group. At the end of the session, groups with fewer than five check marks received a reward. At the beginning of the program, game sessions were announced and tangible rewards (e.g., stickers) were given immediately following the session. As the program became more familiar to students, sessions started unannounced and less tangible rewards were given (e.g., extended recess). In addition, the time between the session and the granting of rewards was extended. The program lasted for two years in the first and second grades.

After one year, experimental students were rated as less aggressive and shy than control students by teachers and peers. Positive effects of the program were most evident among students rated as highly aggressive at baseline. Positive effects of the intervention were maintained through sixth grade for boys, with the highest baseline ratings of aggression at first grade entry (Kellam et al., 1994).

In a long-term follow-up when study participants were between ages 19 and 21, Kellam et al. (2008) and Petras et al. (2008) assessed program effects on a range of important life-course outcomes. Significant reductions in rates of violent and criminal behavior were found among males in the highest risk group compared to their control counterparts (34% vs. 50%). Also, significant reductions in rates of drug abuse/dependence disorders were found among males overall (19% vs. 38%) and in the highest risk group (29% vs. 68%) compared to their control counterparts.

PEERS AND COMMUNITY

Peer-focused programs recognize that association with friends who engage in delinquent behavior or drug use is one of the strongest risk factors for delinquency and drug use. Peer-focused programs to prevent offending are ostensibly designed with two related aims: to reduce the influence of delinquent friends and increase the influence of prosocial friends. Farrington and Welsh (2007) found that there are no outstanding examples of effective intervention programs for delinquency and later offending based on peer risk factors. The most hopeful programs involve using high-status conventional peers to teach children ways of resisting peer pressure; this is effective in reducing drug use (Tobler et al., 1999).

The most important prevention program whose success seems to be based mainly on reducing peer risk factors is the Children at Risk program (Harrell et al., 1999), which targeted high-risk adolescents (average age 12) in poor neighborhoods of five U.S. cities. Eligible youths were identified in schools and were randomly assigned to experimental or control conditions. Initial results of the program were disappointing (Harrell et al., 1997), but a one-year follow-up showed that, according to self-reports, experimental youths were less likely to have committed violent crimes and used or sold drugs (Harrell et al., 1999). Unfortunately, there has been no longer-term follow-up of this program. Similarly, there are no known peer-focused prevention programs with follow-ups of offending outcomes in early adulthood.

Community-based prevention covers a wide array of programs, including after-school, mentoring, and youth and resident groups. These programs hold wide appeal among the public and political leaders alike, but are often among the first programs to lose funding in times of federal or state budget cuts (Butterfield, 2003). This state of affairs has hampered the knowledge base on the effectiveness of this type of prevention.

Gottfredson et al. (2004) concluded that there is insufficient evidence to support claims that after-school programs are effective in preventing delinquency or other problem behaviors, but those that "involve a heavy dose of social competency skill development . . . may reduce problem behavior" (p. 256). Jolliffe and Farrington's (2008) systematic review and meta-analysis of 18 mentoring programs found this to be an effective approach to preventing delinquency. The average effect across the studies corresponded to a significant 10% reduction in offending. The authors found that mentoring was more effective in reducing offending when the average duration of each contact between mentor and mentee was greater, in smaller scale studies, and when mentoring was combined with other interventions. Not one of the studies included in these reviews or others have measured the impact on offending in the early adult years.

Communities That Care (CTC) and other comprehensive community initiatives bring together key stakeholders to target a range of risk factors with programs that have demonstrated effectiveness in preventing delinquency, substance abuse, and serious offending. Findings from a large-scale randomized controlled trial involving 24 communities in seven states in the United States and more than 4,400 students show that CTC reduces targeted risk factors and delinquent behavior community-wide (Hawkins et al., 2008a, 2009). Specifically, the initiation of delinquent behavior, alcohol use, cigarette use, and smokeless tobacco use was significantly reduced in CTC compared with control communities between grades 5 and 8. In grade 8, the prevalence of alcohol and smokeless tobacco use in the last 30 days, prevalence of binge drinking in the past two weeks, and the number of different delinquent behaviors committed in the past year in grade 8 were significantly lower in CTC communities than in control communities. However, at this time, there are no known community-based prevention programs with follow-ups of offending outcomes in early adulthood.

INDIVIDUAL

Individual-based prevention programs target risk factors for offending that are found within the individual. Here, we set out to review a range of interventions that target individual-level risk factors for offending and are implemented in early childhood, adolescence, and early adulthood. In early childhood, preschool intellectual enrichment programs are relevant. In early and later childhood, social skills training or social competence programs, which generally target the risk factors of impulsivity, low empathy, and self-centeredness, have been used. Substance abuse and mental health are two transition issues of special relevance to ex-offenders in early adulthood. Individual-level support includes mental health services and substance abuse treatment. Few studies in these areas have measured the impact on offending in early adulthood. Indeed, only in the case of preschool intellectual enrichment programs are there some evaluations with long-term follow-ups on offending.

Preschool intellectual enrichment programs are generally targeted on the risk factors of low intelligence and attainment. As noted by Duncan and Magnuson (2004, p. 105), "Child-focused early-education intervention programs are designed to provide economically disadvantaged children with cognitively stimulating and enriching experiences that their parents are unlikely to provide at home." Improved cognitive skills, school readiness, and social and emotional development are the main goals of these programs (Currie, 2001).

Three preschool programs have measured the impact on offending in early adulthood. These include the Perry Preschool, the Child-Parent Center program in Chicago, and the Carolina Abecedarian Project. In the Perry Preschool project, carried out in Ypsilanti, Michigan, 123 children were allocated (approximately at random) to experimental and control groups. The experimental children attended a daily preschool program, backed up by weekly home visits, usually lasting two years when children were between ages 3 and 4. The aim of the "plan-do-review" program was to provide intellectual stimulation, to increase thinking and reasoning abilities, and to increase later school achievement (Schweinhart & Weikart, 1980).

This program had long-term benefits. Berrueta-Clement and colleagues (1984) showed that, at age 19, the experimental group was more likely to be employed, more likely to have graduated from high school, more likely to have received college or vocational training, and less likely to have been arrested. By age 27, the experimental group had accumulated only half as many arrests as the controls—an average of 2.3 compared to 4.6 arrests (Schweinhart et al., 1993). Also, they were more likely to have graduated from high school, had significantly higher earnings, and were more likely to be homeowners. More of the experimental women were married, and fewer of their children were born out of wedlock.

The most recent follow-up of this program, at age 40, which included 91% of the original sample, found that the program continued to make an important difference in the lives of the participants (Schweinhart et al., 2005). Compared to the control group, program group members had significantly fewer lifetime arrests for violent crimes (32% vs. 48%), property crimes (36% vs. 58%), and drug crimes (14% vs. 34%), and were significantly less likely to be arrested five or more times (36% vs. 55%). Improvements were also recorded in many other important life-course outcomes. For example, significantly higher levels of schooling (77% vs. 60% graduating from high school), better records of employment (76% vs. 62%), and higher annual incomes were reported by the program group compared to the controls.

The Child-Parent Center (CPC) program provides disadvantaged children, ages 3 to 4, with high-quality, active learning preschool supplemented with family support. It also provides the children with the educational enrichment component into elementary school, up to age 9. The program is located in 24 centers in high-poverty neighborhoods across Chicago.

A rigorous, nonrandomized, controlled design was used to evaluate the program, and the initial sample comprised more than 1,500 children. Evaluation of the preschool intervention found that, compared to the control group, those who received the program were significantly less likely to be arrested for any offense (17% vs. 25%), multiple offenses (10% vs. 13%), and violent offenses (9% vs. 15%) by the time they were aged 18 (Reynolds et al., 2001). The CPC program also produced other benefits for those in the experimental compared to the control group, including a significantly higher rate of high school completion (50% vs. 39%). A more recent evaluation when participants were age 24 (Reynolds et al., 2007) found that the experimental group had significantly lower rates of felony arrest (17% vs. 21%) and lower rates of incarceration (21% vs. 26%).

The Carolina Abercedarian Project targeted children born to low-income, multirisk families. A sample of 111 children aged 3, mostly African-American (98%), were randomly assigned either to receive full-time preschool childcare (focusing on the development of cognitive and language skills) or not. Families of children in both the experimental and control groups received supportive social services as needed (Campbell et al., 2002). At age 21, 104 of the participants were interviewed, and it was found that fewer of the experimental compared to the control participants (but not significantly so) reported being convicted of a misdemeanor offense (14% vs. 18%) or a felony offense (8% vs. 12%) or had been incarcerated (14% vs. 21%). It was also found that significantly fewer of the experimental participants were regular marijuana users, significantly fewer had become a teenage parent, significantly more had attended college or university, and they had significantly higher status jobs.

LABOR MARKET

Here, we review interventions that target key socioeconomic risk factors for offending that are implemented in late adolescence and early adulthood. (For the impact of employment/unemployment on offending, see Horney et al., Chapter 4, this volume.) A key focus is on programs that aim to increase the employment of individuals or populations at risk of serious offending. Bushway and Reuter (2006) found two employment strategies to be especially effective in reducing serious offending: intensive, residential training programs for at-risk youth, and ex-offender job training for older males no longer under criminal justice supervision.

Intensive, residential training programs for at-risk youth. Among job training and education programs for at-risk youth, Bushway and Reuter (2006, p. 214) observed that "very few evaluations of these programs measure change in criminal behavior, simply because crime prevention is not generally a primary objective and its measurement requires substantial and complex additional data collection." Job Corps is the only one of these programs that has demonstrated desirable effects on offending in early adulthood. LaLonde (2003) found that Job Corps is also the only one of these programs that has demonstrated desirable effects on subsequent earnings.

Job Corps is a nationwide program in the United States that is designed to improve the employability of at-risk young people (ages 16 to 24) by offering a comprehensive set of services, including vocational training, basic education (the ability to obtain a high school education), and health care. Each year, Job Corps serves more than 60,000 new participants at a cost of approximately $1.5 billion. It is administered by the Department of Labor. On average, youths are enrolled in the program for eight months. In a three-year follow-up (post-program) of a large-scale randomized experiment involving 15,400 individuals, Schochet et al. (2008) found that participation in Job Corps resulted in significant reductions in criminal activity, improvements in educational attainment, and greater earnings. Program participants had an average arrest rate of 29% compared to 33% for their control counterparts. An analysis of tax data showed that earnings gains were sustained for the oldest participants eight years post-program.

YouthBuild U.S.A. is another national job training program for disadvantaged, unemployed young people (ages 16 to 24). Each year, the program serves more than 7,000 new participants at 225 sites across the country. The program's focus is on building or renovating affordable housing, and through this young people learn skills in carpentry and construction. It also provides educational services—for example, to achieve a high school diploma or prepare for college—and promotes the development of leadership skills. The program was recently the subject of two large-scale implementation studies (Abrazaldo et al., 2009; Hahn et al., 2004). An impact evaluation has not yet been carried out.

Ex-offender job training for older males no longer under criminal justice supervision. Bushway and Reuter (2006) note that maturation (i.e., aging-out of crime) may reduce the propensity of offending among some older adult ex-offenders who are eligible for these programs, but compared to some of their younger counterparts, "these individuals may be finally ready to take advantage of training programs that are offered" (p. 219).

Once again, there are very few evaluations that have measured the impact of these programs on offending. Bushway and Reuter (2006) identified two rather old programs (both implemented in the 1970s) that were effective in reducing offending in early adulthood: the Supported Work program (Piliavan & Masters, 1981) and the Baltimore Life Experiment (Mallar & Thornton, 1978). Uggen's (2000) analyses of the Supported Work program found that it was highly effective in reducing offending and improving employment for ex-offenders over the age of 26, but not for younger participants.

RESTORATIVE JUSTICE

As an emerging intervention, restorative justice may also be important during the transition from juvenile delinquency to adult offending. It serves as a nonpunitive strategy that seeks to address a range of issues that produce conflict between offender and victim (as well as the supporters of either) and, hence, reconcile the parties. Restoration rather than retribution or punishment is at the heart of the restorative justice approach. Sherman (2003, p. 11) describes the methods of restorative justice as "any means that can produce reconciliation between victims, offenders and their supporters, minimizing anger, and leaving all satisfied that they have been treated fairly while justice has been done." Family group conferencing, mediation, and circle sentencing are some examples.

Experimentation on restorative justice approaches has been especially rigorous (see McGarrell & Hipple, 2007; Sherman & Strang, 2007; Sherman et al., 2005). Unfortunately, a search of the literature identified only one study with a measure of offending in early adulthood. Bergseth and Bouffard (2007) compared restorative justice programming to traditional court processing in a quasi-experimental study involving 330 youthful offenders. Whenever possible, the program attempted to facilitate face-to-face conferences between the parties. Control group members were chosen based on matching characteristics to the treatment group members. Study participants had a mean age of 14.7 years at the time of intervention. A four-year follow-up, when study participants were on average aged 18.7, included only 106 participants. Compared to traditional court processing, referral to restorative justice was associated with a marginally significantly lower likelihood of re-offense at the latest follow-up.

In the years to come, there is the potential for many more studies to assess the effects of restorative justice during this important transitional period. This includes Sherman and Strang's (2007) Reintegrative Shaming Experiments in Australia and their multisite randomized controlled experiment in the United Kingdom.

Similar Program Effects for Juvenile and Adult Offenders

Although relatively few studies have examined the effects of interventions specifically on offenders in the transitional age range spanning juvenile and adult status, there are many studies of the effects of similar intervention modalities on either juvenile or adult offenders. When a particular type of intervention (e.g., cognitive-behavioral therapy) shows similar effects on the re-offending of juveniles and adults, it is reasonable to suppose that those results also apply to offenders at transitional ages. A considerable number of meta-analyses have been done in the last decade or so synthesizing research on the effectiveness of particular intervention modalities for juvenile offenders, adult offenders, or both. Those meta-analyses provide a broad perspective on the extent to which there are similarities and differences in the effects of those interventions on juvenile and adult offenders. The summary of this work provided here draws heavily on the rather comprehensive review conducted by Lipsey and Cullen (2007).

In general, the effects of most intervention modalities on later offending are far more similar than different for juvenile and adult offenders. One of the broadest themes emerging from the meta-analytic reviews is the relative ineffectiveness of correctional sanctions and supervision on recidivism rates of both juveniles and adults. Meta-analyses of the effects of probation or parole supervision and other such intermediate sanctions for adults and juveniles show remarkably similar small net negative effects on subsequent offense rates (Andrews et al., 1990; Aos, 2001; Cleland et al., 1997; Lipsey, 2009; Pearson et al., 1997; Petrosino, 1997; Smith et al., 2002). Similarly, only small mean effects for both juveniles and adults are found in studies of the effects of incarceration, albeit slightly positive (less recidivism) in this instance (Pearson et al., 1997; Smith et al., 2002; Villettaz et al., 2006). Studies of boot camps, as an alternative form of incarceration, also show average effects close to zero that are substantially similar for juveniles and adults (Aos et al., 2001; Wilson et al., 2005b).

By contrast, interventions that might be characterized as "therapeutic," that is, those that explicitly promote and support constructive behavior change, show generally positive effects on the re-offending rates of both juvenile and adult offenders. Meta-analyses that provide broad reviews of the hundreds of studies of such interventions find average effects in the range of 10–40% reductions in re-offending rates. Here also there is little evident difference in the net positive effects found in meta-analyses of such programs for juveniles and those for adults

(Andrews et al., 1990; Cleland et al., 1997; Illescas et al., 2001; Lipsey, 2009; Petro-sino, 1997; Latimer et al., 2003).

Within the broad category of therapeutically-oriented interventions for of-fenders, many meta-analyses have summarized the mean effects on re-offending rates for a particular intervention modality or broken out the effects for indi-vidual modalities in a more comprehensive review. There are four broad inter-vention modalities with ample studies of their effects for both juveniles and adults and multiple meta-analyses that have attempted to summarize the effects on re-offending rates found in those studies for juveniles, adults, or both together. These intervention modalities are (a) cognitive behavioral therapy, (b) educa-tional, vocational, and employment programs, (c) drug treatment, and (d) treat-ment for sex offenders. (For a review of treatment in secure settings, see Chapter 7, this volume.)

COGNITIVE BEHAVIORAL THERAPY

The most comprehensive meta-analysis of studies of the effects of cognitive behav-ioral therapy (CBT) on re-offending rates was Landenberger and Lipsey (2005). They found overall positive effects representing an average of about 22% reduc-tions in re-offending rates. Studies with juvenile samples and those with adult samples were included and no significant difference was found between the mean effects for these two subsets of studies. Similar overall findings were reported in other meta-analyses of CBT that included both juvenile and adult studies (Wilson et al., 2005a; Pearson et al., 2002) and in meta-analyses of particular types of CBT with juveniles or adults (Aos et al., 2001; Tong & Farrington, 2006). Based on these findings, there is no reason to expect CBT to be any less effective with offenders in the transitional age range.

EDUCATIONAL, VOCATIONAL, AND EMPLOYMENT PROGRAMS.

The most comprehensive meta-analysis of programs in this category, at least with regard to the number of studies included, was by Pearson and Lipton (1999a). They included both juvenile and adult studies and found a modest average effect repre-senting a reduction of about 10% in the re-offending rate. However, they did not investigate whether the mean effects differed for the juvenile and adult offenders. Wilson et al. (2000) conducted a very thorough meta-analysis of educational, vocational, and work programs for adult offenders and found a mean effect corresponding to about a 20% reduction in the re-offending rate. Smaller scale meta-analyses of the effects of such programs for adults by Aos (2001) and Visher et al. (2005), on the other hand, found smaller effects on the order of 6% and 2% re-offense reductions, respectively. The only meta-analyses focusing on programs of this type with exclusively juvenile samples are Lipsey and Wilson (1998) and Lipsey (2009), which is an update of the previous meta-analysis. The first of these found a mean of zero but the update showed a more positive 6% mean reduction in re-offending rates.

The results from these various meta-analyses do not show a consistent pattern but, if we put the most weight on those encompassing the greatest number of studies, there is some indication that educational, vocational, and employment programs, as a group, are somewhat more effective with adult than juvenile offenders. This is plausible given that the average age of the samples in the juvenile studies is around 15, too young for employment issues to be highly salient. Offenders in the transitional age range around 18, however, may find employment issues more pressing and respond to these programs more like the adult offenders. The ambiguity on this point, however, highlights the need for research specifically directed at the effects of employment-related programs for transitional offenders.

DRUG TREATMENT

Substance abuse problems are commonplace among offenders and a significant risk factor for re-offending. Here we focus on the effects of drug treatment programs on general re-offending rates, not the effects on substance use itself though that is an important outcome in its own right. Meta-analyses of the effects of drug and alcohol treatment found in studies of adult offenders (Aos et al., 2001; Pearson et al., 1997), studies of juvenile offenders (Lipsey & Wilson, 1998), and both kinds of studies together (Mitchell et al., 2006; Pearson & Lipton, 1999b) report a range of positive effects from about 4% to 20% reductions in re-offending rates. Within that range, however, there is no clear distinction between the mean effects found for the different samples. In general, therefore, drug treatment appears to be about equally effective for juvenile and adult offenders and thus we would expect similar effects for offenders in the transitional age range.

TREATMENT FOR SEX OFFENDERS

Various different kinds of interventions are used with sex offenders (e.g., CBT, psychotherapy, therapeutic communities). The available meta-analyses of these programs, however, all look broadly at this category of programs rather than focusing on specific interventions. The meta-analyses that encompass the greatest number of studies all include those with either juvenile or adult samples (Gallagher et al., 1999; Hall, 1995; Hanson et al., 2002; Lösel & Schmucker, 2005). These show very similar and quite positive mean effects on general re-offending rates (not restricted to sex offenses), corresponding to 24–36% reductions. Lösel and Schmucker (2005) and Hanson et al. (2002) break out effects for juvenile and adult samples, with Lösel and Schmucker finding somewhat greater effects for juveniles and Hanson et al. finding somewhat greater ones for adults. Hanson et al. tested this difference and did not find it to be statistically significant. Lösel and Schmucker did not report a significance test, but the difference they found may well be non-significant as well.

Meta-analyses restricted to studies with juvenile samples (Aos, 2001; Reitzel & Carbonell, 2006) show inconsistent effects, but encompass very few studies; no meta-analysis focuses only on studies with adults while looking broadly at different sex offender treatments. Thus in this treatment area, as in others summarized earlier, there do not appear to be large differences in the average effects on re-offending rates for juveniles and adults. Here also we would infer that these interventions would produce similar positive effects for offenders in the transitional age group.

What we find overall from the meta-analyses of interventions with juvenile and adult offenders is a great deal of similarity with regard to effects on re-offending rates. For both groups, sanctions and incarceration appear to have essentially negligible or slightly negative effects and therapeutically-oriented programs have generally positive effects. For those intervention modalities applied, studied, and meta-analyzed for both juvenile and adult samples often enough to support relatively robust conclusions, the effects are substantially similar across age. The one possible exception is for the category of education, vocational, and employment programs, which appear to have larger effects for adult samples, but it is those samples that are likely to be most similar to offenders of transitional age. The generalization that follows from these results is that, for programs applicable to both juvenile and adult offenders, the effects on re-offending rates are not highly sensitive to age. Though focused research is needed to develop evidence of the effects of such programs on offenders in the transitional age range, we would expect them to be similar to those found separately for juvenile and adult samples.

Benefits and Costs of Selected Evidence-Based Programs for Juvenile and Young Adult offenders

This section describes the results of an analysis of the benefits and costs of selected well-researched programs intended to reduce criminal re-offending of juvenile and young adult offenders. It is important to note that not all of these evidence-based programs or the individual studies in each program type have measures of offending in early adulthood. The analysis uses the benefit-cost model developed and maintained by the Washington State Institute for Public Policy (WSIPP), the nonpartisan research unit of the Washington State legislature. The model is designed to help the Washington legislature identify evidence-based and economically sound ways to reduce crime and provide Washington taxpayers with a better return on their dollars. WSIPP developed its initial model in 1997; the version described here was constructed in 2009–2010.

BENEFIT-COST ESTIMATES FOR A SET OF SELECTED PROGRAMS

Table 9.1 displays a summary of benefit-cost estimates for a selected set of specific evidence-based programs, or general types of programming, that could be applied to juvenile and young adult offenders. The principal finding from Table 9.1 is that there are a number of well-researched options available to policymakers that can produce benefits that exceed costs. At the same time, however, the full WSIPP analysis indicates the following: not all well-researched programs have been shown to work; some that achieve crime reductions do not produce benefits that exceed costs; and most programs in the field today have probably never even been evaluated rigorously, or at all. Thus, as with any investment decision, caution is advised. Still, for some programs, the WSIPP analysis indicates impressive returns on investment, as indicated in Table 9.1.

For example, one specific well-researched program for juvenile offenders is FFT. This in-home, family-based program costs about $3,100 (in 2009 dollars) per family in Washington and, according to the WSIPP estimates, can be expected to reduce re-offending by about 18%. This reduction translates into $32,200 of long-run benefits to Washington taxpayers and people who do not become victims of crime, yielding an expected net present value of about $29,100 in benefits per participant.

An example of a more general type of program is cognitive-behavioral therapy for adult offenders. The WSIPP findings indicate that the average evaluated cognitive-behavioral program can be expected to reduce re-offending by about 7%, thereby achieving net benefits of $12,300 per participant. An example of a general type of programming with a poor return on investment is intensive supervision of offenders where the focus is simply on increased surveillance, but not increased treatment. WSIPP found only a modest reduction in recidivism (about 2%), and the benefits from this slight reduction fail to exceed increased staffing costs. In contrast, the WSIPP analysis found that intensive community supervision that includes drug or cognitive-behavior treatment produces a positive $12,700 in benefits per participant.

The figures shown in Table 9.1 are "expected-value" estimates. There is, of course, considerable uncertainty in these average return figures. WSIPP's full analysis includes measures of the riskiness in these return-on-investment estimates.

Two straightforward lessons emerge from this benefit-cost analysis. First, there is information available today that can help public policy-makers craft a criminal justice strategy that can both reduce crime and provide taxpayers with a better return on their dollars. Second, the findings support the "treatment principle" and the "risk principle." Evidence indicates that some types of treatment appear to be able to alter criminal behavior, and treatment strategies that focus on higher-risk offenders tend to (but do not always) have higher returns on investment than those that focus on lower-risk offenders.

TABLE 9.1 } Estimates of the benefits and costs of selected evidence-based programs for juvenile and young adult offenders.

Program Name or Type (and whether it is delivered in juvenile (J) or adult (A) correctional settings)	Expected Effect on Crime Outcomes		Benefits and Costs (2009 Dollars)					
	Percent Change in Criminal Re-Offense Outcomes	Number of Studies on Which the Estimate is Based	Total Benefits Per Program Participant	Benefits to Taxpayers	Benefits to Victims	Total Program Costs per Program Participant	Total Benefits Divided by Costs	Total Benefits Minus Costs (Net Present Value)
Multi-dimensional Treatment Foster Care (J)	-18%	3	$59,275	$13,544	$45,731	$7,418	$7.99	$51,857
Functional Family Therapy (J)	-18%	7	$32,248	$8,463	$23,785	$3,134	$10.29	$29,114
Family Integrated Transitions (J)	-10%	1	$33,770	$7,716	$26,054	$10,795	$3.13	$22,975
Adolescent Diversion Project (J)	-28%	6	$21,434	$5,507	$15,927	$2,116	$10.13	$19,318
Multisystemic Therapy (J)	-13%	9	$23,112	$6,065	$17,047	$7,076	$3.27	$16,036
Vocational Education in Prison (A)	-10%	4	$15,470	$4,763	$10,707	$1,296	$11.94	$14,174
Aggression Replacement Training (J)	-9%	4	$15,325	$4,022	$11,303	$1,449	$10.58	$13,876
Intensive Supervision, with Treatment (A)	-18%	11	$20,617	$6,262	$14,355	$7,878	$2.62	$12,739
Education in Prison, basic or post-secondary (A)	-8%	17	$13,128	$4,042	$9,086	$1,055	$12.45	$12,073
Cognitive Behavioral Programs in Prison (A)	-7%	27	$11,204	$3,450	$7,754	$517	$21.69	$10,687

TABLE 9.1 *(continued)*

Program Name or Type (and whether it is delivered in juvenile (J) or adult (A) correctional settings)	Expected Effect on Crime Outcomes		Benefits and Costs (2009 Dollars)					
	Percent Change in Criminal Re-Offense Outcomes	Number of Studies on Which the Estimate is Based	Total Benefits Per Program Partici-pant	Benefits to Taxpayers	Benefits to Victims	Total Program Costs per Program Partici-pant	Total Benefits Divided by Costs	Total Benefits Minus Costs (Net Present Value)
Drug Treatment in Commu-nity (A)	-9%	6	$9,999	$3,037	$6,962	$629	$15.89	$9,370
Drug Treatment in Prison (A)	-6%	21	$10,195	$3,139	$7,056	$1,758	$5.80	$8,437
Restorative Justice, for low risk offenders (J)	-10%	14	$7,820	$2,009	$5,811	$972	$8.04	$6,848
Drug Courts (A)	-9%	67	$9,869	$3,375	$6,494	$4,792	$2.06	$5,077
Employ-ment Training/ Job Asst in Community (A)	-5%	16	$5,238	$1,591	$3,647	$438	$11.96	$4,800
Coordina-tion of Services (J)	-2%	14	$3,402	$893	$2,509	$379	$8.98	$3,023
Intensive Supervision, surveillance only (A)	-2%	23	$1,769	$537	$1,232	$4,144	$0.43	-$2,375

Note: Estimates prepared by WSIPP. All monetary figures are life-cycle present values; the discount rate used was 3%. All figures estimated with the benefit-cost model of the Washington State Institute for Public Policy. The benefits to taxpayers and program costs are estimated for Washington State taxpayers. The benefits to crime victims are estimated with victim cost information representing the United States. All estimates were calculated in April of 2010; investors should be aware that WSIPP revises estimates whenever new information becomes available or when improvements in modeling are undertaken.

Discussion and Conclusions

This chapter reviewed the scientific evidence on effective prevention and inter-vention programs to reduce serious offending in early adulthood. It was inter-ested in the extent to which program effects vary by age and the major domains in which prevention and intervention programs take place: individual, family, school, peers, community, and labor market. Within these contexts, we set out to assess: (1) programs implemented during the later juvenile years (ages 15–17) that have measured the impact on offending in early adulthood (ages 18–29); (2) programs implemented in early adulthood that have measured the impact on offending up to age 29; and (3) programs implemented in early childhood that have measured the impact on offending in early adulthood. Also important to this chapter was an assessment of the effectiveness of restorative justice for young adult offenders as well as the benefits and costs of selected evidence-based programs for juvenile and young adult offenders.

A number of conclusions can be drawn about the state of evidence on the effectiveness of prevention and intervention programs to reduce serious offending in early adulthood. First, there is a paucity of high-quality evaluations of programs that have measured the impact on offending in early adulthood. Whether this is surprising or not, it is disappointing for sure, and we offer some research recommendations below. Second, there are some promising signs that early prevention programs can produce lasting effects on offending and other important life-course outcomes into the early adult years. At the individual level, preschool intellectual enrichment programs look to be especially effective. At the school level, multicomponent programs emphasizing classroom behavior management seem to be promising. Third, there are some promising signs that family-based interventions for adjudicated delinquents that operate outside of the juvenile justice system can reduce offending in early adulthood. These include multi-systemic therapy and multi-dimensional treatment foster care. Fourth, what evidence is available about intervention modalities used with both juvenile and adult offenders indicates that their effects are substantially similar. This generality across the major age divide in juvenile and criminal justice implies that such programs should be effective with young adult offenders as well. Fifth, there are a number of evidence-based programs for juvenile and young adult offenders that can produce monetary benefits that exceed costs.

RESEARCH RECOMMENDATIONS

Related to the overall paucity of high-quality evaluations is the noticeable lack of studies in the domains that are arguably the most important to the transition from late adolescence to early adulthood: peers, community, and labor market. We did not find one study that addressed peer or community risk factors with follow-ups of offending in early adulthood. Prior research has noted the need for future experiments to test the long-term effects of peer-based programs, as well as to investigate the causal effects of peer influence (van Lier et al., 2007; Welsh & Farrington, 2009).

With only a handful of early prevention programs, there is a need for more high-quality and targeted studies. We encourage prevention scientists to pursue funding for ongoing and long-term follow-ups of their studies and, if they have not already done so, to include offending outcome measures. It is also imperative that federal funding agencies recognize that long-term follow-ups of these studies and a new generation of studies can contribute to the advancement of scientific knowledge as well as the improvement of early childhood policies.

Efforts also need to be taken to address the challenges presented by large-scale dissemination of tested and effective prevention and intervention programs. Some of these challenges include insufficient service infrastructure, greater population heterogeneity, and loss of program fidelity (Welsh et al., 2010). While by no means immune to implementation difficulties, Communities That Care, as a well-developed and effective community prevention operating system, has the capacity to ensure that due attention is paid to many of the problems that contribute to the attenuation of program effects once programs are scaled-up or rolled out for wider public use (Hawkins et al., 2010). State or even national efforts such as the provision of technical assistance, skills, and knowledge can also go some way toward helping to address challenges of large-scale implementation.

POLICY RECOMMENDATIONS

Our conclusion that there are some promising signs that early prevention programs can produce lasting effects on offending into the early adult years is evident in two domains. At the individual level, preschool intellectual enrichment programs are especially effective. At the school level, multi-component programs emphasizing classroom behavior management appear to be promising. At this time, little is known about the effectiveness of early family-based prevention programs with respect to offending in early adulthood. There is, however, strong evidence on the effectiveness of early family-based prevention programs in reducing antisocial behavior and delinquency (Greenwood, 2006; Farrington & Welsh, 2007; Piquero et al., 2009). Furthermore, there are some promising developments in community-based prevention of delinquency. The latest findings of Communities That Care (Hawkins et al., 2008a, 2009) provide one such example.

Also important to our conclusion on early prevention is that the desirable effects of these two types of programs are not limited to a reduction in later offending. Results are highly favorable and robust for impacts on other important life-course outcomes, such as education, government assistance (e.g., welfare), employment, income, substance abuse, mental health, and family stability. This should not come as a surprise to many, given that the original impetus of some of these programs was to first and foremost improve early childhood outcomes well before delinquency or later offending could be measured. Indeed, the desirable impact on offending outcomes is sometimes considered a spin-off benefit. This should be of particular interest to policy-makers who are concerned that early prevention provides benefits only in the long-term.

While it is disappointing that there are not more experimental tests of job training programs for at-risk youth and young adults, the importance of the one Job Corps study should not be underestimated. As a robust, nationwide experiment involving more than 15,000 participants and with between three and eight years of follow-up data, its effects—including significant reductions in criminal activity, improvements in educational attainment, and greater earnings (Schochet et al., 2008)—become all the more impressive and relevant to public policy. It may be that the pressing matter for policy-makers should be how to make it even more effective.

Our last three conclusions provide support for the view that some of these intervention modalities can go a long way toward preventing the continuation from juvenile to young adult offending and fostering early desistance. The most effective of these interventions include multi-systematic therapy, cognitive-behavioral therapy, drug treatment, and sex offender treatment. Furthermore, a recent study in the United Kingdom suggests that a number of alternative interventions for young adult offenders (ages 18–24), including restorative justice conferencing, can produce substantial financial savings to society compared to standard criminal justice system practices (Barrow Cadbury Trust, 2009).

Among interventions that take place outside of the juvenile justice system, MST and MTFC show promising results in reducing serious offending in the early adult years. Both are multi-component interventions, but are considered family-based because this domain takes center stage; the parents or foster care parents (in MTFC) are actively involved. Also, both are targeted at the highest risk juvenile offenders, with each considered a last chance to avoid lengthy prison sentences.

Importantly, both MST and MTFC have produced reductions in early adult offending across a range of subgroups of high-risk offenders. For the three MST studies, one was targeted on serious and violent offenders, another on substance abusers, and the other on sex offenders. For the two MTFC studies, one was targeted on serious and chronic male offenders and the other on serious and chronic female offenders. This generalizability of effects adds further weight to the emerging evidence on the effectiveness of these interventions at this important transitional stage. Benefit-cost analyses conducted by the WSIPP show that these two program models can be a worthwhile investment of public resources. Investments in these interventions stand to make a major contribution to reductions in serious offending in early adulthood.

While there remains much work to be done, there are some promising signs that serious offending in early adulthood can be reduced through a number of prevention and intervention programs that take place over the life course. It is certainly the case that prevention and intervention programs have much more to offer our young people and society at-large compared to more punitive responses (see Howell et al., Chapter 8, this volume). That these prevention and intervention program models are not limited to one stage of development or even one domain is an encouraging sign for making inroads at addressing the needs of our at-risk young people today and for prevention scientists and practitioners alike to build on this knowledge base for the years to come.

Acknowledgments

We wish to thank Sandra Wilson for searches of Vanderbilt University's school-based intervention database.

References

Abrazaldo, W., Adefuin, J.-A., Henderson-Frakes, J., Lea, C., Leufgen, J., Lewis-Charp, H., Soukamneuth, S., & Wiegand, A. (2009). *Evaluation of the YouthBuild youth offender grants*. Final report. Oakland, CA: Social Policy Research Associates.

Alexander, J.F., & Parsons, B.V. (1973). Short-term behavioral intervention with delinquent families: Impact on family process and recidivism. *Journal of Abnormal Psychology*, 81, 219–225.

Andrews, D.A., Zinger, I., & Hoge, R.D. (1990). Does correctional treatment work? A clinically relevant and psychologically informed meta-analysis. *Criminology*, 28, 369–404.

Aos, S., Phipps, P., Barnoski, R., & Lieb, R. (2001). *The comparative costs and benefits of programs to reduce crime*. Olympia: Washington State Institute for Public Policy.

Barnoski, R. (2002). *Washington State's implementation of functional family therapy for juvenile offenders: Preliminary findings*. Olympia: Washington State Institute for Public Policy.

Bergseth, K.J., & Bouffard, J.A. (2007). The long-term impact of restorative justice programming for juvenile offenders. *Journal of Criminal Justice*, 35, 433–451.

Berrueta-Clement, J.R., Schweinhart, L.J., Barnett, W.S., Epstein, A.S., & Weikart, D.P. (1984). *Changed lives: The effects of the Perry Preschool Program on youths through age 19*. Ypsilanti, MI: High/Scope Press.

Boisjoli, R., Vitaro, F., Lacourse, E., Barker, E.D., & Tremblay, R.E. (2007). Impact and clinical significance of a preventive intervention for disruptive boys: 15-year follow-up. *British Journal of Psychiatry*, 191, 415–419.

Borduin, C.M., Schaeffer, C.M., & Heiblum, N. (2009). A randomized clinical trial of multisystemic therapy with juvenile sexual offenders: Effects on youth social ecology and criminal activity. *Journal of Consulting and Clinical Psychology*, 77, 26–37.

Bushway, S.D., & Reuter, P. (2006). Labor markets and crime risk factors. In L.W. Sherman, D.P. Farrington, B.C. Welsh, & D.L. MacKenzie (Eds.), *Evidence-based crime prevention* (rev. ed.; pp. 198–240). New York: Routledge.

Butterfield, F. (2003). Proposed White House budget cuts imperil a lifeline for troubled Oregon teenagers. *New York Times*, June 7; available at: www.nytimes.com.

Campbell, F.A., Ramey, C.T., Pungello, E., Sparling, J., & Miller-Johnson, S. (2002). Early childhood education: Young adult outcomes from the Abercedarian Project. *Applied Developmental Science*, 6, 42–57.

Catalano, R.F. (2007). Prevention is a sound public and private investment: Vollmer award address. *Criminology and Public Policy*, 6, 377–398.

Catalano, R.F., Park, J., Harachi, T.W., Haggerty, K.P., Abbott, R.D., & Hawkins, J.D. (2005). Mediating the effects of poverty, gender, individual characteristics, and external constraints on antisocial behavior: A test of the social development model and implications

272 { From Juvenile Delinquency to Adult Crime

for developmental life-course theory. In D.P. Farrington (Ed.), *Integrated developmental and life-course theories of offending* (pp. 93–123). New Brunswick, NJ: Transaction.

Chamberlain, P., & Reid, J.B. (1998). Comparison of two community alternatives to incarceration for chronic juvenile offenders. *Journal of Consulting and Clinical Psychology*, 66, 624–633.

Chamberlain, P., Leve, L.D., & DeGarmo, D.S. (2007). Multidimensional treatment foster care for girls in the juvenile justice system: 2-year follow-up of a randomized clinical trial. *Journal of Consulting and Clinical Psychology*, 75, 187–193.

Cleland, C.M., Pearson, F.S., Lipton, D.S., & Yee, D. (1997). Does age make a difference? A meta-analytic approach to reductions in criminal offending for juveniles and adults. Paper presented at annual meeting of the American Society of Criminology, San Diego, November 1997.

Cook, T.D., & Campbell, D.T. (1979). *Quasi-experimentation: Design and analysis issues for field settings.* Chicago, IL: Rand McNally.

Currie, J. (2001). Early childhood education programs. *Journal of Economic Perspectives*, 15, 213–238.

Duncan, G.J., & Magnuson, K. (2004). Individual and parent-based intervention strategies for promoting human capital and positive behavior. In P.L. Chase-Lansdale, K. Kiernan, & R.J. Friedman (Eds.), *Human development across lives and generations: The potential for change* (pp. 93–135). New York: Cambridge University Press.

Eckenrode, J., Campa, M., Luckey, D.W., Henderson, C.R., Cole, R., Kitzman, H., Anson, E., Sidora-Arcoleo, K., Powers, J., & Olds, D.L. (2010). Long-term effects of prenatal and infancy nurse home visitation on the life course of youths: 19-year follow-up a randomized trial. *Archives of Pediatrics and Adolescent Medicine*, 164, 9–15.

Eddy, J.M., Bridges Whaley, R., & Chamberlain, P. (2004). The prevention of violent behavior by chronic and serious male juvenile offenders: A 2-year follow-up of a randomized clinical trial. *Journal of Emotional and Behavioral Disorders*, 12, 2–8.

Elliott, D.S., Hamburg, B.A., & Williams, K.R. (1998). Violence in American schools: An overview. In D.S. Elliott, B.A. Hamburg, & K.R. Williams (Eds.), *Violence in American schools: A new perspective* (pp. 3–28). New York: Cambridge University Press.

Farrington, D.P., & Welsh, B.C. (2005). Randomized experiments in criminology: What have we learned in the last two decades? *Journal of Experimental Criminology*, 1, 9–38.

Farrington, D.P., & Welsh, B.C. (2006). A half century of randomized experiments on crime and justice. In M. Tonry (Ed.), *Crime and justice: A review of research* (Vol. 34, pp. 55–132). Chicago, IL: University of Chicago Press.

Farrington, D.P., & Welsh, B.C. (2007). *Saving children from a life of crime: Early risk factors and effective interventions.* New York: Oxford University Press.

Gallagher, C.A.,Wilson, D.B., Hirschfield, P., Coggeshall, M.B., & MacKenzie, D.L. (1999). A quantitative review of the effects of sex offender treatment on sexual reoffending. *Corrections Management Quarterly*, 3, 19–29.

Gordon, D.A., Graves, K., & Arbuthnot, J. (1995). The effect of functional family therapy for delinquents on adult criminal behavior. *Criminal Justice and Behavior*, 22, 60–73.

Gottfredson, D.C., Wilson, D.B., & Najaka, S.S. (2002). The schools. In J.Q. Wilson & J. Petersilia (Eds.), *Crime: Public policies for crime control* (2nd ed.; pp. 149–189). Oakland, CA: Institute for Contemporary Studies Press.

Gottfredson, D.C., Gerstenblith, S.A., Soulé, D.A., Womer, S.C., & Lu, S. (2004). Do after school programs reduce delinquency? *Prevention Science*, 5, 253–266.

Gottfredson, D.C., Wilson, D.B., & Najaka, S.S. (2006). School-based crime prevention. In L.W. Sherman, D.P. Farrington, B.C. Welsh, & D.L. MacKenzie (Eds.), *Evidence-based crime prevention* (rev. ed.; pp. 56–164). New York: Routledge.

Greenwood, P.W. (2006). *Changing lives: Delinquency prevention as crime-control policy*. Chicago, IL: University of Chicago Press.

Hahn, A., Leavitt, T.D., McNamara, E.H., & Davis, J.E. (2004). *Life after YouthBuild: 900 YouthBuild graduates reflect on their lives, dreams, and experiences*. Somerville, MA: YouthBuild U.S.A.

Hall, G.C.N. (1995). Sexual offender recidivism revisited: A meta-analysis of recent treatment studies. *Journal of Clinical and Consulting Psychology*, 63, 802–809.

Hanson, R.K., Gordon, A., Harris, A.J.R., Marques, J.K., & Murphy, W., et al. (2002). First report of the collaborative outcome data project on the effectiveness of psychological treatment for sex offenders. *Sexual Abuse*, 14, 169–194.

Harrell, A.V., Cavanagh, S.E., Harmon, M.A., Koper, C.S., & Sridharan, S. (1997). *Impact of the Children At Risk Program: Comprehensive final report*, vol. 2. Washington, DC: The Urban Institute.

Harrell, A.V., Cavanagh, S.E., & Sridharan, S. (1999). *Evaluation of the Children at Risk Program: Results 1 year after the end of the program*. Washington, DC: National Institute of Justice.

Hawkins, J.D., von Cleve, E., & Catalano, R.F. (1991). Reducing early childhood aggression: Results of a primary prevention program. *Journal of the American Academy of Child and Adolescent Psychiatry*, 30, 208–217.

Hawkins, J.D., Catalano, R.F., Kosterman, R., Abbott, R., & Hill, K.G. (1999). Preventing adolescent health risk behaviors by strengthening protection during childhood. *Archives of Pediatrics and Adolescent Medicine*, 153, 226–234.

Hawkins, J.D., Brown, E.C., Oesterle, S., Arthur, M.W., Abbott, R.D., & Catalano, R.F. (2008a). Early effects of Communities That Care on targeted risks and initiation of delinquent behavior and substance abuse. *Journal of Adolescent Health*, 43, 15–22.

Hawkins, J.D., Kosterman, R., Catalano, R.F., Hill, K.G., & Abbott, R.D. (2008b). Effects of social development intervention in childhood 15 years later. *Archives of Pediatrics and Adolescent Medicine*, 162, 1133–1141.

Hawkins, J.D., Oesterle, S., Brown, E.C., Arthur, M.W., Abbott, R.D., Fagan, A.A., & Catalano, R.F. (2009). Results of a type 2 translational research trial to prevent adolescent drug use and delinquency: A test of Communities That Care. *Archives of Pediatrics and Adolescent Medicine*, 163, 789–798.

Hawkins, J.D., Welsh, B.C., & Utting, D. (2010). Preventing youth crime: Evidence and opportunities. In D.J. Smith (Ed.), *A new response to youth crime* (pp. 209–246). Cullompton, Devon, UK: Willan.

Henggeler, S.W., Schoenwald, S.K., Borduin, C.M., Rowland, M.D., & Cunningham, P.B. (1998). *Multisystemic treatment of antisocial behavior in children and adolescents*. New York: Guilford.

Henggeler, S.W., Clingempeel. W.G., Brondino, M.J., & Pickrel, S.G. (2002). Four-year follow-up of multisystemic therapy with substance abusing and substance-dependent juvenile offenders. *Journal of the American Academy of Child and Adolescent Psychiatry*, 41, 868–874.

Howell, J.C. (2009). *Preventing and reducing juvenile delinquency: A comprehensive framework* (2nd ed.). Thousand Oaks, CA: Sage.

Illescas, S.R., Sanchez-Meca, J.S., & Genovés, V.G. (2001). Treatment of offenders and recidivism: Assessment of the effectiveness of programmes applied in Europe. *Psychology in Spain*, 5, 47–62.

Jolliffe, D., & Farrington, D.P. (2008). *The influence of mentoring on reoffending*. Stockholm, Sweden: National Council for Crime Prevention.

Kellam, S.G., & Rebok, G.W. (1992). Building developmental and etiological theory through epidemiologically based preventive intervention trials. In J. McCord & R.E. Tremblay (Eds.), *Preventing antisocial behavior: Interventions from birth through adolescence* (pp. 162–195). New York: Guilford.

Kellam, S.G., Rebok, G.W., Ialongo, N., & Mayer, L.S. (1994). The course and malleability of aggressive behavior from early first grade into middle school: Results of a developmental epidemiologically-based preventive trial. *Journal of Child Psychology and Psychiatry*, 35, 259–282.

Kellam, S.G., Brown, C.H., Poduska, J.M., Ialongo, N.S., Wang, W., Toyinbo, P., Petras, H., Ford, C., Windham, A., & Wilcox, H.C. (2008). Effects of a universal classroom behavior management program in first and second grades on young adult behavioral, psychiatric, and social outcomes. *Drug and Alcohol Dependence*, 95S, 5–28.

LaLonde, R.J. (2003). Employment and training programs. In R.A. Moffitt (Ed.), *Means-tested transfer programs in the United States* (pp. 517–585). Chicago, IL: University of Chicago Press.

Landenberger, N.A., & Lipsey, M.W. (2005). The positive effects of cognitive-behavioral programs for offenders: A meta-analysis of factors associated with effective treatment. *Journal of Experimental Criminology*, 1, 451–476.

Latimer, J., Dowden, C., & Morton-Bourgon, K.E. (2003). *Treating youth in conflict with the law: A new meta-analysis*. Ottawa: Department of Justice Canada.

Lipsey, M.W. (2009). The primary factors that characterize effective interventions with juvenile offenders: A meta-analytic overview. *Victims and Offenders*, 4, 124–147.

Lipsey, M.W., & Cullen, F.T. (2007). The effectiveness of correctional rehabilitation: A review of systematic reviews. *Annual Review of Law and Social Science*, 3, 297–320.

Lipsey, M.W., & Wilson, D.B. (1998). Effective intervention for serious juvenile offenders: A synthesis of research. In R. Loeber & D.P. Farrington (Eds.), *Serious and violent juvenile offenders: Risk factors and successful interventions* (pp. 313–345). Thousand Oaks, CA: Sage.

Lipsey, M.W., & Wilson, D.B. (2001). *Practical meta-analysis*. Thousand Oaks, CA: Sage.

Loeber, R., Farrington, D.P., Stouthamer-Loeber, M., & Raskin White, H. (2008). *Violence and serious theft: Development and prediction from childhood to adulthood*. New York: Routledge.

Lösel, F., & Schmucker, M. (2005). The effectiveness of treatment for sexual offenders: A comprehensive meta-analysis. *Journal of Experimental Criminology*, 1, 117–146.

Long, P., Forehand, R., Wierson, M., & Morgan, A. (1994). Does parent training with young noncompliant children have long-term effects? *Behavior Research and Therapy*, 32, 101–107.

Mallar, C.D., & Thornton, C.V.D. (1978). Transitional aid for released prisoners: Evidence from the Life Experiment. *Journal of Human Resources*, 13, 208–236.

McGarrell, E.F., & Hipple, N.K. (2007). Family group conferencing and re-offending among first-time juvenile offenders: The Indianapolis experiment. *Justice Quarterly*, 24, 221–246.

Mitchell, O., Wilson, D.B., & MacKenzie, D.L. (2006). *The effectiveness of incarceration-based drug treatment on criminal behavior*. The Campbell Collaboration (http://www.campbellcollaboration.org).

Olds, D.L., Eckenrode, J., Henderson, C.R., Kitzman, H., Powers, J., Cole, R., Sidora, K., Morris, P., Pettitt, L.M., & Luckey, D. (1997). Long-term effects of home visitation on maternal life course and child abuse and neglect: Fifteen-year follow-up of a randomized trial. *Journal of the American Medical Association*, 278, 637–643.

Olds, D.L., Henderson, C.R., Chamberlin, R., & Tatelbaum, R. (1986). Preventing child abuse and neglect: A randomized trial of nurse home visitation. *Pediatrics*, 78, 65–78.

Olds, D.L., Henderson, C.R., Cole, R., Eckenrode, J., Kitzman, H., Luckey, D., Pettitt, L.M., Sidora, K., Morris, P., & Powers, J. (1998). Long-term effects of nurse home visitation on children's criminal and antisocial behavior: 15-year follow-up of a randomized controlled trial. *Journal of the American Medical Association*, 280, 1238–1244.

Olds, D.L., Sadler, L., & Kitzman, H. (2007). Programs for parents of infants and toddlers: Recent evidence from randomized trials. *Journal of Child Psychology and Psychiatry*, 48, 355–391.

Patterson, G. (1982). *Coercive family process*. Eugene, OR: Castalia.

Pearson, F.S., & Lipton, D.S. (1999a). The effectiveness of educational and vocational programs: CDATE meta-analyses. Paper presented at annual meeting of the American Society of Criminology, Toronto.

Pearson, F.S., & Lipton, D.S. (1999b). A meta-analytic review of the effectiveness of corrections-based treatments for drug abuse. *The Prison Journal*, 79, 384–410.

Pearson, F.S., Lipton, D.S., & Cleland, C.M. (1997). Rehabilitative programs in adult corrections: CDATE meta-analysis. Paper presented at annual meeting of the American Society of Criminology, San Diego.

Pearson, F.S., Lipton, D.S., Cleland, C.M., & Yee, D.S. (2002). The effects of behavioral/cognitive-behavioral programs on recidivism. *Crime and Delinquency*, 48, 476–496.

Petras, H., Kellam, S.G., Brown, C.H., Muthén, B., Ialongo, N.S., & Poduska, J.M. (2008). Developmental epidemiological courses leading to antisocial personality disorder and violent and criminal behavior: Effects by young adulthood of a universal preventive intervention in first- and second-grade classrooms. *Drug and Alcohol Dependence*, 95S, 45–59.

Petrosino, A. (1997). "What works?" revisited again: A meta-analysis of randomized field experiments in rehabilitation, deterrence, and prevention. Unpublished Ph.D. dissertation. Newark: Rutgers, the State University of New Jersey.

Piliavan, I., & Masters, S. (1981). *The impact of employment programs on offenders, addicts and problem youth: Implications from the Supported Work Program*. Madison, WI: Institute for Research and Poverty Discussion, University of Wisconsin.

Piquero, A.R., Farrington, D.P., Welsh, B.C., Tremblay, R.E., & Jennings, W.G. (2009). Effects of early family/parent training programs on antisocial behavior and delinquency. *Journal of Experimental Criminology*, 5, 83–120.

Reitzel, L.R., & Carbonell, J.L. (2006). The effectiveness of sexual offender treatment for juveniles as measured by recidivism: A meta-analysis. *Sexual Abuse*, 18, 401–421.

Reynolds, A.J., Temple, J.A., Ou, S., Robertson, D.L., Mersky, J.P., Topitzes, J.W., et al. (2007). Effects of a school-based, early childhood intervention on adult health and well-being. *Archives of Pediatrics and Adolescent Medicine*, 161, 730–739.

Reynolds, A.J., Temple, J.A., Robertson, D.L., & Mann, E.A. (2001). Long-term effects of an early childhood intervention on educational achievement and juvenile arrest: A 15-year follow-up of low-income children in public schools. *Journal of the American Medical Association*, 285, 2339–2346.

Rutter, M., Giller, H., & Hagell, A. (1998). *Antisocial behavior by young people*. New York: Cambridge University Press.

Sánchez-Meca, J., Marín-Martínez, F., & Chacón-Moscoso, S. (2003). Effect-size indices for dichotomized outcomes in meta-analysis. *Psychological Methods*, 8, 448–467.

Schaeffer, C.M., & Borduin, C.M. (2005). Long-term follow-up to a randomized clinical trial of multisystemic therapy with serious and violent juvenile offenders. *Journal of Consulting and Clinical Psychology*, 73, 445–453.

Schochet, P.Z., Burghardt, J., & McConnell, S. (2008). Does Job Corps work? Impact findings from the National Job Corps Study. *American Economic Review*, 98, 1864–1886.

Schweinhart, L.J., & Weikart, D.P. (1980). *Young children grow up*. Ypsilanti, MI: High/Scope Press.

Schweinhart, L.J., Barnes, H.V., & Weikart, D.P. (1993). *Significant benefits: The High/Scope Perry Preschool study through age 27*. Ypsilanti, MI: High/Scope Press.

Schweinhart, L.J., Montie, J., Zongping, X., Barnett, W.S., Belfield, C.R., & Nores, M. (2005). *Lifetime effects: The High/Scope Perry Preschool study through age 40*. Ypsilanti, MI: High/Scope Press.

Shadish, W.R., Cook, T.D., & Campbell, D.T. (2002). *Experimental and quasi-experimental designs for generalized causal inference*. Boston: Houghton Mifflin.

Sherman, L.W. (2003). Reason for emotion: Reinventing justice with theories, innovations, and research—The American Society of Criminology 2002 Presidential Address. *Criminology*, 41, 1–37.

Sherman, L.W., & Strang, H. (2007). *Restorative justice: The evidence*. London: The Smith Institute.

Sherman, L.W., Strang, H., Angel, C., Woods, D., Barnes, G.C., Bennett, S., & Inkpen, N. (2005). Effects of face-to-face restorative justice on victims of crime in four randomized, controlled trials. *Journal of Experimental Criminology*, 1, 367–395.

Smith, P., Goggin, C., & Gendreau, P. (2002). *The effects of prison sentences and intermediate sanctions on recidivism: General effects and individual differences*. Ottawa: Solicitor General of Canada.

Tobler, N.S., Lessard, T., Marshall, D., Ochshorn, P., & Roona, M. (1999). Effectiveness of school-based drug prevention programs for marijuana use. *School Psychology International*, 20, 105–137.

Tong, L.S.J., & Farrington, D.P. (2006). How effective is the "Reasoning and Rehabilitation" programme in reducing reoffending? A meta-analysis of evaluations in four countries. *Psychology, Crime and Law*, 12, 3–24.

Tremblay, R.E., Vitaro, F., Bertrand, L., LeBlanc, M., Beauchesne, H., Boileau, H., & David, L. (1992). Parent and child training to prevent early onset of delinquency: The Montréal Longitudinal-Experimental Study. In J. McCord & R.E. Tremblay (Eds.), *Preventing antisocial behavior: Interventions from birth through adolescence* (pp. 117–138). New York: Guilford.

Tremblay, R.E., Pagani-Kurtz, P., Mâsse, L.C., Vitaro, F., & Pihl, R.O. (1995). A bimodal preventive intervention for disruptive kindergarten boys: Its impact through mid-adolescence. *Journal of Consulting and Clinical Psychology*, 63, 560–568.

Tremblay, R.E., Mâsse, L.C., Pagani, L., & Vitaro, F. (1996). From childhood physical aggression to adolescent maladjustment: The Montreal Prevention Experiment. In R.D. Peters & R.J. McMahon (Eds.), *Preventing childhood disorders, substance use, and delinquency*. Thousand Oaks, CA: Sage.

Uggen, C. (2000). Work as a turning point in the life course of criminals: A duration model of age, employment, and recidivism. *American Sociological Review*, 65, 529–546.

van Lier, P., Vitaro, F., & Eisner, M. (2007). Preventing aggressive and violent behavior: Using prevention programs to study the role of peer dynamics in maladjustment problems. *European Journal on Criminal Policy and Research*, 13, 277–296.

Villettaz, P., Killias, M., & Zoder, I. (2006). *The effects of custodial vs. non-custodial sentences on re-offending. A systematic review of the state of knowledge.* The Campbell Collaboration (http://www.campbellcollaboration.org).

Visher, C.A., Winterfield, L., & Coggeshall, M.B. (2005). Ex-offender employment programs and recidivism: A meta-analysis. *Journal of Experimental Criminology*, 1, 295–315.

Wasserman, G.A., & Miller, L.S. (1998). The prevention of serious and violent juvenile offending. In R. Loeber & D.P. Farrington (Eds.), *Serious and violent juvenile offenders: Risk factors and successful interventions* (pp. 197–247). Thousand Oaks, CA: Sage.

Welsh, B.C., & Farrington, D.P. (2009). Early developmental prevention of delinquency and later offending: Prospects and challenges. *European Journal of Developmental Science*, 3, 241–259.

Welsh, B.C., Sullivan, C.J., & Olds, D.L. (2010). When early crime prevention goes to scale: A new look at the evidence. *Prevention Science*, 11, 115–125.

Wilson, D.B., Bouffard, L.A., & MacKenzie, D.L. (2005a). A quantitative review of structured, group-oriented, cognitive-behavioral programs for offenders. *Criminal Justice and Behavior*, 32, 172–204.

Wilson, D.B., Gallagher, C.S., & MacKenzie, D.L. (2000). A meta-analysis of corrections-based education, vocation, and work programs for adult offenders. *Journal of Research in Crime and Delinquency*, 37, 347–368.

Wilson, D.B., Gottfredson, D.C., & Najaka, S.S. (2001). School-based prevention of problem behaviors: A meta-analysis. *Journal of Quantitative Criminology*, 17, 247–272.

Wilson, D.B., MacKenzie, D.L., & Mitchell, F.G. (2005b). *Effects of correctional boot camps on offending.* The Campbell Collaboration (http://www.campbellcollaboration.org).

Wilson, S.J., & Lipsey, M.W. (2007). School-based interventions for aggressive and disruptive behavior: Update of a meta-analysis. *American Journal of Preventive Medicine*, 33, 130–143.

Woolfenden, S.R., Williams, K., & Peat, J. (2002a). Family and parenting interventions for conduct disorder and delinquency: A meta-analysis of randomized controlled trials. *Archives of Disease in Childhood*, 86, 251–256.

Woolfenden, S.R., Williams, K., & Peat, J. (2002b). Family and parenting interventions in children and adolescents with conduct disorder and delinquency aged 10–17. In *The Cochrane Library, issue 4*. Oxford, UK: Update Software.

10

European Perspectives

Martin Killias, Santiago Redondo, and Jerzy Sarnecki

This chapter presents an overview of European research on the transition between juvenile offending and adult crime that is relevant for policy-makers, researchers, and practitioners, including those in North America. First, we will review relevant European longitudinal studies. Next, we present some major cross-sectional studies that provide information about important differences across Europe and the United States. A section on special offenders includes information on homicide, domestic violence, gangs, and the nexus between migration and crime. The next section on evaluation of interventions emphasizes their effectiveness regarding juvenile offenders. In the final section, we look at Europe's highly heterogeneous policy responses to young offenders, including age limits of juvenile penal laws, sentencing (including the use of custody and other sanctions) and drug and alcohol policies.

Understanding Criminal Behavior

Longitudinal studies in Europe. In presenting an overview of European longitudinal studies, we focus on studies that are relevant to the understanding of crime during late adolescence and early adulthood, including studies outside of the field of criminology. In order to facilitate the overview, all European studies are summarized in Table 10.1. Studies based on samples of less than 100, or without results on adolescence including early adulthood (e.g., Saar, 2003; Kuppens et al., 2009; Eisner et al., 2007) are not included.

All European longitudinal studies that looked at the influence of family and childhood factors found that later delinquency, persistence of careers, and seriousness of offenses are largely explained by a dysfunctional family (including lack of orderly and structured activities within the family, Hoeve 2008), early problems at school (Scotland) and a generally unfavorable environment (including parental imprisonment). In this connection, problems arising at mid-childhood (around

TABLE 10.1 } Longitudinal (cohort) studies across Europe

Author(s), year of publication, country	Birth year of cohort, sample	Research questions and methods	Main results
Sarnecki, 1985 (Sweden)	846 boys born 1943–1951 (including 195 official property offenders by age 15 matched with controls). Sample includes 100 boys from a reformatory and their 222 matched pairs	Long-term development of deviance (including drug use) as outcomes of early risk factors. Methods: official records, SRD (2000 variables collected at age 11–15)	(1) At age 15, convicted boys were worse off than controls with respect to personality, family, and school variables. (2) By 35, 7% of men with 1 conviction before 15 had died, 11% of those with 2+ convictions and 13% of those from a reformatory (vs. 1% among remaining sample). For men convicted once before 15, 18% developed drug-addiction by 35 and 24% among those with at least 2 convictions (vs. 2% among other men). (3) Adult drug abuse is strongly related to (multiple) risk factors at age 15. But even among high-risk youths, 60% did not develop substance dependency and live well-adjusted lives.
Janson, 1975, 1984; Stenberg & Vägerö, 2006; Stenberg et al., 2007; Nilsson & Estrada, 2009 (Sweden)	(1) Project Metropolitan (Janson, 1995) included all individuals born in Stockholm in 1953 who still lived there in 1962 (N=13,852) and who were followed until 1983. (2) A probability matched sample out of the original sample was followed until subjects were 48.	4 groups were distinguished: (a) subjects without known criminality; (b) subjects who desisted from crime after age 20; (c) subjects known for offending before and after age 20 ("persisters"); (d) later starters, i.e, subjects with first known offenses after age 20 ("late starters"). Methods: (1) Up to age 30: surveys, at different times; (2) registers at age 48.	Male persisters make up 11% of the cohort, but are responsible for 76% of all youth and 80% of all adult (known) offenses; female persisters make up 1% of the cohort, but commit about 50% of all (known) offenses. Persisters of each gender come from highly problematic childhood conditions. Female persisters live, as adults, under worse conditions than males from similar backgrounds who in their majority live relatively well.
Bergman, 2009; Bergman & Andershed, 2009 (Sweden)	Individual Development and Adaptation (IDA): The sample includes all 1,400 children who, in 1965, were aged 10, 13, and 15 years and who attended primary schools in Örebro. Follow-ups were carried out when cohort was aged 13, 15, 16, 17, 18, 21, 23, and 43.	Development of offending in different groups (nonoffenders, adolescent only offenders, adolescent and adult offenders, adult only offenders). Methods: Surveys and official records.	60% of men and 91% of females have no criminal record, 16% of men and 3% of females have known offenses before age 21 only, 11% of men and 5% of women have known offenses as adults only, and 13% of men and 1.5% of women are recorded both for juvenile and adult offenses. 5% of men have criminal records as children, juveniles, and adults and accounted for two-thirds of all known offenses committed by the entire cohort. More efficient prevention focused on this small group might, thus, prevent a substantial proportion of crime. Life-long persisters came from particularly unfavorable milieus and suffered from disproportionate numbers of risk factors. Late starters were more similar to law-abiding cohort members, but were more often known for hyperactivity, broken homes (females), and marijuana smoking (males).

(continued)

TABLE 10.1 (continued)

Author(s), year of publication, country	Birth year of cohort, sample	Research questions and methods	Main results
Pulkkinen & Hämäläinen, 1995; Kokko & Pulkkinen, 2000; Pikänen et al., 2005 (Finland)	369 subjects attending 12 2nd grade school classes in 1968 in the town of Jyväskylä. They were re-interviewed at age 14, 20, 27, 36, and 42 (in 2001). Retention rate was 90% at 42.	The study is on a wide array of issues, ranging from violence to alcohol abuse and unemployment. Methods: Interviews, teacher ratings.	Teacher-rated aggression at age 8 is related to school maladjustment at age 14, which predicts, directly and through problem drinking and lack of occupational alternatives, unemployment at age 27. Drinking problems are best predicted by early onset of alcohol consumption. Low self-control in childhood and adolescence was a precursor to crime and accidents by age 32, but only among subjects with other adverse life-circumstances.
Kyvsgaard, 2003 (Denmark)	Official Danish databases, with information regarding offense dates, charges, dispositions, confinement records but also basic demographics and the workforce registers. The sample comprises 1/15th of the Danish population from 1979 to 1991 aged 15 and above (>333,000 persons). Of these, nearly 45,000 have a criminal record. Trajectories of the criminal careers are followed over 13 years.	Characteristics of criminal careers – prevalence, individual crime frequency, criminal onset, duration of and desistance from criminal careers, specialization, and escalation in crime seriousness. Methods: Official data on police records, prosecutorial dispositions, and court decisions (convictions).	The study shows a relationship between patterns of prevalence and frequency of offenses and duration of careers and desistance. Furthermore, the study shows that criminal careers of high-frequency offenders are characterized both by specialization and versatility. Finally, crime seriousness is related to individual offending frequency. Careers do not follow the expected pattern of escalating in seriousness with increasing numbers of offenses.
Olweus, 2011 (Sweden)	780 Stockholm boys, first data collected 1950s–1960s.	The relation between bullying at ages 13–16 and offending at ages 16–24.	73 bullies have more convictions (55% vs. 26%) and more violent convictions (26% vs. 5%) than 707 boys not involved with bullying.
(1) Kazemian & Farrington, 2006; (2) Farrington, Ttofi & Coid, 2009; (3) Murray & Farrington 2005; (4) Kazemian, Farrington & Le Blanc, 2009; (5) Zara & Farrington, 2009 (England)	Cambridge Study in Delinquent Development (CSDD): 411 London boys followed from 8 to 48 (i.e., from 1961 to 2001).	Do age of onset and type of offenses predict career length and number of offenses over the lifespan? Methods: Interviews and official records.	(1) Residual career length and number of offenses declined with age, but it is not clear whether this is predicted by age of onset or type of offense. (Lack of accuracy of official records may distort findings.) (2) All subjects become more unsuccessful with age, but persistent offenders show the most unsuccessful lives at 32 and 48. (3) Boys separated from their parents due to parental imprisonment had the highest score of antisocial outcomes at age 32. (4) Social bonds, cognitive predispositions, and behavioral variables (such as drug use) at age 17–18 predict seriousness of offending and de-escalation by age 32. (5) Personal factors such as isolation, nervousness, anxiety, and neuroticism protect against offending under age 21, but not later.

Study	Description	Findings
(1) Wikström, 2009; (2) Wikström, Ceccato, Hardie, & Treiber, 2010 (England)	Explores the impact of crime propensity and criminogenic exposure on individual crime involvement during early to mid-adolescence. Methods: PADS+ questionnaire and data from the small-area community survey (PCS) and the space-time budget.	(1) A person's criminal involvement depends on his propensity to crime and his exposure. Changes in a person's crime involvement are dependent on changes in his propensity and exposure. (2) Youths' activity fields and exposure to criminogenic settings predict criminal involvement.
(1) Smith & Ecob, 2007; Smith, 2004a; (2) Smith, 2004b; (3) McAra, 2004; Smith, 2006a; (4) Smith 2006b (Scotland)	Edinburgh Study of Youth Transition and Crime — Nexus between delinquency and victimization. Methods: Interviews.	(1) Offending and victimization are interrelated and predict each other 3 years later. The nexus is largely explained by being in risky situations and having antisocial friend. (2) Parenting and family functioning at age 13 are good predictors of delinquency at age 15. (3) Attachment to and behavior at school at age 13 predict offending at 15. (4) Desistance was important by 17, but boys from disadvantaged neighborhoods and those caught by the police were more likely to remain delinquents. (5) Typical age of first conviction was 17. Best predictors were exclusion from school (or dropping out), being male, living in deprived neighborhood, serious and persistent offending, and early contacts with the police/criminal justice system.
Verhulst et al., 1985; Bongers et al., 2006; Donker et al., 2003 (Netherlands)	South Holland Study: 2,600 children of Dutch nationality from 13 birth cohorts aged 4 to 16, selected in 1983 from municipal registers. Consent from parents was obtained for 2,076 children. Follow-up every 2 years until 1991 and again in 1997. 1,149 remained in the sample until 1997. What is the trajectory of externalizing behavior (opposition, property, violent and status offenses) across childhood and adolescence? Methods: Interviews (Child-Behavior Checklist) with parents; teacher reports and SRD.	Follow-up of 1991 (Bongers et al., 2006): Contrary to expectation, aggression did not peak at age 13, but was most prevalent among younger children. Physical aggression decreases and is largely resolved by the beginning of adulthood. Gender differences are considerable during childhood, but level off by late adolescence. Property offenses decreased, whereas status violations increased. However, parents may not be aware of many of their (older) children's norm violations (follow-up until 1991). Follow-up of 1997 (Donker et al., 2003): aggressive behavior is more stable than nonaggressive antisocial behavior.

(continued)

TABLE 10.1 (*continued*)

Author(s), year of publication, country	Birth year of cohort, sample	Research questions and methods	Main results
Gerris et al., 1993; Hoeve et al., 2006 (Netherlands)	Child-rearing and family in the Netherlands study: population sample of 788 families, children followed from 9 to 27 (original study in 1990, follow-ups in 1995 and 2000).	The impact of family factors and parenting styles on delinquency in adulthood (comparison with the Pittsburgh Youth Study): Self-reports.	The lack of orderly and structured activities within the family during adolescence was a strong predictor of delinquency in young adulthood after controlling for prior aggression and demographic variables. Authoritarian and authoritative parenting styles, family SES, supervision, punishment, and attachment were not related to delinquent behavior in young adulthood. The attrition rate in the Hoeve et al. study (2006) was 62%.
Meeus & 't Hart 1993; Meeus et al., 2004 (Netherlands)	Utrecht Study of Adolescent Development: representative sample of 3,392 Dutch adolescents aged 12–23 was drawn from a panel of 10,000 households. Out of this sample, 1,300 subjects were randomly selected for the longitudinal study.	How does having an intimate partner influence delinquency? How does this moderate parental influence on delinquency? Methods: Interviews (SRD) at homes. First wave in 1991, waves 2 and 3 in 1994 and 1997.	If an adolescent finds a partner, that partner takes over the role of parents in reducing criminality. For subjects without a partner, parents remain important.
Gavray, 1997 (Belgium)	In 1992, 444 subjects aged 16–21 were sampled for ISRD-1 in the region of Liège (Belgium). Among these, 139 (who agreed to leave their address in 1992) were re-interviewed in 1996 (when they were between 21 and 25).	Development of offending across adolescence. Methods: Interviews (SRD).	Delinquency (including seriousness of offenses and versatility) in 1996 was strongly predicted by abuse of substances in 1992. Leaving school did prevent later offending only if subjects succeeded with integration into the labor market.
Born, 2002 (Belgium)	363 children placed in institutions were followed over time, along with the sample used by Gavray (1997).	The process of desistance from delinquency at late adolescence. Methods: Interviews and official records.	In both samples, delinquency is not adolescence-limited but often continues into adulthood, particularly among adolescents with early substance abuse, victimization in their biography, and high versatility. The end of a delinquent career comes about with entering into social and emotional responsibilities.
Göppinger, 1985; Bock, 2000 (Germany)	"Tübingen" study: Influenced by the Glueck study (1950), 200 prison inmates were matched with 200 men from the same region without known history of offending. The study started in the 1960s.	Understanding differences in trajectories over life between known serious offenders and "normal" men. Methods: Official records and retrospective interviews. Recently, prospective SRD and official records were collected.	Offending is embedded in a long biographic continuity. Early deviance starts during leisure time and later spreads to the professional (educational) sphere. Originally retrospective, the study became gradually prospective in nature.

| Remschmidt & Walter, 2009 (Germany) | "Marburg Study": The sample included 1,009 boys aged 14 in 1971 and who were known offenders in the Marburg district between 1962 and 1971. 347 matched pairs without records had been selected from population registers. Between 1975 and 1977 (when boys were around 22), 263 were interviewed (61 refused). The study has a "catch-up prospective" design. | Six groups were distinguished: (1) boys with at least one known offense prior to age 14 and none prior to age 18; (2) boys with at least one known offense prior to age 14 and at least two offenses by 18; (3) boys with at least 2 offenses prior to age 14 and none by 18; (4) boys with at least 2 offenses before 14 and before 18; (5) boys without known offenses at age 14 and at least 2 offenses prior to age 18; (6) boys without known offenses by age 14 and between 14 and 18. Methods: Interviews (lasting 2–4 hours) with intelligence and personality tests, a questionnaire on parental style of education, biographic data, and SRD. After age 22, criminal records were collected until subjects were 42. | Important risk factors for offending later in life are (in combination) family and social risk factors, personality characteristics, and undiscovered property offenses committed during childhood. |
| Albrecht & Grundies, 2009 (Germany) | "Freiburg cohort study": All juveniles born in 1970, 1973, 1975, 1978, 1985, and 1988 in Baden-Württemberg having at least once been known as suspects or convicted were considered for follow-up. | Development of official offending over adolescence and young adulthood. Methods: Criminal records concerning all members of the cohort are registered in a database. | Convictions reach a maximum between 18 and 22 (7% of cohort members being convicted every year at this age). The rate decreases to 3% after age 33. The results do not support the view of adolescence-limited and life-course persistent career patterns, but suggest that at any given age, some subjects without previous criminal history are convicted for the first time. The proportion of career offenders decreases with age, but is independent of age of onset. The results support the "life-course desistance" model (by Sampson and Laub). |

(continued)

TABLE 10.1 (continued)

Author(s), year of publication, country	Birth year of cohort, sample	Research questions and methods	Main results
Schmidt et al., 2009 (Germany)	"Mannheim longitudinal study": The sample includes 1,444 children born in Mannheim in 1970 who still lived there in 1978. 216 children were randomly selected for regular follow-up interviews (one-third refused). To this reduced ample, 183 children with psychiatric symptoms were added. These 399 subjects were interviewed at 8, 13, 18, and 25. 321 were retained until 25.	Development of offending (among other problems) over adolescence and young adulthood. Methods: Intensive interviews. SRD when subjects were aged 18 and 25.	Family dysfunctions are particularly important at mid-childhood (age 8–13), especially for later chronic offending.
Schumann et al., 2009 (Germany)	"Bremen study": All students born 1971–74 in their final year of 2 lower track schools in Bremen were first interviewed in 1989 (of these, 90% entered an apprenticeship). At wave 2 (1992), 426 former students agreed to be re-interviewed, and at wave 5 (2000), 333. The study was designed as a comparative study to the *Denver Youth Survey*.	Development of offending during the transition from school to apprenticeship and the labor market. Methods: SRD (waves 2–5).	Delinquency was similar in the Bremen and Denver samples at age 14. It dropped more during the following years in the American sample, despite less institutionalized transitions from school to the labor market. Vocational training and having a stable job requiring job qualifications does not reduce delinquency. Possibly including drug use (cannabis) and shoplifting may have reduced differences over time and across countries. Authors wonder whether vocational training may have delayed effects (by age 25?). Only 2% among the Bremen sample experienced pre-trial detention by wave 5, but 20% among the Denver sample were arrested. No deterrent effect was discovered, but pre-trial detention (D) and arrest (U.S.) are not the same!
Boers et al., 2009 (Germany)	"Duisburg study": 3,411 7th-grade students from Duisburg were recruited for a longitudinal SRD-study to start in 2002. The sample was re-interviewed every year until 2006. 1,552 remained in the sample until the last wave.	Development of delinquency through the ages 14–18. Methods: Annual SRD. Rigid data protection laws reduced the retention rate. Students had to note, on their questionnaire, a personal code (instead of their names), which they had to remember during the following waves.	Delinquency is not alone the result of risk factors, but also affects social bonds and may jeopardize successful integration. (Results are preliminary yet.) The study having covered, at every wave, the entire school population and not only those remaining in the panel (i.e., those remembering their personal codes), it is possible to assess to what extent rigid data protection laws affect sample composition. Retention was better among female students in higher tracks with low delinquency scores.

Laubacher et al. (in press) (Switzerland)	In 1971, 6,315 Army conscripts were interviewed during the day of conscription. Sample covered all Swiss males aged 19 living in the Canton of Zurich. Randomly, for half of the sample (3,155) criminal records were checked. 123 had a record at that time (54% property, 28% violent, and 30% drug offenses). Records continued to be checked for these 123 men until they were aged 52 (in 2004).	Development of psychiatric symptoms (and delinquency) over the lifespan. Methods: Interviews (for psychiatric symptoms). Criminal records for delinquency.	(1) Adolescent delinquency is not necessarily episodic (68% had been reconvicted by age 52, of which about one in four was for a violent offense); (2) socio-demographic variables and psychiatric diagnosis (at age 19) are only weakly related to later violent criminality; (3) type of offenses committed during adolescence have high predictive validity, especially for violent offenses; (4) number and seriousness of offenses including versatility at age 19 are important predictors of serious adult offending.
Haas, 2001; Haas et al., 2004; Haas & Killias, 2003; Staubli & Killias (2011) (Switzerland)	Cross-sectional, retrospective study of 21,300 Swiss Army recruits and a random sample of 20-year-old Swiss men not drafted (born 1997).	Explanations of very serious offenses committed at age 20 through past biographic experiences (before age 6, between 6 and 11, and after 12). Methods: Written interviews (questionnaires to be dropped into a ballot box). SRD and victimization over the lifespan.	Results match (including for very serious offenses, such as serious assault, offenses committed with guns, rape, and child abuse) many findings from longitudinal studies on the role of family and socialization variables, protective factors (e.g., a positive relationship with teachers), and versatility vs. specialization. Serious offenders are committing a wide range of offenses. Certain victimizations (including bullying and sexual abuse) have far-reaching consequences (including suicide attempts and violent offending) at age 19.
Caprara, Regalia, & Bandura 2002; Caprara et al., 2007; Paciello et al., 2008 (Italy)	During the school year 1989/90, approximately 400 3rd grade students (aged about 9) from Genzano (suburban town near Rome) were assessed. Three additional cohorts were assessed during the following 3 years. Each cohort was assessed annually until it reached age 14–15 and every second year afterwards until 2008 (when the oldest subjects were 27).	Development of aggression from mid-childhood into young adulthood in relation to self-efficacy by age 20 (366 subjects retained). Methods: Measures of aggressive traits and delinquency from ages 12 to 23. SRD (violence) at waves 3–5. The study was originally designed in collaboration with Albert Bandura and Gerry Patterson.	Irritability and perceived self-regulatory efficacy (measured from age 14 through the item: "How well can you resist peer pressure to drink beer, wine or liquor?") were important predictors of violence at age 20. There was also a high continuity of irritability and offending across adolescence.
Luengo et al., 1994 (Spain)	1,226 adolescents aged 12–17 interviewed in 1989 and one year later.	How do different forms of impulsivity influence antisocial behavior? Methods: SRD and several impulsivity scales.	Non-planning impulsivity (i.e., not caring about consequences of actions) best explains antisocial behavior one year later, and best distinguishes stable nondelinquents from persistent offenders.

age 13) have also been found to be important (Mannheim study). Self-control (or regulatory self-efficacy), irritability and impulsivity were further found to influence later offending and violence (Italy, Spain).

Regarding protective factors, the story is more complex. Beyond social isolation (Cambridge Study in Delinquent Development), attachment to a teacher was a protective factor associated with low offending in two studies (Scotland, Switzerland). Ironically, successful vocational training did not reduce offending in one German study (Bremen), although this may be due to a small sample that did not allow the isolation of more serious offenses. Two studies (Finland, and Duisburg in Germany) looked at the ways the child's behavior affects social bonds and found the relationship to be far from unidirectional. This should be kept in mind in interpreting findings showing higher odds of later offending for those who were excluded from school or caught by the police and, eventually, sanctioned by the criminal justice system (Scotland).

Some European studies have found a significant impact of various opportunities on later offending (Scotland), such as leisure-time activities (including drug use, Belgium), having an intimate partner (the Utrecht study), unemployment (Finland), and neighborhood disadvantage. Life-styles may influence delinquency, but also allow for the possibility of victimization (Scotland).

Some European studies have found career patterns that do not necessarily match the distinction between adolescence-limited and persistent offenders and late starters. According to some studies, late adolescent offenders continue offending long beyond age 30 (Mannheim, Freiburg, Switzerland), particularly among some minorities (Netherlands, Jennissen, 2009). Substantial numbers of people are later convicted without having had a record by age 20 (England, Soothill et al., 2003). Two Swedish studies found that the proportion of offenses committed by persistent criminals is beyond 60% for the most "productive" 5% and 50% for the "top" 1%. Similar results are reported from the Netherlands where only 1.6% of the offenders were versatile serious delinquents who were responsible of 20% to 30% of all offenses committed by the entire cohort (Meeus et al., 2001).

The often invoked "normalization" of delinquent youths during adolescence seems to refer to mostly trivial offenders and offenses (Timmermans, 2009), but not necessarily refer to persistent and serious offending. Blokland and Palmen (in press) found that, among their 1984 birth cohort whose criminal record could be followed up to 2007 (N = 170,891), offending was more prevalent between ages 18 and 23 than before or in the later twenties when desistance from offending became more common. At the same time, however, a substantial proportion of offenders started during early adulthood, and others continued offending, especially among those who were chronic offenders between ages 12 and 23.

Using data on the same cohort (born in 1984), Averdijk, Elffers, and Ruiter (in press) have combined data on re-offending after age 12 and mobility across neighborhoods over time to assess, for the first time in Europe, such effects in a longitudinal perspective. Controlling for a certain number of background variables (such as employment, marriage, and leaving parental households), they found a weak but consistent (positive) effect of neighborhood disadvantage (as measured by the proportion of non-western residents) on offending, but—paradoxically—a small negative effect of mobility on rearrest. They argue that mobility may isolate young offenders from delinquent peers.

Given the costs of longitudinal studies, it should be recognized that retrospective studies, such as the Tübingen (Germany) study comparing prison inmates with non-convicted matched pairs or the Swiss army recruits study using an unusually large sample, offer opportunities to look at very serious offenses in a (retrospective) biographic perspective. The Bremen (Germany) and the Child-rearing and the Family in the Netherlands Study illustrate how much might be gained from combining longitudinal studies across countries. Unfortunately, no longitudinal studies (either in the fields of criminology or in other related fields, such as psychiatry) could be located in Norway, Ireland, Austria, Portugal, Greece, or in former communist countries (with the exception of Estonia). Rather surprising is the absence of any longitudinal study in France. Such a study was prepared by a panel of international experts (including Richard Tremblay) in 2006 (*'Troubles des conduites chez l'enfant et l'adolescent'*) but it was contested on ethical grounds and abandoned (http://www.vie-publique.fr/actualite/alaune/delinquance-depistage-enfance-critique.html).

International (European) studies. Studies on offending during adolescence and young adulthood are dominated by longitudinal research. Macro-level and contextual variables, traditionally, have found more attention in international studies. Cross-national differences in crime rates are considerable and reflect to a large extent crimes among young males. Given Europe's diversity in macro-level variables and the highly fragmented policy responses across the continent, a few notes on international trends may be of interest to American scholars and policy-makers.

The international crime victimization survey (ICVS). This survey was undertaken in 1989, 1992, 1996, 2000, and 2005 in a significant number of European countries (van Dijk et al., 2007). According to these data, robbery increased compared to 1989 (or the earliest available year) in about half of European countries and remained stable (i.e., within a margin of +/- 20%) or decreased in the other half of countries. Assault increased in the vast majority of European countries. Police-recorded assault and robbery, as measured by the *European Sourcebook of Crime and Criminal Justice Statistics* (also known as ESB, 2010, Table 5.2.1), by and large matched ICVS trends. On the other hand, survey-measured and police-recorded property crime decreased after 1995 (Tavares & Thomas, 2008). This was true especially for domestic burglary and motor vehicle thefts. Drug offenses, including drug trafficking, increased more substantially. For American readers, it may be surprising that Europe has not seen a general drop in violent crime.

How can these changes be explained? Unfortunately, ICVS lifestyle measures were too crude to grasp the relevant changes. Outdoor activities (particularly in inner-city areas) increased dramatically in many countries, often way beyond midnight and combined with high consumption of alcohol and other substances. However, the "revolution" of leisure-time activities following the extension of hours of operation of public transportation, the abolition of closing hours for pubs and the "liberalization" of policies regulating the sale of alcoholic beverages was not universal across Europe, but limited to certain countries and cities. The surprisingly different trends in rates of assault and robbery across Europe may well be attributable to the highly variable development of "routine activities" and risky lifestyles. Cross-national comparative research, e.g., based on data from Peterborough (England) and Eskilstuna (Sweden), has shown that differences in lifestyle predict differences in delinquency levels (Wikström & Svensson, 2008).

In many European countries, however, increases in violence, especially among juveniles, is subject to debate, particularly in Scandinavia (Sarnecki, 2009b; Balvig 2006; Kivivuori & Salmi, 2006; BRÅ, 2010), in Germany (Baier et al., 2009), and in the Netherlands (Wittebrood & Nieuwbeerta, 2006). While the rate of young violent offenders known to the police is increasing, self-report and victimization studies (focusing on young people as victims of crime) suggest more stable trends. The favorite explanation for these discrepancies is generally the presumed increase in propensity to report violence to the police and/or more complete recording of violent offenses by the police. According to ICVS data (see ESB, 2010, Table 5.2.3), reporting to the police increased on average in all European countries from 30 to 33% for assault, and from 45 to 49% for robbery. However, surveys may be less suitable to monitor trends in serious injuries that are more regularly reported to and recorded by the police and other services, such as medical emergency centers (Exadaktylos et al., 2007; BRÅ, 2008, p. 100) and insurance companies (Lanfranconi, 2009). Sources of this kind often match trends with police-recorded offenses.

The International Survey on Violence against Women (IVAWS). According to the results of this survey, conducted in 2004 on samples of 2,000 women in nine countries (including Poland, Switzerland, Denmark, and the Czech Republic), the strongest single correlate of partner violence is the male partner's history of nondomestic violence. Men described by female respondents as being sometimes violent outside the home are between two and 12 times more likely to assault their female partner. This finding underlines the importance of general criminal violence in the causation of domestic violence (Lussier, Farrington, & Moffitt, 2009) and the priority its prevention deserves in the context of domestic violence. Next in importance came frequent binge drinking, which varies considerably across Europe (Johnson, Ollus, & Nevala, 2008).

The International Self-reported Delinquency Survey (ISRD-2). The first ISRD survey was conducted in 1992 in 12 countries (Junger-Tas et al., 1994). In 2006, a second survey of this kind was conducted in 30 countries (Junger-Tas et al., 2010). It provides comparative data on most of continental Europe including countries in Central and Eastern Europe. The results show that juvenile delinquency, as assessed by the ISRD-2 self-report instrument, is substantially correlated with national rates of juvenile offenders known to the police according to the ESB 2010 (Enzmann et al., 2010).

Further, the national rates of self-reported delinquency are also quite strongly correlated with several features of school systems. For example, countries having a high standard deviation of their ninth grade students' PISA (the international tests of students' intellectual abilities) performance scores face higher rates of serious (rare) violent offenses, suggesting that low integration of the weakest students (and, thus, a high standard deviation) has a significant impact on students' behavior. This correlation holds in multilevel analyses even when gender, age, migrant status, and several school variables (such as school disorganization, attachment to school, school climate, and students' performance at school) are taken into account (Lucia & Killias, in press).

Beyond schools, the ISRD-2 shows that delinquency—and particularly serious violence—is highly correlated with lifestyles and going out (and hanging around) during late night hours, as well as neighborhood characteristics (Junger-Tas et al., in press). These are among the strongest explanatory variables among the wide array of independent variables that were collected through the ISRD-2. As far as the neighborhood is concerned, this could be related to the possibility of observing deviant situations (including littering, graffiti, and other signs of disorder) that, as a remarkable Dutch experiment revealed, produce not only "imitation," but offenses that are different in nature from those that are observed, such as theft (Keizer, Lindenberg, & Steg, 2008).

Special Offenders

Homicide. The rate of homicide in Western Europe is generally low, i.e., it nowhere exceeds 2 per 100,000 (with the exception of Finland and Scotland) according to police statistics. In Eastern Europe, however, rates are far higher, namely between 6 and 10 per 100,000 during the years 2003–2007 (ESB, 2010, Table 1.1). However, these global rates never tell the full story. Homicide constellations vary greatly across space and time, since homicide includes family killings, murder in connection with robbery or black markets, and terrorist and political homicide. Looking at varying constellations is, therefore, far more helpful to an understanding of the dynamics of this crime. In this respect, research has benefited from national databases on homicide established during the last decade in the Netherlands (Nieuwbeerta & Leistra, 2007), Finland (Kivivuori & Lehti, 2003), and Switzerland (Killias et al., 2009). These data include many details on victims, offenders, and events that allow international comparisons. If street homicide rates are very high in the United States, American rates of domestic homicide are not out of range of other countries, as Table 10.2 illustrates.

In view of these data, it is inappropriate to consider levels of homicide as an expression of a society's "intrinsic violence" and to call the United States a "violent country." Similarly, differences in homicide rates over time and space may be related to variations in homicide constellations, including, in the case of Scandinavia,

TABLE 10.2 } Prevalence of completed intentional homicide (total, within the family including intimate partners, and homicides followed by suicide) in 7 countries (several recent years).

Country	Total per 1 million population	Within the family		Homicide followed by suicide	
		per 1 million population	in % of all homicides	per 1 million population	in % of all homicides
USA	56	7.9	14 %	2.2	3.9
Finland	24	6.9	29 %	1.6	5.8
Canada	20	5.7	29 %	2.0	10
Australia	20	7.0	35 %	1.2	6
Netherlands	15	4.3	29 %	0.5	3.3
Switzerland	10	4.1	43 %	0.9	14
Spain	10	1.8	18 %	n.a.	n.a.

Sources for total and family homicides: USA: Supplementary Homicide Reports, years 1976–2003; Finland: Kivivuori (2001); Canada: Statistics Canada, years 2000–2004; Australia: Mouzos & Rushforth (2003); Netherlands: Leistra & Nieuwbeerta (2003); Switzerland: Killias et al. (2009); Spain: Instituto Nacional de estadística (INE) and Centro Reina Sofía para el Estudio de la Violencia.

Sources for homicide followed by suicide: Liem et al. (2011); Finland: Kivivuori & Lehti (2003); Canada: Statistics Canada. Family Violence in Canada: A Statistical Profile (2005); Australia: http://www.aic.gov.au/publications/current%20series/cfi/161-180/cfi176.aspx; Spain: Instituto Nacional de estadística (INE) and Centro Reina Sofía para el Estudio de la Violencia.

drinking patterns (Lenke, 1990; Sarnecki, 2009b, p. 96). In America, guns are far more often used in street-level murder, whereas the use of guns is less common among European criminal networks, with the exception of the Italian mafias. This is true even in countries with substantial gun ownership rates, such as Finland and Switzerland (Markwalder, 2011). Rarely used in the streets, guns are, however, very often used in domestic homicide in these two countries. Data from the International Survey on Violence against Women (IVAWS) further suggest that the extent of domestic violence is not related to domestic homicide rates. Rather, the presence of deadly instruments at home increases the likelihood of fatal outcomes in cases of family and partner disputes, as well as risks of multi-person killings and homicide followed by the offender's suicide (Liem, Barber, Markwalder, Killias, & Nieuwbeerta, 2011).

According to mortality as well as police statistics, homicides in Europe leveled off after 1997 and the average of police-recorded homicides dropped from 4 to 2 per 100,000 by 2007 (ESB, 2003, 2006, 2010, Tables 1.2.1.4 and 1.2.1.5). Since non-lethal violence did not decrease (see the preceding section), the question remains whether trends in murder rates are influenced by improved medical services, as suggested by American research (Harris et al., 2002; Doerner, 1988).

Domestic violence. Partner violence is a prominent issue in many European countries, including Greece (Papadakaki, Tzamalouka, Chatzifotiou, & Chlioutakis, 2009) and Spain. Although the rates of women battered by their partner in Spain (less than 4% in 2006) was not out of range of other countries (Instituto de la Mujer, 2006), cases of partner violence are far more often recorded by the police in Spain than in other countries. In 2007, the rate per 100,000 was roughly three times the European median (of about 50) and substantially higher than in neighboring Portugal or in Finland (ESB, 2010, Table 1.1). Much more debated than probably in any other country is the nexus between partner violence and partner killing, although Spain's homicide rate is among the lowest in Europe (Table 10.3).

Gangs. Beyond the "revolution" of the leisure-time industry and decreasing parental control over children, the last decades have brought about a switch from *vertical social control* (parents, other adults and superiors) to *horizontal social control* (peers, schoolmates) of the behavior of young people. In two studies in Stockholm (Sarnecki, 2001) and Copenhagen (Sarnecki, 2009a), youth co-offending networks have been studied through official records over several years. The results show that young offenders (up to age 20) often acted in loose and short-lived networks. Co-offending of two or more individuals over a period of more than one year is, according to crime records, extremely uncommon. This research suggests that there may be differences between American and European gangs.

On the other hand, many European cities reported significant gang activity over the last decade (Klein, 1995). Research on this topic has been intensified by the "Eurogang Network" (Esbensen & Lynskey, 2001), an informal group of American and European scholars whose work has influenced the construction of the questionnaire of the International Self-report Study (ISRD-2). Work on gangs in Europe has identified some common features with American models, in particular far higher incidence rates for particularly serious and violent offenses for gang members compared to juveniles who say they do not belong to any group, or who admit to belonging only to an informal group sharing leisure-time activities (Esbensen & Weerman, 2005). This is true for girls as well as boys (Haymoz & Gatti, 2010).

Migration and crime. An issue with a high degree of relevance in Europe is crime by immigrants and in particular by young minority males who grow up in Western Europe. In most European countries—and contrary to the American experience (where migrants are underrepresented in crime)—this group is overrepresented in police and court statistics, especially for violent crime (see, e.g., for the Netherlands, Junger, Wittebrood, & Timman, 2001). This situation has existed over several decades and has apparently worsened over time (Tonry, 1997). Three reasons for this overrepresentation have been proposed: (1) discrimination by the victims (when they decide to report a crime), by the police, and at the following steps within the criminal justice system, (2) disproportionate exposure to problems (such as politically- and ethnically-motivated violence) in the country of origin, and (3) integration problems these groups face in Western Europe. Results of the international self-report studies (Junger-Tas et al., in press) and victims' accounts of offender characteristics, as measured through victimization surveys in England and Wales (Shah & Pease, 1992) and in Switzerland (Killias, 2009), show, however, that the overrepresentation of minorities is present also in victimization surveys and self-report measures of crime. Validity problems of self-report measures seem even to underestimate the size of this

TABLE 10.3 } Percent alien suspects (known to the police) and convicted alien defendants across Europe in 2006.

Country	Bodily injury (assault)		Rape		Robbery	
	% Alien suspects known to the police	% Alien defendants convicted	% Alien suspects known to the police	% Alien defendants convicted	% Alien suspects known to the police	% Alien defendants convicted
Austria	23	24	36	36	42	40
Czech Republic	7	5	16	16	n.a.	n.a.
Finland	8	6	22	24	11	18
France	14	12	14	8	14	n.a.
Germany	21	24	30	35	29	31
Switzerland	49	58	64	68	60	61

Source: ESB 2010, Tables 1.2.2 and 3.1.2.

problem (Junger, 1989). Further studies on how the criminal justice system operates lend only limited support to the discrimination hypothesis (Hood, 1992). One way of assessing possible discrimination within the criminal justice system is to compare the proportion of alien suspects at the police level with the proportion of alien defendants convicted. As Table 10.3 shows, for the countries collecting such data, there is no systematic increase in the proportion of aliens across different stages of justice processing.

The question arises as to what produces these differences. For example, immigrants may be more likely to suffer from lack of *social capital* (Bakker, Walberg, & Bloom, 2005) including school failure, unemployment, social isolation, and concentration in poor and socially disorganized areas of major cites (Junger-Tas et al., in press). The role of social problems is further underlined by self-report surveys showing that delinquency is far less prevalent in some countries of origin (such as Bosnia-Herzegovina; Killias, Maljevic, & Lucia, 2010) than among juveniles from those countries who have grown up in Western Europe. This suggests that violence is not "imported" from the regions of origin, as suggested by culture-conflict theories, but produced locally by difficulties of integration. According to a Swedish study (Hällsten, Sarnecki, & Szulkin, 2010), up to 80% of differences between young native Swedes and young immigrants can be explained by differences in life circumstances.

It has often been observed (and first noted by Dorothy Krall) that children of migrants may have higher crime rates than their parents. A recent Swedish study lends support to the notion of higher criminal engagement of the so-called second generation (Kardell & Carlsson, 2009). Results of the international self-report project, however, find rather little difference between first- and second-generation immigrants in most countries (Junger-Tas et al., 2010). A further controversial issue is whether young migrants are disproportionately victimized. Again, the international self-report project (Junger-Tas et al., 2010) shows that victimization rates were similar or lower for migrant youths in most countries.

In several parts of Europe, illegal migrants—mainly from overseas countries who are earning a living from shadow economy jobs and sometimes episodic crime—are a particularly difficult problem. Many of them are men around the age of 20. So far, this issue has not been systematically addressed in European research.

Evaluations of Interventions

Throughout European countries, several treatment programs have been implemented and evaluated. Many programs have been adapted from models developed in Anglo-Saxon countries. Most prominent are cognitive-behavioral programs including *"reasoning and rehabilitation"* and several variants of SOTP (*Sex Offender Treatment Program),* the main objectives of which are the confrontation with and cognitive restructuring of justifications and excuses commonly used by sex offenders (Hollin & Palmer, 2006). In the following section, we will focus on European reviews of studies on the effectiveness of treatment programs, particularly with respect to adolescent and young adult offenders.

Reasoning and Rehabilitation (R&R) is a pioneering program in the cognitive treatment of offenders. It was developed by Ross and Fabiano (1985) and applied to both juvenile and adult offenders in many countries, including Spain (Alba, Burgués, Lopez, Alcázar Baró, & Garrido, 2007; Redondo, Cano, Álvarez, & Antequera, 2008) and Switzerland (Eisner et al., 2007). The main objective of R&R is to improve the thinking skills of offenders. To that end, the subjects are trained to be more reflective (rather than reactive), to anticipate and plan their responses to problems, and to think more about alternative solutions to interpersonal problems.

There have been numerous evaluative studies of this program with both juveniles and adults. Tong and Farrington (2006) carried out a meta-analysis of the effectiveness of the Reasoning & Rehabilitation program for reducing criminal recidivism, based on 26 comparisons between treated and control groups. On average, treated groups showed a significant recidivism reduction of 14 points. Effectiveness was observed both in community and institutional applications, and for both high-risk and low-risk offenders. One notable exception to the generally positive results of the Reasoning & Rehabilitation program is a Home Office evaluation of Prison programs (Falshaw et al., 2004). In this study, no significant effects were found on reconviction rates. The authors attributed this outcome to problems of implementation related to the program's rapid expansion.

Redondo and Sánchez-Meca (2003) conducted a meta-analysis of 17 European programs developed between 1980 and 2001 that included 2,775 juvenile offenders. This study distinguished between three categories of juveniles: adolescents (age <16), young adults (age 16–21) and mixed groups (youths and adults, with an average age under 29). An overall effect size of r = .18 was obtained, i.e., treated groups had a recidivism rate of 18 points below control groups. The analysis of variance detected a progressive decrease of effectiveness with subjects' age: six programs implemented with adolescents obtained an average effect size of r = .49, eight programs with young adults an effect size of r = .15, and three programs with mixed groups (juveniles and adults) of r = .11. Concerning the type of interventions, the best results were achieved by the three educational programs (r = .42), followed by the five diversion programs (r = .29), the three community-based treatment programs (r = .14), and the four cognitive-behavioral programs (r = .12). Nevertheless, the results of the effectiveness of different categories of programs should be taken with caution because of the small number of studies included in each category, and because the original theoretical foundations are not necessarily reflected in the program's actual contents (Lösel, 1995, 2000).

Garrido, Anyela, and Sánchez-Meca (2006) conducted a meta-analysis on treatment programs with young delinquents (ages 12 to 21) serving sentences in closed institutions or youth prisons. It included 30 experimental or quasi-experimental studies involving control group comparisons or pre-/post-assessments. The overall sample consisted of 2,831 juveniles in the treatment groups and 3,002 subjects in the comparison groups. The programs included psychological treatments (in the categories non-behavioral, behavioral, and cognitive), social and educational interventions, and interventions in therapeutic communities. An overall effect size of d = .14 was obtained, which can be translated into an average recidivism reduction of seven points. Although almost all the interventions achieved favorable results, higher effect sizes were obtained by cognitive-behavioral (d = .21) and cognitive psychological treatments (d = .12).

Lösel & Köferl (1989) published a review on the effectiveness of the socio-therapeutic prisons in Germany where young and adult recidivists with serious personality disorders were treated. These treatments were conducted in accordance with a broad concept of "social therapy" that includes changes in living and institutional conditions, group processes, strengthening contacts and promoting jobs in the community, use of prison permissions, and preparation for release. This review incorporated 16 primary studies with partially overlapping samples. It found that socio-therapeutic prisons reduced recidivism on an average by 11 points in comparison to the expected recidivism following discharge from ordinary prisons. The success of the interventions was modestly associated with the smaller size of the prisons. In the province of Westphalia, the same programs were evaluated through a randomized controlled trial—again with positive, though weaker effects (Ortmann, 2000).

Endrass, Rossegger, Noll, and Urbaniok (2008) presented a systematic review of studies analyzing the effectiveness of treatment approaches with sex and violent offenders. They concluded that the results of meta-analyses in this field must be interpreted with caution because studies were difficult to compare owing to the heterogeneity in the design of the original studies.

Grietens and Hellinckx (2004) summarized five previous meta-analyses, three from North America (Garrett, 1985; Dowden & Andrews, 2000; Lipsey & Wilson,

1998) and two from Europe (Lösel & Köferl, 1989; Redondo, Garrido & Sánchez-Meca, 1997; Redondo, Sánchez-Meca & Garrido, 1999) regarding the effectiveness of treatment with institutionalized juvenile delinquents. They concluded that effect sizes, or average effectiveness, is equivalent to a recidivism reduction of nine percent (with a range of 9% to 31%).

In sum, European reviews on juvenile offender treatments, similar to American reviews, have highlighted that treatments have a modest but significant effect in reducing delinquency (Hollin, 2001; McGuire, 2004). The interventions achieved an average recidivism reduction of about ten points, based on re-offending rates ranging between 50% and 65% (Cooke & Philip, 2001; Cullen & Gendreau, 2006; Lösel, 1996, 1998; McGuire, 2004). The best treatment programs may even achieve reductions of re-offending between 15 and 25 points. In other words, treatment can decrease the expected recidivism rate between a quarter and one-half, depending on the quality of the program. In this way, treatments can help to reduce criminal careers (Israel & Hong, 2006). However, high-quality evaluations including randomized controlled trials are almost nonexistent in Europe in this domain, despite a myriad of projects implemented in many countries. This is true even for the Netherlands where such studies are still lacking (Boendermaker, Deković, & Asscher, in press; Deković, Asscher, Slagt, & Boendermaker, in press).

Criminal Justice Responses

The *European Sourcebook of Crime and Criminal Justice Statistics* (ESB, 2010) contains data from about 40 countries on police-recorded offenses and offenders (back to 1990) on prosecutorial decisions, on convictions, sentences (including length of custodial sentences and alternative sanctions), corrections, and surveys. It documents Europe's wide variation in justice responses and serves as the basis for this report.

Incarceration rates. Incarceration rates vary widely across Europe. The highest rates are found in Russia, with about 700 prisoners per 100,000, and the lowest in Denmark, Finland, Sweden, and Switzerland with roughly about 70. Since prisoners are predominantly young men below age 30, using data for all age-groups is relevant for young adult offenders. In the following section we will look more specifically at the incarceration of minors.

In the international literature, the view prevails that the number of prisoners per population reflects sentencing styles rather than crime rates. With ESB offense-specific data on (1) convicted offenders and (2) length of custodial sentences, it is possible to show that the rate of defendants convicted of murder is a major driving factor for the prison population, given that everywhere in Europe this group is likely to serve very long sentences. The correlation (r), when outliers are eliminated, is substantial (between .52 and .62). Homicide is particularly frequent in Russia and a few other countries in Eastern Europe where incarceration rates are also very high. Earlier analyses (Aebi & Kuhn, 2000) showed that the average length of custodial sentences for offenses such as robbery, domestic burglary, aggravated assault, rape, and drug trafficking is the next important variable in explaining incarceration rates. Sentences for less serious offenses are far shorter than for murder, but the number of defendants is far higher. Again, variety in sentencing practices across Europe is considerable.

However, the use of alternative sanctions (such as community service, electronic monitoring, and fines) explains less than expected of the variation in incarceration rates. Such sanctions are widely used throughout Europe but tend to replace short prison sentences rather than reducing prison time. In a comparative perspective, it is less the number of persons sent to prison than the length of stay that affects overall incarceration rates. Using ESB data and excluding outliers, the correlation between the number of persons entering prisons ('flow') and the incarceration rate ('stock') is weak (r = .17). In conclusion, there may not be much to gain, in terms of controlling or even reducing incarceration rates, by sending fewer people to prison through replacing short custodial sanctions by other punishments.

The preventive potential of Western Europe's policy of using custody only for serious crimes and for limited periods is hard to assess. Systematic reviews suggest that custodial and noncustodial sanctions differ little in re-offending rates (Villet-taz et al., 2006). The same has been found in systematic reviews based on studies comparing custodial sentences of different length (Gendreau et al., 1999). Given this knowledge, and taking the direct (economic) and indirect (human) costs of incarceration into account, Europe's moderate use of prison sentences may be wise and humane, particularly for juvenile and young adult offenders.

Juvenile justice. One of the peculiarities of the American juvenile justice system is the extent to which it allows juvenile justice waivers (see Griffin, Chapter 7, this volume). In Europe, systems vary widely, and some countries (such as the Netherlands, Belgium, Portugal, and Poland) also allow juvenile defendants (above ages 15 or 16) to be treated as adults. Other countries, such as Germany and Austria, do not allow bringing juveniles below age 18 before an adult court to be sentenced under adult law; they even allow young adults (between ages 18 and 20) to be treated under juvenile law and to be tried under the juvenile criminal justice system, although authorities have some discretion in this regard (Table 10.4). These countries, however, allow very long maximum custodial sentences for juveniles below age 18: 10 years in Germany, and 15 years in Austria. Even if defendants aged between 18 and 21 are put on trial before a juvenile court, the sentence they receive may not be different from what defendants of that age might receive under the adult system in other countries.

It is true that young adult defendants in Germany, Switzerland, and Sweden can be sent to special institutions for the treatment of young offenders, but that would also be possible under the adult system in many other countries. An extreme case is Switzerland where the age-limit is strictly 18, but where the maximum sentence

TABLE 10.4 } The minimum age of criminal responsibility in European countries.

Country	Age of criminality responsibility	Full criminal responsibility (adult law can/must be applied)
Albania	14	18
Armenia	14	18
Austria	14	18/21
Belgium	16	16/18
Bulgaria	14	18
Bosnia-Herzegovina	14	18
Croatia	14	18/21
Cyprus	10	16/21
Czech Republic	15	18
Denmark	14	14/18
Estonia	13	18
Finland	15	15/18
France	10/13	18
Georgia	12	18
Germany	14	18/21
Greece	8/13	18/21
Hungary	14	18
Iceland	15	15
Ireland	10	18
Italy	14	18/21
Latvia	14	18/21
Lithuania	14	14/21
Malta	18	18
Moldova	14	18
Netherlands	12	16/21
Norway	15	15
Poland	13	15/18
Portugal	12/16	16/21
Romania	14	18
Russia	14	18/21
Slovakia	14	18/21
Slovenia	14	18/21
Spain	14	18
Sweden	15	15/21
Switzerland	10	18
Turkey	12	15/18
Ukraine	14	18/21
U.K.: England & Wales	10	10/21
U.K.: Northern Ireland	10	17/21
U.K.: Scotland	8/16	16/21

Source: Junger-Tas & Dünkel, 2009. Table 13.1.

for juveniles is one year (only in exceptional cases is this four years). Thus, countries either have low maximum penalties for juveniles (below 18) and apply, in certain circumstances, adult criminal sanctions to juvenile defendants, or they have sanctions for juveniles that are not all too different from what their law provides for adults (Stump, 2003). These policies make it easier to stick to the age-limit of 18 and even to apply juvenile law to young adults (aged 18 to 20).

The case of Scandinavian countries is particularly interesting since they do not allow juveniles below ages 14 or 15 to be held responsible for their offenses in court. Until the end of 2009, the age of legal responsibility in all Scandinavian countries was 15. In Denmark, this age has now been lowered to 14. Juveniles below the age of criminal responsibility are regarded as children and cannot be punished regardless of the seriousness and other circumstances related to their crimes. Police investigations of crimes committed by children are reported to the local social welfare committee, which has to take adequate action, including various types of support and treatment for the young offender and his/her parents. In severe cases, compulsory institutional treatment can be ordered. The decision may be appealed to an administrative court.

Table 10.4 shows that the lowest limits of criminal responsibility are ages 8 and 10, whereas most countries have opted for age 14. Countries with higher age limits often directly apply the adult criminal law to persons that reach the age of criminal responsibility. This is, for example, the case in Scandinavia where persons who are between ages 15 and 17 are treated by and large as adults, but more leniently. Custodial sentences are very uncommon for young people in this age group and are, when imposed, much shorter than for adults who commit similar crimes. Swedish legislation allows sentencing individuals in this age group to treatment in special youth institutions (special approved homes) where the treatment's duration (up to a maximum four years) is determined by the seriousness of the offense, while its form is determined by the nature of the problems that are associated with the offense. The most common reaction to more serious delinquency in the age group ranging from 15 to 17 in Scandinavia is, however, diversion from the justice system under the form of various types of treatment interventions provided by social services. Community service and fines are also common for less serious offenses.

Offenders aged 18 to 20 are treated more leniently than older adults not only in Scandinavia, but also in 18 other European countries (including Austria, Germany, and the Netherlands), as indicated in Table 10.4. An important consequence of having young adults dealt with under juvenile law is that, for example, in Germany (Heinz, 1994) they may benefit from more lenient procedural rules, such as the wide use of diversion. On the practical effects of such interventions, there is either no systematic research or the results are conflicting. Whereas Heinz (2005), for example, considered diversion as a very effective measure, Entorf and Spengler (2008) concluded that its extension undermined the certainty of punishment and increased particularly violent offenses, such as robbery.

TABLE 10.5 } Maximum custodial sentence (in months) available under juvenile criminal law.

Country	Prior to age 14	age 14-15	age 16-17
Albania	custody not available	150 months	150 months
Armenia	custody not available	84 months	120 months
Austria	custody not available	120 months	180 months
Belgium	custody not available	custody not available	detention for life
Bulgaria	custody not available	120 months	120 months
Croatia	custody not available	custody not available	120 months
Czech Republic	custody not available	120 months (15 yrs.)	120 months
Denmark	custody not available	96 months (15 yrs.)	96 months
Estonia	custody not available	120 months	120 months
Finland	custody not available	144 months (15 yrs.)	144 months
France	240 months	240 months	detention for life
Georgia	120 months	120 months	180 months
Germany	custody not available	120 months	120 months
Greece	custody not available	240 months	240 months
Hungary	custody not available	180 months	240 months
Iceland	custody not available	3 months	3 months
Italy	custody not available	360 months	360 months
Netherlands	12 months	12 months	24 months
Poland	custody not available	300 months	300 months
Portugal	custody not available	custody not available	36 months
Russia	custody not available	120 months	120 months
Slovakia	custody not available	72 months	132 months
Slovenia	custody not available	custody not available	360 months
Spain	custody not available	108 months	216 months
Sweden	custody not available	48 months	48 months
Switzerland	custody not available	12 months	48 months
Turkey	144 months	360 months	360 months
Ukraine	custody not available	180 months	180 months
U.K.: England & Wales	detention for life	detention for life	detention for life
U.K.: Northern Ireland	custody not available	custody not available	48 months
U.K.: Scotland	custody not available	custody not available	detention for life

Note: In Czech Republic, Denmark, Iceland, Finland, Sweden, Switzerland, and Poland, the maximum applies to juveniles of 15 (not 14).

Source: Survey conducted for this report among ESB correspondents.

Beyond the age of criminal responsibility, custodial sanctions are available to a greatly variable extent in various countries. As Table 10.5 shows, countries differ as to what age they allow custodial sanctions to be imposed upon minors. The variety is just as great regarding the legally allowable maximum custodial sentences. It should be noted that the definition of custody is ambiguous and may include, in some countries, secure accommodation of juveniles under child protection legislation.

As Table 10.5 illustrates, only five among 31 countries allow custodial sanctions against minors for acts committed before their 14th birthday. After that age (or eventually the 15th birthday), only six countries do not allow custodial sanctions. Thus, two competing systems co-exist in Europe. Some countries allow very long custodial sentences for defendants aged 16 years or older, or they allow—usually from that same age—the use of adult criminal law. The only cases where neither alternative exists are Switzerland and Iceland where the age limit of age 18 is absolutely rigid and where the maximum penalties greatly differ between the juvenile and the adult systems (4 years and 3 months for minors versus life for adults).

A different question is to what extent sanctions that are legally available are actually applied. Table 10.6 gives an overview on how many minors are sentenced to immediate custodial sanctions (as a percentage of all sentenced juvenile defendants), minus those placed in institutions for treatment under a child protection order. Unfortunately, data on young adults are not available.

TABLE 10.6 } Defendants aged below 18 sentenced to immediate custodial sanctions in 2006 (in % of all sanctions imposed), by offense.

	Criminal offenses: Total	Intentional homicide: Total	Bodily injury (Assault): Total	Rape	Sexual abuse of minors	Robbery	Theft: Total
Armenia	20.8						
Austria	14.5	100	5.3	30.0		51.9	13.7
Belgium	3.3					23.5	44.9
Finland	0.6		0.8	25.0	8.3	15.2	0.0
France	9.1	92.6	8.3	37.3			10.7
Georgia	33.9	100	25.0	100		38.5	30.4
Germany	6.3	90.3	6.3	31.6	13.1	23.6	6.9
Hungary	4.2	87.5	2.8	37.5		26.5	2.9
Latvia	25.6	100	32.1	50.0		27.2	29.6
Netherlands	12.0	33.5	7.7	32.2	19.4	31.6	11.8
Portugal	5.5					21.0	
Romania	26.7	93.8	7.4	80.6	11.1	43.9	25.3
Slovakia	7.2	100	3.8		7.4	27.5	8.5
Slovenia	2.2		3.3	50.0		12.0	2.1
Switzerland	1.5		1.1		1.4	3.8	0.5
U.K.: England & Wales	6.6	75.0	13.5	61.2	15.9	32.0	8.4
U.K.: Northern Ireland	7.0		15.5	100		45.5	10.0
U.K.: Scotland	22.8	100	34.8			40.0	19.2

Source: ESB 2010, Tables 3.2.2.

As Table 10.6 illustrates, European countries vary widely as to the extent to which they use imprisonment as a sanction against minors below age 18. Not surprisingly, this produces wide variations also in the numbers of juveniles actually incarcerated. European countries differ greatly as to the extent that they use prison not only for adults, but also for juveniles. Figure 10.1 presents the rate of minors (below age 18) actually imprisoned per 100,000 inhabitants. The highest rates (Netherlands 11 and Russia 9) are far below the American rate of 31 minors incarcerated. Such differences are unlikely to be caused by definitional problems, such as the statistical treatment of institutions that are, legally speaking, not penal institutions, or juveniles placed in pre-trial detention (as a rule, such cases are included here).

Surprisingly, very little research is available on the effects of Europe's highly variable systems of juvenile justice. The same is true for interventions and particularly for treatment institutions designed for juveniles and young adults.

Welfare policies. European and American welfare policies differ substantially and children from poor families may, overall, receive more support in Europe. Unfortunately, little research has been conducted on the effects of welfare policies on crime. The very limited evidence from Germany (Rabold & Baier, 2007) and from Switzerland (Haas & Killias, 2001) suggests that poverty, if its effects are mitigated by welfare, is not accompanied by increased levels of violent and other serious offenses. In Europe, poverty and welfare are not necessarily concentrated in "social housing" or other disadvantaged areas, as is often the case in America (Wikström, 1998).

An intervention program including increased controls and training of unemployed subjects has been evaluated in Denmark through a randomized trial with 5,180 subjects (Andersen, 2010). The treated group committed significantly fewer offenses than the control group that received the standard program for unemployed persons. Since the intervention was not accompanied by increased welfare benefits, the success of the program may be due to increased controls and reduced opportunities to offend (through reduced leisure time) rather than to improved "welfare" in a traditional sense.

Drug and alcohol policies. Drug and alcohol policies vary considerably across Europe. On the continent and particularly in traditional wine-producing countries, alcohol policies are traditionally tolerant, whereas in Scandinavia they were traditionally much more repressive. A lot can be learned from data on change over time. Sweden, for example, is one of the countries where policies have changed several times (Lenke, 1990). There, the homicide rate increased substantially during the period of increasing alcohol consumption in the early nineteenth century, and decreased after severe restrictions were enacted (von Hofer, 2011). When restrictions were gradually repealed during the second half of the twentieth century, violent crime increased again. Following Sweden's admittance to the European Union in 1995, more restrictions on alcohol sales were lifted, but violent crime did not increase as expected. A possible

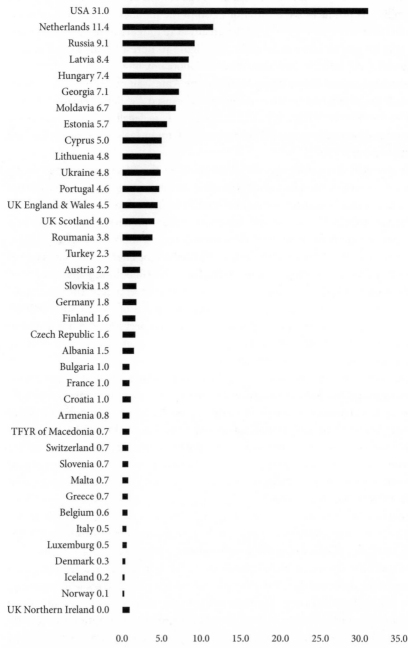

■ Imprisonment rate

FIGURE 10.1 Minors (below 18) incarcerated in Europe (convicted or awaiting trial/sentencing), per 100,000 of the general population in 2006.

Note: The percentage of Dutch incarcerated juveniles under civil law is about 30%.

Source: ESB 2010; U.S. data: Sourcebook of criminal justice statistics.

explanation might be that the "continental" drinking style, characterized by less concentrated but more recreational use, became increasingly popular in Sweden.

With respect to cannabis use, the Netherlands is usually identified as the most liberal country. The Czech Republic, Estonia, Spain, and Switzerland are other countries that liberalized cannabis policies during the 1990s (though in practice more than in law). According to a European survey on drug use (Hibell et al., 2009) and data from the ISRD surveys of 1992 (Junger-Tas, Terlouw, & Klein, 1994) and of 2006 (Junger-Tas et al., 2010), cannabis use among teenagers increased in all these countries by more than 100%, in parallel with the liberalization of cannabis policies. In recent years, however, there are also countries that have experienced a drop in cannabis use, such as Austria, Belgium, France, Germany, Ireland, Italy, Slovenia, Switzerland, the United Kingdom, and Portugal. The top scorers for cannabis use in 2007 were the Czech Republic, Switzerland, and the Netherlands (Hibell et al., 2009).

So far, it is not clear to what extent cannabis use is influenced by policies aimed at restricting availability. In the Netherlands, the lifetime prevalence of cannabis use among students aged 12 to 18 increased since 1988 (when cannabis policies started to be liberalized) from less than 10% to over 20% and subsequently leveled off (Nationale Drug Monitor, 2010, p. 39). A similar natural experiment with important policy shifts was monitored in Switzerland over the last seven years (Chabloz et al., 2010). Population surveys, observation studies, and extensive interviews with police, school, and public health professionals as well as with coffee shop owners and street-level dealers showed that a less tolerant approach, including closing shops where the sale of cannabis was allowed, decreased the availability of cannabis, increased prices, and deeply affected market structures, including lines of distribution (Killias, Isenring, Gilliéron, & Vuille, 2011). Consumption (particularly among those aged 15 to 19) decreased substantially. It is not clear, however, whether similar changes in other countries were the result of parallel shifts in policies—or whether other factors reduced the attraction of a product that might have gone out of fashion.

Plagued by high rates of street-crime among many heroin addicts during the 1990s, several European countries have established programs to administer opiates to long-term users. Such programs have been in operation over several years in Switzerland, Denmark, Germany, and the Netherlands. A recent Campbell review (Egli et al., 2009) addressed the effects on crime among addicts of administering different opiates, including methadone and heroin. Based on randomized trials, the meta-analysis suggests that opiate substitution reduced crime committed by addicts more than the administration of methadone, or therapies based on abstinence. In contrast to these results, Norway, Finland, and Sweden continue to apply very restrictive policies towards narcotics, and there is substantial opposition even to needle exchange programs. From an American point of view, the highly divergent European policies may be as interesting as the fact that substitution therapy seems basically effective in reducing crime committed by addicts.

Conclusions

We found a substantial number of longitudinal studies in 11 European countries. Many of the studies were unpublished or available only in national languages other than English. Most of these studies have found a strong impact of family malfunctioning and other problems during childhood on later offending. Less consistent are the findings regarding the causes of desistance from offending. Some studies have included social correlates of delinquency, such as unemployment, neighborhood, and leisure-time activities, but little is known from European research about criminal career features between ages 15 and 29, and in particular to what extent the results are similar to or different from North America. Further, no research has addressed late onset of offending, or continuity versus discontinuity in offending from the juvenile to the young adult years. Finally, influences of national and legal contexts remain largely unknown.

We also found that European research is often comparative and international. This brings about (and corresponds) to a strong interest in macro-sociological factors. It supports the view that situational changes affect, to a large extent, the volume of crime across space and over time. European data collection initiatives indicate considerable differences (both within Europe and compared to the United States) in rates of homicide and types of responses to crime.

Evaluations of interventions show encouraging results for treatment, but have rarely used sound experimental methods. Research on optimal preventive interventions is largely absent but very much needed. The same is true for prediction methods. Despite their wide use, little is known to what extent predictions turn out to be accurate.

Responses to crime differ greatly across Europe, but generally are more "soft" especially with respect to young offenders. Some of the differences in incarceration rates can be attributed to low homicide rates in Western Europe. Juvenile laws, even in Eastern Europe, are considerably more lenient compared to the United States. It is hard to argue to what extent different "harsh" or "lenient" policies are effective in controlling crime rates. Again, current research does not provide answers about the effects of different age limits, sanctions, and procedural arrangements for juveniles, young adults, and adults on re-offending and financial benefits (or costs) of competing approaches.

To the extent it is available, research has focused on either juveniles (mainly minors) or crime across all age groups, but rarely on young people between the ages of 15 and 29. Much of current general knowledge applies directly to young adults, however, since most offenders known to the police, processed through the criminal justice system, or imprisoned fall into this broad age of transition from adolescence to young adulthood.

Acknowledgments

The authors express their deep thanks to Professor Peter van der Laan for his valuable suggestions and support during the meetings of the study group. They also wish to thank Ana Martínez Catena (University of Barcelona), Lorenz Biberstein, and Nora Markwalder (University of Zurich) for their excellent support during data collection and the preparation of this chapter. Professor Wim Slot has offered invaluable help in locating appropriate Dutch studies.

References

Aebi, M.F. & Kuhn, A. (2000). Influences on the prisoner rate: Number of entries into prison, length of sentences and crime rates. *European Journal on Criminal Policy and Research*, 8, 65–75.

AIC National Homicide Monitoring Program, years 1989–90 to 2006–07. Found under http://www.aic.gov.au/publications/current%20series/cfi/161-180/cfi176.aspx.

Alba, J.L., Burgués, M., López, J., Alcázar, M., Baró, V., Garrido, V., & López, M.J. (2007). El Programa del Pensamiento Prosocial. Versión corta para jóvenes. Tercera aplicación en medio abierto. *Boletín Criminológica*, 98.

Albrecht, H.J. & Grundies, V. (2009). Justizielle Registrierungen in Abhängigkeit vom Alter. *Monatsschrift für Kriminologie und Strafrechtsreform*, 92, 326–343.

Andersen S.H. (2010). Unemployment and crime: On the causal effects of intensified welfare state interventions on unemployed persons' crime rates. Paper presented at the annual meeting of the European Society of Criminology (panel 25). http://www.esc-eurocrim.org/conferences.shtml.

Averdijk, M., Elffers, H., & Ruiter, S. (in press). Disentangling context effects on criminal careers during adolescence and into early adulthood. In R. Loeber, M. Hoeve, N.W. Slot, & P. van der Laan (Eds.), *Persisters and desisters in crime from adolescence into adulthood: Explanation, prevention and punishment*. Aldershot UK: Ashgate.

Baier, D., Pfeiffer, C., Simonson, J., & Rabold S. (2009). *Jugendliche in Deutschland als Opfer und Täter von Gewalt*. Hannover: Kriminologisches Institut Niedersachsen.

Bakker, B.F.M., Walberg, A., & Blom, M. (2005). Jeugdige verdachten. In M. Blom, J. Oudhof, R.V. Bijl, & B.F.M. Bakker (Eds.). *Verdacht van criminaliteit. Allochtonen en autochtonen nader bekeken. Cahier 2005-2* (pp. 45–58). Den Haag: Ministerie van Justitie, Wetenschappelijk Onderzoek en Documentatie Centrum.

Balvig, F. (2006). *Den ungdom! Om den stadigt mere omsiggribende lovlydhed blandt Unge i Danmark. (The youth! About the ever-increasing low-obedience among young people in Denmark)*. Kopenhagen: Det Kriminalpreventive Råd.

Bergman, L.R. (2009). IDA: Individual Development and Adaptation http://www.psychology.su.se/pub/jsp/polopoly.jsp?d=13619&a=70487.

Bergman, L.R. & Andershed, A. (2009). Predictors and outcomes of persistent or age-limited registered criminal behavior: A 30-year longitudinal study of a Swedish urban population. *Aggressive Behavior*, 35, 164–178.

Blokland, A. & Palmen, H. (in press). Criminal career patterns. In R. Loeber, M. Hoeve, N.W. Slot, & P. van der Laan (Eds.), *Persisters and desisters in crime from adolescence into adulthood: Explanation, prevention and punishment*. Aldershot UK: Ashgate.

Bock, M. (2000). *Kriminologie*. München: Vahlen.

Boendermaker, L., Deković, M. & Asscher, J.J. (in press). Interventions. In R. Loeber, M. Hoeve, N.W. Slot, & P. van der Laan (Eds.), *Persisters and desisters in crime from adolescence into adulthood: Explanation, prevention and punishment*. Aldershot UK: Ashgate.

Boers, K., Seddig, D., & Reinecke, J. (2009). Sozialstrukturelle Bedingungen und Delinquenz im Verlauf des Jugendalters. Analysen mit einem kombinierten Markov- und Wachstumsmodell. *Monatsschrift für Kriminologie und Strafrechtsreform*, 92, 267–288.

Bongers, I.L., Koot, H.M., van der Ende, J. & Verhulst, F.C. (2006). Developmental trajectories of externalizing behaviors in childhood and adolescence. In A. Blokland & P. Nieuwbeerta (Eds.). *Developmental and life course studies in delinquency and crime* (pp. 35–52). The Hague: Boom Juridische Uitgevers.

Born, M. (2002). Continuité de la délinquance entre l'adolescence et l'âge adulte. *Criminologie*, 35, 53–67.

BRÅ (2008): *Brottsutveckling i Sverige fram till år 2007 (Crime development in Sweden until 2007)*. Stockholm: Swedish National Council for Crime Prevention (Report 2008.23).

BRÅ. (2010). *Brott bland ungdomar i årskurs nio. Resultat från Skolundersökningen om brott åren 1995—2008 (Crime among young people in grade nine. Results from the school survey on crime years 1995—2008)*. Stockholm: Swedish National Council for Crime Prevention (Report 2010:6).

Caprara, G.V., Paciello, M., Gerbino, M., & Cugini, C. (2007). Individual differences conducive to aggression and violence: Trajectories and correlates of irritability and hostile rumination through adolescence. *Aggressive Behavior*, 33, 1–16.

Caprara, G.V., Regalia, C., & Bandura, A. (2002). Longitudinal impact of perceived self regulatory efficacy on violent conduct. *European Psychologist*, 7, 63–69.

Chabloz, J.-M., Gervasoni, J.-P., Arnaud S., Dubois-Arber F., Vuille, J., & Killias M. (2010). *Monitoring de la problématique du cannabis en Suisse: Etude sentinelle 2004-2008*. Lausanne: Raisons de Santé.

Cohen, L.E. & Felson, M. (1979). Social change and crime rate trends: a routine activity approach. *American Sociological Review*, 44, 588–608.

Cooke, D.J. & Philip, L. (2001). To treat or not to treat? An empirical perspective. In C.R. Hollin (Ed.), *Handbook of offenders assessement and treatment* (pp. 17–34). Chichester, UK: Wiley.

Cullen, F.T. & Gendreau, P. (2006). Evaluación de la rehabilitación correccional: política, práctica y perspectivas. In R. Barberet & J. Barquín (Eds.), *Justicia penal siglo XXI: Una selección de Criminal Justice 2000* (pp. 275–348). Granada: Editorial Comares.

Deković, M., Asscher, J.J., Slagt, M.I. & Boendermaker L. (in press). Effects of early and middle childhood prevention programmes on adult crime. In R. Loeber, M. Hoeve, N.W. Slot, & P. van der Laan (Eds.), *Persisters and desisters in crime from adolescence into adulthood: Explanation, prevention and punishment*. Aldershot UK: Ashgate.

Doerner, W.G. (1988). The impact of medical resources on criminally induced lethality. *Criminology*, 26, 171–179.

Donker, A.G., Smeenk, W.H., van der Laan, P.H., & Verhulst, F.C. (2003). Individual stability of antisocial behavior from childhood to adulthood: Testing the stability postulate of Moffitt's developmental theory. *Criminology*, 41, 593–609.

Dowden, C. & Andrews, D.A. (2000). Effective correctional treatment and violent reoffending: A meta-analysis. *Canadian Journal of Criminology*, 42, 449–467.

Egli, N., Pina, M., Skovbo Christensen, P., Aebi, M.F., & Killias M. (2009). Effects of drug substitution programs on offending among drug-addicts. The Campbell Collaboration (http://www.campbellcollaboration.org).

Eisner, M., Ribeaud, D., Jünger, R., & Meidert, U. (2007). *Frühprävention von Gewalt und Aggression; Ergebnisse des Zürcher Interventions- und Präventionsprojektes an Schulen.* Zürich: Rüegger Verlag.

Endrass, J., Rossegger, A., Noll, T., & Urbaniok, F. (2008). Wirksamkeit von Therapien bei Gewalt- und Sexualstraftätern. *Psychiatrische Praxis*, 35, 8–14.

Entorf, H. & Spengler, H. (2008). Is being soft on crime the solution to rising crime rates? Evidence from Germany, IZA Discussion Paper No. 3710 (University of Frankfurt, Department of Economics).

Enzmann, D., Marshall I., Killias, M., Junger-Tas, J., Steketee, M., & Grusczynska, B. (2010). Self-reported youth delinquency in Europe and beyond: First results of the second international self-report delinquency study in the context of police and victimization data. *European Journal of Criminology*, 7, 159–183.

ESB (2003). *European sourcebook of crime and criminal justice statistics—2003* (2nd ed.). The Hague: Boom Juridische Uitgevers. www.europeansourcebook.org.

ESB (2006). *European sourcebook of crime and criminal justice statistics—2006* (3rd ed.). The Hague: Boom Juridische Uitgevers. www.europeansourcebook.org.

ESB (2010). *European Sourcebook of Crime and Criminal Justice Statistics* (4th ed.). The Hague: Boom Juridische Uitgevers. www.europeansourcebook.org.

Esbensen, F.A. & Lynskey, D.P. (2001). Young gang members in a school survey. In M.W. Klein, H.-J. Kerner, C.L. Maxson, & E.G.M. Weitekamp (Eds.), *The Eurogang paradox* (pp. 93–114). Amsterdam NL: Kluwer Academic.

Esbensen, F.A. & Weerman, F. (2005). Youth gangs and troublesome youth groups in the United States and the Netherlands: A cross-national comparison. *European Journal of Criminology*, 2, 5–37.

Exadaktylos, A.K., Häuselmann, S., & Zimmermann, H. (2007). Are times getting tougher? A six-year survey of urban violence-related injuries in a Swiss university hospital. *Swiss Medical Weekly*, 37, 525–530.

Falshaw, L., Friendship, C., Travers, R., & Nugent, F. (2004). Searching for "What Works": HM Prison Service accredited cognitive skills programmes. *The British Journal of Forensic Practice*, 6, 3–13.

Farrington, D.P., Ttofi, M.M., & Coid, J.W. (2009). Development of adolescence-limited, late-onset, and persistent offenders from age 8 to age 48. *Aggressive Behavior*, 35, 150–163.

Garrett, P. (1985). Effects of residential treatment of adjudicated delinquents: A meta-analysis. *Journal of Research in Crime & Delinquency*, 22, 287–308.

Garrido, V., Anyela Morales, L., & Sáncez-Meca, J. (2006). What works for serious juvenile offenders? A systematic review. *Psicothema*, 18, 611–619.

Gavray C. (1997). Trajectoire déviante à la lisière entre adolescence et âge adulte. *Déviance et Société*, 21, 273–288.

Gendreau P., Goggin C., & Cullen F.T. (1999). *The effects of prison sentences on recidivism.* Ottawa: Solicitor General of Canada.

Gerris, J.R.M, Vermulst, A.A., van Boxtel, D.A.A.M., Janssens, J.M.A.M., van Zutphen, R.A.H., & Felling, A.J.A. (1993). *Parenting in Dutch families: A representative description of Dutch family life in terms of validated concepts representing characteristics of parents, children, the family as a system and parental socio-cultural value orientations.* Nijmegen: Institute of Family Studies, University of Nijmegen.

Glueck, S. & Glueck, E. (1950). *Unraveling juvenile delinquency.* New York. Commonwealth Fund.

Göppinger, H. (1985). *Angewandte Kriminologie. Ein Leitfaden für die Praxis.* Berlin: Springer.

Grietens, H. & Hellinckx, W. (2004). Evaluating effects of residential treatment for juvenile offenders by statistical metaanalysis: A review. *Aggression and Violent Behavior*, 9, 401–415.

Haas, H. (2001). *Agressions et victimisations: Une enquête sur les délinquants violents et sexuels non détectés.* Aarau: Sauerländer.

Haas, H. & Killias, M. (2001). L'assistance sociale—un moyen pour prévenir la délinquance? In G. Étienne, J-L. Chaléard, & A. Dubresson (Eds.), *Mélanges en l'honneur de Jean-Louis Duc* (pp. 157–170). Lausanne: IRAL-UNIL.

Haas, H. & Killias, M. (2003). The versatility vs. specialization debate: different theories of crime in the light of a Swiss birth cohort. In C. Britt & M. Gottfredson (Eds.), *Control theories of crime and delinquency* (pp. 249–273). New Brunswick, NJ: Transaction.

Haas H., Farrington D.P., Killias M., & Sattar G. (2004). The impact of different family configurations on delinquency. *British Journal of Criminology* 44, 520–532.

Hällsten, M., Sarnecki, J., & Szulkin, R. (2010). *Crime as a price for inequality? The delinquency gap between children of immigrants and children to native Swedes.* SULCIS, Stockholm University.

Harris, A.R., Thomas, S.H., Fisher, G.A., & Hirsch D.J. (2002). Murder and medicine: The lethality of criminal assault 1960–1999. *Homicide Studies* 6, 128–166.

Haymoz, S. & Gatti, U. (2010). Girl members of deviant youth groups, offending behavior and victimization: Results from the ISRD2 in Italy and Switzerland. *European Journal on Criminal Policy and Research*, 16, 167–182.

Heinz, W. (1994). Verfahrensrechtliche Entkriminalisierung (Diversion) im Jugendstrafrecht: Zielsetzungen, Implementation und Evaluation. *Neue Kriminalpolitik*, 6, 29–36.

Heinz, W. (2005). Zahlt sich Milde wirklich aus? Diversion und ihre Bedeutung für die Sanktionspraxis, Teil 1, *Zeitschrift für Jugendkriminalrecht und Jugendhilfe*, 16, 166–178, 302–312.

Hibell B., Guttormsson U., Ahlström S., Balakireva O., Bjarnason T., Kokkevi A., & Kraus L. (2009). *The 2007 ESPAD report: Substance use among students in 35 European countries.* Council of Europe (Pompidou Group).

Hoeve, M. (2008). *Parenting and juvenile delinquency.* Nijmegen: Radboud Universiteit.

Hoeve, M., Smeenk, W.H., Loeber, R., Stouthamer-Loeber, M., van der Laan, P.H., Gerris, J.R.M., & Dubas, J.S. (2006). Long-term effects of parenting and family characteristics on delinquency of male young adults. In A. Blokland & P. Nieuwbeerta (Eds.). *Developmental and life course studies in delinquency and crime* (pp. 209–232). The Hague: Boom Juridische Uitgevers.

Hood, R. (1992). *Race and sentencing: A study in the crown court.* Oxford: Clarendon.

Hollin, C.R. (2001). To treat or not to treat? An historical perspective. In C.R. Hollin (Ed.), *Handbook of offender assessment and treatment* (pp. 3–15). Chichester, UK: Wiley.

Hollin, C.R. & Palmer, E.J. (2006). Offending behavior programmes: history and development. In C.R. Hollin & E.J. Palmer (Eds.), *Offending behavior programmes* (pp. 1–32). Chichester, UK: Wiley.

ICVS. International Crime Victimization Survey. Retrieved from http://rechten.uvt.nl/ icvs/.

Instituto de la Mujer (2006). Macroencuesta "Violencia contra las mujeres" (*violence against women*) (2002–2006) (www.inmujer.es).

Israel, M. & Hong, W. (2006). If "something works" is the answer, what is the question? Supporting pluralist evaluation in community corrections in the United Kingdom. *European Journal of Criminology, 3,* 181–200.

Janson, C-G. (1975). *Project Metropolitan: A presentation.* Project Metropolitan Research Report No. 1. Stockholm.

Janson, C-G. (1984). *Project Metropolitan: A presentation and progress report.* Stockholm: University of Stockholm, Department of Sociology.

Janson, C-G. (1995). On Project Metropolitan and the longitudinal perspective. Project Metropolitan Research Report No 40. Stockholm.

Jennissen, R. (2009). *Criminaliteit, leeftijd en etniciteit (Crime, age and ethnicity).* The Hague: WODC (Onderzoek en Beleid 277).

Johnson, H., Ollus, N. & Nevala, S. (2008). *Violence against women: An international perspective.* New York: Springer.

Junger, M. (1989). Discrepancies between police and self-report data for Dutch racial minorities. *British Journal of Criminology, 29,* 273–283.

Junger, M., Wittebrood, K., & Timman, R. (2001). Etniciteit en ernstig en gewelddadig crimineel gedrag. In R. Loeber, N.W. Slot, & J.A. Sergeant (Eds.) *Ernstige en gewelddadige jeugddelinquentie: Omvang, oorzaken, en interventies* (pp. 97–129). Houten: Bohn Stafleu en Van Loghum.

Junger-Tas, J. & Dünkel, F. (Eds.) (2009). *Reforming juvenile justice.* New York: Springer.

Junger-Tas, J., Marshall, I., Enzmann, D., Killias, M., Gruszczynska, B. & Steketee, M. (2010). *Juvenile delinquency in Europe and beyond: Results of the second international self-report delinquency study.* New York: Springer.

Junger-Tas, J., Marshall, I.H., Enzmann, D., Killias, M., Gruszczynska, B. & Stekeete, M. (in press). *The many faces of youth crime.* New York: Springer.

Junger-Tas, J., Terlouw G.-J. & Klein M. (Eds.) (1994). *Delinquent behavior of young people in the Western world.* Amsterdam: Kugler.

Kardell, J. & Carlsson, K.M. (2009). Lagföringar av invandrare och invandrares barn i de olika nordiska länderna. *Nordisk tidskrift for kriminalvidenskab, 96,* 237–261.

Kazemian, L. & Farrington, D.P. (2006). Exploring residual career length and residual number of offenses for two generations of repeat offenders. *Journal of Research in Crime and Delinquency, 43,* 89–113.

Kazemian, L., Farrington, D.P., & Le Blanc, M. (2009). Can we make accurate long-term predictions about patterns of de-escalation in offending behavior? *Journal of Youth and Adolescence, 38,* 384–400.

Keizer, K., Lindenberg, S., & Steg, L. (2008). The spreading of disorder. *Science, 322,* 1681–1685.

Killias, M. (2009). Paradise lost? New trends in crime and migration in Switzerland. In W.F. McDonald (Ed.), *Immigration, crime and justice* (pp. 33–45). Bingley, UK: Emerald.

Killias M., Isenring G., Gilliéron G., & Vuille J. (2011). Do changing policies have an impact on cannabis markets? A natural experiment in Switzerland 2000–2010. *European Journal of Criminology*, 8, 171–186.

Killias, M., Maljevic, A., & Lucia, S. (2010). Imported Violence? Juvenile delinquency among Balkan youths in Switzerland and in Bosnia-Herzegovina. *European Journal of Criminal Policy and Research*, 16, 183–189.

Killias, M., Markwalder, N., Walser, S., & Dilitz, C. (2009). *Homicide and suicide in Switzerland over twenty years (1980–2004): A study based on forensic medicine, police and court files.* Report to the Swiss National Science Foundation no.101312–104167/1.

Kivivuori, J. (2001). Patterns of criminal homicide in Finland 1960–1997. In T. Lappi-Seppälä (Ed.), *Homicide in Finland: Trends and patterns in historical and comparative perspective. National Research Institute of Legal Policy, Publication 181,* Helsinki. National Violent Death Reporting System (NVDRS).

Kivivuori, J. & Lehti, M. (2003). Homicide followed by suicide in Finland: Trend and Social Locus. *Journal of Scandinavian Studies in Criminology and Crime Prevention*, 4, 223–236.

Kivivuori, J. & Salmi, V. (2006). Trends of Self-Reported Juvenile Delinquency in Finland, 1995–2004. In E. Mykkänen (Ed.), *Research report summaries 2005* (pp. 9–16). Helsinki: National Research Institute of Legal Policy.

Klein, M.W. (1995). *The American street gang: Its nature, prevalence, and control.* New York: Oxford University Press.

Kokko, K. & Pulkkinen, L. (2000). Aggression in childhood and long-term unemployment in adulthood: A cycle of maladaptation and some protective factors. *Developmental Psychology*, 36, 463–472.

Kuppens, S., Grietens, H., Onghena, P., & Michiels, D. (2009). Relations between parental psychological control and childhood relational aggression: Reciprocal in Nature? *Journal of Clinical Child and Adolescent Psychology*, 38, 117–131.

Kyvsgaard, B. (2003). *The criminal career: The Danish Longitudinal Study.* Cambridge, UK: Cambridge University Press.

Lanfranconi, B. (2009). *Gewalt unter jungen Menschen. Diskussionsbeitrag auf Basis der Daten der Unfallversicherung nach UVG.* Luzern: SUVA. http://www.unfallstatistik.ch/d/publik/artikel/pdf/Gewalt_d.pdf.

Laubacher, A., Rossegger, A., Endrass, J., Angst, J., Urbaniok, F., & Vetter, S. (in press). Adolescent delinquency and antisocial tendencies as precursors to adult violent offending—A prospective study of a representative sample of Swiss men. *Journal of Offender Therapy and Comparative Criminology.*

Leistra, G. & Nieuwbeerta, P. (2003). *Moord en doodslag in Nederland 1992–2001.* Amsterdam: Elsevier/NCSR.

Lenke, L. (1990). *Alcohol and criminal violence: Time series analyses in a comparative perspective.* Stockholm: Almqvist & Wiksell International.

Liem, M., Barber, C., Markwalder, N., Killias, M., & Nieuwbeerta, P. (2011). Homicide-suicide and other violent deaths in three countries. *Forensic Science International*, 207, 70–76.

Lipsey, M.W., & Wilson, D.B. (1998). Effective intervention for serious juvenile offenders: A synthesis of research. In R. Loeber & D.P. Farrington (Eds.), *Serious and violent juvenile offenders: Risk factors and successful interventions* (pp. 313–345). Thousand Oaks, CA: Sage.

Lösel, F. (1995). The efficacy of correctional treatment: A review and synthesis of metaevaluations. In J. McGuire (Ed.), *What works: Reducing reoffending* (pp. 79–111). Chichester, UK: Wiley.

Lösel, F. (1996). *What recent meta-evaluations tell us about the effectiveness of correctional treatment.* In G. Davies, S. Lloyd-Bostock, M. MacMurran, & C. Wilson (Eds.), *Psychology, law, and criminal justice: International developments in research and practice* (pp. 537–556). Berlín: De Gruyter.

Lösel, F. (1998). Treatment and management of psychopaths. In D.J. Cooke, A.E. Forth, & R.D. Hare (Eds.), *Psychopathy: Theory, research and implications for society* (pp. 303–354). Dordrecht: Kluwer.

Lösel, F. (2000). The efficacy of sexual offender treatment: A brief review of German and international evaluations. In P.J. van Koppen & N. Roos (Eds.), *Rationality, information and progress in law and psychology* (pp. 145–170). Maastricht, NL: Metajuridica.

Lösel, F. & Köferl, P. (1989). Evaluation research on correctional treatment in West Germany: A meta-analysis. In H. Wegener, F. Lösel, & J. Haisch (Eds.), *Criminal behavior and the justice system* (pp. 334–355). New York: Springer.

Lucia, S. & Killias, M. (in press). School systems and their effects on delinquency. In J. Junger-Tas, I.H. Marshall, D. Enzmann, M. Killias, B. Gruszczynska, & M. Stekeete (Eds). *The many faces of youth crime.* New York: Springer.

Luengo, M.A., Carrillo-de-la-Peña, M.T., Otero, J.M., & Romero, E. (1994). A short-term longitudinal study of impulsivity and antisocial behavior. *Journal of Personality and Social Psychology,* 66, 542–548.

Lussier, P., Farrington, D.P., & Moffitt, T.E. (2009). Is the antisocial child father of the abusive man? A 40-year prospective longitudinal study on the developmental antecedents of intimate partner violence. *Criminology,* 47, 741–779.

Markwalder, Nora (2011). *Robbery Homicide: A Swiss and International Perspective.* Dissertation. Zurich: Schulthess (in press).

McAra, L. (2004). Truancy, school exclusion and substance misuse. *Edinburgh Study of Youth Transitions and Crime Research Digest,* 4.

McGuire, J. (2004). Commentary: Promising answers, and the next generation of questions. *Psychology, Crime & Law,* 10, 335–345.

Meeus, W. & 't Hart, H. (1993). *Jongeren in Nederland.* Amersfoort: Academische Uitgeverij.

Meeus, W., Branje, S., & Overbeek, G. (2004). Parents and partners in crime: A six-year longitudinal study on changes in supportive relationships and delinquency in adolescence and young adulthood. In A. Blokland, & P. Nieuwbeerta (Eds.). *Developmental and life course studies in delinquency and crime* (pp. 307–321). The Hague: Boom Juridische Uitgevers.

Meeus, W., Rie, S. de la, Luijpers, E., & Wilde, E. (2001). De harde kern; ernstige gewelddadige en persistente jeugdcriminaliteit in Nederland. In R. Loeber, N.W. Slot, & J.A. Sergeant (Eds.), *Ernstig gewelddadige jeugddelinquentie: Omvang, oorzaken en interventies* (pp. 51–73). Houten, NL: Bohn, Stafleu, Van Loghum.

Mouzos, J. & Rushforth, C. (2003). *Family homicide in Australia. Trends and issues in crime and criminal justice, no. 255.* Canberra: Australian Institute of Criminology.

Murray, J., & Farrington, D.P. (2005). Parental imprisonment: Effects on boys' antisocial behavior and delinquency through the life-course. *Journal of Child Psychology and Psychiatry,* 46, 1269–1278.

Nationale Drug Monitor (2010). *Jaarbericht 2009.* Utrecht: Trimbus-Instituut/The Hague: WODC.

Nieuwbeerta, P. & Leistra, G. (2007). *Lethal violence: Homicide in the Netherlands 1992–2006.* Amsterdam: Prometheus.

Nilsson, A., & Estrada, F. (2009). *Criminality and life-chances: A longitudinal study of crime, childhood circumstances and living conditions.* Department of Criminology, Report series 2009: 3. Stockholm: Stockholm University.

Olweus, D. (2011). Bullying at school and later criminality: Findings from three Swedish community samples of males. *Criminal Behaviour and Mental Health,* 21, 151–156.

Ortmann, R. (2000). The effectiveness of social therapy in prison: A randomized experiment. *Crime and Delinquency* 46, 214–232.

Paciello, M., Fida, R., Tramontano, C., Lupinetti, C., & Caprara, G.V. (2008) Stability and change of moral disengagement and its impact on aggression and violence over the course of adolescence. *Child Development,* 79, 1288–1309.

Papadakaki, M., Tzamalouka, G., Chatzifotiou, S., & Chlioutakis, J. (2009). Seeking for risk factors of intimate partner violence (IPV) in a Greek national sample. *Journal of Interpersonal Violence,* 24, 732–750.

Pitkänen T., Lyyra A.-L., & Pulkkinen L. (2005). Age of onset of drinking and the use of alcohol in adulthood: a follow-up study from age 8–42 for females and males. *Addiction,* 100, 652–661.

Pulkkinen, L. & Hämäläinen, M. (1995). Low self-control as a precursor to crime and accidents in a Finnish longitudinal study. *Criminal Behavior and Mental Health,* 5, 424–438.

Rabold, S. & Baier, D. (2007). Delinquentes Verhalten von Jugendlichen. Zur differentiellen Bedeutsamkeit verschiedener Bedingungsfaktoren. *Kriminalsoziologie + Rechtssoziologie,* 2, 9–42.

Redondo, S., Cano, A., Álvarez, M., & Antequera, M. (2008). Estudio de eficacia del Programa de Intervención para la Mejora del Autocontrol y la Assertivitat en Jóvenes con Medidas Judiciales en Medio Abierto. Memoria de investigación no publicada, Departamento de Personalidad, Evaluación y Tratamientos Psicológicos.

Redondo, S., Garrido, V., & Sánchez-Meca, J. (1997). What works in correctional rehabilitation in Europe: A meta-analytic review. In S. Redondo, V. Garrido, J. Pérez, & R. Barberet (Eds.), *Advances in psychology and law: International contributions* (pp. 499–523). Berlin: De Gruyter.

Redondo, S., Sánchez-Meca, J., & Garrido, V. (1999). The influence of treatment programmes on the recidivism of juvenile and adult offenders: A European meta-analytic review. *Psychology, Crime, and Law,* 5, 251–278.

Redondo, S. & Sánchez Meca, J. (2003). Guía de tratamientos psicológicos eficaces para la delincuencia juvenil. In M. Pérez, J.R. Fernández Hermida, C. Fernández Rodríguez, & I. Amigo Vázquez (Eds.), *Guía de tratamientos psicológicos eficaces III. Infancia y adolescencia* (pp. 183–121). Madrid: Pirámide.

Redondo, S., Sánchez-Meca J., & Garrido, V. (1999b). Tratamiento de los delincuentes y reincidencia: Una evaluación de la efectividad de los programas aplicados en Europa. *Anuario de Psicología Jurídica,* 9, 11–37.

Remschmidt, H. & Walter, R. (2009). *Kinderdelinquenz: Gesetzesverstösse Strafmündiger und ihre Folgen.* Heidelberg: Springer.

Ross, R. & Fabiano, E.A. (1985). *Time to think: A cognitive model of delinquency prevention and offender rehabilitation.* Johnson City, TN: Institute of Social Sciences and Arts.

Saar, J. (2003). Later criminal careers of occupants of juvenile reformatory and penal institutions. *Juridica International,* 8, 100–109.

Sarnecki, J. (1985). *Predicting social maladjustment: Stockholm boys grown up.* Stockholm: Brottsförebyggande rådet (National Council for Crime Prevention).

Sarnecki, J. (2001). *Delinquent networks: Youth co-offending in Stockholm.* Cambridge, UK: Cambridge University Press.

Sarnecki, J. (2009a). Delinquent networks: Youth co-offending. In H.J. Schneider (Ed.), *Internationales Handbuch der Kriminologie Band 2* (pp. 995–1023). Berlin: De Gruyter Recht.

Sarnecki, J. (2009b). *Introduktion till kriminologi (Introduction to Criminology).* Lund: Studentlitteratur.

Schmidt, M.H., Esser, G., Ihle, W., & Lay, B. (2009). Die Bedeutung psychischer und familiärer Faktoren für die Delinquenzentwicklung bis ins Erwachsenenalter. *Monatsschrift für Kriminologie und Strafrechtsreform,* 92, 174–184.

Schumann, K.F., Huizinga, D., Ehret, B., & Elliott, A. (2009). Cross-national findings about the effect of job training, gangs, and juvenile justice reactions on delinquent behavior and desistance. *Monatsschrift für Kriminologie und Strafrechtsreform,* 92, 308–325.

Shah, R. & Pease, K. (1992). Crime, race and reporting to the police. *The Howard Journal,* 31, 192–199.

Smith, D.J. (2004a). Parenting and delinquency at ages 12 to 15. *Edinburgh Study of Youth Transitions and Crime Research Digest,* 3.

Smith, D.J. (2004b). The links between victimization and offending. *Edinburgh Study of Youth Transitions and Crime Research Digest,* 5.

Smith, D.J. (2006a). School experience and delinquency at ages 13 to 16. *Edinburgh Study of Youth Transitions and Crime Research Digest,* 13.

Smith, D.J. (2006b). Social inclusion and early desistance from crime. *Edinburgh Study of Youth Transitions and Crime Research Digest,* 12.

Smith, D.J. & Ecob, R. (2007). An investigation of causal links between victimization and offending in adolescents. *British Journal of Sociology,* 58, 633–659.

Soothill, K., Ackerley, E., & Francis, B. (2003). The persistent offenders debate: A focus on temporal changes. *Criminal Justice,* 3, 389–412.

Statistics Canada, 2000–2004. Retrieved from http://www.statcan.ca.

Statistics Canada. (2005). Family violence in Canada: A statistical profile. Canadian Centre for Justice Statistics, *Years* 1961–2003, 60.

Staubli, S. & Killias, M. (2011). Long-term outcomes of passive bullying during childhood: suicide attempts, victimization and offending. *European Journal of Criminology* 8 (5), 377–385.

Stenberg, S. & Vagerö, D. (2006). Cohort profile: The Stockholm birth cohort of 1953. *International Journal of Epidemiology,* 35, 546–548.

Stenberg, S., Vagerö, D., Österman, R., Von Otter, C., & Janson, C. (2007). Stockholm Birth Cohort Study 1953–2003: A new tool for life-course studies. *Scandinavian Journal of Public Health,* 35, 104–110.

Stump, B. (2003). *Adult time for adult crime.* Mönchengladbach: Forum Bad Godesberg.

Supplementary Homicide Reports (1976–2003); U.S. Department of Justice. Office of Justice Programs. Bureau of Justice Statistics.

Tavares C. & Thomas G. (2008). Crime and criminal justice. *Statistics in focus, 19, Eurostat.*

Timmermans, M. (2009). *Antisocial behaviors: Courses and consequences from toddlerhood to late adolescence.* Ph.D. dissertation. Amsterdam: Vrije Universiteit Faculteit der Psychologie en Pedagogiek.

Tong, L.S. & Farrington, D.P. (2006). How effective is the "Reasoning and Rehabilitation" programme in reducing reoffending? A meta-analysis of evaluations in four countries. *Psychology, Crime & Law*, 12, 3–24.

Tonry, M. (1997). *Ethnicity, crime, and immigration. Comparative and cross-national perspectives (Vol. 21, pp. 1–29).* Chicago IL: University of Chicago Press.

Van Dijk, J., van Kestern J., & Smit P. (2007). *Criminal victimization in international perspective: Key findings from the 2004–2005 ICVS and EU ICS.* Den Haag: Boom.

Verhulst, F.C., Akkerhuis, G.W., & Althaus M. (1985). Mental health in Dutch children: A cross-cultural comparison. *Acta Psychiatrica Scandinavica*, 323, 1–108.

von Hofer, H. (2011). Punishment and crime in Scandinavia 1750–2008. In M. Tonry, & T. Lappi-Seppala (Eds.), *Crime and justice in Scandanavia* (pp. 33–107). Chicago, IL: Chicago University Press.

Villettaz, P., Killias, M., & Zoder, I. (2006). *The effects of custodial vs. non-custodial sanctions on re-offending. A systematic review of the state of knowledge.* The Campbell Collaboration (http://www.campbellcollaboration.org).

Wikström, P.O. (1998). Communities and crime. In M. Tonry (Ed.), *The handbook of crime and punishment* (pp. 269–301). Oxford: Oxford University Press.

Wikström, P.O. (2009). Crime propensity, criminogenic exposure and crime involvement in early to mid adolescence. *Monatsschrift fur Kriminologie und Strafrechtsreform*, 92, 253–266.

Wikström, P.O., Ceccato, V., Hardie, B., & Treiber, K. (2010). Activity fields and the dynamics of crime: Advancing knowledge about the role of the environment in crime causation. *Journal of Quantitative Criminology*, 26, 55–87.

Wikström, P.O. & Svensson, R. (2008). Why are English youths more violent than Swedish youths? *European Journal of Criminology*, 5, 309–330.

Wittebrood, K. & Nieuwbeerta, P. (2006). Een kwart eeuw stijging in geregistreerde criminaliteit. Vooral meer registratie, nauwelijks meer criminaliteit. *Tijdschrift voor Criminologie*, 48, 227–242.

Zara G. & Farrington D.P. (2009). Childhood and adolescent predictors of late onset criminal careers. *Journal of Youth and Adolescence*, 38, 287–300.

11

Overview, Conclusions, and Key Recommendations

Rolf Loeber, David P. Farrington, James C. Howell, and Machteld Hoeve

The preceding chapters by members of the National Institute of Justice Study Group on Transitions between Juvenile Delinquency and Adult Crime have advanced the field in many different ways. The following summaries of the chapters include additional information from corresponding chapters of the Dutch Study Group report on the transition between juvenile delinquency and adult crime (Loeber, Hoeve, Slot, & van der Laan, in press). Therefore, because the following text is integrative and overarching, it contains new information that is not to be found in the preceding chapters.

Section I summarizes the most important points of Chapters 2 to 5 and relevant portions of Chapter 10 (which concerns European issues) by addressing key findings that are relevant for juveniles' transition of offending from adolescence (up to age 17) into adulthood (age 18 onwards). Section I focuses on: (1) criminal careers, including criminal careers of special categories of offenders (e.g., drug dealers, homicide offenders); (2) explanations of persistence and desistance across adolescence and early adulthood; (3) vulnerable populations.

Section II deals with practical issues and covers Chapters 6 to 9 and relevant portions of Chapter 10. The section focuses on six topics: (1) prediction and risk assessments to ascertain the risk of recidivism during the transition period between adolescence and adulthood; (2) legal boundaries between adolescence and adulthood and whether they need to be changed; (3) justice system responses for juveniles and young adults; (4) preventive and remedial interventions outside of the justice system; (5) gender issues; and (6) ethnicity issues. Finally, Section III of this chapter contains the headline conclusions and recommendations for ways forward.

Section I: Criminal Careers, Explanatory Processes, and Vulnerable Populations

The first set of overarching questions in Section I concern criminal careers and ask first: *How common is persistence in and desistance from offending between adolescence and early adulthood, and how common is the onset of offending during early adulthood?* The second set of major questions asks *what explains persistence in and desistance from offending during the transition between adolescence and early adulthood, and what explains the onset of offending during early adulthood?* The third question asks *how well does persistence in and desistance from offending during the transition between adolescence and adulthood map on the minimum legal age of adulthood* (i.e., age 18 in most states)?

The three sets of questions, in conjunction with assessment, legal, and intervention questions addressed in Section II, are essential whether or not a period called "emerging adulthood" (Arnett, 2000) should be designated in which the judicial rules should apply more as they do in adolescence than as in adulthood. Particularly relevant to the discussion around "emerging adulthood" is whether most offending in late adolescence is of short duration and declines naturally; whether legislation should be changed as a result of growing knowledge about adolescent maturation; whether long judicial sentences overreach the naturally occurring decline in offending and consequently are unnecessary and are wasting scarce prison resources (discussed in Section II); and which vulnerable groups are cognitively less competent and take a longer time than others to mature and outgrow delinquency.

I.1. CRIMINAL CAREER PATTERNS, THE AGE-CRIME CURVE, AND PERSISTENCE/DESISTANCE DURING THE TRANSITION BETWEEN ADOLESCENCE AND EARLY ADULTHOOD

We will first review findings on criminal careers between adolescence and early adulthood based on several major longitudinal data sets on the development of offending between ages 15 and 29. The review is based on Piquero, Hawkins, and Kazemian, Chapter 2, this volume; Rosenfeld, White, and Esbensen, Chapter 5, this volume; Blokland and Palmen (in press); and Bijleveld, van der Geest, and Hendriks (in press). The criminal career parameters that are most relevant are prevalence and frequency, persistence and desistance, escalation and specialization, and types of criminal careers from adolescence into early adulthood.

How does the prevalence of offending change between adolescence and early adulthood? Piquero et al. (Chapter 2, this volume) concluded that most studies indicate that the prevalence of delinquency increases from late childhood, peaks in the teenage years (around ages 15–19), and then declines in the early 20s. This age trend is called the *age-crime curve* (Farrington, 1986; Piquero, Farrington, & Blumstein, 2007, Fig. 8.1), which is universal in known populations of youth.

However, age-crime curves may vary in significant ways. For example, the age-crime curve for violence tends to peak later than that for property crime (Blokland & Palmen, in press; Piquero et al., Chapter 2, this volume). Studies also show that the age-crime curve for girls peaks earlier than for boys (Blokland & Palmen, in press; Farrington, 1986; Elliott et al., 2004). The curve is also higher and wider for young males (especially minorities) growing up in the most disadvantaged compared to advantaged neighborhoods (Fabio et al., 2011; Elliott, Pampel, & Huizinga, 2004).

Important for our understanding of the transition between adolescence and adulthood is the right-hand tail of the age-crime curve. The higher and longer that tail, the more this indicates that there is a population of youth who may not have outgrown delinquency or who may have started offending during adulthood. It should be understood, however, that the typical age-crime curve is a cross-sectional prevalence curve and not an indicator of individuals' persistence or desistance in offending. Information about persistence and desistance derives from longitudinal follow-up data and is the key for understanding age-normative vs. delayed outgrowing of delinquency (see Section 1.2.2).

There are several other caveats about the age-crime curve that may influence conclusions drawn from it. For example, self-reported delinquency shows an earlier peak than official records (Piquero et al., Chapter 2, this volume). This may reflect the fact that juvenile offending at a young age (as evident from self-reports) may not be identified by the police or there may be a delay in arrest, and as a consequence these offenses remain undetected in official records until a later age (Piquero et al., Chapter 2, this volume). Another important methodological caveat is that most published age-crime curves based on official records consist of aggregate data from different age cohorts. Only the follow-up of the same participants in longitudinal data can provide us with an estimation of the age-crime curve independent of cohort effects (see, e.g., Loeber, Farrington, Stouthamer-Loeber, & White, 2008).

In summary, the down-slope of the age-crime curve varies between different populations of young people, but often extends from adolescence into adulthood. It is important to realize that the majority of serious forms of crime—including violence—take place in the period of down-slope of the age-crime curve. Since most of the violence is directed at same-age victims, it is not surprising that the age period 16 to 24 is also a high-risk period for violent victimization (e.g., Kershaw, Nicholas, & Walker, 2008; Truman & Rand, 2010).

All available age-crime curves show that the legal age of adulthood at 18 (or for that matter ages 16 or 17 in some states) is not characterized by a sharp change (or decrease) in offending at exactly that age and has no specific relevance to the down-slope of the age-crime curve. Serious offenses (such as rape, robbery, homicide, and fraud) tend to emerge after less serious offenses of late adolescence and early adulthood. Even for serious offenses, however, there is no clear dividing line at age 18. Steinberg et al. (2009, p. 583) concluded that "The notion that a single line can be drawn between adolescence and adulthood for different purposes under the law is at odds with developmental science".

What is the typical age of onset of specific categories of offenses? It is important to establish which types of delinquent acts on average emerge during the transition between adolescence and early adulthood. Findings reported by Rosenfeld and colleagues (Chapter 5, this volume) on special categories of offenders (homicide offenders, gang members, drug dealers, and those carrying weapons) revealed that on average the age of onset of gang membership, drug use, weapon carrying, and drug dealing occurred during adolescence (ages 13 to 17). They also summarized the sequences of the average ages of onset among major categories of offenses. The average age of onset sequence was, first, gang membership (15.9), followed by marijuana use (16.5), drug dealing (17.0), gun carrying (17.3), and hard drug use (17.5). Other studies also support the finding that the onset of gang membership mostly occurs early rather than late in adolescence. A large majority of youths who join gangs do so at very early ages, typically between 11 and 15, and ages 14–16 are the peak ages for gang involvement (Howell, 2011). In contrast, most homicides are single events and are committed in the 19 to 24 age-window. It should be noted, however, that the age of onset may cover a wide range. For instance, about one-quarter of the onset of drug dealing in the Pittsburgh Youth Study (PYS) took place during early adulthood (ages 18 to 25).

How does the frequency of offending (by active offenders) vary over this age range? Piquero and colleagues (Chapter 2, this volume) concluded that the annual frequency of offending is higher for nonviolent rather than violent forms of delinquency. The frequency of offending usually peaks round ages 17–19, and remains stable only among a small number of offenders over time (this is because most criminal careers are only 5–10 years in duration). However, Blokland and Palmen (in press) found that the average frequency of offending was stable over time, as Blumstein et al. (1986) argued.

How does co-offending vary over this age range? Criminologists rightly have stressed that much offending during the juvenile years occurs in the company of others (Reiss & Farrington, 1991). At the same time, it is clear that changes in co-offending occur, particularly during the transition years between adolescence and adulthood. Piquero et al. (Chapter 2, this volume) reviewed the empirical studies and concluded that there were few studies for that period, especially based on self-reported delinquency. Using official data from the Cambridge Study in Delinquent Development in South London, the authors found that, like the age-crime curve, the age-co-offending curve peaked in the late teenage years. The results also showed that the frequency of co-offending decreased with age, primarily because individual offenders changed and became less likely to offend with others (not because group offenders dropped out).[1] Just over half of the total crimes committed by persistent offenders (those males who had each committed at least 10 offenses by age 40) were committed alone. Thus, co-offending is typical during the adolescent to early adult years, but it tends to decrease subsequently and change to solo offending.

What is known about the continuity in offending (persistence as opposed to desistance) from childhood to adulthood? Much has been written about life-course persistent offenders (Moffitt, 1993), but there are actually few longitudinal datasets that can address this issue. There is no doubt that juvenile offending predicts the probability of offending in early adulthood. Piquero et al. (Chapter 2, this volume) concluded that there was a strong continuity in offending from adolescence to adulthood. Le Blanc and Fréchette (1989) found that "from 30 to 60% of adolescents arrested by the police or convicted by a court will have a criminal record as adults" (p. 83). They also warned that criminal activity during adolescence does not mean "the seeds of an assured stability" of offending into adulthood (p. 85).

Against the backdrop of continuity, there is also evidence that (according to official records of convictions) the probability of recidivism decreases from the teenage years to the twenties. In order to assess continuity in offending, Piquero et al. (2007) examined convictions between different age periods, from 10–15 through 36–40 in the Cambridge Study in Delinquent Development, which is a prospective longitudinal survey of over 400 London males. They found that 67% of recorded offenders at 10–15 were also recorded offenders at 16–20 (compared to only 17% of those who were not convicted at 10–15 who were recorded offenders at 16–20). In contrast, only 40% of males convicted at 16–20 were reconvicted at 21–25, and only 33% of males convicted at 21–25 were reconvicted at 26–30 (Farrington et al., 2006). In this sample, the median age of the first conviction was 17, whereas the median age of the last conviction was 25, suggesting that many offenders desisted naturally in their early twenties (Farrington, in press).

The finding of decreasing recidivism rate with age is also reported by Prime et al. (2001) who, based on a national sample of English males born in 1953, found that the fraction of male offenders who were reconvicted within five years decreased from 42% at age 17 to 16% at age 25. For female offenders, the fraction reconvicted decreased only from 23% at age 17 to 19% at age 25. This finding corresponds to the fact that the decrease in the age-crime curve after the peak is much steeper for males than for females.

While the prevalence of offending and the probability of recidivism decrease from the teenage years to the twenties, it does not necessarily follow that the average residual length (in years) of a criminal career (up to the age of desistance) or the average residual number of offences in a criminal career would decline similarly. However, Kazemian and Farrington (2006) investigated these quantities in the Cambridge Study, based on official records of convictions, and found that the average residual length of a criminal career and the average residual number of offenses decreased steadily with age. The average residual career length decreased from 8.8 years for offenders at age 18 to 6.1 years for offenders at age 25, and the average residual number of offences decreased from 5.4 at age 18 to 3.8 at age 25. These quantities should be taken into account by judges who sentence young offenders, because these quantities could be predicted by the age of the offender, the serial number of the conviction, the time since the last conviction, and the age of onset of offending.

There are large individual differences in a juvenile offender's likelihood of becoming a persistent offender into adulthood. In general, those juveniles who start offending prior to age 12, compared to those who start at a later age, are more likely to become juvenile offenders who persist into early adulthood (Loeber & Farrington, 2001). Using best-estimate methods of self-report and official records, Stouthamer-Loeber (2010) found that in the PYS, 52% to 57% of juvenile delinquents continued to offend during early adulthood (ages 20–25), but that this dropped by two-thirds to 16% to 19% in the next five years.[2]

This decrease in offending with age has also been documented in a follow-up study of 1,354 adolescents adjudicated for serious offenses in Philadelphia (Philadelphia County, PA) and in Phoenix (Maricopa County, AZ). Mulvey and colleagues (2010) found that "the general trend among these offenders is to reduce their level of involvement in antisocial activities" (p. 18). Almost six out of 10 members of this sample evidenced very low levels of involvement in antisocial activities during the *entire* three-year follow-up period, and less than 9% of the sample consistently reported high levels of offending (p. 19). It can be argued that this is not necessarily inconsistent with the notion of continuity in offending over time. Continuity refers to similarities in the ordinal position of people over time and is quite compatible with changes in the level of offending. Thus, it is possible to observe continuity in the rank of ordering of offending alongside a change in the level of offending.

Not all offense types have the same years of persistence. Findings reported by Rosenfeld and colleagues (Chapter 5, this volume) show that drug dealing and possessing weapons had the highest likelihood of duration/persistence into early adulthood, while gang membership had a shorter duration. However, among the drug offenses, marijuana use has the longest duration, continuing two to four times longer than serious theft and violence. These findings are in line with Le Blanc and Fréchette's report (1989) that the median age of termination of offending was the highest (age 21.6) for drug trafficking. They also found that minor offenses (such as vandalism, shoplifting, and motor vehicle theft) tended to cease before age 18.

Rosenfeld et al. (Chapter 5, this volume), using U.S. data, found that child abusers start at an older age compared to peer and adult abusers, but this group persisted for a longer period in adulthood. Bijleveld and colleagues (in press) distinguished between "hands-on" young sex offenders (thus, excluding exhibitionists), those who abused children, and those who abused peers. The authors concluded that child abusers offended less often and less frequently than peer abusers.

In summary, studies show that about 40–60% of juvenile offenders persist into early adulthood, but the percentage of persisters substantially decreases afterwards. Since desistance from offending is the inverse of persistence, 40–60% of the juvenile offenders desist from offending by early adulthood. The rates of persistence and desistance are not immutable. As we will see later, interventions outside of the justice system can improve young persons' desistance from offending between adolescence and early adulthood.

To what extent is there adult-onset of offending between ages 18 and 29? Piquero et al. (Chapter 2, this volume) reviewed several studies on the adult-onset of offending and concluded that there is a substantial number of adult-onset offenders (sometimes amounting to 10–30% of all officially recorded offenders). For example, McGee and Farrington (2010) in the Cambridge Study found that 11% of all convicted offenders were first convicted at age 31 or older. However, there are wide variations in the estimates (see also Blokland & Palmen, in press). Findings indicate that a late onset of offending is more common among females than males. Fontaine and colleagues' review of antisocial trajectories (2009) reported that a proportion of women start their delinquent or criminal career in adulthood. They noted that it is unclear to what extent late-onset females are "truly problem free earlier in life" (p. 375).

Killias and colleagues in Chapter 10 emphasize that some longitudinal studies in Europe have reported that a proportion of late-onset offenders continued offending beyond age 30. However, precise numbers of adult-onset offenders depended on the nature of measurement (e.g., self-reports vs. official records) and on the seriousness of offenses included. One study (Stouthamer-Loeber, 2010) used a combination of self-report and official records of moderate and serious delinquency and in the PYS found that, by age 25, 17.0% of a school-based sample of young males who offended between ages 17 and 25 were late-onset offenders. However, this percentage depends considerably on the criterion for what is considered delinquency. If less serious offenses are included, this has an impact on the identification of the percentage of early adult offenders. Blokland and Palmen (in press) reported on subjects detained by the police, thus not convicted for delinquency. The authors found that nearly half of the young adult offenders did not have a juvenile record, a finding that is concordant with the report of Blumstein et al. (1986). However, Zara and Farrington (2010) found that 23% of offenders up to age 50 were first convicted at age 21 or later.

What is known about escalation versus de-escalation in the seriousness of offending during this age range? In general, studies show that the prevalence of serious offenses accelerates during late adolescence and early adulthood, reflecting the fact that the transition between adolescence and adulthood denotes a period of increasing severity of offenses and an increase in lethal violence (e.g., Farrington, 2003; Le Blanc & Fréchette, 1989; Loeber & Farrington, 1998). Serious offenses include violence and homicide, drug dealing, and gun or weapon carrying (Loeber et al., 2008).

However, the prevalence of these serious outcomes in early adulthood varies greatly between cities and rural areas. It is also typical that individuals in the process of desistance during late adolescence and early adulthood de-escalate the severity of their offending. In summary, the period between late adolescence and early adulthood is characterized by an increasing severity of offending in a minority of delinquents, and a decreasing severity of offending in others whose offending decreases during that period (Le Blanc & Fréchette, 1989). This process of escalation for some young males and de-escalation for others is usually not complete for all juvenile delinquents by age 18 but extends into early adulthood.

What types of criminal careers can most usefully be distinguished between ages 15 and 29? Criminal career types are defined as classes of individuals who share a specific pattern of development of offending over time. Individual level criminal trajectories tend to have varied shapes compared to the aggregate age/crime curve (see also Piquero, 2008). Moffitt's notion that there are two types of criminal careers, early onset life-course delinquents and late-onset adolescent-limited delinquents, has been qualified by recent research (Moffitt, 2006) and reviews (e.g., Piquero, 2008). For example, Moffitt (2006) formulated additional types of low-level chronic offenders and adult-onset antisocial individuals. Actually, it has become clear that several subgroups of offenders are identifiable, and new research in Rochester, New York, shows that there may be as many as eight trajectory groups (Thornberry, 2005), although most research has revealed four to six distinguishable groups (Loeber et al., 2008).

Piquero and colleagues' review of developmental trajectories in Chapter 2 (this volume) indicates that the offending career for one group of individuals shows a steep decrease in crime after a peak in adolescence, while for others desistance from offending is far more gradual and extends into early adulthood; a third group may show an almost low and flat rate of offending for much of adulthood; also, a fourth group will show an increase in offending during early adulthood. Thus, there is evidence of different types of offending patterns, and that these patterns intersect age 18 at different phases of the delinquency career, and that for some that career extends into or starts in adulthood.

When is the peak period of desistance? It is not often recognized that desistance processes operate throughout the period of the age-crime curve. For example, a proportion of youth in the PYS with onset of delinquency in middle childhood (ages 7–9) desisted soon after and the same was true for those who started offending during late childhood (10–12), early adolescence (13–16), and so on. However, this raised the question: *do youth with different ages of onset share a period in which desistance becomes more common?* Analyses based on the PYS data indicate that, although there is an inverse relationship between age of onset and persistence (Loeber & Farrington, 2001), most of the desistance of different age-at-onset groups takes place during late adolescence and early adulthood (Stouthamer-Loeber, Pardini, & Loeber, 2009), which reinforces the fact that what is most needed now is to explain this massive desistance during this transition period (reviewed in Section II.2).

The findings by Le Blanc and Fréchette (1989, Table 5.2) concur. The authors followed up two samples of male adolescents: one based on a representative sample, the other based on an adjudicated sample. Juveniles whose self-reported offending started at ages 7 or 8 tended to be active offenders for a median of 12 years (thus, continued to offend up to ages 19–20), whereas those who began offending between ages 9 and 10 had a delinquency career of a median of 9 years (thus ending also around the same age), while those who started offending between ages 11 to 16 had an active delinquency career with a median of 5 to 8 years, thus also ending at ages 16–23. When official records of offending were the criterion, the results were basically replicated but with slightly shorter offending durations than for self-reported delinquency. Thus, desistance processes for 50% of the youth in the two samples occurred a few years after the youth turned age 18.

The results of the Stouthamer-Loeber et al. (2009) and the Le Blanc and Fréchette (1989) studies indicate the irrelevance for desistance processes of the legal age of adulthood at age 18. The findings imply that many youthful offenders, including those already in contact with the court, cease offending soon after age 18. Thus, many young people who offend at ages 18 to 20 and who are now fed into the adult justice system and are therefore more likely to receive longer sentences than in the juvenile justice system, would have been likely to desist in the next few years in any case.

In summary, delinquency career research has informed the field about onset, persistence and desistance patterns relevant for understanding the transition between juvenile delinquency and adult crime. This period is a watershed in terms of distinctive pathways for some juvenile delinquents to become adult criminals and for other youth to desist from offending. A third, less studied group, becomes adult-onset offenders without a significant juvenile delinquency career (often these include individuals engaging in fraud). The key questions that future research on desistance can clarify are: how much desistance occurs during the young adult period (e.g., ages 18–25), and how does the probability of desistance vary with age? If desistance is very high during the 18–25 year-old period, this would be a good argument for delaying severe punishment until after age 25.

I.2. EXPLANATORY PROCESSES

In Chapter 1 we distinguished between 10 possible processes that are thought to explain offending between adolescence and early adulthood, and particularly explain differences among young people in the age-crime curve (see Figure 1.1). Almost all of these processes have been reviewed in the preceding chapters (but see also Kazemian & Farrington, 2010). The processes are:

1. Early individual differences in self-control (discussed in Chapter 3).
2. Brain maturation (Chapters 3, 5, and 8).
3. Cognitive changes (decision-making to change behavior; Chapter 3).
4. Behavioral risk factors (disruptive behavior and delinquency) and behavioral protective factors (nervousness and social isolation; Chapter 3).

5. Exposure to social risk and protective factors (family, peers, school; Chapter 3).
6. Mental illnesses and substance use/abuse (discussed in this section).
7. Life circumstances (e.g., getting married, becoming employed; Chapter 4).
8. Situational context of specific criminal events, including crime places and routine activities (Chapter 4).
9. Neighborhood (e.g., living in a disadvantaged neighborhood, and the concentration of impulsive and delinquent individuals in disadvantaged neighborhoods; Chapter 4).
10. Justice response (e.g., transfer to adult court, longer sentences; Chapter 8).

The present chapter adds relevant information to the preceding chapters and evaluated the putative explanatory processes by addressing three empirical questions: (a) *Does each process explain persistence in offending from adolescence into adulthood?* (b) *Does each process also explain desistance during that period?* And (c) *Does each process explain the onset of offending during early adulthood?*

It should be noted that the aforementioned processes map to some degree onto the five theoretical orientations presented by Thornberry and colleagues (Chapter 3, this volume): static or population heterogeneity models (early individual differences in self-control), dynamic or state dependence models (behavioral risk and protective factors), social psychological theories (cognitive changes), the biosocial perspective (brain development and change in impulsivity), and the developmental psychopathology perspective (including mental illness and exposure to risk and protective factors).

1. Early individual differences in self-control. Thornberry and colleagues (Chapter 3, this volume) called attention to individual differences in self-control that are presumed to emerge relatively early in life and are thought to be stable over much of the life-course. The individual difference framework can also be conceptualized as a population heterogeneity model because subsets of individuals differ in self-control, and associated with that is their probability of becoming serious offenders between adolescence and early adulthood.

Although popular in criminology (e.g., Gottfredson & Hirschi, 1990; Jolliffe & Farrington, 2010), the early individual differences framework lacks agreement among scholars about the exact nature of the underlying construct. Loeber and Pardini's review (2008) showed that many scholars focused on different underlying constructs thought to be central to individual differences. There is little agreement on whether poor self-control, reckless behavior, impulsivity, poor executive functioning, or sensation-seeking are the important constructs (see also Jolliffe & Farrington, 2009), and there is even less agreement on how best to quantify them independently of disruptive child behavior and delinquency. Also, the assumed stability of the underlying constructs across the life course is often untested and is rarely based on a follow-up of the same individuals over time (but see Piquero, Jennings, & Farrington, 2009, 2010a). Another possible flaw is the fact that individual differences in, for example, self-control, do not easily map onto the age-crime curve, especially on the up-slope of the curve representing the increase of offending from childhood (ages 7–12) to middle adolescence (ages 13–16) *and* the down-slope of the age-crime curve representing the decrease of criminal activities from late adolescence (ages 17–19) into early adulthood (ages 20–25). Further, the individual differences approach usually pays lip-service to brain maturation from childhood to early adulthood (but see Moffitt, 1993).

The conceptualization of individual differences has been applied but not empirically tested in relation to late-onset or adult-onset offending. For example, one plausible explanation by Megargee (1966) of late-onset violence without antecedent patterns of aggression rests on the concept of "overcontrol." Blackburn (1993) summarized the concept and stated that "overcontrolled offenders . . . have strong inhibitions, and aggress only when instigation (anger arousal) is sufficiently intense to overcome inhibitions" (p. 238). In support of the notion of over-control, Pulkkinen (1982) found that highly submissive girls were at risk for developing conduct problems later in life. However, several uncertainties remain. First, it is unclear to what extent adult-onset offenders are truly problem-free earlier in life. Second, we are not aware of effective screening devices that identify adult-onset offenders.

In summary, the individual differences approach is much better at explaining persistence in offending than desistance from offending on the basis of "stable" individual differences. Further, the individual differences approach usually does not attempt to explain adult-onset offending, and the traditional individual differences approach assumes stability of key underlying factors and does not take into account that an underlying construct such as self-control is malleable and that it can change as a result of social interactions and systematic interventions (Piquero et al., 2009, 2010). In addition, Lewis et al. (2008) have shown that changes in self-regulation resulting from treatment of 8–12 year-old boys with behavior problems are accompanied by changes in specific areas of the brain. Thus, self-control and impulsivity processes are far from immutable, and changes in these processes can be related to changes in brain functioning.

> 2. *Brain maturation.* The critical issue is whether mental maturation and the associated emergence of internal controls are related to brain maturation and whether both correspond to the down-slope of the age-crime curve. In brief, an improved understanding of individual differences would suggest something like the following. Young people differ in the speed of brain maturation (see Thornberry et al., Chapter 3, this volume), and this brain maturation, accompanied by social learning, causes improved internal controls. These improved controls become evident through a decrease in risk-taking behaviors, reckless behavior, and sensation-seeking, and advances in problem-solving, future orientation, and

decision-making. Improved controls are thought to reduce deviant behavior, including the commission of delinquent acts, and increase prosocial behaviors.

Prior et al. (2011) carried out a very useful literature review in their report entitled *Maturity, Young Adults and Criminal Justice*. They found that physical maturity (the completion of puberty) usually occurred by age 12 or 13, while intellectual maturity was usually complete by age 18. However, the higher executive functions of the brain, such as planning, verbal memory, and impulse control, were not usually fully developed until age 25. They concluded that "the human brain is not mature until the early to mid-twenties" (p. 8).

There are several pieces of research that fit these conclusions. There is increasing evidence that the brain continues to develop during childhood into early adolescence, including ongoing myelination (e.g., Giedd et al., 1996; Sowell et al., 2001), and into adulthood when white matter increases and synapses are pruned. Research also shows that "the dorsal lateral prefrontal cortex, important for controlling impulses, is among the latest brain regions to mature without reaching adult dimensions until the early 20s" (Giedd, 2004, p. 77). The importance of white matter is underscored by the finding that decreased white matter is significantly more common among boys with psychopathic tendencies compared to controls (De Brito et al., 2009). Biological changes in the prefrontal cortex during adolescence and the early twenties lead to improvements in executive functioning, including reasoning, abstract thinking, planning, anticipating consequences, and impulse control (Sowell et al., 2001).

The data on brain development, although mostly cross-sectional, is much in line with behavioral evidence that reckless behaviors tend to decrease as late as early adulthood, as is evident from data on the incidence of car accidents, even when controlling for the number of miles traveled (Foss, 2002). This is widely recognized by insurance companies whose premiums for car insurance for young drivers up to about age 25 are dramatically higher than for older drivers. It is also recognized by car rental companies who either do not rent cars to people under age 25 or levy a surcharge for drivers under that age.

The idea of improved behavioral controls that emerge between late adolescence and early adulthood is also evident from psychological research. For example, Steinberg et al. (2009) investigated time perspective, planning ahead, and anticipation of consequences among individuals between the ages of 10 and 30 (Figure 11.1). Although this was a cross-sectional study, the results suggest that the ability to plan ahead improves dramatically between early adolescence and the early 20s along with the anticipation of consequences, while time perspective improves slightly less in that same period. In addition, a recent meta-analysis concluded that children's and adolescents' coping repertoires increase with age, including planful problem-solving, more diverse distraction techniques, positive self-talk, and intentional self-regulation of emotions (Zimmer-Gembeck & Skinner, 2011).

In general, psychosocial capacities that improve decision making and risk taking—such as impulse control, emotion regulation, delay of gratification, and resistance to peer influence—continue to mature well into young adulthood (Steinberg, 2004).An additional key piece of evidence derives from longitudinal research in which the same individuals are followed up over time. In general, longitudinal research shows that childhood impulsivity measured by ratings made by adults (as early as age 5) is significantly predictive of violence (Jolliffe & Farrington, 2009). Corresponding to the thesis that young individuals differ not just in their stable traits over time, but also in their developmental maturation, research based on the PYS (Loeber et al., 2011) shows that individual differences in cognitive impulsivity, as measured by young males' performance on several psychometric tasks at age 13, map onto individual differences in the age-crime curve. Individuals tested at age 13 were divided into four quartiles on the index of cognitive impulsivity. Particularly relevant outcome parameters are the height and width of the curve for arrest for delinquent acts, with the width indicating a delayed outgrowing of delinquency. The startling results in Figure 11.2 show that individuals scoring one standard deviation over the mean on cognitive impulsivity had the highest prevalence of arrest for delinquent acts throughout adolescence into early adulthood (ages 12–26), but from age 23 onward their prevalence of arrest became very similar to those scoring one standard deviation below the mean on cognitive impulsivity. Again, the results indicate the irrelevance of the legal age of 18 divide for these outgrowing processes, even for those at the highest level of impulsivity.

It should be noted that Loeber et al. (2011) also reported a significant interaction between cognitive impulsivity and intelligence. For boys with low IQ, cognitive impulsivity did not have additional impact on arrest. However, for boys with a higher IQ, cognitive impulsivity was associated with a greater escalation in the

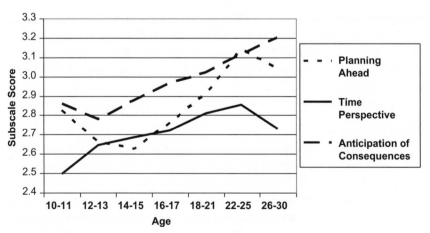

FIGURE 11.1 Planning ahead, time perspective, and anticipation of future consequences improves between ages 10 and 25.

Steinberg et al., 2009.

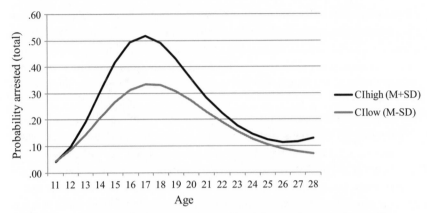

FIGURE 11.2 Cognitive impulsivity measured at age 12 and the age-crime curve for arrest for delinquency; CI = Cognitive impulsivity; M = mean; SD = standard deviation.
Loeber et al., 2011.

prevalence of arrest for offending during early adolescence, followed by a more rapid decline in offending as boys entered early adulthood.

Yet another piece of evidence contradicts the assumed stability of underlying traits with the development of offending. Piquero et al. (2009) reviewed the evidence that several intervention programs both improve self-control and reduce delinquency in young people. The reviewed programs targeted those up to age 10 and showed that juveniles' self-control is malleable as a result of systematic interventions. Less well-documented is how well interventions promoting self-control apply to older populations.

In summary, the central issue is not whether there are stable individual differences between individuals in their cognitive control and their delinquent acts. Instead, the key question is: to what extent do *individual differences balloon over time and then deflate?* Thus, the age-crime curve with its increase, peak, and then decrease in prevalence *and,* possibly, severity over time should be related to within-individual differences in brain and cognitive development. However, brain and cognitive development have not been related to adult-onset offending.

> *3. Cognitive changes.* Cognitions, such as particular ways of thinking, are implicated in the prediction of delinquency and desistance from offending (see also Kazemian & Farrington, 2010). For example, research shows that cognitions such as deviant attitudes, particularly tolerance to violence, tend to increase during adolescence and predict later offending (Zhang, Loeber, & Stouthamer-Loeber, 1997). Further, a positive attitude to delinquency is negatively predictive of desistance (meaning it is predictive of persistence;

Stouthamer-Loeber et al., 2006). In the Cambridge Study in Delinquent Development, Farrington and Hawkins (1991) found that anti-establishment attitudes at age 18 predicted persistence rather than desistance of offending between ages 21 and 32.

Often individuals who stop offending report changes in their thinking, including an increased emphasis on the negative effects of a delinquent lifestyle. Whereas some argue that brain maturation causes behavioral change, including a decrease or cessation of offending, others posit that cognitive changes are necessary requirements for desistance (see Thornberry et al., Chapter 3, this volume). For example, Sampson and Laub (1990) in their age-graded conceptualization of desistance postulated that individuals' investment in conventional (adult) roles reduces offending and encourages desistance. In a different vein, Giordano, Cernkovich, and Rudolph (2002) hypothesized that offenders need to make a cognitive shift to accept the view that their deviant lifestyle is undesirable and involves too high a cost, and in the process they adopt a different self-image and adjust their life accordingly. Although these cognitive changes sound plausible, we are still far away from integrating brain changes with cognitive changes, establishing their temporal order, and demonstrating that both lead to desistance from offending.

In summary, some cognitive factors, such as positive attitudes to delinquency, are predictive of delinquency and are presumed to be correlated with persistent offending. The research on cognitions that are predictive of desistance from offending is scarce. As mentioned, some scholars propose that positive changes in cognitions are necessary elements in criminals' decisions to change course and desist from crime (see Thornberry et al., Chapter 3, this volume). Although plausible, it is far from clear to what extent such cognitive changes relate to brain maturation, or to what comes first. It is also unclear to what extent cognitive changes may underlie adult-onset offending.

4. *Behavioral risk and protective factors.* It is well known that the best predictor of future behavior is past behavior (Farrington, 2003; Loeber & Dishion, 1983). This applies to disruptive behavior during childhood and adolescence, including oppositional behavior and conduct problems, which tend to predict later delinquency (Loeber, Burke, Lahey, Winters, & Zera, 2000). It is also well-established that earlier forms of delinquency predict later offending (see studies reviewed by Piquero et al., Chapter 2, this volume). For example, in the Cambridge Study in Delinquent Development, the odds that a young person with officially recorded delinquency between ages 10–15 would become an officially recorded delinquent during ages 16–20 were 9.7. Piquero et al. (Chapter 2, this volume), also using data from the United States, concluded that early arrest for juvenile offenses, frequent arrests, and arrests over several years during adolescence were each significantly associated with criminal activity during adulthood, and this applied to both males and females.

The notion that earlier behavior helps to explain the persistence of offending has received much support in the empirical literature (Farrington, 2003). At the same time, several empirical studies have attempted to explain why many youth *do not* commit serious crime. There is good support for the notion that children and adolescents who score higher on nervousness (or qualify for an anxiety disorder) are less likely to commit delinquent acts than those who score low on that factor (e.g., Zara & Farrington, 2009, 2010; O'Brien & Frick, 1996; Joyal, Dubreucq, Gendron, & Millaud, 2007). Analyses based on conviction data from the Cambridge Study in Delinquent Development showed that late-onset offenders (i.e., those who were first convicted from age 21 onwards), compared to early onset offenders and nonoffenders were significantly more neurotic at ages 8–10, and were characterized more by social isolation and withdrawal (Zara & Farrington, 2009, 2010). Parent-rated nervousness of the boys and self-reported neuroticism functioned as protective factors in the first two decades, but these factors subsequently lost their protective power (i.e., for adult convictions).

Turning to desistance by juvenile offenders, there is far less support for deviant behaviors (or nervous behaviors) predicting desistance from offending. Those who have not escalated to the most serious offenses are more likely to desist and more likely to do so early than those who have escalated to serious levels of offending. In the Cambridge Study in Delinquent Development, Farrington and Hawkins (1991) found that high nervousness at ages 8–10 was negatively related to offending, but among the offenders high nervousness predicted persistence rather than desistance between ages 21 and 32 (see also Hodgins, De Brito, Chhabra, & Côté, 2010). Further, there is very limited evidence that earlier behavioral risk factors explain the onset of offending during the early adult years (Zara & Farrington, 2009, 2010).

   5. Explanatory social risk and protective factors. Studies generally agree that a multitude of explanatory risk and protective factors in the social environment (thus, excluding the person's prior conduct problems and delinquency) predict later offending (Thornberry et al., Chapter 3, this volume). Scholars often categorize the explanatory risk and protective factors in terms of domains: family, peer, and school, with some distinction within the family domain between parents' child-rearing practices and family demographics. The review by Thornberry and colleagues shows that juveniles' exposure to these risk domains tends to change with age and development, with peer and school influences following the influences of family factors (see also Childs, Sullivan, & Culledge, 2010; Loeber et al., 2006).

Generally, the higher the number of different risk factors, the higher the probability of later offending, even when earlier disruptive behavior and delinquency are not taken into account (Farrington, 1997; Loeber et al., 2008). This supports the notion that individuals' exposure to risk factors is predictive of persistence in offending from adolescence into adulthood.

Findings reported by Rosenfeld and colleagues (Chapter 5, this volume) reveal that most risk factors for violent and general delinquency have also been found in relation to special categories of offenses, including homicide. Research shows that more homicide offenders compared to violent offenders are exposed to known risk factors and thus, that risk factors explaining homicide are quantitatively rather than qualitatively different from risk factors explaining violence (Loeber & Farrington, 2011; Loeber et al., 2005). In addition, a comparison between juvenile rapists and violent offenders showed that risk factors for rape are similar to those for other violent offenses (Van Wijk et al., 2005).

Increasingly, studies show that protective factors are associated with desistance by known delinquents (Stouthamer-Loeber, Loeber, Stallings, & Lacourse, 2008). However, the power of protective factors to explain desistance varied with the timing of desistance. Stouthamer-Loeber and colleagues (2008), who examined a large array of protective factors, concluded that in the PYS, "desistance in the downslope of the age-crime curve was more difficult to predict than on the basis of childhood factors than persistence occurring at earlier ages" (p. 306). Specifically, *none* of the protective factors measured either in early adolescence (ages 13–16) or late adolescence (ages 17–19) predicted desistance in early adulthood (ages 20–25).[3]

In contrast, several "explanatory" risk factors (e.g., family on welfare) and several deviant behaviors (e.g., high alcohol use, drug dealing, gang membership, and gun carrying) measured during early or late adolescence impeded the probability of desistance in early adulthood. That earlier deviant behaviors are negatively associated with later desistance is not that surprising and may reflect the persistence of individual differences over time. The fact that none of the protective factors predicted desistance during early adulthood gives us pause. It remains to be seen whether this is an odd finding or whether this is concordant with the overriding influence of brain maturation on desistance during this period of life.

> 6. *Mental illness and substance use/abuse.* Thornberry and colleagues (Chapter 3, this volume) considered several forms of mental health problems in the context of offending; here we will concentrate on psychiatric disorders. There is a popular perception that mental illnesses increase the risk of recidivism (Cuellar, McReynolds, & Wasserman, 2006; Doreleijers & Fokkens, 2010). This is supported by survey studies showing that mental illnesses are more common among delinquents, especially those in juvenile institutions (e.g., Teplin, McClelland, Abram, & Weiner, 2005). This may not mean, however, that mental illnesses cause offending or that they predict persistence of offending between adolescence and early adulthood. Even if there is a causal link, it remains to be seen whether mental illnesses explain more than a minority of those who persist in their delinquency between adolescence and early adulthood. For example, Odgers et al. (2007) found that by age 32 a higher percentage of life-course persistent conduct-disordered males in the Dunedin Multidisciplinary Health and Development Study, compared to those with childhood-limited conduct disorder,

qualified for one or more psychiatric disorders, including major depressive disorder, cannabis dependence, other drug dependence, and post-traumatic stress disorder.

Our understanding of mental illnesses as causes of offending is also important from a legal and a court processing point of view. Impulsivity combined with mental illness is thought to deprive an individual "of the ability to understand the [delinquent] act . . . or causes the individual to lose the ability to control his or her actions" (Ogloff, 1997, p. 67).

The finding by Odgers et al. (2007) of a high prevalence of mental illness among life-course persistent offenders is in line with results from mental health surveys showing that mental illness is more common among delinquent inmate populations, including those incarcerated in jails and prisons. Further, the studies show a higher rate of comorbid psychiatric disorders among incarcerated populations (e.g., McReynolds et al., 2010; Teplin, Abram, McClelland, Dulcan, & Mericle, 2002; Vreugdenhil, 2003; Wasserman, McReynolds, Schwalbe, Keating, & Jones, 2010; see also Hoge et al., Chapter 6, this volume). On the other hand, the percentage of juveniles or young adults who are certified mentally incompetent to stand trial because of a psychiatric condition is small, but the proportion with impairments in understanding and reasoning is larger for juveniles than for adults (Grisso et al., 2003). The key questions for this volume are whether persistent offending between adolescence and early adulthood is "caused" by single or multiple psychiatric disorders, whether there are psychiatric disorders that can explain desistance from offending, and whether any psychiatric disorder predicts adult-onset offending.

Which psychiatric disorders are common among delinquent youth, and which of the disorders involve deficits in behavioral, cognitive, and emotional controls? Since Conduct Disorder (CD) symptoms (such as bullying, physical cruelty, or theft) largely overlap with delinquency and often precede delinquent offending, it goes without saying that many delinquents qualify for a diagnosis of Conduct Disorder. Therefore, the explanation of persistence in offending because of CD is largely tautological and does not do us much service. However, some evidence suggests that CD increases the risk for precocious transitions to adulthood (e.g., early home leaving or full-time employment) either via high school-dropout (Capaldi & Stoolmiller, 1999) or early initiation of sexual intercourse. Although accelerated transition to adulthood is itself linked to adverse mental health consequences (Ge et al., 2001), the role of CD in these transitions has not been well documented.

Other disorders with cognitive control problems include Attention Deficit–Hyperactivity Disorder (ADHD) and, in adulthood, Antisocial Personality Disorder, possibly Boderline Personality Disorder, and Impulse-Control Disorder, not otherwise specified (American Psychiatric Association, 2005; Hucker, 1997). ADHD in early studies was seen as an important precursor to CD and Antisocial Personality Disorder, but research findings tend to agree that ADHD does not predict the other two disorders once earlier CD is taken into account (see review by Loeber, Burke, Lahey, Winters, & Zera, 2000). Although there is some research on ADHD and the prediction of delinquency (e.g., Satterfield et al., 2007), we do not know of studies that have examined the extent to which ADHD explains persistence in offending among juvenile delinquents. Yet, as mentioned, one set of ADHD symptoms—impulsivity—appears relevant for the prediction of the age-crime curve.

Other major disorders that are common among delinquents, especially among female offenders, are depression (Wasserman et al., 2010) and Post-traumatic Stress Disorder (PTSD; Kerig & Becker, 2010; Wasserman & McReynolds, 2011). Depression tends to follow rather than precede the onset of conduct problems and delinquency, and whereas delinquency predicts depression, depression did not predict delinquency in early adulthood (e.g., Siennick, 2007). For these reasons, it is not plausible that depression is a causal factor for the persistence of offending between adolescence and adulthood. In addition, the absence of depression is not known to be associated with desistance from offending. In the same vein, the presence of PTSD is not known to account for individuals' persistence in or desistance from offending between adolescence and early adulthood.

It has been hypothesized that psychoses are more common among delinquents than nondelinquents. For example, a Dutch survey by Vreugdenhil (2003) showed that in juvenile institutions 32% of the offenders showed psychotic disorders. Schizophrenia and particularly paranoia have been linked to offending and violence (American Psychiatric Association, 1994; Joyal et al., 2007). However, the prevalence of schizophrenia is very low and typically develops between the late teens and the mid-thirties (American Psychiatric Association, 1994). We have not identified studies showing that schizophrenia prior to age 18 is associated with persistence in offending from adolescence into adulthood, or that it predicts the onset of violence in adulthood. Bipolar disorder (sometimes called manic-depressive disorder), which is rare and usually has an onset in early adulthood, has been linked to violence in adulthood (Fazel, Lichtenstein, Grann, Goodwin, & Längström, 2010). However, it is unclear whether this disorder in adolescence predicts persistent offending into adulthood or adult-onset offending.

Turning to substance use, research findings are consistent in showing that criminal offenders report higher rates of substance use, and substance users and abusers report higher rates of offending compared to nonusers (Rosenfeld et al., Chapter 5, this volume). Of all substances, alcohol use especially is known to disinhibit and predict violence (White, Jackson, & Loeber, 2009). However, at least one study failed to show that frequent alcohol use, marijuana use, or any hard drug use distinguished persisters from desisters of serious delinquency in early adulthood (Stouthamer-Loeber, Wei, Loeber, & Masten, 2004). On the other hand, McReynolds et al. (2010) found that the combination of substance use and affective disorders were especially predictive of recidivism among adolescent females in the care of probation authorities. Importantly, Chassin et al. (2010) reported that frequent alcohol and marijuana use by serious juvenile offenders predicted lower psychosocial maturity six months later. For boys, those with the highest level of marijuana use showed the smallest increase in psychosocial maturity.

In summary, a range of psychiatric disorders is common among arrested and incarcerated populations of young offenders, and frequent alcohol and drug use are implicated in a delay in psychosocial maturity. Mental illness, however, is *not* a common explanation of, for example, violence. Joyal and colleagues in their review of studies concluded that between 85% and 95% of violence in communities is not related to major mental disorders (Joyal et al., 2007).

However, the fact is that most young offenders compared to nonoffenders have mental health problems. This has major implications for justice processing, including the need to screen for psychiatric disorders, substance use disorders, and dependence. The Mentally Ill Offender Treatment and Crime Reduction Act of 2003 (S. 1194/H.R. 2387) "claims that collaborative service programs between mental health treatment and justice systems can reduce the number of individuals in correctional facilities and improve public safety" (Cuellar et al., 2006, p. 199). Thus, there is an urgent need to eliminate the possibility that young people with mental illnesses are fed into those areas of the justice system that do not assess and service their mental health needs (McReynolds et al., 2010; Wasserman et al., 2003). Several programs in and outside of the justice system (e.g., MST) for juveniles and young adults are known to reduce psychiatric symptoms and recidivism (Cuellar et al., 2006; Henggeler, Cunningham, Picrel, Scheonwald, & Brondino, 1996).

In addition, the justice system is in a strong position to divert alcohol or drug abusing youth to a Drug Court and require them to undergo treatment for their dependence or addiction, particularly when such treatment can speed up psychosocial maturation and improve self-control processes. Evaluation studies in this area are much needed (Cuellar et al., 2006; Howell et al., Chapter 8, this volume; Wasserman et al., 2003).

The above issues are important independently of the question of whether mental disorders have causal effects on offending and are implicated in the persistence of offending from adolescence into early adulthood. Our review indicates that, despite popular perceptions of a causal connection between psychiatric illnesses in young people and their risk of recidivism (Cuellar et al., 2006), there is a lack of evidence that for a significant number of juvenile offenders common mental illnesses have causal effects on the persistence in offending from adolescence into adulthood. On the other hand, certain combinations of psychiatric disorders appear particularly important for recidivism. More plausible is that cognitive impairments, including cognitive impulsivity, are germane to a range of psychiatric disorders and that these impairments are somehow responsible for the variations in offending in a subgroup of young delinquents.

We did not find evidence that the cessation of mental illness explained desistance from juvenile offending in adolescence. Further, there is a scarcity of findings explaining adult-onset offending by means of earlier mental illness. However, it is not implausible that there are subgroups of offenders for whom the preceding conclusions do not apply. Sherman and colleagues (1997) concluded that factors such as a safe place to live, a job that pays, and a social network have a better predictability for desistance than does the degree of psychopathology. A multistate study of released inmates (Baer, Bhati, Brooks, Castro, La Vigne et al., 2006) found that their most immediate needs were finding and maintaining legitimate job opportunities, treatment of serious mental and physical illness, stable housing arrangements, and restoring and rebuilding noncriminal family and social networks. In addition, Baer et al. (2006) stressed that ex-offenders often have to overcome the effects of the economic deprivation that characterizes the communities to which they return, which compounds the personal challenges and burdens that they face.

Irrespective of the question of whether substance use or psychiatric disorders have a causal impact on offending during the transition between adolescence and early adulthood, there is much agreement that screening for mental illness is necessary in the justice system to ensure that alternative measures to long sentences and incarceration are meted out to young people who are mentally ill (see further Section II.1).

> *7. Life circumstances.* Horney and colleagues (Chapter 4, this volume) reviewed the evidence of the impact of life circumstances, such as marriage and employment, on offending. It is common in the criminological literature to emphasize changes in individuals' life circumstances, such as marriage and parenthood, as critical factors for the reduction of offending during the transition from adolescence into adulthood, and that these changes in life circumstances can help to explain the down-slope of the age-crime curve. The review by Horney and colleagues (Chapter 4, this volume) focused especially on the short-term effects on offending of marriage and romantic relationships, parenthood, employment, and leisure activities.

Marriage and cohabitation. Horney et al. (Chapter 4) showed that for males, marriage on average is linked to a reduction in criminal behavior and substance use, but the evidence for females is less clear. The effect of formalized relationships on offending appears greater than that of nonmarital relationships. Why marriage is associated with a reduction of delinquency seems to depend partly on spending less time with friends and partly on social bonding with a partner. However, the favorable potential of marriage is negated when individuals choose an antisocial partner.

Parenthood. Many of the most serious delinquents have children by different partners and are not permanently involved with former partners or their joint offspring (Wei, Loeber, & Stouthamer-Loeber, 2002). It may well be that the critical factor in reducing offending is not the presence of children in a relationship, but whether the parents are living with their children (Murray & Murray, 2010). Horney et al. in Chapter 4 concluded that, overall, the effects of parenthood are not as robust as those of marriage and appear stronger for a reduction in substance use than for a reduction in offending.

Employment. Horney et al. (Chapter 4, this volume) also reviewed the impact of employment on offending during the transition from adolescence to adulthood. Generally, studies indicate that employment is associated with a reduction of crime and substance use in adulthood. However, studies on employment during adolescence, which is a time when delinquency peaks, have found either a deleterious effect or a beneficial effect of work on offending. It may well be that job stability, job characteristics and job satisfaction are playing a mediating role, but the results of studies are mixed in these respects.

Several well-designed studies have examined the negative effects of the criminal justice system on adult employment outcomes (see Bushway & Reuter, 2002), but high-quality studies on juvenile offenders are lacking, leaving unresolved questions such as the temporal sequence between dropout, criminal activity, juvenile justice system involvement, and unemployment (e.g., Bernburg & Krohn, 2003). Bernburg and Krohn (2003) concluded that "aside from mediating mechanisms, it is evident that court appearance hinders educational attainment, increasing the probability of dropout." High school–dropout, in turn, may set in motion a number of negative outcomes including unemployment and increased criminal involvement' (p. 478). We are very concerned about increasing unemployment among young people and what effect that may have on broadening the age-crime curve for successive cohorts with high unemployment in their early twenties. We will return to employment in Section II.4 when discussing the effectiveness of job training programs on offending.

In summary, findings on employment and its possible impact on offending are less consistent than those on marriage. Specifically, not all studies support the notion that employment fosters desistance from offending and/or substance use. More consistent is the finding that periods of unemployment are associated with higher offending in juveniles and adults alike (e.g., Farrington et al., 1986).

Leisure activities. During the transition from adolescence into early adulthood, major changes usually take place in the pattern of leisure activities, including involvement with peers. Such changes include declines in the time spent riding in a car for fun, visiting with friends, going to parties, spending evenings out for amusement and recreation, and other joint peer activities. One of the best studies, done by Osgood et al. (1986), concluded that adults' decreased control over juveniles' behavior outside the home is accompanied by juveniles' increased spending of leisure time with deviant peers. Horney et al. (Chapter 4, this volume) in their review of the empirical literature concluded that there are consistent findings that a change in leisure activities reduces offending during the transition between adolescence and early adulthood. However, more needs to be known about which specific activities are most critical in this respect.

In summary, there is reasonably consistent evidence that marriage and employment on average are associated with a reduction in offending, but there are gender differences in the effects. Some studies have examined youth's precocious transitions through several types of life circumstances, including early school leaving. For example, Bosick (2009) found that "juvenile offenders are especially likely to transition precariously by exiting school early and becoming early parents, and with the notion that those who do not couple these precarious transitions with early entry into steady employment, independent residence and marriage will be particularly likely to continue offending into adulthood" (p. 132).

Unfortunately, the study of the impact of life circumstances on reducing delinquency is plagued by methodological limitations which have been addressed only in a minority of studies. Key limitations are the relative lack of within-individual (as opposed to between-group) analyses to show how individuals' rates of offending change from before to after a change in a life circumstance. Further, life circumstances research is limited by selection effects in that those who marry may already differ from those who do not marry in terms of delinquency propensity and/or exposure to known criminogenic risk factors. Several researchers (e.g., King et al., 2007; Theobald & Farrington, 2009) have used propensity score matching to deal with selection effects in within-individual analyses of the effects of marriage.

Moreover, effect sizes of changes in life circumstances, such as marriage, often are small (e.g., Theobald & Farrington, 2009). Siennick and Osgood (2008) in their review of the impact of life circumstances on crime concluded that "they have little direct bearing on whether role transitions can explain the age-crime curve" (p. 161). In fact, many of the life circumstances, such as marriage or full-time employment, often occur late into the down-slope of the age-crime curve, where they could still cause a decrease in offending.

> *8. Situational contexts.* Most of the studies on putative explanations of offending have focused on factors that are somewhat distal to the criminal events. For that reason, it is important to consider the impact of more proximal and situational effects on offending and whether situational contexts change from adolescence to early adulthood. Examples of such situational effects are the presence of bystanders in high-risk criminal situations (peers vs. others) and the carrying of weapons. Horney and colleagues (Chapter 4, this volume) concluded that in the absence of studies covering the transition between juvenile delinquency and adult crime there is little known about which situational context changes are associated with desistance in offending during that period.

Crime hot spots. Horney et al. (Chapter 4, this volume) summarized studies showing that crime is concentrated in certain hot spots in cities (e.g., bars), and this applies to juvenile and adult crime. However, government rules regulating the minimum age of allowable alcohol consumption are likely to affect the presence of crime hot spots around bars. Juveniles are known to hang out at other places, and it is reasonable to speculate that there is a shift in hot spots that takes place from adolescence into early adulthood. How shifts in hot spots in the community affect individuals' persistence or desistance between juvenile delinquency and adult crime is far from clear.

> *9. Neighborhoods.* Horney and colleagues (Chapter 4, this volume) summarized the large literature on neighborhood effects on offending. Studies

agree that the highest level of crime occurs in the worst neighborhoods. Persistent offending is more common in disadvantaged than in advantaged neighborhoods. Scholars postulate that structural factors (such as concentrations of poverty) and social processes (including social disorganization) of neighborhoods are among the possible causes of neighborhood differences in crime levels. Thus, it is probable that neighborhood contexts are important in the explanation of young people's persistence in and lack of desistance from offending both at an individual and at an aggregate level. This notion is reinforced by analyses executed by Averdijk, Ellfers, and Ruiter (in press) showing that moving to another neighborhood is associated with a decrease in individuals' offending. However, in an American experiment that moved families out of poverty-stricken neighborhoods, girls benefitted but boys did not (Popkin, Leventhal, & Weismann, 2010).

As mentioned, cognitive impulsivity can be measured at a relatively young age, and certainly prior to the peak in the age-crime curve. Lynam et al. (2000) documented that impulsive individuals (including cognitively impulsive individuals) are concentrated in the most disadvantaged neighborhoods (Lynam et al., 2000). This finding corresponds to another, important finding, namely that the age-crime curve is higher and broader for youth living in disadvantaged neighborhoods than for those in advantaged neighborhoods (Fabio, Cohen, & Loeber, 2011).

We mentioned previously that cognitively impulsive individuals, compared to more controlled individuals, tend to have a higher and broader age-crime curve and that they show a delayed outgrowing of delinquency (Figure 11.2). We posit that the concentration of impulsive and delinquent individuals in disadvantaged neighborhoods stimulates co-offending and also victimization of both delinquents and non-delinquents. In that contagion process, crime and particularly violence is fueled over and above the effect caused by each individual, and at a higher aggregate level than for impulsive and delinquent individuals living in more advantaged neighborhoods.

The concentration of impulsive and delinquent individuals in the most disadvantaged neighborhoods means that there are larger numbers of young people who show delayed outgrowing of delinquency. This delayed outgrowing occurs in environments with high exposure to known criminogenic risk factors, which tend to be concentrated in disadvantaged neighborhoods as well (Horney et al., Chapter 4, this volume) and which are likely to support offending and impair desistance from crime.

10. Justice response. It can be argued that the down-slope of the age-crime curve is at least partially influenced by ways that the justice system—both for juveniles and young adults—is assumed to reduce offending. Interventions through the justice system such as sanctions, including lengthy sentences, incarceration, and transfer of juveniles to the adult court, may all influence delinquency careers and recidivism. Some of these measures are known to increase rather than decrease recidivism. These aspects are discussed in Section II.

Summary of the explanatory factors. As mentioned in Chapter 1, it should be understood that the explanatory frameworks which we reviewed typically cover different age periods in the childhood to early adult time window (see Figure 1.3) and, consequently, may deal with slightly different, but interrelated outcomes. Thus, early individual differences are thought to become manifest after birth and consolidate during the first eight to 10 years (e.g., Gottfredson & Hirschi, 1990), whereas direct exposure to risk factors increases, but also changes, during childhood and adolescence (Thornberry et al., Chapter 3, this volume; Childs, Sullivan, & Culledge, 2010; Loeber et al., 2006), and changes in life circumstances—such as marriage—typically accelerate from late adolescence and early adulthood onward. There are secular changes in many countries showing that more young people than in the past postpone leaving the family home, entering into marriage, and bearing children. However, Hayford & Furstenberg (2008) concluded that there is little evidence that deviant behaviors typical of adolescence manifest themselves later.

As reviewed above, early individual differences appear related to self-control and brain development, and normal maturational processes often are not yet complete by age 18. Yet, as reviewed in Section II.2, age 18 currently serves in most states as the dividing line between adolescence and adulthood (Griffin, Chapter 7, this volume; see also Killias, Chapter 10, this volume for differences among European countries). Research indicates that individuals with early cognitive impulsivity tend to have a higher and wider age-crime curve, which may help to explain the fact that desistance from delinquency is delayed in these youth. Whereas risk factors tend to explain a lower probability of desistance from offending during the period between adolescence and early adulthood, the evidence for protective factors explaining desistance is far from clear. Importantly, very few of the 10 processes reviewed are buttressed by data to explain adult-onset offending.

Which of the 10 processes are implicated in juveniles' persistence in or desistance from offending into adulthood? We concluded that, according to current evidence, the following processes are implicated in persistence: early individual differences, behavioral risk factors, individuals' exposure to risk factors, delayed brain maturation, justice response in the form of incarceration, and possibly, the concentration of impulsive and delinquent individuals in disadvantaged neighborhoods. Thus, persistence processes can be explained by risk and protective factors, with the understanding that protective factors have their own significant contributions and that the protective factors are not necessarily the inverse or the absence of risk factors.

In contrast, desistance from offending between adolescence and adulthood can be facilitated by favorable individual differences early in life, exposure to few behavioral risk factors and, possibly, cognitive changes, but evidence for exposure to protective factors is less clear. Also, early brain maturation, the presence of cognitive changes, and several contextual changes (including marriage) are associated with desistance. Unfortunately, the sparse research on adult-onset offending provides little guidance on which factors explain why some individuals who were nondelinquent during adolescence become adult offenders.

In the absence of meta-analyses documenting effect sizes, it remains unclear which of the different processes associated with persistence (or desistance) are the most important across studies. Further, none of the published longitudinal studies has ascertained the relative contribution of each of the 10 processes from childhood through early adulthood. Kazemian and Farrington (2010) point out the need to integrate objective and subjective types of explanation for desistance from crime.

In those instances in which the explanatory processes of desistance are malleable, we do not know which of the processes can be changed early in life, and which of the processes, once changed, will produce the highest yield in lowering persistence of juvenile offending into adult crime. We will return to this when reviewing the effectiveness of preventive and remedial interventions (Section II.4).

What are the legal implications of knowledge of explanatory processes? Importantly, *none* of the aforementioned processes for which we have some evidence that they may operate during the transition between adolescence and early adulthood clearly map onto the age 18 dividing line, which is the most widely accepted distinction between adolescence and adulthood, and between the jurisdiction of the juvenile and the adult justice systems. Instead, the arbitrary age distinction of 18 appears irrelevant to most of the above processes that are ongoing around that age, including brain maturation. This leaves open the question whether it is a deterrent for juveniles to know that adult laws, with their typically heavy sanctions, will eventually apply to them. Such a lack of awareness would not be surprising given that the cognitive and behavioral maturation of the majority of juveniles is far from complete until they reach at least early adulthood.

I.3. VULNERABLE POPULATIONS

Youths reach adulthood at different ages (e.g., Foster, Flanagan, Osgood, & Ruth, 2005) and they differ in their rates of cognitive maturation. *Which categories of youth are likely to mature more slowly in their cognitive ability to control their behavior and take longer than others to desist from delinquency?* Bijleveld et al. (in press) reviewed new research findings on vulnerable groups, including youth formerly in juvenile institutions and low intelligence youth. The authors showed that both groups had longer criminal careers and were convicted more often than comparison youth.

Youth of low intelligence require special attention, not just because they are often less competent to understand court proceedings, but also because, compared to more intelligent youth, they tend to score higher on cognitive impulsivity and are more often charged with delinquent offenses (Koolhof, Loeber, Wei, Pardini, & Collot d'Escury, 2007).

The following questions pertain to vulnerable populations of youth:

Do vulnerable populations have different and longer delinquency careers? Bijleveld and colleagues (in press) found that men with a low intelligence (IQ below 85) continue to have high conviction rates until they are in their thirties at least (see also Rutter, Quinton & Hill, 1990). Differences between women with low intelligence and women with average or high intelligence are smaller. Zara and Farrington (2009) showed that adult-onset offenders, compared to nonoffenders, had a lower IQ.

Do vulnerable groups experience more atypical life transitions between adolescence and early adulthood? Bijleveld et al. (in press) also found that men and women who were placed in residential care in their childhood on average are less successful in making the transition to adulthood, but compared to nonvulnerable youth some of them make transitions at an atypically early age. For example, motherhood is relatively early for such females, as is marriage. Whereas marriage as well as parenthood reduced offending for the vulnerable men, no effect was found for the vulnerable females. In addition, researchers found that males with a low intelligence (IQ below 85) tended to marry less often than intellectually normally functioning males. On the other hand, females with a low intelligence tended to marry more often.

While vulnerable males performed less well in the labor market compared to males in the general population, vulnerable females did not differ much from other low-educated Dutch females. Low-educated females did not participate at high rates in the labor market, but instead have often chosen to be housewives or mothers. Compared to controls, the vulnerable groups, especially those of low intelligence (IQ below 85) made late transitions into employment and were less likely to be employed. Thus, vulnerable populations of young people tend to experience key adult life transitions differently, but it is less clear whether changes in life circumstances reduce offending and have a reforming effect in the same way as they do for less vulnerable populations.

Examples of other vulnerable groups that need to be studied are those formerly in foster care (Courtney, 2009), early school-dropouts, youth from disadvantaged neighborhoods (for the latter, see Fabio, Cohen, & Loeber, 2011; Lynam et al., 2000), and homeless youth (Hagan & McCarthy, 2005). There is documentation that vulnerable groups take longer to outgrow delinquency than more advantaged groups (see also Foster, Flanagan, Osgood, & Ruth, 2005). We will return to the important issue of vulnerable populations when reviewing the role of justice during the transition between adolescence and early adulthood.

Section II: Practical Issues

This section focuses on six practical topics: (1) Prediction and risk assessments to ascertain the risk of recidivism during the transition period between adolescence and adulthood; (2) Legal boundaries between adolescence and early adulthood and whether these need to be changed; (3) Responses of the justice system; (4) Prevention and intervention; (5) Gender issues; and (6) Ethnicity issues.

II.1. PREDICTION AND RISK ASSESSMENTS TO ASCERTAIN THE RISK OF RECIDIVISM DURING THE TRANSITION PERIOD BETWEEN ADOLESCENCE AND ADULTHOOD

Which risk assessment should be used with young offenders? Hoge and colleagues (Chapter 6, this volume) reviewed studies in North America on risk assessments used to inform the sentencing of juveniles. Risk assessments are carried out by mental health professionals or by others, such as probation officers, intake officers, or youth workers, and the results are taken into consideration by judges. This is consistent with the more individualized, rehabilitative approach of the juvenile court. Risk assessment instruments are also used with juveniles and adults in institutional settings (including mental health settings) to inform release decisions. Consequently, the main aim of many instruments is to predict the probability of re-offending.

Risk assessment is rarely used to inform the sentencing of adults (including young adults), because of the more punitive, retributive approach of the adult criminal court, even when the probability of recidivism is low due to a projected decrease in offending as part of the down-slope of the age-crime curve. We argue that risk assessment instruments should be used to inform the sentencing of young adult offenders.

Hoge and colleagues (Chapter 6, this volume) distinguished between four types of risk assessment. First, unstructured clinical assessments depend on the unguided collection of information and the formulation of a judgment about the level of risk through subjective interpretation of the information. Research has shown that unstructured clinical assessments have poor reliability and validity. Second, static actuarial measures are based on static (unchanging) historical risk factors such as aspects of a person's previous criminal record. Actuarial measures are often superior to unstructured clinical assessments in predicting re-offending and violence (e.g., Quinsey, Harris, Rice, & Cornier, 1998), but actuarial instruments are not useful for intervention planning or for assessing individuals' progress (Hoge & Andrews, 2010). Third, static/dynamic actuarial measures (risk/needs assessments) include both static and dynamic risk factors and are both theoretically and empirically grounded. They are better than static actuarial measures because they can be used for intervention planning and for assessing individuals' progress. Fourth, structured professional judgment (SPJ) tools are based on static and dynamic risk factors (and strengths and protective factors) but the evaluator can use discretion in generating a final risk estimate. Often, a summary risk rating (SRR) is given (Low, Moderate, or High). The idea is to improve clinical judgment by adding structure, and to improve actuarial decision-making by adding a rater's discretion. Generally, the SPJ instruments are considered to be the most useful, and they are at least as accurate as actuarial measures.

What are the most useful instruments with juveniles? Hoge and colleagues reviewed the major juvenile assessment tools, including the Youth Level of Service/Case Management Inventory (YLS/CMI), the Structured Assessment of Violence

Risk in Youth (SAVRY), the Washington State Juvenile Court Assessment (WSJCA), the North Carolina Assessment of Risk (NCAR), and the Psychopathy Checklist: Youth Version (PCL:YV).

Comparisons of the most commonly used tools (YLS/CMI; SAVRY; PCL:YV) suggest that they have rather similar predictive accuracy. The main measure of predictive accuracy is the AUC (Area under the ROC curve), which roughly measures the probability of a prediction being correct (e.g., the probability that a re-offender will score higher than a non-reoffender). AUC measures are typically of the order of .65–.70. It would also be useful to focus on false positives and false negatives and their relative prediction costs (see, e.g., Kraemer, 1992).

Low intelligent youth especially pose a challenge to the justice system (see Howell, Chapter 8, this volume). Key questions relating to this are: *Are vulnerable youth competent enough to understand judicial and court proceedings that affect their future? Are there assessments in place in the court to ascertain their competency? Are such assessments routine and do they have an impact on court proceedings?*

Other categories of vulnerable youth with slower or impaired maturation are youth with one or more mental illnesses involving deficits in cognitive, behavioral, and emotional controls. Examples are those who qualify for a diagnosis of ADHD, depression, drug addiction or dependence (Hussong, Curran, Moffitt, Caspi, & Carrig, 2004), or Antisocial Personality Disorder. These and other disorders are discussed in more detail in Section I.2.

What are the most useful instruments with adults? Hoge and colleagues also re-viewed the major adult assessment tools, including the Classification of Violence Risk (COVR), the Historical-Clinical-Risk Management-20 (HCR-20), the Violence Risk Appraisal Guide (VRAG), the Level of Service Inventory-Revised (LSI-R), and the Psychopathy Checklist-Revised (PCL-R). As with the juvenile tools, comparisons of these assessment devices suggest that they have similar predictive accuracy. However, SPJ tools such as the HCR-20 seem to be the best option because of their usefulness in intervention planning and assessing individuals' progress.

Which instruments can be used with young adults? No risk assessment instrument has been specifically designed to be used with young adults, although the adult tools are used with young adults as well. Hoge and colleagues (Chapter 6, this volume) carried out a re-analysis of existing risk assessment evaluation data to investigate predictive accuracy during young adulthood (defined here as ages 18–25). The most impressive result was that the HCR-20 was a good predictor of both general re-offending (AUC = .73) and violence (AUC = .82) within this age range. In survival analyses focusing on time to re-offending, the Hazard ratios were of the order of 1.14–1.15, showing that a 1-point increase in the total score predicted a 14%–15% increase in the likelihood of re-offending. Hoge and colleagues concluded that their results indicated that both juvenile and adult assessment tools predicted re-offending during young adulthood.

What items should be included in risk assessment instruments? Hoge and colleagues (Chapter 6, this volume) usefully summarized the items included in 10 major risk assessment instruments (five for juveniles and five for adults). Many static factors were commonly included, such as an early age of onset of offending, a history of violence, a history of joblessness, a history of school suspensions/expulsions (personal factors) and criminality in the family, parental conflict, mental illness in the family, low family income, high-crime neighborhood (contextual factors). Dynamic factors included impulsivity, hostility, drug abuse, alcohol abuse, mental illness (personal factors) and poor parenting, parent-youth conflicts, lack of family supports, negative peer associations (contextual factors). Strengths/protective factors were often included in the juvenile instruments, including a prosocial attitude, good social skills, job stability, educational achievement, positive attitude towards authority/treatment (personal factors), and stable/cohesive family, supportive parents, positive peer associations (contextual factors). All of these kinds of items could be considered for inclusion in a risk assessment instrument for young adults.

Hoge and colleagues (Chapter 6) pointed out that about two-thirds of juvenile offenders met the criteria for one or more psychiatric disorders, even after excluding CD. They especially emphasized ADHD and psychopathic features (callous-unemotional traits). They concluded that it was crucial for risk assessment instruments to include items on impulsivity, attention problems, sensation-seeking, low empathy, low remorse, and callousness, all of which were strongly related to chronic offending.

Earlier we mentioned the role that cognitive impulsivity may play in forecasting the age-crime curve (see Section I.2). However, we are not aware of assessment instruments that have incorporated psychometric test results on cognitive impulsivity together with information on other known predictors of delinquency. In general, there is a need to have assessments of psychosocial maturity (Helyar-Cardwell, 2009a) that are sensitive to change as a result of naturally occurring maturation or as a result of interventions aimed at improving self-control and decreasing cognitive and behavioral impulsivity.

How does the predictive accuracy of risk assessment instruments vary with age, gender, and race? Hoge and colleagues (Chapter 6, this volume) pointed out the importance of risk factors varying with age (Odgers, Vincent, & Corrado, 2002; see also Thornberry et al., Chapter 3, this volume). However, it seems likely that many risk factors that are important in the later juvenile years (15–17) would still be important in the early adult years. Hoge and colleagues also reported that several instruments (e.g., YLS/CMI, HCR-20, VRAG, and LSI-R) have high predictive accuracy across gender, race, and countries. However, the predictive validity of the WSJCA was higher for boys and Caucasians than for girls and minorities; the NCAR was not predictive for Caucasian girls, and the association "between PCL-R scores and recidivism likely was moderated by several factors (e.g., race, gender, institutional setting, and country)."

Summary of screening instruments. Well-researched screening instruments are available to assess juveniles' competence to stand trial, and for sentencing and release. However, there are no screening devices available that discriminate between offenders with different developmental trajectories of offending during the period between adolescence and early adulthood. New initiatives are required to generate and validate assessment devices to ascertain cognitive maturity so that this can be measured at an earlier age than entry into the justice system.

In addition, little is known about the prediction of young adult-onset offending, or about continuation of offending from the juvenile to the young adult years, Hoge and colleagues call for longitudinal studies to investigate these topics. They also call for *post hoc* re-analyses of existing longitudinal studies to score risk assessment tools (retrospectively) using variables measured in the dataset. The authors also suggest that a new risk assessment instrument, based on the SPJ approach, should be devised for the young adult years, and to investigate its predictive accuracy using self-reports as well as official records, and focusing on numbers, seriousness, and cost of offenses in a five-year follow-up period rather than merely the probability of recidivism in a short follow-up period. In any new instrument strengths and protective factors as well as static and dynamic risk factors should be measured.

For the present, we believe that many current risk assessment instruments that are used with juveniles or adults (especially those based on the SPJ approach, such as the HCR-20) can be used with young adults. We suggest that these instruments should be used to inform the sentencing of young adults and their allocation to intervention programs. Efforts should be made to assess the effects of using risk assessment instruments on sentencing and re-offending. In particular, cost-benefit analyses should be carried out to investigate if the use of these instruments saves money for taxpayers, for example by reducing re-offending and/or the prison population.

II.2. LEGAL BOUNDARIES OF ADULTHOOD

What are the legal age boundaries between juvenile and adult justice systems in different states? In most states, the adult justice system jurisdiction begins at age 18, while for other states this applies to age 17 or even as low as age 16 (see Griffin, Chapter 7, this volume). In most states, a juvenile court may continue to exercise dispositional jurisdiction over an adjudicated youth until the youth reaches the 21st birthday, and some states (e.g., Pennsylvania) have separate correctional institutions for young adult offenders. The California Department of Juvenile Justice continues to have jurisdiction over juveniles until the 25th birthday (T2A— International Norms & Practices).

Changes in legislation. It can be argued that changes in legislation regarding the legal age of adulthood are warranted to deal with the large numbers of juvenile offenders who continue to offend into adulthood. To address this issue, four strategies have been proposed by politicians and researchers: (a) raising the legal age at which the adult justice system becomes applicable; (b) lowering the legal age at which adult justice becomes applicable; (c) increasing sanctions, particularly by means of legislative offense exclusion, minimal length of sentences, and longer incarceration; and (d) the creation of special courts for young adult offenders. It should be understood that whereas the first and third options can be advanced in unison, the second option is inherently the opposite of the first option. Three key questions in discussions about legal age changes are: *Are legal boundaries related to young people's development of cognitive control (or lowered impulsivity)? Is the justice system relevant to improving young people's cognitive control or is young people's development of cognitive control impervious to the juvenile and adult justice system? What is the usefulness of legislation stipulating minimum or longer sentences for young offenders?* This last question is particularly acute because of the long delays common between arrest, sentencing, and incarceration during the time that many young offenders would be likely to have completed the majority of their offending and be on the down-slope of their age-crime curve.

(a) *Raising the legal age for juveniles at which the adult justice system becomes applicable.* Several States (Connecticut, Illinois) have raised the legal age for juveniles to be dealt with in the adult court (Secret, 2011) or are considering this (Massachusetts, Wisconsin, North Carolina). It can be argued that raising the age of juvenile jurisdiction (from 16 to, for example, 18) will have benefits, even if these benefits are limited to misdemeanors and low-level felonies. The costs and benefits of this strategy are chronicled in a report commissioned by the North Carolina General Assembly (Henrichson & Levshin, 2011). The motivation for the report was based on research findings showing cognitive and behavioral differences between adolescents and adults, a national consensus to treat juveniles in the justice system differently than adults, and an improved awareness about the life-long negative consequences of juveniles' criminal conviction in the adult court. Some of the highlights of the report are:

- Recidivism rates among youth ages 16–17 under the juvenile justice system are expected to be 10% lower than the rates of similar youth currently handled by the criminal justice system.
- Raising the adult jurisdiction age from age 16 to 18 for misdemeanants and low-level felons is anticipated to accrue $97.9 million in long-term benefits over the cost for each successive annual cohort of youths aged 16 and 17.
- From the taxpayer and government view, the policy change will have a net annual cost of $49.2 million (that is a cost of $70.9 million to justice agencies minus $21.7 million in benefits to the criminal justice system).

In summary, there are considerable benefits but also costs to raising the legal age of adulthood.[4] The report does not include cost-benefit assessments of first-time more serious felony offenders. It can be expected that raising the age of adulthood will have greater benefits than those reported here. An English report concluded that "diversion from trial under adult law to trial under juvenile law following maturity assessment is likely to produce cost saving to society . . ." of £420 per offender (Barrow Cadbury Trust, 2009, p. 3). More cost-benefit analyses are needed to quantify the yields of legally raising the age of juvenile jurisdiction to age 21 or 23 or even 25, which is our favored recommendation.

It should be recognized that such a change may have repercussions on other age-related legislation, particularly the right to bear arms. The majority of the homicides in the United States are committed by adolescents and young adults (Heide, 1999). Currently, federal law prohibits ownership of handguns to individuals aged 21 and under. Thus, illegal access to guns overlaps with a period of development in which cognitive maturity is incomplete and violence increases. The challenge is to adjust the legal age of carrying a gun to be more concordant with what is known about the course of cognitive impulsivity and the age-crime curve.

(b) *Lowering the legal age at which adult justice becomes applicable.* The majority of states have legislation stipulating that the upper age of adolescence is age 17, while several states set this upper age at 16 or 15. This legal distinction governs the differential operation of the juvenile and the adult justice systems. *Would the lowering of the age of adulthood, for example to age 16, decrease young people's offending and lower the crime rate of populations of young individuals?*

The watershed between juvenile and adult justice has major implications about how young people are dealt with in the courts and in institutions. As detailed by Howell and colleagues (Chapter 8, this volume), the adult compared to the juvenile justice system is more punitive and more focused on retribution. Typically, diversion from judicial proceedings is available to juveniles but not to adults. Rehabilitation services during incarceration (such as education and job training) often are unavailable in adult prisons, and to a degree are more common in juvenile institutions. Community-based services following adjudication tend to be more available for juvenile than for adult offenders (Mulvey, Schubert, & Chung, 2007). Further, most juvenile offenses can be erased from the record at age of majority, but this does not apply to adult records. Thus, an adult record remains attached to the person for the remainder of his/her life and usually imposes limits on employability in a range of professions, may restrict access to educational grants, and prohibit residence in public housing.

The following are some startling facts about existing legal barriers that returning inmates experience (Legal Action Center, 2004, p. 8): Most states allow employers to deny jobs to people who were arrested but never convicted of a crime, and most states allow employers to deny jobs to anyone with a criminal record, regardless of how long ago or the individual's work history and personal circumstances. Most states also ban some or all people with drug felony convictions from being eligible for federally funded public assistance and food stamps. In addition, most states make criminal history information accessible to the general public through the Internet, making it extremely easy for employers and others to discriminate against people on the basis of old or minor convictions, and deny, for example, employment or housing. Many public housing authorities deny eligibility for federally assisted housing based on an arrest that never led to a conviction. Moreover, all but two states restrict the right to vote in some way for people with criminal convictions. In summary, lowering the age to which adult crime applies has major implications as to how young people are treated during periods of incarceration and for decades after release.

There are precedents for the lowering of the age of adulthood by law. Until 1988, the minimum age of adulthood in the Netherlands was 21, which was then lowered to age 18 (Doreleijers & Fokkens, 2010). It might be argued that further legislative action lowering the age when adult justice becomes applicable (e.g., from age 18 to 16) may have distinct advantages. Among the putative advantages are possible deterrent effects by means of communicating to juveniles that there are more serious consequences to their offending than those that are applied by the juvenile court. However, we are not aware of any evidence that such an attempt at deterrence reduces young people's rate of offending or contributes to their desistance from delinquency. Another putative advantage of absorbing more youth into the adult justice system is to provide a release valve to juvenile court judges in handling the toughest cases.

However, from a legal perspective, the lowering of the current age limit would not be acceptable under International Human Rights Law and would inevitably result in even more public scrutiny by authoritative international bodies, such as the UN Committee on the Rights of the Child (this treaty has not been ratified by the U.S. government). There are distinct disadvantages to lowering the legal age of adulthood. Mention has been made of the paucity of rehabilitative programs in the adult compared to the juvenile justice system, the increased exposure of juveniles to adult criminals in the criminal justice system, and the stigma of having an adult conviction over a juvenile one in terms of reentry into society and engagement in the work force. In addition, lowering the age of adult jurisdiction increases costs for the adult justice system, particularly since here longer sentences than are common in the juvenile court are applied.

Although we have identified only one cost-benefit study of changing the age of adult jurisdiction (Henrichson & Levshin, 2011), we anticipate that such a move can have major negative cost effects. While the juvenile system has more assessment and treatment, the adult justice system is characterized by longer sentences; therefore major cost increases can be expected associated with longer incarceration periods for a new influx of young people into the adult justice system. Besides the daily incarceration costs, this may lead to a need to increase the capacity of prisons, new construction of prisons, and higher long-term staffing costs.

The other critical litmus test is whether legislative change to an earlier threshold to adult justice will lead to both a reduction of individuals' persistence in offending and in offending volume for populations of young people. The answer is that there is no empirical evidence for such a reduction in outcome. Also, it can be strongly argued that the lowering of the adulthood threshold is counter to what we know about adolescent development, particularly brain maturation and improved cognitive control over behavior. The evidence that we reviewed above (Section I.2) indicates that lowering the threshold for the jurisdiction of the adult court restricts options for rehabilitation and does not map at all on what is known about age-normative developments in brain maturation during the transition between adolescence and adulthood.

Moreover, the fact that brain maturation is delayed in some categories of vulnerable youth (e.g., low intelligence boys and girls) implies that these groups disproportionally will be the recipients of more serious sanctions in the adult compared to the juvenile court. Further, such implementation is counter to the principle of competency to stand trial, understand court proceedings, and benefit from the positive counsel of court officials. Finally, lengthier sanctions administered in the adult court aimed at young offenders, based on our understanding of normative outgrowing of delinquency in young populations, will have no bearing on lowering the age-crime curve. In summary, if lowering the age of adulthood is advocated, legislators need to take into consideration the age-crime curve, costs and benefits, and the need to screen vulnerable populations who take longer than others in their brain maturation and their outgrowing of the age-crime curve.

> (c) *Increasing sanctions, particularly by means of legislative offense exclusion, transfer of juveniles to the adult court, longer sentences, and longer incarceration.* In their attempts to deal with crime, legislators often respond to (or generate themselves) calls for increasing sanctions, including higher minimum and longer sentences, and legislation to exclude certain offense categories from the jurisdiction of the juvenile court and transfer juvenile delinquents who committed such offenses to the adult court, effectively placing juveniles under the jurisdiction of courts for adult offenders (see Howell and colleagues, Chapter 8, this volume). Legislators' motivations for such legislative changes are often driven by public pressure and notions of retribution rather than by beliefs in rehabilitation or by empirical findings on recidivism and the age-crime curve.

Most research shows that there is no evidence that lengthening the period of incarceration provides practical benefits in terms of reducing recidivism for serious offenders (Lipsey & Cullen, 2007; Loughran et al., 2012; Mulvey, 2011). A mistaken but common assumption by advocates of longer sentences is that the rate of offenders is constant and therefore, locking the person up will reduce "street" crime and make communities safer. However, the assumption of a constant rate of offending is erroneous for offenders in the transition between adolescence and adulthood when typically their rate of offending declines (see Piquero et al., Chapter 2, this volume). This is in line with conclusions drawn by Loughran et al. (2009), who stated that lengthening sentences, for example, by legislative exclusion of certain offense categories from the jurisdiction of the juvenile court into the hands of the adult court, is unlikely to reduce recidivism among young serious offenders.

What are the laws in different states regarding transfer of juveniles to the adult criminal court? All states have laws allowing the transfer of juveniles to the adult court, by judicial waiver, statutory exclusion, or prosecutorial discretion (see Griffin, Chapter 7, this volume). There are also juvenile blended sentencing laws that allow juvenile courts to impose criminal sanctions under some circumstances, or allow juvenile court judges to impose both juvenile and suspended adult sanctions on certain categories of offenders. A juvenile subject to such a combination sentence remains in the juvenile correctional system only conditionally, with the sword of Damocles of a criminal sentence encouraging cooperation and discouraging future misconduct hanging over his/her head. Conversely, there are reverse waiver laws that permit criminal courts to send transferred youth back to juvenile court for trial or disposition, and criminal blended sentencing laws that authorize criminal courts to impose juvenile dispositions.

Currently, there is no evidence that legislative exclusion of certain offenses from the juvenile court and transfer of juveniles to the jurisdiction of the adult court promotes desistance, reduces recidivism, increases public safety, is cost neutral or even has a positive benefit: cost ratio. Given the lack of replicated proof of its effectiveness, we suggest that legislative exclusion is not a viable alternative at this point in time.

    (d) *The creation of special courts for young adult offenders as separate entities between the juvenile and the adult court.* As Dunkel and Pruin (2012) point out, the International Association of Penal Law in 2004 passed a final resolution stating that the applicability of the special provisions for offending by juveniles could be extended up to the age of 25. In Germany since 1953, all young adults aged 18–21 have been transferred to the jurisdiction of the juvenile courts, which allows the needs of the young adult to be taken into account and allows rehabilitative measures to be used. Whether the young adult receives a juvenile or adult sanction depends on such factors as whether the moral and psychological development of a young adult is like a juvenile and whether the offence is like a juvenile crime (e.g. spontaneous, unplanned, motivated by anger). Thus, practice in Germany conforms to the 2003 Council of Europe recommendation that young adult offenders under 21 should be treated in a way comparable to juveniles when the judge is of the opinion that they are not as mature and responsible for their actions as full adults (Dunkel & Pruin, 2012).

Some other European countries, including Sweden and Austria, have separate young adult sentencing provisions and separate institutions for 18–21 year-olds (see Transition to Adulthood Alliance, 2010). The Netherlands, the Scandinavian countries, and the countries of the former Yugoslavia have special provisions for young adults within the general criminal law or provide for the possibility of avoiding the requirements of the adult law or reducing adult sentences. In Switzerland, young adults can be treated as juveniles until they are aged 25. In Sweden, there is "youth mitigation" up to age 21. In Finland, all those who committed their crime under age 21 are regarded by the prison service as juveniles.

Offenders aged 18 to 20 are dealt with more leniently than older adults not only in Scandinavia, but also in 18 other European countries (including Austria, Germany, and the Netherlands). A practically important consequence of having young adults dealt with under juvenile law is that, for example, in Germany, they may benefit from more lenient procedural rules, such as the wide use of diversion. On the effects of such interventions, there is either no systematic research or the results are conflicting.

In England and Wales, as in the United States, the legal treatment of offenders changes dramatically when they reach their eighteenth birthday. Instead of being dealt with in the youth justice system, which focuses more on rehabilitation, they start being dealt with in the adult criminal justice system, which focuses more on punishment. However, there are some special provisions for young adult offenders, defined as those between ages 18 and 20 inclusive. In particular, these offenders are not sent to a prison but to a young offender institution, and their incarceration sentences must be followed by statutory supervision. At age 21 offenders are considered to be fully adult and fully responsible for their actions.

Because of concern about the legal treatment of young adult offenders in England and Wales, the Barrow Cadbury Trust established an independent Commission on Young Adults and the Criminal Justice System in 2004, and this produced the report *Lost in Transition* (Barrow Cadbury Trust, 2005). The Commission highlighted the problems attending the fact that every offender aged 18 or over was regarded as an adult and that judges applying sentences were under no obligation to take account of the immaturity of offenders aged 21 or older. The Commission argued against using birthdays as an arbitrary indicator of adulthood, and considered that, ideally, there should be only one English criminal justice system for offenders of all ages that took account of the needs and maturity of offenders of different ages.

More realistically, the Commission argued for special provisions for young adult offenders that took account of their immaturity and malleability. It recommended that Transition to Adulthood (T2A) teams should be established in each local criminal justice area to oversee the treatment of young adult offenders and ease their transition between the youth and adult justice systems. It argued that most young adult offenders would naturally desist from crime in their twenties as they matured. Because criminal justice system treatment allegedly made them more likely to offend, there should be presumptions in favor of diversion and against custody for young adult offenders. The Commission pointed out that nearly 70% of incarcerated 18–20 year-olds were reconvicted within two years of release, although (in the absence of some comparison condition) this statistic in itself does not necessarily prove that young offender institutions are ineffective or damaging. The Commission also recommended that judges applying sentences should be required to take account of the emotional maturity of young adult offenders, and that specialists in the National Offender Management Service should submit an assessment of an offender's maturity to the court.

In 2009, the Transition to Adulthood Alliance (www.t2a.org.uk) published *A New Start* (Helyar-Cardwell, 2009a) and the *Young Adult Manifesto* (Helyar-Cardwell, 2009b). The *Manifesto* recommended that young adult offenders aged 18–24 should be recognized as a distinct category. It advocated that the government should consider how maturity and developmental stage could be taken into consideration in the sentencing of young adults, and should pilot a maturity assessment instrument for use by the criminal justice system. The *Manifesto* also recommended more diversion of young adults from the courts, increased use of restorative justice, the abolition of short sentences for nonviolent offenders, and more support in the community to deal with drug, alcohol, mental health, and employment problems of young adult offenders (see Allen, 2012).

Several states in the the United States have begun softening their juvenile "get tough" laws. This may be a suitable time to revisit public policies and make them more amenable to major juvenile justice system reforms pertaining to adolescent and young adult offenders. Three sets of reasons, discussed below, support creating such special courts: (i) excessive punishment of youth who land in the adult justice system; (ii) youthfulness as a mitigating factor; and (iii) the developmental needs of young people.

> i) *Excessive Punishment.* In the past 20 years, virtually every state has lowered the eligible legal age of juvenile transfer and has created additional pathways to adult courts, including statutory exclusion, prosecutorial direct file, or mandatory waiver hearings, which remove judicial discretion from the transfer process (Feld, 2000; Griffin, Chapter 7, this volume; Howell, 2009). Although the Supreme Court's diminished responsibility rationale in *Roper* and *Graham* categorically treated youthfulness as a mitigating factor in sentencing, criminal court judges perversely treat it as an aggravating factor when they sentence youths tried as adults. The consequences for juvenile offenders have been devastating. Perhaps the clearest example is the "juvenile penalty" that researchers have identified—that is, *juvenile offenders sent to adult court are more likely to be incarcerated and to receive lengthier sentences compared with their young adult counterparts* (Kurlychek & Johnson, 2004, 2010; Steiner, 2009; see also Kupchik, 2006, 2007). In addition, a larger proportion of juveniles convicted of murder receive LWOP (life without parole) sentences than do adult murderers (Feld, 2008). The "juvenile status" penalty can be seen in nationwide sentencing patterns. In a federal Bureau of Justice Statistics study (Brown & Langan, 1998), transferred juveniles convicted of felonies were given longer prison sentences than adults. Transferred juveniles were sentenced to prison for a maximum of nine years on average, compared with seven years for under-18 adults (as defined by

state statutes) and five years for adults 18 and older. Similar disparities persist in more recent studies (Kurlychek & Johnson, 2010). These inequities demonstrate the inability of the criminal justice system to treat juvenile offenders fairly and apply a reasonable measure of proportionality to their cases.

ii) *Immaturity and youthfulness as mitigating factors.* The second set of factors center around the unique diminished capacities of juvenile and young adult offenders. In *Roper v. Simmons*, the Supreme Court offered three reasons why states could not punish youths whom they found to be criminally responsible as severely as adults:

- First, juveniles' immature judgment and lesser self-control caused them to act impulsively and without full appreciation of consequences and thus reduced their culpability.
- Second, juveniles are more susceptible than adults to negative peer influence, which further diminishes their criminal responsibility.
- Third, juveniles' personalities are more transitory and less well-formed than those of adults and their crimes provide less reliable evidence of "depraved character."

For these reasons, youths' diminished responsibility requires mitigated sanctions to avoid disfiguring penalties and provide room to reform. The Supreme Court in *Graham v. Florida* reaffirmed the need for mitigated sentences and parole eligibility for youths who did not commit murder. Research suggests that these diminished capacities are present in juvenile and young adult offenders up to approximately age 25 (Feld, 2008; Loeber et al., 2008; Mears & Travis, 2004).

Many European countries, including Sweden, Germany, Austria and others have long had separate young adult sentencing options and separate institutions for 18–21 year-olds (see Killias et al., Chapter 10, this volume). For example, in Germany since 1953, all young adult offenders ages 18–21 have been transferred to the jurisdiction of the juvenile courts, which can sentence according to juvenile law if the young adult has the maturity of a juvenile or if his/her personality is still developing. Austria and Lithuania introduced a similar system in 2001. The Netherlands, Scandinavian countries, and countries of the former Yugoslavia have special provisions for young adults. In Switzerland, young adults can be treated as juveniles until they are over age 25. In Sweden, there is "young mitigation" up to age 21. In Finland, all those who committed their crime under age 21 are treated as juveniles by the prison service (Transition to Adulthood Alliance, 2010).

United States practices often differ from those in the above European countries. Criminal courts seldom use community corrections options and other advanced rehabilitation techniques (Tonry, 1999a, 1999b). Day fines, very popular in European countries for punishment of minor or moderate crimes, are seldom used in the United States. Prosecutorial fines are widely used in Germany and Holland but not in the United States. Many other countries use sentences of community service, scaled to the seriousness of the crime, as an alternative to incarceration; in the United States, only minor offenders are given such sentences. Systematic reviews and synthesis of findings from the implementation of these enlightened laws, policies and practices should provide a useful research foundation for development of similar models in the United States and elsewhere.

iii) *Developmental needs of young people.* Developmental needs undergird the second set of factors that support the creation of Young Offender Courts. Persons in late adolescence (ages 16–19), and early adulthood (ages 20–25) have special developmental needs (Loeber & Farrington, 1998; 2001; Loeber et al., 2008) that cannot be met in criminal courts. These include (Mears & Travis, 2004, p. 16):

- Programs that focus on developing capabilities associated with successful transitions to adulthood, such as life skills, education, and vocational and educational training (see Welsh et al., Chapter 9, this volume). Programs in these areas should build on the resiliency and strengths unique to each youth.
- This effort to tailor programs to the unique circumstances of each young person should also take into account age, gender, race/ethnicity and the distinctive racial, ethnic, and cultural dimensions of the communities to which they will return if confined. They also should take account of any mental or substance abuse disorders or disabilities that might impede a successful transition to the community.
- One of the key strategies in promoting positive youth development is to engage, early in the incarceration period, community groups, family members, and service providers who can begin to build the positive connections that will support the young person following release. These strategies should focus on providing a continuum of care and must be consistently implemented and, where appropriate, sustained for at least six months to a year, a period when the risk of recidivism and return to prison is highest.

In summary, a variety of legal and practical strategies have been proposed, each of which varies in its advantages and disadvantages, and known or unknown costs and benefits. In reality, however, officials in the juvenile and the adult legal systems have considerable leeway, and vary in their practices from jurisdiction to jurisdiction.

II.3. RESPONSES OF THE JUSTICE SYSTEM

There are many uncertainties attached to the ways that the justice system for young people, whether in the juvenile or adult justice system, is thought to reduce recidivism of known offenders. We address here some key questions.

What is known about the relative effectiveness of the juvenile and criminal justice systems in reducing recidivism? Howell and colleagues (Chapter 8, this volume) reviewed the evidence on this topic. First, they pointed out that arrests, convictions, and imprisonment of youth and adults often lead to an increase in offending (see e.g., Huizinga & Henry, 2008; Killias, Aebi, & Ribeau, 2000; Nieuwbeerta, Nagin, & Blokland, 2009). Sending youth to adult prisons usually increases rather than decreases recidivism (see e.g., Kupchik, 2006). Second, they concluded that juveniles transferred to the adult court are more likely to re-offend, re-offend more quickly and at higher rates, and commit more serious offenses than do juveniles retained in the juvenile justice system (see e.g., Bishop & Frazier, 2000). Third, they cited a finding by the Centers for Disease Control Task Force (McGowan et al., 2007) that juveniles who experience the adult justice system commit more violent crimes following release than juveniles retained in the juvenile justice system. Fourth, they concluded that changes in transfer laws and practices do not produce a specific or a general deterrent effect (see e.g., Redding, 2008).

It is clear that the rehabilitative approach of the juvenile justice system is more successful with juveniles than the retributive approach of the adult criminal justice system. Therefore, it is likely that a more rehabilitative approach might also be more successful with young adult offenders.

What is the justification for special treatment of young compared to adult persons? The main justification for the special treatment of juvenile offenders is that youths have diminished responsibility and culpability because they are immature, have greater impulsivity, lower self-control, poorer cognitive abilities, less appreciation of the consequences of their actions, and a generally poorer ability to make decisions. Furthermore, youths are more susceptible to influences by peers and their offending is less likely to indicate ingrained criminal habits. Howell and colleagues (Chapter 8, this volume; see also Section I.2) point out that psychosocial capacities that improve decision-making and moderate risk-taking—such as impulse control, emotion regulation, delay of gratification, and resistance to peer influence—continue to mature well into young adulthood (see Steinberg, 2004).

Howell and colleagues (Chapter 8, this volume) also point out that the same developmental characteristics that diminish youths' criminal responsibility also reduce their adjudicative competence, or ability to understand legal proceedings. Adjudicative competence is especially problematic for those with low intelligence, mental impairment, or mental illness.

Many of the arguments about diminished responsibility and adjudicative competence can apply to young adult offenders. It would be important for any special sentencing and treatment programs for young adult offenders to be based on an assessment of competency and responsibility, and to be rigorously evaluated using randomized experiments.

In light of all the empirical evidence reviewed by Howell and colleagues, we recommend that experiments be mounted to assess the likely effectiveness of special sentencing and treatment provisions for young adult offenders. There may be resistance to this from legislators who are worried about being seen as "soft on crime." However, if a more juvenile-like rehabilitative approach proves to be more effective than the adult retributive approach in reducing the re-offending of young offenders that would be in the interest of taxpayers (lower cost), young persons (constructive futures), and a safer society at large.

II.4. PREVENTION AND INTERVENTION OUTSIDE OF THE JUSTICE SYSTEM

One of the recent advances in criminology and public health is the advent and evaluation of programs to prevent conduct problems and delinquency, or to intervene once conduct problems become apparent. The major advantage of such programs tends to be that they are often implemented earlier than justice programs. The crucial question is whether programs outside of the justice system reduce the probability of delinquency and, particularly, the persistence of offending between adolescence and early adulthood (see Welsh et al., Chapter 9, this volume; Boendermaker, Deković, & Asscher, in press).

How effective are family-based programs during toddlerhood in reducing offending during the young adult years? Welsh and colleagues (Chapter 9) examined early childhood education in the context of home visits during pregnancy and infancy as part of a randomized experiment by Olds and colleagues to evaluate the Elmira (NY) Nurse Family Partnership program. At age 15, children of the higher risk mothers who received home visits incurred significantly fewer arrests than controls. A further follow-up at age 19 found that the daughters of mothers (but not their sons) who had received home visits incurred fewer arrests and convictions. In summary, there is tentative evidence of benefits of early interventions in childhood for preventing delinquency. However, it is not clear whether children who received early intervention committed fewer offenses during the adult years.

How effective are individually-based programs during childhood in reducing offending during the young adult years? The Perry Preschool Program in Ypsilanti, Michigan, shows that an early cognitively-based intellectual enrichment program can have long-term beneficial effects. Children were randomly assigned either to receive the program at ages three and four or to be in a control group. A long-term follow-up showed that, at age 19, the experimental group was less likely to have been arrested, and more likely to be employed and to have graduated from high school (Berrueta-Clement et al., 1984). By age 27, the experimental group had only half as many arrests as the controls (Schweinhart & Weikart, 1993).

Similarly, the Child-Parent Center (CPC) in Chicago provides disadvantaged children, aged 3–4, with a high-quality, active learning preschool supplemented by family support. A controlled evaluation of the program showed that, up to age 18, the CPC children were significantly less likely to be arrested, both for any offense and for violence (Reynolds et al., 2001). Up to age 24, the CPC children had significantly lower rates of felony arrest and incarceration, both of which are likely to have occurred in the young adult years (Reynolds et al., 2007).

In the Carolina Abercedarian Project, children aged 3 were randomly assigned either to receive full-time preschool childcare (focusing on the development of cognitive and language skills) or to be in a control group. Up to age 21, significantly fewer of the experimental children were convicted, and fewer were regular marijuana users.

In summary, the best programs of early interventions during childhood that included nontreatment controls have yielded reductions in offending that extended into adulthood.

How effective are school-based interventions in reducing young adult offending? Welsh and colleagues (Chapter 9, this volume) highlighted results from the Seattle Social Development Project (SSDP), which combined parent training, teacher training, and skills training for children, beginning at age 6. At age 27, the intervention group scored significantly better on educational and economic attainment, mental health, and sexual health, but not on substance abuse or offending (Hawkins et al., 2008).

In the Montreal Longitudinal-Experimental Study, aggressive/hyperactive boys age 6 were randomly assigned either to receive social skills training with their parents receiving management training or to be in a control group. In a follow-up to age 24, Boisjoli et al. (2007) found that the experimental boys were less likely to have a criminal record than the control boys (22% compared to 33%).

Welsh and colleagues (Chapter 9) also cited evidence that the Good Behavior Game (GBG) has long-term desirable effects on offending. This uses a classroom behavior management strategy that is designed to foster learning by teaching children to regulate their own and their classmates' behavior. In an experiment in Baltimore, first-grade students were randomly assigned either to the GBG or to a control condition. A long-term follow-up to ages 19–21 showed that GBG participants had less violent and criminal behavior and fewer drug abuse/dependence disorders (Petras et al., 2008).

In summary, some but not all of the school-based interventions have led to a reduction in offending even during the transition between adolescence and early adulthood. Replication of the best programs is much needed.

How effective are interventions with older juvenile delinquents (ages 14–17) in preventing continuation into young adult offending? Welsh and colleagues (Chapter 9, this volume) pointed out that there is good evidence that Multisystemic Therapy (MST) is effective in preventing later offending. In a long-term follow-up between ages 14 and 28 of a randomized experiment, Schaeffer and Borduin (2005) found that MST participants had lower recidivism rates (50% versus 81%), including lower rates of rearrest for violent offenses (14% versus 30%). MST participants also had 57% fewer days of confinement in adult detention facilities.

Similarly, a long-term follow-up between ages 15 and 22 of an experiment on Functional Family Therapy (FFT) showed that it was effective in preventing continuation into young adult offending (Gordon et al., 1995). Only 9% of FFT participants were rearrested compared with 41% of controls (who received probation services). Also, there is evidence from shorter-term follow-ups (from approximately ages 15 to 17) that Multidimensional Treatment Foster Care (MTFC) is effective in preventing re-offending (Eddy et al., 2004; Chamberlain et al., 2007).

Killias and colleagues (Chapter 10, this volume) review several meta-analyses of the effectiveness of European programs with juvenile and young adult offenders. They concluded that "reasoning and rehabilitation" is generally effective in decreasing recidivism by about 14% (Tong & Farrington, 2008). A meta-analysis of 17 European programs by Redondo, Sánchez-Meca, and Garrido (2003) found that recidivism was decreased by 18% overall, that educational and diversion programs were the most effective, and that the programs worked better with juveniles than with young adult offenders. A later meta-analysis of treatment programs for serious delinquents by Garrido, Angela, and Sánchez-Meca (2006) concluded that recidivism was decreased by 7% overall, and that cognitive-behavioral programs were the most effective.

Do early interventions lower the age-crime curve? One of the limitations of evaluation studies is the absence of yearly follow-ups of treated and nontreated individuals during adolescence and early adulthood. For that reason, published evaluation studies have not been able to show the degree to which interventions lowered the age-crime curve. To resolve this, Loeber and Stallings (2011) used longitudinal data from the PYS to simulate the impact of an intervention on the offending by at-risk youths. Simulation can be compared with asking the question "What if . . ." one aspect of the dataset were changed, what impact would that have on future offending? To address this, the authors modeled first the efficacy to screen for high-risk individuals and then to apply a treatment that "knocked out" youth who otherwise would have been at risk of committing serious delinquency. To identify high-risk boys a screening risk score was computed from data collected at the first assessment for each of the three cohorts at ages 7, 10, and 13, for the youngest, middle, and oldest cohorts, respectively (Loeber et al., 2008). This screening score included conduct problems and delinquency as reported by the boys and their parents and teachers. The intervention modeled was inspired by the best intervention programs available (Lipsey & Wilson, 1998), evaluated by the comparison of an experimental sample receiving the intervention versus a control sample not receiving the program (or receiving an alternative program). Loeber and Stallings (2011) took as a conservative criterion a success rate of 30%.

Figure 11.3 shows the comparison between the age-crime curve for serious delinquency without the "intervention" and the curve with the "intervention." The intervention was associated with a substantial reduction in serious delinquents by one-fifth to one-quarter (21.5% and 27.6% for the youngest and oldest cohort, respectively), especially from ages 11 to 21. Other results (not shown in Figure 11.3) indicate that the intervention was also associated with a decrease of 20% in the prevalence of arrest by the police, a 35% lower prevalence of homicide offenders and homicide victims, and a 29% reduction in the weeks of incarceration. Thus, the modeled intervention had a substantial benefit of lowering the age-crime curve by reducing the prevalence of self-reported serious offenders, officially recorded homicide offenders, and homicide victims during adolescence and early adulthood, and had benefits for the justice system by greatly reducing arrests and convictions.

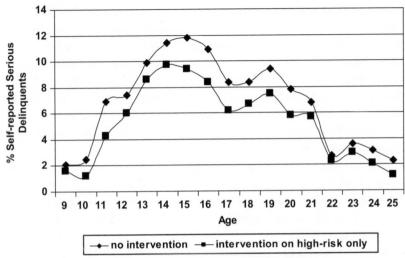

FIGURE 11.3 Age-crime curve of serious self-reported delinquency before and after simulated intervention on high-risk participants (PYS; youngest and oldest cohorts).
(Loeber & Stallings, 2011).

Summary of the interventions outside of the justice system. There are many intervention programs available outside of the justice system that reduce recidivism and prevent persistence of offending from adolescence into early adulthood. Preliminary results indicate that interventions may lower the age-crime curve. Much needed are programs for low intelligence youth to reduce their impulsivity (Koolhof et al., 2007).

How effective are labor market interventions in reducing young adult offending? Welsh et al. (Chapter 9, this volume) concluded that the nationwide Job Corps program, which is designed to improve the employability of at-risk youth aged 16–24, is effective in reducing offending and in improving educational attainment (Schochet et al., 2008). Similarly, the supported work program was effective in reducing offending and improving employment for ex-offenders over the age of 26 (Uggen, 2000). Killias and colleagues (Chapter 10, this volume) reported a recent large-scale employment experiment in Denmark that showed that increased control and training of unemployed persons caused a significant decrease in offending. Thus, there is substantial evidence that labor market interventions reduce offending during the transition between adolescence and early adulthood.

How effective is restorative justice in reducing young adult offending? Welsh and colleagues (Chapter 9, this volume) found one evaluation of restorative justice with a measure of offending in early adulthood. Bergseth and Bouffard (2007) compared restorative justice with traditional court processing. In a follow-up between ages 15 and 19, on average, referral to restorative justice predicted a slightly lower rate of re-offending.

Do programs have similar effects on juveniles and adults? If a program has similar effects on juveniles and adults, it is likely to have the same effect on young adults, even if it has not been evaluated with young adults specifically. Welsh and colleagues (Chapter 9, this volume) concluded that, generally, programs do have similar effects on juveniles and adults. This was true for cognitive-behavioral therapy (Landenberger & Lipsey, 2005), drug treatment programs (Mitchell et al., 2006), and sex offender treatment programs (Hanson et al. 2002). However, educational, vocational, and employment programs seemed to be more effective with adults than with juveniles, according to Welsh and colleagues; the review of European programs by Redondo et al. (2003) concluded that they were more effective with juveniles than with young adults.

What is known about the financial benefits and costs of different interventions that might reduce offending in the young adult years? Based on research conducted by the Washington State Institute for Public Policy (WSIPP), Welsh and colleagues (Chapter 9, this volume) concluded that the financial benefits of programs often outweigh their costs. This was true, for example, of MTFC ($8 saved per $1 expended), FFT ($10 saved per $1 expended), MST ($3 saved per $1 expended), vocational education in prison $12 saved per $1 expended), cognitive-behavioral therapy in prison ($22 saved per $1 expended), drug treatment in prison ($6 saved per $1 expended), and employment training in the community ($12 saved per $1 expended). Thus, it seems clear that many programs not only reduce offending in the young adult years but also save a lot of money in the long run.

What can be learned about scale enlargement of programs? Key to the introduction of effective programs, however, is scale enlargement in which a proven program is adopted at a regional, state, or national scale. Welsh et al. (2010) have discussed this in great detail, and they pointed out that some of the greatest challenges concern insufficient service infrastructure, greater population heterogeneity, and loss of program fidelity (see also Dodge, 2009). As Ogden and Amlund-Hagen (in press) show, the experience of introducing nationwide programs for young people to reduce recidivism in Norway may "serve as a model and inspiration for large-scale implementation of evidence-based practice combining 'top-down' and 'bottom-up' initiatives, both in the child and adolescent services and in the correctional system" (p. 11 in ms.). Implementation was facilitated by the perception of decision-makers that therapeutic approaches to the process of change appeared more effective than correctional sanctions administered by the justice system.

II.5. GENDER ISSUES

A substantial proportion of offenders are girls and women with problems and needs that often are different from those of boys and men. In addition, it is debatable to what extent delinquency careers and causes of delinquency are the same for each gender, and whether programs are equally effective for males and females. This section addresses several key questions on gender-related issues.

How do criminal career features vary with gender? It is widely known that crime rates in males are higher than in females. It is less well known, however, to what extent trajectories of criminal behavior in females are different from those in males. Piquero et al. (Chapter 2, this volume) concluded that usually the age-crime curve for girls peaks earlier than that for boys. However, gender differences in adolescent offending are relatively small at ages 14–15 (Moffitt, Caspi, Rutter, & Silva, 2001; Van der Laan & Blom, 2006). Persistence in crime is less likely in females compared to males. Blokland and Palmen (in press) also found that although the group of persistent female offenders is small, it seems that they were as criminally active as their male peers during late adolescence. Kempf-Leonard and colleagues (2001) reported that, similar to males, a small proportion of life-course female offenders account for a large proportion of adult crimes. Little is known about adult-onset female offenders and whether there are any markers of late onset that are present earlier in life.

Are different theories of criminal behavior needed for each gender? Thornberry and colleagues (Chapter 3, this volume) summarized the main theories about offending in the transition between adolescence and early adulthood. It was not until feminist criminologists began to criticize mainstream theories for focusing exclusively on male criminal behavior (Daly & Chesney-Lind, 1988) that scholars began to investigate potential explanations of gender differences in delinquency, referred to as the gender gap, and potential explanations of female delinquency. These feminist scholars argued for gender sensitive theories of crime (Miller & Mullins, 2009). However, others have stated that explanations of criminal behavior in males can be applied to females as well. For example, control theory argues that some females are more likely to engage in delinquency because they have weaker bonds to society and, according to labeling theory, because they have been informally labeled as delinquents by parents or teachers (Agnew, 2009). Unquestionably, there are gender differences in the prevalence of risk factors, but the key issue is whether there are gender differences in the strength of associations with offending. Moffitt et al. (2001) did the most extensive study of this by far and concluded that generally there are few gender differences in strength of associations.

Research on gender differences in risk factors for delinquency has been inconsistent. Several studies revealed that the same risk factors apply to boys as to girls (Junger-Tas, Ribeaud, & Cruyff, 2004; Moffitt et al., 2001), while others did find gender differences (Hay, 2003; Kroneman, Loeber, Hipwell, & Koot, 2009; Van de Rakt, Weerman, & Need, 2005). A recent European review of risk factors for female adolescents and young adults shows that many shared risk factors exist that explain delinquency in both males and females, but many unique factors that explain female delinquency have also been found (Wong, Slotboom, & Bijleveld, 2010). Females were more at risk for criminal behavior if they were affected by negative life events and physical abuse by parents. Moffitt et al. (2001) also reported that boys are more exposed to neurobiological risk factors that increase the risk of persistent offending. Moffitt et al. (2001) concluded that females mature slightly earlier than males and as a consequence girls may associate with older male peers. Peer influence may therefore explain the relatively early peak in delinquency in girls.

Comparing findings on risk factors for female delinquency in the United States and Europe, Wong et al. (2010) concluded that some findings from the United States could not be generalized to Europe. For example, a single parent family appeared to be a risk factor for female offending in the United States, but less consistently in Europe. It should be noted that the vast majority of European studies were cross-sectional and therefore further research is necessary to establish unique risk factors in females. Moreover, the authors did not compare female adolescents with female young adults, and therefore it is unclear whether unique female risk factors exist during the transition from adolescence to young adulthood.

Are genetic and biological influences the same for each gender? Hodgins, de Brito, Simonoff, and Viding (2009) in their review of neurological factors noted that the impact of explanatory factors in a person's environment on stable antisocial behavior differed by gender, with genetic factors being more important for girls, while antisocial behavior in boys was largely mediated by explanatory factors (D'Onofrio et al., 2007). However, the genetic and neurological transmission is far from clear. Whereas the MAOA gene has consistently been implicated in persistent male antisocial behavior and aggression, the results are inconsistent for females, and the same applies to the serotonin transporter (5-HTTPLR) and to low cortisol levels (Hodgins et al., 2009).

Do life events, life transitions, situational factors, and neighborhood factors have different effects on each gender? There is some evidence to suggest that life events and situational factors have different effects for males and females. For example, Horney et al.'s review (Chapter 4, this volume) shows that marriage has been associated with lower levels of crime in males. Some studies, however, found that the link between marriage and crime is weaker for females than for males (note that Theobald and Farrington, 2010, reported in the Cambridge Study in Delinquent Development that females, like males, decreased their offending after getting married). An explanation could be that women, more than men, are likelier to marry to a criminal partner (Bersani, Laub, & Nieuwbeerta, 2009) because there are more criminal men than criminal women (Farrington, Barnes, & Lambert, 1996). This is consistent with findings that stronger associations have been found between a deviant romantic partner and criminal behavior for females than for males (Horney et al., Chapter 4, this volume). Furthermore, stronger links have been found between parenthood and desistance from crime in females than in males. With regard to employment, there is some evidence to suggest that job satisfaction is more strongly associated with lower levels of criminal behavior in males than in females. However, findings on the relationship between employment and crime are not very consistent (Horney et al., Chapter 4). Finally, neighborhood factors may affect girls differently from boys (e.g., (Popkin et al., 2010).

Clearly, further investigation on gender differences in effects of contextual factors is needed, since prior research suggests that context changes may affect males and females differently (Horney et al., Chapter 4, this volume).

Are psychiatric disorders more common among young female than male offenders? The prevalence of mental illnesses among young females in the juvenile and adult justice system is higher than for males. This also applies to the prevalence of comorbid (co-occurring) conditions, which is higher among incarcerated females than males (see summary in, e.g., Hipwell & Loeber, 2006). However, studies are rare on the differential recidivism rates of males and females with one or more mental disorders. An exception is the study by McReynolds et al. (2010), which found a four-times higher recidivism rate for girls compared to boys with comorbid substance use and affective disorder who were referred to the Texas probation authorities.

How does the predictive accuracy of risk factors, needs, and protective factors vary with gender? Hoge and colleagues (Chapter 6, this volume) reviewed a range of screening devices to guide sentences, alternative referrals or placements, and release from institutions. They noted that screening devices often differ in their validity for each gender. Van der Put and colleagues (2011) analyzed potential gender differences in risk factors in adolescents (up to age 18) on re-offending within two years (up to age 20). They found that most static and dynamic risk factors were predictive of recidivism for both boys and girls. However, female-specific factors were found to be particularly prevalent in the family domain and concerned the following dynamic risk factors: parents with judicial contact, alcohol and/or drug abuse by parents, being a victim of abuse, and alcohol or drug abuse by the adolescent herself. Furthermore, problems in the family were found domain was found to accumulate more for girls. Family-related problems were serious and concerned abuse and court custody cases (Van der Put et al., 2011). To what extent gender differences exist in risk factors, needs, and protective factors during the transition to young adulthood is unknown. Hoge and colleagues (Chapter 6, this volume) concluded that, in general, more information about risk, needs, and protective factors associated with criminal activity during this transition period is required for both males and females. This also raises the question as to what extent instruments are accurate in assessing the risk of recidivism in females.

How effective is juvenile versus adult court treatment for each gender? Once girls are placed on probation—typically for status offenses, such as running away or liquor law violations—subsequent probation violations and minor misbehaviors tend to propel them toward confinement (Acoca, 1998; Chesney-Lind, 1997). Girls are far more likely than boys to be held in detention centers for minor offenses. When girls are placed in confinement, they are often subjected to further victimization in the form of emotional abuse, emotional distress from isolation, physical and sexual abuse, threats, and intimidation by staff.

Slotboom and Bijleveld (2007) interviewed women who were imprisoned and had children. The women reported many problems in relationships with other detainees, prison employees, loneliness, psychological problems, health problems and problems with health care. In addition, they were dissatisfied with their daily activities in prison and they had troubles with parenthood. Also, children of female detainees had problems, including low levels of general well-being, internalizing and externalizing problem behavior, a disturbed family life and neglect (Ezinga & Hissel, 2010). Thus, it appears that young mothers have many problems when they are imprisoned. Despite the existence of a few special facilities for this group, conditions for these women do not seem to show improvement over the years. In conclusion, much evaluation research remains to be done to show which interventions are effective for females in juvenile jails and in adult prisons.

Are interventions outside of the justice system differentially effective with each gender? Research has shown that gender specific interventions are rare and that studies on the effectiveness of regular interventions with females are scarce (Hipwell & Loeber, 2006; Zahn, Day, Mihalic, & Tichavsky, 2009). However, a recent meta-analysis concludes that generic types of program services (e.g., cognitive-behavior therapy, individual counseling, and the like) are about equally effective with males and females (Lipsey, 2009). Hipwell and Loeber (2006) show that there is some evidence to suggest that interventions specifically designed to address female delinquency and multimodal interventions can be effective for female adolescents.

Deković, Asscher, Slagt, and Boendermaker (in press) and Welsh et al. (Chapter 9, this volume) found a few differences in effects between males and females. In Deković et al.'s review of the international literature, they show that long-term effects of early and middle childhood prevention programs on young adults depend among other things on the characteristics of participants. The effects of the Good Behavior Game program were significantly larger for males than for females. Piquero et al. (2009) found that early intervention programs to improve self-control had, on average, a larger effect size for girls than boys. They also found that the average effect size for the reduction of delinquency was larger for females than males. In summary, there are inconsistent findings on the effects of treatment programs for each gender, and much research in this area is needed to ensure that interventions become more predictably applicable to either males or females.

II.6. ETHNICITY

There are many agreements and some misunderstandings about the importance of race/ethnicity in the transition between adolescence and early adulthood. For ease of exposition, we will focus on African-American and Caucasian young males. Studies show that African-American males show an earlier and higher peak in the age-crime curve than either African-American females or Caucasian males and females. Homicide offending and homicide victimization are much higher among African-American than Caucasian young males (Anderson & Smith, 2005; Fox & Zawitz, 2007).

Tracy and Kempf-Leonard (1996) have provided the most relevant information about continuity in offending from the juvenile to the adult years, using official records collected on over 27,000 individuals from the 1958 Philadelphia Birth Cohort followed up to age 26 (see Piquero et al., Chapter 2, this volume). African-American male delinquents (45%) were somewhat more likely to persist into adult offending than Caucasian males (37%) or Hispanic males (36%). African-American female delinquents (14%) were more likely to persist than Caucasian females (9%) or Hispanic females (5%). Also, African-American male nondelinquents (19%) were slightly more likely to have an adult-onset of offending than Hispanic males (17%) or Caucasian males (11%), and African-American female nondelinquents (4%) were slightly more likely to have an adult-onset of offending than Hispanic female nondelinquents (2%) or Caucasian female nondelinquents (1%). The probability of persisting in adult offending increased with the number of juvenile offenses regardless of race/ethnicity.

Race/ethnicity differences in offending might be explained by race/ethnicity differences in risk factors. Loeber and Farrington (2011) showed that African-American boys were more deprived than Caucasian boys on socioeconomic/demographic factors, such as a broken home, a family on welfare, a bad neighborhood, and a young mother. Other analyses of the PYS data have shown that, once other social and structural factors are taken into account, race does not predict violence (Loeber et al., 2011; see also Huizinga et al., 2006) or homicide offending (Loeber & Farrington, 2011).

Even though the prevalence of violence is much higher among African-American compared to Caucasian young males, screening instruments to assess the risk of recidivism are equally effective for the two ethnic groups (see Hoge et al., Chapter 6, this volume). The same applies to prevention and intervention programs (Welsh et al., Chapter 9, this volume). This is in sharp contrast to the justice system: African-American males at all levels of the legal system are overrepresented in arrest, conviction, and incarceration levels (see Howell et al., Chapter 8, this volume). This also means that more juvenile African-American male delinquents than Caucasian male delinquents end up in the criminal justice system. However, it is unclear how much of this difference reflects differences in offending and how much of it reflects differences in official processing.

Section III: The Headlines

We started out with Arnett's thesis that there is a period called "emerging adulthood" (Arnett, 2000) between adolescence and adulthood. We do not think that such a term is useful for future legal purposes because it will be difficult if not impossible to create a new terminology in legal statutes. On the other hand, in regard to offending the period between adolescence and early adulthood is unique in two ways. First, the number of juvenile and young adult offenders decreases with age as is evident from the down-slope of the age-crime curve, which usually does not flatten out until early adulthood. Second, the period between adolescence and early adulthood is unique in that, on average, juveniles' cognitive and behavioral maturation, as shown by their impulsivity and sensation-seeking, is not complete at ages 16, 17, or 18, the ages at which most states stipulate that adulthood starts. Thus, two major indicators of adulthood, that is, lowered offending and lowered impulsivity, do not map at all on current definitions of the minimum age of adulthood.

We posit that there is nothing magical about a legal calendar age of adulthood and that it is based on assumptions rather than on evidence. That young people tend to be more impulsive and that the majority grow out of this during early adulthood is well recognized by many commercial organizations, including car insurance and rental companies. It is perplexing why many politicians appear to ignore adolescents' naturally declining propensity to commit crime and naturally improving cognitive maturity. It is also remarkable that whereas many legislators promote changes in evidence-based and cost-effective policies in multiple areas of government, scientific findings about the intersection between the age-crime curve and juveniles' maturational development often are ignored in legislation and the practice of juvenile and adult law (Doreleijers & Fokkens, 2010).

Legislators and policy-makers can learn from research findings showing normative decreases in impulsivity and offending during adolescence and early adulthood, and that these changes do not map well on current legal statutes governing the point when juvenile justice ends and adult justice begins. This means that many young persons who engage in impulsive forms of offending are directed away from juvenile justice—with its emphasis on rehabilitation—to adult justice with its more punitive justice and longer sentences, resulting in longer periods of incarceration, usually without rehabilitative programs. The situation is especially dire for vulnerable young men and women, such as those with low intelligence who, compared to youth with higher intelligence, often take longer to mature cognitively and behaviorally. Another vulnerable category is offenders with serious mental health disorders. Keeping vulnerable and less-vulnerable young offenders in adult prisons beyond their propensity to offend is comparable to keeping patients with physical ailments in hospital beyond their time of recovery. Both examples are economically wasteful and unjust from a humanistic point of view.

There are two other reasons why more legislators and researchers should focus on young adulthood. First, this is a period in which a minority of the juvenile offenders will persist in their delinquency and become adult offenders. Second, another group will experience adult-onset offending. During this time some individuals may become violent, while others start engaging in "new" forms of crime such as fraud, trafficking in humans, identity theft, cyber-criminality, electronic forms of economic crimes, and prostitution.

There is no single "silver bullet" solution to the problems addressed in this volume. We have the following recommendations for a strategic plan for legislators, policy-makers, the judiciary, and other individuals working with juveniles in and outside the juvenile and adult courts:

- All sentencing decisions should take account of young adults' reduced competence to understand court proceedings and reduced culpability because of poor maturation. Thus, a "reduced competency" and a "reduced maturity" consideration should be applied when sentencing youth under current law.
- Transfer of juveniles to the jurisdiction of the adult court should not occur for youths of low intelligence and youths who are cognitively immature.
- Life without parole should be abolished for offenses committed during childhood, adolescence, and early adulthood.
- Four types of screening devices need to be routinely used in the court to optimize fair decision-making, including decision-making for vulnerable populations of youth:
  - Screening devices to ascertain juvenile offenders' risk of recidivism.
  - Screening instruments to assess young people's competence to stand trial.
  - Screening instruments to assess young people's mental health.
  - Screening instruments to assess young people's cognitive immaturity (this category of assessment tools is currently in greatest need of being validated).
- Drug- and alcohol-using juvenile offenders should be routinely referred to a Drug Court and drug treatment and not processed in the regular juvenile courts.
- Given the fluidity of youths' cognitive and emotional maturity, we strongly urge elimination of arbitrary definitions of age of adulthood in the justice system and that serious consideration be given to establishing Young Offender Courts for youth between ages 18 and 25, modeled after the cited British examples. Once the most practical and effective models are identified, these should be established in every major U.S. city and thus obviate the need for transfer laws.
- It is not widely recognized that self-control (as the opposite of impulsivity) is malleable and can be acquired through systematic training (see, e.g., Piquero et al., 2010). There are many proven intervention programs outside of the justice system that show that self-control is malleable and that the programs can improve self-control. Thus, it appears that maturation processes can be accelerated and that youth with delayed maturation can "catch up." The programs can be applied at different youthful ages, certainly prior to the minimum age of criminal responsibility, which is on average age 12, although this varies from state to state (Loeber & Farrington, 2001).

- Thus, the adult justice system should be a last, rather than a first, resort to deal with impulsive juveniles and young adults.

Based on what has been documented in this volume, we advocate a three-pronged approach to achieve necessary improvements. First, we advocate interventions with impulsive youth at a young age, well before contact with the justice system. We believe that the benefits of reduced impulsivity and improved self-control by young people go way beyond offending and include many other positive outcomes as well (e.g., academic achievements, contacts with peers and parents, intimate relations).

Second, we call for justice programs in each state to use the knowledge amassed by scholars in this volume and elsewhere to investigate how justice can be applied more fairly on the basis of what is known about youngsters' maturational development, and reduce unnecessarily severe and long sanctions for those whose offending is likely to diminish or cease soon.

Third, we advocate a forward-looking administrative model in both the juvenile and adult criminal justice systems that bases program placements and supervision levels upon objective risk and needs assessments, and supports individualized case management plans focused on improving future behavior, rather than punishing past behavior. Use of this forward-looking administrative framework and advanced management tools should increase the capacity of state juvenile justice systems to more effectively control and rehabilitate adolescents on the verge or at high risk of becoming transition offenders (Howell and colleagues, Chapter 9, this volume).

We conclude that young adult offenders aged 18–24 are more similar to juveniles than to adults with respect to features such as their executive functioning, impulse control, malleability, responsibility, susceptibility to peer influence, and adjudicative competence. Therefore, we make the following policy recommendations (some of which are alternatives):

1. Changes in legislation are warranted to prevent large numbers of juvenile offenders becoming adult criminals. We recommend raising the minimum age for referral of young people to the adult court to age 21 or 24 so that fewer young offenders are dealt with in the adult criminal justice system. There are several advantages: fewer young offenders will be incarcerated, fewer of them will be exposed to the criminogenic influences of incarceration, and more of them can receive alternative, noncustodial, and rehabilitative sanctions. We expect that, consequently, the number of adult prisoners will decrease and considerable savings for taxpayers will accrue. To prompt legislative change, we recommend cost-benefit analyses to quantify the benefits of legally raising the minimum age of adult jurisdiction to 21 or 24. Such cost-benefit analyses have been executed abroad but not yet in the United States, although there have been cost-benefit analyses in the United States of the effects of raising the minimum age from 16 to 18 (Henrichson and Levshin, 2011). As mentioned, an English report concluded that 'diversion from trial under adult law to trial under juvenile law following maturity assessment is likely

to produce cost saving to society . . .' of £420 per offender (Barrow Cadbury Trust, 2009, p. 3). More analyses are needed to quantify the monetary costs and benefits of legally raising the age of juvenile jurisdiction to age 21 or 24, which is our favored recommendation.

2. Alternatively, special courts for young adult offenders aged 18–24 could be established on an experimental basis in a small number of areas (building on the experience of the United Kingdom Transition to Adulthood Alliance: see www.t2a.org.uk). Three reasons support creating special courts for young adult offenders: (i) preventing excessive punishment of young people who land in the adult justice system; (ii) youthfulness as a mitigating factor; and (iii) the developmental needs of young people. The focus should be on rehabilitation rather than retribution. Since juveniles who are transferred to adult courts tend to receive more severe sentences and tend to have higher recidivism rates than those in juvenile courts, we expect that these special courts would decrease recidivism and decrease incarceration, and consequently save taxpayer money. In addition, they should be designed to have fewer ongoing stigmatizing effects than the adult criminal courts.

3. A third option is to set up special correctional facilities for young adult offenders and include programs such as cognitive-behavioral therapy, drug treatment, restorative justice, mentoring, education and vocational training, and work release. In most states, a juvenile court may continue to exercise dispositional jurisdiction over an adjudicated youth until the youth reaches the twenty-first birthday, and some states (e.g., Pennsylvania) have separate correctional institutions for young adult offenders. The California Department of Juvenile Justice continues to have jurisdiction over juveniles until the twenty-fifth birthday (Transition to Adulthood Alliance, 2010). Most research shows that there is no evidence that either longer sentences or lengthening the period of incarceration provides benefits in terms of reducing the recidivism of serious offenders.

4. There could be a 'reduced maturity consideration' for young adult offenders: a decrease in the severity of penalties that takes account of young persons' lesser culpability and diminished responsibility. Along that line, death sentences and life without parole sentences should be abolished for young adult offenders.

5. There should be risk/needs assessments and screening of young adult offenders to guide the selection of appropriate dispositions and interventions. This screening should assess topics such as executive functioning and impulse control, in addition to risk factors such as low intelligence. Young adult offenders with substance use problems should be diverted to drug courts, and those with mental health problems should be dealt with by mental health professionals.

6. There should be evidence-based programs for young adult offenders in the community and after release, including multisystemic therapy, cognitive-behavioral therapy, drug treatment, restorative justice, mentoring, educational

and vocational training programs, and programs such as Communities That Care (see Farrington and Welsh, 2007). Employment and relationship programs should be offered to encourage desistance, as well as other programs aimed at reducing disorderly transitions such as not graduating from high school and single teenage parenthood. Other useful programs are those aiming to reduce opportunities for offending, such as 'hot spots policing' and situational crime prevention, and reducing gang membership and drug dealing (especially targeted on high-crime neighborhoods). In addition, in light of the long-term positive effects of early nurse home-visiting, parent training, and family-based programs, these also should be more widely implemented and followed up to assess their effects on young adult offending.

In summary, all of these initiatives should be rigorously evaluated, in randomized experiments or high-quality quasi-experimental studies, and cost-benefit analyses should be carried out. Age, gender, and racial/ethnic differences in the effectiveness of programs should be studied.

We urge the U.S. federal government to develop an action plan to implement the key recommendations in this volume to assist states in changing their statutes and practices so that justice is applied more fairly and with more knowledge of how youth develop into mature adults. We believe that, in efforts to effect improvements in the safety of citizens and communities, our approach offers more hope and more benefits than does the implementation of longer sentencing of young people in the adult justice system. The litmus test will be whether concerted preventive and remedial interventions in and outside of the justice system can lower and shrink the age-crime curve for future generations of young people.

Notes

1. The average number of offenders per offense decreased steadily with age from age 10 onwards.

2. Stouthamer-Loeber (2010) also found that out of the PYS's youngest cohort only 2.8% of the young males continued to offend (defined as moderate to serious forms of delinquency) from late childhood (ages 10–12) into early adulthood; and only a slightly higher percentage (3.6%) continued to offend from early adolescence (ages 13–15) to early adulthood. Thus, relatively few young males were childhood-onset delinquents who persisted in their offending into adulthood, and about the same percentage became adolescent-onset offenders who also persisted into adulthood. Thus, only small numbers of young males could be characterized as "life-course" persisters, at least into early adulthood.

3. In contrast, several protective factors (such as parents' good supervision and the youth's high perceived likelihood of getting caught when delinquent) measured at middle childhood (ages 7–9), late childhood (ages 10–12), or early adolescence (ages 13–16) predicted desistance during early adolescence (ages 13–16) and/or late adolescence (ages 17–19) (Stouthamer et al., 2008, Table 9.7). The results are at variance with an earlier report on the same data showing that desistance in early adulthood from *persisting* offending up to age 19 was predicted by several protective (called promotive) factors, including

low physical aggression, the youth's high perceived likelihood of getting caught when delinquent, and having many skills for getting a job (Stouthamer-Loeber, Wei, Loeber, & Masten, 2004).

4. As of March 17, 2011, the recommended change died in the finance committee, due to the high price tag that would come with the proposed change.

References

Acoca, L. (1998). Outside/inside: The violation of American girls at home, on the streets, and in the juvenile justice system. *Crime and Delinquency*, 44, 561–589.

Agnew, R. (2009). The contribution of mainstream theories to the explanation of female delinquency. In M. Zahn (Ed.), *The delinquent girl* (pp. 7–29). Philadelphia, PA: Temple University Press.

Allen, R. (2012). Young adults and the English criminal justice system: the policy challenges. In F. Lösel, A. Bottoms & D.P. Farrington (Eds.), *Young Adult Offenders: Lost in Transition* (pp. 156–170). London: Routledge.

American Psychiatric Association (1994). *Diagnostic and statistical manual of mental disorders* (4th ed.). Washington, DC: American Psychiatric Association.

American Psychiatric Association (2005). *Diagnostic and statistical manual of mental disorders* (4th ed., text revision). Washington, DC: American Psychiatric Association.

Anderson, R.N., & Smith, B.L. (2002). Deaths: Leading causes for 2002. *National Vital Statistics Report*, 53, 1–92.

Arnett, J.J. (2000). Emerging adulthood: A theory of development from the late teens through the twenties. *American Psychologist*, 55, 469–480.

Averdijk, M., Elffers, H., & Ruiter, S. (in press). Disentangling context effects on criminal careers during adolescence and into early adulthood. In R. Loeber, M. Hoeve, N.W. Slot, & P. van der Laan (Eds.), *Persisters and desisters in crime from adolescence into adulthood: Explanation, prevention and punishment*. Aldershot UK: Ashgate.

Baer, D., Bhati, A., Brooks, L., Castro, J., La Vigne, N., Mallik-Kane, K., Naser, R. Osborne, J., Roman, C., Roman, J., Rossman, S., Solomon, A., Visher, C., & Winterfield, L., (2006). *Understanding the challenges of prisoner reentry: Research findings from the urban institute's prisoner reentry portfolio*. Washington, DC: Justice Policy Center.

Barrow Cadbury Trust (2005). *Lost in transition*. London: Author.

Barrow Cadbury Trust (2009). *Economic analysis of interventions for young adult offenders*. London: Author.

Barrow Cadbury Trust and International Center for Prison Studies. (2011). *Young adults and criminal justice: International Norms and Practices*. London, UK: Author.

Bergseth, K.J., & Bouffard, J.A. (2007). The long-term impact of restorative justice programming for juvenile offenders. *Journal of Criminal Justice*, 35, 433–451.

Bernburg, J.G., & Krohn, M.D. (2003). Labeling, life chances, and adult crime: The direct and indirect effects of official intervention in adolescence on crime in early adulthood. *Criminology*, 41, 1287–1318.

Berrueta-Clement, J.R., Schweinhart, L.J., Barnett, W.S., Epstein, A.S., & Weikart, D.P. (1984). *Changed lives: The effects of the Perry Preschool Program on youths through age 19*. Ypsilanti, MI: High/Scope Educational Research Foundation.

Bersani, B.E., Laub, J.H., & Nieuwbeerta, P. (2009). Marriage and desistance from crime in the Netherlands: Do gender and socio-historical context matter? *Journal of Quantitative Criminology*, 25, 3–24.

Bijleveld, C., van der Geest, V., & Hendriks, J. (in press). Vulnerable youth on pathways to adulthood. In R. Loeber, M. Hoeve, N.W. Slot, & P. van der Laan (Eds.) *Persisters and desisters in crime from adolescence into adulthood: Explanation, prevention and punishment*. Aldershot UK: Ashgate.

Bishop, D.M., & Frazier, C.E. (2000). Consequences of transfer. In J. Fagan, & F.E. Zimring (Eds.), *The changing borders of juvenile justice: Transfer of adolescents to the criminal court* (pp. 227–276). Chicago IL: University of Chicago Press.

Blackburn, R. (1993). Psychopathic disorder, personality disorders and aggression. In C. Thompson, & P. Cowen (Eds.), *Violence, basic and clinical science* (pp. 101–118). Oxford: Butterworth Heinemann.

Blokland, A.A.J., & Palmen, H. (in press). Criminal career patterns from adolescence to early adulthood. In R. Loeber, M. Hoeve, N.W. Slot, and P. van der Laan (Eds.), *Persisters and desisters in crime from adolescence into adulthood: Explanation, prevention and punishment*. Aldershot UK: Ashgate.

Blumstein, A., Cohen, J., Roth, J.A., & Visher, C.A. (1986). *Criminal careers and "career criminals."* Washington, DC: National Academy Press.

Boendermaker, L., Dekovic, M., & Asscher, J.J. (in press). Intervention. In R. Loeber, M. Hoeve, N.W. Slot, & P. van der Laan (Eds.), *Persisters and desisters in crime from adolescence into adulthood: Explanation, prevention and punishment*. Aldershot: Ashgate.

Boisjoli, R., Vitaro, F., LaCourse, E., Barker, E.D., & Tremblay, R.E. (2007). Impact and clinical significance of a preventive intervention for disruptive boys: A 15-year follow-up. *British Journal of Psychiatry*, 191, 415–419.

Bosick, J.S. (2009). Crime and the transition to adulthood: A person-centered analysis of at-risk boys coming of age in 1940s Boston, 1970s London, and 1990s Pittsburgh. Unpublished Ph.D. dissertation, Harvard University, Cambridge, MA.

Bosick, S.J. (2009). Operationalizing crime over the life course. *Crime and Delinquency*, 55, 472–496.

Brown, J.M., & Langan, P.A. (1998). *State court sentencing of convicted felons, 1994*. Washington, D.C.: U.S. Department of Justice, Bureau of Justice Statistics.

Bushway, S., & Reuter, P. (2002). Labor markets and crime risk factors. In L. Sherman, D. Farrington, B. Welsh, & D. MacKenzie (Eds.), *Evidence-based crime prevention* (pp. 198–240). New York: Routledge.

Capaldi, D.M., & Stoolmiller, M. (1999). Co-occurrence of conduct problems and depressive symptoms in early adolescent boys: III. Prediction to young-adult adjustment. *Development and Psychopathology*, 11, 59–84.

Chamberlain, P., Leve, L.D., & DeGarmo, D.S. (2007). Multidimensional treatment foster care for girls in the juvenile justice system: 2-year follow-up of a randomized clinical trial. *Journal of Consulting and Clinical Psychology*, 75, 187–193.

Chassin, L., Dmitrieva, J., Modecki, K., Steinberg, L., Cauffman, E., Piquero, A.R., Knight, G.P., & Losoya, S.H. (2010). Does adolescent alcohol and marijuana use predict suppressed growth psychosocial maturity among male juvenile offenders? *Psychology of Addictive Behaviors*, 24, 48–60.

Chesney-Lind, M. (1997). *The female offender: Girls, women, and crime*. Thousand Oaks, CA: Sage

Childs, K.K., Sullivan, C.J., & Culledge, L.M. (2010). Delinquent behavior across adolescence: Investigating the shifting salience of key criminological predictors. *Deviant Behavior*, 32, 64–100.

Courtney, M.E. (2009). The difficult transition to adulthood for foster youth in the U.S.: Implications for the state as corporate parent. *Social Policy Report*, 23, 3–18.

Cuellar, A.E., McReynolds, L.S., & Wasserman, G.A. (2006). A cure for crime: Can mental health treatment diversion reduce crime among youth? *Journal of Policy Analysis and Management*, 25, 197–214.

Daly, K., & Chesney-Lind, M. (1988). Feminism and criminology. *Justice Quarterly*, 5, 497–538.

Dekovic, M., Asscher, J.J., Slagt, M.I., & Boendermaker, L. (in press). Prevention programmes in early and middle childhood and their effect on adult crime. In R. Loeber, M. Hoeve, N.W. Slot, & P. van der Laan (Eds.), *Persisters and desisters in crime from adolescence into adulthood: Explanation, prevention and punishment*. Aldershot: Ashgate.

De Brito, S. A., Mechelli, A., Wilke, M., Laurens, K.R., Jones, A.P., Barker, G.J., Hodgins, S., & Viding, E. (2009). Size matters: Increased grey matter in boys with conduct problems and callous-unemotional traits. *Brain: A Journal of Neurology*, 132, 843–852.

Dodge, K.A. (2009). Community intervention and public policy in the prevention of antisocial behavior. *Journal of Child Psychology and Psychiatry*, 50, 194–200.

D'Onfrio, B.M., Slutske, W.S., Turkheimer, E., Emery, R.E., Harden, K.P., Heath, A.C., Madden, P.A.F., & Martin, N.G. (2007). Intergenerational transmission of childhood conduct problems: A children of twins study. *Archives of General Psychiatry*, 64, 820–829.

Doreleijers, T., & Fokkens, J.W. (2010). Inderjarigen en jongvolwassenen: Pleidooi voor een evidence based strafrecht. *Rechtsreeks*, 2, 1–47.

Dunkel, F. & Pruin, I. (2012). Young adult offenders in juvenile and criminal justice systems in Europe. In F. Lösel, A. Bottoms, & D.P. Farrington (Eds.), *Young adult offenders: Lost in transition* (pp. 11–38). London: Routledge.

Eddy, J.M., Whaley, R.B., & Chamberlain, P. (2004). The prevention of violent behavior by chronic and serious male juvenile offenders: A 2-year follow-up of a randomized clinical trial. *Journal of Emotional and Behavioral Disorders*, 12, 2–8.

Elliott, D.S., Pampel, F., & Huizinga, D. (2004). *Youth violence: Continuity and desistance. A supplemental report to Youth Violence: A report of the Surgeon General*. Boulder, CO: Center for the Study and Prevention of Violence, Institute of Behavior Science, University of Colorado.

Ezinga, M., & Hissel, S. (2010). *Wellbeing and behavior of the children of incarcerated mothers*. Paper presented at the annual meeting of the American Society of Criminology, San Francisco, CA.

Fabio, A., Cohen, J., & Loeber, R. (2011). Neighborhood socioeconomic disadvantage and the shape of the age-crime curve. *American Journal of Public Health*, Dec; 101 Suppl 1:S325–32. Epub 2011 Jul 21.

Farrington, D.P. (1986). Age and crime. In M. Tonry, & N. Morris (Eds.), *Crime and justice: An annual review of research* (Vol. 7, pp. 189–250). Chicago IL: University of Chicago Press.

Farrington, D.P. (1997). A critical analysis of research on the development of antisocial behavior from birth to adulthood. In D.M. Stoff, J. Breiling, & J.D. Maser (Eds.), *Handbook of antisocial behavior* (pp. 234–240). New York: Wiley.

Farrington, D.P. (2003). Key results from the first 40 years of the Cambridge Study in Delinquent Development. In T.P. Thornberry, & M.D. Krohn (Eds.), *Taking stock of delinquency: An overview of findings from contemporary longitudinal studies* (pp. 137–183). New York: Kluwer-Plenum.

Farrington, D.P. (2012). Childhood risk factors for young adult offending: Onset and persistence. In F. Lösel, A. Bottoms, & D.P. Farrington (Eds.), *Young adult offenders: Lost in transition* (pp. 48–64). London: Routledge.

Farrington, D.P., Barnes, G.C., & Lambert, S. (1996). The concentration of offending in families. *Legal and Criminological Psychology*, 1, 47–63.

Farrington, D.P., Coid, J.W., Harnett, L.M., Jolliffe, D., Soteriou, N., Turner, R.E., & West, D.J. (2006). *Criminal careers up to age 50 and life success up to age 48: New findings from the Cambridge Study in Delinquent Development*. London: Home Office (Research Study No. 299).

Farrington, D.P., Gallagher, B., Morley, L., St Ledger, R.J., & West, D.J. (1986) Unemployment, school leaving and crime. *British Journal of Criminology*, 26, 335–356.

Farrington, D.P., & Hawkins, J.D. (1991). Predicting participation, early onset and later persistence in officially recorded offending. *Criminal Behaviour and Mental Health*, 1, 1–33.

Farrington, D.P., & Welsh, B.C. (2007). *Saving children from a life of crime: Early risk factors and effective interventions*. New York: Oxford University Press.

Fazel, S., Lichtenstein, P., Grann, M., Goodwin, G.M., & Langström, N. (2010). Bipolar disorder and violent crime: New evidence from population-based longitudinal studies and systematic review. *Archives of General Psychiatry*, 67, 931–938.

Feld, B. (2000). *Cases and materials on juvenile justice administration*. New York: West Group.

Feld, B. (2008). A slower form of death: Implications of Roper v. Simmons for juveniles sentenced to life without parole. *Notre Dame Journal of Law Ethics and Public Policy*, 9, 26–40.

Fontaine, N., Carbonneau, R., Vitaro, F., & Barker, E.D. (2009). Research review: A critical review of studies on the development trajectories of antisocial behavior in females. *Journal of Child Psychology and Psychiatry*, 50, 363–385.

Foss, R. (2002). Liscensing. Translating Injury Prevention Research into Action: A Strategic Workshop, Dallas, Texas (February 1).

Foster, M.E., Flanagan, C., Osgood, D.W., & Ruth, G.R. (2005). The transition to adulthood for vulnerable youths and families: Common themes and future directions. In D.W. Osgood, M.E., Foster, C. Flanagan, & G.R. Ruth (Eds.), *On your own without a net: The transition to adulthood for vulnerable populations* (pp. 375–409). Chicago IL: University of Chicago Press.

Fox, J.A. & Zawitz, M.W. (2001). *Homicide trends in the United States*. Washington, DC: US Bureau of Justice Statistics.

Ge, X., Conger, R.D., & Elder, G.H. (2001). Pubertal transition, stressful life events, and the emergence of gender differences in adolescent depressive symptoms. *Developmental Psychology*, 37, 404–417.

Giedd, J.N. (2004). Structural magnetic resonance imaging of the adolescent brain. *Annals of the New York Academy of Sciences*, 1021, 77–85.

Giedd, J.N., Rumsey, J.M., Castellanos, F.X., Rajapakse, J.C., Kaysen, D., Vaituzis, A.C., Vauss, Y.C., Hamburger, S.D., & Rapoport, J.L. (1996). A quantitative MRI study of the corpus callosum in children and adolescents. *Developmental Brain Research*, 91, 274–280.

Giordano, P.C., Cernkovich, S.A., & Rudolph, J.L. (2002). Gender, crime, and desistance: Toward a theory of cognitive transformation. *American Journal of Sociology*, 107, 990–1064.

Gordon, D.A., Graves, K., & Arbuthnot, J. (1995). The effect of functional family therapy for delinquents on adult criminal behavior. *Criminal Justice and Behavior*, 22, 60–73.

Gottfredson, M.R., & Hirschi, T. (1990). *A general theory of crime.* Stanford, CA: Stanford University Press.

Grisso, T., Steinberg, L., Woolard, J., Cauffman, E., Scott, E., Graham, S., Lexcan, F., Reppucci, N.D., & Schwartz, R. (2003). Juveniles' competence to stand trial: A comparison of adolescents' and adults' capacities as trial defendants. *Law and Human Behavior*, 27, 333–363.

Hagan, J., & McCarthy, B. (2005). Homeless youth and the perilous passage to adulthood. In D.W. Osgood, E.M. Foster, C. Flanagan, & G.R. Ruth (Eds.), *On your own without a net: The transition to adulthood for vulnerable populations* (pp. 178–201). Chicago, IL: University of Chicago Press.

Hanson, R.K., Gordon, A., Marques, J.K., Murphy, W., Quinsey, V.L., & Seto, M.C. (2002). First report of the collaborative outcome data project on the effectiveness of psychological treatment for sex offenders. *Sexual Abuse*, 14, 169–194.

Hawkins, J.D., Brown, E.C., Oesterle, S., Arthur, M.W., Abbott, R.D., & Catalano, R.F. (2008). Early effects of communities that care on targeted risks and initiation of delinquent behavior and substance abuse. *Journal of Adolescent Health*, 43, 15–22.

Hay, C. (2003). Family strain, gender, and delinquency. *Sociological Perspectives*, 46, 107–135.

Hayford, S.R., & Furstenberg, F.F. (2008). Delayed adulthood, delayed desistance? Trends in the age distribution of problem behaviors. *Journal of Research on Adolescence*, 18, 285–304.

Heide, K.M. (1999). *Young killers: The challenge of juvenile homicide.* Thousand Oaks, CA: Sage.

Helyar-Cardwell, V. (2009a). *A new start: Young adults in the criminal justice system.* London: Transition to Adulthood Alliance.

Helyar-Cardwell, V. (2009b). *Young adult manifesto.* London: Transition to Adulthood Alliance.

Henggeler, S.W., Cunningham, P.B., Pickrel, S.G., Schoenwald, S.K., & Brondino, M.J. (1996). Multisystemic therapy: An effective violence prevention approach for serious juvenile offenders. *Journal of Adolescence*, 19, 47–61.

Henrichson, C., & Levshin, V. (2011). *Cost-benefit analysis of raising the age of juvenile court jurisdiction in North Carolina.* New York: Vera Institute of Justice.

Hipwell, A.E., & Loeber, R. (2006). Do we know which interventions are effective for disruptive and delinquent girls? *Clinical Child and Family Psychology Review*, 9, 221–255.

Hodgins, S., De Brito, S.A., Chhabra, P., & Coté, G. (2010). Anxiety disorders among offenders with antisocial personality disorders: A distinct subtype? *Canadian Journal of Psychiatry*, 55, 784–791.

Hodgins, S., de Brito, S., Simonoff, E., Vloet, T., & Viding, E. (2009). Getting the phenotypes right: An essential ingredient for understanding aetiological mechanisms underlying persistent violence and developing effective treatments. *Frontiers of Behavioral Neuroscience*, 3. doi:10.3389/neuro.08.044.2009.

Hoge, R., & Andrews, D. (2010). *Evaluation for risk of violence in juveniles.* New York: Oxford University Press.

Howell, J.C. (2009). *Preventing and reducing juvenile delinquency: A comprehensive framework* (2nd ed.). Thousand Oaks, CA: Sage.

Howell, J.C. (2011). *Understanding and combating gangs in America.* Thousand Oaks, CA: Sage.

Hucker, S.J. (1997). Impulsivity in DSM-IV impulse-control disorders. In C.D. Webster, & M.A. Jackson (Eds.), *Impulsivity: Theory, assessment, and treatment* (pp. 195–311). New York: Guilford Press.

Huizinga, D., & Henry, K.L. (2008). The effect of arrest and justice system sanctions on subsequent behavior: Findings from longitudinal and other studies. In A. Liberman (Ed.), *The long view of crime: A synthesis of longitudinal research* (pp. 220–254). New York: Springer.

Huizinga, D., Thornberry, T.P., Knight, K.E., Lovegrove, P.J., Loeber, R., Hill, K., & Farrington, D.P. (2006). *Disproportionate minority contact in the juvenile justice system: A study of differential minority arrest/referral to court in three cities.* Report to the Office of Juvenile Justice and Delinquency Prevention. Access: http://www.ncjrs.gov/pdffiles1/ojjdp/grants/219743.pdf

Hussong, A.M., Curran, P.J., Moffitt, T.E., Caspi, A., & Carrig, M.M. (2004). Substance abuse hinders desistance in young adults' antisocial behavior. *Development and Psychopathology, 16,* 1029–1046.

Jolliffe, D., & Farrington, D.P. (2009). A systematic review of the relationship between childhood impulsiveness and later violence. In M. McMurran, & R. Howard (Eds.), *Personality, personality disorder, and violence* (pp. 41–62). New York: Wiley.

Jolliffe, D., & Farrington, D.P. (2010). Individual differences and offending. In E. McLaughlin, & T. Newburn (Eds.), *The Sage handbook of criminological theory* (pp. 40–55). Thousand Oaks, CA: Sage.

Joyal, C.C., Dubreucq, J-L., Gendron, C., & Millaud, F. (2007). Major mental disorders and violence: A critical update. *Current Psychiatry Reviews, 3,* 33–50.

Junger-Tas, J., Ribeaud, D., & Cruyff, M.J.L.F. (2004). Juvenile delinquency and gender. *European Journal of Criminology, 1,* 333–375.

Kazemian, L. & Farrington. D.P. (2006). Exploring residual career length and residual number of offenses for two generations of repeat offenders. *Journal of Research in Crime and Delinquency, 43,* 89–113.

Kazemian, L., & Farrington, D.P. (2010). The developmental evidence base: Desistance. In G.J. Towl, & D.A. Crighton (Eds.), *Forensic psychology* (pp. 133–147). New Jersey: Wiley Blackwell.

Kempf-Leonard, K., Tracy, P.E., & Howell, J.C. (2001). Serious, violent, and chronic juvenile offenders: The relationship of delinquency career types to adult criminality. *Justice Quarterly, 18,* 449–478.

Kerig, P.K., & Becker, S.P. (2010). From internalizing to externalizing: Theoretical models of the processes linking PTSD to juvenile delinquency. In S.J. Egan (Ed.), *Post-traumatic stress disorder (PTSD): Causes, symptoms, and treatment* (pp. 33–78). Hauppauge, NY: Nova Science.

Kershaw, C., Nicholas, S., & Walker, A. (2008). *Crime in England and Wales 2007/08.* London: Home Office. www.homeoffice.gov.uk/rds/pdfs08/hosb0708.pdf.

Killias, M., Aebi, M., & Ribeaud, D. (2000). Does community service rehabilitate better than short-term imprisonment? Results of a controlled experiment. *Howard Journal of Criminal Justice, 39,* 40–57.

King, R.D., Massoglia, M., & Macmillan, R. (2007). The context of marriage and crime: Gender, the propensity to marry, and offending in early adulthood. *Criminology, 45,* 33–65.

Koolhof, R., Loeber, R., Wei, E.H., Pardini, D., & Collot d'Escury, A. (2007). Inhibition deficits of serious delinquent boys of low intelligence. *Criminal Behaviour and Mental Health*, 17, 274–292.

Kraemer, H.C. (1992). Measurement of reliability for categorical data in medical research. *Statistical Methods in Medical Research*, 1, 183–199.

Kroneman, L.M., Loeber, R., Hipwell, A.E., & Koot, H.M. (2009). Girls' disruptive behavior and its relationship to family functioning: A review. *Journal of Child and Family Studies*, 18, 259–273.

Kupchik, A. (2006). *Prosecuting adolescents in adult and juvenile courts.* New York: New York University Press.

Kupchik, A. (2007). The correctional experiences of youth in adult and juvenile prisons. *Justice Quarterly*, 24, 247–270.

Kurlychek, M.C., & Johnson, B.D. (2004). The juvenile penalty: A comparison of juvenile and young adult sentencing outcomes in criminal courts. *Criminology*, 42, 485–517.

Kurlychek, M.C., & Johnson, B.D. (2010). Juvenality and punishment: Sentencing juveniles in adult criminal court. *Criminology*, 48, 725–758.

Le Blanc, M., & Fréchette, M. (1989). *Male criminal activity from childhood through youth: Multilevel and developmental perspectives.* New York: Springer.

Landenberger, N.A., & Lipsey, M.W. (2005). The positive effects of cognitive-behavioral programs for offenders: A meta-analysis of factors associated with effective treatment. *Journal of Experimental Criminology*, 1, 451–476.

Legal Action Center (2004). After prison: Roadblocks to re-entry. A report on state legal barriers facing people with criminal records. http://www.lac.org/lac/main.php?view=law&subaction=4.

Lewis, M.D., Granic, I., Lamm, C., Zelazo, P.D., Stieben, J., Todd, R.M., Moadab, I., & Pepler, D. (2008). Changes in the neural bases of emotion regulation associated with clinical improvement in children with behavior problems. *Development and Psychopathology*, 20, 913–939.

Lipsey, M.W. (2009). The primary factors that characterize effective interventions with juvenile offenders: A meta-analytic overview. *Victims and Offenders*, 4, 124–147.

Lipsey, M.W., & Cullen, F.T. (2007). The effectiveness of correctional rehabilitation: A review of systematic reviews. *Annual Review of Law and Social Science*, 3, 297–320.

Lipsey, M.W., & Wilson, D.B. (1998). Effective intervention for serious and violent juvenile offenders: A synthesis of research. In R. Loeber, & D.P. Farrington (Eds.), *Serious and violent juvenile offenders: Risk factors and effective interventions* (pp. 313–345). Thousand Oaks, CA: Sage.

Loeber, R., Burke, J.D., Lahey, B.B., Winters, A., & Zera, M. (2000). Oppositional defiant disorder and conduct disorder: A review of the past 10 years, part I. *Journal of the American Academy of Child & Adolescent Psychiatry*, 39, 1468–1484.

Loeber, R., & Dishion, T. (1983). Early predictors of male delinquency: A review. *Psychological Bulletin*, 94, 68–99.

Loeber, R., & Farrington, D.P. (Eds.) (1998). *Serious and violent juvenile offenders: Risk factors and successful interventions.* Thousand Oaks, CA: Sage.

Loeber, R., & Farrington, D.P. (Eds.) (2001). *Child Delinquents: Development, intervention and service needs.* Thousand Oaks, CA: Sage.

Loeber, R., & Farrington, D.P. (2011). *Risk factors, prediction, and prevention from childhood.* New York: Springer.

Loeber, R., Farrington, D.P., Stouthamer-Loeber, M., & White, H.R. (2008). *Violence and serious theft: Development and prediction from childhood to adulthood*. Mahwah, NJ: Lawrence Erlbaum.

Loeber, R., Hoeve, M., Slot, N.W., & van der Laan, P. (Eds.) (in press), *Persisters and desisters in crime from adolescence into adulthood: Explanation, prevention and punishment*. Aldershot UK: Ashgate.

Loeber, R., Menting, B., Lynam, D., Moffitt, T., Stouthamer-Loeber, M., Stallings, D., Farrington, D. P., & Pardini, D. (2011). Cognitive impulsivity and intelligence as predictors of the age-crime curve: Findings from the Pittsburgh Youth Study. Manuscript submitted for publication.

Loeber, R., & Pardini, D. (2008). Neurobiology and the development of violence: Common assumptions and controversies. *Philosophical Transactions of the Royal Society of Biological Sciences*, 363, 2491–2503.

Loeber, R., Pardini, D., Homish, D.L., Wei, E.H., Crawford, A.M., Farrington, D.P., Stouthamer-Loeber, M., Creemers, J., Koehler, S.A., & Rosenfeld, R. (2005). The prediction of violence and homicide in young men. *Journal of Consulting and Clinical Psychology*, 73, 1074–1088.

Loeber, R., Slot, W., & Stouthamer-Loeber, M. (2006). A three-dimensional, cumulative developmental model of serious delinquency. In P.-O.H. Wikström, & R.J. Sampson (Eds.), *The explanation of crime: Context, mechanisms, and development* (pp. 153–194). Cambridge, UK: Cambridge University Press.

Loeber, R., & Stallings, R. (2011). Modeling the impact of interventions on local indicators of offending, victimization, and incarceration. In R. Loeber & D.P. Farrington (Eds.), *Risk factors, prediction, and prevention from childhood* (pp. 137–152). New York: Springer.

Loughran, T.A., Piquero, A.R., Fagan, J., & Mulvey, E.P. (2012). Differential deterrence: Studying heterogeneity and changes in perceptual deterrence among serious youthful offenders. *Crime and Delinquency*, 58, 3–27. Advance online publication. DOI: 10.1177/0011128709345971.

Lynam, D.R., Caspi, A., Moffitt, T.E., Wikström, P-O., Loeber, R., & Novak, S. (2000). The interaction between impulsivity and neighborhood context on offending: The effects of impulsivity are stronger in poorer neighborhoods. *Journal of Abnormal Psychology*, 109, 563–574.

McGee, T.R. & Farrington. D.P. (2010). Are there any true adult onset offenders? *British Journal of Criminology*, 50, 530–549.

McGowan, A., Hahn, R., Liberman, A., Crosby, A., Fullilove, M., Johnson, R., Moscicki, E., Price, L., Snyder, S., Tuma, F., Lowy, J., Briss, P., Cory, S., Stone, G., & Task Force on Community Preventive Services. (2007). Effects on violence of laws and policies facilitating the transfer of juveniles from the juvenile justice system to the adult justice system: A systematic review. *American Journal of Preventive Medicine*, 32, 7–28.

McReynolds, L.S., Schwalbe, C.S., & Wasserman, G.A. (2010). The contribution of psychiatric disorder to juvenile recidivism. *Criminal Justice and Behavior*, 37, 204–216.

Mears, D.P., & Travis, J. (2004). Youth development and reentry. *Youth Violence and Juvenile Justice*, 2, 3–20.

Megaree, E.I. (1966). Undercontrolled and overcontrolled personality types in extreme antisocial aggression. *Psychological Monographs*, 80, 1–29.

Miller, J., & Mullins, C.W. (2009). Feminist theories of juvenile delinquency. In M. Zahn (Ed.), *The delinquent girl* (pp. 30–49). Philadelphia, PA: Temple University Press.

Mitchell, O., Wilson, D.B., & MacKenzie, D.L. (2006). The effectiveness of incarceration-based drug treatment on criminal behavior. The Campbell Collaboration (http://www.campbellcollaboration.org).

Modecki, K.L.(2008). Addressing gaps in the maturity judgment literature: Age differences and delinquency. *Law and Human Behavior*, 32, 78–91.

Moffitt, T.E. (1993). Adolescence-limited and life-course-persistent antisocial behavior: A developmental taxonomy. *Psychological Review*, 100, 674–701.

Moffitt, T.E. (2006). Life-course-persistent and adolescent limited antisocial behavior. In D. Cicchetti, & D.J. Cohen (Eds.), *Developmental psychopathology: Risk, disorder, and adaptation* (Vol. 3, pp. 570–598). New York: Wiley.

Moffitt, T.E., Caspi, A., Rutter, M., & Silva, P.A. (2001). *Sex differences in antisocial behaviour: Conduct disorder, delinquency, and violence in the Dunedin Longitudinal Study.* Cambridge, UK: Cambridge University Press.

Mulvey, E.P., Schubert, C.A., & Chung, H.L. (2007). Service use after court involvement in a sample of serious adolescent offenders. *Children and Youth Services Review*, 29, 518–544.

Mulvey, E.P., Steinberg, L., Piquero, A.R., Besana, M., Fagan, J., Schubert, C., & Cauffman, E. (2010). Trajectories of desistance and continuity in antisocial behavior following court adjudication among serious adolescent offenders. *Development and Psychopathology*, 22, 453–475.

Mulvey, E.P. (March, 2011). Highlights from pathways to desistance: A longitudinal study of serious adolescent offenders. *OJJDP Juvenile Justice Fact Sheet*.

Murray, J., & Murray, L. (2010). Parental incarceration, attachment and child psychopathology. *Attachment and Human Development*, 12, 289–309.

Nieuwbeerta, P., Nagin, D.S., & Blokland, A.A.J. (2009). Assessing the impact of first-time imprisonment on offenders' subsequent criminal career development: A matched samples comparison. *Journal of Quantitative Criminology*, 25, 227–257.

O'Brien, B.S., & Frick, P.J. (1996). Reward dominance: Associations with anxiety, conduct problems, and psychopathy in children. *Journal of Abnormal Child Psychology*, 24, 223–240.

Odgers, C., Vincent, G.M., & Corrado, R.R. (2002). A preliminary conceptual framework for the prevention and management of multi-problem youth. In R.R. Corrado, R. Roesch, S.D. Hart, & J. Gierowski (Eds.), *Multi-problem violent youth: A foundation for comparative research on needs, interventions, and outcomes* (pp. 116–129). Amsterdam: IOS Press.

Odgers, C.L., Caspi, A., Broadbent, J.M., Dickson, N., Hancox, R.J., Harrington, H., et al. (2007). Prediction of differential adult health burden by conduct problem subtypes in males. *Archives of General Psychiatry*, 64, 476–484.

Ogden, T., & Amlund-Hagan, K. (in press). Systems oriented interventions in Europe. In R. Loeber, M. Hoeve, N.W. Slot, & P. van der Laan (Eds.), *Persisters and desisters in crime from adolescence into adulthood: Explanation, prevention and punishment*. Aldershot: Ashgate.

Ogloff, J.R.P. (1997). A legal perspective on the concept of "impulsivity." In C.D. Webster, & M.A. Jackson (Eds.), *Impulsivity: Theory, assessment, and treatment* (pp. 63–81). New York: Guilford.

Osgood, D.W., Gold, M., & Miller, C. (1986). *For better or for worse? Peer attachments and peer influence among incarcerated adolescents*. Paper presented at the annual meeting of the American Society of Criminology, Atlanta, GA.

Petras, H., Kellam, S.G., Brown, C.H., Muthén, B.O., Ialongo, N.S., & Poduska, J.M. (2008). Developmental epidemiological courses leading to antisocial personality disorder and violent and criminal behavior: Effects by young adulthood of a universal preventive intervention in first- and second-grade classrooms. *Drug and Alcohol Dependence*, 1, S45–S59.

Piquero, A.R. (2008). Taking stock of developmental trajectories of criminal activity over the life course. In A. Liberman (Ed.), *The long view of crime: A synthesis of longitudinal research* (pp. 23–78). New York: Springer.

Piquero, A.R., Farrington, D.P., & Blumstein, A. (2007). *Key issues in criminal career research: New analyses of the Cambridge Study in Delinquent Development.* Cambridge, UK: Cambridge University Press.

Piquero, A.R., Jennings, W.G., & Farrington, D.P. (2009) *Effectiveness of programmes designed to improve self-control.* Stockholm: National Council for Crime Prevention. Available from www.bra.se (choose English language pages) (2009).

Piquero, A.R., Jennings, W.G., & Farrington, D.P. (2010). On the malleability of self-control: Theoretical and policy implications regarding a general theory of crime. *Justice Quarterly*, 27, 803–834.

Popkin, S.J., Leventhal, T., & Weismann, G. (2010). Girls in the 'hood: How safety affects the life chances of low-income girls. *Urban Affairs Review*, 45, 715–744.

Prime, J., White, S., Liriano, S. & Patel, K. (2001). *Criminal careers of those born between 1953 and 1978.* London: Home Office (Statistical Bulletin 4/01).

Prior, D., Farrow, K., Hughes, N., Kelly, G., Manders, G., White, S., & Wilkinson, B. (2011). *Maturity, young adults and criminal justice.* Birmingham, UK: Institute of Applied Social Studies, School of Social Policy, University of Birmingham.

Pulkkinen, L. (1982). Self-control and continuity from childhood to late adolescence. In P. Baltes, & O. Brim (Eds.), *Life span development and behavior* (Vol. 4, pp. 64–102). San Diego, CA: Academic Press.

Quinsey, V.L., Harris, G.T., Rice, M.E., & Cormier, C.A. (1998). *Violent offenders: Appraising and managing risk.* Washington, DC: American Psychological Association.

Redding, R.E. (2008). *Juvenile transfer laws: An effective deterrent to delinquency?* Office of Justice Programs, U.S. Department of Justice.

Redondo, S., Sánchez-Meca, J., & Garrido, V. (2003). Crime treatment in Europe: A review of outcome studies. In J. McGuire (Ed.), *Offender rehabilitation and treatment: Effective programs and policies to reduce re-offending* (pp. 113–142). Chichester, UK: Wiley.

Reiss, A.J., & Farrington, D.P. (1991). Advancing knowledge about co-offending: Results from a prospective longitudinal survey of London males. *Journal of Criminal Law and Criminology*, 82, 360–395.

Reynolds, A.J., Temple, J.A., Robertson, D.L., & Mann, E.A. (2001). Long-term effects of an early childhood intervention on educational achievement and juvenile arrest: A 15-year follow-up of low-income children in public schools. *Journal of the American Medical Association*, 285, 2339–2346.

Reynolds, A.J., Temple, J.A., Ou, S-R., Robertson, D.L., Mersky, J.P., Topitzes, J.W., & Niles, M.D. (2007). Effects of a school-based, early childhood intervention on adult health and well-being: A 19-year follow-up of low-income families. *Archives of Pediatrics and Adolescent Medicine*, 161, 730–739.

Rutter, M., Quinton, D., & Hill, J. (1990). Adult outcomes of institution-reared children: Males and females compared. In L.N. Robins, and M. Rutter (Eds.), *Straight and devious pathways from childhood to adulthood* (pp. 135–157). Cambridge, UK: Cambridge University Press.

Sampson, R.J., & Laub, J.H. (1990). Crime and deviance over the life course: The salience of adult social bonds. *American Sociological Review*, 55, 609–627.

Satterfield, J.H., Faller, K.J., Crinella, F.M., Schell, A.M., Swanson, J.M., & Homer, L.D. (2007). A 30-year prospective follow-up study of hyperactive boys with conduct problems: Adult criminality. *Journal of the American Academy of Child and Adolescent Psychiatry*, 46, 601–610.

Schaeffer, C.M., & Borduin, C.M. (2005). Long-term follow-up to a randomized clinical trial of multisystemic therapy with serious and violent juvenile offenders. *Journal of Consulting and Clinical Psychology*, 73, 445–453.

Schochet, P.Z., Burghardt, J., & McConnell, S. (2008). Does Job Corps work? Impact findings from the National Job Corps Study. *American Economic Review*, 98, 1864–1886.

Schweinhart, L.J., & Weikart, D.P. (1993). Success by empowerment: The High/Scope Perry Preschool Study through age 27. *Young Children*, 49, 54–58.

Secret, M. (March 5, 2011). States prosecute fewer teenagers in adult court. *New York Times*.

Sherman, L., Gottfredson, D., MacKenzie, D., Eck, J., Reuter, P., & Bushway, S. (1997). *Preventing crime: What works, what doesn't, what's promising*. Washington, DC: National Institute of Justice.

Siennick, S.E. (2007). The timing and mechanisms of the offending-depression link. *Criminology*, 45, 583–615.

Siennick, S.E., & Osgood, D.W. (2008). A review of research on the impact on crime of transitions to adult roles. In A.M. Liberman (Ed.), *The long view of crime: A synthesis of longitudinal research* (pp. 161–187). New York: Springer.

Slotboom, A., & Bijleveld, C. (2007). Wat er in je hoofd en je hart zit weet niemand: Gedetineerde vrouwen in Nederland. *Justitiële Verkenningen*, 4, 72–88.

Soderstrom, I.R., Castellano, T.C., & Figaro, H.R. (2001). Measuring mature coping skills among adult and juvenile offenders: A psychometric assessment of relevant instruments. *Criminal Justice and Behavior*, 28, 300–328.

Sowell, E.R., Delis, D., Stiles, J., & Jernigan, T.L. (2001). Improved memory functioning and frontal lobe maturation between childhood and adolescence: A structural MRI study. *Journal of the International Neuropsychological Society*, 7, 312–322.

Spanjaard, H.J.M., van der Knaap, L.M., van der Put, C.E., & Stams, G.J.J.M. (in press). Risk assessment and the impact of risk and protective factors. In R. Loeber, M. Hoeve, N.W. Slot, & P. van der Laan (Eds.), *Persisters and desisters in crime from adolescence into adulthood: Explanation, prevention and punishment*. Aldershot UK: Ashgate.

Steinberg, L. (2004). Risk taking in adolescence: What changes, and why? *Annals of the New York Academy of Sciences*, 1021, 51–58.

Steinberg, L., & Cauffman, E. (1996). Maturity of judgment in adolescence: Psychosocial factors in adolescent decision making. *Law and Human Behavior*, 20, 249–272.

Steinberg, L., Cauffman, E., Woolard, J., Graham, S., & Banich, M. (2009). Are adolescents less mature than adults? Minors' access to abortion, the juvenile death penalty, and the alleged APA "flip-flop." *American Psychologist*, 64, 583–594.

Steiner, B. (2009). The effects of juvenile transfer to criminal court on incarceration decisions. *Justice Quarterly*, 26, 77–106.

Stouthamer-Loeber, M. (2010). *Persistence and desistance in offending*. Unpublished report. Life History Research Program, University of Pittsburgh, Pittsburgh, PA.

Stouthamer-Loeber, M., & Loeber, R. (2002). Lost opportunities for intervention: Undetected markers for the development of serious juvenile delinquency. *Criminal Behaviour and Mental Health*, 12, 69–82.

Stouthamer-Loeber, M., Loeber, R., Stallings, R., & Lacourse, E. (2008). Desistance from and persistence in offending. In R. Loeber, D.P. Farrington, M. Stouthamer-Loeber, & H.R. White, *Violence and serious theft: Risk and promotive factors from childhood to early adulthood* (pp. 269–308). Mahwah, NJ: Erlbaum.

Stouthamer-Loeber, M., Wei, E., Loeber, R., & Masten, A.S. (2004). Desistance from persistent serious delinquency in the transition to adulthood. *Development and Psychopathology*, 16, 897–918.

Teplin, L.A., Abram, K.M., McClelland, G.M., Dulcan, M.K., & Mericle, A.A. (2002). Psychiatric disorders in youth in juvenile detention. *Archives of General Psychiatry*, 59, 1133–1143.

Teplin, L.A., McClelland, G.M., Abram, K.M., & Weiner, D.A. (2005). Crime victimization in adults with severe mental illness: Comparison with the National Crime Victimization Survey. *Archives of General Psychiatry*, 62, 911–921.

Theobald, D., & Farrington, D.P. (2009). Effects of getting married on offending: Results from a prospective longitudinal survey of males. *European Journal of Criminology*, 6, 496–516.

Theobald, D. & Farrington, D.P. (2010). Should policy implications be drawn from the effects of getting married on offending? *European Journal of Criminology*, 7, 239–247.

Thornberry, T.P. (2005). Explaining multiple patterns of offending across the life course and across generations. *Annals of the American Academy of Political and Social Science*, 602, 156–195.

Tong, J., & Farrington, D.P. (2008). Effectiveness of "reasoning and rehabilitation" in reducing reoffending. *Psicothema*, 20, 20–28.

Tonry, M. (1999a). Parochialism in the U.S. sentencing policy. *Crime and Delinquency*, 45, 48–65.

Tonry, M. (1999b). Why are U.S. incarceration rates so high? *Crime & Delinquency*, 45, 419–437.

Tracy, P.E., & Kempf-Leonard, K. (1996). *Continuity and discontinuity in criminal careers*. New York: Plenum.

Transition to Adulthood Alliance (2010). *Young adults and criminal justice: International norms and practices*. London: Author.

Truman, J.L., & Rand, M.R. (2010). *Crime victimization, 2008 (NCJ 231327)*. Washington DC: US Department of Justice.

Uggen, C. (2000). Work as a turning point in the life course of criminals: A duration model of age, employment, and recidivism. *American Sociological Review*, 65, 529–546.

van der Laan, A. M., & Blom, M. (2006). *Jeugddelinquentie: Risico's en bescherming (Juvenile delinquency: Risks and protection)*. The Hague: WODC.

van der Laan, P.H., van der Laan, A.M., & Hoeve, M. (in press). Offending from adolescence to adulthood and justice response at the juvenile-adult interface. In R. Loeber, M. Hoeve, N.W. Slot, & P. van der Laan (Eds.), *Persisters and desisters in crime from adolescence into adulthood: Explanation, prevention and punishment*. Aldershot UK: Ashgate.

van der Put, C.E., Deković, M., Hoeve, M., Stams, G.J.J.M., van der Laan, P.H., & Langewouters, F.E.M. (2011). Risk assessment of girls: Are there any sex differences in risk factors for re-offending and in risk profiles? *Criminal Justice and Behavior*, 38, 248–262. Advance online publication. doi: 10.1177/0011128710384776.

van der Rakt, M., Weerman, F., & Need, A. (2005). Delinquent gedrag van jongens en meisjes: Het (anti) sociale kapitaal van vriendschapsrelaties. *Mens en Maatschappij*, 80, 329–354.

van Wijk, A., Loeber, R., Vermeiren, R., Pardini, D., Bullens, R., & Doreleijers, T. (2005). Violent juvenile offenders compared with violent juvenile nonsex offenders: Explorative findings from the Pittsburgh Youth Study. *Sexual Abuse: A Journal of Research and Treatment*, 17, 333–352.

Vreugdenhil, C. (2003). *Psychiatric disorders among incarcerated male adolescents in the Netherlands*. Dissertation. Amsterdam: Vrije University.

Wasserman, G.A., Jensen, P.S., Ko, S.J., Cocozza, J., Trupin, E., Angold, A., Cauffman, E., & Grisso, T. (2003). Mental health assessments in juvenile justice: Report on the consensus conference. *Journal of the American Academy of Child and Adolescent Psychiatry*, 42, 752–761.

Wasserman, G.A., & McReynolds, L.S. (2011). Contributions to traumatic exposure and posttraumatic stress disorder in juvenile justice youths. *Journal of Traumatic Stress*, 24, 422–429.

Wasserman, G.A., McReynolds, L.S., Schwalbe, C.S., Keating, J.M., & Jones, S.A. (2010). Psychiatric disorder, comorbidity, and suicidal behavior in juvenile justice youth. *Criminal Justice and Behavior*, 37, 1361–1376.

Wei, E.H., Loeber, R., & Stouthamer-Loeber, M. (2002). How many of the offspring born to teenage fathers are produced by repeat serious delinquents? *Criminal Behaviour and Mental Health*, 12, 83–98.

Welsh, B.C., Sullivan, C.J., & Olds, D.L. (2010). When early crime prevention goes to scale: A new look at the evidence. *Prevention Science*, 11, 115–125.

White, H.R., Jackson, K.M., & Loeber, R. (2009). Developmental sequences and comorbidity of substance use and violence. In M.D. Krohn, & A.J. Lizotte (Eds.), *Handbook on crime and deviance* (pp. 434–468). Dordrecht, NL: Springer.

Wong, T.M.L., Slotboom, A-M., & Bijleveld, C.C.J.H. (2010). Risk factors for delinquency in adolescent and young adult females: A European review. *European Journal of Criminology*, 7, 266–284.

Zahn, M.A., Day, J.C., Mihalic, S.F., & Tichavsky, L. (2009). Determining what works for girls in the juvenile justice system. *Crime and Delinquency*, 55, 266–293.

Zara, G., & Farrington, D.P. (2009). Childhood and adolescent predictors of late onset criminal careers. *Journal of Youth and Adolescence*, 38, 287–300.

Zara, G., & Farrington, D.P. (2010). A longitudinal analysis of early risk factors for adult-onset offending: What predicts a delayed criminal career. *Criminal Behaviour and Mental Health*, 20, 257–273.

Zhang, Q., Loeber, R., & Stouthamer-Loeber, M. (1997). Developmental trends of delinquent attitudes and behaviors: Replications and synthesis across domains, time, and samples. *Journal of Quantitative Criminology*, 13, 181–215.

Zimmer-Gembeck, M.J., & Skinner, E.A. (2011). Review: The development of coping across childhood and adolescence: An integrative review and critique of research. *International Journal of Behavioral Development*, 35, 1–17.

INDEX